U2 Live! *a concert documentary*

GW00360665

OMNIBUS PRESS
LONDON / NEW YORK / SYDNEY

Pimm Jal de la Parra

CREDITS

Copyright © 1994 Pimm Jal de la Parra
This edition Copyright © 1994 Omnibus Press
(A Division of Book Sales Limited)

Text Edited by Chris Charlesworth
Picture Research by Pimm Jal de la Parra
Design by Lemm & Ten Haaf,
Amsterdam, Holland
Electronic Publishing by Martien Holtzappel

ISBN: 0.7119.3666.8
Order No.: OP47526

Exclusive Distributors:
Book Sales Limited
8/9 Frith Street
London W1V 5TZ, UK

Music Sales Corporation
257 Park Avenue South
New York, NY 10010, USA

Music Sales Pty Limited
120 Rothschild Avenue
Roseberry, NSW 2018, Australia

To the Music Trade only:
Music Sales Limited
8/9 Frith Street
London W1V 5TZ, UK

Printed & bound in Singapore.

A catalogue record for this book is available from the British Library.

PICTURE CREDITS:

U2 LIVE: A CONCERT DOCUMENTARY

Literally hundreds of people have helped me with this book in one way or another. I owe a great deal of gratitude to Caroline van Oosten de Boer and Kathy Lonquist for many years of loyal support. When I started *U2 Collectormania* magazine in 1987 they were there from the start and soon became indispensable forces, translating and proof-reading most of my writing and helping in many other ways both on the magazine and this book.

I am grateful to the following for doing extensive research, each concentrating on one particular year or tour, and making contributions to the text along the way: Monika Habner, Guido Matena, Guido Heygele and Jeroen van Meggelen. Thanks also to Guido Matena for helping me with editorial work and for offering invaluable advice. For feeding copy into the computer I thank Jeroen Eygelaar, Sandra Verkruisen, Gerian Alofs, Sandra van der Laan, and Gonnie Herfst.

This book wouldn't exist if U2 didn't have such a loyal and dedicated fan base. Through *Collectormania* magazine and meetings at U2's concerts I've gotten to know many people who have delved into their own U2 collections for the benefit of this book, sending me newspaper clippings, pictures, and memorabilia, much of which has been used. They have also shared their own memories and experiences of seeing U2 in concert, supplying me with information about live appearances from all over the world that I wouldn't otherwise have known. I am grateful to each and every one of you:

FROM HOLLAND: Annelies de Haan, Geraldo van Kessel, Jessica Snabel, Jolanda Meijboom, Barbara Koedooder, Willy Tonis, Sander Wiersma, Suzanna Bronger, Hans van de Berg, Corla Supèr, Leo de Cort, Siem Boon, Arnaut Nanning, Wendy Smit, Marjan Kuipers, Roy Lith, H. Prins, Karen Dashorst, Laura Rooymans, Mariel Otten, M. Vinke, Marc van der Vliet, Marieke Groen, Janet van de Werken, Arno Lammerts, Jacob Kugel, G. Hauser, Sandra Jong, Corine Brouwer, Petra Vethman, Marja and Robin Scheermeijer.

BELGIUM: Bart Moons, Eric Naulearts, Christ Devos, Joris van Eeckhoven, Gerd van Poucke, Kristien Druyts, Rudy Serpentier, Peter Thoelen, Ann Neumuller, Frank Janssens, Erik Hoebeke, Mirella Bisschop, Kristiaan Janssens, Genevieve Senden.

UNITED KINGDOM: Tony Pearson, Tony Coyle, Mark and Wendy Chatterton, James Motley, Nick Bradburn, Phil Stickels, Kevin Reilly, Matthew McDonald, Mark Lloyd, Andrew Roy, John Harris, Nigel Dunn.

IRELAND: Patrick Lynch, Derek Carroll, Declan Bates, Shane Henry.

GERMANY: Florian Küpper, Kay Bauersfeld, Anne-Marie Zietz, Karsten Radau, Dorothea Reuter, Bianca Dieckmann, Ursula Wielitzka, Violetta Opitz, Patrick Musial, Björn Lampe, Kristin Enseling, Sandra Radmacher, Vera Holzhauer, Pascal Moog, Sandra Holzfuss, Ute Hammermann.

AUSTRIA: Manuel Stuttler.

SWITZERLAND: Jessica Stetzenmeyer, Laure Backelard.

PORTUGAL: Luis Miguel Cruz Alves.

FRANCE: Charles Fernandez, Corinne Nonnotte, Anne-Marie Burtin, Helène Borrelli, Jordane Simha, David Delacencellerie, Joseph Moua, Anne Gauthier.

SPAIN: Esther Aliaga, Santi Herranz Martin.

SWEDEN: Elpida Sarridou and Pang, Nils Windahl, Mats Johansson, Anna K. Ekholm, Adam Kahsai-Rudebeck, Jaan Blomberg.

NORWAY: Anne-Gro Tveita.

FINLAND: Anne Mikkonen, Hannu Nyström, Kati Mäkipää, Anu Nousiainen, Antti Rimminen.

ITALY: Luca Cattini, Mauro Coscia, Emanuele Campion, Elena Piccioni.

ARGENTINA: Linda Wiske.

AUSTRALIA: Glenn Shambrook, David Perry, Joe Lazzaro, David Fowler.

NEW ZEALAND: Eleanor Simmonds.

JAPAN: Rie Nonomura.

CANADA: Cindy Anderson, Shannon Colby, Michel Tremblay, B. Lee.

USA: Karen Key, Jim Rinaldi, Jan Pietraszek, Minerva Velasquez, Scott Zumsteg, Carolyn Adams, Chris Trimm, Kevin Rainwater, Tanya Penson, Sherece Lamke, Maggie Gibson, Kelly Stockman, Mark Saarinen, Victor Campos, Timothy Healy, Wendy Wylo, Cindy Masry, Tania Berger, Deborah Cohen, Margaret Mathews, Patricia Birkholz, Peggy Tuten, Margaret O'Rourke, Archie Pugh, Amanda Newcomer, Rebecca Morgan, Carla Koch, S. Kathleen Maki, Rita Ann Spaletti, Sandi Wheeles, Isabella Campora, Kelley Harrison, Quintin C. Mecke III, Debra Miller, Melissa Hunt, Sue Zuege, Kristel Barnes, David D. Kim, Kathy Shoemaker, Christine Clugh, Wanda Stone, Chris Dicke, Kimberley Mitchell, Denise Greenstein, Stacey Mitchell, Kate Mulligan, Liza Post, Heather Sargent, Chris Cassino, Darren Jaffe, Christine Borkowski, Beth Hart, Abby Aldrich, Lori Mills, Jon Haagenson, Sara Rusmisel, Christine LoFranco, Amy Beckberger, David Lindsay, Meri Dresser, Jon Finafrock, Hilda Cedillo, Tammy Leinenbach, Donna Souza, Judy Chen, Scott Calzia, Jennifer Franklin, Shereen Walker, J. Felicia Chavez, Wendy Munn, Jennifer Lynn Sharp, Joseph Kusner, Dana L. Miller, Lezia Lozowy, Barbara Ann Ferrette, Eddie Veltman, Annette Wright, Adam Doti, Hilary Smith, Roland Young, Stephanie Griest, Jeff Kempton, Matthew Kistenmacher, Alex Seazzu, Nancy Moran, Deanna Doerr, Sonia Ann Moss, Sue Weber, James Naughton, Kathy Mooney-Smith, Stephen & Marianne Houk, Carole Johnson, and Jennifer Danner of *Patriot News* newspaper.

I have quoted from articles that originally appeared in the following newspapers and magazines: *Hot Press, New Musical Express, Melody Maker, Sounds, Record Mirror, Rolling Stone, The Boston Globe, The Washington Post, The Denver Post, The Oregonian, The Daily Cardinal, Smash Hits, Minneapolis Star & Tribune, Expressen, Phoenix Gazette, Juke, Sydney Herald, The Irish Times, Trouser Press, Philadelphia Daily News, Philadelphia Inquirer, Courier Post* and *Detroit Free Press*.

I have consulted the following books, all of which supplied invaluable insight into early or rare U2 live appearances or gave general background information:

- 'The U2 File: A Hot Press U2 History', edited by Niall Stokes (Omnibus Press, 1985)
- 'Three Chords And The Truth', by Niall Stokes and the editors of Hot Press magazine (Omnibus Press, 1989)
- 'U2: The Early Days - Another Time Another Place' with text by Bill Graham and photos by Patrick Brocklebank, James Mahon and Hugo McGuinness (Mandarin Paperbacks, 1989)
- 'Unforgettable Fire - The Story Of U2' by Eamon Dunphy (Viking, 1987)
- 'Wide Awake In America' by Carter Alan (Boxtree Limited, 1992).

Very Special Thanks goes out to: Jurgen MaaB, Mary Cipriani, Tom Goos, Jan Michaels, Linda Lenting, and all the photographers listed on page 2. Thanks also to Dave Brolan at Omnibus Press, and my editor Chris Charlesworth for bearing with me. Lots of love to my family and all my friends; thanks for all support, meals, beers, talks, laughs, patience. Most thanks of all to my China Girl and The Pasha, without whom...

Pimm Jal de la Parra, July 1994

During the past 17 years U2 have played nearly 1,000 concerts to millions of people all over the world. Starting out as a group of teenage friends, they have grown to become one of the most successful and critically acclaimed rock bands ever.

The strength and diversity of U2's live performance accounts largely for their huge, loyal following. I am one of the many who was pulled in along their rise to global success. Throughout the years I've enjoyed following their musical development and observing the way in which their songs and music have reflected the times in which they live and their own personal evolution, from adolescent issues and love-torn melancholy to the far greater problems of the world at large. Inner struggles combined with their impressions from around the world have emerged through their songs and set the themes for their shows.

Between 1982 and 1994 I attended 47 U2 concerts in 11 different countries, and virtually every night has been different. Travelling around Europe to see the shows, I have found that the quality of U2's performance on any given night is very much shaped by the circumstances and events that surround them. A crowd's enthusiasm is capable of inspiring U2, and if the interaction is well channelled and the band hit their stride, it can be a hugely uplifting experience. When it goes wrong or things simply don't click, an anger-fuelled show can have riveting results as U2 push themselves to the very brink to fight their frustrations.

In 1987 I founded *Collectormania: An International Magazine For U2 Fans And Collectors* as a way of releasing my enthusiasm and bridging the gap with others around the world. Though I have published an average of only one issue per year so far, *Collectormania* has been received with open arms by an increasing number of fans. One of the magazine's main features has been detailed reports from U2's concerts around the world, with readers contributing information about shows they have attended.

This book has been put together in much the same way. The information herein stems from the archives of fans throughout the world, from their experiences of seeing U2 live as well as my own. They have also supplied me with photographs and memorabilia collected on tour, much of which is reproduced here.

Further information has been culled from magazine articles, newspaper reviews, and from circulating recordings from concerts, radio interviews and TV appearances. Analysing many hundreds of hours of audio and video tapes enabled me to quote exact conversations and monologues and study rare versions of songs, all the while tasting the atmosphere at specific shows. Documenting every single change in song lists, and noting live sessions or duets with other artists, this book aims to trace the musical meandering which defines U2's career and which has thrilled audiences for nearly two decades.

Support acts and attendance figures are mentioned where known. If (P) follows the attendance figure, it means it is the *precise* number of fans attending, as officially published by trade magazines like *Billboard*. Otherwise the figure is an estimate based on the seating capacity of venues or data from newspaper reports. In the case of multiple shows, the figures are totals. Complete set lists are printed when radically different, otherwise a reference is made to a previous list.

Impressive as U2's concerts can be, memories are bound to fade as time goes by. If this book enables you to recall any of the sights, smells and sounds of your personal experiences of seeing U2 in concert, and if fans draw pleasure from tracing the band's live career, then I have achieved my goal.

As I wind up my final typescript, I feel like I'm coming home from a three-year long trip that started in the nightclubs of Dublin, and eventually took me through the mainland of Europe, the vast open plains of America and the stadia of sunny Australia. To everyone holding this book – have a pleasant journey.

Pimm Jal de la Parra, July 1994.

Updates to this book will appear in *Collectormania* magazine until the next edition is published. To receive information about *Collectormania*, or any comments about the book, please write, including an International Reply Coupon, to:

Pimm Jal de la Parra
PO Box 9652
1006 GD Amsterdam
Holland

AUTUMN 1976. DUBLIN, MOUNT TEMPLE COMPREHENSIVE SCHOOL

A group of school friends calling themselves Feedback perform Peter Frampton's *Show Me The Way* at a talent contest at Mount Temple Comprehensive School. They are Adam Clayton, Paul Hewson (aka Bono), Larry Mullen and Dave Evans (aka The Edge) and their messy, ten-minute performance receives a rapturous applause.

"There was, from the very start, the evidence I believe of a spark," Bono would recall four years later in an interview with Neil McCormick of *Hot Press*, the Dublin-based Irish arts magazine. "We walked up on that stage, I was playing guitar, and when I heard that D-chord, I got some kick. When I heard that D-chord it was like starting up a motorbike. There was something very special there.

"And the audience went wild! And I think we might as well forget the actual piece because that wasn't important, but it was the first thing I ever sang well. That was a very special concert, that was one of the best concerts of our lives. And we built ourselves around that spark. I'll tell you, it was like four blind kids blustering away, and there was the evidence of just a little light in the corner and we started to work towards that. Getting to grips with our instruments, getting to grips with performance. And the light was getting clearer."

The first ever performance by the group that would become U2 came at the end of several months in which the four teenagers became acquainted with each other and with their instruments. Their first meeting was initiated by the drummer, 15-year-old Larry Mullen, who pinned a note on the school notice board seeking guitarists to form a band. Larry had been drumming since he was nine, and had some experience of playing in bands, albeit of the marching variety. He played in the Artane Boys Band and the Post Office Workers' Band, but now he wanted to form his own rock group. Initially, Larry approached Adam Clayton, a fellow pupil who owned a bass guitar, and he agreed to go to Larry's house on the appointed day. Larry thought Adam was such a cool looking guy that he wanted him in the group regardless of how well – or, indeed, whether – he could play.

Several pupils responded to the note, including brothers Dave and Dik Evans, who had guitars that were either self built (Dik) or bought for £1 at a jumble sale (Dave); Peter Martin, a friend of Larry's, who brought his guitar and an amplifier; Ivan McCormick, a friend of Peter's, who brought an electric guitar; and another pupil, Paul Hewson. They talked about music for hours in Larry's kitchen, then the seven guys plugged their instruments into Peter's amp and tried to play some of the songs they had boasted about.

Opened in 1972, Mount Temple was a revolutionary school by conservative / Catholic Irish standards. It was the first non-denominational, co-educational school in Dublin: Catholics mixed with Protestants, boys mingled with girls, there was no school uniform. A liberal educational policy emphasised individual growth, and encouraged creative expression. The teachers allowed the group to rehearse in a classroom on Saturday afternoons.

Early rehearsals showed that Larry and Dave already knew how to handle their instruments. Larry's experience was obvious. Ivan could not play, so Dave took over his electric guitar, leaving Ivan with the £1 acoustic that was barely audible. Adam's cool attitude and use of hip band-circuit jargon impressed the others. Peter and Ivan were soon phased out. Though Paul, soon to be called Bono, insisted he had mastered the guitar, he couldn't play at all but he instinctively took control of the rehearsals, organising the others and inspiring them to produce music from their instruments. With Dave and Dik on guitars, Adam on bass and Larry on drums, the group realised the only vacancy for Paul was that of vocalist. It was a position that would eminently suit his leadership qualities and dominating presence.

As things started to fall into place, they rehearsed extensively, trying to play The Rolling Stones' *Jumping Jack Flash*, David Bowie's *Suffragette City*, and other favourites. Though not always succeeding in actually playing the tunes, the five guys all enjoyed making the impressive noise that came from their instruments so much that they officially declared themselves a band: Feedback.

AUTUMN 1976. DUBLIN, ST. FINTAN'S SCHOOL

Dik did not play at the Mount Temple performance, but he is present at the band's second live appearance at St. Fintan's School. Having changed their name to The Hype, after David Bowie's backing band before The Spiders, they play a version of The Moody Blues' *Nights In White Satin*. Aided by Stella, Ivan's sister, and her friend Orla on backing vocals and flute, Bono has to hold his microphone towards them because their mike breaks down halfway through.

FALL 1976 - EARLY 1978

Still attending school, the group rehearse as often as possible. Though all have differing personalities, there is a certain chemistry which lifts their encounters to an exciting and inspiring level. While they have fun spending time with each other and are rapidly becoming genuine friends, they continue to develop both as musicians and as a unit. Though they are all deeply interested in music, they don't approach it too seriously. The fun aspect is just as important as their creative ambitions.

It becomes more serious when Adam is expelled from school and decides he wants to devote all his time and energy to the band. Besides working on his musical skills, he becomes involved in promoting the band, but faces obstructions and practical difficulties. Due to the country's conservatism and Catholic morality, being in a rock group is looked down upon by many sections of the community. Apart from a handful of bands, Thin Lizzy, Horslips and The Boomtown Rats, the Irish rock scene is virtually non-existent. Showbands have dominated Irish music for years, and enjoyed huge success by playing safe cover versions of old evergreens. National radio rarely plays rock music, and venues are scarce. The lack of infrastructure makes it extremely difficult for young bands to develop and get a foot on the ladder to international recognition.

Being able to rehearse at school is a bonus, but Adam shrewdly uses his spare time collecting information on other aspects of the music business. He rings up musicians within the small local rock scene asking advice about equipment, how to get gigs, who to contact and anything else that might come in useful. Eager to learn all the angles, the band soak up every bit of knowledge to help them in any way whatsoever, and grab every opportunity to promote themselves. Adam even sends fake fan-messages to the classified sections of big-selling British music papers like *New Musical Express* just to get their name out.

Performing live wherever possible, the band display a vibrant, untainted enthusiasm on stage, and a fervent desire to be heard. As singer and main communicator, Bono bubbles over with spirit, unable to keep still or assume the same pose for longer than a few seconds. His hyperactive behaviour is fuelled by a need to communicate with his audience. Though occasions to play live are as scarce as the number of people that attend, word about The Hype slowly starts to spread around town.

EARLY 1978. DUBLIN, McGONAGLE'S

The Hype support Revolver in one of the main rock clubs in Dublin, playing several Stranglers and Sex Pistols covers.

MARCH 16, 1978. DUBLIN, PROJECT ARTS CENTRE

The Hype headline a midnight show to celebrate St. Patrick's Day, the Irish holiday. Festivities go on until deep in the night.

MARCH 17, 1978. LIMERICK

After just a few hours sleep, The Hype catch a train to Limerick on the west coast of Ireland and perform at a talent contest co-sponsored by Harp Lager, *Evening Press* and CBS Records. Having read about a competition for best pop band with £500 and a demo session as the first prize, Larry has convinced the rest of the band to enter and see what happens. The contest consists of a couple of rounds in which bands have to play before a jury only, and after each round losing bands are eliminated. Bono's throat is sore as result of his uncontrolled singing the night before. He apologises to the jury, claiming he has laryngitis but assuring them that although he can't sing properly, the songs are good. Nevertheless, The Hype make it to the final round, which takes place before a live audience. Their frantic three-song performance wins the first prize, leaving a far more accomplished band, the East Coast Angels, as runners-up.

Besides winning £500, one of the members of the jury, Jackie Hayden, marketing manager of the Irish division of CBS Records, arranges for The Hype to do a short demo session at Keystone Studios, with a possible recording contract to follow. The session is messy and uninspired, and doesn't impress CBS headquarters in London when they hear the tape. Though unwilling to offer the band a contract, one CBS executive sees their potential and suggests they do another, proper demo session later in the year.

The Limerick victory increases the band's belief in their future. Adam hunts down any potentially useful contact even more fiercely, pestering families of busy people who are difficult to reach to extract their home numbers. Once he has the number, he doesn't hesitate to phone as early as 6am to catch people before they're unreachable again.

Thin Lizzy leader Phil Lynott advises Adam to find a manager and record a good demo tape to send to people in the business. Adam phones Bill Graham, an influential journalist writing for *Hot Press* magazine. Their meeting results in an article in *Hot Press*. Graham will prove to be an important link for the band to the music press, as he will rave about the band while following their progress.

Taking care of the band's business and promotional matters as well as being a member of the band proves too hard for Adam. They decide they need a real manager, someone who can handle all their business affairs, promote their best interests and spread the word. Adam phones Bill Graham again, this time to ask if he knows anyone suitable for the job.

Graham suggests Paul McGuinness, a friend from his English college days. Graham knows that McGuinness has experience in the film business and for some time has been interested in managing a young band right from the start, rather than becoming involved with an existing band who may have lost some of their enthusiasm. McGuinness is interested in guiding a group and creating situations in which they can work, as well as inventing ways of how their music can be presented to an audience. Bill Graham spends weeks trying to persuade McGuinness to take on the job, but McGuinness is sceptical and needs time to think about it.

MARCH 1978. HOWTH, COMMUNITY CENTRE

Shortly after the Limerick victory, The Hype play a farewell show for Dik Evans who is quitting the band. He walks off halfway through the concert, and the four remaining members become U2, a name suggested by Steve Averill, singer of Irish punk band The Radiators, who has become one of their main advisors. U2 play a cover version of Thin Lizzy's *Dancing In The Moonlight*. Dik will later join The Virgin Prunes.

MAY 25, 1978. DUBLIN, PROJECT ARTS CENTRE

Paul McGuinness sees U2 live for the first time and decides to become their manager. He is attracted by their honesty and openness, their enthusiasm, ambition, and eagerness to learn. He recognises that they are true friends and considers this a good base on which to build, more important at this stage than their actual performing abilities which he thinks leave a lot to be desired.

New cover versions often played in this period include Wire's *Mannequin*, Neil Young's *Heart Of Gold*, and several Bay

Adam, Larry, Bono, The Edge. August 21, 1979

City Rollers' tunes. Growing increasingly dissatisfied and bored with doing covers, they now start to develop their own sound and songs, inspired by their friendship. Though they like the energy that the current wave of punk music contains, they resent the cynical, negative attitudes of the punk bands. They want to make music that will genuinely arouse emotions, music that combines the excitement of bands like The Who with the sensitivity of artists like Neil Young.

Original U2 songs developed in the course of 1978 include *Alone In The Light, False Prophet, The Magic Carpet, Another Time, Another Place, Inside Out, Stories For Boys, Concentration Cramp,* and *Boy-Girl.* Most are characterised by sharp riffs on Edge's distinctive, chiming guitar, harmonic melodies that invite sing along participation, and a solid, fast paced rhythm section. Adolescent issues like sexuality and insecurity set the mood for most of their songs which are often written from the point of view of an innocent boy, or through the eyes of a confused and frustrated teenager. Bono will often adapt his stage antics to the moods of the songs, and lyrics are often altered on the spur of the moment.

A new song which Bono wrote on the morning of May 10, his 18th birthday, is *Out Of Control,* an exuberant, energetic song which deals with the realisation that the two major events in life - birth and death – are beyond choice or decision. Another outstanding song is the rousing *Street Missions,* which slows down halfway through as Edge plays a lengthy solo to introduce a dreamy air to its conclusion. The lyrics deal with spiritual longing: "I need something... I need someone... I need you..." Edge's background singing echoes in perfect harmony with Bono's lead vocals.

JULY 31, 1978. DUBLIN, McGONAGLE'S

U2 support Modern Heirs and headliner Revolver. Scheduled at the bottom of the bill, Paul McGuinness, in one of his first actions as U2's manager, insists that his band do not perform before the crowd arrive. He suggests a switch with Modern Heirs. Though he doesn't get this plan through, the hall manager delays the start of the show to allow the crowd to arrive before U2 take the stage.

SUMMER, 1978. DUBLIN, LIBERTY HALL

U2 play a benefit show for the Contraception Action Campaign, protesting against Ireland's contraception laws, which forbid the sale of condoms and other contraceptives. A whole range of cardboard banners at the back of the stage carry slogans like, 'FREE LEGAL AND SAFE CONTRACEPTION', and 'NO DISCRI-MINATION AGAINST "ARTIFICIAL" CONTRACEPTIVE USERS'. Halfway through their set, the band are interrupted by women from the campaign who make speeches.

Later in the year, U2 headline a benefit show for the 'Rock Against Sexism' group in Dublin's Magnet Bar. Only 50 people turn up.

SEPTEMBER 9, 1978. DUBLIN, TOP HAT BALLROOM

■   Attendance: 2,500
U2 support The Stranglers and get a £50 fee. Playing for their biggest crowd so far, the show is a major test and a good opportunity to expose themselves. They have no dressing room of their own, so they change behind the stage. Because they could not do a soundcheck, Edge's guitar stutters during the show and he breaks a string. Stranglers' fans get annoyed and throw lighted cigarettes.

SEPTEMBER 18, 1978. DUBLIN, PROJECT ARTS CENTRE

U2 and The Virgin Prunes share the bill. Bono joins the Prunes for a few songs.

OCTOBER 1978. CORK, ARCADIA BALLROOM

U2 play their first headlining show outside Dublin in Cork, the country's second largest city. Being top of the bill with three other bands from Dublin performing, U2 finally hit the stage after midnight but only 200 of the 2,000 plus crowd are left. They still receive U2 with enthusiasm.

LATE 1978. CROFTON AIRPORT HOTEL

Only six people turn up, three of whom think a different band are playing.

DECEMBER 1978. DUBLIN, THE STARDUST

U2 play as support to The Greedy Bastards, a band made up of members of Thin Lizzy and The Sex Pistols. U2's set is uninspired and marred by technical problems.

JANUARY 3, 1979. DUBLIN, McGONAGLE'S

Thanks to word of mouth, U2 play to a sellout crowd.

FEBRUARY 3, 1979. DUBLIN, McGONAGLE'S (AFTERNOON) DUBLIN, TRINITY COLLEGE (EVENING)

FEBRUARY, 1979. DUBLIN, PROJECT ARTS CENTRE

■   'Dark Space Festival' line up: The Mekons, Terri Hooley and

The Good Vibrations, The Vipers, Throbbing Gristle, Public Image, Virgin Prunes, U2, D.C. Nien, The Blades, The Atrix U2 perform at a weekend-long festival, with numerous Irish bands appearing. Several members of the London music press attend, and the bands are eager to expose themselves at their best. U2 get frustrated as their set is marred by bad acoustics and bursts of feedback from their amplifiers.

U2 don't get any mention in the reviews. A couple of weeks later, Bono borrows some money to take the boat to London, where he visits the offices of various major record companies, and music papers like *New Musical Express*, *Melody Maker*, *Sounds* and *Record Mirror*. Plugging U2, Bono drops off copies of demo-tapes and urges writers to see U2 when they play in London some time soon.

MAY, 1979. DUBLIN, DANDELION CAR PARK

U2 play the first of six Saturday afternoon gigs during the spring and summer at the Dandelion, a disused indoor car park. Situated next to the Gaiety Green flea market beside St. Stephen's Green, the shows are attended by large crowds, including many youngsters under 18 who can't see U2 in clubs because of the licensing laws. Entry to the Dandelion is 50 pence or £1. On a small wooden stage with basic lighting and amplification, U2 play energetic shows that establish their name in the Dublin scene. They will eventually become legendary events in the U2 saga.

As the crowds at the Dandelion grow with each show, Bono improves his skill at controlling, stirring up, and surprising audiences, and he learns to use inconveniences to his advantage. At the first show, a power failure cuts off Adam and Edge's instruments. While the power is being restored, Bono invites a guy on stage to hum him the bassline and shows another guy how to perform a vocal interpretation of Edge's part. While Larry continues to play and his two pupils' voices stand in for the instruments, Bono improvises lyrics until power is restored.

Bono's improvisation increases the crowd's focus on the stage, instead of leaving them to wander off for a drink while the problems are fixed. With some lessons in dramatic expression under his belt, Bono uses his miming skills to illustrate several songs. For *Boy-Girl*, a song about adolescent confusion, he asks for a cigarette, then nervously trots around the stage like a youngster having a secret smoke for the first time.

Some of the Dandelion shows see the beginnings of U2 stage rituals that will re-appear throughout their career. At one show, Paul McGuinness hands Bono the first of what will become many hundreds of bottles of champagne with which to celebrate the night, toast the audience and spray into the crowd during the encore. These shows strengthen McGuinness' belief in the band. As he sees them progress and the crowds swell, he realises the importance of live performance for U2, and that the key to success is building up a following through their concerts.

MAY, 1979. DUBLIN, TRINITY COLLEGE

U2 perform a free, lunch-time gig on the stairs of the college that attracts more and more students with each song performed. Most stay to listen even when it starts to rain.

JUNE 7, 14, 21, 28 1979. DUBLIN, McGONAGLE'S

As a publicity stunt, U2 play four Thursday night 'Christmas In June' shows at McGonagles during the month of June. Dubbed 'The Jingle Balls', Christmas decorations are draped all over the stage, slides are projected at the side, and Santa Claus masks hang at the rear, making for a bizarre atmosphere.

JULY, 1979. HOWTH, YOUTH CLUB

AUGUST, 1979. HOWTH, YOUTH CLUB

The wide area around this suburb of Dublin is plastered with publicity posters. The show attracts around 250 youngsters. U2 play a powerful, hour-long set that includes *The Magic Carpet*, *Stories For Boys* and a new song called *Silver Lining*, among many others. The band come out to talk with some of the audience afterwards.

AUGUST, 1979. DUBLIN, DANDELION CAR PARK

The last show at the Dandelion includes *Out Of Control*, *In Your Hand*, *Concentration Cramp*, *Shadows And Tall Trees*, *The Magic Carpet* and *The Fool*. Critics note U2's specific sound. Declan Lynch writes in Hot Press: 'Dave Edge is a superlative guitarist and he'll improve so much, being so young, being so bright, so good. U2 have created a unique and identifiable sound of their own. It's a good sound, one that's adding nuances to pop and metal, without being either one exclusively.'

AUGUST 21, 1979. DUBLIN, THE BAGGOT INN

■ Support: The Blades

This show is attended by several record company talent scouts from London. The show fails to persuade any of them to offer U2 a contract, but it does impress Dave McCullough of *Sounds* magazine, who has come over from London to report on the Irish music scene, and becomes one of the first members of the UK press to support U2.

SEPTEMBER 1979. DUBLIN, PROJECT ARTS CENTRE

U2 play two shows in support of Patrick Fitzgerald. On the first night, U2 face hostility from a group of punks who threaten to invade the stage. Bono removes a shoe to ward them off before they are evicted.

SEPTEMBER 1979

U2 release their first record, a three-song EP dubbed 'U2-3', on CBS Ireland. Unavailable anywhere else in the world, the 7" contains *Out Of Control / Stories For Boys / Boy-Girl*. The recordings stem from a CBS session last December. It brings the band their first chart success in Ireland, selling all 1,000 copies of the 12" version and doing well in its 7" edition.

OCTOBER 5, 1979. CORK, OPERA HOUSE

■ Set: *Stories For Boys / The Speed Of Life / Cartoon World / The King's New Clothes / Inside Out / Another Time, Another Place / Boy-Girl / Out Of Control /* encore: *Glad To See You Go*

This is U2's television début, on RTE. The TV presenter announces the band: "Tonight is my pleasure to introduce to you a new, young, four-piece band from Dublin, and their music has been described as, and I quote: 'A unique brand of tight, melodic, energetic rock'. They just released a new single, and they're tipped for greater things, so sit back and put your hands together and welcome: U2."

Opening with *Stories For Boys*, the band's pent-up excitement results in a chaotic version with the instruments stumbling over each other. *The Speed Of Life* betrays Larry's background in marching bands. Before *Cartoon World*, Bono tells the crowd that the band have been warned that it might be scary performing on TV. He looks straight into the TV cameras: "I know one thing: I can see some people at home, through that camera there, and maybe the camera there, and maybe that one here. And I watch that television programme, and I can see Kevin, and I can see Morla, and I can see Bobby, and uncle Jack, and auntie Barbra, and uncle Teddy, and Joy and Alison. And Norman, and me dad. Hello!" *Cartoon World* portrays the sheer dullness working nine-to-five on the same job day after day, with weekend visits to the pub as the only escape. Bono holds the crowd, urging them to raise their hands and put them down

The Baggot Inn, August 21, 1979

again, encouraging them to cheer, then hushing them when they become too loud. Bono announces *Another Time, Another Place* as being about a dream he had once. The track is played much rawer and louder than the eventual album version, but is similar in arrangement. Without interrupting his singing, Bono wanders into the crowd to take a seat in the first few rows. "You might wonder why we shouldn't stay under the little piece here in front of the drum kit," he says afterwards. "I was just seeing what it's like watching him [Edge] play his guitar sitting down like you are. It's quite strange..." *Boy-Girl* is dedicated to "boys and girls and all their sweethearts." Standing on top of a chair amid the crowd, he talks to the guy next to him. "Have you got a sweetheart? Do you love her? Do you really love her? Are you going to marry her?" The audience laugh as the guy turns pink with embarrassment.

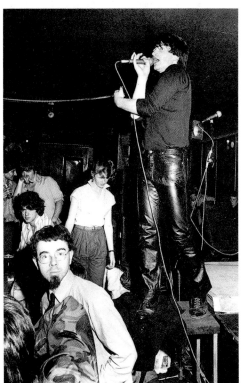

In foreground: Dik Evans

The crowd shout for more even before the band have left the stage. Bono assures them, "You didn't have to work that hard! Look at all these guys rushing up the front. This one was written by a fool. It's not *The Fool*. It's a Ramones number, it's called *Glad To See You Go*. I want everybody from the back up here, c'mon!" With the crowd rushing the stage, U2's powerful rendition brings the show to a frenzied end.

In November, *Record Mirror*, a UK music paper, gives U2 their first cover story outside Ireland. Bono tells Chris Westwood: 'I believe that perfect beauty can be harmful. Did you ever notice that the really beautiful girl in the school was never all that together because she got things handed to her? Perfection is

unreal, everybody's un-perfect... but you've got these heroes on TV – and this is the first TV generation, if you like – people being bombarded with perfect images. Superman, Bionic Man, the girl from the perfume ad, and everyone playing let's pretend. Everything should be pointed towards the individual, making them think for themselves. If people could just pull off that layer, that mask, that macho man image...'

Chris Westwood: 'The thing that makes Bono and U2 so believable is their awareness of vulnerability, both in themselves and in other individuals. They see acceptance of this as central to the very concept of harmony, unity and self-belief.'

Bono: 'I'm an outgoing sort of person, I want to take everything and break everything. I want people in London to see and hear the band. I want to replace the bands in the charts now, because I think we're better.'

LONDON CLUB TOUR 1979

In December 1979, U2 visit London for their first dates outside Ireland. Having lived out of each other's pockets for years, they are broke and borrow £3,000 from friends and family to finance the tour. The trip is an all-or-nothing attempt to ignite press support and stir record companies in the hope of a contract.

DECEMBER 1, 1979. WEST HAMPSTEAD, MOONLIGHT CLUB

As support for The Dolly Mixtures, U2's set includes *Concentration Cramp, The Dream Is Over, Shadows And Tall Trees,* and *Inside Out.*

Dave McCullough writes in *Sounds* magazine: 'U2's lead singer Bono is tense and anxious about the band's first gig outside their native Ireland. While the gear is set up he stands with the rest of the band around the side of the stage. Guitarist Dave Edge's hand is in plaster following a car crash, and they don't know how he'll cope. U2's feeling of tension comes from a feeling close to bursting with an urgent need to get their music across. U2 are about four people. Their music has minimum distortion and their songs reflect the strength of the four individuals. There's a kind of naïve, rushing feeling about their music...'

DECEMBER 2, 1979. EARL'S COURT, NASHVILLE ROOMS

U2 open for Secret Affair, with 25 people in the audience.

DECEMBER 3, 1979. CLAPHAM, 100 CLUB

DECEMBER 4, 1979. ISLINGTON, HOPE & ANCHOR

The band are billed as 'The U2's'. Dozens of press and record company people come out of curiosity, mainly as a result of Bono's lobbying earlier in the year but also prompted by positive press reviews. Only nine actual paying customers turn up. Halfway through the show, Edge breaks a string and the band are so distraught they leave the stage, not to return.

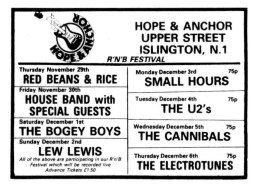

DECEMBER 5, 1979. COVENT GARDEN, ROCK GARDEN

U2 support The Dolly Mixtures. U2 are billed in *Melody Maker's*

gig guide as 'V2'. Their set includes *Twilight, Shadows And Tall Trees* and *Boy-Girl.* The show gets a rave review in *Record Mirror.*

DECEMBER 7, 8, 1979. CAMDEN, ELECTRIC BALLROOM

Two shows in which U2 open for The Talking Heads and Orchestral Manoeuvres In The Dark.

DECEMBER 11, 1979 CANNING TOWN, BRIDGE HOUSE

■ Support: Idiot Dancers

Melody Maker try to correct their earlier mistake and bill U2 as 'UR'.

DECEMBER 12, 1979. UXBRIDGE, BRUNEL UNIVERSITY

U2 open for The Photos.

DECEMBER 14, 1979. CAMDEN, DINGWALLS

DECEMBER 15, 1979. HARROW ROAD, WINDSOR CASTLE

After the last London club date, U2 return to Dublin disappointed because they had blown it in front of the record company people at the Hope & Anchor.

JANUARY 15, 1980. DUBLIN, RTE STUDIOS

U2 perform *Stories For Boys* live on national TV for the 'Late Late Show'. Bono sings "There's a late late show" instead of "TV show" in the second line. U2 win five categories in *Hot Press* magazine's readers' poll, beating established favourites such as Thin Lizzy and The Boomtown Rats, evidence of the impact they are making on the Irish music scene.

Encouraged by this, U2 tour Ireland throughout January and February, playing small venues in every nook and cranny of the country to reinforce their status as the most exciting live band on the rise. It coincides with the release of their second single, *Another Day.*

FEBRUARY, 1980. BELFAST, QUEEN'S UNIVERSITY

FEBRUARY, 1980. TULLAMOORE, BRIDGE HOUSE

■ Attendance: 650
■ Set: *Silver Lining / The Speed Of Life / The Magic Carpet / Stories For Boys / Trevor / Another Time, Another Place / Another Day / The Dream Is Over / Pete The Chop / Cartoon World / Jack In The Box / Shadows And Tall Trees / A Day Without Me / Twilight / Boy-Girl*

This set list is representative for most shows on the Irish tour. *The Magic Carpet* is preceded by Bono calling out "Judith, can you hear me, can you see me?" followed by the opening line, "Life on a distant planet", which often leads reviewers to refer to this track as either *Judith* or *Life On A Distant Planet.* The song *Trevor* is about a guy who smiles all the time because he wants to live forever. *Pete The Chop* is a rousing number that U2 will eventually re-record in late 1982 during the 'War' sessions. Renamed *Treasure (Whatever Happened To Pete The Chop),* it will be released as B-side of the 1983 *New Year's Day* single. The backing remains the same, though *Treasure's* lyrics are completely different to the original *Pete The Chop.*

FEBRUARY, 1980. CORK, COUNTRY CLUB

■ Set includes: *Cartoon World / Boy-Girl / Out Of Control / Trevor / Twilight / Another Day / The Dream Is Over / Shadows And Tall Trees*

Paul Morley reviews the show for *New Musical Express*: 'Bono is adored. He dangerously treads the fine line between being adulated rock star and parodying that role. He controls fights and calms down a stage invasion. He's never sure whether to patronise the audience for their stupidity, understand and gee them on, cool them down or join in. In the end he does it all and more. Acting, hurting, fighting. His performance is unruly but riveting.

"I'm not yet fully in control of my own performance," he will tell me. "I'm not sure which way it's going to go when I hit that stage. It could go any way. There have been times when I have been really frightened and could hardly sing. I hardly looked up. Like when I can't get anything out of the hall, the audience, I turn into myself, close my eyes and try to find something in there.

"I'm frightened of the responsibility of standing in that space. Sometimes I don't want to be on that stage. Sometimes I can be really happy. Other times I am mean and nasty, and there are

times when I haven't got complete control of myself but I do want some sort of discipline. I haven't got that yet. I would like to take any situation and get something out of it. You can't always do that, but you must try."

FEBRUARY, 1980. TULLERMENY, GARDEN OF EDEN CLUB

The day after the Cork show U2 play in support for Tony Steven's Showband in Tullermeny, a small village 70 miles from Dublin. Paul Morley reports for *NME*: 'The U2 opening blast is exhilarating. There is a minimal response from the audience. A few lost souls wander aimlessly down to the front and stare up at Bono's frantic, manic animation, briefly bemused. Some gently sway. Sat along the front of the stage bored looking girls can't even be bothered to turn around and see what all the commotion is about. The audience peer at U2 like they're looking at animals in the zoo. They're not used to this intimidating energy, the volume, Bono's mobile passion. Momentarily curious, some wander away. Those that do dance

Cork

could be dancing to anything.

'The performance hardly captures the depth of U2, the potential massive yet subtle assault. Bono has nothing to bounce off, just a blandness; he gets frustrated, slows down, misses cues, annoys the group. Larry shouts at him for his indulgence, and Bono admits he lacked the discipline to sell himself, the ability to attack positively the disinterest.'

Bono responds after the show: "I felt ashamed because we didn't work. Tonight we could have shown what rock & roll can do, but we failed."

FEBRUARY 26, 1980, DUBLIN, NATIONAL STADIUM

■ Attendance: 2,400; sellout
■ Set: same as Tullamoore, with *Pete The Chop* and *The Dream Is Over* switching places, plus *Out Of Control* after *Boy-Girl*.

The Irish tour climaxes with a major show at one of the largest venues in Dublin. Though Paul McGuinness was initially hesitant, unsure whether U2 were ready to playing the National Stadium, he was encouraged by their Irish agent Dave Cavanagh and the convincing *Hot Press* poll results. The show marks the first time that an Irish home-based band sells out the National Stadium. It is recorded by RTE radio for broadcast at the end of the year.

U2 play with confidence, knowing that a respresentative of Island Records is present to offer them a recording contract. Throughout the show, Bono makes remarks about U2's imminent break-through. Announcing *Another Day*, he says, "I think we've shown a lot of people what we can do. This is our new single, it's out on the CBS label, it won't be out on CBS label for long, I can tell you that story there. Things will not be the same in this city for us..."

After the show, in their dressing room, U2 are offered a deal by Bill Stewart, talent scout for Island Records, who had seen the band play London last December. He and Island's press officer Rob Partridge are very impressed, and U2's *Hot Press* poll victory further increases their belief in the band. Island Records president Chris Blackwell is also keen to sign U2. Though details of the contract have yet to be finalised, Island will agree to the band's insistence on having total artistic control: U2 will deliver their records complete with sleeve artwork and Island will release them without interfering with U2's finished product in any way. After negotiations, Island offer U2 a world-wide contract for four albums over the next four years, after which Island will have options. During the first 12 months, Island will issue three U2 singles and their début album.

At the Country Club

Dublin, April 17, 1980

MARCH 19, 1980. LONDON, ACKLAM HALL

■ 'Sense of Ireland Festival', third night, line-up: U2, Berlin, Virgin Prunes

U2 perform at the third night of the 'Sense Of Ireland Festival', organised to showcase Irish talent. Numerous Island Records' executives come to check out U2 before the contracts are signed. This time, the band don't fail to impress; four days later the contracts are signed.

The Sense of Ireland
PRESENTS

THE SOUNDS OF IRELAND

— OPENING SPECIAL —

SUN. 16th MARCH 7.30 p.m.

Venue **THE TEARJERKERS**
MOONDOGS • RUDI
PLUS GUESTS   ADM. £3

MON. 17th MARCH 7.30 p.m.

THE **LYCEUM**

RORY GALLAGHER

ADM. £4   PLUS SPECIAL GUESTS

ST. PATRICK'S NIGHT 17th MARCH

Venue BRITISH DEBUT
THE ATRIX
D.C. NIEN
ADM. £3   PLUS GUESTS

WED. 19th MARCH 8 p.m.

ACKLAM
HALL
BERLIN
U2 • VIRGIN PRUNES   ADM. £2

IRELAND HAS MADE AN EXTRAORDINARILY CREATIVE AND INNOVATIVE CONTRIBUTION TO THE INTERNATIONAL MUSIC SCENE: THE S. OF I. IS THUS PARTICULARLY HAPPY TO PRESENT BOTH THE PIONEERING RORY GALLAGHER AND THE FRESHEST AND BEST OF THE NEW BANDS — NORTH AND SOUTH THE FLOW OF PERFORMING TALENT CONTINUES

11 O'CLOCK TICK TOCK TOUR: UNITED KINGDOM, SPRING 1980

The track *11 O'Clock Tick Tock*, previously called *Silver Lining*, is released as a single on May 23, 1980, backed with the song *Touch*, which used to be called *Trevor*. Produced by Martin Hannet, it's U2's first release for Island Records. In support, U2 do a UK club tour that will see them play outside London for the first time. The audiences are usually 100-200 strong.

WIP 6601

U2

THEIR NEW SINGLE

11·O·CLOCK·TICK·TOCK

ON SALE NOW!

PRODUCTION
MARTIN HANNETT

TOUR DATES

MAY

```
22 · LONDON · HOPE & ANCHOR
23 · LONDON · MOONLIGHT CLUB
24 · SHEFFIELD · UNIVERSITY
26 · BRIGHTON · NEW REGENT
27 · LONDON · ROCK GARDEN
28 · BRISTOL · TRINITY HALL
29 · BIRMINGHAM · CEDAR BALLROOMS
30 · LONDON · NASHVILLE
31 · MANCHESTER · POLYTECHNIC
```

JUNE

```
2 · NUNEATON · 77 CLUB
3 · NOTTINGHAM · BOAT CLUB
4 · MANCHESTER · BEACH CLUB
5 · LEEDS · FAN CLUB
6 · DUDLEY · JB'S
7 · LONDON · MARQUEE
8 · LONDON · HALF MOON
```

ISLAND

Ballymun, April 17, 1980

MAY 22, 1980 LONDON, HOPE & ANCHOR

■ Support: Fashion

MAY 23, 1980 LONDON, MOONLIGHT CLUB

■ Support: Fashion

MAY 24, 1980. SHEFFIELD, UNIVERSITY

■ Support: Fashion

MAY 26, 1980. BRIGHTON, NEW REGENT

■ Support: Fashion

MAY 27, 1980. LONDON, ROCK GARDEN

■ Support: Fashion

MAY 28, 1980. BRISTOL, TRINITY HALL

■ Support: Fashion

MAY 29, 1980. BIRMINGHAM, CEDAR BALLROOM

■ Support: Fashion

To establish contact, Bono jumps into the crowd and is followed by Edge and Adam, who move beyond the reach of their guitar-cables. The plugs shoot out, leaving only Bono and Larry audible until they get it together again.

MAY 30, 1980. LONDON, NASHVILLE

■ Support: Fashion

MAY 31, 1980. MANCHESTER, POLYTECHNIC

■ Support: Fashion

JUNE 2, 1980. UNEATON, 77 CLUB

■ Support: Fashion

JUNE 3, 1980. NOTTINGHAM, BOAT CLUB

■ Support: Fashion

JUNE 4, 1980. MANCHESTER, BEACH CLUB

■ Support: Fashion

JUNE 5, 1980. LEEDS, FAN CLUB

■ Support: Fashion

JUNE 6, 1980. DUDLEY, J.B.'S

■ Support: Fashion

JUNE 7, 1980. LONDON, MARQUEE CLUB

■ Support: Fashion
U2's first show at the famous Marquee Club, London.

JUNE 8, 1980. LONDON, HALF MOON CLUB

■ Support: Fashion
After the UK tour, U2 commence work on their first album, to be released by Island Records in the fall. With Steve Lillywhite as producer, the band work at Windmill Lane Studios in Dublin,

recording a selection of the 30 or so songs they have been playing in the last two years, and improving tracks they had earlier recorded as demos.

JULY 10, 1980. LONDON, CLARENDON HOTEL

■ Attendance: ca. 200; (capacity 500)
■ Support: Midnight & The Lemon Boys, Medium Medium
The show is attended largely by journalists and Island Records' staff. Because of the low number of actual paying customers, the atmosphere is strained. Bill Graham writes in *Hot Press*: 'The circumstances of environment and audience make for a struggling, emotionally naked gig. There's nothing inaccurate or unfeeling about the band's playing but the confrontation between band and the worldiest audience of the tour has its moments when the dare-devil comes close to desperation. With wild determination, Bono keeps bringing his toys to them, keeps demanding 'Look at this' but the chemistry is odd and you know he knows it. The audience have come to measure U2 against their building reputation as 'at least this week's thing' and won't be willed into enjoyment.

'Despite a small crowd bopping around the front, Bono just can't feel the audience. Suddenly out of the unsettled climate wafts a moment of sublime dignity. A sequence of guitar chords - the linking passage between two new songs, *An Cat Dubh* and *The Heart Of A Child (Into The Heart)* steadily spirals upwards and for once the echoing acoustics assist. Soothing, a peace offering, this vision of unwasted youth transforms the mood and when the song is over there's a muted, sighing cheer of recognition. Such

sweet thunder! Doubt diminishes, though Bono's still fraught on the encore *I Will Follow* and a triplet of fans joins them on stage. One wears a T-shirt of Sid Vicious, the man whose manipulated inauthentic self-detonating rebellion represents everything U2 stand against. A small stubborn step forward for U2 has been achieved.'

JULY 11, 1980. LONDON, HALF MOON CLUB

Good crowd participation inspires the band to deliver a powerful performance. The show is a milestone for U2, as it's the first time they've sold out a concert venue in the United Kingdom.

JULY 12, 1980. LONDON, MOONLIGHT CLUB

Paul McGuinness gets the band a bottle of champagne to celebrate their progress: this show is sold out as well, with 200 people locked outside without tickets. U2's touring is beginning to bear fruit as word is spreading through town and the band establish a small London following.

JULY, 1980. LONDON, MARQUEE CLUB

U2 play as support to The Photos.

JULY 27, 1980. DUBLIN, LEIXLIP CASTLE

■ Attendance: 15,000
■ 'Dublin Festival 1980'; line-up: John Olwan, Moondogs, Skafish, Q-Tips, Squeeze, U2, The Police
■ Set includes: *Another Day / 11 O'Clock Tick Tock / Shadows And Tall Trees / A Day Without Me / Twilight*
U2 play their first show at an open-air festival before a large crowd.

JULY 28, 1980. DUBLIN

■ 'Dublin Festival 1980'; 'Dalymount Festival'

Clarendon Hotel

THE 'BOY' TOUR, LEG 1: UNITED KINGDOM, EUROPE, FALL 1980

With the work on their first album, called 'Boy', finished and release set for October, U2 embark on a lengthy UK tour to announce its release and preview the songs. Stretching throughout the country, U2 reach many places for the first time, as well as playing dates in Holland and Belgium in between. Wanting a more visual stage presentation, the concerts are illustrated by a large backdrop showing the sleeve of the upcoming 'Boy' album, with seven-year old Peter Rowan as the symbol of innocence and purity.

SEPTEMBER 6, 1980. COVENTRY, GENERAL WOOLFE

SEPTEMBER 7, 1980. LONDON, LYCEUM BALLROOM

- Attendance: 1,500
- Line-up: The Books, The Au Pairs, Delta 5, U2, Echo & The Bunnymen
- Set: 11 O'Clock Tick Tock / I Will Follow / Stories For Boys / An Cat Dubh / Into The Heart / A Day Without Me / Twilight / Electric Co. / 11 O'Clock Tick Tock

U2 perform before Echo & The Bunnymen in one of the main London rock venues. Knowing how cynical a London audience can be, Bono is insecure about facing a large crowd who haven't come primarily for them. "I don't know how you feel about people like ourselves. We're sort of giving out a lot of our flesh and passion. I was told you didn't like that sort of thing, so I tried hard to think, well, I better keep it steady or..." The crowd offer practically no response throughout the show, leaving a frustrated Bono to make sarcastic remarks. When he points out The Edge during his solo in Electric Co., Bono confronts the crowd's lack of reaction by twitching his fingers and demanding, "Check! Attention!" A powerful version of 11 O'Clock Tick Tock ends the show as it had started, but gets hardly any applause. Bono drops the microphone on the floor as the band leave the stage.

SEPTEMBER 8, 1980. LONDON, MARQUEE CLUB

This is the first of four Monday evening shows at the Marquee.

SEPTEMBER 9, 1980. BRISTOL, BERKELEY

SEPTEMBER 11, 1980. HULL, WELLINGTON CLUB

SEPTEMBER 12, 1980. SCARBOROUGH, TABOO CLUB

- Support: Midnight & The Lemon Boys
- Set: 11 O'Clock Tick Tock / I Will Follow / Touch / An Cat Dubh / Into The Heart / A Day Without Me / Twilight / Electric Co. / Things To Make and Do / Stories For Boys / Boy-Girl / Out Of Control / encore: 11 O'Clock Tick Tock

"Somebody told me you would be a difficult audience, but I don't believe that," Bono calls out optimistically after the opening song. The small crowd are very quiet. Only a few clap when a song has finished. Bono sighs, "Look, I'm not asking you to crack skulls here, but..." A rousing version of Out Of Control leaves hardly any impression either, but the band come back for an encore nevertheless.

SEPTEMBER 13, 1980. LEEDS, QUEEN'S HALL

- Attendance: 4,000
- 'Futurama Festival'; line-up: Eaten Alive By Insects, Soft Cell, The Distributors, Music For Pleasure, Y?, Vena Cava, Blah Blah Blah, Modern English, I'm So Hollow, Acrobats Of Desire, Altered Images, The Mirror Boys, Guy Jackson, Clock DVA, Wasted Youth, Simple Minds, U2, League Of Gentlemen, Bill Nelson, Robert Fripp, Siouxsie & The Banshees.

In Melody Maker, Lynden Barber writes that there is an unpleasant atmosphere surrounding the festival. 'Despite the conditions, U2 perform brilliantly, throwing themselves maniacally into their set, lifting the audience's emotions out of their depressing physical surroundings. U2 play truly great rock music which inspires the heart. They make Echo & The Bunnymen sound as stupid as their name.'

SEPTEMBER 15, 1980. LONDON, MARQUEE CLUB

- Support: Vision Collision

SEPTEMBER 16, 1980. PLYMOUTH, FIESTA SUITE

- Set: The Ocean / 11 O'Clock Tick Tock / I Will Follow / Touch / An Cat Dubh / Into The Heart / A Day Without Me / Twilight / Electric Co. / Things To Make And Do / Stories For Boys / Boy-Girl / Out Of Control

SEPTEMBER 17, 1980. PENZANCE, DEMELZAS

SEPTEMBER 18, 1980. TOTNES, CIVIC HALL

SEPTEMBER 19, 1980. STROUD, MARSHALL ROOMS

- Support: Midnight & The Lemon Boys

SEPTEMBER 21, 1980. WOLLASTON, NAG'S HEAD

SEPTEMBER 22, 1980. LONDON, MARQUEE CLUB

- Support: Jane Kennaway & Strange Behaviour, Jerry Floyd

SEPTEMBER 23, 1980. SHEFFIELD, LIMIT CLUB

SEPTEMBER 24, 1980. BIRMINGHAM, BOGART'S

SEPTEMBER 25, 1980. LIVERPOOL, BRADY'S

SEPTEMBER 26, 1980. BIRMINGHAM, CEDAR BALLROOM

SEPTEMBER 27, 1980. COVENTRY, POLYTECHNIC

SEPTEMBER 29, 1980. LONDON, MARQUEE CLUB

SEPTEMBER 30, 1980. BRIGHTON, POLYTECHNIC

SEPTEMBER, 1980. LONDON, MAIDA VALE STUDIOS

- Set: I Will Follow / Electric Co. / An Cat Dubh / Into The Heart
Recorded for Richard Skinner's programme.

OCTOBER 2, 1980. LEEDS, FAN CLUB

OCTOBER 3, 1980. RETFORD, PORTERHOUSE

OCTOBER 4, 1980. LONDON, SCHOOL OF ECONOMICS

OCTOBER 5, 1980. LONDON, HALF MOON CLUB

OCTOBER 7, 1980. NOTTINGHAM, BOAT CLUB

OCTOBER 9, 1980. MANCHESTER, POLYTECHNIC

OCTOBER 11, 1980. LONDON, KINGSTON POLYTECHNIC

In an interview in early October, Bono tells Dave McCullough of *Sounds*: "When I was thirteen I had a vision of myself standing in front of thousands of people. I wasn't even sure I was going to be in a group, I thought I might be a politician or something, but I knew one day I was going to be standing in front of many thousands of people. I have seen this vision come truer and truer. It's ridiculous, for instance, that U2 are where they are now, considering that four years ago we couldn't play our instruments..."

OCTOBER 14, 1980. HILVERSUM, HOLLAND, KRO STUDIOS

■ Set: *11 O'Clock Tick Tock / I Will Follow / Touch / An Cat Dubh / Into The Heart / A Day Without Me / Twilight / Electric Co. / Stories For Boys / Boy-Girl / Out Of Control /* encore: *11 O'Clock Tick Tock*

U2's first performance on the Continent of Europe is for Dutch radio with a small studio audience present. Bono is well aware he is reaching many people through the broadcast. "We're from Dublin, we're a group called U2, we're glad to be here. We release our first album, titled 'Boy', the next week, and you should make sure your record holder has one." Recorded on the 14th, the show is aired the next day. Bono is very aware of that as well, as he says at the end, "We're going now. You can see us in an hour's time at the Milkyway I think." The first version of *11 O'Clock Tick Tock* is not broadcast.

OCTOBER 15, 1980. AMSTERDAM, HOLLAND, THE MILKYWAY

■ Attendance: 500
■ Set: *The Ocean / 11 O'Clock Tick Tock / I Will Follow / Touch / An Cat Dubh / Into The Heart / A Day Without Me / Twilight / Electric Co. / Things To Make And Do / Stories For Boys / Boy-Girl /* encore: *11 O'Clock Tick Tock*

The band get a good response from a moderately enthusiastic crowd and play a powerful set that does not remain unnoticed by the Dutch music press.

OCTOBER 16, 1980. GRONINGEN, HOLLAND, VERA

■ Set includes: *The Ocean / 11 O'Clock Tick Tock / I Will Follow / Touch / An Cat Dubh / Into The Heart / A Day Without Me / Electric Co.*

OCTOBER 17, 1980. APELDOORN, HOLLAND, GIGANT

Bono catches a cold and has trouble finishing the show.

OCTOBER 18, 1980. BRUSSELS, BELGIUM, KLARICK

U2's début in Belgium is marred by the 'flu.

OCTOBER 19, 1980. LONDON, LYCEUM BALLROOM

■ Attendance: 1,500
■ Line-up: The Last Words, Discharge, U2, Slade
Having just returned from their brief Continental trip, the band deliver a tired performance at the Lyceum which receives a stream of negative reviews.

The first Continental gig: The Milkyway

OCTOBER 20, 1980

U2's first album, 'Boy', is released in the UK and Ireland.

NOVEMBER 7, 1980. EXETER, UNIVERSITY

After almost three weeks off, the UK tour to promote 'Boy' continues. The album will reach No. 52 in the UK charts; the *I Will Follow* single doesn't dent the Top 40. Playing mostly universities and rock clubs with a few hundred people in attendance, the itinerary includes several London shows, as well as return visits to venues already played in September.

NOVEMBER 8, 1980. SOUTHAMPTON, UNIVERSITY

NOVEMBER 9, 1980. LONDON, MOONLIGHT CLUB

NOVEMBER 11, 1980. CANTERBURY, KENT UNIVERSITY

■ Set: *Stories For Boys / The Ocean / 11 O'Clock Tick Tock / Touch / An Cat Dubh / Into The Heart / Another Time, Another Place / Electric Co. / Things To Make And Do / Twilight / I Will Follow / Father Is An Elephant*

A revised set opens with *Stories For Boys* and includes the melodic song called *Father Is An Elephant*, which will be performed only a couple of times.

NOVEMBER 12, 1980. BRADFORD, UNIVERSITY

NOVEMBER 13, 1980. SHEFFIELD, LIMIT CLUB

NOVEMBER 14, 1980. KIDDERMINSTER, TOWN HALL

NOVEMBER 15, 1980. BRISTOL, POLYTECHNIC

NOVEMBER 18, 1980. READING, UNIVERSITY

■ Support: Medium Medium

NOVEMBER 19, 1980. WOLVERHAMPTON, POLYTECHNIC.

■ Support: Medium Medium

NOVEMBER 20, 1980. BLACKPOOL, POLYTECHNIC

NOVEMBER 21, 1980. EDINBURGH, NITE CLUB

■ Attendance: 400; sellout
■ Set (incomplete): *Stories For Boys / The Ocean / 11 O'Clock Tick Tock / Touch / An Cat Dubh / Into The Heart / Another Time, Another Place / Cry-Electric Co. / 11 O'Clock Tick Tock / The Ocean / Father Is An Elephant*

The tour reaches Scotland. "This is our first time in your country, it's sold out, we're very flattered," Bono calls out. In the UK press, 'Boy' has been getting rave reviews, but the tour has reaped mixed response. "Don't believe everything you read in the papers," Bono stresses. "Make up your own mind."

Electric Co. is preceded by a brief, sharp edged guitar bit that from now on will be played every time the song is performed. Called *The Cry*, Bono sings, "So many, so many cry, so many cry... so many eyes, so many eyes, in somebody's eyes. So many cry, but I can't see why or what for," followed by the soaring intro to *Electric Co.* (*The Cry's* guitar riff will later show up on the 'October' album as the opening chords of the track *Is That All?*) Bono dedicates *Father Is An Elephant* to his father.

NOVEMBER 22, 1980 LIVERPOOL, BRADY'S

NOVEMBER 24, 1980. COVENTRY, POLYTECHNIC

NOVEMBER 26, 27, 1980. LONDON, MARQUEE CLUB

■ Support: Jerry Floyd & Friends
'Only a blind man and the dead could ignore the passion and charisma generated by singer Bono,' Gavin Martin writes in *New Musical Express*. 'The very essence which underpins the perfor-

mance is an electric vibrancy between the stage and the dance floor. It's something loads of groups try for but only a few can achieve. Bono carries it to the edge of the stage, crouches and curls upwards, writhing like a tiger and uncoiling like a snake through a forest of outstretched arms and pawning hands. It's unique spectacle and a unique feeling: the only comparison I can think of is with some old Iggy Pop footage once shown on Old Grey Whistle Test.'

NOVEMBER 28, 1980. BIRMINGHAM, ASTON UNIVERSITY

■ Set: *Stories For Boys / The Ocean / 11 O'Clock Tick Tock / Touch / An Cat Dubh / Into The Heart / Another Time, Another Place / Cry-Electric Co. / Things To Make And Do / Twilight / I Will Follow / encore: 11 O'Clock Tick Tock / The Ocean / Father Is An Elephant*

NOVEMBER 29, 1980. STOKE, KEELE UNIVERSITY

NOVEMBER 30, 1980. BRIGHTON, JENKINSON'S

DECEMBER 1, 1980. LONDON, HAMMERSMITH ODEON

U2 team up with The Talking Heads to play in their support for two London dates and a show in Paris.

DECEMBER 2, 1980. LONDON, HAMMERSMITH PALAIS

DECEMBER 3, 1980. PARIS, FRANCE, BALTARD PAVILION

■ Attendance: 1,200
■ Set: *11 O'Clock Tick Tock / An Cat Dubh / Into The Heart / Another Time, Another Place / Cry-Electric Co. / Things To Make And Do / Twilight / I Will Follow / encore: 11 O'Clock Tick Tock*

At their first performance in France, Bono attempts to address the crowd in their own language. "Uhm, let me see... nous appelle U2, et we sont... er... is that alright?" The Talking Heads fans respond to U2 reasonably well. "We're going to New York tomorrow, so we'll say hello for you."

THE 'BOY' TOUR, LEG 2: AMERICA, DECEMBER 1980

With their first album in shops throughout Europe, and critics recognising the purity and passion of their music, the time has come for U2 to stretch their wings out to the rest of the world. In Ireland and the UK, U2 have slowly but surely managed to build a following through their live performances. There is no reason to think that this method will not work in the United States, the country where rock & roll originated thirty years ago and where most of today's popular music is produced. America is also the largest market in the world for records.

Frank Barsalona, the head of Premier Talent, the biggest booking agency in America, agrees to represent U2 in the United States. Barsalona has never seen or even heard U2, but is persuaded to work with them by Island Records' boss Chris Blackwell. U2 will need to tour America intensively. The country is fragmented: each state and each city has its own audience, its own newspaper, and every type of music on its own radio stations. You can be famous in Texas, but people in the other 49 states may never have heard of you. Conquering America will therefore require constant touring in all the major cities. For now, Barsalona books a small series of gigs around the East coast, some of which are in support of other bands. The mini-tour is meant to gain U2 their first American fans and ignite some publicity which should pave the way for a much larger, nation-wide tour early in the new year.

DECEMBER 6, 1980. NEW YORK, NY, THE RITZ

Because a show planned for the previous night at the Penny Arcade in Rochester, NY, is cancelled, U2 find themselves in one of the country's most prestigious venues for their American début. Originally a dance hall, The Ritz is filled with outgoing people dancing, drinking and having a good time while they occasionally glance at whoever is playing. As U2's set progresses, they slowly get through as more and more people get into the music and quit their conversation to watch.

Up in the balcony observing U2, Frank Barsalona goes wild with enthusiasm as he sees the critical New York crowd applauding the show. Realising he has booked a winner, Barsalona rushes into the dressing room after their set to congratulate them.

DECEMBER 7, 1980. WASHINGTON, DC, BAYOU CLUB

■ Attendance: 200

DECEMBER 8, 1980. BUFFALO, NY, STAGE ONE

U2 open for the Buffalo-based trio Talas.

DECEMBER 9, 1980. TORONTO, CANADA, EL MOCAMBO

The news of John Lennon's murder in New York the night before inspires an angry and emotional performance. U2's début show in Canada gets ecstatic reviews in the papers.

DECEMBER 11, 1980. NEW YORK, NY, MUDD CLUB

DECEMBER 12, 1980. PROVIDENCE, RI, MAIN EVENT

DECEMBER 13, 1980. BOSTON, MA, PARADISE THEATER

■ Attendance: 150; (capacity 500)
■ Set: *11 O'Clock Tick Tock / An Cat Dubh / Into The Heart / Another Time, Another Place / Cry-Electric Co. / Things To Make And Do / Twilight / I Will Follow / encore: 11 O'Clock Tick Tock / encore: Out Of Control*

U2 support Detroit band Barooga before a small but enthusiastic crowd. Bono sings a line of John Lennon's *Give Peace A Chance* in *Electric Co*. "I would like to tell you that we're called U2, and we're not just another English band passing through," he says. "We're only really coming into the country to see what the place and the people are like, and we're coming back here next year. But this tour has been better than we expected, thank you very much!" The crowd hoot for another encore. Though U2 are the support act, most of the crowd leave after their set. Around 40 people remain to see Barooga, some of whom are members of U2 and their crew.

DECEMBER 14, 1980. NEW HAVEN, CT, TOAD'S PLACE

DECEMBER 15, 1980. PHILADELPHIA, PA, BIJOU CAFE

DECEMBER 17, 1980. BELFAST, ULSTER HALL

One show in Northern Ireland is followed by four Irish dates.

DECEMBER 18, 1980. GALWAY, LEISURELAND

DECEMBER 19, 1980. SLIGO, BAYMOUNT

DECEMBER 20, 1980. CORK, DOWNTOWN KAMPUS

DECEMBER 22, 1980. DUBLIN, TV CLUB

■ Support: Microdisney

JANUARY, 1981. BELFAST, QUEEN'S UNIVERSITY

- Set: *The Ocean / 11 O'Clock Tick Tock / An Cat Dubh / Into The Heart / Another Time, Another Place / Cry-Electric Co. / I Will Follow / A Day Without Me / Out Of Control.*

U2 and Stiff Little Fingers perform for a BBC Northern Ireland TV special. "A month ago we hadn't played Belfast properly, I regret that," Bono tells the crowd. Curiously, he wears a headband and a big fur coat for the first few songs. During *Out Of Control* he jumps into the audience and sings on while he is touched and grabbed from all sides. He tries to climb back on stage but trips and falls flat on his face. *The Ocean, 11 O'Clock Tick Tock, Cry-Electric Co.* and *Out Of Control* will be broadcast on August 12.

JANUARY 24, 1981. GLASGOW, STRATHCLYDE UNIVERSITY

- Attendance: 1,000; sellout
- Support: Altered Images
- Set: *The Ocean / 11 O'Clock Tick Tock / Touch / An Cat Dubh / Into The Heart / Another Time, Another Place / Cry-Electric Co. / Things To Make And Do / Stories For Boys / Twilight / I Will Follow / 11 O'Clock Tick Tock / The Ocean.*

Before *Twilight* Bono points to the 'Boy' backdrop. "This here is Peter... I'll tell you about Peter. We're going to the USA next week and Peter isn't allowed in there." The 'Boy' album sleeve has been deemed unsuitable for America because some narrow minds in the record industry think that the pure image of a young boy might associate the band with paedophilia or child pornography. 'Boy' will be released in America in March in a different sleeve from the European album but U2 will use the backdrop during their concerts. Bono dedicates *Twilight* to Peter.

JANUARY 25, 1981. EDINBURGH, VALENTINO'S CLUB

- Support: Altered Images

JANUARY 26, 1981. YORK, UNIVERSITY

- Attendance: 1,300
- Support: Altered Images

JANUARY 27, 1981. MANCHESTER, POLYTECHNIC

- Support: Altered Images

JANUARY 28, 1981. NORWICH, UNIVERSITY OF EAST ANGLIA

- Attendance: 900
- Support: Altered Images

JANUARY 29, 1981. NORTHAMPTON, IRON HORSE

- Support: Altered Images
- Set: same as Glasgow, with *Out Of Control* at the end instead of *11 O'Clock / The Ocean.*

A few songs into the set, someone comes onstage with an announcement for the audience: "Could you go back a little bit, we've got a very weak stage!"

JANUARY 30, 1981. LOUGHBOROUGH UNIVERSITY

- Support: Altered Images

Lyceum Ballroom

JANUARY 31, 1981. ST. ALBANS, CITY HALL

- Attendance: 1,000
- Support: Manic Jabs

FEBRUARY 1, 1981. LONDON, LYCEUM BALLROOM

- Attendance: 1,000; sellout
- Line-up: Red Beat, Thompson Twins, Delta 5, U2
- Set: *The Ocean / 11 O'Clock Tick Tock / Touch / An Cat Dubh / Into The Heart / Another Time, Another Place / Cry-Electric Co. / Things To Make And Do / Stories For Boys / Twilight / I Will Follow / Out Of Control / All Along The Watchtower / encore: 11 O'Clock Tick Tock.*

This show is a convincing sellout. "Tonight is the end of a complete stage for U2, with regards. A year ago when we came over here we played in support at some very small places; there were 700 people that were left outside tonight..." Surprisingly, U2 play a raw and noisy version of Bob Dylan's *All Along The Watchtower*, sung with Pete Wylie of the band Wah Heat! who is announced by Bono as "one of the new breed".

FEBRUARY 9, 1981. SWEDISH TV: 'MANDAGSBÖRSEN'

- Set: *11 O'Clock Tick Tock / I Will Follow*

On their first TV appearance in Scandinavia U2 perform *11 O'Clock* and *I Will Follow* live in the studio. Bono does some promotional work: "We're called U2, we're from Dublin. We're playing later at the Underground. We released our first album in Sweden, it's called 'Boy'."

FEBRUARY 9, 1981. STOCKHOLM, SWEDEN, UNDERGROUND

FEBRUARY 10, 1981. BRUSSELS, BELGIUM, BEURSSCHOUWBURG

This show is recorded for the TV Programme 'Rock Follies'. Five songs are broadcast four days later.

FEBRUARY 11, 1981. AMSTERDAM, HOLLAND, PARADISO

- Attendance: 600; (capacity 1,000)
- Support: Bugs

Tickets cost 7,50 Guilders. U2 give a strong performance in the Dutch capital's best known rock temple. Earlier in the day Bono and Edge hung out with a photographer in an inner-city bar where Bono played a few tunes on the piano.

FEBRUARY 12, 1981. THE HAGUE, HOLLAND, PAARD VAN TROJE

- Attendance: 500
- Set: *The Ocean / 11 O'Clock Tick Tock / Touch / An Cat Dubh / Into The Heart / Another Time, Another Place / Cry-Electric Co. / Things To Make And Do / Stories For Boys / Twilight / I Will Follow / encore: 11 O'Clock Tick Tock / The Ocean / encore: Out Of Control*

The band soundcheck extensively during the afternoon, playing *I Will Follow* and an instrumental version of *11 O'Clock Tick Tock*. After some jamming they do *An Cat Dubh* and *Into The Heart*, during which Bono checks out the hall's acoustics and sight lines from all angles. The show is recorded for Dutch radio and TV. Unfortunately, after the rigours of the previous evening's show followed by a night on the town, U2 appear somewhat tired. "Tonight can be very special... it's up to you," Bono says, none too inspired by the relatively quiet audience. It takes until *I Will Follow* for the audience to catch on. During *11 O'Clock* Bono dances a jig with a girl from the audience. A second encore of *Out Of Control* is played with fervour, inspiring the crowd to jump up and down. "I'm just waking up!" Bono shouts.

FEBRUARY 13, 1981. ROTTERDAM, HOLLAND, DE LANTAARN

FEBRUARY 14, 1981. SITTARD, HOLLAND, STADSSCHOUWBURG

FEBRUARY 15, 1981. HAMBURG, GERMANY, ONKEL PO'S CARNEGIE HALL

■ Set: *11 O'Clock Tick Tock / Touch / An Cat Dubh / Into The Heart / Another Time, Another Place / Cry-Electric Co. / Things To Make And Do / Stories For Boys / Twilight / I Will Follow /* encore: *Out Of Control / 11 O'Clock Tick Tock / The Ocean*

"We're called U2 and we come from Dublin, Ireland. We haven't played in a place like this for a while, so close," Bono says. "Can you understand me?" The concert starts slowly but the audience liven up towards the end. "When we started to play places like this, it was like audition time for people who'd come and see us," Bono says in the encore. "Well, we don't want to play any more auditions. There's a lot of people here, I think, who like what we're doing. I would like to see those tables moved away, and then we'll play an encore. It'll be very good for everybody." "Move the tables away!" someone in the audience yells. "You don't mind, do you?" Bono asks. "This is the first time in your country, and we wanna do it right." With more space to move around freely, the crowd finally get to their feet during *Out Of Control*.

FEBRUARY 17, 1981. BERLIN, GERMANY, KANTKINO

FEBRUARY 18, 1981. MUNICH, GERMANY, SUGAR SHACK

FEBRUARY 19, 1981. GENEVA, SWITZERLAND, SALLE DU FAUBURG

FEBRUARY 20, 1981. LYON, FRANCE, ECOLE NATIONAL DES TRAVAUX

FEBRUARY 21, 1981. PARIS, FRANCE, LE PALACE

FEBRUARY 28, 1981. UK TV: 'OLD GREY WHISTLE TEST'

■ Set: *The Ocean / 11 O'Clock Tick Tock / I Will Follow*
This is U2's début on the BBC's long running TV rock show. Against the 'Boy' backdrop, the band play well, but look a little out of place in a TV studio with its small audience and bright lights. "Hello... I'm the singer with U2... this is *11 O'Clock Tick Tock*," Bono announces timidly.

Amsterdam bar, February 11, 1981

THE 'BOY' TOUR, LEG 3: AMERICA, SPRING 1981

The quick December trip has stirred some media attention in America. Progressive music fans on the East coast have noted their name and read favourable reviews. Island Records release 'Boy' in America in March, with distribution by Warner Brothers, coinciding with a lengthy tour that will see U2 play rock clubs throughout the country. Warner Brothers finance the tour. They see the band's potential and are convinced that many people will like to buy the album. In the absence of nationwide radio airplay, the best way for the band to build a following is to expose themselves and play as many shows to as many people as possible.

Determined to conquer America, the band are eager to confront audiences that yet don't know them. Frank Barsalona, the head of Premier Talent, books venues known for presenting young, progressive bands. Interviews are granted to any magazine or paper that's interested. U2 and their entourage travel by bus, which, because of the enormous distances, means more time is spent just sitting in the tour bus than anything else. They often have to leave straight after a gig, travelling all night in order to make it to the next town in time. Driving through the vast open spaces of America inspires the band and Bono spends many hours writing, scribbling notes for songs and lyrics in a booklet.

MARCH 3, 1981 (TWO SHOWS). WASHINGTON, DC, BAYOU CLUB

■ Attendance: 500
■ Set: *The Ocean / 11 O'Clock Tick Tock / Touch / An Cat Dubh / Into The Heart / Another Time, Another Place / Cry-Electric Co. / Things To Make And Do / Stories For Boys / Twilight / I Will Follow / Out Of Control*
Harry Sumrall writes a positive review in the *Washington Post* the next day. 'Forget the other groups. Remember U2. The Dublin-based group appeared last night at the Bayou and this city's perception of New Wave may never be the same. Tearing away at the crowd with searing guitar solos and jittery, electronically echoed vocals, U2 also brought to their

performance a sense of refinement that has been lacking in rock for some time... U2, like The Police and The Clash, are taking New Wave to the next, higher, musical level. Their music is still simple, but never simplistic – and simply marvellous.'

Wide awake in America

MARCH 4, 1981. PHILADELPHIA, PA, BIJOU CAFE

- Attendance: 250
- Set: *The Ocean / 11 O'Clock Tick Tock / Touch / An Cat Dubh / Into The Heart / Another Time, Another Place / Cry-Electric Co. / Things To Make And Do / Stories For Boys / Twilight / I Will Follow /* encore: *Out Of Control / 11 O'Clock Tick Tock / The Ocean*

The Ocean and *11 O'Clock Tick Tock* are both played twice, opening and closing the show. "We played here a while ago," Bono says, referring to their December show. "And we told them that we weren't just another English band passing through and that we intend to come back here. Well, we are back, and thank you for coming!" Later Bono says that they had been warned about American radio's conservative attitudes and that it would be hard to get airplay. "I really believe that's gonna change, especially here in Philadelphia; you got some good radio here. The good news is that our first album 'Boy' has just got into the charts today – it's at 135, which is a start."

MARCH 5, 1981. ALBANY, NY, J.B. SCOTT'S

- Attendance: 400
- Support: Mission of Burma

MARCH 6, 1981 (TWO SHOWS). BOSTON, MA, PARADISE THEATER

- Attendance: 1,000; sellout
- Support: La Peste
- Set first show: same as Philadelphia.

As in Washington DC, U2 play two shows on one night. Both Paradise shows have sold out, following the band's successful opening show for Barooga back in December. Local radio station WBCN has been supporting U2 ever since, playing

tracks from 'Boy' and advertising the shows.

At the first show, Bono remarks that much good music has come out of Boston and that tonight's, as well as the previous night's, support band come from the city. He mentions speaking with Mission of Burma's singer about the way new American bands help each other out and appreciate each other. A far cry from the situation in Dublin, Bono explains, where bands don't give each other the time of day. The crowd are highly enthusiastic over U2's blistering set, and scream for *Out Of Control* when the band come back for the encore.

The show is recorded and used for promotional purposes by Warner Brothers, who feel the power of U2's live performance should be emphasised to increase radio interest. They supply DJ's throughout the country with a promotional album containing the live recording.

Officially, several songs from the recording are used as B-sides of singles. *Out Of Control* appears on the B-side of the American *I Will Follow* single, released in April 1981. In July, the single *Fire / J. Swallow* is released in the UK and Ireland, with a limited edition issued as a double pack, and a second 7" disc with *Cry-Electric Co.* and *11 O'Clock Tick Tock* from the Boston show is given away free. *11 O'Clock Tick Tock* and *The Ocean* are used on the 12" version of the single also issued on CD in early 1992. In October 1981, *I Will Follow* from this show appears on the B-side of the *Gloria* single.

- Set second show: *Twilight / 11 O'Clock Tick Tock / I Will Follow / An Cat Dubh / Into The Heart / Another Time, Another Place / Cry-Electric Co. / Things To Make And Do / Stories For Boys / Boy-Girl / Out Of Control / 11 O'Clock Tick Tock / I Will Follow*

Surprisingly, *Twilight* opens the show and *Boy-Girl* is added after a long absence.

MARCH 7, 1981. NEW YORK, NY, THE RITZ

- Attendance: 1,600
- Support: Our Daughter's Wedding
- Set: same as Philadelphia.

U2's New York début in December has raised curiosity and the Ritz is as good as sold out. Bono asks why everybody has come to the dance hall this Saturday night. "We were told that it doesn't matter who you are, people are here for the booze, is that right?" "Noooo!" the audience cry. "These people are here to see us, OK. Maybe some of you don't know who we are. Well, hello, I'm Bono, I'm the singer, this is The Edge, the guitar player, this is Adam, this is Larry, this is the Ritz, this is *Out Of Control*, thank you!"

MARCH 9, 1981. MONTREAL, CANADA, LE CLUB

MARCH 10, 1981. OTTAWA, CANADA, BARRYMORE'S

MARCH 11, 1981. TORONTO, CANADA, MAPLE LEAF BALLROOM

MARCH 14, 1981. SAN DIEGO, CA, GLOBE THEATER

- Set: same as Philadelphia.

MARCH 15, 1981. RESEDA, CA, COUNTRY CLUB

- Attendance: 600; sellout
- Set: *The Ocean / Twilight / I Will Follow / 11 O'Clock Tick Tock / An Cat Dubh / Into The Heart / Another Time, Another Place / Cry-Electric Co. / Things To Make And Do / Stories For Boys / Boy-Girl / Out Of Control /* encore: *11 O'Clock Tick Tock / The Ocean /* encore: *I Will Follow / A Day Without Me*

A changed set includes *Boy-Girl* and *A Day Without Me*. The progressive local radio station KROQ has been playing U2's music for weeks and has announced their coming to the Los Angeles area, which largely contributes to this concert selling out. The audience look on expectantly but after 30 minutes the ice is broken.

MARCH 16, 1981. ANAHEIM, CA, WOODSTOCK

- Attendance: 12; (capacity 400)

Nobody realises U2 are playing another concert in the LA metropolitan area and only a dozen people show up.

MARCH 18, 1981. SAN JOSE, CA, STATE COLLEGE AUDITORIUM

- Attendance: 2,000; (capacity 1,000!)
- Support: Romeo Void
- Set: *The Ocean / 11 O'Clock Tick Tock / I Will Follow / An Cat*

Dubh / Into The Heart / Another Time, Another Place / Cry-Electric Co. / Things To Make And Do / Stories For Boys / Boy-Girl / Out Of Control / encore: A Day Without Me / 11 O'Clock Tick Tock / The Ocean

The cigarette act

Howie Klein reviews the show in a local newspaper: 'The auditorium in the Student Union of San Jose State was probably built to hold about a thousand people. No one at the school figured a relatively unknown band from Dublin, Ireland would draw nearly twice as many anxious fans as the room could properly hold. They did. And it seemed that each and every one of them wanted to dance – vigorously – on the earthquake-proof floor, which is built on springs and is capable of vibrating the entire building with the right stimulus. U2 was definitely the right stimulus. If their album tends towards an arty presentation of their abstract and spiritual – even subtle and delicate material, their live show was every bit as aggressive, direct and powerful.

'For a band whose members pride themselves on their fiercely guarded individualism, onstage they are a remarkably well-coordinated unit. They are precision players, perfectionists. The Edge, an extraordinarily inventive and tastefully colorful guitarist, sounds like he's grinding away on two or three axes simultaneously. It tends to make for a big sound, a psychedelically resurgent sound. The rhythm section, drummer Larry Mullen and bassist Adam Clayton, are the backbone of material that is quirky and diverse enough so that one never loses sight of the fact that a real flesh and blood experience is transpiring.

'Lead singer Bono was all over the stage, putting every ounce of energy into communicating on many levels. (Who expects this from such a sensitive poet?) His songs concern that very special time of personal evolution when a boy starts to become a man. The band has an exquisitely spiritual way of dealing with the subject, with lyrics and music interwoven to get across the same point.

'I don't remember whether they did three or four encores. I just remember getting the distinct impression that if they hadn't called it off, the audience would have probably gotten them to do the whole set over again.'

MARCH 19, 20, 1981. SAN FRANCISCO, CA, THE OLD WALDORF

- Support: Romeo Void
- Attendance: 1,200; sellout

MARCH 22, 1981. PORTLAND, OR, FOG HORN

A successful, energetic, sold out show. Later, in the dressing room, the band receive guests and afterwards Bono discovers that somebody has stolen his briefcase containing his notebook with song ideas and lyrics for the next album.

MARCH 23, 1981. SEATTLE, WA, ASTOR PARK

MARCH 24, 1981. VANCOUVER, CANADA, COMMODORE BALLROOM

- Attendance: 1,000

MARCH 26, 1981. SALT LAKE CITY, UT, NEW FACES CLUB

MARCH 28, 1981. DENVER, CO, RAINBOW MUSIC HALL

- Attendance: 1,400; sellout
- Set: same as Reseda, with *A Day Without Me* after *Out Of Control* instead of at the end.

"I'd just like to say we are not just another English band passing through. First of all we're Irish, and we're spending about three months here, so that's not passing through." The Denver audience are open to U2. After thunderous applause the band return for an encore of *A Day Without Me*, for which Bono straps on a guitar. "This is where I get to play guitar... Stop laughing!"

The local concert promoter, Chuck Morris, is very impressed with the concert and the next day he takes U2 and their manager to the Red Rocks Amphitheater, high up in the Rocky Mountains, where big concerts take place during the summer. "You'll play here some day," he assures the young band.

MARCH 30, 1981. LUBBOCK, TX, THE ROX

The first of four shows in Texas. At one show Paul McGuinness asks the club owner to pay the band in cash. The club owner pulls a gun, insisting that U2 accept payment by cheque, just like everybody else.

MARCH 31, 1981. AUSTIN, TX, THE CLUB FOOT

APRIL 1, 1981. HOUSTON, TX, CARDI'S

APRIL 2, 1981. DALLAS, TX, BIJOU

APRIL 3, 1981. OKLAHOMA CITY, OK, QUICKSILVER'S

APRIL 4, 1981. TULSA, OK, CAINES BALLROOM

APRIL 6, 1981. KANSAS CITY, MO, UPTOWN THEATER

- Support: Romeo Void
- Set: *The Ocean / 11 O'Clock Tick Tock / I Will Follow / An Cat Dubh / Into The Heart / Another Time, Another Place / Cry-Electric Co. / Things To Make And Do / Stories For Boys / Boy-Girl / Out Of Control / encore: A Day Without Me / 11 O'Clock Tick Tock / The Ocean / I Will Follow*

After passing through Texas and Oklahoma the tour reaches the

Mid-West. Bono regularly improvises during most shows, replacing lyrics with new words that come to mind. *Another Time, Another Place* is dedicated to those on the balcony of the theatre. By law they are not allowed downstairs – where alcohol is sold – because they are under 21. "You can't come down here because you're under 21, is that right? Well, earlier on this afternoon the gentleman promoter came up to me and he told me I couldn't go down here either 'cause I'm under 21, and so is everybody here." Bono tries extra hard to reach the people up there. "Now, this is something we can do – everybody on the top floor... show me, I wanna see you!" he shouts after an exceptionally loud *Out Of Control*. *I Will Follow* closes the show and leaves the audience in a state of frenzy.

APRIL 7, 1981. ST. LOUIS, MO, WASHINGTON UNIVERSITY GRAHAM CHAPEL

- Attendance: 600
- Set: same as Kansas City.

Bono remarks that he has heard there are a lot of people here tonight who have read about the band and come to check them out. After the first encore of *A Day Without Me* the audience applaud the band for several minutes and they return for another three songs.

APRIL 9, 1981. MINNEAPOLIS, MN, UNCLE SAM'S

- Attendance: 1,000

U2 do an extensive soundcheck during the afternoon, fiddling around with new melodies and snippets of lyrics that Bono has thought up during shows or on the tour bus.

APRIL 10, 1981. AMES, IA, FILLMORE

APRIL 11, 1981. CHICAGO, IL, UNIVERSITY OF CHICAGO INTERNATIONAL HOUSE

- Set: *The Ocean / 11 O'Clock Tick Tock / I Will Follow / An Cat Dubh / Into The Heart / Another Time, Another Place / Cry-Electric Co. / Things To Make And Do / Stories For Boys / Boy-Girl / Out Of Control / Twilight / I Will Follow / A Day Without Me / 11 O'Clock Tick Tock / The Ocean*

Because tickets cost only $1 and include free beer, many students come out of curiosity. The next day Bono is interviewed on WNVR radio: "What I was impressed with last night was, and this is very important to us, is that we were playing to an audience who basically didn't know who the hell we were. And they were making up their mind before our eyes, and I can see them making up their mind. And I'm seeing it dawn on them that the music isn't what they see. You know, they think, young band from England/Ireland area: they're a new wave band, so they put us up with Blondie or The Police, or other bands that they associate as being new wave. We're not a 'new wave' band, we're not a 'punk' band. I don't know what the hell we are, we are just U2. We're individual, and whatever they thought about their preconceptions, they were wrong. It's an interesting process to watch."

APRIL 12, 1981. CHICAGO, IL, PARK WEST

- Attendance: 1,100; sellout
- Set: same as the night before, but *A Day Without Me* replaces *The Ocean* at the end.

APRIL 14, 1981. MADISON, WI, MERLING'S

APRIL 15, 1981. MILWAUKEE, WI, PALM'S

APRIL 17, 1981. CINCINNATI, OH, BOGART'S CLUB

- Attendance: 800

The girlfriends of Bono, Edge and Larry arrive from Ireland to join the tour and this inspires a powerful, joyous concert during which a new song, *I Fall Down*, is premièred.

APRIL 18, 1981. DETROIT, MI, HARPO'S

- Attendance: 1,400
- Set: *The Ocean / 11 O'Clock Tick Tock / I Will Follow / An Cat Dubh / Into The Heart / Another Time, Another Place / Cry–Electric Co. / I Fall Down / Things To Make And Do / Stories For Boys / Boy-Girl / Out Of Control / Twilight / I Will Follow / encore: 11 O'Clock Tick Tock / The Ocean / encore: A Day Without Me*

The gig almost sells out despite the lack of local radio support. U2's first performance in the infamous Motor City is a big success with a willing audience served a 70-minute show, fifteen minutes longer than usual during this period. "This is for me girlfriend!" Bono says, introducing *Another Time, Another Place*. After *Electric Co.* there is a technical problem. "One, two, check... Hello, we're called U2, we're from Dublin, Ireland. And this microphone isn't working for now. Is that OK?" The audience don't mind. "You alright, Joe?" Bono asks their new sound engineer Joe O'Herlihy, who has arrived to reinforce U2's

permanent crew. Bono announces the new song *I Fall Down*. "This has never been perf... oh, yeah, well, it was performed last night once. This is the *second* time this is being performed." It is a raw, guitar-dominated song, very different from the eventual studio version which will be recorded later in the year. The lyrics are only partly written. The venue is bigger than they are used to and it bothers Bono that he cannot see the people at the back. "This is *Stories For Boys*, and this is where we wanna see people closer!" He goes into the audience during *11 O'Clock* and some fans get up on stage to dance.

SON OF BAMBOO presents From Ireland The DETROIT PREMIERE of
U2
SATURDAY APRIL 18 1981 9pm
"A breathtaking surge of freshness and energy to lift our emotions over the edge." — Melody Maker
Hear their debut LP "BOY" on Island Records
APPEARING AT
HARPO'S
HARPER AT CHALMERS, DETROIT 823-6400
TICKETS $4.00
available in advance at the Harpo's Box Office, Sam's Jams (Ferndale), Dearborn Music, Peaches (Frasier), and Schoolkids (Ann Arbor).
design Gary Grimshaw A SON OF BAMBOO Production

APRIL 19, 1981. COLUMBUS, OH, THE AGORA

APRIL 20, 1981. CLEVELAND, OH, THE AGORA

- Attendance: 1,000

On September 22, 1972 David Bowie started his first major American tour in Cleveland, introducing his Ziggy Stardust alter-ego and reaping sensational success. "So, this is where Bowie made it big," Bono remarks during this concert.

APRIL 21, 1981. PITTSBURGH, PA, THE DECADE

- Set: *The Ocean / 11 O'Clock Tick Tock / I Will Follow / I Fall Down / An Cat Dubh / Into The Heart / Another Time, Another*

Edge and Ellen Darst in Cleveland

Place / Cry-Electric Co. / Stories For Boys / Boy-Girl / Out Of Control / I Will Follow

"It's good that we can actually see the people in the back tonight, it's been a bit of a problem in the last few days," Bono says. Someone in the front is mucking about. "Please stop the water pistol... it's a lady," Bono laughs. The following day U2 take off for the Bahamas for a short break and to record a new song, *Fire*, with their producer Steve Lillywhite at Compass Rose Studios in Nassau for their next single.

MAY 2, 1981. GAINESVILLE, FL, RATHSKELLER - UNIVERSITY OF FLORIDA

MAY 3, 1981. TAMPA, FL, END ZONE

MAY 4, 1981. HALLENDALE, FL, THE AGORA

MAY 6, 1981. ATLANTA, GA, THE AGORA

- Attendance: 1,300

A show at The Ram's Head in Birmingham, AL, for March 7 is cancelled.

MAY 8, 1981. NEW ORLEANS, LA, OL' MAN RIVER'S

- Set: *The Ocean / 11 O'Clock Tick Tock / I Will Follow / I Fall Down / An Cat Dubh / Into The Heart / Another Time, Another Place / Cry-Electric Co. / Things To Make And Do / Stories For Boys / Boy-Girl / Out Of Control / encore: 11 O'Clock Tick Tock / I Will Follow*

During the day the band stroll through the wrought-iron decked streets of New Orleans' historic French Quarter, where Dixieland jazz has its origins and where there are dozens of clubs and bars in which authentic jazz and blues musicians have performed for decades. "We went down a street called Bourbon Street," says Bono. "I met an old man and he took his teeth out! You've got some very strange traditions around here..."

A youth in front spits towards the stage. "Hold on a second!" Bono yells at the start of *Electric Co.*, and asks Joe to turn the houselights on. "I wanna show you something. This is what they call a 'real' punk," he says sarcastically. "I'll tell you why he's a real punk... because he read about it in the papers. He wears a suit, it's a uniform. He spits! Because he read about it. He does a lot of things because he read about it. We can hold up the show because he's spitting, but I don't think we should do that any longer." Bono does not hold with punks very much, ever since he discovered that The Sex Pistols' punk ethos had been merely a gimmick of Malcolm McLaren. The Edge continues with *Electric Co.* "So shut up or get out!" Bono sneers at the guy. The incident has a beneficial effect on the show, as Bono's anger stirs up the power of the songs and he works extra hard to connect with the rest of the crowd.

MAY 9, 1981. MEMPHIS, TN, POETS

MAY 11, 1981. DENVER, CO, RAINBOW MUSIC HALL

- Attendance: 1,400; sellout
- Set: *The Ocean / 11 O'Clock Tick Tock / I Will Follow / I Fall Down / An Cat Dubh / Into The Heart / Touch / Another Time, Another Place / Cry-Electric Co. / Things To Make And Do / Stories For Boys / Boy-Girl / Out Of Control*

The promoter feels that he can sell out The Rainbow again, only six weeks after the first concert, and convinces U2 to return. The audience are wild with excitement and Bono confronts them with the reputation of Mid-Western cities: "You're not supposed to act like this; you're supposed to be laid-back, you know!" Halfway through *Boy-Girl* Bono informs the audience that John Travolta has been asked to play the part of Jim Morrison in a forthcoming film about The Doors. He reminisces about the film 'Saturday Night Fever' and sings a few lines of Chubby Checker's *Let's Twist Again.* ("Like we did last summer...") The show is recorded by local radio KEZY.

MAY 13, 1981. SANTA MONICA, CA, CIVIC CENTER

- Attendance: 3,000
- Support: Suburban Lawns

U2 return to California to consolidate their rapidly growing support in the LA area. Bono mentions that he had seen Ted Nugent play the Sports Arena the night before, and apes Nugent's stage behaviour, joking about the clichés Nugent had spouted: "Hey, it's great to be back in L.A.!", or "Thank you Los Angeles, you're the greatest!"

MAY 15, 1981. SAN FRANCISCO, CA, CALIFORNIA HALL

- Set: *The Ocean / 11 O'Clock Tick Tock / I Will Follow / I Fall Down / An Cat Dubh / Into The Heart / Touch / Another Time, Another Place / Cry-Electric Co. / Things To Make And Do / Stories For Boys / Boy-Girl / Out Of Control / Twilight / I Will Follow / A Day Without Me / 11 O'Clock Tick Tock / The Ocean*

Busta Jones. Palladium, May 29, 1981

MAY 19, 1981. TORONTO, CANADA, RYERSON THEATER

U2's touring is clearly successful. During the month of May, they return to many areas they had played at the start of the tour, but this time the venues are bigger.

MAY 20, 1981. ROCHESTER, NY, RED CREEK

MAY 21, 1981. BUFFALO, NY, UNCLE SAM'S

MAY 22, 1981. SYRACUSE, NY, CITY LIMITS

MAY 23, 1981. ALBANY, NY, J.B. SCOTT'S

- Attendance: 400

MAY 24, 1981. HAMPTON BEACH, NH, CLUB CASINO

MAY 25, 1981. PROVIDENCE, RI, CENTER STAGE

MAY 27, 1981. NEW HAVEN, CT, TOAD'S PLACE

- Attendance: 600; sellout
- Set: *The Ocean / 11 O'Clock Tick Tock / I Will Follow / I Fall Down / An Cat Dubh / Into The Heart / Another Time, Another Place / Cry-Electric Co. / Things To Make And Do / Stories For Boys / Boy-Girl / Out Of Control / encore: Twilight / I Will Follow / encore: A Day Without Me / Fire*

Bono thanks everyone for coming and asks whether there are any present who had also been at the December show. Many fans raise their hands or shout out. "You couldn't have all been there, I think there was about 10 people there," Bono says,

laughing. During *Boy-Girl* he sees someone wearing a Monkees' T-shirt and sings a few lines from The Monkees' *I'm A Believer:* "When I saw your face, I'm a believer..." U2 floor the audience with *I Will Follow* which receives an enormous response. "Are you usually this loud? We're gonna try something special. We got a single coming out in England in about two weeks time and this has never been performed before." *Fire,* the new song recorded in Nassau in late April is premièred. "See you in the fall," Bono shouts at the end.

In the afternoon Bono, The Edge and Larry were interviewed by Ken Shelton for WBCN radio. "I can't even remember what home looks like," said Bono. "We've been touring here so long. It's very important for us to tour, because, you know, a lot of bands put out records and then sit back and wait for it to happen. We want to play to people face to face and let them make up their own mind.

"There is a new album planned at the moment, in fact we're obsessed by it. It'll be out in October. We're going home next week to start working on that for a month and we'll record in July."

MAY 28, 1981. BOSTON, MA, METRO

- Attendance: 1,250; sellout
- Set: *The Ocean / 11 O'Clock Tick Tock / Touch / I Will Follow / I Fall Down / An Cat Dubh / Into The Heart / Fire / Another Time, Another Place / Cry-Electric Co. / Things To Make And Do / Stories For Boys / Boy-Girl / Out Of Control / Twilight / I Will Follow*

A speedy return to Boston after the two March shows goes a long way towards increasing U2's rapidly growing support in this town. A piper opens the show. Bono announces *I Fall Down:* "We've been travelling for the last few months on a bus across your country, and in the back of the bus, this was found. It's called *When I Fall Down.*" They also play *Fire,* mentioning that it is only the second time they have played it live. Inspired by the night before, Bono again sings part of *I'm A Believer* in *Boy-Girl* and continues to do so on several subsequent occasions.

MAY 29, 1981. NEW YORK, NY, PALLADIUM

- Attendance: 3,400; sellout
- Set: *The Ocean / 11 O'Clock Tick Tock / Touch / I Will Follow / I Fall Down / An Cat Dubh / Into The Heart / Fire / Another Time,*

Pink Pop, U2's first big festival show

Another Place / Cry-Electric Co. / Things To Make And Do / Stories For Boys / Boy-Girl / Out Of Control / encore: Twilight / I Will Follow / 11 O'Clock Tick Tock

U2 share the bill with The Teardrop Explodes, who open the show. Again there is an intro on bagpipes. During *I Will Follow* some joker throws a box of mice on stage. "I don't know who's throwing little white rats on stage, but you've got the wrong band," says Bono, referring to Dublin's Boomtown Rats. The poor creatures run around the stage in panic, some dying of heart attacks on the spot.

The prestigious Palladium is the biggest venue U2 have played in America so far. "We've only played here twice before, that was at a place called The Ritz. Have you heard of that? This is much bigger. I can't really work out the seats..." During the bridge of *Electric Co.* Bono sings a part of *New York, New York.*

Before *11 O'Clock Tick Tock* the band welcome a guest: bassist Busta Jones, who had worked with Talking Heads on their 1980/81 tour and had now recorded his own album. Bono explains, "We played two dates in London and Paris with the Talking Heads, that's when we met him. He's just a man for the studio actually. Right, what can we play?" Busta plays a long solo.

MAY 30, 1981. AMERICAN TV: 'THE TOMORROW SHOW'

This show, broadcast on June 4, marks U2's first major appearance on American television. *I Will Follow* and *Twilight* are played live in the studio in New York, and Bono unnerves the camera crew by walking in and out of the lights and the cameras' viewfinders. Afterwards host Tom Snyder asks Edge: "Why do they call you The Edge... I mean, what the heck, sir?" Edge: "Well, you know, my real name is Johnny Carson but I just didn't think that would get me on the show." Snyder concludes: "Judging by what people have written about these fellas, we will be hearing a great deal of The U2 in this country in the years to come..."

MAY 31, 1981. ASBURY PARK, NJ, FAST LANE

U2's first major American tour ends with a sell out concert on the New Jersey shorefront made famous by Bruce Springsteen. They have played no fewer than 60 concerts during the previous three months.

JUNE 4, 1981. SALFORD, ENGLAND, UNIVERSITY

- Support: Altered Images

FRIARS — MAXWELL HALL AYLESBURY
SATURDAY JUNE 6th 7.30p.m.
THE FRIARS AYLESBURY 12th BIRTHDAY PARTY
U2 + ALTERED IMAGES
Tickets £3.25 from Earth Records, Aylesbury; Scorpion, High Wycombe; Old Town Records, Hemel Hempstead; F.L. Moore, Dunstable & Luton; D.J. Holland, Leighton Buzzard & Bletchley; Hi-Vu, Buckingham; Music Market, Oxford or £3.25 at door on night (i.a.) Life membership 25p. W. Cup TV in Aston Hall. Stories for boys.

JUNE 6, 1981. AYLESBURY, ENGLAND, FRIARS CLUB

- Support: Altered Images

JUNE 8, 1981. GELEEN, HOLLAND, SPORTPARK

- Attendance: 50,000; sellout
- 'Pinkpop Festival' line-up: New Adventures, U2, Fischer Z, Madness, Michael Schenker Group, The Pretenders, Ian Dury & The Blockheads
- Set: *The Ocean / 11 O'Clock Tick Tock / I Will Follow / An Cat Dubh / Into The Heart / Another Time, Another Place / Cry-Electric Co. / Stories For Boys / Boy-Girl / Out Of Control / encore: Twilight / I Will Follow*

With a crowd of 50,000, the 12th edition of the Pinkpop Festival is a sellout and U2 hold their own in front of an audience of this size for the first time. Bono appears surprised by the enormous applause that *11 O'Clock Tick Tock* receives. "You're not supposed to know who we are! Thank you very much!" After 10 previous impressive performances in Holland the Dutch audience did know who U2 was. This performance strengthens their status as one of the best and most exciting new live acts around and is a key element in the great success they will enjoy in The Netherlands.

Inaugurated by Annelies de Haan in March 1981, Holland was the first country to have its own U2 fan club and members of the club are po-going up front. "We have some friends in the front. I think we have friends all over the field," says Bono. "More than we expected! Uhm... can you understand me? Do you speak English?" "Yeeaaahhh," is the response from all parts of the field. U2 are delighted to discover that their music retains its strength in such a large arena. Nine days later the entire show is broadcast on Dutch radio.

JUNE 9, 1981. LONDON, ENGLAND, HAMMERSMITH PALAIS

- Attendance: 1,500; sellout
- Support: Altered Images, This Heat
- Set: *Carry Me Home / Twilight / I Will Follow / I Fall Down / An Cat Dubh / Into The Heart / Fire / Another Time, Another Place / Cry-Electric Co. / Things To Make And Do / Stories For Boys / Boy-Girl / Out Of Control / encore: 11 O'Clock Tick Tock / The Ocean / encore: I Will Follow*

U2 open by playing an uptempo, drum-dominated song they haven't performed before: *Carry Me Home.* "Home is where the heart is, carry me home," Bono sings intensely. It is unclear whether this was a U2 song or a cover version; they haven't performed it since. The audience lap it up and with *I Will Follow* there is no holding back. "We used to play on a Monday night meeting here in London at a place called The Marquee," Bono says. "It's an old story – a lot of people said we could never take that atmosphere into a bigger place. Well, it's here now!"

U2 preview new material in the form of *I Fall Down* and *Fire*, which will be released as a single in a few weeks. Bono dedicates *Stories For Boys* to a cousin of his. Bruce Springsteen, having just completed the English leg of his 'River' tour, postpones his return to America in order to attend this concert. He watches from the wings and meets the band after the show.

Bono & Bruce

U2 start recording their new album in Windmill Lane Studios in July. As his notes have been stolen in Portland and he can't manage to get anything down on paper, Bono ends up improvising most of the lyrics.

AUGUST 16, 1981. DUBLIN, IRELAND, SLANE CASTLE

- Line up: Sweet Savage, Rose Tattoo, The Bureau, Hazel O'Connor, U2, Thin Lizzy
- Set: *With A Shout / Twilight / I Will Follow / I Threw A Brick Through A Window / An Cat Dubh / Into The Heart / Gloria / Rejoice / October / Stories For Boys / Boy-Girl / Out Of Control / encore: Fire / 11 O'Clock Tick Tock*

Having nearly completed their studio work, U2 play their only Irish show of the year supporting Thin Lizzy at Slane Castle, just outside Dublin in County Meath. U2 première five new songs from the upcoming 'October' album, starting off with a rousing

With A Shout, which is introduced with a thundering drum roll from Larry, but is vocally too demanding for Bono, who has trouble keeping up with the high pace. While recording the album, he has been making up lyrics on the spot because his notes had been stolen. At this show he is still in the improvisatory mood as on all the new songs the words are completely different from the eventual album versions. In *I Threw A Brick Through A Window* he improvises around its theme of an adolescent eyeing his mirror image in a shop window and not liking what he sees. Bono's words are barely intelligible but sound good melodically. "This is a new song, it's called *Gloria And Gloria*," he announces. It's one of the new songs that captures the spiritual nature of the new album. During the bass solo Bono has trouble hearing himself. He asks Edge, "Can you hear anything? I can't – I got all these echoes in my ear!"

"You haven't heard this one before, neither have we: *Rejoice*." Its lyrics contain references to Dublin's housing problems, where old buildings in the centre of town are being pulled down and people are moved to the outskirts. *October*, the title track of the album, displays U2's musical expansion as it features Edge playing a long, atmospheric piano intro before Bono joins in. "October, when I fall down, it's all I got..." he sings. He makes a remark about some of the press that are present. "I'd like to tell you about a special sort of people. They're called reporters, and they come with notes and pens in their hands. And they find somebody like that guy over there, who's throwing the bottles in the air. And then they take a photograph of him and print the photograph. And then you *all* are throwing the bottles, do you see what I mean?" During the encore *Happy Birthday* is sung for Aisling, Edge's girlfriend. There is good audience participation, but at the back of the field people are sitting down. Bono urges, "Up on your feet, this is not Woodstock!"

AUGUST 23, 1981. LONDON, ENGLAND, PARIS CINEMA STUDIO

■ Set: *11 O'Clock Tick Tock / I Will Follow / An Cat Dubh / Into The Heart / With A Shout / Twilight / Out Of Control / Rejoice*

U2 play a 30-minute set for a small studio audience for the BBC radio 'In Concert' series. *11 O'Clock Tick Tock* starts out of tune, Bono forgets the lyrics to *I Will Follow* and during *Into The Heart*, his shaky voice enters at totally the wrong point. He tries to break the tension: "We were told you would be Japanese tourists, but..." Nobody laughs. Where old and trusted songs flop, a new, difficult live song – *With A Shout* – is played tighter and more energetically than before. The show will be aired on October 3.

AUGUST 24, 1981. ODEL, ENGLAND, GREENBELT ARTS AND MUSIC FESTIVAL

■ Attendance: 20,000
■ Set: *11 O'Clock Tick Tock / I Will Follow / An Cat Dubh / Into The Heart / With A Shout /* encore: *Fire*

U2 make an unannounced appearance at this Christian festival in the village of Odel, some 50 miles north of London. "From our new record, released in October, this is *With A Shout!*" The track gets lost in a muddle but appeals to the crowd. While the band are heading for the dressing room, the announcer comes onstage: "Absolutely amazing! Let's hear it for U2! Do you want to hear more?" The band come back to play *Fire*, which had given U2 their first British chart single just a few weeks ago. Bono remarks, "This is the first time we've ever played to a Christian audience, but you're just as rowdy and as noisy as everyone else!"

AUGUST 29, 1981. GATESHEAD, ENGLAND, INTERNATIONAL STADIUM

■ Attendance: ca. 7,500
■ 'Rock On The Tyne Festival' line up: The Polecats, Pauline Murray and The Invisible Girls, Doll By Doll, Huang Chung, U2, Elvis Costello and The Attractions, Ian Dury and The

Blockheads
■ Set: *With A Shout / 11 O'Clock Tick Tock / I Will Follow / An Cat Dubh / Into The Heart / Another Time, Another Place / Cry-Electric Co. / I Threw A Brick / Stories For Boys / Out Of Control /* encore: *I Will Follow / Fire*

Although the organisers of this two-day festival are hoping for an attendance of 20,000 each day, only 15,000 turn up in all. Things don't click within the band; Adam and Larry often play out of synch and Bono forgets many of the lyrics.

AUGUST 31, 1981. EDINBURGH, SCOTLAND, COASTERS

■ Support: Boots For Dancing
■ Set: *With A Shout / Twilight / I Will Follow / An Cat Dubh / Into The Heart / Another Time, Another Place / I Threw A Brick / Cry-Electric Co. / Things To Make And Do / Stories For Boys / Boy-Girl / Out Of Control /* encore: *Fire*

With the Simple Minds' *Love Song* still on the PA, U2 burst loose with *With A Shout* for a 50-minute party, during which the audience sing along to every song. Several people get crushed in the crowd. "There's a 10-year old girl down there getting squashed." The girl is rescued from the crowd and at Bono's request she is brought onstage for a quick talk before *Another Time, Another Place*. To this day, *Things To Make And Do* has not been played again.

THE 'OCTOBER' TOUR LEG 1: UNITED KINGDOM, EUROPE, FALL 1981

U2 have scheduled 18 UK shows before doing some Continental dates to promote the new 'October' album, which is due for release on October 12. The album will enter the UK charts at No. 11; the *Gloria* single also makes the charts. Most dates are at universities or rock clubs with capacities around 2,000. Ticket prices are £2.50 for Leicester, and £3.00 for all others.

The stage gear has been augmented by a piano, while the lighting includes a row of fierce spotlights on the floor of the stage, shining up obliquely into the audience. A similar array of spots hang on both sides of the drum kit. Besides green, orange and purple, much use is made of white lights with different degrees of brightness. The 'Boy' backdrop is not utilised for this tour.

OCTOBER 1, 1981. NORWICH, UNIVERSITY OF EAST ANGLIA

■ Support: Wall of Voodoo
■ Set: *Gloria / Another Time, Another Place / Cry-Electric Co. / An Cat Dubh / Into The Heart / Rejoice / I Threw A Brick / I Will Follow / I Fall Down / October / Twilight / Out Of Control /* encore: *Fire /* encore: *11 O'Clock Tick Tock / The Ocean*

Edge plays piano on *I Fall Down*, replacing the rough guitar sound

that dominated the song at early versions during the American tour. With the new album not available yet, the crowd are unfamiliar with its songs. U2 play somewhat cautiously.

OCTOBER 2, 1981. NOTTINGHAM, ROCK CITY

■ Support: Wall of Voodoo
■ Set: same as Norwich

The audience rejoice in U2's return to their city and sing the first part of I Will Follow without Bono. The new songs are well received but cannot live up to the popularity of the old favourites.

OCTOBER 3, 1981. SALFORD, UNIVERSITY

■ Support: Wall of Voodoo
■ Set: *Gloria / Another Time, Another Place / Rejoice / An Cat Dubh / Into The Heart / I Threw A Brick / Cry-Electric Co. / I Fall Down / October / With A Shout / I Will Follow / Twilight / Out Of Control /* encore: *Fire / 11 O'Clock Tick Tock / The Ocean*

'The gentleman selling beer downstairs says the tiles are falling off downstairs, and asks if you're gonna jump, if you can take off your shoes," says Bono. The audience just get wilder.

OCTOBER 4, 1981. GLASGOW, TIFFANY'S

■ Attendance: 1,500; sellout
■ Support: Comsat Angels
■ Set: same as Salford.

Bono picks up a guitar for *I Fall Down* and asks the audience not to laugh at his inadequate playing. His singing lacks passion, he isn't very active physically and none too talkative either. There is even an awkward silence when he mutters, "We're called U2" after *I Will Follow*. He has said this before at festivals and in American clubs; this show, however, has sold out and the Glasgow audience are well aware of who they had paid to see. Bono cannot think of anything to fill up the silence. "These last nights I haven't been able to say much," he says during the encore. "I'll say it in other ways."

OCTOBER 6, 1981. COVENTRY, WARWICK UNIVERSITY

■ Support: Comsat Angels
■ Set: *Gloria / Another Time, Another Place / Rejoice / An Cat Dubh / Into The Heart / I Threw A Brick / Cry-Electric Co. / I Fall Down / October / Stories For Boys / I Will Follow / Twilight / Out Of Control /* encore: *Fire / 11 O'Clock Tick Tock / The Ocean*

With A Shout is replaced by *Stories For Boys*.

OCTOBER 7, 1981. LEICESTER, POLYTECHNIC

■ Support: Comsat Angels
■ Set: same as Coventry.

OCTOBER 8, 1981. SHEFFIELD, LYCEUM

- Set: same as Coventry.

The concerts improve as the tour progresses. Here, U2 are warmly received and they play an excellent set during which the new songs in particular are played convincingly. After *Electric Co.* Bono tells the audience that a member of the crew has just become a father.

OCTOBER 9, 1981. NEWCASTLE, MAYFAIR

- Attendance: 2,100
- Support: Comsat Angels

OCTOBER 10, 1981. LIVERPOOL, ROYAL COURT THEATRE

- Attendance: 1,500
- Support: Comsat Angels
- Set: same as Coventry, but with *Fire* as the last song.

OCTOBER 12, 1981. BRIGHTON, TOP RANK

- Attendance: 2,000
- Support: Comsat Angels
- Set: same as Coventry.

The audience are not too vocal, so Bono does his best to encourage more participation. During *11 O'Clock Tick Tock* he hands the microphone to the audience which results in wild shouting.

OCTOBER 13, 1981. PORTSMOUTH, LOCARNO

- Support: Comsat Angels

OCTOBER 14, 1981. BBC RADIO SESSION: KID JENSEN

- Set: *Boy-Girl / With A Shout / I Threw A Brick Through A Window / Scarlet*

This session is recorded during the day and airs in the evening. Jensen introduces *With A Shout* as *With A Shot*, perhaps misled by a circulating misprint of the 'October' sleeve on which the song is named as such. The producer of the show adds some background claps and other sounds, and *I Threw A Brick* in particular does not sound genuinely live. The version of *Scarlet* is rare: to this day it is the only time this song is played live. "A very mysterious number there," Jensen says after the song.

OCTOBER 14, 1981. CARDIFF, TOP RANK

- Attendance: 1,900
- Support: Comsat Angels

OCTOBER 16, 1981. STOKE, KING'S HALL

- Support: Comsat Angels

OCTOBER 17, 1981. BRACKNELL, SPORTS CENTRE

BRACKNELL SPORTS CENTRE

U2
+ Special Guests

COMSAT ANGELS

7.30 pm Saturday 17th October

Tickets £3, available from Sports Centre, Quicksilver, Reading and usual agents.

- Attendance: 2,000
- Support: Comsat Angels

After the show members of the band come into the venue to talk with some Dutch and Irish fans who are following the tour.

OCTOBER 18, 1981. BRISTOL, LOCARNO

- Attendance: 2,500
- Support: Comsat Angels
- Set: same as Coventry.

OCTOBER 19, 1981. BIRMINGHAM, LOCARNO

- Support: Comsat Angels
- Set: same as Coventry

A good 60-minute concert with a hyper-energetic *Rejoice*. At the end of *Into The Heart* there is a minor technical hitch, so Larry has to wait to start *I Threw A Brick*. A roadie comes to the rescue. "You can see how professional we are now," Bono grins.

OCTOBER 20, 1981. LEEDS, TIFFANY'S

- Support: Comsat Angels
- Set: *Gloria / Another Time, Another Place / I Threw A Brick / An Cat Dubh / Into The Heart / Rejoice / Cry-Electric Co. / I Fall Down / October / Stories For Boys / I Will Follow / Twilight / Out Of Control /* encore: *Fire / 11 O'Clock Tick Tock / The Ocean*

Rejoice and *I Threw A Brick* swap places. A lot of the songs sound stiff as Edge and Larry make numerous mistakes. *Another Time, Another Place* is interrupted owing to a brawl in the audience. "One more from you, and we're getting off this stage, OK!" Bono says angrily, then requests security to look after the victim.

OCTOBER 21, 1981. HEMEL HEMPSTEAD, PAVILION

- Set: same as Leeds.

The fanatical audience are a bit too wild and a brawl erupts. Bono interrupts *I Threw A Brick* and asks the audience to stop pushing.

OCTOBER 24, 1981. DEINZE, BELGIUM, BRIELPOORT

OCTOBER 25, 1981. HERENTHOUT, BELGIUM, ZAAL LUX

- Attendance: 400; (capacity 600)

Before the concert, U2 appear on a live show called 'Generation 80' on the Belgian/French station RTBF 1. They lipsynch to *I Fall Down* at the start of the show and *Gloria* at the end.

OCTOBER 26, 1981. PARIS, FRANCE, ELYSEE MONTMARTRE

- Attendance: 3,500
- Set: same as Leeds, but with *Fire* as the final song.

OCTOBER 28, 1981. LEIDEN, HOLLAND, STADSGEHOORZAAL

- Attendance: 800
- Set: *Gloria / Another Time, Another Place / Rejoice / An Cat Dubh / Into The Heart / I Threw A Brick / Cry-Electric Co. / I Fall Down / October / Stories For Boys / I Will Follow / Twilight / Out Of Control*

tour bus

people. We don't want them, right? We wanna get on with this. Is there anybody here who wants to hear what we're doing, or should we just go now?" Some weak cheers satisfy the band; *I Will Follow* is essayed for the third time. They finish the set with all their energy, but there is no reason for an encore.

NOVEMBER 4, 1981. BERLIN, GERMANY, METROPOL

- Attendance: ca. 350; (capacity 2,000)
- Set: *Gloria / Another Time, Another Place / I Threw A Brick / An Cat Dubh / Into The Heart / Rejoice / Cry-Electric Co. / I Fall Down / October / Stories For Boys / I Will Follow / Twilight / Out Of Control / encore: 11 O'Clock Tick Tock / The Ocean*

U2's first appearance on the 'Rockpalast' concert series on German TV is far from perfect. The audience look on solemnly which puts a fatal stamp on the course of the show. Bono, irritable from the night before, becomes extremely frustrated as

Larry's present

OCTOBER 29, 1981. TILBURG, HOLLAND, DE HARMONIE

OCTOBER 30, 1981. AMSTERDAM, HOLLAND, PARADISO

- Attendance: 1,000; sellout
- Support: Phantom Limb
- Set: same as Leeds.

U2 play an overwhelming concert in which a guy from the crowd is pulled onstage to sing along. The show is recorded for Dutch radio. It reaches a climax at midnight, as Bono announces: "Tonight is very special, because the last teenager, our drummer, has just become 20 years old," and leads the crowd singing *Happy Birthday*. Back in their dressing room, the band celebrate further and drown Larry with presents, one of which is a radio-steered truck that Bono had bought earlier in the day in a toy shop.

OCTOBER 31, 1981. ARNHEM, HOLLAND, STOKVISHAL

- Attendance: 400; sellout

NOVEMBER 1, 1981. ROTTERDAM, HOLLAND, DE LANTAARN

- Attendance: 400

NOVEMBER 3, 1981. HAMBURG, GERMANY, FABRIK

- Set: *Gloria / Another Time, Another Place / I Threw A Brick / An Cat Dubh / Into The Heart / Rejoice / Cry-Electric Co. / I Fall Down / October / Stories For Boys / I Will Follow / Twilight / Out Of Control*

U2 share the bill with The Psychedelic Furs but for reasons unclear they do not play. Rumour has it that they refused to play because they had not had time to do a soundcheck. Most of the audience have come for the Furs. "Sorry for the delay, the piano broke down, things like that," Bono explains but the damage is

done. Halfway through *Gloria* something is thrown onstage. Bono stops the song. "In Dublin, people who come to our concerts show people that start throwing things the way out. I expect that here, or we leave the stage."

U2 toil to break through the hostile, oppressing tension. "Right," Bono says firmly. "The atmosphere in here has got to change. You've been sold a dummy tonight; you expected to see two bands, there's one band. It's not our fault, it's not The Psychedelic Furs' fault. They wanted to be here. This is called *I Fall Down*. Let's break through this!" During *I Will Follow* a few hooligans work off their irritation on bystanders, and the band stop the song. "This isn't a circus, right? Hey you! Shall I tell you something about violence? I come from a country where violence is real, not pretend violence." Edge starts *I Will Follow* again, and Bono shouts as if possessed, "And again! We start from the beginning! We go up, we go *up*, *I Will Follow*!!" Ten seconds later, things go wrong again. "Look, there's some people back here who wanna eat you up. They're called security

Paradiso

Control, the DJ addresses the radio listeners. "Pandemonium at the Orpheum Theater tonight, the crowd's going crazy, U2 are leaving the stage but you know they'll be back. This is absolutely incredible, the response here... Well, U2 consider Boston their home away from home, really. The place is going nuts! The crowd is on their feet, and I hope you're diggin' it at home. Listen to the clapping hands, people who appreciate good music... that's Boston, Massachusetts for ya. They're coming back onstage! I see The Edge..."

NOVEMBER 15, 1981. NEW HAVEN, CT, TOAD'S PLACE

■ Attendance: 600; sellout

NOVEMBER 17, 1981. PROVIDENCE, RI, CENTER STAGE

Before the concert, Lou Papineau of *The NewPaper* conducts an interview with Adam.

Lou Papineau: "Is each show different or do you dig a rut?"

Adam Clayton: "No, I think each show is different, and I think it improves. A lot of people say when you're playing every night you just lose the feel; I don't agree with that. With a band like U2, every night the feel is different, but it's great all the time."

LP: "Does your performance depend on the audience's reaction?"

AC: "Yeah, obviously whatever way you play a gig is apt to counterpoint the feedback you're getting from the audience. If they're disinterested, it makes you play a certain way – it makes you play a lot harder, a lot more aggressively, until you've won them over. Whereas if they're on your side right from the start, then I think you're a bit more creative and sensitive and relaxed."

LP: "Were you surprised with your success? Were you prepared for it?"

AC: "I think in a way we were surprised, but at the same time, you don't get involved in a business like this unless you really believe that what you've got to say is worthwhile. We didn't enter into it in a naïve way. We were well aware of the stakes. I think if you're going to get into rock & roll you've got to be perfectly sure that from that day you start doing it, you know what you want and where you're going. And though we've never gone through that period of 'paying our dues' for 10 years, we were perfectly prepared to do that if it was necessary, because we believed in what we were doing. But it has happened as fast as we wanted it to. It's great for it to come through like that."

Adam goes on to explain that the band are happy with the new record. It was a different approach, there were more individual songs, a more diverse sound than on 'Boy'.

LP: "Were the songs written on the road?"

AC: "Yeah, funnily enough, all the rough drafts, all the ideas came together on the road at soundchecks. Basically what we do when we finish a tour is we go away for a couple of days and listen to all the tapes of soundchecks, little bits that we've put down. Then we put them all together and start working with the ideas. That's how 'October' came about."

---

he tries in vain to get a reaction. "We're not used to doing auditions or playing on stages like this; you and us will break that!" Roadie Steve Iredale comes on stage to hand Bono his guitar. "This is Steven, everybody," he announces but there is no response whatsoever. "It's a custom in our country, clapping hands," Bono says sarcastically. In *I Fall Down* he sings, "I feel like nothing to say, I think I'll go home... I think I don't like this show," and kicks over his microphone stand at the end. This show is broadcast on WDR TV on March 6, 1982.

THE 'OCTOBER' TOUR, LEG 2: AMERICA, FALL 1981

The single *Gloria* receives scant airplay on nationwide radio stations, whose rigid, conservative line is a hard nut to crack for a new band like U2. Several college radio stations, however, admire the group for making such a non-commercial record and regularly play several of its songs, as well as keeping students informed about upcoming local shows and ticket details. It helps increase interest in U2, as does the support of a new cable TV station that was established in August and broadcasts a steady diet of music. The arrival of MTV will change the face of rock and pop promotion in the decade to come, making videos mandatory for any band with international ambitions. U2 have made a video clip for *Gloria*, which MTV plays often. In several cities U2's following has outgrown clubs, so theatres are booked, allowing U2 to reach many more people.

NOVEMBER 13, 1981. ALBANY, NY, J.B. SCOTT'S

■ Attendance: 400; sellout

After the two shows here in spring the club is packed. The 'October' album has entered the *Billboard* album chart six days earlier at number 181.

NOVEMBER 14, 1981. BOSTON, MA, ORPHEUM THEATER

■ Attendance: 2,000; sellout
■ Support: David Johansen
■ Set: *Gloria / Another Time, Another Place / I Threw A Brick / An Cat Dubh / Into The Heart / With A Shout / Rejoice / Cry-Electric Co. / I Fall Down / October / Stories For Boys / I Will Follow / Twilight / Out Of Control /* encore: *Fire / 11 O'Clock Tick Tock / The Ocean*

The show is broadcast live on WBCN, the first American radio station that gave U2 airplay back in 1980. "Good evening Boston!" the announcer calls out. "You know the show's a sellout!? Your grandmother can't get in the door tonight! We're broadcasting this show live on WBCN. Your screams, your cheers will be heard live in stereo! Put your hands together for U2!"

The band receive a deafening welcome befitting homecoming heroes, barely a year after their first performance in a half-full Paradise Theater. "Let's go, this is *Gloria!*" shouts Bono, and the show is on, the band throwing all their power and passion into a memorable concert. "I suppose you got a lot of people that come and they say, 'Hey, it's good to be back in Boston'. Well, I couldn't say it like that, but we really mean it," Bono remarks.

When the band leave for the dressing room after *Out Of*

NOVEMBER 18, 1981. PHILADELPHIA, PA, RIPLEY'S MUSIC HALL

- Set: same as Boston.

"This is when I try to be a musician," Bono says, picking up a guitar for *I Fall Down*. "You have five minutes to find out I'm not! But I have nervous hands, nervous energy, I have to hold on to *something*!" U2 floor the audience but Bono works up such a sweat he feels tight in the chest during *I Will Follow*. In the bridge he sings, "I can't breathe, I need some air..." and a roadie promptly finds him a fan. "...Aaahhh, thank you."

NOVEMBER 20, 21, 22, 1981. NEW YORK, NY, THE RITZ

- Attendance: 4,800; sellout
- Set third night: same as Boston, with the addition of *I Will Follow*, which is played for the second time that night after *The Ocean*.

U2's following in New York is growing so fast the three Ritz shows all sell out. The audience on the final night are largely unfamiliar with U2 and have come to check out the band. All day U2 had been recording a new song in the Kingdom Sound Studio on Long Island. As a consequence the group seem tired and barely manage to get the audience up from their seats. "This is far too late for everybody to be up..." says Bono disappointedly during the encore. The day after is again spent in the studio finishing the recording, but band are not satisfied with the session and never release the track.

NOVEMBER 24, 1981. PASSAIC, NJ, HITSVILLE NORTH NIGHTCLUB

NOVEMBER 25, 1981. ASBURY PARK, NJ, HITSVILLE SOUTH NIGHTCLUB

- Attendance: 700; sellout
- Set: *Gloria / Another Time, Another Place / I Threw A Brick / An Cat Dubh / Into The Heart / With A Shout / Rejoice / Cry-Electric Co. / I Fall Down / October / Stories For Boys / I Will Follow / Twilight / Out Of Control / encore: Fire / 11 O'Clock Tick Tock / The Ocean / I Will Follow*

"We ended our last tour here; I think there's a lot more people here this time, thank you!" During Edge's solo in *Electric Co.* Bono assaults the piano, playing a few tunes made up on the spot. He lets himself fall into the crowd and floats backwards on the sea of outstretched hands before he is pushed back on stage. "I want to go for a swim... I'll meet you down at the beach in half an hour after this, OK?" Bono says before *Out Of Control*, during which he again plays the piano. The second performance of *I Will Follow* is an added bonus for the over-excited crowd.

NOVEMBER 28, 1981. LOS ANGELES, CA, HOLLYWOOD PALLADIUM

- Attendance: 4,200; (capacity 4,400)
- Support: Romeo Void

A Day Without Me is included for the first time since New Haven on May 27, and proves to be a suitable song to follow *I Threw A Brick*; eventually these songs will segue into one another every time they are played. Bono comments on *Rejoice*: "In Dublin they're pulling the houses down in the city centre and they're putting the people out of the city centre and throwing them away in districts outside of the city like if they were something not human. But I say: rejoice!"

NOVEMBER 29, 1981. SAN FRANCISCO, CA, WARFIELD THEATER

- Support: Garland Jeffreys
- Set: same as Asbury Park, plus *A Day Without Me* after *I Threw A Brick*, and minus *I Will Follow* at the end.

The fact that the New York audience have mostly remained seated bugs U2. "Good evening; you can stand up now," Bono says as he comes onstage. They play as energetically as possible, in an effort to get the people off their backsides. It pays off. "I was kinda frightened when I saw all the seats," Bono confesses. "Then I realised that these seats were made for standing, so thank you." He replaces the usual *Send In The Clowns* bit in *Electric Co.* with a brief *I Left My Heart In San Francisco*. Later, he urges the audience to call radio stations to request U2's music.

DECEMBER 1, 1981. ATLANTA, GA, THE AGORA

- Attendance: 1,300
- Set: same as Asbury Park.

DECEMBER 2, 1981. NASHVILLE, TN, VANDERBILT UNIVERSITY

DECEMBER 4, 1981. DETROIT, MI, ROYAL OAK MUSIC THEATER

- Set: same as Asbury Park, minus *Stories For Boys* and the reprise of *I Will Follow* at the end.

Bono explains that he is happy that everybody has come to see them. "We thought everyone else was going to go see that other great Irish rock & roll band, The Rolling Stones or something..." "Booooo!" shout the Detroit audience. (The Stones played the Silverdome a few days earlier.)

DECEMBER 5, 1981. GRAND RAPIDS, MI, FOUNTAIN ST. CHURCH

- Set: *Gloria / Another Time, Another Place / I Threw A Brick / An Cat Dubh / Into The Heart / With A Shout / Rejoice / Cry-Electric Co. / I Fall Down / October / I Will Follow / Twilight / Out Of Control / encore: 11 O'Clock Tick Tock / The Ocean*

The tour reaches a few remote areas of Michigan state where bands seldom play. The audience, however, are well acquainted with U2 and shout requests. "You're not supposed to have heard of us out here!" Bono says. "Well, we have!" someone yells. *11 O'Clock Tick Tock* has a gospel-twist to it because the audience join in, singing its "Lalalala" chorus for a long time. "This is a church, let's sing," Bono urges and continues the community singing.

DECEMBER 6, 1981. CHICAGO, IL, PARK WEST

- Attendance: 1,100

DECEMBER 7, 1981. EAST LANSING, MI, DOOLEY'S

DECEMBER 8, 1981. CLEVELAND, OH, THE AGORA

- Attendance: 1,000; sellout
- Set: *Gloria / Another Time, Another Place / I Threw A Brick / A Day Without Me / An Cat Dubh / Into the Heart / With a Shout / Rejoice / Cry-Electric Co. / I Fall Down / October / Stories For Boys / I Will Follow / Twilight / Out Of Control / encore: Fire / 11 O'Clock Tick Tock / The Ocean*

A few hours before the show the town is hit by a massive blizzard, covering the streets with an eight-inch thick white carpet. "We thought you all would stay home with all the snow," says Bono. "Nooo!" the audience reply. "You're on the radio tonight!" College station Case Western Reserve University's WRUW broadcasts the show.

DECEMBER 10, 1981. BUFFALO, NY, UNCLE SAM'S

- Support: S.Y.T. featuring Jack Cassidy and Pauline and the Perls.
- Set: same as Grand Rapids, but *Fire* replaces the last two songs.

DECEMBER 11, 1981. WASHINGTON, DC, ONTARIO THEATER

- Support: Bow Wow Wow
- Set: same as Grand Rapids.

DECEMBER 12, 1981. HARTFORD, CT, STAGE WEST

DECEMBER 13, 1981. LIDO BEACH, NY, MALIBU BEACH NIGHT CLUB

"This is *Rejoice*," Bono announces exuberantly, but Edge is not ready yet. "Uhm, actually, this is not *Rejoice*, this is The Edge tuning up, so... This is where it all breaks down, where all professionalism and years of touring just leave you lying there destructed. What can I say? There's people nodding their heads in agreement. How are you? My name is Bono, this is The Edge, this is Adam, this is Larry, this is U2... and this is *Rejoice*." Bono has plans. "Because this is our last night we couldn't go home without having a sort of a party. So we're all going for a swim afterwards, so..."

U2's last American show of the year is recorded by WLIR radio. The band will be back in February to tour areas neglected during this trip. Next on the schedule are two shows in London before going home for Christmas and a couple of weeks off.

DECEMBER 20, 21, 1981. LONDON, ENGLAND, LYCEUM BALLROOM

- Attendance: 4,000; sellout
- Support: The Alarm
- Set both nights: *Gloria / Another Time, Another Place / I Threw A Brick / A Day Without Me / An Cat Dubh / Into The Heart / With A Shout / Rejoice / Cry-Electric Co. / I Fall Down / October / I Will Follow / Twilight / Out Of Control / encore: Fire / 11 O'Clock Tick Tock / The Ocean*

The shows receive a stream of overwhelmingly positive reviews. Gill Pringle starts her review in *Record Mirror* with: 'U2 played the gig of 1981 and words fail me. Everyone is hugging each other as they stumble outside and the night air is singing with snatches of song.'

Karen Swayne writes in *Sounds*: 'What can I say? That U2 were an experience that defies the written word? That the atmosphere was one of sheer jubilation? Or maybe just that if you missed them live, you missed one of the most joyous and inspiring events of the year.

'Imagine the Lyceum transformed into a hall of celebration, where U2's followers could gather to pay tribute to the band they know should have been much, much bigger in 1981. We were overwhelmed by their music and lifted by their feeling, and the world outside seemed a million miles away as we were carried into a land of passion and beauty.'

JANUARY 23, 1982. GALWAY, IRELAND, LEISURELAND

The 'October' tour resumes with three shows in Ireland. A concert in Belfast is cancelled because of the bad state of the venue's floor.

JANUARY 24, 1982. CORK, IRELAND, CITY HALL

In their own country U2's popularity has grown vastly since the festival at Slane Castle the previous August. Before this Cork show a large group of fans approach Bono requesting autographs, something he isn't used to. "They didn't want to talk; they wanted bits of me," Bono later tells *Hot Press* magazine. "They wanted me to write my name down on scraps of paper. Incidents like that did make me think about the whole thing – we're not into that gladiators, dinosaur rock thing."

JANUARY 26, 1982. DUBLIN, IRELAND, ROYAL DUBLIN SOCIETY HALL

- Attendance: 5,000; sellout
- Two support acts.

Tomorrow is performed for the very first time, accompanied by Vincent Kilduff on uillean pipes, who also plays on the album. It is the first time the RDS Hall is used for a rock concert, and the first time U2 play a hall this size in their own right.

THE 'OCTOBER' TOUR, LEG 3: AMERICA, WINTER/SPRING 1982

The tour is in jeopardy when Warner Brothers, disappointed by sales of the 'October' album, hesitate to pump more money into promoting U2. After having entered the Billboard charts at 181, the album peaked at 104 and is now rapidly on its way down. Their booking agency Premier Talent comes up with the idea to have U2 play in support for The J. Geils Band, who are at the height of their fame with a worldwide hit, *Centerfold*, a platinum-selling album and a sellout arena tour. Having U2 on this tour would expose them to large crowds of people, which could boost album sales and win fans for them. J.Geils singer Peter Wolf thinks it's an excellent idea. He had seen U2 play Boston and thinks they have an intensity that will befit their support. Warner Brothers continue to finance U2's own tour before they will team up with J. Geils on March 3 in Florida.

FEBRUARY 11, 1982. NEW ORLEANS, LA, S.S. PRESIDENT RIVERBOAT

- Attendance: 1,500; sellout

- Support: RZA
- Set: *Gloria / Another Time, Another Place / I Threw A Brick / A Day Without Me / An Cat Dubh / Into The Heart / Rejoice / Cry-Electric Co. / I Fall Down / October / Stories For Boys / I Will Follow / Twilight / Out Of Control /* encore: *Fire / 11 O'Clock Tick Tock / The Ocean.*

This unusual show is in the ballroom of an old Mississippi steamboat where the captain's cabin serves as U2's dressing room and the deck as a stage. The big local rock station has neglected to mention the show, but a college station has generated interest and the gig sells out. Just before the support band's set, the boat casts off and sets sail down the Mississippi. "This is the first time we've ever played a venue and the venue left!" says Paul McGuinness as the riverboat cruises down America's biggest natural waterway. Not until the end of U2's set does the boat dock.

Stimulated by the bizarre location, the band play a strong show. *With A Shout* is dropped from the tour just when the song has been mastered. A journalist from Britain's *New Musical Express* is present to report on U2's progress and he brings with him the Dutch photographer Anton Corbijn. This is U2's first meeting with Corbijn, who will go on to create many of U2's best known images, and in the afternoon they do a long photo session together on the deck of the boat.

FEBRUARY 13, 1982. AUSTIN, TX, OPRY HOUSE

- Attendance: 3,000; sellout

Four concerts in Texas all sell out.

I Fall Down

FEBRUARY 14, 1982. SAN ANTONIO, TX, CARDI'S

- Attendance: 3,000; sellout

FEBRUARY 15, 1982. HOUSTON, TX, CARDI'S

FEBRUARY 16, 1982. DALLAS, TX, CARDI'S

In the afternoon Bono hears Neil Young's *Southern Man* on the radio. Written as an anti-redneck tirade, the band rehearse the song during the soundcheck and play it live that evening for the first time. Because Bono hardly knows the lyrics, he asks whether anyone in the audience knows them and duets with a fan on stage.

FEBRUARY 17, 1982. OKLAHOMA CITY, OK, JAMMIE'S

FEBRUARY 19, 1982. ST. LOUIS, MO, NIGHT MOVES

FEBRUARY 21, 1982. MINNEAPOLIS, MN, FIRST AVENUE

- Attendance: 1,000
- Set: same as New Orleans, minus *Stories For Boys* and, after *The Ocean, Southern Man* and *I Will Follow* are played as extra encores.

Before *I Threw A Brick Through A Window*, a talkative Bono explains that the song was conceived the year before in this very venue, as was *Stranger In A Strange Land*. "We did them on the stage in the afternoon when we came in to see if everything was working," he tells the crowd. He dedicates *Out Of Control* to Jim, one of the truck drivers, who had turned 32, and sings "Happy birthday to you, you were born in a zoo", and similar nonsense. Bono is obviously in high spirits. "I wanna dance with EVERYBODY!" he yells enthusiastically, before inviting a fan on stage for a joyful link-your-arms dance during *11 O'Clock Tick Tock*, a gesture that will soon become a nightly ritual. The mood comes down for *The Ocean* which indicates the end of the show. The audience are far from sated, cheering so loudly that the band return. "Again, this is for you, Jim! This is for some of the older members of the audience. We just heard it on the radio, we think we can play it..." *Southern Man* is played, again with a guy from the crowd coming on stage to sing. Though he sings way off key, the crowd love the duet. *Southern Man* takes more than five minutes and when the frantic audience refuse to call it a day, U2 eventually come back to hit them over the head with a rousing *I Will Follow*.

FEBRUARY 22, 1982. MADISON, WI, HEADLINERS

- Attendance: 1,000 ; sellout
- Support: The Vers
- Set: same as New Orleans, plus *Southern Man* as final encore, again with a member of the audience on vocals but this time Adam takes the spotlight to close the song on his own with a long bass solo.

Avram Rosen reviews this show in the *Daily Cardinal*: 'By the fifth song, *An Cat Dubh*, the intensity of the performers and the crowd, which had been building since the concert began, rose to such levels it seemed that something must break. As the guitar segue began between *An Cat Dubh* and *Into The Heart*, it seemed like all of Headliners was pushed into a state of transcendence. The well-behaved crowd, made up of a lot of out-of-towners became stoned from the music. The rest of the songs, with few exceptions, maintained this feeling. The music itself wasn't psychedelic, but the effect it had on the crowd was.'

FEBRUARY 23, 1982. CHAMPAIGN, IL, UNIVERSITY OF ILLINOIS AUDITORIUM

- Support: Combo Audio
- Set: same as New Orleans, plus *Southern Man* as extra encore at the end.

Bono grabs a camera from a photographer in the front to capture the audience on film. The encores are a veritable party. "I wanna dance with you!" Bono yells and dances with a fan during *11 O'Clock Tick Tock*. Bono interrupts the audience's 'singing' to do a few lines of *Give Peace A Chance*. "What we are saying, is give peace a chance..." Just as in Dallas and Minneapolis, U2 return after the houselights have gone on to surprise the audience with *Southern Man*.

STAR COURSE
★ ★ ★ ★ ★ PRESENTS ★ ★ ★ ★ ★
U-2
UNIVERSITY OF ILLINOIS AUDITORIUM
23 FEB 1982 URBANA, IL
TUESDAY
8:00 P.M.

FEBRUARY 25, 1982. KANSAS CITY, MO, UPTOWN THEATER

This concert includes the first performance of *A Celebration*, a new song which U2 had recorded around Christmas for a UK single release on March 22.

FEBRUARY 27, 1982. DENVER, CO, RAINBOW MUSIC HALL

■ Attendance: 1,500; sellout

FEBRUARY 28, 1982. FORT COLLINS, CO, COLORADO STATE UNIVERSITY LINCOLN COMMUNITY CENTER

■ Attendance: 2,000

MARCH 3, 1982. FORT MEYERS, FL, LEE COUNTY ARENA

■ Attendance: 6,336 (P); sellout
This is U2's first of 14 concerts supporting The J. Geils's Band. They have insufficient time for their soundcheck and have to leave it to the roadies. They also have to get used to a new situation, new surroundings, and the size of the venue. For the first time in their career they are playing an arena. As support act they have only limited playing time, so they shorten the set to 45 minutes. They play a somewhat reserved show but are reasonably well-received by the audience.

MARCH 4, 1982. WEST PALM BEACH, FL, AUDITORIUM

■ Attendance: 6,200 (P); sellout
■ Set: *Gloria / I Threw A Brick / A Day Without Me / An Cat Dubh / Into The Heart / Rejoice / Cry-Electric Co. / I Fall Down / I Will Follow / Twilight / Out Of Control*
U2 feel more at home tonight with Bono announcing most songs for an enthusiastic audience. During the transition from *An Cat Dubh* to *Into The Heart* he improvises, "We've been waiting, we've been waiting all day, for you...," followed by Edge's sensitive solo that receives a screaming response from the audience.

MARCH 5, 1982. TAMPA, FL, CURTIS HIXON HALL

■ Attendance: 7,600 (P); sellout
■ Set: same as West Palm Beach, plus *11 O'Clock Tick Tock* at the end.
"We come from a place called Dublin in Ireland. Any Irish here tonight?" asks Bono. To his great surprise people respond from all over the arena. "You can't all be Irish!" The audience become so involved that U2 could be the headlining act. "Is this good, when you light your lighters?" Bono asks, watching a sea of tiny

flames light up in front of him after *Into The Heart*. He thanks the audience for their hospitality. This night it becomes clear that the concept works. The J. Geils audience are very receptive as U2's music goes down well.

MARCH 6, 1982. TALLAHASSEE, FL, LEON COUNTY ARENA

■ Attendance: 6,217 (P); sellout
After the show Adam, Bono and Larry are walking outside when they hear a garage-band playing nearby. Curious, they go to listen, get to talking and the band persuade them to play *I Will Follow*, which results in a messy collaboration.

A show at Jacksonville University for March 7 is cancelled.

MARCH 10, 1982. KNOXVILLE, TN, UNIVERSITY OF TENNESSEE

After their set, U2 attend a Rod Stewart concert, arriving in time to see the second half of the show.

MARCH 11, 1982. ATLANTA, GA, CIVIC CENTER

■ Attendance: 10,000
■ Set: same as West Palm Beach, minus *Twilight*.

MARCH 12, 1982. MEMPHIS, TN, NORTH HALL AUDITORIUM

■ Attendance: 3,691 (P); (capacity 4,333)
At midnight it is Adam's 22nd birthday and after the concert an old acquaintance takes the band to Miller's Cave, a local club run by two brothers who also have a band, The Miller Brothers. They put up a sign saying 'Happy Birthday Adam'. The Miller Brothers play a few songs in honour of Adam and the band, and later that night U2 take the stage themselves, playing drunken versions of *Southern Man* and *Out Of Control*.

MARCH 13, 1982. LOUISVILLE, KY, GARDENS

■ Attendance: 7,000

MARCH 14, 1982. INDIANAPOLIS, IN, CONVENTION CENTER

■ Attendance: 10,500
The J. Geils tour has a week-long break after this concert and U2 use the time to play a few clubs and theatres on the east coast on their own.

MARCH 16, 1982. AMHERST, MA, UNIVERSITY OF MASSACHUSETTS BOWKER AUDITORIUM

MARCH 17, 18, 1982. NEW YORK, NY, THE RITZ

■ Attendance: 3,200; sellout
■ Set first night: *Gloria / Another Time, Another Place / I Threw A Brick / A Day Without Me / An Cat Dubh / Into the Heart / Rejoice / Cry–Electric Co. / I Fall Down / October / Tomorrow / I Fall Down / Twilight / Out of Control / encore: Fire / 11 O'Clock Tick Tock / The Ocean.*
Originally, U2 planned to join in the annual St. Patrick's Day parade down Fifth Avenue, playing live on a large float, so that thousands of people would have seen them in the streets but

shortly before the parade, IRA member Bobby Sands dies as a result of his hunger strike in prison. The organisers of the parade want to turn the event into a tribute to Sands and because it thus acquires political meaning, U2, unwilling to be part of an IRA showpiece, pull out. These two shows at the Ritz are organised quickly, so that their stay in New York will not be wasted. They sell out rapidly and in welcoming the audience Bono explains what happened in the afternoon. "Actually, it's quite surprising that we made it here, because we were nearly arrested today. We had a really sweet lady photographer called Lynn Goldsmith and she was taking us around and was making us get into the parade and we weren't really invited. Some people were pushing us away. But we're here now and it looks great."

After *Rejoice* Bono spots two people waving flags. One is a Celtic (football) supporter who proudly waves his banner. The other waves an Irish tricolour, probably to show that he is Irish as well. "There's only one part of the Irish flag that really concerns me and that's the white bit," Bono tells him.

Adam's dark, ominous bass lines introduce *Tomorrow*. It is only the second live performance of the song. Edge plays the intro on tin whistle. During *11 O'Clock* Bono says that it bothers him that Americans generally have a distorted image of the Irish, a 'cartoon' image. He insists that not all of them walked the streets with either a bottle or a petrol bomb in their hand.

- Set second night: same as previous night, plus *Southern Man* and *A Celebration* as final encores.

This second show is the longest U2 performance to date: 80 minutes. After *Rejoice* Adam's birthday receives attention for the third time in one week when Bono lies, "What do you think of a bass player who's reached the fine age of 22 yesterday?" and sings *Happy Birthday* to Adam. After *Electric Co.* Bono talks about the first time they played here, in December 1980. "I wasn't sure what was going on, because I was looking over people at the balcony and I kinda felt: Oh, well, you know, they're coming to look and see as if we were a circus or something, but we weren't. And now, we came back here because this is right for us to do this. Last night and tonight have just proved that it can happen in here. It's been really good! I met somebody about a week ago, when we were in this restaurant in Florida, and he said: `Hey, I saw you at the Ritz. I was one of the guys up on the balcony, when you started shouting at me.' He said that he got up off his ass and he 'got into it', whatever that means. I think it means something good, to me anyway."

The show gets the crowd up from their seats. Bono reacts, "Hey, will you look at this, a standing ovation, wow! Oh boy, crazy!" He says that it will take a while before U2 will return, because they have been on tour for so long. He points out Edge's jaw as proof: "The Edge's mother doesn't even remember what he looks like. He's even grown a beard, look at this! I'm all against facial hair myself!" *Southern Man* is performed together with Garland Jeffreys, who happens to be in town. Neither of them knows the lyrics. "We don't know the words but we hope you understand," Bono sings, and changes the song into a conversation. "Now, tell me Garland, how are you these days?" "Pretty good, Bono!" "When I first met him," Bono says, "he said: You got two months left to keep singing the way you do. So, then I tried singing like him." They jam for a while before Bono thanks Garland for his presence. The band return for a festive extra encore of *A Celebration* to wind up two successful shows.

MARCH 19, 1982. GARDEN CITY, NY, NASSAU COUNTY COMMUNITY COLLEGE BALLROOM

MARCH 20, 1982. PROVIDENCE, RI, BROWN UNIVERSITY – ALUMNAE HALL

MARCH 21, 1982. PHOENIX, AZ, NIGHTCLUB

Brown Concert Agency presents
U2

Plus Special Guests
8 P.M. THIS Saturday
(March 20)
Alumnae Hall, Brown
$5.50 with Brown undergraduate ID
$6.50 general public

TICKETS ON SALE NOW AT:
Brown Student Activities Office
Also at: **Midland Records** [Thayer Street and Mall],
Strawberries [Providence] and **Record Town** [Prov.]

U2 fly to Phoenix where a few days later the tour with The J. Geils Band will resume. Tonight U2 go to a nightclub and some members end up jamming with a local singer/guitar player who is performing.

MARCH 25, 1982. PHOENIX, AZ, COLISEUM

- Attendance: 13,000

Resumption of J. Geils tour. In *Rock Bill* magazine of April 1983 Adam speaks to journalist Robert Blau: "We were opening for J. Geils in Phoenix, Arizona. The promoter came to our dressing room and said, 'You're nice guys, but I feel it's my duty to tell you that the audience is very heavy down there. It's very much a sport to bottle off the opening act very viciously. It's a game to see how long it takes to get you off stage. Bob Seger lasted about four songs. Tom Petty... same thing.' We knew we could take that kind of a fight. By the end of the night we had played two encores."

MARCH 26, 1982. SAN DIEGO, CA, SPORTS ARENA

- Attendance: 12,000

MARCH 27, 1982. LOS ANGELES, CA, SPORTS ARENA

- Attendance: 12,000

MARCH 29, 30, 1982. SAN FRANCISCO, CA, CIVIC CENTER

- Attendance: 15,000
- Set second night: *Gloria / I Threw a Brick / A Day Without Me / An Cat Dubh / Into the Heart / Rejoice / Cry–Electric Co./ I Will Follow / encore: Out Of Control / encore: 11 O'Clock Tick Tock.*

These are the last two shows supporting The J. Geils Band. The first night U2 are confronted with jeering for the first time. The second night goes better for them. After *Rejoice* Bono recognises someone in the audience: "This is a very special lady whom I just found over there... because we've been here four times now, and those four times she's been here!" The band work hard, throwing their last reserves of energy into the show. The audience are ecstatic. "This is our last show of the tour... what a way to go!" Bono says elatedly. A bit of *Give Peace A Chance* ends the show. U2 say goodbye to The J. Geils Band but agree to meet at The Rolling Stones concert in Dublin, where J. Geils will be opening. U2 have plans to tour Canada, Australia, Japan and even India, but they decide not to. After two years of virtually continuous touring, it is time for some well-earned rest. In an interview with Kid Jensen (BBC Radio) Bono says, "You've got to do a bit of living because if you don't do any living there's no real life to put into your music."

MAY 14, 1982. HATTEM, HOLLAND, 'T HEEM

- Support: Powerplay
- Attendance: 1,500; sellout
- Set: *Gloria / Another Time, Another Place / I Threw A Brick / A Day Without Me / An Cat Dubh / Into The Heart / Rejoice / Cry – Electric Co. / I Fall Down / October / I Will Follow / A Celebration / Twilight / Out Of Control / encore: Fire / 11 O'Clock Tick Tock / The Ocean / encore: Southern Man*

After a few weeks off, U2 step into the spotlight again to perform for 'Countdown In Concert' for Dutch TV. The

GLORIA
ANOTHER TIME
BRICK
DAY WITHOUT
AN CAT DUBH
INTO THE HEART
REJOICE
CRY /ELEC CO
FALLDOWN
OCTOBER
FOLLOW
CELEBRATION
TWILIGHT
CONTROL

Hattem set list

president of the fan club taught Bono to say in Dutch, "I wish I could speak Dutch, but I'll never manage that; welcome everybody," but Bono's attempt to greet the frantic audience in their own language is as pathetic as it is funny. The festive concert ends with *Southern Man*, during which Bono is joined by one of the show's photographers who happens to know the lyrics. *Another Time, Another Place* has not been performed since.

Six songs from the show make it into the TV special when it is aired on July 7, stirring up Dutch interest in U2.

Fragments of the interview that Kees Baars has done some days prior to the show are included. Asked when U2 started as a band, Edge replies: "Five minutes ago." Larry takes over: "Yeah, I think about twenty minutes ago... but as a band we've been together for about four, five years now. We came together in Dublin, as sort of just friends, and it's been growing and evolving ever since."

Baars: Is it hard to start a band in Ireland?
Larry: "Yeah, there are a lot of bands in Dublin at the moment, and there are very few places to play, so most bands have to actually move out to London, or Holland..."
Baars: Because of the political situation in Ireland, is it so that people expect more from you than only entertainment? Do they expect a sort of message?
Bono: "There's a lot of people that expect a lot of things from U2, and people will never get what they expect. People would like us to be a political mouthpiece, a punk mouthpiece, or whatever; people have been trying to put us into sort of little boxes for years. And we're not, we're just U2, we speak just as we are. The lyrics are autobiographical. We became more aware of the political situation when we actually left Ireland. Growing up in Ireland we weren't even aware, it was so close, we were blind to the situation."
Larry: "I think there's some confusion as well – there isn't actually any political violence in Dublin, where we come from, it's all in the North of the country, and you find most of the bands from the North tend to write about political issues and that, but we're not really involved. The violence is not on our doorsteps, it's about 50 miles up the road."
Bono: "It's hard when you realise that 50 miles from where you walk, you're a dog. There are people being murdered in the name of God... you know, it makes me feel very ill. As I said, growing up I didn't even think about it, but now we think about it. Our music is to try and break down barriers, whether they'd be between religious barriers, or musical barriers, whether people think I'm into punk rock, I'm into heavy rock: we're here to break down barriers, whatever they are. And that's what our music stands for."
Baars: What's the meaning behind the title 'October'?
Bono: "October... it's an image. I think we've been through the Sixties, and we've been through a time where things were in full bloom. We had fridges, and cars, we sent people to the moon, and everybody thought how great mankind was. And now, as we go through the Seventies and through the Eighties, it's a colder time of year, and it's after the harvest: the trees are stripped bare. You can see things, and we finally realise that maybe we weren't so smart after all, now that there's millions of unemployed people, now that we've used the technology that we've been blessed with, to build bombs for war machines, to build rockets, whatever. So October is an ominous word, but also it's quite lyrical..."
Baars: Is it more realistic than pessimistic, as some people said?
Bono [speaking animatedly, swinging his arms]: "It's not pessimistic at all, this band stamps on pessimism, we're anti-cynics. We try to be realistic, I think there's a realism there. We're not really into that sort of plastic trip, and I feel that 'October' is an optimistic record, because through it there is a joy. You know, it says, 'It's falling it's falling, and outside the

building come tumbling down, but inside a child on the ground says he'll do it again. What am I to do, what am I supposed to say? He says he'll change the world, but I say, I rejoice.' You know, *don't* let it bring you down. I'm sick and tired hearing bands on stage complaining. There's a bitterness in them, in their lives. They're repeating these clichés about, We're out of work... we've nothing to do; whatever it is. We say: fight it, rejoice, go for it! Don't let it bring you down. That's another cliché... look, you've started me off now..."

Jumping in on this, Island Records release the version of *I Will Follow* from the show as a single in July. Wrapped in an attractive picture sleeve, this becomes U2's first hit single in Holland, peaking at Number 12 in the charts. Since it is only released in Holland it makes for a much sought-after collector's item.

MAY 15, 1982. UK TV: 'SOMETHING ELSE'

■ *Rejoice / I Will Follow / With A Shout*
The day after the Hattem show U2 perform three songs in a TV studio in London for the programme 'Something Else' which will be aired a week later. *With A Shout* has not been performed live since.

MAY, 1982. UK TV: 'GET SET FOR SUMMER'

■ *Gloria / A Celebration / Rejoice*

JULY 1, 1982. LEIDEN, HOLLAND, GROENOORDHALLEN

■ Attendance: 12,000; sellout
■ Line-up: U2, Tom Tom Club, Talking Heads
■ Set: *Gloria / I Threw A Brick / A Day Without Me / An Cat Dubh / Into The Heart / Rejoice / Cry – Electric Co. / I Fall Down / I Will Follow / Out Of Control /* encore: *Fire / 11 O'Clock Tick Tock / The Ocean*
U2 open for The Talking Heads and bassist Tina Weymouth's spin-off hobby band Tom Tom Club. The Alarm are supposed to appear as the first act, but the announcement that they will not play doesn't seem to bother anyone. With thousands of U2's fanatical Dutch fans pushing to get to the front and singing along en masse from the moment *Gloria* starts, the concert seems an intimate U2-only occasion. The band play an exuberant and energetic set and seem to have retained their fluent concert rhythm after a few weeks of rest. While singing *Give Peace A Chance* during *11 O'Clock Tick Tock* Bono urges the crowd to sing along.

JULY 2, 1982. ROSKILDE, DENMARK, FESTIVAL GROUNDS

■ Attendance: 25,000
A series of big outdoor festival shows begins with the annual Roskilde festival outside Copenhagen. In an attempt to reach out to the huge audience on the wide open field Bono climbs onto the iron fence that separates the crowd from the stage. While singing *Electric Co.* he desperately tries to get a firm grip but is hindered by a thick layer of barbed wire. "I better watch myself," he mumbles and has more success when he jumps onto the small photographer's platform during *Out Of Control* and dances with a female photographer. The show is recorded for Danish TV.

JULY 3, 1982. TORHOUT, BELGIUM, FESTIVAL GROUNDS

■ Attendance: ca. 25,000; (capacity 60,000)
■ Festival line-up: Allez Allez, The Members, U2, Steve Miller Band, Mink DeVille, Tom Tom Club, Talking Heads, Jackson Browne

Torhout Festival

The Torhout/Werchter double festival is held on two fields in the villages of Torhout (near the coast) and Werchter (some 30 km Northeast of Brussels), with the same artists on the bill both days.

Bono has strained his voice at the two previous shows and to compensate tries even harder to diminish the physical distance to the large crowd. During the guitar solo in *Electric Co.* he starts climbing the gigantic stage construction, holding on to its aluminium poles. Once at the top, Bono sings his distorted version of *Send In The Clowns*: "Two... three... four... two... three... four... why must I hide from myself, when I need the

crowd; bring on the crowd, I love this crowd..." While Edge continues his solo, Bono makes his way back onstage accompanied by the amazed audience's applause. Later, he jumps offstage to shake hands with members of the audience and climbs on the fence, singing on while he stands on the edge, held upright by people in the front.

Several people in the audience bring white flags and are waving them frantically, some have messages written on them, some are plain white. Bono acknowledges the flags and after gesturing to someone to pass his up to him, accepts a big flag and takes it onstage.

and mumbles, "never again". The white flag comes in handy for *11 O'Clock Tick Tock*: Bono's rendering of *Give Peace A Chance* during this song is now illustrated with a symbol that everyone understands.

Bono's sensational, breathtaking stunts during the festival show his desire to reach out to the people and on both days lift

The first flag

JULY 4, 1982. WERCHTER, BELGIUM, FESTIVAL GROUNDS

- Attendance: ca. 35,000; (capacity 60,000)
- Festival line-up: Allez Allez, The Members, U2, Steve Miller Band, DeVille, Tom Tom Club, Talking Heads, Jackson Browne
- Set: *Gloria / I Threw A Brick / A Day Without Me / An Cat Dubh / Into The Heart / Rejoice / Cry – Electric Co. / I Fall Down / I Will Follow / Out Of Control / 11 O'Clock Tick Tock / The Ocean / Fire*

"About this time yesterday afternoon, at the other site, I lost my voice, so if anybody finds it, if they could bring it around to the side of the stage." Bono's voice has become worse, but he gives it everything he has. He doesn't stand still for a second, fights playfully with Adam or Edge, dances with the cable-holding girl from the TV crew, or reaches out to accept gifts from fans. During *I Threw A Brick* he picks up a white flag with 'U2' written in red on it, and uses it as a prop throughout the rest of the show. With all eyes and cameras focused on the singer, Bono again climbs the scaffolding during *Electric Co.* Back onstage he looks up, as if he doesn't believe what he has just done, laughs

spirits among the crowd. Combined with the exuberant energy of the music and the symbolism of the white flags, U2 make a big impression on the audience and the media. At the same time Bono's actions demonstrate to himself that these are powerful gestures that are capable of getting his ideals across to a large audience. It inspires him and suggests many ideas for the future.

The festival is filmed and audio taped by ID-TV and broadcast in several Dutch and Belgian radio and TV programmes. In addition, *Fire, I Threw A Brick* and *A Day Without Me* are issued by Island Records on the second 7" record that is given for free in the *New Year's Day* double-pack single, released in January 1983, and its 12" version. In 1992, the 12" is made available as a CD single.

JULY 18, 1982. DUBLIN, IRELAND, PUNCHESTOWN RACECOURSE

- Festival line-up: Big Self, De Danann, Simple Minds, Paul Brady, U2, Rory Gallagher
- Set: *Gloria / I Threw A Brick / A Day Without Me / An Cat Dubh / Into The Heart / Rejoice / Cry – Electric Co. / I Fall Down / I Will Follow / Out Of Control / encore: Fire / 11 O'Clock Tick Tock / The Ocean*

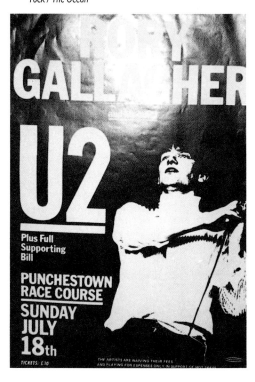

The Irish magazine *Hot Press* celebrates its fifth anniversary by organising a rock festival. Bono tells the crowd, "Last night we played a special gig for some lads in Shop Street. I said today that this one was gonna be for you, because in the centre of our city they're pulling the buildings down. This is *Rejoice*, and we will rejoice, this afternoon!" He climbs the scaffolding during *Electric Co.*, eliciting cheering from the crowd. During the encore Bono is joined onstage by his wife-to-be Alison Stewart. Dublin-based disc-jockey/media bandit B.P. Fallon is watching the show from the wings, and Bono drags him onstage for a quick duet of *Give Peace A Chance* during *11 O'Clock Tick Tock*.

JULY 31, 1982. GATESHEAD, ENGLAND, INTERNATIONAL STADIUM

- Attendance: 12,500
- Festival line-up: Lords Of The New Church, Gang of Four, The Beat, U2, The Police
- Set: *Gloria / I Threw A Brick / A Day Without Me / An Cat Dubh / Into The Heart / Rejoice / Cry–Electric Co. / I Will Follow / Out*

Of Control / encore: A Celebration / 11 O'Clock Tick Tock / The Ocean

Though U2's participation in the Glastonbury festival has already been announced, and the band are rumoured to play at about every other festival in the UK during the summer, Gateshead is the only one they actually perform at. Like the previous year the stadium is far from being sold out.

Hugh Fielder writes in *Sounds*: 'U2 took advantage of the day's upswing to reinforce the numerous claims made on their behalf to be 'the next big thing'. Currently cooped up in the country getting their third album together, they exploded with a barrage of pent-up energy that no amount of pastoral activity can fulfil. Bono demonstrated his sudden sense of release, quite literally, by scaling the PA stack beside the stage and crowning it

with a white flag plucked from the audience, singing *Electric Co.* all the while. "There's only one flag and that's a white flag," he announced with what was a defiantly peaceful fervour for these aggressive times. The *A Celebration* encore had an irresistible force born of a group chemistry that's bubbled into the most precious of rock & roll commodities: 'charisma.'

During The Police's performance, Bono joins Sting on *Invisible Sun*. Rock programme 'The Tube' film the show.

AUGUST 3, 1982. VILAR DE MOUROS, PORTUGAL

At their first concert in southern Europe, U2 perform a 70-minute set which includes *Gloria, Rejoice, I Fall Down, Fire* and *A Celebration*.

AUGUST 7, 1982. TURKU, FINLAND, RUISROCK FESTIVAL

- Set: *Gloria / I Threw A Brick / A Day Without Me / An Cat Dubh / Into The Heart / Rejoice / Cry – Electric Co. / I Fall Down / A Celebration / 11 O'Clock Tick Tock / The Ocean / encore: I Will Follow / Southern Man*

The audience at U2's first performance in Finland are unfamiliar with their music but enjoy it nevertheless. The relaxed and joyous atmosphere reminds Bono of another festival. "So, here we are in Woodstock, yes? People have been telling me about Woodstock, I never knew it could happen again, this is wonderful!" During *Rejoice* Bono sings bits of Bob Dylan's *Like A Rolling Stone* and in *Electric Co.*, while climbing the scaffolding, a piece of *Let's Twist Again* shows up. "When I was younger I used to be afraid of heights," Bono says later. "So, I used to climb up on the bridges over the railway lines and kinda push myself into doing things I wasn't very good at. That's why I joined a rock & roll band!" The performance of *Southern Man* is very long as Bono sings together with someone from the crew and adds lines of *Waiting For The Man*, ending their last show of the summer. U2 continue work on their third album.

THE PRE-'WAR' TOUR: UNITED KINGDOM, EUROPE, DECEMBER 1982

After the summer shows U2 had begun working on their next album. Throughout August, September and October, songs were written, recorded and mixed at Windmill Lane Studios in Dublin with Steve Lillywhite producing. On the first day of December, U2 start a four-week, 20-date tour which serves as a warm-up for a major tour in the New Year and gives the band an opportunity to preview some of the key songs of the new album, which is called 'War' and scheduled for release in February 1983.

The stage set-up has three large white flags positioned at the back, with air-blowers on the floor to set the flags flying at given moments. These props had proven their symbolic value during the summer shows, and are now used because they capture the theme of the 'War' album: surrender. Covered by a red carpet, the stage has a riser to house the drum kit and keyboards. This pre-'War' tour starts with six UK shows, then moves to the Low Countries and Scandinavia before ending with a string of Irish dates.

DECEMBER 1, 1982. GLASGOW, TIFFANY'S

- Attendance: 1,500; sellout
- Set: *Out Of Control / Twilight / I Threw A Brick / A Day Without Me / An Cat Dubh / Into The Heart / Surrender / Sunday Bloody Sunday / Cry-Electric Co. / I Fall Down / October / New Year's Day / Gloria / I Will Follow / encore: 11 O'Clock Tick Tock / The Ocean / encore: A Celebration / Fire*

Out Of Control gets the show off to a frenzied start. Bono welcomes the audience and explains it's the band's first gig after several months in the studio. "We've never invited so many people along to a rehearsal before," he says. Introducing the first new song, *Surrender*, he says it's one of the two songs on the new album about New York City and it's the album's theme song. Besides Edge's choppy guitar it has a chilling steel-guitar solo. Bono tries to get the crowd to sing along to the catchy chorus. The second new song opens with Larry's fierce, rattling, march beat. Bono announces, "This is a song called *Sunday Bloody Sunday*," while the audience listen silently. Dealing with the troubles in Northern Ireland, it refers to the events of November 21, 1920, when fourteen civilians were shot by soldiers during a Gaelic football match as a reprisal for the assassination of eleven British officers and soldiers. It also refers to the day in 1972, when another Bloody Sunday occurred in

Londonderry as British soldiers fired in panic at a crowd of Irishmen during a protest march. *Sunday Bloody Sunday*, the song, confronts the listener with the consequences of opposing religious beliefs. It asks when the atrocities will stop ("How long must we sing this song") but offers an optimistic undertone ("Tonight, we can be as one."). The crowd receive the song reasonably well.

During the guitar solo in *Electric Co.*, Bono repeats the climbing stunt practised at the summer festivals, as he will continue to do. With the crowd following his every move all the way up to the balcony, it strengthens the sense of unity that reigns in the hall and provides sensation to match the explosive energy of the music. Standing on the edge of the balcony, he sings on while continuing to hold people's hands. During the *Send In The Clowns* bit, Bono explains that he recently met the members of Simple Minds and expresses his disgust with the meaningless music currently flooding the UK charts. "Glasgow is famous for Simple Minds. And it's bands like Simple Minds and U2 that are gonna show this blibberty-blop where to go! Because I am sick and tired of turning on the television and seeing this 'wallpaper music' on the television, on the radio. I wanna go over to them and say 'What are you saying to me? You're saying nothing!'"

Before *I Fall Down*, Bono reveals that during the rehearsals Edge had to listen to their own records to remember the old songs. Edge, however, plays the song flawlessly while Bono sings the wrong words at the wrong moment. "This should be on the shops on New Year's Day – this is called *New Year's Day*." This is the third new song premièred tonight, and is chosen as the first single from 'War'. The band are forced to end it prematurely as Edge's amplifier suddenly emits loud feedback. While he explains that the guitar needs some time to be fixed, Bono invites fans onstage if they have something from the heart to say. Nobody makes the first move. "Nobody has got anything to say?" When the house lights go up and Bono tries again, a guy climbs onstage to shout something aggressive. The next guy just swears at some people. "Is there *anybody* that has something to say?", Bono urges. A girl comes on to wish her friend luck with something. "Now, *she's* got something to say!"

During the encore Bono receives a bottle of champagne. "This is from some friends of yours, from the lads in Simple Minds, thanks!" Bono pours cups for the band and for some in the audience. He sings "We wish you a merry Christmas and a happy New Year" a few times during *11 O'Clock Tick Tock*, which he will do throughout the month in this song.

DECEMBER 2, 1982. MANCHESTER, APOLLO THEATRE

- Attendance: 2,400; sellout
- Support: The Alarm
- Set: *Out Of Control / Twilight / Surrender / I Threw A Brick / A Day Without Me / An Cat Dubh / Into The Heart / Sunday Bloody Sunday / Cry-Electric Co. / I Fall Down / October / New Year's Day / Gloria / I Will Follow /* encore: *Fire / A Celebration / 11 O'Clock Tick Tock / The Ocean /* encore: *I Will Follow*

A bunch of fans following the tour are allowed in to watch the soundcheck, as at most shows of the December tour. The three new songs are well-received. *Sunday Bloody Sunday* again causes problems and halfway through the band forget what comes next. *New Year's Day* is dedicated to "the people who seem to be travelling along with us." After *A Celebration*, Edge takes off his guitar and leaves the stage. "Edge – we're not going!" Bono shouts. "Give him his guitar." The fans continue cheering so long that U2 come back again to play *I Will Follow* for the second time that night.

DECEMBER 3, 1982. LEICESTER, DE MONTFORT HALL

- Attendance: 2,500; sellout
- Support: The Set

- Set: *Out Of Control / Twilight / Surrender / I Threw A Brick / A Day Without Me / An Cat Dubh / Into The Heart / Sunday Bloody Sunday / Cry-Electric Co. / I Fall Down / October / New Year's Day / Gloria / I Will Follow /* encore: *Fire / A Celebration / 11 O'Clock Tick Tock / The Ocean*

Introducing the new song *Sunday Bloody Sunday*, Bono tells the crowd, "You'll never hear it on the radio" because of its lyrics. While Bono climbs to the balcony during *Electric Co.*, the spotlight operators have trouble locating him. "Hey, spotlight, I'm over here, on the right hand side! Aah, wonderful..." During *A Celebration* too many fans climb onstage to dance and are sent back by security.

DECEMBER 4, 1982. BIRMINGHAM, ODEON

- Attendance: 2,500; sellout
- Support: The Alarm
- Set: same as Manchester, but *A Celebration* is played after *The Ocean* and instead of the second performance of *I Will Follow*, *Sunday Bloody Sunday* is played for a second time.

Bono sings in a restrained manner because his throat is bothering him. During the second performance of *Sunday Bloody Sunday* he throws one of the white flags into the audience. Several fans try to grab it as a souvenir which results in some pushing. Bono interrupts the song and shouts, "When I throw a white flag into the audience, I don't expect anybody to fight for the white flag!"

DECEMBER 5, 1982. LONDON, LYCEUM BALLROOM

- Attendance: 1,500; sellout
- Support: Zerra 1, The Alarm
- Set: same as Leicester.

The smoke machines irritate Bono's throat as he is still suffering from a virus. "I have to confess to you that I haven't been feeling all right... Not more smoke *please*, forget about the smoke!"

DECEMBER 6, 1982. LONDON, HAMMERSMITH PALAIS

- Attendance: 2,000; sellout
- Support: Zerra 1, The Alarm
- Set: same as Leicester.

Bono makes an appearance during The Alarm's set to join Mike Peters singing the Bob Dylan classic *Knocking On Heaven's Door*, which Peters had taught Bono. Besides the lyrics, the song appeals to Bono because its simple chords are easy to play but still make for a powerful, compelling song.

U2's show is recorded for radio and finds the band in good form. "For a long time I have been frightened to write about where I live, Ireland, and its problems. This is called *Sunday Bloody Sunday*. This is not a rebel song." Bono dedicates *I Fall Down* to a U2 fan. "I received a letter about five minutes before the concert. It's about a boy called Duncan. Duncan didn't write it. It says Duncan is dying, he's in a coma. This is for you, Duncan..." Bono changes the lyrics in reference to Duncan to give him hope; Duncan dies on the night of the show. During *11*

O'Clock Tick Tock Bono dances the can-can with two girls who have jumped onstage.

DECEMBER 8, 1982. UTRECHT, HOLLAND, MUZIEKCENTRUM VREDENBURG

- Attendance: 2,000; sellout
- Support: Zerra 1
- Set: same as Leicester.

An impatient U2 fan bombards the opening act with fruit and yoghurt. Bono's voice is in full strength again after a day's rest. Tonight's version of *Sunday Bloody Sunday* is convincing as Bono gets the crowd to sing "No more" as an expression of disgust at the horrific images the song evokes. He tells the buoyant crowd of the public's initial reservations about U2: "When we were a garage-band from garage-land, they said that we had a spark but that we could never take it out of a small room, that we could never make it into a big hall, that we wouldn't be able to survive..." He proudly looks around the theatre, from the people in the front to those far up in the balcony. "I love this!" When the crowd sing along with the bit of *Merry Christmas* in *11 O'Clock Tick Tock*, the band stop playing to listen to the crowd.

DECEMBER 9, 1982. GRONINGEN, HOLLAND, MARTINIHAL

- Attendance: 5,000; sellout
- Set: same as Leicester.

The enthusiastic crowd clap and sing along with every single song. Bono briefly interrupts *Fire* as a little brawl erupts in the audience.

DECEMBER 10, 1982. MECHELEN, BELGIUM, VOLKSBELANG

- Attendance: 2,000; sellout

The atmosphere in the hall is hot and humid due to bad air-conditioning. Bono tells the crowd that he got the idea for the white flags during the Werchter festival in the summer. After the show Adam, Larry and Bono come out to chat with fans in the hall.

DECEMBER 11, 1982. DEINZE, BELGIUM, BRIELPOORT

- Support: Angry Voices

Someone throws a small smoke bomb on stage during the support band. U2 start their concert energetically but are hindered by a guy in the front pushing and provoking people around him for no reason. "Listen you," Bono shouts, "If you don't stop using violence, I can have some people throw you

Copenhagen

out! I come from a country where people use violence... and it's real, so don't pretend." He points to the white flags on stage. "Do you know what that is? This is a white flag which means peace!" Confused and annoyed, the band proceed with the show.

DECEMBER 12, 1982. GENK, BELGIUM, LIMBURGHAL

The show is marred by bad acoustics. Edge has the flu but manages to play.

DECEMBER 14, 1982. COPENHAGEN, DENMARK, FALKONER TEATRET

- Attendance: 3,000
- Set: same as Leicester, but *Gloria* and *I Will Follow* switch places.

Fiddle-player Steve Wickham, who has contributed to two songs on the upcoming 'War' album, appears onstage and gets a grand introduction from Bono, who says the band have become very attached to Steve. He plays violin during *Into The Heart* and *Sunday Bloody Sunday*. The band feel they are not succeeding in turning the theatre into a small room as the crowd are not very lively. To effect a breakthrough, Bono invites the audience up onstage to dance during *11 O'Clock Tick Tock*. After initial hesitation, several people get up and in the end around 100 members of the audience jam the stage. Adam climbs up on one of the speakers.

DECEMBER 15, 1982. STOCKHOLM, SWEDEN, KONSERTHUSET

- Attendance: 2,000

- Set: same as Leicester.

Both crowd and critics consider the show a success. U2 use their stay in Sweden to shoot the video clip for *New Year's Day*, which will be released as the first single off the 'War' album in January 1983. U2 select photographer Anton Corbijn, whom they first met in New Orleans in February, to shoot photographs for the inside of the album's fold-out record sleeve and for publicity purposes.

DECEMBER 16, 1982. OSLO, NORWAY

DECEMBER 18, 1982. CORK, IRELAND, CITY HALL

DECEMBER 19, 1982. GALWAY, IRELAND, LEISURELAND

- Support: Blue in Heaven

DECEMBER 20, 1982. BELFAST, NORTHERN IRELAND, MAYSFIELD LEISURE CENTRE

- Attendance: 3,000; sellout

With Belfast the battleground for the minor civil war between Protestants and Catholics, and often the scene of IRA assaults to protest against British presence in Northern Ireland, U2 are keyed-up about the performance and concerned about how *Sunday Bloody Sunday* will go down. The first half hour of the concert is tense. Edge's amplifier blows up and has to be replaced in the middle of a song. When it's time for *Sunday Bloody Sunday*, Bono nervously tells the crowd it's a song especially written for them and stresses that it's not a (pro-IRA) rebel song. He promises that if they don't like it, U2 will never play it in Belfast again. The crowd listen to the stomping beat and confrontational, but optimistic, lyrics and scream their heads off in enthusiasm at the end of the song. Only two or three guys boo and leave the hall. The band are relieved and rejoice with the crowd for the rest of the show.

DECEMBER 22, 23, 24, 1982. DUBLIN, IRELAND, S.F.X. CENTRE

- Attendance: 3,600; sellout
- Support: (1st night) Big Thorp, (2nd night) Zerra 1, (3rd night) Blue in Heaven

Three shows in U2's hometown end the December tour with every night a different support act. Fiddle-player Steve Wickham makes a guest appearances at the shows, as does Vincent Kifduff who plays uillean pipes on some songs.

Supporting their new single, *New Year's Day*, U2 playback to a version recorded live earlier that day.

THE 'WAR' TOUR, LEG I: UNITED KINGDOM, WINTER/SPRING 1983

Starting in Scotland, the new tour will see U2 zigzagging their way through the UK. All 19 shows originally announced have sold out, and another nine are added to the schedule, which includes return visits to several cities. The band are eager to go on the road and present their new songs. The tour is intended to maintain the character of the album. 'War', released on February 28, is the band's vision of political conflicts throughout the world, as well as on personal inner struggles they have been experiencing. The album deals with battles between the sexes, lovers, and religions, but surrender is the theme that dominates.

Both musically and lyrically, the songs are spikier than before, more straightforward and less atmospheric than the two previous albums, but still contain a richness and diversity on all fronts. With 'War', U2 fight the enormous surge of 'wallpaper music' that has been dominating the British charts the last few years. Music made by machines rather than by genuine artists, with TV presentation revealing that the bands have spent more time on shaping their haircuts than on trying to invest some substance or personality into the lyrics. U2 want to replace those bands in the charts, and are highly pleased that *New Year's Day* has reached No. 9, giving them their first Top 10 single in the UK.

FEBRUARY 26, 1983. DUNDEE, CAIRD HALL

- Attendance: 2,500; sellout
- Support: The Nightcaps
- Set: *Gloria / I Threw A Brick Through A Window / A Day Without Me / New Year's Day / Out Of Control / Sunday Bloody Sunday / Cry–Electric Co. / I Fall Down / October / Tomorrow / Two Hearts Beat As One / Seconds / Fire / 11 O'Clock Tick Tock / I Will Follow / encore: Party Girl / Surrender / Like A Song / 40.*

The photo from the 'War' record sleeve is used as a backdrop for the stage, just like the 'Boy' cover had served as a prop in

1980/81. The pure child has now grown up, looks at the world and is angry and scared by what he sees. As at the December shows, there are three white flags at the back of the stage to indicate the show's theme.

Gloria is the opening song throughout the UK tour, an old favourite that gets the show off to a rousing and celebratory start. *I Threw A Brick* segues into *A Day Without Me*. *Sunday Bloody Sunday* is played with vigour, Larry's fierce drum beat and Edge's guitar playing matching the lyrics in intensity. The white flags fly up to contrast the dark red spotlights and dry ice that illustrate this song. Bono picks up one of the flags to march across the stage, taking it with him when he climbs the balcony during *Electric Co.*. The crowd love Bono's antics. Back on stage, he comments, "Sometimes it feels like a long way from here to the back of a building like this. Sometimes you have to show an audience how much you want to get across; I hope you understand."

October serves as a breather in the set, the piano delicately played by Edge alone in the spotlight. Larry caresses the cymbals for *Tomorrow*, Adam produces dark and grim bass sounds, while Edge plays the intro melody on tin whistle. The song has been performed on just two occasions before but now has a fixed spot in the set. It is vocally demanding for Bono but he finds a way of delivering it with emotion without straining his voice too much.

Several songs are premièred tonight. *Two Hearts Beat As One* describes inner struggles, trying to cope with the left or right, right or wrong, but finding unity nevertheless. *Seconds* has Edge making his live début both singing lead and playing acoustic guitar. Bono does background vocals on this song about the nuclear arms race between world powers. *Seconds* is followed by *Fire*, which will turn out to be the last time U2 ever play it.

Party Girl, originally titled *Trash, Trampoline And The Party Girl*, is another first this night. It is not on the 'War' album, and has featured only on the B-side of the 1982 *A Celebration* single. Bono introduces it as being the first and probably last time U2 play it. The band have trouble with the high-paced *Like A Song*, and will consequently drop it from their set. The closing song of 'War', *40*, is chosen to end the show as well, with Adam and Edge swapping their instruments. The song takes the hopeful aspect of *Sunday Bloody Sunday* further, repeating the line "How long to sing this song", in a long, hymn-like version that subdues the crowd. Clannad's *Theme Of Harry's Game* is played over the PA as the crowd leave the theatre.

There are several first-night mistakes here and there, but on the whole the tour opening is a big success. Though several of the new songs confront the crowd with aspects of war and struggle, the overall feeling U2 manage to implant in the audience is that of harmony.

FEBRUARY 27, 1993. ABERDEEN, CAPITOL THEATRE

- Attendance: 2,000; sellout
- Support: The Nightcaps

FEBRUARY 28, 1983. EDINBURGH, PLAYHOUSE

- Attendance: 3,000; sellout
- Support: The Nightcaps
- Set: *Gloria / I Threw A Brick / A Day Without Me / Seconds / New Year's Day / Sunday Bloody Sunday / Cry–Electric Co. / I Fall Down / October / Tomorrow / Twilight / Out of Control / 11 O'Clock Tick Tock / I Will Follow / encore: Party Girl / Surrender / encore: A Celebration / 40.*

By this time there are a good few changes in the set. *Out Of Control* is moved forward, likewise *Seconds*, which was song number twelve in Dundee, and is now played fourth. *Two Hearts Beat As One* is left out and *A Celebration* is played as an encore. During *Electric Co.* Bono briefly strays, segueing into The Doors' *Break On Through*. The Scottish audience sing along enthusiastically to every single song. After the show, while

Clannad's outro music plays over the PA, they keep on singing the chorus of *40*, "How long to sing this song," for a long time.

MARCH 1, 1983. NEWCASTLE, CITY HALL

- Attendance: 2,150; sellout
- Support: The Nightcaps
- Set: *Gloria / I Threw a Brick / A Day Without Me / Seconds / New Year's Day / Sunday Bloody Sunday / Cry–Electric Co. / I Fall Down / October / Tomorrow / Twilight / Out of Control / encore: Party Girl / A Celebration / 11 O'Clock Tick Tock / I Will Follow / 40.*

Slowly but surely U2 discover where in the set each song is best suited. *Surrender* disappears. *11 O'Clock Tick Tock* and *I Will Follow* are now used as encores, and *Out Of Control* brings up the rear of the regular set. As at most shows on this tour Bono explains that his biggest ambition is to "break through into you". But tonight he adds, "Sometimes we don't succeed."

MARCH 2, 1983. LANCASTER, UNIVERSITY

- Attendance: 1,600; sellout
- Support: The Nightcaps
- Set: same as in Newcastle, plus the re-appearance of *Two Hearts Beat As One* after *Seconds*.

A better and more spirited show than the previous night. "I think this is working, yes?" Bono sounds relieved. Many songs are introduced, and before *Twilight* Bono, referring to the location of this show, mentions that he also went to university, albeit for only two weeks.

MARCH 3, 1983. LIVERPOOL, ROYAL COURT THEATRE

- Attendance: 1,500; sellout
- Support: The Nightcaps
- Set: same as Lancaster, but the order of encores differs: *11 O'Clock Tick Tock / I Will Follow / Party Girl / A Celebration / 40*

The crowd are happy to see U2 again and sing along to every single song. During *Twilight*, Bono sings lines from *Too Shy*, a current hit by Kajagoogoo, and a typical example of the kind of band that U2 want to replace in the charts, a band who hide behind their haircuts to make a quick buck.

MARCH 4, 1983. HANLEY, VICTORIA HALL

- Attendance: 1,500; sellout
- Support: The Nightcaps
- Set: same as Lancaster, minus *A Celebration*, which has disappeared from the basic set.

After a slow start in which the band lack power and Bono hardly speaks to the crowd, the band finally get things rolling with a thundering *Out Of Control* during which Bono sings some lines from Echo & The Bunnymen's *The Cutter*, one of the few tracks in the current charts that he does like, followed by a joyous encore. At the end of *40* Bono slowly sings some lines from *Sunday Bloody Sunday* before ending with "How long to sing this song."

MARCH 6, 1983. PORTSMOUTH, GUILDHALL

- Attendance: 2,000; sellout
- Support: The Nightcaps
- Set: same as Lancaster, minus *A Celebration* and *Two Hearts Beat As One*, but plus *Surrender* after *Tomorrow*.

Before *Sunday Bloody Sunday* Bono expresses his annoyance with a journalist who wrote that the songs did not do anything for him. Bono quotes some lines from the song and delivers an extra-aggressive and emotional version.

MARCH 7, 1983. BRISTOL, COLSTON HALL

- Attendance: 2,100; sellout
- Support: The Nightcaps
- Set: *Gloria / I Threw a Brick / A Day Without Me / Seconds / Surrender / New Year's Day / Sunday Bloody Sunday / Cry–Electric Co. / I Fall Down / October / Tomorrow / Two Hearts Beat As One / Twilight / Out Of Control /* encore: *Party Girl / 11 O'Clock Tick Tock / I Will Follow / 40.*

After fluctuating to and fro at the previous shows, two songs find their fixed spots in the set: *Surrender* is now played after *Seconds* and *Two Hearts Beat As One* after *Tomorrow*. During *Surrender* Bono sings snippets of Michael Jackson's *Billie Jean*, which he will repeat practically every night on the UK tour. There is a special guest in the audience tonight: an inmate from a Devon remand centre who has escaped for the evening to attend U2's concert. Afterwards he returns to the centre.

MARCH 8, 1983. EXETER, UNIVERSITY

- Attendance: 1,800
- Support: The Nightcaps

The escaped prisoner pleads with the authorities to allow all the inmates to attend the Exeter show and permission is granted. "It was amazing when we all met them afterwards," Bono says later in an interview. "Some of them looked really villainous, but they were all well behaved."

MARCH 9, 1983. POOLE, ARTS CENTRE

- Attendance: 1,500
- Support: The Nightcaps

MARCH 10, 1983. BIRMINGHAM, ODEON

- Attendance: 1,400; sellout
- Support: The Nightcaps
- Set: same as Bristol.

When U2 return for the encore, Bono confesses that the band was initially hesitant about moving from clubs to theatres, but he now feels they are no longer afraid of the increase in audience size. After *Party Girl* he announces that the 'War' album has just entered the UK charts at No. 1 and wants to celebrate with champagne. He has problems opening the bottle and asks for the "strongest man in the building". U2's tour manager Dennis Sheehan comes on stage but can't open the bottle either. A drum roll by Larry builds up excitement while someone from the audience comes on stage for another unsuccessful attempt to uncork the thing. "Fuck the champagne," Edge probably thought as he goes straight into *11 O'Clock Tick Tock*.

Karen Swayne reviews this show in *Sounds* magazine: 'After going well and truly over the top a year or so ago when I last reviewed U2, I was determined that this time I wouldn't get too carried away. Problem is, I'd forgotten just how overwhelmingly good they can be; their ability to send tingles down my spine remains undiminished and their skill at breaking down barriers between band and audience has never been better. Against a backdrop of three white flags and the face of the Boy (in 1983 his eyes are suspicious and fearful), U2 rejoiced in life and love. They conveyed a warmth that is increasingly rare in these cynical times where a worthless bunch of singing hairdo's can hit the top of the charts. U2's honesty alone makes them a band to trust and to treasure.'

MARCH 11, 1983. CARDIFF, ST. DAVID'S HALL

- Attendance: 3,000; sellout
- Support: The Nightcaps
- Set: same as Bristol.

Bono interrupts *A Day Without Me*: "Somebody in the front row...

Tyne Tees Studio, 'The Tube'

stop spitting!" He threatens to have the culprit thrown out, which is met with cheers from a few of the victims. *I Fall Down* is dedicated to someone called Rizzy. "He's not here anymore," Bono says sadly, "I love him." *11 O'Clock Tick Tock* makes for a more cheerful ending of the show. Bono dances with a girl from the audience and asks her name. "Ladies and gentlemen: from Holland on the mainland, this is Marie!" For Edge, born in Wales, this is a kind of a homecoming, and for the occasion Bono asks the audience to sing for Edge. "A song of your choice!" Suggestions fly. "I'm gonna select one member from the audience to lead you in song." Bono invites a girl on stage who starts to sing *Land Of My Fathers,* and the entire crowd join in.

MARCH 13, 1983. BRIGHTON, TOP RANK

- Attendance: 2,000
- Set: same as Bristol, only *Cry–Electric Co.* and *Sunday Bloody Sunday* swop places, and *Knocking On Heaven's Door* is played before *40.*

Adam celebrates his 23rd birthday, and throughout the show Bono makes sure that everybody knows. "Will you welcome the birthday boy!" he shouts and sings *Happy Birthday* with the audience. "I think I know what he wants," Bono sings during *Party Girl*, and asks Adam, "What do you want, man? I tell you what you want. He wants a present! He wants some sort of gift. Do you want a drink? Get the boy a drink!" Dennis Sheehan then brings a bottle of champagne and a birthday cake on stage. Steve Iredale brings on some presents, including a silk morning coat and slippers. While Adam accepts the gifts, Bono picks up

the bass and plays a funky solo, with the audience singing *Happy Birthday* again.

During the encore *Knocking On Heaven's Door* is played, together with Mike Peters, the singer of The Alarm, and his saxophonist joining in. Peters had taught Bono the song that December past. At that time, in London, Bono sang along to The Alarm's own performance of the Dylan classic; now the roles are reversed. It is the first time U2 play this song and Bono does not yet know all the lyrics, but Mike stands by him.

MARCH 14, 1983. LONDON, HAMMERSMITH ODEON

- Attendance: 3,000; sellout
- Support: The Nightcaps
- Set: Same as Bristol but with snatches of *Billie Jean, Too Shy* and *The Cutter* here and there.

The security is strict to the point of annoyance, with fans constantly being asked to show their ticket every time they leave their seats to get a drink or go to the toilet, and this leads to irritation in the audience. U2 play a rather tentative show and never really warm up. With many journalists attending to report on U2's first London show this year, some less than positive reviews appear the following week.

MARCH 15, 1983. IPSWICH, GAUMONT THEATRE

- Attendance: 1,600; sellout
- Support: The Nightcaps

■ Set: same as Bristol. *Sunday Bloody Sunday* is announced as "a song of hope". *Tomorrow* is sung very emotionally. When the band come back on stage for the encore, Bono says he liked the show and that they will be back here again. However, this was to be U2's first and last show in Ipswich.

MARCH 16, 1983. NEWCASTLE, TYNE TEES TV STUDIOS

■ Set: *Gloria / New Year's Day / Sunday Bloody Sunday / 40 / I Will Follow*

A live session for 'The Tube' includes performances by Big Country, The Undertones, and U2. Bono is interviewed briefly before starting a five song set in front of a small studio audience. U2's official fan club in the UK, 'U2 Info', has invited fifty members from the Newcastle area to attend. The group perform before the 'War' backdrop and the flags and there is a catwalk running into the crowd which Bono frequently uses. During *I Will Follow* around 25 fans jump on stage, resulting in a joyous dance across the catwalk. Two days later the first three songs are broadcast, while *I Will Follow* is aired on June 24, 1983. The performance of *40* remains unshown.

MARCH 17, 1983. SHEFFIELD, CITY HALL

■ Attendance: 2,300; sellout
■ Support: The Nightcaps
■ Set: same as Bristol, plus *Gloria* and *A Celebration* after *I Will Follow*.

A super-enthusiastic audience see U2 perform a great show in which the band reward the fans for their warm reception by playing *Gloria* a second time that night during the encores. Bono compliments the venue, calling it the best building in England and stating that "it has a great passion". They pull out *A Celebration* for the first time since Liverpool on March 3, playing it wildly and joyously. It is to be the last time U2 will ever play the song.

MARCH 18, 1983. LEEDS, UNIVERSITY

■ Attendance: 1,500; sellout
■ Support: The Nightcaps
■ Set: same as Bristol.

The show begins late and Bono apologises. "We just wanted to make it right for you. This could be the best concert of our lives," he says optimistically, but it is not to be. The spark isn't there and Bono makes a tired impression. He adds a short bit of *Loch Lomond* to *Two Hearts Beat As One*, which adds something extra even though they aren't in Scotland where the song originated. *Two Hearts Beat As One* also includes snippets of *Let's Twist Again*.

MARCH 19, 1983. MANCHESTER, APOLLO THEATRE

■ Attendance: 2,400; sellout

■ Support: The Nightcaps
■ Set: same as Bristol.

Bono reminisces about U2's performance in this town three years earlier. "We played a room at the top of a building; it was a place called the Beach Club and I loved this place." Lines from The Doors' Break *On Through* pop up in *Electric Co.*

MARCH 20, 1983. DERBY, ASSEMBLY ROOMS

■ Attendance: 1,500; sellout
■ Support: The Nightcaps

This is the last show with The Nightcaps. The Alarm and Big Country take over for the last couple of shows.

MARCH 21, 1983. LONDON, HAMMERSMITH ODEON

■ Attendance: 3,000; sellout
■ Set: same as Bristol.

There is no support act and the band are back at the Hammersmith Odeon for a better show than the one the week before. Fiddler Steve Wickham plays along on *Sunday Bloody Sunday* at this concert and the following evening, contributing a sensitive intro to *Tomorrow*. Bono tells everyone that they got to know Wickham after Edge met him at a bus-stop in Dublin.

MARCH 22, 1983. LONDON, HAMMERSMITH PALAIS

■ Attendance: 2,000; sellout
■ Support: The Alarm
■ Set: same as Bristol.

The busy tour schedule is taking its toll on the band with Bono sounding somewhat sad and a little lost. During *I Fall Down* he sings, "Don't you know this is a cry for help... I don't know what I'm doing here..." During *Twilight* the smoke from the smoke machine becomes too much. "Turn off that stupid smoke!" he shouts. At the end of *Out Of Control* he improvises, "All I want is you... all I want is you..." The audience pick up on this for a while.

Five minutes of rest in the dressing room do wonders. During the encores the show takes a bizarre turn when Bono picks a guy from the audience during *Party Girl* and builds the entire song around him. "I know a boy, a boy called Party," Bono sings directly to the guy and introduces him to the audience. "This is Party, by the way. What's your name?" "John." "John's gonna sing for you!" The audience cheer but never get to hear John.

Bono restarts *Party Girl* and deviates from the original lyrics at the end of the song. "I know a boy, a boy called Joe, and his girl called Jill, they climbed down the hill and they sat on the hill, that's Joe and Jill..." Bono continues, in spoken voice: "So, one day Joe and Jill were walking down the street. I think it was the King's Road, was it? Yeah, and Joe and Jill were spotted, and people would say, Hey, you're Joe and Jill. And he said, Yeah man, this is me. I'm Joe, and this is my girlfriend Jill, how did you know that? And they said, well, we saw you... we saw U2, and *you* were on stage!" "So, what do you think being up here, you like it?" John loves it. Bono carries on singing: "And this is turning into some kind of party, I don't know what to say, you wanna sing this? Well, hold on a second... sometimes I don't know the words!" Giving it a thought Bono recites the text, with the crowd repeating every word.

MARCH 24, 1983. GLASGOW, TIFFANY'S

■ Attendance: 1,500; sellout
■ Support: The Alarm
■ Set: same as Bristol. Maintaining a Glasgow tradition, they do a snippet of *Loch Lomond*, during *A Day Without Me*.

"So, here we are in the capital of Great Britain," Bono says to the boisterous crowd, but some don't like the joke. As U2 start *Seconds* two guys jump on the stage, one of whom shouts 'Fuck off!' into the microphone. Roadie Steve Iredale has trouble removing them, so Bono helps him and Larry runs forward to lend a hand as well. Bono asks the audience to behave and not spoil the show. "Tonight is a celebration!" he shouts exuberantly. The joyous atmosphere is so strong that the ugly incident is soon forgotten. Before *Two Hearts Beat As One*, Bono tells the audience, "People expect me to know the answers, asking me things. I don't know, I don't know which is right, wrong. Just *Two Hearts Beat As One*." Snippets of The Alarm's *Blaze Of Glory* are included in *Out Of Control*.

Except for five songs, the whole show is broadcast on local FM radio.

MARCH 25, 1983. LIVERPOOL, ROYAL COURT THEATRE

■ Attendance: 1,500
■ Support: The Alarm
■ Set: same as Bristol.

As the UK tour nears its end, it returns to some venues that had already been played earlier in the month. Tonight the audience are electrified... perhaps too much so. Before *Sunday Bloody Sunday* Bono tries to calm down fans who are pushing and shoving in the front. "No bursts of violence of any sort, right?" he demands, then introduces *Sunday Bloody Sunday*: "People said that we couldn't write a song like this next song. They said that we didn't live in Derry or Belfast, we live in Dublin. Well, the bombs may not go off in Dublin but they are made there and I'm opposed to any kind of violence. I feel that we have a right to sing this song, called *Sunday Bloody Sunday*."

MARCH 26, 1983. NEWCASTLE, CITY HALL

- Attendance: 1,600
- Support: The Alarm
- Set: same as Bristol.

Steve Iredale

Newcastle sees a cheerful Bono talking throughout the show. Before *Surrender* he says, "We made an LP called 'War', but the theme of the record is very much surrender. We're trying to talk about friction and what frictions are bad and stepping on people's toes and I kind of thought that surrender was a kind of principle, not just a white flag." During *Electric Co.* Bono says he feels great performing for this crowd. After the song he stumbles over his words as he tries to explain that he hopes that in the future he will be better at expressing himself. "I find it's very difficult to explain what's going on, especially if somebody is talking like this." Bono's self-knowledge is met with laughter and applause. He intends to say more but is stopped by Edge who starts *I Fall Down*.

MARCH 27, 1983. BIRMINGHAM, ODEON

- Attendance: 1,400
- Support: Big Country
- Set: same as Bristol.

MARCH 28, 1983. NOTTINGHAM, ROYAL CENTRE

- Attendance: 1,000
- Support: The Perfect Crime, Big Country
- Set: same as Bristol.

The security crew of the Royal Centre treat the enthusiastic fans far too roughly and Bono stops the show on two occasions to help people in distress. "Excuse me sir, is there some sort of trouble?" he says sarcastically, confronting a bouncer during *A Day Without Me*. He asks a fan if he's OK, and continues the show. After *New Year's Day* Bono shouts "Stop, hold it, lights on!" to his crew, and rescues a girl from the rough hands of the bouncers, pulling her on stage to let her have her say. She complains openly about the way she has been treated. Bono addresses the bouncers. "These people are paying your wages," he yells, pointing at the audience.

Out Of Control is dedicated to those who attended U2's first gig in Nottingham, in June 1980 at the Boat Club. "I think it was about four people there. I played that concert on my bare feet because I lost my suitcase, is that right?" Before *Party Girl* Bono

thanks The Perfect Crime and Big Country calling them "the other two headlining bands".

MARCH 29, 1983. LONDON, HAMMERSMITH PALAIS

- Attendance: 2,000; sellout
- Support: Big Country
- Set: same as Bristol, plus *Knocking On Heaven's Door* before *40*.

For the last UK show of the tour the band give their all before enjoying a few days' rest. *Two Hearts Beat As One* includes short bits of *Let's Twist Again*. *Electric Co.* has Bono doing *Yankee Doodle Dandy*, and *Billie Jean* again shows during *Surrender*. After that song Bono says, "I was gonna say that it is our ambition to make this large building a small room. I'm not even gonna say it... it has happened. Thank you!"

Together with Mike Peters from The Alarm and Stuart Adamson from Big Country, U2 play a messy but inspired *Knocking On Heaven's Door* in which Bono improvises heavily and which sees the three singers taking turns singing lead.

MARCH 31, 1983. UK TV: 'TOP OF THE POPS'

U2 appear on 'Top Of The Pops' to playback to a version of *Two Hearts Beat As One*, their new single, that was recorded live earlier in the day. Bono climbs on the balcony to embrace a girl and inserts *Let's Twist Again* in the song.

APRIL 3, 1983. BOURGES, FRANCE, FESTIVAL DE PRINTEMPS

- Attendance: 5,000
- Festival line-up: The Gun Club, U2
- Set: *Gloria / I Threw A Brick / A Day Without Me / Seconds / Surrender / New Year's Day / Sunday Bloody Sunday / Cry-Electric Co. / I Fall Down / October / Tomorrow / Two Hearts Beat As One / Twilight / Out Of Control / encore: 11 O'Clock Tick Tock / I Will Follow / 40*

This festival takes place in a large circus tent. During the soundcheck in the afternoon, a few fans from England and Holland who are following the tour see U2 go through a new song with Edge on drums. That night U2 play a tight show for a reserved audience.

THE 'WAR' TOUR, LEG 2: NORTH AMERICA, SPRING 1983

In America, nationwide radio programming is still very conservative, rarely deviating from mainstream, and generally avoiding anything progressive or relatively unknown. U2's American tour becomes a crusade against both the conservative style of radio programming, and the music that fills most of it. Emphasising it more than on the UK leg, advertisements for the tour aggressively read 'U2 DECLARE WAR'. Dubbed as 'The War On Boring Music', U2 want to break the radio format open to allow more space for themselves, as well as for contemporaries and

future bands that are unlikely to suit the 'safe' programming formula.

With the 'War' album, U2 are already starting to achieve that. Backed by MTV, who put the clip for *New Year's Day* in their 'heavy rotation' schedule, the single achieves considerable airplay, but had only reached No. 53 in the *Billboard* singles chart. Still, mainly due to the new fans that U2 have gained through their consistent touring of the last few years, 'War' has been selling very well. The album had entered the *Billboard* chart at No. 91, and jumped to 19 in its fifth week, before the tour had even begun. Catering to people's tastes, radio programmers are obliged to play its tracks regularly. The airplay results in a healthy surge of new fans, as the straightforward nature of the music appeals to the American public.

Tickets for the tour are selling well. Besides playing 2,000-seat theatres, the ten-week American tour will also see U2 perform at a few open-air festivals, as well as expanding their reach by playing small university auditoriums for a few hundred students in towns the band had never visited before. The 'War' album eventually reaches No. 12, and will linger around in the Top 20 throughout the duration of the tour, an unprecedented commercial and critical success for U2.

APRIL 23, 1983. CHAPEL HILL, NC, KENAN STADIUM

- Attendance: 4,000
- 'The Carolina Concert For Children' line-up: The Producers, U2, Todd Rundgren
- Set: *Gloria / I Threw A Brick / A Day Without Me / New Year's Day / Sunday Bloody Sunday / Cry-Electric Co. / I Fall Down / October / Tomorrow / 11 O'Clock Tick Tock / I Will Follow*

U2 start their American tour by participating in The Carolina Concert For Children, a benefit for Unicef. Because relatively few tickets are put on sale, the stage is in the middle of the field and only one side of the stadium is used. Heavy rainfall forces the crowd to hide under umbrellas but U2 work hard to overcome the conditions. There is a 60-foot long causeway from stage centre that leads towards the stands, and Bono runs to and fro, jumping off the ramp towards the audience. During *Electric Co.* he sings amidst the crowd then climbs into one of the towers and plants a white flag on top.

U2's performance gets an ecstatic review from Rick Miller in a local newpaper: 'Finally, forty feet in the air, "safely" perched on top of the billowing canopy, flag in hand, rain drenching him, Bono smiled and topped off his impromptu, lunatic ascent with perfect, genius-inspired lyrics: "I'm singing in the rain..." The

U2 DECLARES WAR!

Enlist now to join the fight against boring
music with "WAR", the new album from U2.
Featuring the single, "NEW YEAR'S DAY".

U2 ON TOUR:

Island Records
On Cassette

mesmerized, delighted crowd joined in: "What a glorious feeling,
I'm happy again." I think that's where the tears were felt. Here is
this happy maniac, playing human lightning rod with a white flag

KENAN STADIUM
CHAPEL HILL, N.C.
Admission $10.00
APR 23 1983
Sat, Apr. 23, 1983, 8:00 P.M.
The Carolina Concert For Children
Featuring
TODD
RUNDGREN

of peace on the first day of the tour, just to break through to us.
There are no words for the warmth of the thrill that U2 gave the
crowd. I surrendered to U2 and I know I'm not alone.'

APRIL 24, 1983. NORFOLK, VA, CHRYSLER HALL

- Set: *Gloria / I Threw a Brick / A Day Without Me / Seconds /
Surrender / New Year's Day / Sunday Bloody Sunday / Cry-
Electric Co. / I Fall Down / October / Tomorrow / Two Hearts
Beat As One / Twilight / Out Of Control / encore: 11 O'Clock
Tick Tock / I Will Follow / 40*

APRIL 25, 1983. COLLEGE PARK, MD, RITCHIE COLISEUM

- Set: same as Norfolk, minus *New Year's Day*
The energetic show drives the crowd crazy. Bono interrupts
Sunday Bloody Sunday when a brawl erupts in front of the stage.
"You see that?" he shouts, pointing to the flags at the back of the
stage. "That's a white flag!"

APRIL 27, 1983. AUBURN, NY, CAYHUGA COUNTY COMMUNITY COLLEGE GYM

- Attendance: 500
- Support: Robert Ellis Orrall
Bono climbs up the stage set during *Electric Co.* and plants a
white flag between the speakers. On his way back he loses
balance and almost falls down.

APRIL 28, 1983. ROCHESTER, NY, INSTITUTE OF TECHNOLOGY ICE RINK

- Set: same as Norfolk, with *New Year's Day* moved to follow
Tomorrow
"When we came here three years ago," Bono explains after
Seconds, "we were trying to make a point of telling people that
we weren't just another English fashion band passing through.
I tried to explain to people that, one: we were an Irish band, and
two: we were here to stay. We meant what we said." Bono
emphasises his statement in a loud voice and continues to do so
at practically every show of the tour. Singing a bit of *Billie Jean*
during *Surrender* he encourages the crowd to participate but gets
little response. A girl from the audience hands Bono an Irish flag.
"This lady has brought me a gift for which I'm very thankful of,"
he says. "But it's something that caused a lot of trouble for
where I come from, and that's why I only believe in the white flag."

APRIL 29, 1983. DELHI, NY, STATE UNIVERSITY OF NEW YORK

APRIL 30, 1983. PROVIDENCE, RI, BROWN UNIVERSITY

- Set: same as Norfolk, with *New Year's Day* played after
Tomorrow, and *Party Girl* as first song of the encore.
Bono introduces *I Fall Down*: "Sometimes we have been
criticised for trying to maybe take too much out of rock & roll.
Sometimes people just want rock & roll to be like, 'Get up off
your arse and dance'. Well, I think there's a lot more in the heart
of rock & roll. Sometimes we fail but at least we try..."
Introduced as "a song we do on special occasions", *Party Girl*
makes its début in the USA. Bono dedicates *40* to George
Skaubitis of Warner Brothers, U2's distributor for America for
the 'Boy' and 'October' albums, who is present at the show even
though U2 are now being distributed by Atlantic Records.

MAY 1, 1983. STONY BROOK, NY

At the soundcheck Bono sings *White Christmas*, the title song of
the Bing Crosby movie. During the show he jumps on the back
of a guy in the audience, and sings on from there.

MAY 3, 1983. PITTSBURGH, PA, FULTON THEATER

MAY 5, 6, 1983. BOSTON, MA, ORPHEUM THEATER

- Attendance: 5,600 (P); sellout
- Set second night: U2 turn the set completely around, with
Out Of Control replacing *Gloria* as opening song, and *An Cat
Dubh* and *Into The Heart* return to the set for the first time
since December 1982. *Tomorrow* has disappeared and to
date has never been performed again.
The night before the Boston shows, U2 were interviewed by
Carter Alan for WBCN radio during which they announce their
intention to gradually move from theatres to sports arenas.
Adam reveals that U2 will play their first headlining arena show
at the Centrum in Worcester, near Boston, on June 28. Sales of
the 11,000 tickets will start on May 10, just days after the
Orpheum shows.
Though U2 have their doubts, they no longer resent the
idea of playing 10-15,000 capacity ice hockey arenas. "If we stay
in small clubs," Bono tells *Trouser Press* magazine, "we'll develop
small minds, and then we'll start making small music." The
Boston area is chosen because it was the first place in America
to support U2. Local concert promoter Don Law feels confident
about ticket sales. Since U2's first Boston show as support act at
the Paradise Theater in December 1980, the pattern of audience
growth has been consistent. In March 1981 U2 played two
sellout shows at the 500 capacity Paradise, followed by a concert
at the 1,500 capacity Metro just two months later. That
November, a further increase in venue was made by playing to
2,800 fans at the Orpheum Theater, and now U2 sell out two
shows at that same theatre.
After a successful first night, the second show is even
better. The show is recorded for radio, as was U2's previous
appearance here in November 1981. It is one big party from the
moment the band burst into *Out Of Control*. "You may leave your
seats now, Boston," Bono calls, giving the sign for the crowd to
abandon their seats and make their way to the front. The
security are concerned but the fans behave well. Highlights of
the show include a funky *Two Hearts Beat As One* during which
Bono sings *Let's Twist Again* with the audience, then lets himself
fall into the crowd to be carried on their outstretched hands.
Electric Co. features the thrill-seeking singer shaking hands with
people on the balcony but not letting go, urging them to pull him
up. Spurred on by the crowd, Bono is hauled onto the balcony,

after which he asks for a flag. Dennis Sheehan hands him one and he sings *Send In The Clowns*, followed by a tightrope act on the railing of the balcony before making his descent back to the stage. *11 O'Clock Tick Tock* is later put on the live EP 'Under A Blood Red Sky'.

MAY 7, 1983. ALBANY, NY, STATE UNIVERSITY OF NEW YORK MAYFEST

■ Festival line-up: Robert Hazard, David Johansen, U2
■ Set: *Out Of Control / Twilight / An Cat Dubh / Into The Heart / Surrender / Two Hearts Beat As One / Seconds / Sunday Bloody Sunday / Cry-Electric Co. /* encore: *New Year's Day / Gloria / I Will Follow / 40*

U2 take part in university festivities and play a 13-song, 50-minute set on the campus field in beautiful spring weather. They are announced with fervour but get little response from the students. Bono sees it as a challenge and shouts, "This afternoon we're gonna set this place on fire!" During *Two Hearts Beat As*

One he spurs on the crowd to sing *Let's Twist Again* but nobody seems to know the words. Bono's stunt of climbing the scaffolding during *Electric Co.* and placing the white flag on top of the stage does the trick and gets a huge applause.

MAY 8, 1983. HARTFORD, CT, TRINITY COLLEGE

■ Attendance: 500; sellout
■ Set: same as Albany.

Again U2 play on a campus field. During *Electric Co.* Bono takes a flag, jumps down and runs to a building behind the stage. Unaware of his intentions, the band are forced to stretch the song another five minutes. When he finally comes back he is exhausted as he tried to get to the roof of the building but access was blocked by a closed door. Unwilling to tell the audience this, he instead points to the building and claims he has shown the white flag to everyone inside.

MAY 10, 1983. NEW HAVEN, CT, WOOLSEY HALL AT YALE UNIVERSITY

■ Support: Dream Syndicate

It's Bono's 23rd birthday and a festive show is guaranteed. At his request a small square stage has been set up in front of the main one, sticking out like a promontory, enabling Bono to get closer to the audience than usual. It also makes it easier for fans to approach the stage. A wild girl jumps Bono from the side, almost dragging him into the crowd. Later, when no fewer than four women beset him, Bono takes his time chatting with them and snapping their picture as they sit down on the monitors. This takes too much time for Edge's liking and he puts down his guitar and picks up a magazine instead. Dennis Sheehan comes on to bring Bono a big birthday cake, as he had done for Adam in Brighton, and the audience burst into *Happy Birthday*.

MAY 11, 1983. NEW YORK, NY, PALLADIUM

- Attendance: 3,400; sellout
- Support: Dream Syndicate
- Set: *Out Of Control / Twilight / An Cat Dubh / Into The Heart / Surrender / Two Hearts Beat As One / Seconds / Sunday Bloody Sunday / Cry-Electric Co. / I Fall Down / October / New Year's Day / Gloria / I Threw A Brick / A Day Without Me / encore: 11 O'Clock Tick Tock / I Will Follow / 40*

"There's somebody over here who says 'Fuck the British'," Bono says halfway through the show, sounding both surprised and sad. "I think that's stupid. Now, that's why we're here." The crowd are rowdy, with fans at the back trying to get closer to the stage. Bono interrupts *I Will Follow* when fans get squashed and asks for everyone to move back. "I'm sorry, this is my fault," he says. Later, there is a discussion in the U2 camp about playing all-seat theatres where the crowd often don't have enough space to jump around.

MAY 12, 1983. PASSAIC, NJ, CAPITOL THEATER

- Attendance: 2,000
- Support: Dream Syndicate
- Set: same as New York, minus *I Threw A Brick / A Day Without Me*, plus *Party Girl* as first song of the encore.

"...The music that they make, is gonna hit you right here, so please welcome from Ireland: U2!" the announcer calls out, banging his chest. *Out Of Control* starts explosively and Bono urges the fans to "leave your seats now", which is taken to heart. A few songs into the show, dozens of photographers block the audience's view, resulting in wild pushing in the front and fans being wedged tight. Bono intervenes. "I really need this row here," he says, indicating the photographers' pit. "The filming of the show is great, but I'm gonna invite the photographers and the cameramen onstage, so

we can have people here. Is that OK?" Security people help the photographers onstage and position them at the side, while fans take their place up the front and offer grateful applause.

MAY 13, 14, 1983. PHILADELPHIA, PA, TOWER THEATER

- Attendance: 6,000; sellout
- Support: Dream Syndicate

U2's long trek through the States continues with two spirited shows in the legendary Tower Theater in Upper Darby. The first show is superb with Bono jumping onto the front seats and creating a frenzy as he lets surrounding fans sing some lines. The show is partly aired on local FM radio.

- Set second night: *Out Of Control / Twilight / An Cat Dubh / Into The Heart / Surrender / Two Hearts Beat As One / Seconds / Sunday Bloody Sunday / Cry-Electric Co. / I Fall Down / October / Gloria / I Threw A Brick / A Day Without Me / New Year's Day / encore: Party Girl / 11 O'Clock Tick Tock / I Will Follow / 40*

MAY 16, 1983. BUFALLO, NY, SHEA CENTER

- Support: Dream Syndicate
- Set: same as Philadelphia 14th, with *Gloria* and *New Year's Day* swapping places.

The cheerful nature of the show changes when security manhandles fans for pushing and Bono tries to calm everybody down. The enthusiasm is so charged that it endangers others and gets out of hand during *I Will Follow*. "There is never any trouble at a U2-concert!" Bono shouts to the people pushing up at the front.

MAY 17, 1983. TORONTO, CANADA, MASSEY HALL

- Attendance: 2,689 (P); sellout
- Support: Dream Syndicate
- Set: *Out Of Control / Twilight / An Cat Dubh / Into The Heart / Surrender / Two Hearts Beat As One / Seconds / Sunday Bloody Sunday / Cry-Electric Co. / I Fall Down / October / I Threw A Brick / A Day Without Me / New Year's Day / Gloria / encore: Party Girl / 11 O'Clock Tick Tock / I Will Follow / 40*

Four young women invade the stage during the encore, flinging themselves around Bono and almost knocking him down. Bono remarks they are not at a Duran Duran concert, then performs a square-dance with two girls on each arm before he borrows a press-photographer's camera to capture the girls on film.

MAY 19, 1983. CLEVELAND, OH, MUSIC HALL

- Attendance: 3,000; sellout
- Support: Dream Syndicate
- Set: same as Toronto, minus *Party Girl*.

MAY 20, 1983. DETROIT, MI, GRAND CIRCUS THEATER

- Support: Dream Syndicate
- Set: same as Toronto.

Tonight's version of *Electric Co.* is riveting with an outstanding guitar solo and Bono running around the theatre and shaking hands while improvising lyrics. After the song he talks about wanting to turn the building into a small room and concludes, "I think tonight we've done that." The band stop playing halfway through *I Fall Down* because of crowd disturbances. "Quiet, OK?! Look: white flags on stage. It's a lot of bullshit, people are jumping on other people's heads," Bono says, disillusioned by all the audience trouble over the last few weeks. Near the end of the show he seeks confirmation that tonight the band succeeded in creating unity. "A small room, this evening, yes?" he asks desperately, but gets little response. "YES?!!" he repeats. "Yeaahh!!" the answer finally resounds.

MAY 21, 1983. CHICAGO, IL, ARAGON BALLROOM

- Attendance: 4,000
- Support: Dream Syndicate

While in Chicago, U2 visit the Chicago Peace Museum, which exhibits `The Unforgettable Fire', a collection of paintings and drawings made by survivors of the Hiroshima and Nagasaki nuclear bombings of August 1945. The artworks capture the fear felt after the immensely destructive atomic blasts had destroyed everything and everybody around them. The images impress the band, as does the Museum's devotion to the life of Martin Luther King and his non-violent struggle for black civil rights in America. After the tour, U2 will donate one of the white flags and the stage backdrop used on the tour to the Peace Museum for an exhibition called `Give Peace A Chance' which displays items from numerous artists who promote peace through their music, including Bob Dylan, Joan Baez, and Yoko Ono.

MAY 22, 1983. MINNEAPOLIS, MN, NORTHRUP AUDITORIUM

- Attendance: 3,674 (P)
- Support: Dream Syndicate
- Set: *Out Of Control / Twilight / An Cat Dubh / Into The Heart / Surrender / Two Hearts Beat As One / Seconds / Sunday Bloody Sunday / Cry-Electric Co. / I Fall Down / October / New Year's Day / I Threw A Brick / A Day Without Me / Gloria / encore: Party Girl / 11 O'Clock Tick Tock / I Will Follow / 40*

In the afternoon U2 do an extensive soundcheck and play an as yet unknown song. The show that night is powerful and enjoys perfect band/audience interaction without any trouble. "Thank you, what can I say? Wonderful!" Bono responds. Lines from the Simple Minds' track *Glittering Prize* ("Shine a light, shine a light on me") are included in *Electric Co.* The show gets a favourable review in the *Minneapolis Star and Tribune*. Staff writer Jon Bream describes Bono as 'a curious frontman, this young man named Paul Hewson. He looks like a chubby Ron Wood of The Rolling Stones...'

MAY 25, 1983. VANCOUVER, CANADA, QUEEN ELISABETH THEATER

- Attendance: 2,845 (P); sellout
- Support: Dream Syndicate

MAY 26, 1983. SEATTLE, WA, PARAMOUNT THEATER

■ Attendance: 3,000
■ Set: same as Minneapolis.

After a rowdy start with a fight in the audience during *Sunday Bloody Sunday*, the show takes a funny turn when Bono recalls, "I remember when we used to make demo-tapes and send them out to record companies and radio stations. Some said that we were great, some said we were not so great, but we kept on making these tapes. This song is about trying, it's called *I Fall Down*." Halfway into the song he stops singing to tell the crowd what happened prior to the show: "Earlier on, in the hotel, somebody from this city rang me. He woke me up, sort of hassled me, saying that his band was the greatest band in the world. He reminded me about the way *we* used to work!" The audience laugh, then Bono asks if the caller in question is present. He is, so the guy comes on stage and Bono makes him an offer he can't refuse: "You wanna play drums?" The guy nods and amidst loud cheers from the audience some roadies bring extra drums onstage and the guy picks up the rhythm of *I Fall Down* and happily drums along.

MAY 27, 1983. PORTLAND, OR, PARAMOUNT THEATER

■ Attendance: 2,500; (capacity: 2,750)

Breaking barriers

U2's stage act makes a great impact throughout America, receiving good press in every state they visit. 'Irish U2 heading for stardom' reads the headline in *The Oregonian*. The reviewer calls U2's show 'the best concert of 1983 so far: solid music played rhythmically and well, a positive stage attitude that recognised audience input, excellent sound and lights...'

(In March, U2 were advertised to appear at the Schüttorf festival in Germany on May 28th, but they never performed there on this date.)

MAY 30, 1983. DEVORE, CA, GLEN HELEN REGIONAL PARK

■ Attendance: ca. 125,000

■ 'US Festival', third day; line-up: Little Steven & the Disciples of Soul, Berlin, Quarterflash, U2, Missing Persons, The Pretenders, Joe Walsh, Stevie Nicks, David Bowie.
■ Set: *Gloria / I Threw A Brick / A Day Without Me / An Cat Dubh / Into The Heart / New Year's Day / Surrender / Two Hearts Beat As One / Sunday Bloody Sunday / Cry-Electric Co.* / encore: *I Will Follow / 40*

U2 play the final day of the US Festival in the Glen Helen Regional Park in Devore, near San Bernardino. With headliner David Bowie playing his first American concert in five years and some 125,000 people in attendance, U2 perform for the largest crowd in their career. The three-day event is marred by two people dying on the second day in drugs-related incidents and a total of 150 people arrested for violent behaviour, while 130 are injured. So much money is spent on the fees of all 33 acts that the festival has to sell 800,000 $25 tickets to break even. Since only 500,000 show up over three days, an enormous loss is suffered. On the opening day there is an argument with The Clash over their fee and they announce from the stage that they are performing under force. During U2's show Bono jumps in on this, saying, "Nobody twisted my arm to come here. I'm here because I want to be here!"

Lines from The Beatles' *Dear Prudence* are included in *A Day Without Me* while *40* includes the chorus of *Give Peace A Chance*. Bono is in a boisterous mood and tries to connect with the audience as much as possible. After letting himself fall into the crowd and joining the TV cameraman on the crane during *Surrender*, he climbs 120 feet up the stage scaffolding and greets the masses below from the edge of the roof. On his way back the canvas on the roof starts ripping but he gets back safely. Bono's stunt succeeds in attracting attention of the 125,000 present but within the U2 entourage there is concern for his safety and he is warned not to go too far in the future. The whole show is aired on radio while some songs are also broadcast on TV.

JUNE 1, 1983. SAN FRANCISCO, CA, CIVIC AUDITORIUM

■ Attendance: 6,359 (P); (capacity 8,000)
■ Support: Romeo Void, The Alarm
■ Set: same as Minneapolis.

One song into the set, Edge's guitar malfunctions and Bono sings, "Who needs guitar, we don't need a guitar..." to fill up the gap. Edge gets huge cheers when his guitar works again but when he milks the moment by playing a long solo, it breaks down again. "For the first time in five years we've got a breakdown," Bono states, and asks the audience if it's OK if they just start again. Eventually finishing *Out Of Control*, Edge's guitar is

thoroughly checked while Bono tries to kill time. "Uhm, does anyone know any jokes...?" At the end of the show he refers to the technical problems and seems grateful to the crowd. "There's a lot of cities in the world that if you started a concert and these machines broke down, that would be the end of it. Tonight it was only the start for us; thank you for trusting us."

JUNE 3, 1983. SALT LAKE CITY, UT

JUNE 5, 1983. DENVER, CO, RED ROCKS AMPHITHEATER

■ Attendance: 9,000; sellout
■ Set: same as Minneapolis.

The show is videotaped by the crew of the British TV rock programme 'The Tube'. Directed by Gavin Taylor, it is released on video cassette and becomes one of the top selling concert videos ever.

The original plan had been around for some time. Paul McGuinness thought it would be a great idea to capture the power of a U2 performance on video in order to convince more people of the band's qualities, while at the same time documenting the first few years of their career. Denver has been one of the first American cities to embrace U2 right from the start; back in 1981, the concert promoter had taken U2 to see

the Red Rocks site, assuring them that one day they would play there. Located two miles up in the Rocky Mountains, Red Rocks is a natural amphitheater wedged between towering sandstone cliffs. Since U2's continuing success enables them to fill Red Rocks, this might be the occasion to film the show. Its atmospheric setting would supply a unique backdrop to the concert.

However, U2 had no money to invest in the project and costs would be high due to the logistical difficulties caused by the location. To capture the surroundings to full advantage, the rocks would have to be lit up. A mobile recording unit was required for the sound. A helicopter would film from the air. U2 were only just beginning to receive income from album sales and live shows, but they didn't have the $250,000 that the production required.

Paul McGuinness found concert promoter Barry Fey, who presented U2's shows in the Southwest, and their record company Island Records, willing to invest, in return for a business interest. A joint production company called 'U2 At Red Rocks Associates' was set up, the three parties each absorbing one third of the cost, thus sharing the risk, and receiving one third of all eventual profits from TV rights and video sales. For radio, rights were sold to NBC, who would fit the show into their live concert series 'The Source'.

Incessant rain caused problems during the days before the show, hampering the building of the stage and jeopardising the

safety of the crew who were installing the lighting system and sound equipment. All tickets had been sold, but doubts arose over whether the audience would actually show up if the rain kept pouring down.

Barry Fey rings up McGuinness on the day of the show, and because it is still pouring urges him to cancel the shoot and film one of the upcoming indoor shows instead. He feels it would be better than shooting a sad, rain-drenched affair with hardly any people in attendance. But if the shoot is postponed, all monies invested will be lost. Having put all their energy into the pre-production, and with their minds focused on the show, U2 and

Paul McGuinness don't want to hear of cancelling. Both the show and the shoot will go ahead as planned.

Late in the afternoon, with rain still bucketing down and the amphitheater shrouded in a blanket of thick fog, fans start appearing from the hills. They are in rain gear, carrying food and hot drinks, and are in high spirits, and they assume the show will go ahead as there has been no announcement otherwise. While the crew try to keep the cameras and the stage gear dry, the place rapidly fills up. Just before showtime, the rain finally stops. The scheduled performances by The Divinyls and The Alarm are cancelled. Three torches placed on the rocks are lit, forming a triangle of light over the stage. With the camera and lighting crew in position, U2 are announced: "Bob Dylan did it – they called it 'Hard Rain' and made a movie – and that's what you got right here, so you're all part of history. Ladies and gentlemen, a warm welcome please, from Dublin, Ireland: U2!"

U2 enter the stage to tremendous applause. From the moment they burst into *Gloria*, all worries fade away. They play with more vigour than ever, determined to reward the crowd for waiting for hours in the rain, and inspired by the adverse conditions to play the best show of their lives for those who will see the video. Attacking every song fiercely, the energy of the music infects the crowd, whose combined body heat transforms the moisture into clouds of steam as the show progresses. The Tube camera crew film from the side of the stage, from among

the crowd, and from helicopter. During *Electric Co.* Bono climbs on the roof of the stage to plant a white flag on top, his silhouette cast against a backdrop of misty, reddish light reflected from the rocks. In *New Year's Day*, he sings "under thunderclouds and rain," instead of "under a blood red sky", the line that would turn out to become the title of the video.

The footage pleases the band enormously. The Tube camera team have recorded one of the most blistering shows on the tour. Besides showing the energy of the band and their music, the video captures the crowd's spirit and enthusiasm, undiminished by their long wait in the rain. It is tangible proof of U2's strong bonding with their audience. Combined with the attractive setting which lends a mystical feeling to the event, it gives the video footage a quality that would not have been achieved if filmed in a regular concert setting.

The footage will turn out to be a powerful marketing tool for the band. Besides the video release, a wide variety of edits are made for several TV programmes, while several clips are used for promotional purposes. On radio, 'The Source' broadcasts the show on July 8, 1983. On TV, the American cable pay-channel Showtime broadcasts 12 songs, and soon after, a nine-song compilation is made for MTV. A third version of the show with 13 tracks is put together for the video, with two songs, *I Threw A Brick* and *A Day Without Me*, which were not featured in the TV versions. For the video, the six tracks excluded are: *Out Of Control, Twilight, An Cat Dubh, Into The Heart, Two Hearts Beat As One* and *I Fall Down*. Called 'U2 Live At Red Rocks: Under A Blood Red Sky', the video will be released in November 1983, coinciding with the low-priced mini-live album 'Under A Blood Red Sky', which includes only two of the actual Denver tracks: *Gloria* and *Party Girl*. The video will become a best-seller, while the numerous TV broadcasts, which succeed in catching the attention and interest of vast numbers of people, act as regular advertisements for U2.

JUNE 6, 1983. BOULDER, CO, COLORADO STATE UNIVERSITY

- Support: The Divinyls, The Alarm
- Set: *Gloria / I Threw A Brick / A Day Without Me / An Cat Dubh / Into The Heart / New Year's Day / Surrender / Two Hearts Beat As One / Seconds / Sunday Bloody Sunday / Cry-Electric Co. / A Hard Rain's Gonna Fall /* encore: *11 O'Clock Tick Tock / I Will Follow /* encore: *40*

Admission for this show is free. Paul McGuinness had planned the concert as a potential substitute in case the Denver date was cancelled or if heavy rainfall spoiled the show. Otherwise, this show in nearby Boulder would serve as a present to anyone who wants to see U2.

Opening with *Gloria*, U2 play a loose and relaxed show with a lot of fans that were at Red Rocks in the audience, as well as many that come out of curiosity after hearing good reports. Bono is very talkative and inserts numerous lines and melodies that come to mind into many songs. In *A Day Without Me* he refers to the Rocky Mountains and in *Two Hearts Beat As One* he sings a long text with "Nobody knows where my baby goes" as the main line. "There's only one thing that could follow last night and that's tonight," Bono says. "And just for this occasion I'm gonna bring back The Alarm, a band you're gonna hear about in the future, we're gonna play something special for you." He explains that The Alarm came into U2's dressing room before the show with the idea of doing a song together. As The Alarm come onstage with their instruments, they play *A Hard Rain's Gonna Fall*, a quiet folk song written by Bob Dylan, with Bono and Mike Peters taking the vocals.

JUNE 7, 1983. WICHITA, KS

JUNE 8, 1983. KANSAS CITY, MO, MEMORIAL HALL

- Attendance: 3,000
- Set: same as Minneapolis.

The show starts far too late and Bono apologises, explaining that his laundry was temporarily lost at the hotel and the band decided to wait for its return instead of having him perform naked. Before I *Fall Down* Bono sings some lines of The Beatles' *A Hard Day's Night* while strumming the guitar.

Cleveland Music Hall

JUNE 9, 1983. TULSA, OK

JUNE 10, 1983. NORMAN, OK, LLOYD NOBLE CENTER

- Attendance: 2,000; (capacity 13,000)
- Set: same as Minneapolis, minus *Party Girl, I Threw A Brick* and *A Day Without Me*.

The show is optimistically booked for this 13,000-seat venue but only sells 2,000 tickets. The theatre-sized audience move in close to the stage. Bono recalls that at U2's previous show in Oklahoma (February 17, 1982) someone gave him a pair of earplugs and asks if that person is here, proposing a meeting backstage. U2 play a good show, which to date is their last in this State.

JUNE 11, 1983. AUSTIN, TX, THE MEADOWS

- Support: The Alarm
- Set: *Out Of Control / Twilight / An Cat Dubh / Into The Heart / Surrender / Two Hearts Beat As One / Seconds / Sunday Bloody Sunday / Cry-Electric Co. / I Fall Down / October / New Year's Day / Gloria /* encore: *Party Girl / 11 O'Clock Tick Tock / I Will Follow / 40*

U2 play the seventh consecutive show without a day off. After *Twilight* Bono says, "From the first time we came to this city it was clear that this was an important place for us. Sometimes you play to an audience and you're not too sure if they fully understand what the excitement of the music is about. People always misunderstand this group. They're putting us into one box or the other. We're called U2, all right?" The crowd are silent and seem to wonder what Bono is on about.

JUNE 13, 1983. DALLAS, TX, BRONCO BOWL

- Support: The Alarm
- Set: same as Austin, minus *Party Girl*.

Bono's voice is strained from the heavy tour schedule, and he admits that he wasn't sure if he would be able to sing tonight, but claims it wouldn't have made a difference because the crowd sing along so well.

JUNE 14, 1983. HOUSTON, TX

- Support: The Alarm

JUNE 17, 1983. LOS ANGELES, CA, SPORTS ARENA

- Attendance: 9,633 (P); (capacity 12,000)
- Support: The Alarm
- Set: same as Austin.

After performing at numerous theatres and university auditoriums, U2 play their first headlining show at a sports arena. The show was added to the tour schedule when tickets for Worcester, which was originally to be U2's first arena show, were selling rapidly. Though the Sports Arena is not filled to capacity, sales of 9,633 tickets indicate that U2 are on the verge of breaking big in America.

"A few weeks ago we played in a large field about 50 miles from here," Bono says, referring to the US Festival. "Now we play in a large sports-complex. It's our ambition tonight to turn this large building into a small room." He gets an overwhelming response and adds, "And I think that maybe we've already done that..." Like at the smaller venues, the crowd are frenzied and push to the front. Their size somewhat intimidates the band. "You have a word in your vocabulary that we don't use and you do so much, called 'party'; tonight I want a party," Bono says amid much cheering during *Two Hearts Beat As One*. "But," he continues, "our kind of party is different to a lot of other people's kind of parties. Nobody breaks their legs at our party." He urges the rowdy crowd to move back and *Sunday Bloody Sunday* is interrupted for this reason.

As usual, Bono leaves the stage with a white flag during *Electric Co.* and climbs on the balcony. Though this stunt has always worked well, unifying the band and the audience, the LA crowd try to grab Bono. Hundreds of people push to get to him, while others close by get their hands on him and don't let go. He breaks loose and runs, but everywhere he goes people want to grab him. Meanwhile *Electric Co.* ends and the band start *I Fall Down*, Bono tries to make his way back to the stage and tells the crowd to stay back. "Julie says, I want you to stay back, Julie says, you know I'm finding it hard to breathe," he sings, but the crowd hysterically chase him down. Bono gets desperate and motions he will jump off the balcony if they don't stop jostling him. In a state of panic he indeed jumps 20 feet down into the arms of those below. Screaming with excitement people below now rush over to touch him and when, out of self-protection, Bono pushes someone, the guy pushes back and it almost results in a fight. Tour manager Dennis Sheehan comes to the rescue and with all his might pulls the singer back to the stage. Their clothes are ripped to shreds and the aluminium flag pole is broken in two along the way.

U2's first arena show is a complete disaster and in the dressing room afterwards the other members of the band and the crew express their anger at Bono. After ample warnings about the potential danger of his climbing, it has finally backfired with disastrous results. It is decided that for his own and the crowd's safety he will no longer climb balconies.

The incident generates much publicity and puts U2 in a negative light. Later, Bono comments in an interview with *Rolling Stone* magazine: "I lost my senses completely... Somebody could have died at that concert, it was a real sickener for me. It's meant a total re-evaluation of what we are about live. We don't need to use a battering ram. It has to be down to the music."

JUNE 21, 1983. ORLANDO, FL, JAI ALAI FRONTON HALL

- Attendance: 3,029 (P); (capacity 3,500)
- Support: The Alarm
- Set: same as Austin.

A few days off in Florida allow the band to recover after the

debacle in Los Angeles. Snippets of *Singing In The Rain* are included in *Two Hearts Beat As One*. *I Fall Down* is interrupted because of heavy pushing in the front. "You see the white flags that we have at the back of the stage? That means nobody gets hurt when we play!" It's a hot night in Florida and the air-conditioning isn't at its best. "Have you any air to breathe down there?" Bono asks during the encore. "Well, if you have, just breathe it this way, OK?"

JUNE 22, 1983. TAMPA, FL, CURTIS HIXON CENTER

- Attendance: 3,702 (P); (capacity 4,000)
- Support: The Alarm
- Set: same as Austin.

Bono discovers a banner in the audience. "U2, the next biggest thing," he reads sarcastically, not wanting to be labelled as the umpteenth band that happens to be hot for a while until the next one comes along. The press have used that term for U2 far too many times. "We knew that already. One thing that really makes me sick is when people say kind of, 'Oh listen, we're into U2 because it's fashionable to be into U2.' That really bugs me because that implies going out of fashion, and we have no intention of doing that."

JUNE 23, 1983. MIAMI, FL

- Support: The Alarm

JUNE 24, 1983. JACKSONVILLE, FL

- Support: The Alarm

JUNE 25, 1983. ATLANTA, GA, CIVIC CENTER

- Attendance: 8,000
- Support: The Alarm

- Set: same as Austin.

Bono avoids the high notes because he has a sore throat. He includes bits of *Be Bop A LuLa* in *Two Hearts Beat As One* and, as in Kansas City, sings the first lines of *A Hard Day's Night*. A bad cough prevents him from extending the song. Bono cautiously starts singing *I Fall Down* instead, but halfway through picks up The Beatles' song again, accompanied only by Larry's quiet drumming, turning in a unique version.

JUNE 27, 1983. NEW HAVEN, CT, COLISEUM

- Attendance: 5,695 (P); (capacity 9,000)
- Support: Marshall Crenshaw, The Alarm
- Set: same as Austin.

"The last time we were here it was my birthday," Bono recalls. The late insertion in the tour schedule of an arena show in a city already played, indicates U2's fast rising popularity. An extra support act is added to help ticket sales, but though the crowd are bigger than on most dates, the show doesn't come close to selling out.

JUNE 28, 1983. WORCESTER, MA, CENTRUM

- Attendance: 10,329 (P); (capacity 11,000)
- Support: The Alarm
- Set: same as Austin.

With tickets priced at $9.50 and $11.50, the show generates $116,145 which is around five times U2's average takings on this tour and is their highest gross for a headlining show yet. With 10,329 people in attendance, it's also the biggest crowd U2 has pulled in their own right to date. Early in the show Bono remarks that the Boston area is a home away from home for the band. Steve Wickham makes a special appearance to play violin during *Sunday Bloody Sunday*. Before *Party Girl* Bono announces that sales of the 'War' album have passed 500,000 copies in America, earning U2 their first gold album in the States. "Tonight we're throwing a party!" he shouts to the cheering crowd. During the song he gets mobbed by about a dozen cheerful women who climb on stage, one of whom handcuffs herself to the strap on one of his boots. Dennis Sheehan cuts him loose. The girls are excited to be onstage but behave respectfully. "In any other city of the world we would have a riot right now," Bono says, good naturedly. The show is a morale boost for the band after the LA debacle since it proves that U2's show *can* work in an arena with a big crowd and still retain the festive mood of the smaller places.

JUNE 29, 1983. NEW YORK, NY, PIER 84

- Support: The Alarm
- Set: same as Austin, minus *Party Girl*.

The finale of the American tour is an open-air show on a large parking lot at the docks, next to a huge storage depot. (This is U2's first car park show since the days of the Dandelion Green in 1979.) The show is the initiative of NY concert promoter Ron Delsener who, in the Seventies, used to organise low-priced shows at the Wolman skating rink in Central Park. His new series of annual shows at Pier 84 finds itself in its third year with U2 and The Alarm performing. Miller Beer sponsors the event which enables Delsener to keep ticket prices low. The bizarre location and beautiful weather enhance the atmosphere. Eyeing a helicopter flying overhead during *Out Of Control* Bono adds lyrics about objects flying in the sky and the sun going down on New York riverside. After *Twilight* he says that rock stars are often rewarded with girls or caviar after a show (called 'the rider' in the music industry, he explains), but reveals U2 have other stimulants: "We told the promoter we wouldn't play unless they had an aircraft-carrier parked beside the gig and a blue sky!"

A TV crew film some songs for a news item and are

With Jim Kerr at Werchter

dragged on stage by Bono during *New Year's Day*. "Are you at the news? Come on here, film these people," he says, and while the crowd cheer Bono makes clear again why the tour is dubbed the 'War on Boring Music': "These people are here because they are sick to the teeth of what they're hearing on the radio and TV. They're here because they believe in rock & roll, like I do – not wallpaper music…"

The Pier is the last, the 48th, concert of the American tour which draws a total of 175,000 people, an average of around 3,725 a night, plus an additional 125,000 at the US Festival. The tour grosses around $1,750,000 and marks the first time that U2 make money from touring.

JULY 2, 1983. TORHOUT, BELGIUM, FESTIVAL GROUNDS

- Attendance: 30,000; (capacity 60,000)
- Festival line-up: The Scabs, John Cale & Band, Warren Zevon, The Eurythmics, Simple Minds, U2, Peter Gabriel, Van Morrison

ROCK TORHOUT
zaterdag 2 juli
samedi juillet
Aanvang 11 u
Début h

ROCK WERCHTER
zondag 3 juli
dimanche juillet
Aanvang 11 u
Début h

HUMO

THE SCABS
JOHN CALE & BAND
WARREN ZEVON
EURYTHMICS
SIMPLE MINDS
U2
PETER GABRIEL
VAN MORRISON

- Set: *Out Of Control / Twilight / An Cat Dubh / Into The Heart / New Year's Day / Surrender / Two Hearts Beat As One / Seconds / Sunday Bloody Sunday / Gloria / encore: 11 O'Clock Tick Tock / I Will Follow / 40*

After two days off the band are back in Europe to perform at the Torhout / Werchter double festival where they played the previous year. Before *Sunday Bloody Sunday* Bono comments about the many flags sticking out of the crowd, a tradition that started at this festival a year ago. Besides white ones, there are also some advertising flags. "Who's Coca-Cola, are they playing here?" he jokes. "We have chosen white flags. Last year somebody threw me a white flag on this stage. I haven't let it go since, it's up there. We are proud to be Irish and yet we're not so territorial as to bandy about that flag." The audience don't respond. "I'm not very good in making speeches. I'm gonna have to make a speech at Edge's wedding next week… I probably won't do very well there either!" [Edge will marry Aisling O'Sullivan on July 12.]

JULY 3, 1983. WERCHTER, BELGIUM, FESTIVAL GROUNDS

- Attendance: 40,000; (capacity: 60,000)

- Festival line-up: The Scabs, John Cale & Band, Warren Zevon, The Eurythmics, Simple Minds, U2, Peter Gabriel, Van Morrison
- Set: same as Torhout, minus *Seconds*, and *New Year's Day* is played after *Two Hearts Beat As One*.

Bono thanks the large crowd for having U2 on the festival two years in a row. In the encore he says he's honoured to share the stage with all the great artists that are on the bill. He thanks Jim Kerr of Simple Minds, who promptly comes onstage, and Bono celebrates their meeting by shaking a bottle of champagne, spraying the band and the audience and having a sip themselves. During *11 O'Clock Tick Tock* Bono sings the chorus of the Simple Minds song *Someone, Somewhere, In Summertime*. Members of Simple Minds are watching U2's performance from up in the scaffolding on the side of the stage. Jim Kerr comes on again to sing along on his composition, and at the end of a joyous session he introduces the members of U2 to the audience. Before the final song Bono thanks the U2 crew, "people who've been with us through the whole year and whose lives I made probably quite difficult." He singles out drums technician Tom Mullally whose birthday it is. "Come here Tom!" Bono yells, but Tom is hesitant and the crowd chant "We want Tom!" after which he comes onstage and the audience sing *Happy Birthday* for him. After *40* they continue to sing "How long to sing this song" for such a long time that Bono comes back and picks up the song again, accompanied by Annie Lennox of The Eurythmics and, somewhat later, Dave Stewart.

Though the shows have their moments, both performances at Torhout and Werchter are criticised for the band trying too hard to prove themselves to the crowd. Bono seems stuck in the

mannerism adopted during the American tour, shouting that they're called U2 and making exaggerated gestures with the flags, which most of the crowd have already seen the year before.

AUGUST 14, 1983. DUBLIN, IRELAND, PHOENIX PARK RACECOURSE

- Attendance: 20,000; sellout
- 'A Day at the Races'; line-up: Perfect Crime, Steel Pulse, Big Country, The Eurythmics, Simple Minds, U2
- Set: *Out Of Control / Twilight / An Cat Dubh / Into The Heart / Surrender / Two Hearts Beat As One / Seconds / Sunday Bloody Sunday / Cry-Electric Co. / I Fall Down / October / New Year's Day / I Threw A Brick / A Day Without Me / Gloria / encore: Party Girl / 11 O'Clock Tick Tock / I Will Follow / encore: 40*

After Simple Minds have finished the impressive support, DJ Dave Fanning announces U2 for their only domestic show of the year: "…In six short months they've conquered the world! Do you wanna see the very best in live music?! Then let's hear it, a great welcome home for U2!" Larry and Adam start *Out Of Control* before Fanning is even finished and immediately bring the crowd to hyper-excitement. The show is a memorable reunion with some 20,000 fans and friends celebrating U2's homecoming in beautiful summer weather.

During *Surrender* Bono improvises lyrics that don't make sense, then sings, "I try too hard, sometimes I fall on my face, I just make up a song and I don't know why…" Several fans are waving flags and Bono asks someone to pass on his Irish tricolour. "There's been a lot of talk about this flag, and about

this next song," Bono announces, and the audience cheer knowing that *Sunday Bloody Sunday* is next. During the song, Steve Wickham joins the band to play fiddle and stays for *Electric Co.* as well. Bono climbs the scaffolding, which excites those seeing U2 for the first time but attracts criticism from fans who've already seen Bono do it (at Punchestown the previous summer and at the December shows) and feel his behaviour is getting repetitive.

The show includes several personal notes. *I Fall Down* is dedicated to Jim Reilly, drummer of Stiff Little Fingers, whose brother Thomas was shot in Belfast the previous weekend.

Somewhat later Bono drags his father, Bobby Hewson, out of the wings for his first appearance on a U2 stage. *Party Girl* is played in Ireland for the first time, during which Bono announces, "I don't think Edge even realises that today is his birthday..." While the audience cheer, Edge looks on completely bewildered since his 22nd birthday was six days earlier. Bono sings *Happy Birthday* with the crowd and dedicates *Party Girl* to Edge's wife Aisling. *Give Peace A Chance* is included in *11 O'Clock Tick Tock*. As in Werchter, Annie Lennox joins Bono,

improvising around the chorus of *40*, after which the crowd keep singing "How long to sing this song" for some 15 minutes before slowly making their way out of Phoenix Park.

AUGUST 20, 1983. ST. GOARSHAUSEN, GERMANY, LORELEY AMPHITHEATRE

- ■ Attendance: 22,000; sellout
- ■ 'Loreley Festival'; line-up: Dave Edmunds, U2, The Stray Cats, Joe Cocker, Steve Miller
- ■ Set: *Out Of Control / Twilight / An Cat Dubh / Into The Heart / Surrender / Two Hearts Beat As One / Seconds / Sunday Bloody Sunday / Cry-Electric Co. /* encore: *Gloria / New Year's Day /* encore: *I Will Follow / 40*

U2 play their only German show of the year on the banks of river Rhine at the Loreley Festival, which is aired live on WDR TV and radio in the 'Rockpalast' concert series. It marks the first time that U2 perform on live TV. Early in the show Bono is not his usual buoyant self and acts nervously and somewhat confused. Hardly anyone in the audience is familiar with U2 and the festive aspect that usually dominates their shows is absent. The band work hard to conquer the crowd but signs of tour-exhaustion are evident. Bono climbs on the fence between the audience and the stage during *Surrender* and while he tries to retain his balance, he falls backwards on the concrete floor. When he climbs back he swings over to the other end and falls onto the outstretched arms of the crowd. He sings some lines of *Ein Bisschen Frieden*, Nicole's winning song of the 1983 Eurovision Song Contest, then moves into *Midnight Hour* before falling down again. A swinging and hard-hitting version of *Two Hearts Beat As One* manages to break the ice. Slowly but surely the audience grow more enthusiastic and Bono seems relieved to be getting a grip on the show. Though he had sworn off his wild actions after the Los Angeles incident, Bono grabs a flag and makes his way safely through the audience during Edge's guitar solo in *Electric Co.* to sing on from the lighting tower at the back of the field. At the end of *40* Bono waves goodbye but as he walks off, he suddenly turns around when he hears the crowd softly sing, "How long... to sing this song..." Staring at the audience, the band realise the show has still worked after its shaky start.

Afterwards Bono and Edge are interviewed by 'Rockpalast' TV presenter Alan Bangs. Bono is very tired and confesses he found it very hard to perform for an open-air crowd and at the same time have TV cameras capture his every move for millions of people at home.

The show and the broadcast have a direct result on U2's

popularity as their distributor for Germany registers a significant rise in record sales the following months. Sensing that a breakthrough in Germany is imminent, they release studio versions of two successful songs of U2's set, *40* and *Two Hearts Beat As One*, as a Germany-only single in November 1983. *40* is named as *40 (How Long)* and a sticker is stuck to the picture sleeve saying: 'The discovery of Loreley 1983'.

Surprisingly, five songs of this show, *I Will Follow, Sunday Bloody Sunday, Cry-Electric Co., New Year's Day* and *40*, are put on the 'Under A Blood Red Sky' mini-live album, released in November 1983. Though the record accompanies the video recorded at Red Rocks Amphitheater in Denver, U2 prefer the audio tapes of the Loreley show since they like the way several songs have evolved, and thus choose them over the recordings of Denver. On 'Under A Blood Red Sky', producer Jimmy Iovine has added more echo, background singing and crowd noise to the original recordings to enhance the atmosphere.

AUGUST 21, 1983. OSLO, NORWAY, KALVOYA FESTIVAL

- ■ Attendance: 15,000
- ■ 'Kalvoya Festival'; line-up: U2, Joe Cocker
- ■ Set: same as St. Goarshausen.

Bono takes a refreshment on the hot summer afternoon. "This is salt water," he remarks surprisedly. "Do you drink that around here? We drink Guinness, that's much better." The crowd don't know U2 very well but receive them enthusiastically and cheer when Bono tells them about the white flag being the most important one. U2's last show of the summer ends with the band coming back after *40* to join the crowd again in their peaceful clapping and singing of the song's chorus.

Later in the day the band hold a press conference and explain they've come a full circle and need to move on.

Adam: "We've done three records with Steve Lillywhite and really, to keep the energy, we have to inject ourselves with something different than going back to home ground."

Bono: "It's very easy to become a parody of yourself. We work in a sort of improvisation. The Edge would play his guitar, and we'd say, 'Hey, don't play that, that sounds too much like U2.' And we'd say, 'But we *are* U2!' We must develop new areas. Those first three records are part of a whole, and we feel it's finished. We feel that U2 are to disband. Today was the last U2 gig. I'm not talking about the end of U2 – I'm talking about the start of U2. U2 is just beginning. This is the end of a cycle."

Adam: "We're just going into the studio to write new material and we're gonna come back with something slightly different

30,000 at Torhout

than what we've been doing up to now. It's too early to say what that's going to be..."

Bono: "We will be an aggressive rock & roll band. We want contrast. Highs and lows. I want U2 to make the loudest, angriest record we ever made, and yet at the same time we want it to be sensitive and atmospheric." Bono explains that up to now the lyrics have been autobiographical and hints at the future as he expresses his disgust for 'wallpaper' music. "You hang it on the wall, it's beautiful but it says nothing, it's just emptiness. Last night Adam and I were talking about our aspirations. We do make, and we will continue to make, soul music. Not soul music with black singers – soul music is not about the instruments you play. Soul music is when you reveal, rather than conceal. Soul music is when you bring what's on the inside to the outside."

Referring to the last phase of the 'War' tour and the last couple of shows in particular, Bono says, "We've been knocking on a door for the first few years, and we broke down the door, but we're still knocking. And that's stupid. We try to break down the barrier between the stage and the audience, but sometimes in our efforts we go over the top. In order to get across to a large crowd of 20,000 people, you sometimes exaggerate yourself, and we become cartoons. In that respect, we have failed at times. It's so hard to relax; sometimes I feel like I've got a strait-jacket on and I don't know what to do. But today we relaxed and it was incredible."

SEPTEMBER 23, 1983. THE ALARM: NEW YORK, NY, THE RITZ

Bono makes an appearance with The Alarm to sing along on

Knocking On Heaven's Door, which Mike Peters had taught Bono to play in December 1982 at Hammersmith Palais.

OCTOBER 23, 1983. THE ALARM: DUBLIN, IRELAND, UNIVERSITY

For the fifth time in a year Bono and Mike Peters share the stage singing *Knocking On Heaven's Door*. Bono comes on towards the end of the song and both singers' long improvisations and passionate singing stretch the song to twice its length. "I was so blind I could not see, Mike Peters had spoken to me. I read in the paper that he was no good: I said, knock knock knocking on heaven's door," Bono sings, and makes up lyrics which involve the other band members.

After some rest and working out ideas for the next album, U2 head off for Japan for their first concerts in Asia. Though in their heads they are already in their next phase, they play six shows in Japan that still belong to the old phase. Plans to tour Australia and New Zealand are postponed.

NOVEMBER 16, 1983. HONOLULU, HI

On their way to Japan the band stop over in Hawaii for a short vacation and a one-off concert. Already deep into the work for the next album they try a few new songs and musical ideas during the soundcheck.

NOVEMBER 22, 1983. OSAKA, JAPAN, FESTIVAL HALL

■ Set: *Out Of Control / Twilight / An Cat Dubh / Into The Heart / Surrender / Two Hearts Beat As One / Seconds / Sunday Bloody Sunday / Cry – Electric Co. / I Fall Down / October / New Year's Day / Gloria /* encore: *Party Girl / 11 O'Clock Tick Tock / I Will Follow / 40*

U2's first concerts in Japan have sold out weeks in advance. The basic set remains unchanged. Making allowance for the fact that not many Japanese can speak English, Bono takes time over his announcements, and exaggerates his articulation. "Tonight – is – the – first – night – of – our – first – Japanese – tour. I – hope – there – are – many – more – to – come." The Japanese audience, known for its reticence, politely clap in time with the songs. Any show of emotion, like hysterical screaming, is pernicious. Bono inserts some lines of Marvin Gaye's *Sexual Healing* into *Two Hearts Beat As One*.

U2 show up in a TV show for a brief interview, after which they perform *New Year's Day* live in the studio. Edge's guitar breaks down, resulting in a chaotic, improvised version.

NOVEMBER 23, 1983. NAGOYA, JAPAN

NOVEMBER 26, 27, 28, 29, 1983. TOKYO, JAPAN, SUN PLAZA HALL

■ Set all four nights: same as Osaka.
During the first show, Bono comments on the TV appearance. "On the weekend we played a TV show. I think we entered the world of show business. I don't think it worked out for us." He says U2 are not about 'show business', they are in Japan because

they want to be. Bono sings lines of *Jingle Bells* during *Two Hearts Beat As One* and wishes the crowd a happy Christmas. Several times during the 1982 American tour, Bono had invited a member of the audience on stage to help sing *Southern Man*; on the first Tokyo show, Bono asks someone to play guitar on *I Fall Down*. The audience look on in surprise as a guy climbs on stage and is instructed by Bono how to play the song. This is highly unorthodox to the Japanese who are used to considerably more formality during concerts.

Instead of playing along to *I Fall Down*, the guy realises he will never get a chance like this again and plays Deep Purple's *Smoke On The Water* and some hard rock tunes. Bono fills in, singing "Smoke on the water, fire in the sky," and improvises some lines and melodies before getting back to *I Fall Down*. The crowd let their hair down, screaming loudly, proving that involving a member of the audience in the show works well in breaking barriers between artist and audience.

After the tour, Bono comments in an interview: "Japan was very interesting. I have a lot of respect for the people although we had to get used to them. The fans react very differently there. When you leave after a show by car there are hundreds of screaming fans. You get a police escort and there are at least five taxis with fans following, so that it becomes a sort of race, everybody trying to reach the hotel the first. When the taxis drive next to you and you look who's in the back, there's nobody there... until they suddenly stick their heads out and start taking your photo. We didn't like it at first, we were somewhat cynical. I don't think these people can express themselves another way. According to the response they really liked us and that surprised us somewhat. The tour was sold out way in advance!"

DECEMBER 18, 1983. LONDON, ENGLAND, VICTORIA APOLLO

- Attendance: 2,000; sellout
- 'The Big One' line-up: Hazel O'Connor, Mari Wilson, Ian Dury and Chas Jankel, Elvis Costello, Paul Weller and The Style Council, The Alarm, U2
- Set: *I Will Follow* / *11 O'Clock Tick Tock* / *Seconds* / *Sunday Bloody Sunday* / *Knocking on Heaven's Door* / *New Year's Day* / *40*

With US President Ronald Reagan situating cruise missiles in military bases all over Europe, the arms race between the Soviet Union and the United States reigns supreme. Both sides spend billions of dollars and roubles fabricating nuclear arms, pointing them at each other as a 'deterrent'. All over Europe people take to the streets to show their fear and concern about this insane and perilous game of bluff poker. Though they are keeping a low profile while working on their next record, U2 decide to participate in this peace concert organised by the Campaign of Nuclear Disarmament to protest against American nuclear missiles at Greenham Common. The show includes three or four song sets by all the artists and sketches and comedy turns by actors who "wished to confirm their commitment to peace", according to the press release. Ticket prices range between £6 and £18, the proceeds going to CND.

At the end of The Alarm's set, Mike Peters announces U2, who play a short set of some of their most powerful and lyrically appropriate songs. Edge sings a moving version of *Seconds*, its anti-nuclear lyrics never more appropriate. Mike Peters comes out to join Bono on *Knocking On Heaven's Door*.

MAY - AUGUST 1984. DUBLIN, SLANE CASTLE / WINDMILL LANE STUDIOS

U2 record their new album with Brian Eno and Daniel Lanois as producers. Ideas for new songs have been materialising since the American tour in 1983 and by the time the tour reached Japan, the band has a clear picture of what they wanted. Recording sessions start in the ballroom of Slane Castle on May 7, moving four weeks later to Windmill Lane Studios. The work is complete on August 5.

A 45-minute video documentary about the recordings is made by Barry Devlin, a friend of U2's, which is put on the video, 'The Unforgettable Fire Collection', released in 1985.

JULY 8, 1984. BOB DYLAN: DUBLIN, IRELAND, SLANE CASTLE

Bob Dylan plays an open-air concert in the grounds of Slane Castle, where U2 recorded material for their new album in May. Bono appears during the bluesy *Leopard Skin Pillbox Hat*. Before the show Dylan asked if he knew the lyrics to the song. "Yeah, sure," Bono bluffed. He gets a kick out of sharing the stage with Dylan but in fact doesn't know any of the lyrics and just hums and bawls along. He is familiar with *Blowing In The Wind*, which is played as the final song, and sings the chorus as well as a whole verse.

THE UNDER AUSTRALIAN SKIES TOUR 1984

Having just finished mixing the new album and shooting a video for its first single, *Pride*, U2 hastily prepare for their first Australian tour, scheduled to start in New Zealand on August 24. Plans to visit the Antipodes were first discussed in 1982, and the band had intended to play there in late 1983, but were too worn out from touring to see it through.

In America and Europe it has taken U2 years to build up their audience step-by-step; in Australia, however, they will start by playing sports arenas right away. Originally, three concerts have been planned in both Sydney and Melbourne, and one each in Adelaide, Perth and Brisbane, but as all the shows sell out quickly, another six are added. The last international act to tour Australia was Culture Club, who took the country by storm. With less hullabaloo U2 sell twice as many tickets in less time. 'U2's music has meaning, and they're not the sort of band to let that meaning become obscured by tacky marketing or glossy production,' *The National Times* states.

Partly responsible for the incredible demand for tickets is the

best-selling Red Rocks video. Although U2's albums have sold well in Australia, it is the video that has introduced U2 to a wider audience as one of the most exciting and compelling live bands around, and has built up anticipation to see U2 in concert.

The tour finds the band in a transitional phase. As Bono will say during the tour, "In some ways it's like a joint between the past of U2 and the future of U2." The 'Under A Blood Red Sky' album and video have closed off the 'War' era. The new work has been completed, but has not yet been released. Through lack of time, the band have not yet been able to translate the new songs to a live situation, and as they have never played Australia before, U2 decide to play the 'War' tour set. They can practise their new songs during sound checks and gradually introduce them into the show.

AUGUST 29, 1984. CHRISTCHURCH, TOWN HALL

The first of four concerts in New Zealand.

AUGUST 31, 1984. WELLINGTON, SHOW BUILDING

- Set: *Gloria* / *I Threw A Brick Through A Window* / *A Day Without Me* / *An Cat Dubh* / *Into The Heart* / *Surrender* / *Two Hearts Beat As One* / *Seconds* / *Sunday Bloody Sunday* / *Cry-Electric Co.* / *I Fall Down* / *October* / *New Year's Day* / *Pride* / *Out Of Control* / encore: *Party Girl* / *11 O'Clock Tick Tock* / *I Will Follow* / encore: *40*

The atmospheric new instrumental *4th Of July* is played over the PA and for the entire tour serves as an introduction and a cue for the band to take their places on stage. Bono greets the audience enthusiastically and with *Gloria* the show is off to a rousing start. "A few days ago we weren't too sure if we remembered how to play," Bono says after *A Day Without Me*. During rehearsals for the tour, he had forgotten some of his guitar riffs and had to go out to buy U2 albums to refresh his memory. At any rate, U2 have lost none of their force and their ambition hasn't changed either. "Well, this is quite a hay-barn," Bono says. "Tonight, you and we will turn it into a living room."

Some lines from *Midnight Hour* are included in *Surrender*, and Bono improvises on *Two Hearts Beat As One*: "Yes I feel so good, I think I got you in my blood. Oh give me the moonlight, oh give me the girl. I belong to the moonlight, and she belongs to me. We belong with each other... you see, I can't stop to dance..." During *New Year's Day* there is a minor problem with a microphone which is solved quickly by guitar technician Steve Rainford. ("Steve's about the only good thing from Liverpool," Bono claims.) *Pride*, the only new song in the set, is played tightly

and is well-received. It will be released as a single a week later, prefacing the upcoming album which is set for release early October. *Party Girl* is the playful element in the set, and *11 O'Clock Tick Tock* and *I Will Follow* get the audience jumping. For this tour, *40* has again been chosen to calm down the audience at the end of the show. Bono is a bit unsure as to whether the performance has been a success. "It's very hard to make music in this place and I hope and pray that we made it tonight." The contented audience cheer and sing along to *40*.

SEPTEMBER 1, 2, 1984. AUCKLAND, LOGAN CAMPBELL CENTRE

■ Set first night: same as Wellington.

Besides U2's regular crew, hired for the entire tour, some extra hands are needed in each town. In Auckland one of the additional hands is Greg Carroll. He stands out from the others because he is quick, attentive, he works hard, and is a fun guy to be with. He seems to be the perfect choice for a permanent

stage-roadie, fulfilling the difficult task of watching over Bono from the edge of the stage, making sure his mike-lead doesn't get stuck somewhere or that he doesn't trip over things thrown onstage. Paul McGuinness offers Greg a job and he accepts. Bono is pleased about this and during the show tells the audience about Greg and thanks him for accepting the job.

■ Set second night: *Out Of Control / Twilight / An Cat Dubh / Into The Heart / The Unforgettable Fire / Surrender / Two Hearts Beat As One / Seconds / Sunday Bloody Sunday / Cry- Electric Co. / I Fall Down / October / New Year's Day / Pride / Gloria /* encore: *Party Girl / 11 O'Clock Tick Tock / I Will Follow / 40*

Concert audiences in Auckland are known to be rowdy; all too often shows are upset by disturbances. After only a few minutes, blows are exchanged amid the pushing and jostling at the front. The band stop during *Out Of Control*. "We haven't come a long way to see you crack heads here!" Bono yells.

"A lot of the songs that we're playing for you tonight will probably never be played again. In some ways it's very good to be able to just celebrate these songs with people we haven't played them to before. This is one such piece of music, this is *An Cat Dubh*." After the Australian tour, songs such as *An Cat Dubh*, *Into The Heart* and *Twilight* will yield to more recent work. To this day, U2 have never performed these songs again.

One of the new songs displacing the old is *The Unforgettable Fire*, which premières tonight. The only song in the set that hints at U2's new direction, the audience listen to it attentively while The Edge conjures up its ethereal intro on keyboards. Bono has difficulty reaching the high notes and sings a few of the lines in a whisper. He diverges from the studio version, singing "Stay till your heart beats through" in long bursts, and then gets the audience to sing along to that.

Bono is handed a guitar before *I Fall Down*. "Well, at least I pretend to play, you know," he jokes. "All I need is about two chords. I know two – this one is an F, right? This is an A-minor. I really like the A-minor because a lot of my favourite songs are in A-minor." Bono starts strumming *Southern Man*. "Remember that one by Neil Young? Southern man better keep your head up," he sings, but stops after that. "I only know two chords!"

"Tonight is our last night in this country. I'm not happy either about that. I've made some very good friends, seen some very good places, drunk some very good water, some very good beer. And some very good champagne! Sing this song with me, this is *40*."

SEPTEMBER 4, 5, 6, 8, 9, 1984. SYDNEY, ENTERTAINMENT CENTRE

■ Attendance: 60,000; sellout
■ Support: Matt Finish

For the first time in their career U2 are scheduled to play the same venue five times within a week. On September 4, dozens of reporters and photographers turn up to report on U2's first concert under Australian skies. The elated audience give U2 an overwhelming reception. The band burst forth with *Gloria*, but technical malfunctions with The Edge and Adam's instruments ruin the song. Bono apologises while Adam's bass is inspected by a roadie. During *Surrender*, Edge is forced to replace his guitar, so Bono hastily improvises to fill in the gap. The band work hard to conquer the problems and repeat *Gloria* in the encore. "Let's get it right this time!" Bono shouts, and dances with a fan who has sneaked through the security lines.

The reviews of the first concert are generally positive. *The Sydney Herald* points out that it is to U2's credit that the technical problems did not harm the development of the concert. 'U2's honesty was evident when the band experienced problems with the bass guitar. Lead singer Bono just stopped the show and he told the audience of the problems.'

In *Juke* magazine Simon Mayhard and Christie Eliezer describe the audience's devotion. 'So when was the last time you saw an audience continue to sing a song five minutes after the band's finished that song and quit the stage? That's exactly what happened after *40*.' However, Mayhard and Eliezer felt that the

ideals of the songs went a bit too far at times: 'Passionately held religious beliefs in rock are fine, in their sense of fair play and spirituality, but they become a drag when they present a static demeanour to the overall concept. Cripes, who wants to 'surrender' in these sad, pathetic days? Who's Bono kidding?

'Nevertheless, a chord is struck. The bond formed is so strong and tight that the band's accessibility becomes a gospel meeting (save for the usual overzealous fool roadies using too much roughness in handling kids who've been asked to celebrate by Bono). Huge auditoriums holding 12,000 people turn into extended living rooms.

Melbourne, September 13, 1984

'The reprise of *Gloria* was stunning, a celebration with Bono doing an impromptu jig with a fan who broke onto the stage. You walked out impressed by their sensitivity to human and socio-political issues, fascinated by their technique and passion within and without the music. But to surrender? Not us, sorry.'

■ Set second and fourth shows: *Gloria / I Threw A Brick Through A Window / A Day Without Me / An Cat Dubh / Into The Heart / The Unforgettable Fire / Surrender / Two Hearts Beat As One / Seconds / Sunday Bloody Sunday / Cry-Electric Co. / I Fall Down / October / New Year's Day / Pride / Out Of Control / encore: Party Girl / 11 O'Clock Tick Tock / I Will Follow / 40*
At the fourth show, a girl jumps on stage during *Two Hearts Beat As One* and hides behind Larry's drum kit before she is finally caught by the security guards. Bono runs over to take her by the hand and dance with her. At the beginning of *Out Of Control* another girl climbs onstage and, with his arm around her, Bono sings, "They make children, yes, like *this* one. Ladies and gentlemen: this is Kathy!" he tells everyone. *11 O'Clock Tick Tock* includes a bit of *Give Peace A Chance*, in which the band stop to let the audience finish the song.

■ Set fifth show: same as second night in Auckland.
The Australian tour has run smoothly until now, but the first crowd disturbance occurs during *Gloria*. Bono stops the song for a while but remains calm. "You OK? Everything's cool... All week there's been no trouble, these security people have been really good, so..." With the house-lights on and Clannad's *Theme From Harry's Game* accompanying the audience to the exits after *40*, the band return to pick up the song again. The lights dim and the chanting audience are treated to a few more minutes, ending a long week in Sydney.

SEPTEMBER 11, 1984. BRISBANE, FESTIVAL HALL

■ Attendance: 7,000; sellout

SEPTEMBER 13, 14, 15, 17, 18, 1984. MELBOURNE, SPORTS AND ENTERTAINMENT CENTRE

■ Attendance: 35,000; sellout
Like Sydney, Melbourne has effortlessly sold out its five shows. A sixth concert is considered for the 19th, but does not take place. U2 are once again received ecstatically and several fans succeed in invading the stage. Besides girls running after Bono, during the first show a big skinhead lifts him in his arms and holds him dangerously close to the edge of the stage. Afterwards they do a little dance together.

■ Set third show: same as the second night in Auckland.
The concert gets off to a curious start when the band go into *Out Of Control* and Larry, in a state of confusion, bangs out the first rolls of *Gloria*. He corrects himself immediately.

■ Set fourth show: *Wire / Gloria / I Threw A Brick / A Day Without Me / An Cat Dubh / Into The Heart / The Unforgettable Fire / Surrender / Two Hearts Beat As One / Seconds / Sunday Bloody Sunday / Cry-Electric Co. / A Sort Of Homecoming / October / New Year's Day / Pride / Out Of Control / encore: Party Girl / I Will Follow / 40*
Two new songs are premièred: *A Sort Of Homecoming* and *Wire*, which, surprisingly, opens the concert. The *4th Of July* intro has barely ended when Edge's rasping guitar work surprises the fans who have been at the previous nights. *Wire* is played loud as thunder and sung aggressively, which has its consequences: "I'd just like to ask you to bear with me a little bit tonight," Bono says before *An Cat Dubh*. "My throat's a bit sore, but I don't mind if you don't mind. The band think it's good this way; that will shut me up for a while." During *The Unforgettable Fire* Bono again sings, "Stay, till your heart beats through," and gets the audience to sing along, resulting in a long version of a song that will ultimately allow no room for such improvisation. Afterwards Bono says, "I sometimes wish that it was possible in a place like this to be able to converse, to talk to all of you people. Speaking is not just about the words, about whether you've got your voice or you lost your voice, it's about something much more important than that. I hope tonight we'll prove that music, which is the action, speaks louder than the words." Bono has just read the review of the first Sydney concert in *Juke* magazine. "Everyone's talking about this next song; in the paper about this song they said, 'How can this man suggest that we surrender in times like this?' or something." The band burst forth in *Surrender*, to the sound of thunderous applause. "To you I surrender! Dance with me!" Bono pleads, seemingly hurt by the review. Unlike the record, the live version of *A Sort Of Homecoming* starts with The Edge playing the intro acoustically, and the rest of the band join in after the first verse.

SEPTEMBER 20, 21, 1984. ADELAIDE, APOLLO ENTERTAINMENT CENTRE

■ Attendance: 10,000; sellout

SEPTEMBER 23, 24, 1984. PERTH, ENTERTAINMENT CENTRE

■ Attendance: 14,000; sellout
Two good shows in the Western Australia capital end U2's tour. In the course of the month the 'Boy', 'October', 'War' and 'Under A Blood Red Sky' albums have climbed the charts and the *Pride* single reached Number 4. Bono thanks the crew, the fans, the band and everyone else for the past four successful weeks, and he promises to return soon.

OCTOBER 1, 1984

U2's fourth album, 'The Unforgettable Fire', is released worldwide.

'THE UNFORGETTABLE FIRE' TOUR, LEG 1: EUROPE, FALL 1984

The European tour is originally planned to start in Rotterdam, Holland, on October 1, the day the album is released, with another 16 shows planned for the rest of the month. Ticket sales for several shows have already begun when, at the last moment, U2 postpone the tour for a few weeks because they need more time to rehearse the new songs and to attune the show to the new record.

Named after the exhibition of paintings by survivors of the nuclear bombings of Hiroshima and Nagasaki which the band visited in Chicago in 1983, 'The Unforgettable Fire' album title also applies to most of the songs' subject matter in a broader sense of the word.

The album honours two men who both exuded, but were also consumed by, an 'unforgettable fire'. Martin Luther King fought for black civil rights in America in the Fifties and Sixties with such passion and force that he became a spiritual leader for Afro-Americans suffering from discrimination. He was eventually shot dead in public. Elvis Presley possessed the ability to warm the hearts of millions through his voice, a fire which continues to burn long after he became the victim of the pressure of massive success, and the drugs he used to escape from its demands. The theme of drug addiction and its destructive effect show up in the tracks *Wire* and *Bad*.

Musically, the album contrasts rhythmic, uptempo arrangements with atmospheric, orchestrated pieces. Producer Brian Eno has helped U2 create soundscapes that evoke images for the listener. Partly recorded in the ballroom of Slane Castle, the music has a rich sound benefiting from its natural acoustics. Enhanced by lyrics open to many interpretations, the album is very 'visual', as the band members will say in interviews.

For the tour, U2 adapt their show to the dreamy nature of the album, and they try to transform its visual inspiration into the show. The stage presentation will be subtle, depending on moods transcending from the music and lighting, rather than from Bono's stage antics.

The original tour dates were: Rotterdam (October 1), Copenhagen (4), Oslo (5), Stockholm (6), Hamburg (8), Düsseldorf (10), Offenbach (11), Munich (12), Bologna (14), Milan (15), Lausanne (17), Lyon (18), Marseille (19), Barcelona (21), Toulouse (22), Rennes (24), Paris (25).
The Lyon, Marseille and Paris dates remain unchanged, while the rest are either postponed until early 1985, or cancelled altogether.

The show was postponed

OCTOBER 18, 1984. LYON, FRANCE, ESPACE TONY GARNIER

- Attendance: 17,000
- Set: *MLK / The Unforgettable Fire / Surrender / Two Hearts Beat As One / Seconds / Sunday Bloody Sunday / Cry-Electric Co. / Bad / Indian Summer Sky / October / New Year's Day / Pride /* 11 O'Clock Tick Tock / I Will Follow / encore: *Gloria* / encore: *40*

U2 will travel clockwise through France for six shows within a week. Since they had played only a total of five shows in the country before, the French know U2 mainly from the Red Rocks video, which had been a big seller. Following Bono's example during that Denver performance, many in the audience bring along white flags. Where the crowd expect a thundering show *à la* Red Rocks, U2 – somewhat ironically – have already departed the phase that attracted the crowd's interest in the first place.

After a rapturously received entrance, the band bravely open with *MLK* to emphasise their change, but the slow, dreamy tribute to Dr. King is drowned out completely by the crowd's deafening cries. It is immediately obvious that this song is too delicate to open with. The versions of the other new songs are vulnerable and are generally not well received by the crowd. *The Unforgettable Fire* is aided by programmed instrumentals on sequencer, as the string arrangements of the album version are impossible to play live within the band's four-instrument complement. The sequencer supplies *Bad* with the chiming, rattling sound that sets the rhythm. The song's first live performance is short and fragile, as Bono softly whispers the climactic "I'm wide awake" bit instead of singing it passionately as he will in the future.

During *The Unforgettable Fire*, slides with Japanese writings and lithographs from the original 'Unforgettable Fire' exhibition are projected onto a white backdrop. Six long white banners are let down from the ceiling for *New Year's Day*. The portrait of Martin Luther King is projected during *Pride*. These visuals have the double function of illustrating the songs, as well as bridging the physical distance to the crowd now that Bono doesn't run around the stage.

The slides, however, confuse tonight's crowd, who are disappointed that Bono doesn't climb the balcony. Bono tries to explain to the crowd that he wishes he could speak their language, but hopes to "be able to speak through the music".

The songs from 'War' are recognised and loudly sung along with, but it's not until the end of the show that old favourites like *11 O'Clock Tick Tock* and *I Will Follow* turn the crowd's confusion into celebration. When the houselights are lit and Clannad's *Theme Of Harry's Game* resounds, crowd response to the show is mixed. Some sing "How long to sing this song", while others boo.

OCTOBER 19, 1984. MARSEILLE, FRANCE, STADIUM

- Attendance: 8,000

■ Set: 11 O'Clock Tick Tock / I Will Follow / The Unforgettable Fire / Surrender / Two Hearts Beat As One / Seconds / Sunday Bloody Sunday / Cry-Electric Co. / Bad / October / New Year's Day / A Sort Of Homecoming / Pride / encore: Party Girl / Gloria / 40

The set is totally changed, with 11 O'Clock Tick Tock and I Will Follow opening the show so the audience have an opportunity to release their pent-up excitement before the new songs are introduced. During The Unforgettable Fire the audience have a hard time restraining their enthusiasm and seem relieved when golden oldies like Two Hearts Beat As One and Sunday Bloody Sunday are played, hollering along as loud as hell.

OCTOBER 20, 1984. TOULOUSE, FRANCE, PALAIS DES SPORTS

■ Attendance: 7,000; sellout
■ Set: 11 O'Clock Tick Tock / I Will Follow / The Unforgettable Fire / Wire / Surrender / Two Hearts Beat As One / Seconds / Sunday Bloody Sunday / Cry-Electric Co. / October / New Year's Day / Pride / encore: A Sort Of Homecoming / Gloria / 40

With only 15 songs, this is a short, 70 minute show. Wire is added to the set, A Sort Of Homecoming has moved to the encore while Party Girl and Bad, which needs more rehearsing, are left out. Gloria is dedicated to ticketless fans listening outside.

OCTOBER 22, 1984. BORDEAUX, FRANCE, PATTINOIRE

■ Attendance: 7,500
■ Set: 11 O'Clock Tick Tock / I Will Follow / MLK / The Unforgettable Fire / Surrender / Two Hearts Beat As One / Seconds / Sunday Bloody Sunday / Cry-Electric Co. / Bad / Indian Summer Sky / October / New Year's Day / Pride / encore: A Sort Of Homecoming / Gloria / encore: Party Girl / 40

Slowly but surely the new show begins to take shape; in Bordeaux a full 18-song set is played. MLK has returned, after its unfortunate première in Lyon. Bad still sounds rickety because Bono cannot handle the demanding "I'm wide awake" part, while Indian Summer Sky lacks the edge it has on record.

The band checked out the town the previous night and stumbled on a fun fair. "There was this big wheel, and we went to the top of it and could see all over the city of Bordeaux," Bono says excitedly, implying that usually they have no time for such outings. "When you travel a lot, you go in and out of hotels, another room, more people and more people, you just forget

that..." He stammers, realising this is a problem that fans will have difficulty relating to. "We've a pretty good job actually. Well, this is for some of you who maybe don't feel so good, but I'm sure you will – this is a song called 40. Comprenez moi?"

OCTOBER 23, 1984. NANTES, FRANCE, ST. HERBLAIN

■ Attendance: 8,000
■ Support: Big Audio Dynamite
■ Set: 11 O'Clock Tick Tock / I Will Follow / Wire / MLK / The Unforgettable Fire / Surrender / Two Hearts Beat As One / Seconds / A Sort Of Homecoming / Sunday Bloody Sunday / Cry-Electric Co / Bad / Indian Summer Sky / October / New Year's Day / Pride / encore: Party Girl / Gloria / encore: 40

Searching for the right balance in the show, A Sort Of Homecoming is now played earlier in the set as the band feel it's unsuitable as an encore. After three uptempo songs, MLK is the first breather in the show, but the Nantes audience don't appreciate the ambient piece and coercively clap hands.

After the concert Adam Sweeting of Melody Maker asks

Adam whether it is a challenge to play new material for a new audience. Adam: "There's an awful lot of people all around the world that want to see us, and why should we just end up playing for London and New York who see everyone who comes through? I like to be able to tour in other places. It's not always fun, it's not always together, but you have to accept that as part of the problems of going to these places."

OCTOBER 25, 1984. PARIS, FRANCE, ESPACE BALLARD

■ Attendance: 12,000
■ Support: The Alarm
■ Set: same as Nantes, minus Indian Summer Sky.

Sultry and wet are the key words for this show, which takes place in a large circus tent. The 12,000-strong crowd are so packed together that condensation saturates the air, almost resulting in raincloud formations inside the tent. Outside, rain comes down in buckets and penetrates the tarpaulin which affects the instruments. Though the roadies desperately try to cover the equipment with plastic, Edge's guitars are out of tune while a fragile song like The Unforgettable Fire comes to nothing due to malfunctioning keyboards. "If I could speak your language, I would tell you the way I feel right now, which is that this group, and this audience, deserve better than this place. And I don't mind being rained-out on the stage, let it rain! The sun is coming out for us tonight," Bono says. "Let it rain on me, let it rain on the sea, I like it when the rain comes down," he sings in Two Hearts Beat As One, managing to give an optimistic twist to the inconveniences. The rain is not altogether without danger. 40 is hastily played after Bono receives a warning from the technicians that the PA has become so wet it's likely to explode.

OCTOBER 27, 28, 1984. BRUSSELS, BELGIUM, VORST NATIONAAL

■ Attendance: 16,000; sellout
■ Support: The Alarm
■ Set first night: same as Nantes.

Although numerous band and crew members have caught colds in Paris, the tour really lifts off when it reaches the Low Countries. 'The Unforgettable Fire' has already turned gold both in Holland and Belgium, where it stands at Number One in the charts. This audience have seen the band go through many phases and welcome the new material, being appropriately quiet for MLK while Wire makes them release their energy as much as I Will

Follow does. The show as a whole has become more balanced. The sound level during the first concert is so loud it shakes houses in the vicinity of the venue and the Brussels Seismological Institute identify the tremors as being from an earthquake. When asked for a reaction, Bono blames Adam's heavy basslines.

■ Set second night: same as Nantes, minus *Indian Summer Sky*. Much to the audience's pleasure, Bono remembers the Torhout and Werchter festivals well: "You know that these festivals are world-famous? A lot of the groups talk about it and like to play here, from Simple Minds, to Talking Heads, Pretenders, you name them." Before *40* he says: "Just one story that I was told yesterday – I think everybody here has to join the army at some point, is that right? Well, this particular person spent the last week in a barracks under arrest for wearing his 'War' T-shirt. They actually lock you up in a cell, just for one of these. I wish you well in all your efforts to stop all that nonsense."

OCTOBER 30, 31, 1984. ROTTERDAM, HOLLAND, SPORTPALEIS AHOY

■ Attendance: 16,000; sellout
■ Support: The Alarm
■ Set both nights: same as Nantes, minus *Indian Summer Sky*.

Tickets sell out within two hours. U2 play two of the best shows of the tour so far. The atmosphere is excellent and all songs are played with full conviction, with extra lines and improvisations added to several songs. On the first night Bono finally masters the dramatic "I'm wide awake" part in *Bad*, making the despair and hope of the album's version come alive in concert. He tries to repeat the Dutch lines that he learned in Hattem in 1982, saying that he wished he could speak Dutch but couldn't manage it. Indeed, his pronunciation has become even worse.

The second night the audience sing *Happy Birthday* for

Larry's 23rd birthday, while Bono sprays champagne all over him. "Two years ago, again today," he shouts, referring to the Paradiso show in 1981. "I've said this before, but I will say it again: this is the first place that gave U2 the time of day, this country, these people. We went from Ireland to England, and after that, Holland."

NOVEMBER 2, 3, 1984. LONDON, ENGLAND, BRIXTON ACADEMY

■ Attendance: 9,000; sellout
■ Support: The Waterboys
■ Set both nights: same as Nantes.
U2's first UK tour since the spring of 1983 gets an awkward

Soundcheck at Barrowlands. Background: Charlie Burchill

start. The crowd at Brixton Academy are aggressive. Several fights erupt in the front and the atmosphere is closer to hostility than celebration. Bono doesn't know what to do to restore order but says it's good that the UK tour starts here, because, "I think this is really a good place... also very good people." Realising his remark is rather misplaced, some songs later Bono confusingly tries again to break the tense atmosphere by telling the crowd about his paradoxal bond with the city of London: "I feel like I've got to say something, just that we be loose and everything. I'm not actually sure what I should say but... this is a very big city, London, it's a city I love very much. It didn't always feel this way, I used to fight with this city a lot. When the band was just beginning we were getting on the train and going on a boat and coming to London and it was just such a big city for me, and I was a little nervous and frightened. I think I probably still am, even tonight, a little nervous and frightened of this city. I just hope that this music can break this down, and make this place work for us tonight. I'm not trying to make a speech or anything, I just wanna make this a good concert."

During *Pride* Bono stops the song when fights continue and several people from the crowd climb onstage. "I just wanna explain something. Last year was really a good year for us. You climb to some sort of a peak, you reach there, you don't know where you're going to because there is no other land, you gotta switch peaks, switch mountains or something. We're trying to begin again here in front of you and I just feel that..." Bono gives up as the crowd jeer and whistle. "Just thanks for coming, for God's sake," he mumbles and starts *Pride* anew.

At the second show things aren't much better and again Bono tries to bond with the crowd by praising the city and its people in a situation that doesn't suit it. This being the start of the UK tour, reporters for most periodicals are present. Most reviews aren't positive and Bono's rambling is attacked and ridiculed. David Quantick writes in *New Musical Express*: 'The most boring band in the world. There may be groups equally as dull, but I fail to see how any of them can be worse.'

NOVEMBER 5, 1984. EDINBURGH, SCOTLAND, PLAYHOUSE

■ Attendance: 5,000; sellout
■ Support: The Waterboys
■ Set: same as Nantes, minus *Indian Summer Sky*.
The enthusiastic Scottish audience sing and clap along continuously, often out of time. At the start of *Bad*, Edge experiences some technical problems. "Take your time Edge, take your time... is on my side," Bono sings, improvising his way towards The Rolling Stones song. He drags production manager Steve Iredale onstage during *Party Girl* and announces it's his birthday.

NOVEMBER 6, 7, 1984. GLASGOW, SCOTLAND, BARROWLANDS

■ Attendance: 5,000; sellout
■ Support: The Waterboys
■ Set both nights: same as Nantes, minus *Indian Summer Sky*.
U2 get an incredibly warm reception and play two energetic shows in the smallest venue of the tour. Hundreds of ticketless fans wait at the door for a chance to slip inside. Tickets had sold out amazingly fast, leaving thousands of fans complaining that U2 should have booked a bigger venue. During the second show Bono hands out cups of water to people who are getting squashed in the front. Others are thirsty as well and chant to the melody of *Here We Go*, "Over here, over here, over here..." During the soundcheck in the afternoon, Simple Minds guitarist Charlie Burchill pops up for a chat and during the show plays along on *40* while his whole band watch from the back. Bono dedicates *40* to them and afterwards the audience turn around and applaud them when a spotlight points them out.

NOVEMBER 9, 10, 1984. MANCHESTER, ENGLAND, APOLLO THEATRE

- Attendance: 6,000; sellout
- Support: The Waterboys
- Set first night: same as Nantes.

Bono mentions that *11 O'Clock Tick Tock* was "born" in Manchester, and recalls that the city was one of the first in Britain to support U2. "We drove up in a van from London and played in a little room," he says amid yelling from the audience. "You couldn't have been there, there was only about three people there," he laughs. Again they call something. "Oh, you were the three, I see…"

- Set second night: same as Nantes, minus *Indian Summer Sky*.

Since U2 want to put together a mini-LP with some remaining songs from the 'Unforgettable Fire' sessions combined with some live recordings from the tour, both Manchester shows are professionally recorded, as are the next three shows in Birmingham and Wembley.

Peter Martin reviews the show for *Smash Hits* magazine: 'Inside the Apollo, I feel an anticipation, an excitement rarely felt at concerts – a genuine atmosphere that was willing the night to be great. Some fans dart out of their seats and rush to the front of the stage. Others follow but are stopped by the dreaded bouncers. Still, it's impossible to dampen spirits. I now know why most bands have given up trying to talk about the importance of their music, because sometimes it's just impossible to avoid all the awful clichés about "honesty" and "integrity" and "power" and "passion" and "commitment". Those *are* the areas U2 work in – there's no getting away from it.

'During *Sunday Bloody Sunday* one lad got dragged out of the hall and plonked in the street. After the song Bono shouted for someone to go out and get him, find out his name and bring him backstage. He constantly keeps an eye on the fans, checking there's no one getting crushed…

'About an hour after the show Bono emerges from the stage door and is immediately swamped by fans. As he finds out he's blocking the equipment removal he steadily ushers his merry throng around the corner, perching himself on the bonnet of a car. Questions ranged from 'give us a kiss' to more serious enquiries into the band's politics and ideals. After 30 minutes of constant autograph signing and chatting he is forced to go – he's holding up the entire tour coach. The more understanding majority just step back and let him go but one girl gets a bit carried away and takes a grab at his bum.

'Back on the coach Bono wags his finger at her but she's quite shameless and just gestures that she couldn't resist. He tries to suppress a smile. And with that it's back to the hotel to talk to even more fans.'

NOVEMBER 12, 1984. BIRMINGHAM, ENGLAND, NATIONAL EXHIBITION CENTRE

- Attendance: 11,000; sellout
- Support: The Waterboys
- Set: *11 O'Clock Tick Tock* / *I Will Follow* / *Seconds* / *Sunday Bloody Sunday* / *Cry-Electric Co.* / *I Fall Down* / *MLK* / *The Unforgettable Fire* / *Wire* / *Bad* / *October* / *New Year's Day* / *Pride* / *Gloria* / encore: *Two Hearts Beat As One* / *Party Girl* / encore: *40*

The order of the songs is changed, with *Wire* now being played after *The Unforgettable Fire*, which will remain there for the rest of the tour. Remarkable is the inclusion of *I Fall Down* and the absence of *Surrender* and *A Sort Of Homecoming*.

With 11,000 fans in attendance it's the biggest hall U2 play in the UK to date. Not everyone is pleased. Longtime fans feel the band are selling out while others cannot see them simply because they are unable to travel to any of only five cities the tour visits. During the UK leg of the 'War' tour, U2 played 28 theatre shows in four weeks for 55,000 people. On this tour, that same number of people is reached with 10 shows in half the time. Criticism that playing venues like the NEC will harm the

quality of the performance is unfounded. Tonight's heart-stopping version of *Bad* is later included on the mini-album 'Wide Awake In America', released in May 1985.

NOVEMBER 14, 15, 1984. LONDON, ENGLAND, WEMBLEY ARENA

- Attendance: 20,000; sellout
- Support: The Waterboys
- Set both nights: *11 O'Clock Tick Tock* / *I Will Follow* / *Seconds* / *Sunday Bloody Sunday* / *Cry-Electric Co.* / *A Sort Of Homecoming* / *MLK* / *The Unforgettable Fire* / *Wire* / *Bad* / *October* / *New Year's Day* / *Pride* / *Gloria* / encore: *Party Girl* / *Two Hearts Beat As One* / encore: *40*

U2's two nights at the famous Wembley Arena are superb and manage to impress those writers who had criticised the Brixton shows. On the second night, Bono vigorously responds to those who had questioned his sincerity. "I really gotta watch what I say actually – people in the papers really don't like it when I talk to you. And I can understand. Sometimes people come into this city and they say, 'Yeah, we really want to be in this city, and we really want to be on stage'. The only difference is, when we say it, we mean it."

The shows ignite further interest in seeing U2, but with the band scheduled to tour America, there is no chance of additional UK shows. Rumours fly that U2 will be back to play the UK 'some time next year'.

During the soundcheck of the second show, U2 record *A Sort Of Homecoming*, and as they prefer this version over those recorded during the actual shows, the soundcheck version ends up on the mini-LP 'Wide Awake In America'. Audience sound is mixed in to suggest the song was actually recorded in concert. Originally intended as an America-only mini-LP, 'Wide Awake In America' is released on CD worldwide in 1987. The soundcheck version of *A Sort Of Homecoming* also appears on the B-side of *The Unforgettable Fire* single, released in May 1985.

NOVEMBER, 21, 1984. DORTMUND, GERMANY, WESTFALENHALLE

- Attendance: 15,000; (capacity 17,000)
- 'RockPop in Concert' line-up: The Waterboys, Spandau Ballet, U2, Bryan Adams, Talk Talk
- Set: *11 O'Clock Tick Tock* / *I Will Follow* / *Sunday Bloody Sunday* / *Cry-Electric Co.* / *A Sort Of Homecoming* / *MLK* / *The Unforgettable Fire* / *Bad* / *October* / *New Year's Day* / *Pride* / *Gloria* / *40*

U2 play a blistering 13-song set for German TV. During *Electric Co.* Bono runs up the slope of the cycling track left of the stage and sings a bit of *Amazing Grace*. He becomes irritable during *Pride* when the cameraman pushes his camera almost into Bono's face. Bono points at the audience and tactfully turns the camera in their direction. The show, less three songs, is aired on January 12, 1985.

'THE UNFORGETTABLE FIRE' TOUR, LEG 2: NORTH AMERICA DECEMBER 1984

DECEMBER 1, 1984. PHILADELPHIA, PA, TOWER THEATER

- Attendance: 3,000; sellout
- Support: The Waterboys
- Set: *11 O'Clock Tick Tock* / *I Will Follow* / *Seconds* / *Sunday Bloody Sunday* / *Cry-Electric Co.* / *A Sort Of Homecoming* / *MLK* / *The Unforgettable Fire* / *Wire* / *Bad* / *October* / *New Year's Day* / *Pride* / encore: *Gloria* / *Party Girl* / *Two Hearts Beat As One* / *40*

Preceding a major American tour in the spring of 1985, U2 do a quick round of the bigger cities to preview their new show and ignite interest in next year's concerts. Several shows are booked at sports arenas while most take place at theatres. Ticket demand for the Tower has outstripped supply many times over and U2 could easily have sold out an arena show in Philadelphia. As this situation occurs in the other cities that house the smaller shows as well, it indicates that this may be the last time that U2 will play these intimate theatres.

"I think it's about four years since we first came to Philadelphia," Bono recalls, and starts a new tradition introducing the next song. "We played in a small club to about ten people; I just hope those ten people are here tonight. This is for us *A Sort Of Homecoming*." It's the first of six new songs off 'The Unforgettable Fire' which are all received well by the highly enthusiastic crowd.

"I seem to have lost my voice a little bit," says Bono as he fails to reach the high notes in *The Unforgettable Fire*, and repeats an old joke, asking anybody who finds it to bring it around to the back of the stage. Improvising in *Two Hearts Beat As One*, Bono quotes Donna Summer, singing "Love, love to love you baby" a couple of times.

DECEMBER 2, 1984. WORCESTER, MA, CENTRUM

- Attendance: 11,058 (P); sellout
- Support: The Waterboys
- Set: *11 O'Clock Tick Tock* / *I Will Follow* / *Seconds* / *MLK* / *The Unforgettable Fire* / *Wire* / *Sunday Bloody Sunday* / *Cry-Electric Co.* / *A Sort Of Homecoming* / *Bad* / *October* / *New Year's Day* / *Pride* / encore: *Party Girl* / *Gloria* / *40*

The song order changes and *Two Hearts Beat As One* is omitted. Tonight's show marks the first time U2 completely sell out an arena in America. Even with over 11,000 tickets available, it has been hard to get them. Hundreds of ticketless fans try to listen to the show outside the venue. Bono thanks the crowd for the great reception and says they are playing for those outside as well. Before the final song he says, "Last year when we came here, we were very frightened of playing in places like this. It was when we played here last year that we changed our minds, because it was our ambition to just turn this place into a living room and I think we have done that here tonight. I hope it worked out for you, it really worked out for us."

DECEMBER 3, 1984. NEW YORK, NY, RADIO CITY MUSIC HALL

- Attendance: 5,874 (P); sellout
- Support: The Waterboys
- Set: same as Worcester.

The show sells out in a new RCMH record of just 18 minutes. U2 donate all profits to Amnesty International to help launch their 'Stop Torture Week'. A high profile atmosphere precedes the show, with Amnesty representatives, dozens of special guests and reporters from influential newspapers and magazines in attendance. Radio City Music Hall is an old but chic theatre only occasionally used for rock concerts, and from the moment the show opens hundreds of fans leave their seats and make their way to the front, cramming the aisles and blocking the view for those in the front rows. Fans stand on their seats to see better, forcing everybody behind them to do the same. Unused to this, the Radio City security guards panic and become aggressive as they try to get the crowd to back off.

Frustrated at his inability to control the crowd, one bouncer actually beats up a fan during *I Will Follow*. Larry sees this and angrily jumps up from behind his drum kit in mid-song. Edge throws off his guitar and rushes to the front of the stage. "Where the hell are we?!" Bono shouts, taking the crowd's side. "The last time we were here, this city just began for us. We won't have it spoiled now, or any mistreatment to our people. These are our people!" he yells to the security guards. "And if anybody spoils, it's our fault, we make the music… it's rock &

roll, not cabaret!"

The audience are enraptured; the press and Amnesty officials are shocked. It seems ironic that an aggressive bouncer manhandles a fan just for being too enthusiastic during a benefit show for an organisation that is struggling to ban violence and human injustice from this world.

Taking positions to pick up *I Will Follow* again, Edge finds his guitar broken into two pieces on the floor. He gets a replacement and the show continues. "As you know this concert tonight is a benefit for Amnesty International," announces Bono. "All over the world these people are protecting human rights, looking after people who can't look after themselves. This next song is dedicated to one such man, a man whose pride was not in himself, but in the name of love: the Reverend Martin Luther King, the song *Pride*."

During a sweeping *Gloria*, the energy of the mass becomes so intense that dozens of fans get hurt. Trying to escape the crush, several fans climb onstage. The band stop playing. "Just move back here, be on your best behaviour for a second," Bono pleads. Two fans in the front remain rowdy. "Why are you here? You're not here for the same reason I'm here if you won't move back. Because only one thing will be destroyed tonight, and that's the barrier between the stage and the audience! And that's not a physical thing. We feel as close to those people as to these people," Bono says, pointing to the back and to those in the front, emphasising that people need not push. The band resume *Gloria*, but as the crowd's enthusiasm remains dangerous, the hall manager decides to stop the show. The house lights are turned on and a string of security guards go on stage to push the crowd back. *Gloria* is stopped again. "We don't want any security people on the stage," Bono spits, and in a last attempt urges the audience to behave. "If you move back the guards are gonna leave. Move back! If you've got a problem with it, you wait around the front and we'll give you your money back, OK? If everybody just pushes back, we're OK." The crowd co-operate by singing "move back, move back..." to those who are still restless. The band pick up *Gloria* for the third time and after a quick version of *40* leave the stage eagerly.

DECEMBER 5, 1984. WASHINGTON, DC, CONSTITUTION HALL

- Attendance: 3,000; sellout
- Support: The Waterboys
- Set: same as Worcester up to the encore, then: *Gloria / Party Girl / Two Hearts Beat As One / 40*

During *I Will Follow* those in the front push each other around. "Normally when this group hits the stage, people start dancing with the others," Bono says. "Why is this not possible in this prestigious place?" The show continues in festive spirit without any more disturbances. During the encore Bono introduces "the greatest living guitar roadie in the world... bring on Steve Rainford, it's his birthday today," and sings *Happy Birthday* with the crowd.

J.D. Considine reviews the show in *The Washington Post:* 'Midway through a rousing rendition of *Sunday Bloody Sunday*, a cry for peace inspired by the Bloody Sunday riots in Northern Ireland, singer Bono broke off to lead the crowd in a chant of "No more, no war!" A girl at the foot of the stage reached up to hand the singer a small bouquet; Bono accepted the flowers, then lifted the girl onto the stage, embracing her as if in demonstration of the brotherhood the song was advocating.

'Moments like that are what live rock & roll is all about, and they happen too infrequently these days. More common by far is blind adulation and passive acceptance, in which the stars are cheered merely for walking on stage. There was a fair bit of that, too, in U2's concert. There were times when the applause in response to the Edge's guitar flourishes made it impossible to hear what he was playing, and Bono even earned cheers for simply loosening his shirt.'

DECEMBER 7, 1984. TORONTO, CANADA, MASSEY HALL

- Attendance: 2,800; sellout
- Support: The Waterboys
- Set: same as Worcester.

Bono refers to U2's first Toronto show at the El Mocambo four years ago, claiming only *40* people were there. Throughout the show the balcony shakes as a result of the mass of excited dancing people, and actually moves up and down 10 inches to the rhythm of the music. Many in the crowd are completely hysterical and scream through quiet songs like *MLK*. During the intro to *A Sort Of Homecoming* Bono gets fed up with their hysteria. "Could you stop screaming, this is not The Beatles or The Bay City Rollers! I think the majority of the people here understand that." During *Party Girl* several girls from the audience come on stage and run towards Bono while another grabs Edge around the waist and kisses him all over. Bono remarks, "I think they've got the wrong group here. I can never think of myself as a pop star or anything like that."

Though Bono is uncomfortable dealing with this new level of hysteria, he receives every girl who runs on stage with open arms, thus preventing security guards from dragging them off. By embracing or dancing with them for a while, Bono has found a way of spiritually and physically breaking down the barrier between stage and audience that is more subtle than his dangerous climbing of previous years.

DECEMBER 8, 1984. DETROIT, MI, FOX THEATER

- Attendance: 5,000; sellout
- Support: The Waterboys
- Set: same as Worcester.

Another show is hopelessly sold out. Ticket sales have been chaotic, with fans standing in line for two days, and thousands of fans are left disappointed. Scalpers make the most of this situation and sell $13 tickets for three to ten times their face value. Hundreds pay big bucks and desperately try to get to the front, which is already crammed. The energy of U2's music sweeps up the fans and while most are happy to dance and jump around, others push their way to the front which inevitably leads to problems. During *Sunday Bloody Sunday* a riot erupts from the pushing. "Hold the spotlight over here – I won't have any fighting at a U2 concert! Just calm down in there," Bono demands, then desperately screams *"Calm down!"* as some guys in the front just can't be contained. Bono becomes disillusioned. "You know what this song is about, *Sunday Bloody Sunday*? It's a call not to violence, it's a call to the opposite... Are you listening to the song?!"

With the chaos at Radio City and a near riot in Washington DC fresh in their memories, and ticket scalpers taking advantage of the band's success, it becomes clear that U2 have definitely outgrown the theatres. Not only does the level of their current success enable them to fill sports arenas, U2 find themselves in a situation where continuing to play theatres in the future would be asking for trouble.

Dear Detroit,
Thanks for a sold out show. And for those of you who couldn't get tickets for this show, we promise we'll be back again in the spring. See you then.
With great affection,

U2

SPRING DATES TO BE ANNOUNCED SOON

DECEMBER 9, 1984. CLEVELAND, OH, MUSIC HALL

- Attendance: 3,000; sellout
- Support: The Waterboys

While leaning over into the audience to accept a white flag, a woman tries to grab the towel around Bono's neck. Bono pulls it back, briefly disappears back stage, returns with a pair of scissors

Cleveland

Equal shares

and cuts the towel in two. He goes over to the woman and gives her one half, then walks to the other end of the stage to give someone else the other half.

DECEMBER 11, 1984. CHICAGO, IL, ARAGON BALLROOM

- Attendance: 5,500 (P); sellout
- Support: The Waterboys
- Set: same as Worcester.

The band play an inspired show to a highly vocal crowd. Bono sings *Bad* so intensely that he runs out of air and has to cut the song short in order to catch his breath. During *Pride* he improvises about Elvis Presley and John Lennon. *Gloria* is briefly interrupted as Bono sees someone in the crowd in difficulty. Stretching *40*, singing "How long to sing this song" with the crowd for several minutes, he urges to "sing it for the Chicago Peace Museum," host of the 'Unforgettable Fire' exhibition, after which U2 named their album.

DECEMBER 15, 1984. SAN FRANCISCO, CA, CIVIC AUDITORIUM

- Attendance: 8,472 (P); sellout
- Support: The Waterboys
- Set: same as Worcester.

DECEMBER 16, 1984. LOS ANGELES, CA, LONG BEACH ARENA

- Attendance: 13,974 (P); sellout
- Support: The Waterboys
- Set: same as Worcester.

A successful final night to this US mini-tour with no crowd problems whatsoever. Edge is dubbed Eddie van Edge by Bono during the guitar solo in *Party Girl*, at the end of which Bono gets tour manager Dennis Sheehan on stage while claiming the U2 road crew to be the best in the world and that "behind every successful man there is another successful man. Merry Christmas to you all, we'll see you in the spring time!"

JANUARY 5, 1985. SIMPLE MINDS: GLASGOW, SCOTLAND, BARROWLANDS

During along version of *New Gold Dream* singer Jim Kerr tells the audience in his thick Scottish accent, "For the second time tonight, we make history. One, because there's a mobile recording outside and you're in here. And two, I have to tell you a story. This guy uhm, (many in the audience scream "Bono!") this guy turned up at my door... A peculiar fellow indeed. He said to me, I wanna join the band. I said, you can. He says, I've come all the way from Ireland to have a good job. I said, can ya sing? And he said, yeah, I think so. You can judge... *All the way from Dublin: Bono!!*" The band increase volume and Bono enters amid immense cheering from the 4,000 strong crowd. "He is my friend, till the bitter end," Bono and Jim sing alternately, before continuing with snippets of Al Green's *Take Me To The River* and The Doors' *Light My Fire* with both singers excelling in long vocal outbursts.

'THE UNFORGETTABLE FIRE' TOUR, LEG 3: EUROPE, WINTER 1985

After a five week break, 'The Unforgettable Fire' Tour resumes, with replacement shows for those cancelled in October 1984, and a couple of extras. There are a total of 13 concerts in Europe, which see U2 tour Germany properly for the first time and making their very first visit to Italy.

JANUARY 23, 1985. DRAMMEN, NORWAY, DRAMMENSHALLE

- Attendance: 7,000
- Set: *11 O'Clock Tick Tock / I Will Follow / Seconds / MLK / The Unforgettable Fire / Wire / Sunday Bloody Sunday / Cry-Electric Co. / A Sort of Homecoming / Bad / October / New Year's Day / Pride / Gloria /* encore: *Party Girl / Two Hearts Beat As One / 40*

The set has changed in one aspect: *Gloria* is now the last song before the encore in which *Two Hearts Beat As One* shows up again. The audience aren't all that familiar with the songs. Bono refers to their previous performance in Norway on August 21, 1983, at the Kalvoya Festival. "We felt there was a connection between the audience and the stage that was quite unique that day. We're not on beautiful hills now, we're in a tin box," and says he hopes he can create intimacy in here as well. During the encore the audience actually sing along and the band seem to have attained their goal.

JANUARY 25, 1985. STOCKHOLM, SWEDEN, ISSTADION

- Attendance: 10,000
- Set: same as Drammen.

Mans Ivarsson reviews the concert for the Swedish newspaper *Expressen*: 'A your-arms-around-me dance on the stage of the Isstadion in front of 10,000 overcome fans as the singer Bono asked a girl from the crowd for a dance. That was the highlight of Irishmen's U2 rock mass yesterday. Rock mass? Yes, there was such an overflow of traditional rock symbols and gestures that it almost looked like a religious ritual. The fans had lighters, sparklers, flags and an enormous enthusiasm. U2's skill to caress and bait a rock crowd is not far removed from Bruce Springsteen's. Bono makes a big effort for the people in the bad seats and he occasionally is almost down in the crowd, flattering

us for our good English and thanking us deeply for coming. Sing for John Lennon, sing for Elvis Presley, Jimi Hendrix – Bono and U2 not even for a moment let us forget that they represent the good guys in rock. Sure they are pleasant even if it can get a little bit too cute. But the music is hardly cute. It's hard, hypnotic rock with Edge, the remarkable guitarist, as the leader. I don't understand how he does it, but his tones are like a never ending shooting star, forever glittering against a dark and cold backdrop...'

JANUARY 26, 1985. GOTHENBURG, SWEDEN, SCANDINAVIUM

- Attendance: 8,000
- Set: same as Drammen.

"Well, I think we haven't been in this country for maybe too long. I'll hope the next time is sooner rather than later... people have been very kind to us, maybe over-kind. We try not to forget when we played to 10 people, let alone 10,000 people. Thank you."

JANUARY 28, 1985. HAMBURG, GERMANY, CONGRESS CENTRE

- Attendance: 5,000; sellout
- Support: Belfegore
- Set: same as Drammen.

Belfegore, a trio from Düsseldorf, join the U2 bandwagon to support them on most of the shows, but are not accepted well by the audience. During U2's set, however, the atmosphere is excellent. There are none of the disturbances that have marred the two 1981 concerts in this town. Bono remembers those rowdy performances: "Well, this is our first serious, proper, respectable long-time tour of your country. I wonder what went wrong when we were here before, but I hope that what went wrong is now going right."

The night before the concert, the band took a stroll around the infamous Reeperbahn, the heart of Hamburg's red-light district. Bono dedicates *Bad* to "some people I fell in love with last night, some girls, some very nice and very pretty girls. They can't be with us tonight, because they are working girls. This song is for them, this is called *Bad*." He sings an intense version

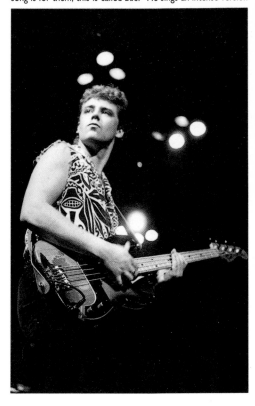

of the song that segues into The Velvet Underground's *Waiting For The Man*.

Bono refers to the Loreley show on August 20, 1983, where most of the songs on 'Under A Blood Red Sky' stem from. "This is a song that sort of belongs to you people – you put it on the record, it's your voices, taken from the Rockpalast concert. This is the song *40*."

JANUARY 29, 1985. OFFENBACH, GERMANY, STADTHALLE

- Attendance: 3,500
- Support: Belfegore
- Set: same as Drammen.

Bono sings part of *Wooden Heart* during *Electric Co*. Introducing *Bad* he says it is his ambition to talk about things, songs, anything, during concerts, well aware of the fact that he is prone to losing track of his thoughts while speaking. Again he dedicates *Bad* to the working girls in Hamburg.

JANUARY 31, 1985. COLOGNE, GERMANY, SPORTHALLE

- Attendance: 8,000; sellout
- Support: Belfegore
- Set: same as Drammen.

During *Pride* a girl from the audience runs on stage and clings to Bono, refusing to let go. He escapes from her firm grip, lifts her over his shoulder, brings her to the edge of the stage and helps her back into the audience. There is an exceptionally long performance of *40*, during which all but Larry leave the stage twice only to return and play on. Bono asks several people on the balcony to stop throwing sparklers down into the audience.

FEBRUARY 1, 1985. MANNHEIM, GERMANY, MUSENSAAL

- Attendance: 2,500; sellout
- Support: Belfegore
- Set: same as Drammen, but the encore is: *Party Girl* / *Gloria* / *Southern Man* / *40*.

The German tour is running smoothly. "I was telling people last night that we never, ever, in our wildest dreams expected to be made feel so much at home as we have this last week in Germany. For many years when we came and played here, we felt that something was beginning for us, we felt that some sort of spark was trying to ignite. Well, this week, we just felt that it just exploded, it's great! The only thing is, I'm going to have to spend some time with an English–German dictionary, so that I can speak to you a lot better. Actually, if I wanted to do it right I'd like to spend some time with an Irish–German dictionary." A wild performance of *Wire* follows with loud cock-a-doodling from Bono at the start, and long final bellowing of: "... I give you rope, here's the rope, now swing on it... Need a pocket for the dough, money for hope, money for rope." Echo enhances the dramatic effect of the last words.

Before *A Sort of Homecoming*: "Sometimes if I feel that my voice is sore, or if I feel that I can't sing, I can feel very awkward, but you people are doing enough singing so that I don't care if I can't sing. Tonight, we wanna make this small hall like a big hall," Bono says, laughing, realising that he is turning things around. *Party Girl* ends with a long improvisation that could easily have been a song in itself. The highlight of the evening is *Southern Man*, played for the first time since 1982 and the only time on the entire 'Unforgettable Fire' tour. Bono accompanies himself on guitar during the first verse after which the band join in to play a ragged version.

FEBRUARY 2, 1985. MUNICH, GERMANY, RUDI–SEDLMAYERHALLE

- Attendance: 5,500
- Support: Belfegore
- Set: *11 O'Clock Tick Tock* / *I Will Follow* / *Seconds* / *Indian Summer Sky* / *MLK* / *The Unforgettable Fire* / *Wire* / *Sunday Bloody Sunday* / *Cry–Electric Co.* / *A Sort of Homecoming* / *Bad* / *October* / *New Year's Day* / *Pride* / encore: *Party Girl* / *Gloria* / *40*

The set features *Indian Summer Sky* for the first time since Manchester and it is played more competently than before. *Two Hearts Beat As One* is dropped and *Gloria* is moved to the encore again. Bono's voice is going downhill. During *Bad* he tries in vain to sing the "I'm wide awake" part, and a bit later during *New Year's Day* his vocal cords seem to have given up completely. "Sorry," Bono sighs, and he struggles through *Pride* and *Party Girl*. "This is the end of 'The Unforgettable Fire Week'," he says at the close, "and this is also the end of my voice... so long!"

FEBRUARY 4, 1985. MILAN, ITALY, PALAZZETTO DELLO SPORT

- Attendance: 3,000; sellout
- Set: same as Munich.

Travelling through Europe in the middle of winter is not easy. Trucks with equipment regularly get stuck in the snow, often causing delays. Just before U2 arrive in Italy they discover some prankster has put sugar in a few of the trucks' tanks. The band barely make it in time to play this concert. There is no time for a soundcheck.

"Buona sera Milano!" Bono shouts, "la prima, ma non ultima volta!" ("the first, but not the last time!"). The audience are well acquainted with the songs and make clear they have waited a long time for U2's Italian début. The band are *very* well received and each song is lapped up hysterically.

FEBRUARY 5, 6, 1985. BOLOGNA, ITALY, TEATRO TENDA

- Set first night: same as Munich, minus *Indian Summer Sky* and plus *Knocking On Heaven's Door* before *40*.

Each song is sung by the temperamental audience. A long version of *Bad* sees snippets of *Waiting For The Man, Sympathy For The Devil, Ruby Tuesday*, and, for the first time *Take Me To The River* pass in review. *Knocking On Heaven's Door* is played for the first time this tour, with plenty of improvisation as Bono still does not know the lyrics.

- Set second night: same as Drammen.

Bad is again introduced with the story of Hamburg's working girls, but now, during the opening bars of the song, Bono expands it a little further. He approaches a lady and asks her for her price. "He said, how much do you feel like tonight; well, I feel like 50 DeutschMarks tonight. I say, I think you're worth a lot more than 50 DM. She says, I'm 60 DM then. Well, I say, you're worth much more than 60 DM. She says, 100 DM. And I say, that's *bad*..."

FEBRUARY 8, 1985. ZURICH, SWITZERLAND, HALLENSTADION

- Attendance: 10,000
- Support: Belfegore

- Set: *11 O'Clock Tick Tock / I Will Follow / Seconds / MLK / The Unforgettable Fire / Wire / Sunday Bloody Sunday / (break) / Sunday Bloody Sunday / Cry–Electric Co. / Bad / October / New Year's Day / Pride / encore: Knocking On Heaven's Door / Gloria / encore: 40*.

"Well, if I lose my voice tonight, if I can't sing for you tonight, I hope you can sing for me." This is serious. During *Sunday Bloody Sunday* Bono sounds as if someone is switching him on and off by remote control. "I'm sorry," he rasps after the song. "I think we're gonna have to break for some time because we've come a long way to play you the best concert of our lives, not the second best. So we must go now, we see you in ten minutes." The band leave the stage and return after 20 minutes. "Well, tonight I hope we make very good friends, because this is what friendship's about. For you only, the second time we play *Sunday Bloody Sunday*." It does not sound much better, and Bono struggles through the rest of the show. *A Sort of Homecoming* is dropped and they skip entire parts of *Bad*.

During the encore, before *Knocking On Heaven's Door*, Bono thanks the audience for their understanding. "To sing is a very intimate thing, and if you feel that you can't give, you feel very open, very naked. So for you, we're gonna play you a song that gives me great strength, but also a song that we never played in front of people, never." Though not exactly true, Bono feels like he has failed and wants to give the audience the feeling they are getting something special. He uses his last reserves and Edge contributes a heartfelt backing vocal.

FEBRUARY 10, 1985. PARIS, FRANCE, PALAIS DES OMNISPORTS DE BERCY

- Attendance: 16,000; sellout
- Support: Belfegore
- Set: *11 O'Clock Tick Tock / I Will Follow / Seconds / MLK / The Unforgettable Fire / Wire / Sunday Bloody Sunday / Cry–Electric Co. / A Sort of Homecoming / Bad / October / New Year's Day / Pride / encore: Knocking On Heaven's Door / Gloria / encore: 40*.

This time they don't play in a leaking tent, but in the large sports arena of Bercy, the largest venue of the tour up until then. There are 16,000 people in attendance, including many fans from The Netherlands, Germany, Ireland and the UK who have travelled with organised bus tours. Bono's voice seems OK again. "I can sing!" he shouts during the first song. That he really can sing becomes obvious during *Knocking On Heaven's Door* when he includes a passionate improvisation: "Well, I got a feeling deep inside of me; I can't explain it all the time. I don't know the words, and sometimes I don't know the tune, sometimes I feel that I'm knocking on heaven's door."

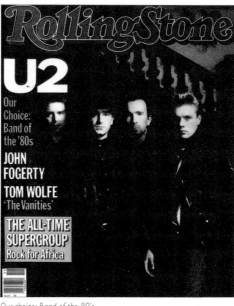

Our choice: Band of the 80's

'THE UNFORGETTABLE FIRE TOUR' LEG 4: AMERICA, WINTER/SPRING 1985

Tickets for U2's first all-arena tour of North America disappear just as quickly as at the December tour. Though the move to arenas enables the band to reach crowds five to six times as big as at theatres, many are still left without tickets. Word of mouth through their fan base accounts for an explosive rise in numbers of people that now want to see U2. Having attended previous shows, fans go again, and convince their friends to experience it as well. They are also responsible for healthy sales of 'The Unforgettable Fire'. Though the *Pride* single didn't get further than No. 33 in the charts, and media response to the album had been mixed, 'The Unforgettable Fire' reached No. 12, and turned gold three months after its release. Shortly before the tour is to begin, its consistent sales pass one million copies, giving U2 their first American platinum disc. A week later, 'War' tops the million-sales mark as well. Both albums, as well as 'Under A Blood Red Sky', will continue to sell well throughout the tour.

U2's battle to build their audience is won. They now face another battle: to retain their privacy. In every town, masses of people congregrate at the hotels where they are staying, hoping for some personal encounter. Though the band members often take time to chat and sign autographs, it becomes increasingly difficult as the crowds swell. Though generally well-behaved and genuinely interested in talking, fan behaviour regularly goes over the top; blocking hotel entrances, hysterically screaming on seeing any of the band or desperately trying to touch them. Bodyguards responsible for the band's safety often have a hard time whisking them off from the hotel to the venue and back again.

The band decide to utilise the full capacity of the arenas, includ-

ing the seats behind the stage. Going "360" (degrees), as they say in the business jargon, requires an uncluttered stage so as to leave uninterrupted views from the sides and behind the stage. Besides the amplifiers attached to the ceiling, the white stage backdrop that was used in Europe disappears, and the slide projections that gave the European performances such a special atmosphere are consequently not used.

FEBRUARY 25, 1985. DALLAS, TX, REUNION ARENA

■ Attendance: 13,000; sellout
■ Support: Red Rockers
■ Set: 11 O'Clock Tick Tock / I Will Follow / Seconds / MLK / The Unforgettable Fire / Wire / Sunday Bloody Sunday / Cry-Electric Co. / A Sort of Homecoming / Bad / October / New Year's Day / Pride / encore: Party Girl

America is ready for U2, and vice versa. The band are greeted with hysterical screaming when they hit the stage during *4th Of July*. They play solid and with conviction. Without the slide projections, the crowd's focus is more on the band. Dozens of fans manage to make it past security and run onstage, but Bono handles it well, embracing them, motioning to the security guards it's OK, and gracefully leading them back into the crowd. A hazardous incident occurs during *Gloria* when a man in the front row screams and points an object, which seems to be a gun, at Bono. Security quickly catch him. Bono interrupts the show angrily, asks for quiet and shouts to the man to shut up because he is disturbing the concert.

FEBRUARY 26, 1985. AUSTIN, TX, FRANK ERWIN CENTER

■ Attendance: 11,633; sellout
■ Support: Red Rockers

FEBRUARY 27, 1985. HOUSTON, TX, THE SUMMIT

■ Attendance: 14,000
■ Support: Red Rockers
■ Set: same as Dallas, with *Knocking On Heaven's Door* instead of *Party Girl*.

Bono flatters the audience. "I used to think that Texas was a part of the United States; now I know that the United States is just a part of Texas." He incorporates *Do They Know It's Christmas* into *40*, singing the chorus very slowly: "Feed... the... world... let... them... know... it's... Christmas... time... feed... the... world... let... them... know... it's... spring... time... today..."

MARCH 1, 1985. PHOENIX, AZ, COMPTON TERRACE

■ Attendance: 23,000; sellout
■ Support: Red Rockers
■ Set: 11 O'Clock Tick Tock / I Will Follow / Seconds / MLK / The Unforgettable Fire / Pride / Sunday Bloody Sunday / Cry-Electric Co. / A Sort of Homecoming / Bad / October / New Year's Day / Pride / encore: Knocking On Heaven's Door / Gloria / 40

U2's first headlining show in Phoenix is also the only open air concert of the 1985 American tour and, with 23,000 people present, it is the largest audience they have drawn on their own

strength to date. As this isn't an arena but a wide open plain, the distance between the stage and the audience is now too big. Thousands of fans are pushing to get to the front where the pressure becomes unbearable. This situation has often occurred in theatres but even the fact that there is now much more space to move doesn't seem to help. With a crowd of such threatening size, the situation becomes more dangerous than ever before.

A representative of the promoter comes onstage to announce the band, but first urgently requests one and all to stop pushing. "OK Phoenix, are you ready? From Dublin, Ireland: U2!!" "We've been away for far too long," Bono says when he arrives on stage, and the crowd go crazy. They are jumping up and down during *11 O'Clock Tick Tock*, swaying from left to right, back to front, crushing dozens of people against the metal barriers. The band hold out for a moment but when Bono spots an aggressive guy elbowing people and punching someone in the face during *The Unforgettable Fire*, he sees red. "HOLD IT! NOW HOLD IT RIGHT THERE!" he screams. His blood is boiling. "We don't EVER have trouble at a U2 concert!" The disturbance escalates as more people get involved. "Hold it! The two of you and your friends – one walk that way and the other walk that way. You both meet each other in another place!" Bono sounds disappointed. "Now, we expected something special tonight. We didn't expect as many people, we are very proud to be here. WE can prove that in Phoenix Arizona, rock & roll can do what the politicians can't do! And that is: that we bring people together. BRING people TOGETHER!" Bono sighs in exasperation and takes a moment to catch his breath while things calm down a bit in the front. "That's the end of the ceremony. I love being here tonight, and I'm not going home with anybody damaged. This is a song we only play once a night, but tonight we play it twice. This is *Pride (In The Name Of Love)*." This is *Wire's* spot in the set but they hope that *Pride's* peaceful lyrics might calm the audience. Bono tries hard to restore order. "Now, if everyone just takes a step back, just everybody, one yard, starting at the back. One yard ... All right." His intervention is successful. Step by step people shuffle back and those in front get a bit more breathing space.

Tense, but determined to make it work, U2 continue. At the beginning and end of *A Sort of Homecoming* Bono sings "Pom pom pom, satellite of love, pom pom, satellite of love" a few times, quoting the Lou Reed song. Before *40* Bono takes a breath of relief. "Before we go, I'd like to say that to my knowledge nobody has been hurt, and that feels really good. I mean, you Southern people are a little wild... but so are we Irish, you know!"

MARCH 2, 4, 5, 1985. LOS ANGELES, CA, SPORTS ARENA

■ Attendance: 45,071 (P); sellout
■ Support: Red Rockers
■ Set first night: same as Houston.

Not surprisingly the first of these LA shows is a timid affair. The previous night has made the band uneasy, and taken its toll on Bono's voice.

■ Set second night: same as Dallas, plus *Surrender* and *Two Hearts Beat As One* after *Seconds*.

Surrender has not been played since Manchester in November, *Two Hearts* since Cologne. "Well, people at the back, you're gonna feel like you're at the front tonight," are Bono's words of welcome at the start of a powerful, spirited concert. Someone throws a large bouquet of flowers at Bono, who then hands them out to the audience one by one. He starts *Bad* with a few lines of The Beatles' *Norwegian Wood*: "I once had a girl, or should I say, she once had me... she showed me her room, isn't that good, Norwegian wood..." Edge's mother attends the concert, and for the solo in *Party Girl* Bono introduces Edge as 'Mrs. Edge's 'little boy'.

A local group has organised a 'food drive' at the third concert and food will be collected in the lobby for handing out

to the many homeless and poor of Los Angeles. Bono promotes the initiative. "Tomorrow night we have a thing called the Food Drive – you bring food, you put it in bags, and some very, very starving people will get that food, tomorrow night." Before *40* Bono says: "I hope we make it clear that this music, and these people, are bigger than this place."

■ Set third night: same as Houston.
Still somewhat hoarse, Bono asks the crowd to help him out, which they do. Halfway through *Knocking On Heaven's Door*, he urges further participation by asking all guitar players in the crowd to put up their hands. Fans stick out their arms here and there throughout the arena. Bono brings one guy onstage, hands him a guitar, and shows him the chords to the song. When the guy has mastered the chords, Larry picks up the beat, and Bono, Edge and Adam move to the side of the stage to leave the guest guitarist alone at centre stage in the spotlights, happily enjoying five minutes of fame while the crowd roar their approval. Starting a new tradition, the band come back to produce a joyful climax before the guy bows and goes back into the audience.

MARCH 7, 8, 1985. SAN FRANCISCO, CA, COW PALACE

■ Attendance: 29,000; sellout
■ Support: Red Rockers
■ Set first night: same as Houston.

Seconds is powerfully played, with Bono announcing over the opening chords, "This is a message to the President; a message to Ronald Ray-gun. We make enough noise here, you can hear us in The White House in Washington. This is a song called *Seconds*. You see, Ronald, it takes a second to say goodbye..." After the song Bono urges those in the front to look after themselves. Cow Palace is general admission, whereas at all the other shows chairs have been placed on the floor, as is common practice in America. Because of the heavy pushing, many who are short of breath or claustrophobic have to be pulled out of the audience.

It is flowers in L.A., but something else in San Francisco: "Everybody keeps throwing their shoes up on stage. I mean, what is this? There's no business like shoe-business?" To introduce *Bad*, Bono tells the audience, "You know, we come from Dublin City. Dublin is not always a fair city. This song is written about one particular person, but it's probably written about many, many more, it's probably even written about myself. This song is inspired – on the street where I live a lot of people... you know, I joined a rock & roll band, they joined the dole queue, and some of them didn't even get as far as the dole queue. This is for them, this is for those of them that fell in love with a very dangerous lover – that lover was the drug heroin, and this is the song *Bad*."

Throughout the entire tour *Bad* has been one of the emotional highlights of the show, sung intensely, often desperately and always unpredictably. The end, drawn out, includes snippets of other artists' songs. Here *Norwegian Wood*, *Ruby Tuesday*, and also *Waiting For The Man* get their turn, followed by *Sympathy For The Devil* ('Pleased to meet you... I hope you guess my name.').

Another high point is *Knocking On Heaven's Door*, which Bono introduces: "You know, it doesn't seem long ago that we were 16 and 17 and we were just playing to one person or maybe 10 people. It's just great to play to so many thousands of people now. There's probably a lot of young bands out there,

garagebands from garageland. If you're playing for one person or two people, you give them as much as you give to anybody here. We don't need stadiums and large PA's and fancy equipment – you don't need that. It has taken me seven years to learn that all you need is maybe three or four chords and you can write a song, a song like this man wrote. This song gives us a lot of strength, I dedicate it to the man who wrote it." The song is recognised from the first notes Bono strums on the guitar, and is performed in a lengthy, passionate version with another guest appearance from a rock-star-to-be from the crowd.

■ Set second night: Same as Dallas, again plus *Surrender* and *Two Hearts Beat As One* after *Seconds*.

Hours before the show, panic in the U2 camp arises when Larry suffers from intense pain in his left hand and feels he won't be able to do the show. It has swollen because of intensive use. Being rushed to hospital, a doctor examines him and tells Larry to take the next two weeks off in order to give his hand complete rest. Larry explains that it's out of the question, seeing the intensive touring schedule ahead. The doctor produces a plaster for Larry to keep his hand in, which can be removed for the duration of the gigs. Pain killers will have to carry him through the rest of the tour until he can be treated.

Larry manages to play the show. During *Surrender* Bono sing the chorus of Wilson Pickett's *Midnight Hour*, and during *Electric Co.*, "Well, if you're going to San Francisco, be sure to wear flowers in your hair...", followed by a long fragment of *Amazing Grace*, which replaces the *Send In The Clowns* quote on this tour. "I used to think it was impossible to play such a large place and still have this feeling of smallness and intimacy. I hope you people at the back don't feel left out, because you're just as close to the music. It's not about being close to the musicians, the music's much more important, I think. Anyway, The Edge has got smelly feet, you know."

MARCH 11, 1985. HONOLULU, HI, NEAL BLAISDELL CENTER ARENA

■ Attendance: 8,178 (P); (capacity 8,850)
■ Support: Red Rockers

This is the smallest venue U2 play on this tour but it doesn't sell out. Bono says that he is proud to play a song that was developed during U2's last visit to Hawaii, in November 1983: *Pride*. The band have a few days off, a welcome rest for Bono's voice.

MARCH 17, 1985. DENVER, CO, McNICHOLS SPORTS ARENA

■ Attendance: 17,475 (P); sellout
■ Support: Red Rockers
■ Set: same as Dallas.

Instead of *4th Of July*, *Amazing Grace* is played as an introduction by three kilt-wearing bagpipers. For this is St. Patrick's Day, the Irish holiday which, as Adam tells *The Denver Post* newspaper that afternoon... "seems to be celebrated much more flamboyantly here than in Dublin." Journalist G. Brown asks Adam if March 17 means something to him. "Back home, St. Patrick's Day is basically an opportunity to miss work and spend a lot of time in the pub. I mean, I don't know St. Patrick, I've no strong feelings about him. So I don't think the concert will be special for us in that sense, but I'm sure everyone will be aware of the occasion."

With the now world-famous Red Rocks concert in the back of everybody's mind, expectations in the Mile High city run high. As he hits the stage, Bono says: "One mile is not enough, we're going up and we're never coming down!" St. Patrick's Day

clearly makes the audience even more exuberant, but Bono uses the occasion to make a more serious point while introducing *Sunday Bloody Sunday*. "We are proud of our country, but the good thing is that I never wanna be so proud of my country that I'd take another man's life."

U2 bring the show to a jovial climax with Bono singing the old Dublin favourite *Molly Malone*: "Oh Dublin fair city, where the girls are so pretty, I first set my eyes on sweet Molly Malone…" The audience are invited to sing along, but don't know the lyrics. They are more familiar with *Party Girl* and holler "Hey, hey" to the beat of the music, just like two years earlier at Red Rocks. It is this performance which has made the song famous and established it as a crowd favourite. Bono reminisces about that show. "Well, I noticed it's not raining in here this time. When we played Red Rocks I'll always remember that rain, that was the sunniest rain I ever felt." U2 will never forget the spirit of the audience, Bono says, and he also thanks concert promoter Barry Fey, who has booked U2 for the amphitheater and now McNichols. A long version of *40*, with snippets of *Do They Know It's Christmas* and *We Are The World*, end the show. With the houselights on and the audience singing "How long to sing this song" while they make their way to the exits, there is an incident near the stage.

Reviewer Chris Deutsch writes: 'Right in the middle of the crowd, in front of the stage, a fight had broken out, which lasted several minutes. Two people were wrestling over a stick drummer Larry Mullen had tossed out at the show's end. A few chairs were knocked over as the two went after the stick, and a few other people got involved trying to break up the fight, before it was all over. It proved that, while U2 have come a long way blending peace and harmony with rock & roll, there are people who still have an equally long way to go.'

MARCH 19, 1985. MINNEAPOLIS, MN, AUDITORIUM

- Attendance: 9,000; sellout
- Support: Red Rockers
- Set: same as Houston.

Minneapolis was one of the first cities in America where U2 drew a relatively large audience."The first time we played this city, well, I don't think the records were on the radio. I don't think many people in the United States were even aware that this group existed, but a thousand people came in Minneapolis! It's good to see so many people here tonight. We are a long way from home, and we thank you for making us feel so much at home. *A Sort of Homecoming*."

Bono's speech introducing *Bad* changes somewhat during this period: "This song is written about a friend of mine, somebody who meant a great deal to me, somebody I used to play football with, just spent a lot of time with. He was much younger than me. I joined this band and he didn't join very much at all. In fact on his 21st birthday his girlfriend gave him enough heroin to kill him. This song is written for him, it's written for any of you also. This song is *Bad*."

Knocking On Heaven's Door is again dedicated to its author, and to young bands in Minneapolis. No fewer than four guitarists audition before Bono finds one who can play the song.

MARCH 21, 22, 1985. CHICAGO, IL, UNIVERSITY OF ILLINOIS PAVILION

- Attendance: 21,256 (P); sellout
- Support: Red Rockers
- Set first night: same as Houston.

CBS, the American TV station, film a few songs for a news item on the concert. During the bridge of *I Will Follow*, Bono walks over to their cameraman. "Is this CBS news? You wanna see some people, you come up here and see these people." Bono pulls the cameraman on stage and points out the audience to him. "You see, these people are 'our' people," he proclaims dramatically, "And this is a big place… but this music and these people are much bigger than this place!" It makes the news the next evening.

"I wanna tell you about the group that opened for us today," says Bono before *40*. "I wanna tell you about The Red Rockers, they've been on tour since we began. These fellas just reminded us what the good things are about being in a group and

if they are out there, if they would come up here and sing this song with us. It's their last night on the tour." The Red Rockers join in *40*.

- Set second night: same as Dallas, plus *Surrender* and *Two Hearts Beat As One* after *Seconds*, and, surprisingly, minus *Party Girl*.

MARCH 23, 1985. DETROIT, MI, JOE LOUIS ARENA

- Attendance: 17,000; sellout
- Support: Lone Justice
- Set: same as Houston.

An Irish flag is thrown onstage during *Electric Co.* Bono picks it up, drapes it over the mikestand and throws it to someone in the audience after the song. A wrong move. Fans jostle each other to get hold of the flag. "Hey listen, stop fighting about that flag," Bono says, annoyed. "That's what all the trouble is, don't you understand that?"

MARCH 25, 1985. CLEVELAND, OH, RICHFIELD COLISEUM

- Attendance: 17,000; sellout
- Support: Lone Justice
- Set: same as Houston

Wire is played highly energetically, and is introduced by Bono as being "the hypodermic needle" of the 'Unforgettable Fire' album. Demonstrating the four chords that make up *Knocking On Heaven's Door*, Bono hopes that inviting a guy from the crowd to play along will inspire local bands. "Next time we come back to Cleveland: a hundred new groups!"

Knocking On Heaven's Door

MARCH 27, 1985. MONTREAL, CANADA, FORUM

- Attendance: 15,000; sellout
- Support: Lone Justice
- Set: *11 O'Clock Tick Tock* / *I Will Follow* / *Seconds* / *Two Hearts Beat As One* / *MLK* / *The Unforgettable Fire* / *Wire* / *Sunday Bloody Sunday* / *Cry–Electric Co.* / *A Sort of Homecoming* / *Bad* / *October* / *New Year's Day* / *Pride* / encore: *Knocking On*

Heaven's Door / *Gloria* / *40*.

Two Hearts Beat As One is back in the set for a couple of shows. Bono is not so talkative and omits his regular speeches. No guitarist is invited onstage.

MARCH 28, 1985. TORONTO, CANADA, MAPLE LEAF GARDENS

- Attendance: 17,000 (P); sellout
- Support: Lone Justice
- Set: same as Montreal.

"Well it's a long way from the El Mocambo," is Bono's one-liner before *11 O'Clock Tick Tock*, referring to the first club U2 played here, back in December 1980. *MLK* is sung against a backdrop of thousands of tiny flames from lighters. During *Electric Co.* Bono accepts an Irish flag from someone in the audience and drapes it around himself to the loud approval of the audience. After singing *Amazing Grace* he throws the flag into the audience and while fans scramble to get their hands on it, he calls to them to stop fighting over the flag, as he did in Detroit.

During an extended version of *40* Bono grabs a spotlight, and shines it over the outstretched arms of the audience.

MARCH 30, 1985. OTTAWA, CANADA, CIVIC CENTER

- Attendance: 9,000; sellout
- Support: Lone Justice
- Set: same as Montreal.

APRIL 1, 1985. NEW YORK, NY, MADISON SQUARE GARDEN

- Attendance: 19,000; sellout
- Support: Lone Justice
- Set: same as Montreal.

April Fool's Day is a memorable day for U2. It is their first concert in the most prestigious arena in New York. If you can crack this nut, you're right up there with the Greats. It is said that no matter how well you play in Kansas or Dallas or wherever – Madison Square Garden is where you have to prove yourself. The media are massively represented and high expectations make for a tense atmosphere. U2's management pour oil on the flames by flying over large numbers of Irish press to cover the event as well as a delegation of family and friends to share a great moment for U2 and for Ireland.

"So, this is Madison Square Garden," Bono sighs to the deafening roar of 19,000 fans. "It's eh… well, real big!" The show is excellent but no better or more special than other good shows on the tour. The audience surrender just as everywhere else. Still, the New York show is inflated to triumph stature because, as they have proved again and again, U2 are able to handle the enormous pressure that the concert/media event entails. They are not intimidated but believe in their show as it is and in the loyalty of the audience they have built up over the years.

The next day U2 hold a press conference in the New York Berkshire Hotel. They slyly use their New York triumph and the presence of the Irish media to announce an important concert: a big Croke Park stadium show in their hometown Dublin on June 29. This will be the first time that U2 headline a stadium concert. The announcement is cleverly contrived because it coincides with excellent reviews of the New York show. U2's mega-success in America appeals to the Irish imagination. It enlarges the band's status in their own country and turns Croke Park into an event not to be missed. Tickets go on sale soon after.

APRIL 2, 1985. PROVIDENCE, RI, CIVIC CENTER

- Attendance: 13,349 (P); sellout

usually scans the audience for new talent, he gives his speech about those four chords that "are more important than all these amplifiers that sometimes don't work."

APRIL 3, 1985. UNIONDALE, NY, NASSAU VETERANS' MEMORIAL COLISEUM

- Attendance: 15,000; sellout
- Support: Lone Justice
- Set: same as Dallas: *11 O'Clock Tick Tock / I Will Follow / Seconds / MLK / The Unforgettable Fire / Wire / Sunday Bloody Sunday / Cry–Electric Co. / A Sort of Homecoming / Bad / October / New Year's Day / Pride / encore: Party Girl / Gloria / 40*

During *I Will Follow* Bono accepts a letter from a fan in front. "You want me to open this?" He opens the envelope. "There's a guy here, he wants to be in the band... I can't blame him, it's a good job! I wasn't good at anything else, you know."

He introduces *Wire*: "When we were making 'The Unforgettable Fire', we had two extremes in our mind. We wanted an album that would make us feel so at rest, and at the same time we wanted to make a record that captured the real anger of what we saw around us. And so, there are two sides to 'The Unforgettable Fire'. This is the other side, this is the needle in the record, this is *Wire*."

APRIL 8, 1985. LANDOVER, MD, CAPITAL CENTER

- Attendance: 15,000; sellout
- Support: Lone Justice
- Set: *11 O'Clock Tick Tock / I Will Follow / Seconds / MLK / The Unforgettable Fire / Wire / Sunday Bloody Sunday / Cry–Electric Co. / A Sort of Homecoming / Bad / October / New Year's Day / Pride / encore: Knocking On Heaven's Door / Gloria / 40*

Capital Center, situated just outside Washington DC, sees the next major crowd disturbance. Thousands of fans dance on the floor of the arena, swept up in a rush of euphoria, but security insists that everyone remains seated. However, restraining the ecstatic audience proves difficult, and frustrated security men become increasingly rough. Fans who move to the front are manhandled back to their seats. During the bridge of *I Will Follow* Bono states: "Well, of course it's OK to come to the front! These people have paid to celebrate, and tonight we WILL celebrate! And when I see T–shirts with 'Crowd Control', I

- Support: Lone Justice
- Set: *11 O'Clock Tick Tock / Seconds / MLK / The Unforgettable Fire / Wire / Sunday Bloody Sunday / Cry–Electric Co. / Knocking On Heaven's Door / A Sort of Homecoming / Bad / October / New Year's Day / Pride / encore: Gloria / 40.*

Two Hearts Beat As One is dropped because Bono strained his voice in Madison Square Garden. Technically things aren't up to scratch either. Bono introduces *A Sort of Homecoming*, but when Edge is supposed to come in, nothing but static resounds. He tries again in vain. "If you'll give me a guitar, I'll play," says Bono. Edge looks up in surprise. "It's OK, if we're not gonna play that one, we'll play something else." A roadie brings an acoustic guitar and Bono starts to play *Knocking On Heaven's Door* which is normally saved for the encore. During the bridge, when he

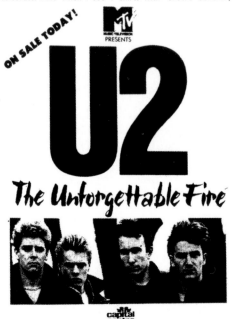

but is not here tonight, and that's because she's dead. Her name is Beth Lieberman. I dedicate this song to you, Beth ... This is *Pride (In The Name Of Love)*." During the bridge he asks the audience to "Sing it for Jimi Hendrix... sing it for John Lennon... for Jim Morrison... for Brian Jones... for Janis Joplin... for James Dean... for Elvis Presley... for Beth Lieberman."

APRIL 10, 1985. HAMPTON, VA, COLISEUM

- ■ Attendance: 10,000; sellout
- ■ Support: Lone Justice
- ■ Set: same as Landover.

This concert is chock full of atmosphere, thankfully without problems in the audience. Before *A Sort of Homecoming* Bono thanks the security people at the venue for their civilised behaviour. "It's good to see security people that treat people like human beings," he says, relieved.

Originally, a concert has been planned for April 13 at the 9,500 capacity War Memorial Auditorium in Rochester, NY. Tickets have already gone on sale (price: $11.50) but the show is postponed, to be cancelled altogether shortly after, probably because a third show is added at the Meadowlands Arena.

APRIL 12, 14, 15, 1985. EAST RUTHERFORD, NJ, MEADOWLANDS ARENA

- ■ Attendance: 61,715 (P); sellout
- ■ Support: Lone Justice
- ■ Set first night: same as Landover.

"I want to dedicate this to ... well, I was watching television the other night, in New York, in a hotel room and I saw on the news, there were some students at Columbia University who were sitting on the steps, trying to do something about what is happening in South Africa. So I went down to the campus, to the University and met some good people there. I dedicate this song to Nelson Mandela, this is *Pride, (In The Name Of Love)*." *Wire* from the show is included in a report for 'The Old Grey Whistle Test' on BBC Television, aired on April 23.

- ■ Set second show: *Gloria / I Threw a Brick Through A Window / A Day Without Me / MLK / The Unforgettable Fire / Two Hearts Beat As One / Seconds / Sunday Bloody Sunday / Cry–Electric Co. / A Sort of Homecoming / Bad / October / New Year's Day / Pride / encore: 11 O'Clock Tick Tock / I Will Follow / 40.*

U2 play a set reminiscent of the 'War' tour, opening with *Gloria* and doing *11 O'Clock* and *I Will Follow* as encores. With three nights at Meadowlands, U2 realise that many fans will see all three shows so this set would ring the changes. *I Threw A Brick* and *A Day Without Me* had not been played since Australia. During *A Day Without Me* Bono segues into The Beatles' *Dear Prudence*.

- ■ Set third night: same as Uniondale.

Back to the regular set but with a strong finale. "Well it's been three nights here in New Jersey," Bono acknowledges. "This is the last night in a whole series of dates in and around New York." He explains that after some reservations he at last feels at home in New York and he thanks the audience for their hospitality. "It's hard to know what to say without repeating yourself. You always repeat yourself again. You say what you mean, you tell the truth. At one stage, when we first came to New York, we were really frightened of playing large arenas like this. We thought that it just belonged to all the groups that we didn't wanna belong to. And that is until we saw one person play in Wembley Arena in London, and that shames our feeling about these buildings. You know this person very well, his name is Bruce Springsteen." This becomes a cue for the shouts of 'Brooooooce' that occur at all Springsteen concerts. "We saw Springsteen and his E. Street Band and we just saw someone who could turn these large buildings into small, intimate places. We feel very much that that's what happened over the last tour

don't like that word at all! Because our crowd can control themselves, thank you very much."

The band's irritation makes for a highly energised show, with short extra lines added to several songs. In *The Unforgettable Fire* Bono repeatedly sings, as he did during the Australian tour, "Stay, till your heart breaks through," taking Edge by surprise to the extent that he messes up his keyboard playing. Bono starts an aggressive version of *Wire* with the chorus of The Doors' *Break On Through*. During *Electric Co.* He sings *Amazing Grace* as well as *Wooden Heart*.

During Bono's "Come on down" bit at the end of *Bad* he motions the audience to move to the front, provoking the bouncers. Several fans who get on stage are saved from the claws of the irritated bouncers by Bono, who expands *Bad* by encouraging the audience to sing along.

The police arrive at Capital Center. After the concert Production Manager Steve Iredale, who has signed the contracts, is held responsible for a disturbance of the peace and arrested. He has to be bailed out.

APRIL 9, 1985. PITTSBURGH, PA, CIVIC ARENA

- ■ Attendance: 15,000; sellout
- ■ Set: same as Uniondale.

After *Wire* somebody from the audience throws Bono a T-shirt which offends him. "I wanna show you something," he says. "I wanna show you a T-shirt. It's a T-shirt that refers to my country, the country where I grew up in. And it's a T-shirt that seems to suggest that arms and bombs are the solution to what's going on in my country. I tell you, it's NOT the solution. So take the T-shirt and shove it." An aggressive *Sunday Bloody Sunday* follows.

As an intro to *A Sort of Homecoming* Bono says: "This next song is not written about my country, or any country. It's written about the hope that one day we may all share the same country. Maybe there will be no more flags, maybe we'll have just one flag. And maybe that flag will be a white flag."

Bono sounds morose while introducing *Pride*. "This song I dedicate to somebody who bought tickets for tonight's concert

and I hope you feel the same way. This is a song that... often when you write songs, you think you write them about someone else but you're really writing about yourself. It's a song called *Bad*."

APRIL 16, 18, 19, 1985. WORCESTER, MA, CENTRUM

■ Attendance: 37,416 (P); sellout
■ Support: Lone Justice
■ Set first night: same as Landover, plus *Two Hearts Beat As One* after *Wire*.

After having played to a full house here in December, these three Centrum shows sell out in half a day. Promoter Don Law tries to get U2 to play a fourth concert on April 17, but the band decide against it as they need a day's rest in their busy schedule.

The fact that there is a demand for a fourth concert reflects U2's incredible popularity in the Boston area. The fans here are among U2's most fanatic in America. Brett Milano discusses the audience in his review for the *Boston Globe*: 'U2 attracts one of rock & roll's most devoted audiences. A U2 crowd does more than jump and shout: they bring Irish flags and peace banners, they drop to dead silence in the slow numbers, they sing in perfect time when singer Bono leads a chant. The band return the warmth, making the audience feel like an important part of the show.'

The same audience almost become victims of disaster. During *Wire*, a lighting rig on Adam's side of the stage begins to slip from its perch above the audience, threatening to fall into the front rows. Adam notices it, keeps his cool and whispers into Bono's ear. The band stop playing, Bono consults a technician and roadies climb up to tighten the cables and make the lighting rig secure. Bono urges the audience to move out of the way for safety's sake, and tries to calm everyone down to avoid panic. "They need 20 minutes to fix this with steel cable and stuff. Don't worry. We're gonna have a rock & roll concert even if we have to wait all night." Twenty minutes or so later everybody is allowed back into their seats. U2 resume the show with *Two Hearts Beat As One*, not originally on the set list.

■ Set second show: Gloria / I Threw A Brick Through A Window / A Day Without Me / I Fall Down / MLK / The Unforgettable Fire / Two Hearts Beat As One / Seconds / Sunday Bloody Sunday / Cry–Electric Co. / A Sort of Homecoming / Bad / October / New Year's Day / Pride / encore: Party Girl / I Will Follow / 40.

Just as at the second Meadowlands show the alternate set is played, with a few changes. *Party Girl* replaces *11 O'Clock*, making it the only concert of the tour where this song is not played. Bono again segues into *Dear Prudence* during *A Day Without Me*, integrating a complete verse. The Massachusetts audience always react well to U2. "Well, it's no secret that this whole Boston/Worcester area is important to U2. And because of the

way things are between us and you, because we arrived here in a station wagon five years ago and this city took notice - this city took notice before even we took notice! - we wanna play a song for you we haven't played in a long time. This is *I Fall Down*." People immediately recognise the opening bars and clap along *en masse*. It has not been performed since.

After *Electric Co.* there is a curious moment when Bono sees a little boy in the front row. He invites him onstage and gives him a big red balloon. "Just wanna make a gift," he says, and asks the boy his name. He is too shy, but his father wants to say something. "Be cool with this," says Bono, throwing his microphone to him. "He's my son, his name is Ever Peaceful," Dad explains, and throws it back. Bono is surprised. Ever Peaceful? In the meantime the red balloon has burst and Bono mumbles something about balloons not being what they used to be. He promises Ever to give him a new present and then carries on with the show.

As always, *Party Girl* is played in festive spirit, with Bono challenging the audience to sing along and opening a bottle of champagne. He hesitates with the bottle. "I think we should open it, shouldn't we?" "Yeeeaaahh!" the audience holler. "Oh no we shouldn't," Bono says with a touch of irony, "remember, we're a really serious political group, OK!" He aims his remarks at the press, who often emphasise the political aspects of U2 too much and ignore the other aspects. He opens the bottle and sprays the first few rows. He brings Ever Peaceful and his father and mother on stage, and a crew member comes to hand Ever a big surprise box, compensating for the burst balloon. Inside, Ever finds a teddy bear. Bono pours champagne for the parents. The association of champagne and family inspires him to spontaneously sing the melancholy *Auld Lang Syne*: "Should old acquaintance be forgot..." He stops after one line, but the 12,500 fans pick it up and loudly finish the verse. It is a moving moment in one of the best concerts of the tour. Bono raises his glass. "I drink to you, thank you, good night!"

■ Set third night: same as Landover.

Peculiarly, *Drowning Man* is played over the PA before U2 hit the stage, instead of *4th Of July*. This is also true for the next four shows. U2 have never played that song live.

APRIL 20, 1985. HARTFORD, CT, CIVIC CENTER

■ Attendance: 15,505 (P); sellout
■ Support: Lone Justice
■ Set: same as Uniondale.

Additional shows are added in Hartford and Philadelphia due to strong ticket demand, but because other events are taking place at both venues around the same time U2 cannot play consecutive nights and end up travelling to and from both cities twice.

As at some earlier shows, an Irish flag is thrown at Bono, and he throws it back into the audience after a while. Bounty

hunting fans try to snatch the flag with a little bit too much enthusiasm, and so yet another brawl starts in the audience. "There's people over there fighting over that flag – well, you've come to the wrong concert, OK! There's been enough fighting over flags!" Bono shouts.

The Detroit incident had been genuine, but it seems as if Bono staged it at later concerts, when the situation called for it, to make a point and do it dramatically. With this he confronts the audience with itself, and criticises the often blind hysteria that U2 face during this American tour.

APRIL 22, 1985. PHILADELPHIA, PA, SPECTRUM ARENA

■ Attendance: 18,455 (P); sellout
■ Support: Lone Justice
■ Set: same as Landover.

During *Electric Co.* Bono sings a snippet of John Lennon's *Happy Christmas (War Is Over)* instead of *Amazing Grace*.

APRIL 23, 1985. HARTFORD, CT, CIVIC CENTER

■ Attendance: 15,505 (P); sellout
■ Support: Lone Justice
■ Set: same as Landover, plus *Two Hearts Beat As One* after *I Will Follow*.

Back in Hartford, the band seem tired but work hard. Bono gets a kick out of the mass of people and during the bridge of *I Will Follow* he asks for the house lights so he can see everybody. "This song says it all for us, about the way we feel about you, the way we feel about being on a stage in front of such a crowd of people; this is *Two Hearts Beat As One*," he announces, launching into a long and swinging version. "Celebrate good times, come on!" he sings, quoting Kool And The Gang's song. Next, after having sung a complete verse of *Loch Lomond*, Bono says: "When we first played around here, we played in a small club called Toad's to about 10 or 20 people. I'm sure glad there's a lot more here tonight. We used to get angry with ourselves, I used to feel there was no other way out for us, that there was nothing else we could do. And then I found out that we could do rock & roll. We first started making music in a small garage, with a small amplifier. We plugged our guitars in and, well... pretty soon we were plugging in guitars in Connecticut."

This time *Electric Co.* segues into *Give Peace A Chance*, Bono sings the chorus a couple of times, which he hasn't done since 1982.

APRIL 24, 1985. PHILADELPHIA, PA, SPECTRUM ARENA

■ Attendance: 18,455 (P); sellout
■ Support: Lone Justice
■ Set: same as Uniondale, with again the addition of *Two Hearts Beat As One*, this time after *Seconds*.

Sunday Bloody Sunday becomes a community sing-song when Bono asks the audience to join in: "You know the words? I want you to sing something for me. I want you to remember something I could never possibly understand. Something that's much closer to you than it is to me. Because it's 10 years ago since Vietnam. So sing after me: NO MORE. No war!"

During *Party Girl* Bono takes the opportunity to toast the road crew, the audience, and he thanks everybody for taking the trouble to get tickets. "Also, I wanna thank our guest band tonight, Lone Justice, an American band playing American music. I wish the best of luck on them, wherever they're going." It is their last concert on this tour, and to say goodbye, singer Maria McKee sings along to *40*. "Lone Justice for ya!" Bono shouts, and together with Maria he sings a pot-pourri of *40*, *Do They Know It's Christmas* and *We Are The World*. Maria's shrill, fierce voice drowns out Bono, who shouts: "Ladies and gentlemen: Kenny Rogers and Dolly Parton!"

APRIL 29, 1985. ATLANTA, GA, THE OMNI

- Attendance: 12,000; sellout
- Set: same as Landover, plus *Two Hearts Beat As One* after *Seconds*.

During their few days' rest U2 visit the Martin Luther King Center at the invitation of Coretta King, Dr. King's widow. They are very honoured to see the Center and to meet Coretta, who is still very active in the American civil rights movement. Coretta says she is honoured that her husband has been the inspiration for two of U2's songs.

U2's stay in Atlanta is also memorable for another reason. Bono's father has flown over from Ireland to be at the concert and in an interview with *Rolling Stone* magazine (RS 651, March 4, 1993, conducted by Alan Light), he recalls: "I remember I brought him over to the US to see us play, and I told one of the spotlight operators to get ready. I just introduced this guy – 'It's his first time in America, here's my father, he's come to see us play' – and 20,000 people turned around, and he just stands up and gives me the finger. Like, 'Don't do this to me.' I just laughed. He's very cool like that."

APRIL 30, 1985. JACKSONVILLE, FL, MEMORIAL COLISEUM

- Attendance: 9,000
- Set: same as Uniondale.

Warm spring weather presides over a sultry performance. Security is busy handing out cups of water to those squashed in front against the barrier. "Well, there is one thing we're not assured of in Florida, and that's water, so I'd quite like some myself if you could pass me up a glass." Bono quenches his thirst. "You live in a very, very beautiful part of America. Has anyone ever thought that it might be a good place for people to come on their summer holidays... ? Oh, somebody has already thought about it, I see..." During *Bad* he sings part of *Candle In The Wind*, Elton John's tribute to Marilyn Monroe. During *Party Girl* he invites a girl on stage, offers her a seat on a monitor, and gives her a bottle of champagne to uncork. The band have something to celebrate. "The reason that champagne is with us is because tonight we have passed 500,000 people on the United States tour! One half a million..." Bono sounds as if he can hardly believe it. Two years before, during the 'War' tour, U2 played many more concerts in America and did not play to even half the number of people they reached this time. The girl opens the champagne, they have a drink, Bono sings on and embraces her: "This is Sonny and Cher Bono!"

MAY 2, 1985. TAMPA, FL, UNIVERSITY OF SOUTH FLORIDA SUN DOME

- Attendance: 10,907 (P); (capacity: 11,200)
- Support: Red Rockers

Pre-showtime in Tampa

- Set: same as Landover.

Give Peace A Chance appears again in *Electric Co.* and Bono goes into *Amazing Grace* as well. The tour nears its end. "Thanks for making us feel at home," he says. "We've been away so long I think we're forgetting what home looks like! We get so used to this – this is the most familiar part of our day, you know. Every night, when you're travelling and going from city to city, it's THIS: this stage becomes our living room, this becomes our bedroom."

MAY 3, 4, 1985. FORT LAUDERDALE, FL, HOLLYWOOD SPORTATORIUM

- Attendance: 25,000

Two shows in the Miami area close the American tour after ten weeks; forty-one concerts for a total of 578,000 people, many more than Bono announced in Jacksonville. Two weeks of complete rest will follow before the band go back to Europe where they are booked for a few summer festivals.

The European pop festival season starts in mid-spring and practically every promoter is eager to add U2 to their bill as their name guarantees successful ticket sales. The Dutch 'Lochem 7000' festival boldly announces on radio that negotiations with U2 have reached a point where it's practically certain that they will play, but nothing is further from the truth. All in all the band receive twelve invitations to play big festivals but after the exhausting American tour they agree to do just a few.

MAY 25, 1985. ADENAU/KOBLENZ, GERMANY, NÜRBURGRING RACECOURSE

- Attendance: 70,000
- 'Rock am Ring Festival' line-up: Lone Justice, Merle & The Ring, The Alarm, Shakatak, Rick Springfield, Gianna Nannini, Joe Cocker, REO Speedwagon, U2, Chris de Burgh.
- Set: 11 O'Clock Tick Tock / I Will Follow / Seconds / MLK / The Unforgettable Fire / Wire / Sunday Bloody Sunday / Cry-Electric Co. / A Sort of Homecoming / Bad / October / New Year's Day / Pride / Gloria / 40

With their RockPop performance in Dortmund and a series of indoor shows earlier in the year, U2 are finally gaining a foothold in Germany, the third largest record market in the world. Playing a number of German festivals would serve to consolidate their following.

They play the first day of this annual two-day festival at the Nürburgring race-circuit, near the cities of Adenau and Koblenz. Their American support, Lone Justice, open and U2's fellow countryman Chris de Burgh closes the day. Under a warm spring sun around 70,000 people sprawl around the gigantic circuit in miserable conditions: there are far too few toilets, there is a limited food supply, and a serious lack of water. U2 play only an average set that initially can only be seen by those in the front while halfway up the field fans are talking and drinking, with the festival serving as background music. A song such as *MLK* pales into insignificance and when Bono tries to get the crowd to sing "No more" during *Sunday Bloody Sunday*, the response is meagre. He pulls an old stunt by climbing the scaffolding during *Electric Co.* to sing lines of *Give Peace A Chance*. It still works, as those in the back who had not seen the band now see him and and cheer him on.

MAY 26, 1985. STUTTGART, GERMANY, NECKARSTADION

- Attendance: ca. 30,000; (capacity 55,000)
- Festival line-up: Immaculate Fools, The Alarm, Rick Springfield, Joe Cocker, Gianna Nannini, REO Speedwagon, U2, Chris de Burgh
- Set: *11 O'Clock Tick Tock* / *I Will Follow* / *Seconds* / *MLK* / *The Unforgettable Fire* / *Sunday Bloody Sunday* / *Cry-Electric Co.* / *Bad* / *October* / *New Year's Day* / *Pride* / encore: *40*

The show is far from being sold-out, with the stands practically empty. Due to time constraints U2 strike *Wire*, *A Sort of Homecoming* and *Gloria* from the set. The show is better than the day before with active audience participation. Bono sings snippets of *Ruby Tuesday*, *Norwegian Wood* and *Walk On The Wild Side* at the end of *Bad*. During *Electric Co.* Bono goes into the audience to seek contact but ends up back on stage with his clothes ripped to shreds.

MAY 27, 1985. MÜNSTER, GERMANY, FREIGELÄNDE HALLE MÜNSTERLAND

- Attendance: 10,000
- Festival line-up: Rick Springfield, Mink DeVille, Gianna Nannini, Joe Cocker, U2, Chris de Burgh
- Set: same as Stuttgart, plus, remarkably, *Gloria* after *I Will Follow*.

The Alarm are also on the bill but do not perform. This is a failed attempt to launch another annual festival, which turns out to be the last event in this venue, which is actually a huge parking lot. Again, the organisation is bad, the weather too hot and facilities inadequate. The band are tired and it shows. Bono pulls a girl onstage during *Bad* and holds her tight for a long time. Only half the audience stay to watch top-of-the-bill Chris de Burgh. Security guards patrol in and around the site with dogs and shortly after U2's set two fans heading home are bitten by an aggressive dog.

JUNE 1, 1985. BASEL, SWITZERLAND, ST. JACOB'S FUSSBALSTADION

- Attendance: 40,000
- 'Rock in Basel' Festival line-up: Gianna Nannini, The Alarm, Rick Springfield, Joe Cocker, U2, Chris de Burgh
- Set: same as Stuttgart, again plus *Gloria*, now after *Seconds*.

JUNE 3, 1985. BERLIN, GERMANY

U2 intended to give a free show on the Platz der Republik in front of the Reichstag in Berlin, which is near The Wall that so obtrusively divides the communist East from the capitalist West. Through their concert, U2 hoped to unite people from both parts of town for a day, but though the date is printed in the official tour programme, the event eventually doesn't take place as the band experience difficulty in getting it off the ground.

JUNE 22, 1985. MILTON KEYNES, ENGLAND, MILTON KEYNES BOWL

- Attendance: 50,000; sellout
- 'The Longest Day' line up: The Faith Brothers, Spear Of Destiny, Billy Bragg, The Ramones, R.E.M., U2
- Set: *11 O'Clock Tick Tock* / *I Will Follow* / *Seconds* / *MLK* / *The*

Unforgettable Fire / *Wire* / *Sunday Bloody Sunday* / *Cry-Electric Co.* / *A Sort of Homecoming* / *Rain* / *Bad* / *October* / *New Year's Day* / *Pride* / encore: *Party Girl* / *Gloria* / *40*

On the longest day of the year U2 play their only UK show of 1985 at the amphitheatre of Milton Keynes, a booming new town between London and Birmingham. Billed as the 'Longest Day' Festival, it is in fact a U2 show with extended support rather than a festival, as all tickets sell out before even one support act is booked. It's U2's first headlining open-air show in the UK, where their popularity has enjoyed a spectacular growth in just half a year's time. "Well, we started off in a car park, we've ended up in a field," Bono remarks during *I Will Follow*. "The only difference is you, 50,000 of you. And we thank you..."

Bits of *Wooden Heart* and *Amazing Grace* are included in *Electric Co.*, which Bono closes by dramatically crying out, "Ziggy played guitar", the words that David Bowie used to end his song *Ziggy Stardust*. The crowd were drenched by rain during the support acts but are in good spirits. "And this indeed is what makes you the best audience in the world," Bono comments after *Electric Co.*. "I ask myself why people queue up in lines, wait for a long time – and it gets rainy on them. Sometimes I feel that we can never live up to this, and it's true: we can't live up to this, but you just did..."

When Bono introduces, "This is *Bad*," the sequencer that produces the song's opening notes malfunctions and spews forth bursts of feedback. "This is very bad!" he calls out. Technicians try to solve the problem while Bono stalls the crowd. "It's really great to be back in Los Angeles," he quips. "Well, now you know why we don't break down so much, because I don't tell very good jokes. Actually, there was this sandwich that went into a bar..." The crowd groan, while Bono turns to the rest of the band, gesturing that it's too stupid a joke to tell, but tells it anyway: "Right, so this sandwich goes into a bar, and eases his way past a few pork pies and steps up to the waiter and says, 'Waiter, can I have a pint of Guinness?' He says, 'No, I'm sorry, we don't serve sandwiches'." Right. Bono invites someone from the audience to tell a better joke. While the crowd chant "Here we go", a guy about twice Bono's size called Martin gets hoisted onstage and gives Bono a big hug. He reacts, "All right, sunshine, seeing as you're the height you are, you can do the rest of this on your knees, OK!" Martin kneels down but threatens not to tell his joke. Bono states that the whole crowd are waiting for him and their sigh of disappointment puts pressure on Martin. "OK! I'll tell a joke: what's the biggest joke in Great Britain? Wham!" Bono thanks Martin for his contribution and leads him off. "Well, seeing as the concert is broken down, let's play something for the day. You know any Beatles' songs, Edge?" The crowd call out several titles. "Edge – they want you to play that song *Rain*." The Edge carefully hits the first chords and an impromptu version of The Beatles' song which follows actually sounds solid. The song briefly segues into Bob Dylan's *A Hard Rain's Gonna Fall*, then Bono switches back to *Rain* again.

During a second attempt to start *Bad*, the sequencer stutters and then quits altogether. "Anyone knows any more jokes?" laughs Bono, and *Bad* is performed without the sequencer-produced rattling sound that normally accompanies the song.

"We're gonna go away now and write some songs for our next LP," Bono says before *40*. "It means a lot to this group that we can be away for the last six months and that so many people

The Unforgettable Fire

An Exhibition Of Drawings by Survivors
of the Hiroshima & Nagasaki Bombings

Presented by U2 for Dublin Street Carnival
at the GRAPEVINE ARTS CENTRE
June 29 th – July 5 th

open - 11 – 5 Sat. – Sun., 10 – 5 Mon – Fri.

our US tour was meeting Coretta King, wife of Martin Luther King and mother of the whole civil rights movement in America. We met her and Martin Luther King's daughter Jolanda. They invited us into their house and shook our hand and said they were pleased that we should've dedicated two songs from our album to her husband and to her father. Because it's still a big issue in America right now, black civil rights. What I liked about Martin Luther King, what attracted me to him as an Irishman, was that I saw a similar situation in Ireland, the troubles up North, and the way he dealt with it. Because there was a very volatile situation in the Sixties in America between the blacks and whites. And he believed enough in his cause to die for it, but never to kill for it. And I thought that was something – that was a message that maybe people in this country could relate to. Someone who'd give a life, rather than take a life. Does that make any sense?"

JUNE 29, 1985. DUBLIN, IRELAND, CROKE PARK

- Attendance: 57,000; sellout
- Support: In Tua Nua, R.E.M., The Alarm, Squeeze
- Set: 11 O'Clock Tick Tock / I Will Follow / Seconds / MLK / The Unforgettable Fire / Wire / Sunday Bloody Sunday / A Sort of Homecoming / Cry-Electric Co. / Bad / October / New Year's Day / Pride / encore: My Hometown / Out Of Control / Gloria / 40

Tickets for U2's first Irish show since Phoenix Park in 1983 sell out easily. Reports from U2's triumphs abroad have fuelled a national sense of pride and, with the band bringing the 'Unforgettable Fire' exhibition to the people of Dublin, U2 are looked on as national heroes. U2-fever is driven to the maximum. Fans travel from all over the Republic and the North and the show also attracts thousands of fans from the UK, USA and Europe who want to see U2 play their home town. A few hundred tickets are made available on the day of the show which successfully puts the touts out of business. It's U2's first headlining show at a football stadium. DJ Dave Fanning introduces the band: "Now they're back! They have conquered the world. Are you ready for the greatest live rock & roll show you will ever see? Welcome back Bono, Larry, Adam, The Edge: U2!"

When U2 walk onstage the crowd go bonkers and turn the stadium into one big party. "Well, the Jacks are back, and what an All-Ireland we have for you tonight," Bono says proudly. 11 O'Clock Tick Tock opens the homecoming concert in a euphoric atmosphere that will remain throughout the night. The crowd push and jump around so much that huge clouds of sand and dust drift towards the stage.

"This is a song I wish we didn't have to write – but we had

---

still want to come and see us." He thanks the groups performing today, as well as Larry, Adam and The Edge for letting him be in their band. Lines of We Are The World and Do They Know It's Christmas are included in 40, after which a spectacular fireworks display lights up the sky before the 50,000 head home.

In their reviews, the critics agree that U2 made the day and, despite the rain, sent the crowd home happy. In *Sounds* magazine, Gary Bushel writes: 'Even in the miserable drizzle, U2 were so hot I was gulping down malaria tablets. Such power, such passion, such intensity. If we have to have "stadium rock", then thank God we're blessed with a band like U2 who can command this attention and still be a joyous inspirational force, still generate a feeling of community, and still grow. And the greatest thing of all is that they still mean it. I left Milton Keynes' Saturday Muddy Saturday grinning, because mine eyes had seen the real glory of honest Eighties rock, and not groaning because I'd suffered the sight of tired old men living off their laurels and shaming their legacy at Knebworth.'

JUNE 28, 1985. DUBLIN, IRELAND, CROKE PARK

While rehearsing for their highly anticipated homecoming concert, U2's sound volume is so high that it disturbs students taking exams at the Rosmini Community School, which is over half a mile away from Croke Park. The school's caretaker walks

---

up to the stadium to complain and U2, unaware of the problems they are causing, stop right away.

That evening, U2 attend the opening of the 'Unforgettable Fire' exhibition of drawings and paintings by survivors of the Hiroshima and Nagasaki nuclear bombings at the Grapevine Arts Centre. The works are on display for a full week. Though the originals are Japanese art treasures that never leave the country, lithographs and prints of the originals were made for the Chicago Peace Museum where U2 originally saw them while on tour in 1983. U2 organised and paid for the transport of these replicas to Dublin in order to offer their hometown access to the exhibition that had impressed and inspired the band so much.

Bono tells an RTE camera crew: "An enormous exercise for themselves, the fear they felt over the holocaust and the bombs being dropped in Nagasaki and Hiroshima – they just painted. And that's what got me, even more than the paintings: just the idea that people should use art, if you like paint on canvas, to get something out of themselves. I suppose it's a bit like what we do with our music, that's the way we get it out of us. And it stuck on me, and when I was writing the words for *The Unforgettable Fire*, it just came back."

In another room of the Grapevine Arts Centre there is an exhibition about the life of Martin Luther King and his non-violent struggle for black civil rights in America, up to the news reports of his murder. Bono continues: "One of the highlights of

to write it, and we want to play it," Bono announces fiercely, and proclaims: "One day Irishmen will stop fighting with each other over the past. They will live and work together in the present. This is not the future: *Sunday Bloody Sunday*." The enormous cry of emotion sums up 57,000 fans' feelings about their country being torn apart by religion. U2 belt out a savage version that unifies an audience which participate en masse in this song of hope and aggressive pacifism. The stands reverberate from people jumping up and down. This night, the song is all the more meaningful since the original Bloody Sunday happened here in Croke Park, when British soldiers gunned down fourteen civilians at a Gaelic football match on November 21, 1920. Fiddle player Steve Wickham, who performed earlier in the day with In Tua Nua, plays along on the song.

Bono waves an Irish flag he plucked from the audience while singing the chorus of *Give Peace A Chance* during *Electric Co.* *Bad* has references to Dublin City and is dedicated to those suffering from the city's darker side. "For those without jobs, without money, it's a very unfair city, like any other city. Some are broken and beaten down by this – I sing this for you. There's good and bad in every city... this is *Bad*."

Coming back for the encore, Bono says, "Well, they're saying backstage that this is the friendliest crowd they have ever seen in a place like this! Fifty-seven thousand people – no problem! About a year and a half ago I was sitting in a coffee bar with a singer/songwriter that I've got to know. I was talking to him about a song of his that he had written. A song I said that when we play Dublin, I would like to play it for the people of Dublin. He said he would be both proud and pleased that we should do this. His name was Bruce Springsteen, the song is *My Hometown*. This is for my father." Edge plays keyboards on this monotonous song, which has otherwise limited instrumentation. For once Bono actually knows the lyrics of a song he covers. It remains the only occasion U2 has performed it.

Out Of Control, which hasn't been played since the Australian tour steams up the stadium again. It's the oldest song of the night and is played to celebrate the fact that U2 are now performing at stadiums in contrast to the pubs and car parks that hosted the early gigs. By the time U2 perform *40* dusk has set in and the crowd hold lighters to accompany their singing of "How long to sing this song", producing a breathtaking sight as Larry drags out the song for a long time before he finishes the night with a crash on the cymbals. The audience clap and sing for several minutes to reward U2 for the wonderful night they have given them.

At a time when the city of Dublin is plagued by high unemployment, drug abuse and architectural deterioration, the show is a morale boost for U2's Irish fans. Headlining a sellout show at Croke Park only five years after playing small clubs, U2's domestic and international success inspires a whole generation of young bands. U2 have shown that it *is* possible as an Irish band to become successful and break out to the rest of the world without succumbing to the flood of American and British pop music. U2 donate their proceeds of the show, several hundreds of thousand pounds, into the building of rehearsal rooms for young bands that cannot afford expensive equipment and have no place in which to practise. Called The City Centre, it will open in June 1989.

JULY 6, 1985. TORHOUT, BELGIUM, FESTIVAL GROUNDS

- Attendance: 60,000; sellout
- Festival line-up: The Ramones, R.E.M., Lloyd Cole and The Commotions, The Style Council, Depeche Mode, Paul Young and The Royal Family, U2, Joe Cocker
- Set: *11 O'Clock Tick Tock / I Will Follow / Seconds / MLK / The Unforgettable Fire / Wire / Sunday Bloody Sunday / Cry-Electric Co. / A Sort of Homecoming / Bad / October / New Year's Day / Pride /* encore: *Knocking On Heaven's Door / Gloria / 40*

This is the third time U2 play the double festival of Torhout and Werchter, where they have grown from third on the bill to festival headliners. During *I Will Follow* Bono goes over to the

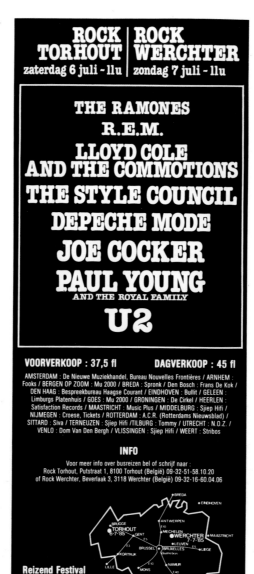

photographers' pit and points at the crowd. "See these people... they make a big, positive noise. We don't have a riot – we have a good feeling. So take that to the cameras and take that to the people at home..." The show is good, with *Knocking On Heaven's Door* one of the highlights. Edge adds an extra, atmospheric piece of piano music to precede *October*; a beautiful, melancholy bit which could be either a leftover tune from the 'Unforgettable Fire' album sessions, or a piece recently composed for a film score that Edge is working on. Before *40* Bono says he's proud to perform on the same stage as the artists on the bill, Joe Cocker in particular, and dedicates *40* to Cocker. Joe Cocker, originally scheduled to appear after Depeche Mode, performs after U2's set for only about half the crowd, since most people are heading home or move to the back of the field to relax and listen to his set around campfires.

JULY 7, 1985. WERCHTER, BELGIUM, FESTIVAL GROUNDS

- Attendance: 60,000; sellout
- Festival line-up: The Ramones, R.E.M., Lloyd Cole and The Commotions, The Style Council, Depeche Mode, Joe Cocker, Paul Young and The Royal Family, U2
- Set: same as Torhout, with *Party Girl* replacing *Knocking On Heaven's Door*, and *Out Of Control* added after *Seconds*.

U2 play their last official performance on the 'Unforgettable Fire' tour before a sellout crowd of 60,000 Belgian, Dutch, French, German and British people. *Out Of Control* makes another rare appearance.

JULY 13, 1985. LONDON, ENGLAND, WEMBLEY STADIUM

- Attendance: 72,000; sellout
- 'Live Aid'; London line up: Status Quo, The Style Council, The Boomtown Rats, Adam Ant, Ultravox, Loudness, Spandau Ballet, Elvis Costello, Nik Kershaw, Sade, Sting, Phil Collins, REO Speedwagon, Howard Jones, Bryan Ferry, Paul Young, Alison Moyet, U2, Dire Straits/Sting, Queen, David Bowie, The Who, Elton John, Kiki Dee, Wham, Paul McCartney, All Star Finale.
- Set: *Sunday Bloody Sunday / Bad*

U2's performance at Live Aid is their most widely exposed to date. Organised by Boomtown Rats' singer Bob Geldof to raise funds for the benefit of the starving in Ethiopia and other African countries, Live Aid became the biggest music festival ever, with the most prestigious line up of stars ever assembled, reaching a combined television audience of 1.5 billion people in over 160 countries.

The festival is a logical extension of the Band Aid project, initiated in November 1984 by Midge Ure and Geldof. Released in December 1984, Band Aid's all-star single Do They Know It's Christmas?, on which Bono and Adam had featured, sold millions of copies, generating £8,000,000 for famine relief. The Band Aid project focused global attention on the famine to the embarrassment of Western politicians responsible for grain mountains going to rot in Europe. Where world leaders fail to tackle these problems successfully, Band Aid's initiative was widely respected and prompted American artists to do something similar. Called United Supporting Artists For Africa, their 'We Are The World' single and album, released in January 1985, was also hugely successful. Like the Band Aid funds, investments were thoughtfully made, concentrating mainly on structural aid, such as the installation of water pumps, but immediate food requirements were not ignored.

Following the success of Band Aid, Bob Geldof spent months organising Live Aid, getting the bill of artists together and trying to persuade broadcasters worldwide to take up the live broadcast and do a telethon to raise funds. When the event is advertised to take place on July 13 at two sites, Wembley Stadium in London and JFK Stadium in Philadelphia, all tickets sell out instantly. Taking place more or less simultaneously, a wide range of artists will perform, gladly responding to Geldof's call. U2 participate, issuing the following statement on the day itself:

'U2 are involved in Live Aid because it's more than money, it's music... but it is also a demonstration to the politicians and policy-makers that men, women and children will not walk by other men, women and children as they lie, bellies swollen, starving to death for the sake of a cup of grain and water.

'For the price of Star Wars, the MX missile offensive-defence budgets, the desert of Africa could be turned into fertile lands. The technology is with us. The technocrats are not. Are we part of a civilisation that protects itself by investing in life... or investing in death?'

The opening fanfare at Wembley blasts out at noon, and Status Quo open the proceedings appropriately enough with *Rockin' All Over The World*. Additional contributions are beamed in via satellite from Melbourne (INXS), The Hague (B.B. King), Belgrade, Moscow, Vienna and Cologne. At five in the afternoon, Bob Geldof welcomes Philadelphia, where the American half commences at 1pm local time. Performances at Philadelphia and Wembley alternate for the rest of the day, enabling fans at both to see all the performers either live or on video screens.

At 17.20pm London time, Jack Nicholson announces U2 from the Philadelphia stage. "...And now, to keep with the international and global feeling that we have, direct from London, a group who's heart is in Dublin, Ireland, whose spirit is with the world, a group that's never had any problem saying how they feel: U2." The band are warmly received by the crowd at Wembley, as well as by those at JFK watching the screens. Dozens of U2 flags stick out from the audience. When Bono announces Sunday Bloody Sunday, the stadium becomes one swaying mass of people. His voice is still powerful after a year on the road, though he has a slight lisp and sounds like he has bitten his tongue. The performance is spirited. Bono bows for Edge doing his solo, takes the onstage cameraman by his arm to point out the crowd, and spurs the crowd on to chant "No more". He announces, "We're an Irish band, we come from Dublin City, Ireland. Like all cities it has its good, and it has its bad. This is a song called *Bad*." Appropriate for a charity event televised all over the world, Bono opens the song with lines from Lou Reed's *Satellite Of Love. Bad* is powerful, with Larry's loud bass drum blasting out the rhythm over the huge sound system. Increasing intensity as the song progresses, Bono looks for a dance partner, gesturing to the crowd below. While dozens anxiously push their way to the front, Bono trots around the stage. He points down to show the security guards which girl to pick out, then impulsively jumps down onto floor level. One girl is finally lifted over the barriers, and she falls into Bono's open arms. The audience roar as they follow their slow dance on the screens. Bono gracefully kisses her hand, leaving her dazed as he climbs back onto the stage. Continuing *Bad*, he sings snippets of *Ruby Tuesday, Sympathy For The Devil,* and *Walk On The Wild Side,* successfully prompting the crowd to sing along. He improvises, "Holly came from Miami, Fla., hitch-hiked all the way across the USA, she could hear the satellite coming down, pretty soon she was in London town... Wembley Stadium, and all the people went Do-do-do-do..." Bono finishes the song and, looking somewhat distraught, walks off. Because *Bad* has lasted 15 minutes, there is no time left to play *Pride* as originally planned.

Later, after memorable performances by Queen, David Bowie and Paul McCartney, Bono joins the exuberant all-star finale for *Do They Know It's Christmas?* Still, Bono leaves the stadium upset, confused about his own performance, and questioning the stupidity of rock & roll while millions are dying from starvation. When he sees his performance on video the next day, his feeling that he blew it is stengthened. He drives around the country, not speaking to anyone for days, until at Newross he meets a sculptor in his late fifties, who is working on a bronze statue. The artist explains it is called 'The Leap' and is inspired by Bono's jump down the stage.

Despite Bono's own feelings, his gesture of breaking through barriers to unite with the audience hits home with millions of people all over the world. Though involving members of their audience has always been an important aspect of U2's live performance, Bono's 'leap' at Live Aid is particularly significant as it clicked with the message of universal brotherhood that surrounded the event and, besides that, one third of the world population was watching.

Having always aimed to get through to people, U2 have now introduced themselves to the world in one go. Instantly winning a lot of new fans, U2's record sales treble in the months that follow and the demand to see them live increases dramatically.

Live Aid itself proves a great success. Ticket sales, television rights, merchandising and the worldwide telethon bring in £60,000,000. The festival ignites a huge collective sense of commitment and understanding for world issues, and will trigger a whole series of events in the years to come.

AUGUST 25, 1985. CORK, IRELAND, LARK BY THE LEE FESTIVAL

- Attendance: 6,000
- Set: an hour-long set includes *I Will Follow, Sunday Bloody Sunday, Gloria, Pride, Knocking On Heaven's Door* and *40*.

U2 make an unannounced appearance at the 'Lark By The Lee' festival before a surprised audience. The band have an affinity with the city of Cork, since many of their road crew come from Cork and in the early days U2 were at times more successful there than they were in Dublin. U2 play a loose and inspired show without their regular lights and smoke machines. The show closes down the 'Unforgettable Fire' phase which had started almost exactly a year earlier in New Zealand.

JANUARY 30, 1986. IRISH TV, RTE: 'TV GAGA'

■ Set: *Womanfish / Trip Through Your Wires / Knocking On Heaven's Door*

Larry and Bono are interviewed for half an hour before U2 play some new songs for a studio audience. After a six-month period in which the band have worked on their new album and contributed to side projects, this is their first major interview in a long time. The interviewer and members of the audience ask a wide variety of questions, ranging in subject matter from U2's beginnings to their recent success in *Rolling Stone* magazine's readers' poll where U2 were voted Band Of The Year 1985, and Best Performance At Live Aid.

Asked what he thinks of young bands wanting to be like U2, Bono says: "Some people come to me and say, 'Hey Bono, I've got a band that sounds just like U2'. You know, then you've really got the wrong end of the stick, because one thing that U2 always stood for was to try to find our own way; they should find *their* own way. Everyone walks and talks differently, everyone has their own original way about them. If they just apply that to their music, their music will be as original."

Recalling Live Aid, Larry says the atmosphere was great, no inflated egos dominating backstage behaviour. Bono explains how someone would storm into a dressing room and yell, "David Bowie – out of here!" and then Bowie saying very quietly, "Oh yeah, sure," while gathering his things. Queen guitarist Brian May came up to Bono: "Wow, you've got a great guitar player in your band. Give my regards to The Hedge..."

Larry and Bono move over to the stage where Adam and Edge are waiting. Bono announces a song called *Womanfish*, while Larry bangs out a thundering, high-paced drum beat and Edge produces a cutting guitar riff. According to Bono, the song is about "a mermaid I met once in America". It has a chorus in a high-pitched voice: "Love is all you need, love is all..." It remains the only occasion this track has been played.

The next song is a rough sketch of a track that will end up on the album. Introduced as *I Tripped Through Your Wires*, it's a bluesy number with Bono playing harmonica. It is played much slower than the eventual album version and has different lyrics. "In this town, begin the rebuilding," sings Bono, referring to the many ruins of rundown houses in Dublin which are not being cleared away. A shabby version of *Knocking On Heaven's Door* ends the performance. Two guys from the audience are invited to take over Bono's and Edge's parts. The guest guitarist plays well but the singer just repeats the song's title over and over again.

MAY 17, 1986. DUBLIN, IRELAND, R.D.S. SHOWGROUNDS

■ Attendance: 30,000; sellout
■ 'Self Aid' Festival; line-up: Brush Shields, Bagatelle, Blue In Heaven, Stockton's Wing, In Tua Nua, Clannad, Big Self, Les Enfants, The Chieftains, Chris Rea, Freddie White, Those Nervous Animals, The Pogues, Cactus World News, Scullion, De Dannann, The Fountainhead, Paul Brady, The Boomtown Rats, Auto da Fe, Moving Hearts, Rory Gallagher, Christy Moore, Elvis Costello and The Attractions, Chris de Burgh, Van Morrison, U2.
■ Set: *C'Mon Everybody / Pride / Sunday Bloody Sunday / Maggie's Farm / Bad*

U2 play their only European concert of 1986 at the Self Aid Festival. Following the spirit of Live Aid, Self Aid is organised to collect money and create jobs to alleviate Ireland's massive unemployment problem, and to stir up hope for a better future through music and celebration. The festival is simulcast on RTE radio and TV, and viewers are invited to donate money in a live telethon, while employers are urged to offer jobs. All monies from donations and ticket sales will go into the Project Fund, which will administer the creation and development of new jobs and opportunities in communities around the country.

The festival concept has been greeted with sharp criticism from the outset. *In Dublin* magazine runs a story titled: 'The

Great Self Aid Farce – Rock Against The People', and uses a photo of Bono on the cover. Members of the press and a considerable number of individuals feel that the whole idea of Self Aid is patronising to the country's 230,000 unemployed, because they are being treated as a charity cause. They say the initiative will take away responsibility from the government, instead of pressurising it to improve the situation. They say that money can't buy jobs that simply aren't there, and that employers may be using the telethon merely to gain publicity for their companies, since, with 50 unemployed people for every vacancy in the country, they would have no trouble filling vacancies anyway. The opposition propagate that 'Self Aid Makes It Worse' instead of the official slogan, 'Make It Work'. However, the feeling among the artists involved is positive: Self Aid will do no harm, and it might do some good.

Starting at noon, Brush Shields opens the festival with a 15-minute performance, the time limit for most bands. With 27 Irish acts performing, it's the biggest ever musical event in Ireland. The organisers use a revolving stage similar to Live Aid, with one half facing the crowd, while on the other half the next band's equipment is being set up. Bob Geldof, who later in the day will play his final show with The Boomtown Rats, creates a commotion in the crowd by simply seeking a seat on the stands. The man responsible for Band Aid, Live Aid, Sport Aid, and the big inspiration behind this particular festival, is respected for his positive actions so much that everyone in the stadium stands to

face 'Saint Bob' and gives him a huge, emotional cheer.

Tension rises as Van Morrison ends a memorable set. The crowd sing the chorus of *40*. Dave Fanning introduces U2: "Everybody in Ireland is watching you right now: from Wexford to Donegal, from Belfast to Kerry, they're all watching a great day. Answer me this: are you happy? ("Yeeaaaahh!!") Are you ready? ["Yeeeaaahh!"] Do you wanna see a band from Dublin? Do you wanna see a band that you know and I know to be the greatest live rock band in the world? Well, they're standing behind me right now: it's Adam, it's Bono, it's Larry, it's The Edge, it's U2!"

Their entrance exhilarates the crowd. Edge starts the guitar riff of the 1959 Eddie Cochran classic *C'Mon Everybody*. U2's stomping version of the rebellious song rocks the socks off the crowd. "A song about pride – don't let them take it away," Bono announces, followed by a grand version of *Pride*. Bono runs around, reaches out, the crowd sway to and fro, guys have their girlfriends on their shoulders, and all 30,000 present sport happy faces. "I don't know what it's like to be out of work, what it's like to be unemployed," he confesses. "I just don't know – since I was 16 I got to join this group, I'm 26 now. I can't imagine what it must be like to stand in line week after week, or to lose your job after ten or twenty years, or worse, never to even have had a job. But there's a lot of you that know just what it's like. Well, let me say: this country belongs to YOU, just as much as it belongs to RTE, just as much as it belongs to CIE, or ESB, and AIB, or the Bank of Ireland. And if you work for AnCO, or if you work for Manpower, if you're paid by the people, you better look after those people. So treat them nice on Monday morning. God bless ya, I love ya." Edge starts *Sunday Bloody Sunday* in a completely new arrangement, softly stroking the strings, which allows Bono to sing the song slower and with more intensity than usual. It paces up into the regular version halfway through.

The band soar into a dark and macabre interpretation of Bob Dylan's *Maggie's Farm*. Larry comes forward to the edge of the stage with a single drum, softly tapping the edge at first and intensifying banging as the song progresses. Adam produces grim bass lines; Edge's guitar shrieks and howls. The song touches Ireland's massive emigration, a direct result of unemployment, then Bono rages at the nuclear disaster that occurred at Chernobyl three weeks ago, and the threat of a similar accident occurring at the Sellafield nuclear plant in the UK: "Temperature rising, the fever is high; I can't see the future, when they're screwing up the sky. The water is heavy, and so is my head. I don't live in Chernobyl, instead I live in Sellafield..." Hinting at Dublin's drug abuse problem, Bono goes into John Lennon's *Cold Turkey*, while backing tapes play political gobbledy-gook and radio reports of the USA's airstrike in Libya.

Bono goes offstage, but quickly returns: "The man back there says we can do one more." He inquires which song to play. Shouts for *New Year's Day* and *Bad* dominate, and *Bad* it is.

C'Mon everybody

Maire, Bono, Bob, Chris - Let's make it work.

Maggie's Farm

With their 15-minute performance of the song at Live Aid still in everyone's memory, U2 now do a version not half as long but equally as majestic. Bono quotes Elton John's *Candle In The Wind*, and adapts the lyrics to the Self-Aid backlash: "They crawled out of the woodwork, onto pages of cheap Dublin magazines..."

As U2 finish their set, the stage is prepared for the big finale, which becomes a tribute to the late Phil Lynott. The remainder of Thin Lizzy play *Don't Believe A Word*, then do *The Cowboy Song* with Bob Geldof singing, and most of the artists on the bill come out for a joyous version of the traditional Irish song *Whiskey In The Jar*, of which Bono sings one verse. When the stage is cleared and everyone thinks the show is over, Bono walks on to announce Paul Doran, the author of *Make It Work*, the anthem penned for this night. The song was released on single as well, with Larry joining in with the 'Self Aid Band'. Christy Moore and Paul Brady join Doran for the song, as do Bono, Chris de Burgh, Geldof and Maire from Clannad, who embrace to sing into one microphone for this spiritually uplifting song.

The press agree that the festival has installed a sense of hope among the Irish people. 'IT WORKED!' read the headlines in the papers. The results from the telethon are far better than the organisers expected: 1,332 jobs are made available, and £552,952 has been collected so far.

'A CONSPIRACY OF HOPE': CONCERTS FOR AMNESTY INTERNATIONAL, AMERICA, 1986.

In June 1986, on their 25th anniversary, Amnesty International goes on the road to focus attention on the fact that human rights are still being violated. Fascist governments all over the world throw people in prison for their beliefs, without any formal charge. Often they are tortured, women are raped, and many eventually 'disappear'. Amnesty International is a worldwide, voluntary movement, independent of any government. Their aim is to establish the release of prisoners of conscience; they advocate fair trials for political prisoners and work on behalf of such people detained without charge or trial. They oppose the death penalty and torture, or other cruel, inhumane or degrading treatment of prisoners. To stand stronger in their actions, and to shake a fist against governments violating human rights, Amnesty needs to raise money, membership and awareness. The 'Conspiracy Of Hope' tour is intended to do all that.

With some 500,000 members in 160 countries, Amnesty has been responsible for the release of between 1,000 and 5,000 prisoners of conscience each year. One of their most powerful and successful methods has been mobilising people to write letters to governments. Every person attending the tour will be handed a sheet of six pre-printed postcards, addressed to specific countries, each demanding the release of one particular prisoner. Amnesty hope that many of those sending postcards will also end up writing letters on a regular basis to create continuity.

U2 were first contacted to take part in August 1985. Jack Healey, director of Amnesty's American division, had seen U2 play Radio City Music Hall and was impressed by the band's passion and commitment. Paul McGuinness had promised Healey at least one

week of the band's time in 1986. With the assurance of U2's participation, Healey contacted Sting, who had performed for Amnesty earlier in his career with The Police, and readily agreed this time as well. Joan Baez, The Neville Brothers, Peter Gabriel, Bryan Adams and Lou Reed all joined in. Although all of these artists (barring Adams) are much further into their careers, U2 are the headlining act and are accepted as such by the others. Several additional artists will join in at some shows, and every night video messages are played between acts. Though it distracts them from work on their new album, U2 are happy to participate in the tour. Only six shows are lined up, but the band know the tour will be memorable and, like Live Aid, could trigger an awareness and idealism that hopefully would contribute to an improvement of world society.

crowd gasping for air. He blindfolds himself, walks to the side of the stage, hands outstretched, climbs on top of the amplifiers and assumes a position as though he is standing before a firing squad. Then, he rips off the blindfold and looks to the crowd, happy to be freed and makes his way safely back on stage. Bono will subsequently do this act most nights on the tour.

In the absence of new songs, another cover version is added: The Beatles' *Help*. The "Isolation, desolation" section in *Bad* is extended with "segregation" and "humiliation". The chorus of the Peter Gabriel song *Biko*, the lament for black leader Steven Biko who was murdered while in custody by South Africa police, is included. As he will do at each show, Lou Reed adds vocals on U2's version of *Sun City*, the song penned by Little Steven to discourage fellow artists from performing for the rich, white community in South Africa. "Twenty-three million can't vote because they're black; we're stabbing our brothers and sisters in the back," they sing. Bob Dylan's *I Shall Be Released* is chosen as the theme song of the tour, introduced by Bono as "A song that says it all," and performed by all artists on the bill to close the five-hour event. They substitute "I" for "They" in the chorus.

During their stay in San Francisco, Bono and Lou Reed visit Balmy Alley in the Mission District of the city, where walls are covered with political graffiti artwork. They meet René Castro, a mural artist from Chile who, because his artwork criticised fascist oppression in his country, had been tortured and held captive in a concentration camp for two years in the mid-Seventies until Amnesty International managed to free him. Castro moved to San Francisco, continuing his artwork, focusing on countries in Central America that suffer from USA's military intervention. Bono and Castro agree to keep in touch.

JUNE 4, 1986. SAN FRANCISCO, CA, COW PALACE

- Attendance: 13,380 (P); sellout
- Line-up: The Neville Brothers, Joan Baez, Lou Reed, Jackson Browne, Peter Gabriel, Bryan Adams, Sting, U2
- Set: *C'mon Everybody / Pride / New Year's Day / Sunday Bloody Sunday / Maggie's Farm / Help / Bad / Sun City* / encore: *I Shall Be Released*

With only 45 minutes on stage each night, U2 select songs appropriate to the context of the show. The crowd rush the stage when the band come on. White flags pop out everywhere, U2 banners are draped over the balcony. Bono announces *C'Mon Everybody* but Edge has guitar problems. Bono unsuccessfully tries to fill up the vacuum by talking. "You've got it together, Edge? I've run out of story!" he calls, before the Eddie Cochran song gets the show rolling. During *Pride* Bono asks the crowd to "sing it for Martin Luther King, and every prisoner in every jail, wrongfully imprisoned." *Sunday Bloody Sunday* is played as the slow, acoustic version performed at Self Aid, and has optimal crowd participation. Larry goes up to the front of the stage with a single drum for *Maggie's Farm*. Tossed a scarf, Bono does a dramatic improvisation which leaves the

JUNE 6, 1986. LOS ANGELES, CA, THE FORUM

- Attendance: 15,944 (P); sellout
- Line-up: Joan Baez, The Neville Brothers, Lou Reed, Jackson Browne, Bob Dylan & Tom Petty and The Heartbreakers, Peter Gabriel, Bob Geldof & Dave Stewart, Bryan Adams, Sting, U2
- Set: *MLK / Pride / New Year's Day / Sunday Bloody Sunday / Maggie's Farm / Help / Bad / Sun City* / encore: *I Shall Be Released*

With the lights dimmed, save for a single spotlight, Bono sings one verse of *MLK*, before Edge starts *Pride* and the lights flash on. It replaces *C'Mon Everybody* as opener for the rest of the tour. The show is attended by a flock of special guests from the Hollywood and music scene, and there are several extra artists performing. Dave Stewart and Bob Geldof do a version of Bob Marley's *Get Up, Stand Up* between acts, while Bonnie Raitt, Don Henley, Joni Mitchell and Maria McKee join the all-star finale of *I Shall Be Released*. At the end Bono thanks concert promoter Bill Graham.

JUNE 8, 1986. DENVER, CO, McNICHOLS SPORTS ARENA

- Attendance: 8,368 (P); (reduced capacity 11,700)
- Line-up: Joan Baez, The Neville Brothers, Lou Reed, Peter Gabriel, Bryan Adams, Sting, U2
- Set: MLK / New Year's Day / Pride / Sunday Bloody Sunday / Maggie's Farm / Bad / Sun City / encore: I Shall Be Released

Pride and New Year's Day switch places for one show. Originally scheduled for Dallas, then Houston, the show in Denver fails to sell out even though the capacity is set low for McNichols standards (the maximum capacity of the arena is 17,000). The atmosphere is excellent nevertheless. Bono remarks after Pride, "For the best kept secret in Colorado you're making a lot of noise!" Bad includes parts of Amazing Grace, Biko and If You Love Somebody, Set Them Free. When coming back onstage for the finale, Bono announces that one of Amnesty's longtime employees celebrates her birthday. "Would you welcome the birthday girl herself: Mary Daly." Bono hands Mary a bouquet and leads the crowd in singing a round of Happy Birthday before Edge commences I Shall Be Released.

JUNE 10, 1986. ATLANTA, GA, RAMADA HOTEL LOUNGE

In Atlanta, the entire Amnesty entourage is booked into the Renaissance Ramada Hotel. After dinner, the company move to the lounge for drinks, and watch a local band. Peter Gabriel's drummer Manu Katche and Lou Reed's guitarist go over to the band and ask if they can play their instruments. No problem. Bono gets up and starts Lou Reed's Sweet Jane, moving towards the bar to sing it right in front of a young lady, making her the centre of his attention. The girl is flattered but whispers to Bono her name is Rose, not Jane. Bono proceeds to sing "Sweet Rose" instead. Later, Joan Baez, Peter Gabriel, The Neville Brothers, Bryan Adams, as well as Larry and Adam, join the jamming and sing rock and blues classics in high spirits for hours. At 4am the hotel manager chases them out of the lounge, so they sing on in the foyer. Lou Reed and Edge had gone to bed early and are sorry to have missed it when they hear about it the next morning.

JUNE 11, 1986. ATLANTA, GA, THE OMNI

- Attendance: 11,592 (P); sellout
- Line-up: Joan Baez, The Neville Brothers, Peter Gabriel, Bryan Adams, Lou Reed, U2, The Police
- Set: same as Los Angeles.

Sting reunites with his former band mates Andy Summers and Stewart Copeland to perform as The Police for the Atlanta, Chicago and Giants Stadium shows. Because they headline with U2 performing before them, Bad ends U2's show and the closing songs Sun City and I Shall Be Released are linked to The Police's set. During a soaring version of Sun City, Bono and Lou Reed belt out the refrain of Reed's song Vicious from his classic 'Transformer' album. After the show, the tour entourage again relax in their hotel lounge and, as a promise from Bono to Lou Reed who had missed the session the night before, everybody takes the stage for another jam session. Bono drags Lou onstage for them to sing Vicious together.

JUNE 13, 1986. CHICAGO, IL, ROSEMONT HORIZON

- Attendance: 16,625 (P); sellout
- Line-up: Joan Baez, The Neville Brothers, Peter Gabriel, Bryan Adams, Lou Reed, U2, The Police
- Set: same as Los Angeles.

The delirious Chicago crowd see U2 perform their best show of the year. During Bono's blindfold act during Maggie's Farm he picks up a spotlight and spins it around, illuminating the crowd. Tonight's version of Bad starts with lines from Norwegian Wood, and includes extended bits of Biko, Candle In The Wind, If You Love Somebody Set Them Free, as well as Marvin Gaye's Sexual Healing. "And when I get that feeling, you know I need sexual healing," he moans, breathing heavily. Sun City ends U2's set. Bono joins The Police for Invisible Sun.

JUNE 14, 1986. NEW YORK, NY, CENTRAL PARK

Giants' Stadium

The day before the final show there is an Anti-Apartheid rally in New York, with marchers from all over town coming together in Central Park. The estimated 60,000-strong crowd are addressed by Reverend Jesse Jackson. Black bands from New York perform between speeches. The rally takes a surprising turn when suddenly the 'Sun City performers' are announced. Peter Gabriel goes onstage to play *Biko*, then Black Uhuru perform, followed by Little Steven and his band who play a hard-hitting version of *Sun City*, during which U2 and most of the other Amnesty performers also take part. *Give Peace A Chance* is included as well.

JUNE 15, 1986. EAST RUTHERFORD, NJ, GIANTS' STADIUM

- Attendance: 50,207 (P); sellout
- Line-up: Joan Baez, The Neville Brothers, Jackson Browne, Peter Gabriel, Bryan Adams, Lou Reed, U2, The Police
- Set: *MLK / Pride / Bad / Sunday Bloody Sunday / Maggie's Farm / Help / Sun City /* with The Police: *Invisible Sun /* all-star finale: *I Shall Be Released*

The show is simulcast on MTV America and the Westwood One Radio Network. The bill is extended to create a 12-hour media event. Every five minutes or so, a toll-free phone number is given out, urging people to join Amnesty, donate money or request further information about the organisation and its cause. ZZ Top, Whitney Houston, Jeff Beck, Pete Townshend, Carlos Santana, Third World, Run DMC, Fela Kuti, Miles Davis, Patti LaBelle, and Sarah Vaughn all make appearances in between the usual acts.

I Shall Be Released. Bono, Peter Gabriel, Fela Kuti, Sting, Bryan Adams

On entering the stage, U2 are initially intimidated by the immense, blinding floodlights that MTV have lit, but *Pride* gets the show in full swing. Once again, Bono proves his ability to carry such a big, important event, turning the crowd into one huge mass of people voicing their disgust at world injustice, at the same time having millions of people at home on the edge of their seats. During *Maggie's Farm* Bono rages at the TV camera, aggressively repeating, "No more!" Nona Hendrix, Little Steven, Ruben Blades and Lou Reed accompany him in a blistering version of *Sun City*, which ends U2's set. Bono joins The Police for *Invisible Sun*, after which everyone on today's bill comes out for *I Shall Be Released*. Dozens of genuine prisoners of conscience come on stage hand in hand, all of them freed by Amnesty, to remind everyone what it is all about.

The six Conspiracy of Hope concerts draw a total of 116,116 people, grossing $4,041,935 for Amnesty, 75% of which is pure profit. In the weeks to follow, the organisation will double its membership in the United States, as over 35,000 apply

as a direct result of the tour and the Telethon. The public send out a combined 100,000 postcards and letters, which pressurize the governments involved and ultimately result in the release of hundreds of prisoners.

JUNE 28, 1986. SIMPLE MINDS: DUBLIN, IRELAND, CROKE PARK

Dublin band In Tua Nua play in support and please the crowd with their version of U2's *Two Hearts Beat As One*. For Amnesty's 25th anniversary, Simple Minds make a substantial financial contribution from their 'Once Upon A Time' tour and also support Amnesty by printing their logo on all tickets for the European tour. *Sun City* is included in their repertoire and during this particular performance, Bono makes a guest appearance. Jim Kerr gives him a hug and sings, "He is my friend, until the bitter end," while Bono receives a huge cheer from the crowd. They sing a medley of *Lovesong, Sun City* and *Dance To The Music* which lasts some 10 minutes.

JULY 8, 1986. WANGANUI, NEW ZEALAND, KAI-IWI MARAE

U2 crew member Greg Carroll is buried at Kai-Iwi Marae close to his hometown of Wanganui, five days after he is killed in a motorcycle accident in Dublin. Running an errand as a favour for Bono, Greg was hit by a car just outside the city centre.

His death is a tragedy for the U2 organisation. Having first met him in Auckland in 1984, Greg became a much loved member of the band's entourage. To pay their last respects, Larry, his girlfriend Ann, Bono and Alison, Joe O'Herlihy and Steve Iredale bring Greg's body to New Zealand, to be buried in Maori tribal tradition. "In the rock & roll business, the higher you climb the lonelier you become, the fewer people there are to turn to," Bono tells a reporter. "In the short time we had together, Greg became flesh and blood. He felt like my brother." At the funeral, Bono reads a poem he has written for him. Later, at the 'last supper', Bono is called up to sing. He delivers emotional versions of *Let It Be* and *Knocking On Heaven's Door*, accompanied by the violinist from a local band.

Back home in Dublin, Bono writes the song *One Tree Hill* about the funeral, naming it after the highest of the volcanic moulds that overlook the city of Auckland. Recording sessions for the new album start on August 1 with Brian Eno and Daniel Lanois producing. Bono spends some time visiting El Salvador and Nicaragua, on the invitation of René Castro. He incorporates his experiences in the new work.

JANUARY 9, 1987. AMSTERDAM, HOLLAND, PARADISO

The Dutch U2 fan club holds a convention with around 600 attending. Adam Clayton interrupts work on the final stages of the new album to make a quick appearance. He goes on stage to accept a gold album which fan club president Annelies de Haan is handing him on behalf of Ariola Records (Island's distributor for Holland). Adam tells how much he appreciates the award, as much as the fact that Holland was one of the first countries where U2 enjoyed success. Adam announces the performance of Irish band Tuesday Blue, who released a single on U2's Mother Records label, and joins them in the encore for a rendition of Them's *Gloria*. After the show he spends half an hour talking to fans, posing for photos, and signing autographs.

Adam in A'dam

MARCH 8, 1987. BELFAST, NORTHERN IRELAND, BALMORAL TV STUDIOS

- Set: *People Get Ready / Southern Man / Trip Through Your Wires / Exit / In God's Country / Pride*

U2 play live in public for the first time in eight months to showcase some new songs from 'The Joshua Tree' for the 'Old Grey Whistle Test', for broadcast three days later. Opening with a cover version of a Curtis Mayfield gospel song, the band's playing sounds shaky with Bono's singing in particular not yet strong enough to carry the songs. Bono plays guitar on a version of Neil Young's *Southern Man*. He introduces *Exit* as "a song about a religious man, a fanatic, who gets into his head the idea he calls 'the hands of love'." The small studio crowd have to get used to the new songs, but *Pride* gets them going.

After the TV recordings, the band go to the Belfast branch of Tower Records, which, like their shops in Dublin and London, opens at midnight to allow fans to be the first to buy 'The Joshua Tree'. The band sign albums and chat with fans. The album reaches platinum status in the UK in its first week of release, selling 300,000 copies and becoming the fastest selling record in the UK of all time.

MARCH 9, 1987

'The Joshua Tree' is released worldwide.

MARCH 13, 1987. DUBLIN, IRELAND, BOLAND'S MILL

Adam celebrates his 27th birthday at Boland's Mill in Dublin, the factory hall where U2 have been rehearsing for the upcoming 'Joshua Tree' tour. A country band play all evening, but at midnight U2 take over the stage and perform *People Get Ready*. The evening is heavy with emotion: their 300+ guests know now that U2 have arrived at a new plateau in their career and that they will be away the rest of the year playing to more fans around the world than ever before.

Fan club convention

the fans on the streets as well as the traffic chaos. *Where The Streets Have No Name* is played three times amid versions of *Sunday Bloody Sunday*, in which Bono inserts lines from the classic *Dancing In The Street*, and *Pride*, during which the Los Angeles police forbid U2 to continue and close down the generators. The crowd continue to sing the song as they slowly fade out.

The stunt is well co-ordinated and supplies ample footage for the video clip, generates publicity for U2 and fuels enthusiasm among fans. It also brings back echoes of The Beatles' final concert, also on a rooftop in a public place, documented in their movie 'Let It Be'. The event makes the news that night. With 'The Joshua Tree' having entered the American *Billboard* chart at No 7 (their first American top ten album) and tickets for the five upcoming shows at Los Angeles Sports Arena long gone, the town is in a state of U2 frenzy like never before. It is a foretaste of the enthusiasm that will accompany U2 in every city and country 'The Joshua Tree' tour will play during 1987.

'THE JOSHUA TREE' TOUR LEG 1: AMERICA, SPRING 1987

APRIL 2, 4, 1987. TEMPE, AZ, ARIZONA STATE UNIVERSITY ACTIVITY CENTER

- Attendance: 25,113 (P); sellout
- Support: Lone Justice
- Set first night: *Where The Streets Have No Name / I Still Haven't Found What I'm Looking For / Gloria / I Will Follow / Bullet The Blue Sky / Running To Stand Still / Exit / In God's Country / A Sort Of Homecoming / Sunday Bloody Sunday / Maggie's Farm / Bad / October / New Year's Day / Pride / encore: People Get Ready / 40*

Fittingly, the tour starts in a city that lies as an oasis in the desert of Arizona, where Joshua trees flourish despite the arid conditions. With the new album named after that cactus species, the Joshua tree has become a symbol for what lies at the heart of the album's songs: a belief in the human spirit, and its ability to survive amid personal, political and economical setbacks.

U2's stay in Tempe is not without its problems. While rehearsing *Bullet The Blue Sky* two days before opening night, Bono fell backwards off the stage and smacked himself in the face with the big spotlight that he uses for the song. His fall was broken by bass technician Fraser McAllister. Thoroughly shaken, Bono finished the song before he was taken to hospital to have his chin stitched up. After going through the entire show several times, the extensive rehearsals and the hot, dry, desert air affect Bono's vocal cords. At the tour première, with 12,500 fans and the world press eagerly awaiting, Bono is unable to sing.

As the house lights dim, the backdrop lights up in red and while the intro of *Where The Streets Have No Name* elicits screams from the crowd, the band come on one by one. "Hello! We missed you," Bono croaks out, and forces his way through the song with a voice that suggests he is at the end of a nine-year tour instead of at the start of a nine-month tour. He screws up the end of the song by doing another verse just when Edge hits the final notes. Before starting *I Still Haven't Found What I'm Looking For*, Bono pleads, "It looks like you have to help me with some singing tonight. It looks like for once, I'm stuck for words..." The audience sing along fervently throughout the show, filling in when Bono's voice cracks or unexpectedly disappears, besides joining in at traditional places in songs.

Bits of the Bob Marley songs *Exodus* and *Three Little Birds* are included in *I Still Haven't Found*. *Bullet The Blue Sky* is visually stunning, with a dozen or so lighting operators up in the rigging circling angry red spotlights over the stage and the crowd. Criticising American military intervention in El Salvador, the number captures the terror Bono felt when, during his trip to the country, he witnessed the bombing of a small village in the farmlands. Bono holds a light on Edge during his soaring guitar solo.

The stage set-up is simple but effective, with all the

MARCH 16, 1987. IRISH TV, RTE: 'THE LATE LATE SHOW'

U2 take part in a special tribute show to celebrate the 25th anniversary of Irish folk band The Dubliners. "I'm very proud to be part of this," says Bono. "I met Ronnie Drew along the road over the years, really love the man. Never met Luke Kelly; I saw him cross O'Connell Street once. Fiery red hair, would have loved to have met him. This is a song that you lot have inspired me with. It's your version of *Springhill Mining Disaster*."

After a delicate intro by Edge, Bono pours his heart and soul into the song, a lament for the victims of a mining disaster at Springhill, in the Canadian Province of Nova Scotia. Written by American folk singer Peggy Seeger and often performed by The Dubliners, its lyrics tell of miners trapped underground singing songs while waiting for a rescue team, trying to stay alive without food and water. "In the town of Springhill you don't live easy, often the earth will tremble and roar. When the earth is restless, miners die. Bone and blood is the price of coal..." At the end of the show, U2 join The Dubliners and The Pogues in a finale.

MARCH 27, 1987. LOS ANGELES, CA, LIQUOR STORE ROOFTOP AT 7TH AVENUE AND MAIN STREET

- Set: *Where The Streets Have No Name (playback) / People Get Ready / In God's Country / Where The Streets Have No Name / Sunday Bloody Sunday / Where The Streets Have No Name / Where The Streets Have No Name / Pride.*

Days before the start of the tour, U2 set up their gear on the roof of a liquor store in downtown Los Angeles to film a video for *Where The Streets Have No Name*, which will be released as a single later in the year. They play along to a tape of the song, then play it live. A radio station mentions the videoshoot on air and, inevitably, they attract the attention of passers-by. Before long thousands from all over town gather to watch the band play *People Get Ready* and *In God's Country* to an evergrowing mass of people who pack the sidewalks and eventually hold up the traffic in the street.

Several cameras on the roofs of nearby buildings and in a helicopter film the mini-concert and capture the enthusiasm of

speakers attached to the ceiling, leaving an unobstructed view of the stage for those at the side or the rear. Bono dedicates *Pride* to Martin Luther King, and refers briefly to the controversy in which the band found themselves on arrival in Arizona. State Governor Evan Mechum wants to abolish the national holiday in honour of Martin Luther King's birthday in Arizona. Stevie Wonder, The Doobie Brothers and other artists decided to cancel their Arizona shows in protest. U2 figured that instead of cancelling, it would be more effective to play and air their views. Before showtime, concert promoter Barry Fey read a statement of behalf of U2, that included the words, "Governor Mechum is an embarrassment to the people of Arizona. We condemn his actions and views as an insult to a great spiritual leader." U2 donated $5,000 to the Mechum Watchdog Committee, which was especially installed to oust the Governor.

Though Bono's defective voice didn't result in the tour première everyone had expected, the press react positively to the show. *The Phoenix Gazette*: 'Flying in the face of defeat is precisely what this band is about, and Bono and company showed a determination and spirit that would have convinced any unbeliever.'

■ Set second night: same as first show up to and including *October*; then: *With Or Without You / Pride /* encore: *MLK / The Unforgettable Fire / People Get Ready*

Originally planned for April 3, the second show is played a day later to allow Bono to recover. His voice has improved. "I can sing!" he calls out happily, but it's still shaky. During *Bad* he can't manage the "I'm wide awake" part and instead seeks a female companion from the audience to dance with. He stretches the song, singing or humming bits from *Ruby Tuesday*, *Sympathy For The Devil*, *Candle In The Wind*, *Walk On The Wild Side*, and even

Bowie's *John, I'm Only Dancing*. *With Or Without You* includes snippets of Joy Division's *Love Will Tear Us Apart*.

"We won't forget the way you've treated us over the last few days and especially when I couldn't sing the other night and people sang for me," Bono says during *People Get Ready*, after which he announces that *Time* magazine is preparing a cover story on U2. "So they brought along their photographer and he's gonna take a picture of us with you." The band line up for the photographer on the edge of the stage, with the crowd functioning as a lively background. Bono asks a guest guitarist up to entertain them while the photographer takes his shots, so a guy comes onstage and picks up *People Get Ready*. When the *Time* photographer is finished, Larry joins in again and the band add another cheerful verse to the song. (The photo does not end up on the cover; a posed group shot taken before the show is used instead.) Throughout the year, Bono will invite a guest guitarist from the crowd for this song, as he used to do for *Knocking On Heaven's Door*.

APRIL 5, 1987. TUCSON, AZ, COMMUNITY CENTER

■ Attendance: 8,032 (P); sellout
■ Support: Lone Justice
■ Set: *Where The Streets Have No Name / I Still Haven't Found / Gloria / I Will Follow / Bullet The Blue Sky / Running To Stand Still / Exit / In God's Country / A Sort Of Homecoming / Sunday Bloody Sunday / Maggie's Farm / Bad / October / With Or Without You / New Year's Day / Pride /* encore: *MLK / The Unforgettable Fire / Lucille / People Get Ready / 40.*

After talk of Bono's throat problems the audience may have been concerned but from the moment the show starts, it is clear

their worries are unfounded. The band play energetically, and are relieved that Bono can carry the show. He runs around the stage, up to his old antics: climbing on things, taking an Irish flag from a fan and tearing it into thirds, then triumphantly waving the white part above his head. Before *Pride* Bono talks of the group's admiration for Martin Luther King, suggesting that his own country had needed a man like him during the past 15 years. While on the subject, Bono sneers at Governor Mechum, passing a quick message up to him: "Boooh!"

The encore is a lot of fun with a new song, *Lucille*, premièred. "As a surprise I'd like to play you a country song that I wrote a few days ago," Bono announces. "I just hope you take it seriously, 'cause I come from Ireland and I don't want people laughing at me." The song has a simple one-two drum track with lyrics about a girl called Lucille who is asked to stay the night, and at the same time is confronted with, "I know our love will last forever, but will our love last the night?"

APRIL 7, 8, 1987. HOUSTON, TX, THE SUMMIT

■ Attendance: 27,251 (P); sellout
■ Support: Lone Justice
■ Set first night: *Where The Streets Have No Name / I Still Haven't Found / Gloria / I Will Follow / Bullet The Blue Sky / Running To Stand Still / A Sort Of Homecoming / Sunday Bloody Sunday / Exit / In God's Country / Bad / October / With Or Without You / New Year's Day / Pride /* encore: *MLK / The Unforgettable Fire / People Get Ready / 40 /* encore: *Trip Through Your Wires / Southern Man.*

Responding to long applause and an enthusiastic chant of "How long to sing this song", U2 return for an extra encore while the

1.

U2
— PLUS —
BUGS

PARADISO ● Wo. 11 Feb.
Entree : F.7.50. & F.2.50. Lidmaatschap
Voorverkoop: Cisca, Nieuwe Muziekhandel & RAF Platen.

2.

4.

3.

1.   U2's first major festival appearance: Leixlip
     Castle, July 27, 1980.

2 & 3. The UK 'October' tour fall 1981.

4.   Rainbow Music Hall, Denver, May 11, 1981

1.

1. Shortly before hitting the stage, Leiden, Holland, July 1, 1982

2. The beginning of the white flag-era: Werchter, July 4, 1982

3. Bono's first break-neck stunt, at Werchter.

4. Backstage at Werchter

5. Utrecht, Holland, December 8, 1982

2.

3.

4.

5.

1.

3.

1 & 2. Performing for Dutch TV in Hattem, May 14, 1982

3.   At the Werchter festival, July 4, 1982

2.

1.

2.

1.   Bono falls into the crowd at the US Festival, May 30, 1983

2 & 3. Dave Stewart and Jim Kerr make guest appearances at Werchter, July 3, 1983

4 & 5. The 'War' Tour in the UK

5.

3.

4.

1.

4.

2.

1, 2, 3 & 4.
'The Unforgettable Fire' tour hits Europe in October 1984

3.

1. Sunday Bloody Sunday in Rotterdam, October 30, 1984
2. You know how to play this? Knocking On Heaven's Door at Madison Square Garden, April 1, 1985
3. With Paul McCartney during the all-star finale of Do They Know It's Christmas at Live Aid.
4. Reaching out to the world; Live Aid, July 13, 1985.

1.

2.

3.

4.

1. U2 belt out Maggie's Farm at Self Aid

2 & 3. Self Aid, Dublin, May 17, 1986

4 & 5. The 'Conspiracy Of Hope' tour

1.

2.

3.

4.

5.

1. Adam outside San Diego Sports Arena, April 13, 1987

2. Bono sings Knocking On Heaven's Door with fans outside the hotel in San Diego, April 14, 1987

3. You too

4. The biggest selling magazine in the world. U2 becomes the fourth rock band ever to make the Time cover

2.

4.

3.

1. Clubs and theatres have become too small.
   With 72,000 fans at Wembley Stadium, June 12, 1987

2 & 3. The 'Joshua Tree' hits Chicago, October, 1987

4. Los Angeles, November 18, 1987

5. We'll be back for an encore

1.

2.

3.

4.

5.

1.

3.

1. The Dalton Brothers support in Los Angeles,
    November 18, 1987

2. Bono gets himself into trouble. San Francisco,
    November 11, 1987

3. Shooting 'Rattle And Hum', Tempe, December 20, 1987

1.

2.

1. Keith Richards guests at Smile Jamaica, London, October 16, 1988

3.

2. Adam with Maria McKee and Maria Doyle at Glastonbury, June 18, 1989

3. Busking at the 'Rattle And Hum' premiere, Los Angeles, November 4, 1988

4. Larry in Sydney on the 'LoveTown' tour, October 20, 1989

1. St. Patrick's Day in Boston Gardens, 1992

2. The Mirror Ball man

3. Bono as the helicopter commander during Bullet The Blue Sky

4. See the burning crosses; Bullet The Blue Sky

5. Zoo TV in Rotterdam, June 15, 1992

3.

2.

1. Satellite Of Love in Dortmund, June 4, 1992

2. Champagne anyone? Trying To Throw Your Arms Around The World

3. Edge in Boston, March 17, 1992

4. Axl Rose and Bono sing Knocking On Heaven's Door in Vienna, May 24, 1992

5. Kiel, June 13, 1992

4.

5.

1. She moves in Mysterious Ways. Rotterdam, May 11, 1993

2. It rained at the 'Zooropa' premiere

3. MacPhisto: Look what you've done to me...

4. The view from the field: Stuttgart, June 6, 1993

1.

2.

3.

1 & 3.
Even Better Than The Real Thing, UK, August 1993.

2.
Salman Rushdie, Wembley Stadium, August 11, 1993

1. Naomi Campbell on stage for Trying To Throw Your Arms Around The World, Dublin, August 28, 1993

2. Galway theatre group Macnass parody U2 at Wembley

3. Love Is Blindness. Dublin, August 28, 1993

Bullet The Blue Sky

APRIL 12, 1987. LAS VEGAS, NV, THOMAS & MACK ARENA

- Attendance: 8,673 (P); (capacity 9,700)
- Support: Lone Justice
- Set: *Where The Streets Have No Name / I Still Haven't Found / I Will Follow / Bullet The Blue Sky / Running To Stand Still / MLK / The Unforgettable Fire / Sunday Bloody Sunday / Exit / In God's Country / Gloria / Bad / October / With Or Without You / New Year's Day / Pride;* encore: *Trip Through Your Wires / People Get Ready / 40.*

Still experimenting with the songs and the order in which they should be played, U2 turn the set completely around. It's the first time they play this city and this is the only show of the Spring leg of the tour that doesn't sell out. Afterwards the band film the promotional video clip for *I Still Haven't Found*, miming the words while they walk around neon-lit casino-filled streets.

APRIL 13, 14, 1987. SAN DIEGO, CA, SPORTS ARENA

- Attendance: 27,937 (P); sellout
- Support: Lone Justice
- Set first night: *Where The Streets Have No Name / I Will Follow / I Still Haven't Found / MLK / The Unforgettable Fire / Bullet The Blue Sky / Running To Stand Still / A Sort Of Homecoming / Sunday Bloody Sunday / Exit / In God's Country / Gloria / Bad / October / New Year's Day / Pride;* encore: *With Or Without You / I Shall Be Released / 40.*

Not having played San Diego since the J. Geils tour in March 1982, U2 add a second show after all 13,500 tickets for the 13th sell out in a Sports Arena record of one hour and 17 minutes. Black market tickets fetch $100. A bizarre moment occurs halfway through *Pride* when Bono closes his eyes and announces that someone is sending him signals, good signals, that he knows who she is, and that she must join him on stage. A woman makes her way up from the middle of the audience and stands on stage, using sign language to translate the words Bono is singing. After the song Bono embraces her and leads her offstage, leaving the audience puzzled as to who she is and how Bono knew she was there.

Bob Dylan's *I Shall Be Released* is played during the encore and while Bono announces the song a fan manages to climb on stage and run towards him. "And here's Bob Dylan now," says Bono. "Sorry Bob, you'll have to go!"

- Set second night: same as previous show, but *Gloria* is played after *With Or Without You,* and *Mothers Of The Disappeared* replaces *40.*

Having entered the *Billboard* album chart at No 7, then moved to No 3, 'The Joshua Tree' jumps to No 1 on April 14. Bono tells the audience about their first American No 1 and admits the band weren't confident that the album and tour would be so successful. "This is the first time we've been out on a long tour with a record for about two years," he says. "It's good to see so many people coming out to see us play. I know that in San Diego they broke some sort of record with the tickets. When you make a record, you've been in a studio, which is like a big black hole, for a few months. When you come out you're kinda dazzled by the light. You put out the record and wonder if anyone is gonna buy it or will come out to see you."

When Edge starts *I Shall Be Released,* Bono announces a special guest: "I wanna thank Lone Justice for playing with us, and if we can find Maria McKee, maybe she'd sing this with me." Maria adds her voice to a thrilling duet, singing the second stanza alone. *Mothers Of The Disappeared* is played for the very first time. Like *Bullet The Blue Sky,* the song is a direct result of Bono's trips to El Salvador and Nicaragua, where he had met with mothers whose children had been the victims of fascist oppression. The song proves a worthy closing song, with Bono singing in a higher register than on the album.

After the show, a group of around 40 fans wait for U2 at the entrance to their hotel, and are delighted when they spend time talking and signing autographs. Offered an acoustic guitar,

Clannad tape that traditionally ends the show is playing and the house lights are up. Those making their way through the exits retrace their steps to hear U2 play *Trip Through Your Wires* and *Southern Man.*

- Set second night: same as first show, minus *People Get Ready* and *Southern Man,* with *40* as the final song.

The tour starts to take shape, with each concert better than the one before. The second show in Houston is superb, with an extended version of *I Still Haven't Found* during which Bono soulfully sings along with the audience. Introducing *A Sort Of Homecoming,* he says: "I've been reading how a lot of people had to leave their homes, their families to find work on other shores. The United States in particular holds a kind of special place for a lot of Irish people. Over the last hundred and more years Irish men and women brought with them songs and stories on the boats and on the planes to the United States and became a part of your music culture, and part of your folk music especially. More and more as I discover American music, blues music and

gospel music, I see a real connection with the music I come from. And so, this is for us truly a sort of homecoming."

After the show, U2 and their entourage move to a nightclub where the band end up playing some acoustic songs live, including Johnny Cash's *I Walk The Line,* Hank Williams' *Lost Highway,* and Bono's newly penned country song *Lucille.*

APRIL 10, 1987. LAS CRUCES, NM, PAN AMERICAN CENTER

- Attendance: 12,500 (P); sellout
- Support: Lone Justice
- Set: same as the first show in Houston, minus *40* and *Southern Man.*

This show is originally planned for El Paso, Texas, then Albuquerque, New Mexico, but is finally booked into a small town near the border of Texas and Mexico, marking the first time that U2 perform in this state.

Bono plays a quick version of *Lucille*, the recently-written country song also performed in Tucson, before he goes up to his room. The fans serenade the band with U2 songs from across the street. Edge appears on the balcony, chats with the fans, then gets a flashlight to introduce Adam and Larry, illuminating their faces. Larry gives a one-man show, taking off his shirt, flexing his muscles, then dropping his pants to flash his bare bottom to the crowd below. Later Bono comes down to join the fans and sits on the edge of a fountain in the little park in front of the hotel. Fans gather around and again somebody hands him guitar to sing *Lucille*, followed by *Knocking On Heaven's Door* and *I Still Haven't Found*.

Afterwards, U2 record a video message for the final edition of the popular rock programme 'The Tube', whose team directed and filmed U2's Red Rocks show. Sitting in their hotel room, Bono addresses the Tube team, saying it's a shame the programme is over, and starts singing an hilarious version of Hank Williams' country song *Lost Highway*. Edge plays acoustic guitar, Larry nonchalantly drums on the sofa, while Adam smokes a cigarette. Halfway into the song, Bono recalls, tongue-in-cheek: "Well, in 1983 we released our third LP. It was called 'War', and it did really well for us. It was the first time we ever made money from playing live, and with that money we decided to make a film of the group live: Red Rocks. It was called 'Under A Blood Red Sky' and was directed by Gavin Taylor. Well done Malcolm Gerrie and the Tube team. They were the first to play it – they played it A LOT. As a result, well, U2 has become the biggest kick-ass rock group in the world. Which was the last thing we wanted to be. What WE wanted to be was a country band, playing country music..." The whole band finish the song as a choir. It is broadcast on April 24.

Tempe, April 4, 1987

emotionally when Bono starts singing *Knocking On Heaven's Door*, another Dylan classic. A long version is played with improvisations from both Dylan and Bono. "You know, I usually make up my own words to Bob Dylan songs, he says he doesn't mind," Bono remarks. "Oh, I do it too!" Dylan adds his unmistakeable nasal voice. "What would be great is if we could take him on tour with us, then he could sing with us every night," Bono teases the crowd. "I'd like to thank you for coming out to see us. When we come back to Los Angeles, we're gonna see a thousand more bands in the streets... We're gonna see more songs like... like *Knocking On Heaven's Door*."

- Set fourth night: same as April 18, minus *Maggie's Farm* and *People Get Ready*, and *Sunday Bloody Sunday* is played before *40*.

- Set last night: *Stand By Me / MLK / Pride / Trip Through Your Wires / I Will Follow / Bullet The Blue Sky / Running To Stand Still / The Unforgettable Fire / Sunday Bloody Sunday / Exit / In God's Country / Electric Co. / October / New Year's Day / Gloria / Bad* / encore: *Where The Streets Have No Name / I Still Haven't Found / With Or Without You / 40*.

U2 surprise their audience for the fifth and final night in Los Angeles. As *Stand By Me* is heard on the intermission tape, the crowd execute Mexican waves, becoming more and more vocal with each wave. Suddenly Bono comes out on stage while the roadies are still working and lights are still on. He grabs the microphone and starts singing along with the tape, then the rest of the band come out and take their positions and as the tape slowly fades out, U2 take the song over live with Bono improvising. "Sing it Edge!" Bono shouts and holds the microphone in front of Edge who doesn't know the lyrics. With the audience screaming in amazement, all lights go out and *MLK* is played in total darkness. Then U2 launch into *Pride* and the show is rolling.

"I know a lot of you went to a lot of trouble to get tickets for tonight," Bono says. "Don't let anyone take advantage of the fact that you are into the music. There's a lot of guys outside charging too much for tickets for U2 concerts; we don't like it." *Electric Co.* is played for the first time this tour and for the first time since October 1980 it is performed without the brief, sharp-edged *The Cry* preceding it. Bono includes lines of The Doors' *Light My Fire* during the climax of the song. He continues to do so throughout the tour.

APRIL 17, 18, 20, 21, 22, 1987. LOS ANGELES, CA, SPORTS ARENA

- Attendance: 74,176 (P); sellout
- Support: Lone Justice
- Set first night: same as first show in San Diego.

With five sellouts at the Sports Arena there still is a shortage of tickets and scalpers take advantage of the huge demand, selling tickets in the streets around the venue for $100 to $200, depending on the position of the seat in the arena.

- Set second night: *Where The Streets Have No Name / I Will Follow / I Still Haven't Found / MLK / The Unforgettable Fire / Bullet The Blue Sky / Running To Stand Still / Exit / In God's Country / Sunday Bloody Sunday / Maggie's Farm / Bad / October / New Year's Day / Pride* / encore: *With Or Without You / Gloria / People Get Ready / 40*.

During the intro of *I Still Haven't Found* Bono recalls the first show U2 played in Los Angeles and says he hopes the few hundred people that were there then are present tonight as well. Halfway through *Sunday Bloody Sunday* he talks about Amnesty International and urges fans to browse around their stand in the arena's lobby. "When you leave the building you

might meet some people from Amnesty International. They're good people, Amnesty International is a good thing. Whether it is Belfast or Beirut, whether it's torture, capital punishment or false imprisonment of prisoners of conscience: say after me one thing... NO MORE!"

- Set third night: same as April 18, with *I Shall Be Released* and *Knocking On Heaven's Door* replacing *People Get Ready*.

"What a week for us," says Bono before *I Still Haven't Found*. "Number 1 on the *Billboard* charts, on the cover of *Time* magazine... I want our records on the radio, I want people to come and see us play, it's good. All this success is something, but the thing about success is that just because we can sing in tune, doesn't mean we got any more answers than you've got. Just a whole pile of questions...

"We were over here earlier with the Conspiracy of Hope tour, we heard Amnesty International *doubled* the amount of people that belong to them, so that's pretty good. We learned the chords to *I Shall Be Released*. I can't remember who wrote it," Bono says, and after the first stanza exclaims, "Will you welcome Bob Dylan!" Accompanied by loud cheering, Dylan arrives on stage for an inspired duet in which Bono appears to know the lyrics better than Bob himself. The audience react

APRIL 24, 25, 1987. SAN FRANCISCO, CA, COW PALACE

- Attendance: 25,785 (P); sellout
- Support: Lone Justice
- Set first night: same as first show in San Diego, minus *I Shall Be Released*, and *Gloria* is played before *40*.

- Set second night: *Where The Streets Have No Name / I Will Follow / Trip Through Your Wires / I Still Haven't Found / MLK / The Unforgettable Fire / Bullet The Blue Sky / Running To Stand Still / Exit / In God's Country / Sunday Bloody Sunday / Electric Co. / Bad / October / Springhill Mining Disaster / New Year's Day / Pride* / encore: *Mothers Of The Disappeared / With Or Without You / 40*.

During the soundcheck in the afternoon U2 rehearse their version of *Silver And Gold*, the song that Bono wrote for the 'Sun City' album and performed acoustically with Keith Richards and Ron Wood helping out on guitar. On the version that U2 rehearse Edge plays a completely different guitar melody than will later appear on U2's studio take of the song.

Big peace demonstrations are held that day in Washington DC and San Francisco, where some 50,000 people march for peace and justice. Many in the audience have been at the march and cheer Bono on as he raps in *Bullet The Blue Sky*: "And there's some people gathered in the streets of San Francisco... how many? One thousand! Two thousand! Three thousand! Four thousand! Five thousand! They don't wanna hear those fighter

Hotel lobby, San Diego

planes. Across the trenches where the children sleep, and to the aisles of the quiet city streets, we gather in a square... how many? Millions. Turn the key and slowly unlock the door... it's our door that's why, and WE hold the key to that lock, and if we can't open it, we're gonna knock it down... I hear a man breathe into a saxophone and through the walls we hear the city groan. Outside it's America, it's San Francisco, yeah!"

Many songs have long introductions. "This is a song inspired by a very dangerous drug called heroin. A drug that has taken the lives of some of my friends, has destroyed areas of the city I come from, has destroyed areas of this city. While rich men put dirty dollars in the back of their pockets, others are lying with hypodermic needles stuck into their veins, stuck into their eyes, stuck into their fingernails... This is *Bad*."

After *October* Bono says, "This next song we've never played before. Well, we played it once, on a TV show called 'The Late Late Show' back home. We were doing a special on a group called The Dubliners, which are the best folk guys out of Ireland. Of course we always really deep down always wanted to be a folkband, so... This song was written by an American, Peggy Seeger, and it's a song that I wish I'd heard on the radio around about the time of the miners' strike in England. It's called *Springhill Mining Disaster*." Larry adds dramatic touches to the song with a single drum and tambourine, while Bono sings a heartbreaking version that keeps the audience silent and still. "Listen to the shouts of the black-faced miners, listen to the calls of the rescue team. We have no water, light or bread, so we're living on songs and hope instead..." The song is a worthy addition to U2's evergrowing list of cover versions; its lyrical contents sit well amidst U2's own songs and its spirit matches the ideas behind 'The Joshua Tree'.

During *Pride* Bono calls a worker for Amnesty International up on stage to state the Amnesty credo and explain what the organisation stands for. During *Mothers Of The Disappeared* Bono asks the audience: "How many people do you think are still in camps, in prison cells across the world for no reason? How many do you think?" He chants, "Four, five, six," counting up to twenty and then by fives up to 100, and then by hundreds up to 500. The audience call out the even figures while Bono

does the uneven figures. Bono thanks the audience and says, "It's not just up to us, it's up to you!" The crowd are impressed. After the show they visit the Amnesty booths in the lobby in large numbers to become members, sign petitions demanding the release of political prisoners or to just donate money which helps Amnesty continue their fight for human rights.

APRIL 29, 1987. CHICAGO, IL, ROSEMONT HORIZON

- Attendance: 16,854 (P); sellout
- Support: Lone Justice
- Set: same as April 25, minus *Electric Co.* and plus *Gloria* before *40*.

While Bono concentrates on singing *Springhill Mining Disaster*, some fans whistle and scream hysterically, causing him to spit out, "Shut up for a second, will ya? Stop whistling 'cause I'm not in The Beatles OK, it's U2 here!" During *Pride* Bono reminisces about the Amnesty tour. "When we came through here on the Conspiracy of Hope tour, I could just feel something happening. People, all the cities, factories, schools and artists – everybody just kinda wakening up or something. It's great!"

APRIL 30, 1987. PONTIAC, MI, SILVERDOME

- Attendance: 51,718 (P); sellout
- Support: Lone Justice
- Set: same as April 13, minus *I Shall Be Released*, and *Gloria* is played before *40*.

U2 play their first headlining stadium show in America in this gigantic, covered stadium just outside Detroit. Although it is the only stadium date of this leg of the tour, it represents the beginning of a new era for U2. Thousands of fans are unpleasantly surprised by the choice of venue, and talk flares up. Many fans are indignant, resenting the band's decision not to do two or three shows in a smaller venue like Joe Louis Arena. Others, however, feel it makes sense, that it's unavoidable for a fast-growing band like U2 to take this step at some point. The choice of venue does not hamper ticket sales. Although the show only sells out completely thirty minutes before the show, all 51,718 tickets are sold.

During *I Still Haven't Found* Bono sees a security guard acting roughly towards a fan and, as usual, he speaks up for the fan and shouts to the guard to take it easy. When the song ends the situation in front of the stage becomes unpleasant as thousands push forward to get the best spot. "Just take it easy in the front, everybody ease back a little bit, OK," Bono says, then continues laughing, "Some people down there look like they smell real bad!

Lucille

TOUR U2 87

Special Guest LONE JUSTICE

THURSDAY, APRIL 30 ● 8 P.M.
PONTIAC SILVERDOME
"Only Michigan Appearance"

TICKETS ON SALE NOW!
AVAILABLE AT ALL TICKETMASTER OUTLETS
TO CHARGE CALL (313) 423-6666
A CELLAR DOOR PRODUCTION

Moving to stadiums

Pushing in the crowd

Got some real body odour problems here!" He suggests people take a step back or even move up along the aisles to create more space for people to breathe. It works. Bono is proud to show the security guards they don't have to interfere. "See, I told them we could look after ourselves..."

The local press find that U2's first American stadium show succeeds in reaching its goal. 'U2 Bring Intimacy To The Silverdome' reads the headline of the review in the *Detroit Free Press*. There is some criticism concerning technical aspects: 'Because U2 are playing arenas on this current US swing, its lighting rig was undersized for a stadium. A larger and more intense system would be in order for future stadium dates. A video screen is a must for those as well. Past the half-way point on the floor, the members of U2 were veritable ants onstage. Having close-ups of the onstage action would only enhance U2's goal of creating a communal spirit in concert. Fortunately, technical inadequacies are the easiest to fix. If the quality of U2's performance remains as high as it was at the Silverdome, there's no doubt the group will be able to put on some of the best rock stadium shows ever.'

MAY 2, 3, 4, 1987. WORCESTER, MA, CENTRUM

■ Attendance: 37,482 (P); sellout
■ Support: Lone Justice
■ Set first night: same as second show in San Francisco, minus *Electric Co.* and *Mothers Of The Disappeared*, and plus *Gloria* before *40*.

"You, in Boston and all around this area, have seen so many Irish people have come over across the Atlantic ocean, these Irish immigrants, they brought with them old Irish folk songs which soon became old American folk songs..." When Bono starts *Springhill Mining Disaster* the crowd are again rowdy and he has to quieten them down before he can sing the song.

■ Set second night: *Where The Streets Have No Name / I Will Follow / I Still Haven't Found / MLK / The Unforgettable Fire / Bullet The Blue Sky / Running To Stand Still / A Sort Of Homecoming / Sunday Bloody Sunday / Exit / In God's Country / Trip Through Your Wires / C'Mon Everybody / Bad / October / New Year's Day / Pride /* encore: *With Or Without You / 40*.

U2 continue to change the set and insert *C'Mon Everybody* which, just like its last performance in San Francisco in 1986, starts out problematically. "Eddie Cochran having a bit of trouble with his foot switches here," Bono jokes. The strong hook of the song is reinforced by Larry's tight drum beats and Edge's gritty guitar sound and it becomes a rocking version with references to Boston in the lyrics. "Another classic trashed by U2," Bono says afterwards. During *Pride* he introduces his cousin A.J., who works as a roadie on the tour, and then points out the film crew of the Irish TV programme 'Today Tonight' who film for a TV special. After the show the TV crew interview fans in the lobby of the arena. "I sang, I laughed, I cried, the whole thing," says one girl. "They bring everyone together; it's not like everyone's in their own little world, like at most concerts," says another. Interviewer: "Some people say, a band from outside this country shouldn't be coming in here and talking about your own domestic politics." A guy reacts fervently: "Today, Americans don't see, they're too isolated. We don't get the Continental view that Europeans get. We only get one influence: America. We have no influences from other parts of the world. You look to the north, well, Canada doesn't give you much, and Mexico is Third World practically. Americans don't even know the geography of Central America – if it wasn't for people coming in from other parts of the world telling us what we're doing there, we'd never know."

■ Set third night: *Stand By Me / Pride / MLK / The Unforgettable Fire / Bullet The Blue Sky / Running To Stand Still / Sunday Bloody Sunday / Exit / In God's Country / Trip Through Your Wires / Electric Co. / October / New Year's Day / Gloria / Bad / encore: Where The Streets Have No Name / I Will Follow / I Still Haven't Found / With Or Without You / 40.*

Opening with *Stand By Me* with the houselights still on works extremely well again, surprising the audience and establishing an atmosphere of exhilaration for the rest of the night. It also indicates that U2 will perform this trick at the last show in cities they play on multiple dates. Bono mentions several times that Boston was the first city in America to support U2 and that they have good memories of their shows at Boston's Paradise Theater in 1980 and 1981. He dedicates *I Will Follow* to the 'Paradise people'.

MAY 7, 8, 9, 1987. HARTFORD, CIVIC CENTER

■ Attendance: 47,327 (P); sellout
■ Support: Lone Justice
■ Set first night: *Where The Streets Have No Name / I Will Follow / I Still Haven't Found / People Get Ready / Trip Through Your Wires / MLK / The Unforgettable Fire / Bullet The Blue Sky / Running To Stand Still / Exit / In God's Country / C'mon Everybody / Bad / October / Springhill Mining Disaster / Sunday Bloody Sunday / New Year's Day / Pride / encore: With Or Without You / Gloria / encore: 40.*

People Get Ready is played early in the set and Bono wants to sing it "for somebody really special to me: my big brother Norman," who is present at the show and who "taught me how to play guitar, he taught me about three or four chords and that's all you need to write it." The audience try to sing along but don't know the words very well, and Bono is surprised an Irishman has to recite the words of an American folk song to Americans.

■ Set second night: same as second show in Worcester, plus *Springhill Mining Disaster* after *October, Mothers Of The Disappeared* after *Pride*, and *Gloria* before *40*.

During *Pride* Bono asks the audience to sing along "for the best road crew in the whole world. I want you to sing this for one man of the road crew: his name is Cody, his lady's name is Jane and they just got a little baby today called Christine Ray. That's the power of love!"

■ Set third night: same as third show in Worcester, but *I Still Haven't Found* is played after *Trip Through Your Wires.*

MAY 11, 12, 13, 15, 16, 1987. EAST RUTHERFORD, NJ, MEADOWLANDS ARENA

■ Attendance: 102,640 (P); sellout
■ Support: Lone Justice
■ Set first night: same as second show in Worcester, plus

Springhill Mining Disaster after *October*, and *Gloria* before *40*. When Bono welcomes the audience with a hoarse "How ya doing?" it sounds as if his voice has suffered too much from his 27th birthday party the night before, but after a few songs he gets in full swing. He reveals that *Trip Through Your Wires* almost didn't make the album, but is glad that it did. After the song he comments on some of the press the band are getting. "People keep saying that this band must be taking themselves too seriously because we look so serious on our photographs and stuff. So, just to prove we don't take ourselves so seriously... have you heard U2 do Eddie Cochran?" Bono is eager to start *C'Mon Everybody*, but again Edge has difficulty starting the song. Bono changes the text: "Well, c'mon everybody let's get to Meadowlands tonight. Well New Jersey's OK and I'm gonna stay here all night..."

Bono asks the exuberant crowd to keep quiet for *Springhill Mining Disaster*, and unlike at some previous shows the crowd really are quiet. The audience are up on their feet the whole night but many sit down to listen to the song. "Hold on a second," Bono says somewhat confused after the song. "I just have to tell you something: I've never seen people sitting down at a U2 concert! This is amazing! And I'm not sure if I like it! Up on your feet!" he calls, probably for the first time in four or five years.

■ Set second night: same as first show in Worcester, plus *Electric Co.* and *People Get Ready* before *Bad*, and minus *Gloria*.

Bono sings *People Get Ready* for someone special: "Her first ever rock & roll concert, and that's Edge's little baby girl called Holly, she's here..." During *40* a girl comes running onstage and embraces Bono. "You see, that's what happens when your record goes to Number 1: you get all the beautiful girls!"

■ Set third night: same as second show in Worcester, minus *C'Mon Everybody.*

■ Set fourth night: *Where The Streets Have No Name / I Will Follow / Trip Through Your Wires / People Get Ready / I Still Haven't Found / MLK / The Unforgettable Fire / Bullet The Blue Sky / Running To Stand Still / Exit / In God's Country /Sunday Bloody Sunday / Maggie's Farm / C'Mon Everybody / Trip Through Your Wires / Bad / October / Springhill Mining Disaster / New Year's Day / Pride / encore: With Or Without You / Gloria / 40*

With 23 songs, the longest of the tour so far, this show is the first of around twenty shows on the tour to be recorded by Jimmy Iovine for possible use on U2's next album. Surprisingly, *Trip Through Your Wires* is played twice. "I wanna do *Trip Through Your Wires* again, I think we played it pretty shit the first time."

Bono's wife is present at the show. During *C'Mon Everybody* he sings: "Well, I got my own baby and she's sitting in the front row good. Well, she says I'm bad, but she knows that I feel so good..."

■ Set last night: same as third show in Worcester, but *I Still Haven't Found* is played after *Trip Through Your Wires*, and *Springhill Mining Disaster* replaces *October*.

Starting with *Stand By Me*, the 'Last Night In Town' set is played to end a successful five-night stint and the first leg of the tour. A few days of rest follow before the band embark on the European tour.

The 29 concerts of the first leg of the tour generate $7,501,329 with a total of 465,452 tickets sold. Only 1,063 tickets remain unsold in Las Vegas, which means the tour is a 99.77% sellout.

'THE JOSHUA TREE' TOUR LEG 2: EUROPE, SUMMER 1987

By the time the tour reaches Europe, 'The Joshua Tree' has sold seven million copies, topped the charts in 22 countries, and is still going strong. U2 appear on magazine covers everywhere; their back catalogue and video sales flourish. The album has propelled U2 from being a band with a large cult-following to a supergroup at the highest level of success. Not wishing to exclude new fans from seeing them, U2 decide to play stadiums, as well as some indoor dates. The United Kingdom is well represented with five open-air concerts and six indoors, while Ireland finally gets plenty of attention with two Croke Park shows, and one each in Cork and Belfast. Dates for the mainland of Europe, however, are

scarce. Only fifteen shows are booked, three each in Germany, Italy and France, two in Holland, and single shows for Spain, Belgium, Switzerland, and Scandinavia. Though most of these are at stadiums, the number of tickets available doesn't come close to meeting the demand.

As a result, ticket sales are beset by public disorder in virtually every country. If tickets go on sale on Saturday, people start queueing on Thursday. When box offices open, it is usually so crowded that people become rowdy, leading to scenes where police have to conduct military-like operations to control crowds. In Holland, all 92,000 available tickets sell out in one hour, with streets so jammed that dozens of people are pushed through shop windows. In Glasgow, some 12,000 people queue at the primary sales outlet for the Edinburgh show, but when it becomes known that there are only 2,500 tickets available, fights erupt. The police use tear gas to break up the crowd, then see their bus turned over and set on fire. More than 250 fans are arrested.

Extra shows are added where possible, but with the European leg already taking all summer, and a four-month American tour set to commence in September, U2 have to protect their valuable days off. On numerous occasions the band fly to and from Dublin in between shows. This enables the band to have some time to themselves in an already exhausting tour, and also allows them to go into the studio and record new songs for the B-sides of the next few singles.

For the open-air shows, the band decide not to use video screens, preferring a minimalistic setting to let the music speak for itself. A huge, blurry image of a Joshua tree is painted on the backdrop that covers the amplifiers and the back of the stage.

A wide variety of bands are selected to play in support, with two to four groups lined up for the outdoor shows to give good value for money.

MAY 27, 1987. ROME, ITALY, STADIO FLAMINIO

- Attendance: 35,000; sellout
- Support: Lone Justice, Big Audio Dynamite, The Pretenders
- Set: *Where The Streets Have No Name / I Will Follow / Trip Through Your Wires / I Still Haven't Found / MLK / The Unforgettable Fire / Bullet The Blue Sky / Running to Stand Still / Exit / In God's Country / Sunday Bloody Sunday / Help / Bad / October / New Year's Day / Pride / encore: With Or Without You / 40*

The first show of the European tour is also U2's first open-air show of the year. The audience give U2 an extremely warm welcome. Bono is suffering from a sore throat but the audience fill in for him.

MAY 29, 30, 1987. MODENA, ITALY, STADIO COMUNALE BRAGLIA

- Attendance: 80,000; sellout
- Support: Lone Justice, Big Audio Dynamite, The Pretenders
- Set first night: *Where The Streets Have No Name / I Will Follow / I Still Haven't Found / MLK / The Unforgettable Fire / Bullet The Blue Sky / Running To Stand Still / Exit / In God's Country / Sunday Bloody Sunday / Maggie's Farm / Bad / October / New Year's Day / Pride / encore: Party Girl / Trip Through Your Wires / Gloria / With Or Without You / People Get Ready / 40*

Bono announces *I Still Haven't Found* in Italian and lets the audience sing half of the first verse. During *Trip Through Your Wires* a football is thrown on stage. Bono asks, "Have you got a good football team here? What are they called? Who is the best player?" The crowd scream several names. "What's his name? THE EDGE?" They play the slow version of *Sunday Bloody Sunday*, as performed in 1986, with Edge playing the intro and Larry and Adam waiting until Bono has sung the first two verses. This version will continue to show up at most concerts the rest of the year. During *People Get Ready* Edge plays bass, and Bono remarks he has never done that on the song before. The guy that comes onstage to play guitar fails to impress and Bono sings, "God have mercy, you're a hopeless guitar player! You even make me feel better, you son of a bitch..."

- Set second night: *Where The Streets Have No Name / I Will Follow / I Still Haven't Found / MLK / The Unforgettable Fire / Bullet The Blue Sky / Running To Stand Still / A Sort Of Homecoming / Sunday Bloody Sunday / Exit / In God's Country / Help / Bad / October / New Year's Day / Pride / encore: Party Girl / With Or Without You / 40*

During *Pride* Bono calls out, "Cantate! La gente Irlandese e quella Italiana hanno spirito vicino." ("Sing it! Irish people and the Italians have a kindred spirit.")

JUNE 2, 1987. LONDON, ENGLAND, WEMBLEY ARENA

- Attendance: 12,000; sellout
- Support: Hurrah!
- Set: same as first night in Modena, plus *C'Mon Everybody* before *Bad*, *Springhill Mining Disaster* after *October*, and minus *People Get Ready*.

When both Wembley Stadium shows sell out, this arena show is added to cater to those who don't want to see U2 in a stadium. This tactic of playing a small venue in the same city where big

'The Joshua Tree' tour reaches Europe

open-air shows are later planned is used in other cities like Paris, Boston and Philadelphia. During the ominous bass intro of *Exit*, Bono again mentions that the song is about "a religious man who became a very dangerous man when he failed to work out the hands of love", but this time adds: "You could call him Ian Paisley, yeah sure! You can put anyone you like in that spot, put me in the spot." With the upcoming elections in the UK in the back of his mind, during *Maggie's Farm* Bono says: "Well, you've got a few days to make up your mind. We sing songs about our country being divided, tonight we sing this song for your country because it also is divided. I'm not going to tell you how to vote, but you will all be voting, won't you? Sing for me: I ain't gonna work on Maggie's farm no more..." During *C'Mon Everybody* Bono makes no secret of his political opinion as he improvises, "Well, I like to hear it good and I like to hear it go real slow / You know I fancy Margaret Thatcher but I think she's gonna have to go..."

JUNE 3, 1987. BIRMINGHAM, ENGLAND, NATIONAL EXHIBITION CENTRE

- Attendance: 11,000; sellout
- Support: Hurrah!
- Set: same as May 29, minus *Party Girl*, *Trip Through Your Wires* and *Gloria*; *People Get Ready* is played after *Maggie's Farm*, followed by *Knocking On Heaven's Door*.

At the end of *People Get Ready* Bono asks his guest guitarist if he's in a band. He is. "Is the whole band here?" The guy says yes and proceeds to call his fellow-band members up on stage. In no time the whole band are onstage and are given some extra instruments. Bono chats with them and together they end up playing a messy version of *Knocking On Heaven's Door* with the guest singer ending the song.

JUNE 6, 1987. GOTHENBURG, SWEDEN, ERIKSBERG

- Attendance: 50,000; sellout
- Support: Lone Justice, Big Audio Dynamite, The Pretenders
- Set: *Where The Streets Have No Name / I Will Follow / I Still Haven't Found / MLK / The Unforgettable Fire / Bullet The Blue Sky / Running To Stand Still / Exit / In God's Country / Sunday Bloody Sunday / Bad / Springhill Mining Disaster / New Year's Day / Pride / encore: Party Girl / With Or Without You / People Get Ready / 40*

This show is originally booked for the Ullevi Stadium but has to be moved because repairs to the stadium, necessitated after 60,000 Bruce Springsteen fans jumped up and down too vigorously two years earlier, are still being carried out. Eriksberg shipyard is chosen as the new location and after two weeks of work on the stage and carpeting, the site is ready. Thousands of fans travel from Denmark, Finland, Norway and all over Sweden to attend U2's only Scandinavian show of the year. Around 500 tickets are put on sale only a few hours before the show as a deterrent to scalpers. The band arrive by plane in the afternoon and fly back to Dublin immediately afterwards for a few days off. Before the show U2 receive a gold record for 'The Joshua Tree' for sales in Sweden. It rains all night which prompts Bono to include snippets of The Beatles' *Rain* at the end of *I Still Haven't Found*. Though the atmosphere is spirited at the front of the stage, halfway down the field the crowd are cold and can't see a thing. The pushing up front becomes really bad and around 1,000 people have to be pulled out of the crowd. U2 fail to ignite the crowd and the evening goes down as one of the least memorable nights on the tour.

JUNE 12, 13, 1987. LONDON, ENGLAND, WEMBLEY STADIUM

- Attendance: 144,000; sellout
- Support (first night): World Party, Spear of Destiny, The Pretenders; (second night): Lone Justice, The Pogues, Lou Reed
- Set first night: *Where The Streets Have No Name / I Will Follow / I Still Haven't Found / MLK / The Unforgettable Fire / Bullet The Blue Sky / Running To Stand Still / Sunday Bloody Sunday / Exit / In God's Country / Trip Through Your Wires / Bad / October / New Year's Day / Pride / encore: Party Girl / Gloria / With Or Without You / 40*

Audience reaction is extremely warm at both these sellout shows at the massive Wembley Stadium, where U2 play for roughly as many people as *all* their UK shows from the previous two tours put together (28 shows in 1983, 10 in 1984, and 1 in 1985).

- Set second night: *Stand By Me / Pride / I Still Haven't Found / MLK / The Unforgettable Fire / Sunday Bloody Sunday / Exit / In God's Country / C'Mon Everybody / Help / Bad / October / New Year's Day / I Will Follow / Gloria / encore: Where The Streets Have No Name / Bullet The Blue Sky / Running To Stand Still / With Or Without You / Party Girl / 40*

The *Stand By Me* opening is premièred in Europe. Edge sings a whole verse. During *Pride* Bono exuberantly reminds the audience of Live Aid: "Two years ago we played on this stage and a great work was done in the name of love. Have you forgotten? I haven't forgotten! So we continue – in the name of love..." Before segueing into Them's *Gloria* during *Exit*, Bono asks, "Do you believe in soul music? I learned this song from a soul singer from Belfast, his name is Van Morrison, song goes something like this... Gloria, G-L-O-R-I-A..."

Bullet The Blue Sky is moved to the encore for all European open-air shows (except for Madrid), in order to take full advantage of lighting conditions. The fiery red spotlights produce a breathtaking sight as they drift over the extensive field and illuminate the crowd. The song ends with, "I was walking through the streets of London, walking through the streets of Kilburn, Brixton and Harlesden, and I felt I was a long way from San Salvador, but still, the sky was ripped open, the rain pouring through the gaping wound, pelting the women and children, waiting in line to the hospitals, waiting in line to pick up money, pelting the women and children who run... who run into the arms of Margaret Thatcher..."

JUNE 15, 1987. PARIS, FRANCE, LE ZENITH

- Attendance: 7,000; sellout
- Support: Lone Justice
- Set: same as June 12, plus Help and Springhill Mining Disaster before Bad, and Sweet Jane after Party Girl.

This is the first of only four indoor shows on the mainland of Europe. Maria McKee comes on stage during Party Girl to serve champagne, and drinks a glass with Bono. "There's no justice like Lone Justice!" he cries, and announces Sweet Jane, Lou Reed's classic and Maria's favourite rock & roll song. "Here's a little song that we learned from this girl," and they burst into a rugged version. Bono and Maria try to outdo each other vocally, and the duet goes into the Stones' Satisfaction and ends with inspired bawling.

JUNE 17, 1987. COLOGNE, GERMANY, MÜNGERSDORFER STADION

- Attendance: 67,000; sellout
- Support: Big Audio Dynamite, Lou Reed, The Pretenders
- Set: Stand By Me / C'Mon Everybody / I Will Follow / I Still Haven't Found / MLK / The Unforgettable Fire / Sunday Bloody Sunday / Exit / In God's Country / Electric Co. / Help / Bad / New Year's Day / Pride / encore: Bullet The Blue Sky / Running To Stand Still / With Or Without You / Party Girl / 40

C'Mon Everybody follows Stand By Me. Electric Co. is played for the first time on the European tour. A second date for the 18th is printed on the official T-shirts but does not take place. Rain and poor organisation lead to a bad atmosphere, and thousands of fans are victims of the promoter's senseless bureaucratic procedure. Those with vouchers have trouble exchanging them for actual tickets as there is only one exchange booth outside the stadium. Irritation is fuelled when, after a long wait, fans are told that in order to obtain their tickets, they need to show identification papers, which most people don't carry with them

to the show. The number on the vouchers is meticulously compared against a list and it all takes far too long and thousands are still queueing in the rain when the gates are opened and the support bands take the stage. Not until the support acts have finished, with the stadium practically full, do the organisers decide that vouchers can serve as tickets. Inside the stadium, several disturbances occur in the audience. A display stand selling candy and sweets is looted and boxes of sweets are thrown into the crowd. Worse, the crowd loudly cheer their 'heroes' on for supplying them with candy for free.

During the show Bono has trouble connecting with the audience and doesn't tell his usual stories. Those in the back of the stadium have trouble hearing the show as the sound is distorted by gusts of wind.

JUNE 21, 1987. BASEL, SWITZERLAND, ST. JAKOB'S STADION

- Attendance: 40,000; (capacity 50,000)
- Support: The Pretenders, Lou Reed
- Set: same as Cologne, plus October after Bad.

Basel is located close to the border with Germany and France and thousands of fans from both countries are present. However, it's the only show of the European tour that fails to sell out.

JUNE 24, 1987. BELFAST, NORTHERN IRELAND, KING'S HALL

- Attendance: 8,000; sellout
- Support: Lou Reed
- Set: same as Cologne, with Where The Streets Have No Name replacing C'Mon Everybody, plus People Get Ready before Help, October after Bad, and minus Party Girl.

Belfast is included in U2's itinerary for the first time since December 1982, and the audience are grateful. Back then, Sunday Bloody Sunday was performed with U2's promise that if the audience didn't like it, they would never play it again. They did like it, and the rest is history. At King's Hall, five years after that emotional performance, the song is as popular as ever and numerous flags show up in the crowd during the song. "You can put down the flags, we don't need any flags... we're sick of all flags!" Bono shouts angrily. It adds a sharp edge to the show without ruining the boisterous atmosphere.

JUNE 25, 1987. IRISH RADIO: DAVE FANNING SHOW

The band appear on Dave Fanning's show for a live interview during which listeners can phone in to ask questions. The 75 minute programme goes down in U2 annals as the 'In The Nude' interview as early in the show Iggy Pop's Lust For Life is aired and the band impulsively react to the line, "He's gonna do another striptease" by dancing wildly and shedding their clothes. They continue the interview stark naked. As Iggy fades out, Fanning remarks, "This is quite strange, actually. The only person without his top off is The Edge – everybody else have their clothes off in the studio, and in fact (Edge) has nothing on from the waist down! Look at Edge's bum! What a bum!"

This establishes a loose atmosphere for the evening and the programme is very funny, with each member of the band demonstrating his sense of humour. Fanning asks if the upcoming Dublin shows will differ from each other. "Yeah, we're gonna put the stage in the other end of the stadium on Sunday," Adam says dryly. Asked by a caller to name his favourite U2 song, The Edge cites Lost Highway and proceeds to sing and play the song live in the studio. Larry drums on the chairs with his fingers and the rest of the band sing second voice, actually turning in a passable version of the Hank Williams' classic. Many callers ask silly questions and the band cleverly juggle the serious with the banal. A girl called Michelle, clearly infatuated with Larry, asks him when he is getting married. "Whooo!" everybody in the studio goes. "Well, no one's asked me yet. I think it's when Ann decides it," Larry answers. "Who's Ann?!" Michelle asks somewhat shocked, unaware that Ann is Larry's long-time girlfriend. "Whoooooo!!" "Well, just tell him I'm available," Michelle says seriously. "Well, you can leave your phone number and I'll give you a ring later on," says Larry. "I'm going to the show on Saturday, can I get up on stage with ya?" Larry: "No problem, if you just stand within the first ten rows, just wave a little flag with just me on it, and I'll instruct Bono to get you, alright?"

More serious questions deal with the consequences of U2's current mega-success and how it changes their lives. Asked his opinion of the immense stream of publicity the band are generating, Edge answers: "It's fantastic, but I'm also bored stiff with just the quantity of trivia that's been written about the band. I mean, it's fantastic, it's great that we get that much recognition, but I don't know how people stick it, to be honest." Larry picks up on this: "You got a good point there. A lot of people think it's us winding it up, but basically it's just the press going on their own initiative, and we don't have that much to do with it. Obviously, a lot of it is good, but there's a little bit of saturation at the moment. You know, we're trying to live here, so the more press that we get here, the more difficult it becomes to actually be a human being in this country. But, you know, if I can say this without sounding like an asshole, it's the

Belfast

Belfast

price you pay, unfortunately."

Fanning asks if the band still have close contact with fans, as they did in the early days. "The only restriction is the number of people that you have to talk to," Edge says. "If you got 5,000 people outside a venue there's no way you can go out, but if you find like 10 or 30 people then we go and talk to them. It still happens, it's just not quite as easy as it used to be." Bono takes up the theme: "There is an element where we are getting a bit cut off, you know. We are separated a bit more now and I don't like it, but we've just gotta live with it. We have to play these big gigs. If we play only small gigs, the ticket touts make a fortune on our fans, and we won't have it like that. So we play the big gigs, it's just the way it goes. It's not important that you might meet 10,000 people. It's important that you meet one person that has something to say to you that's relevant, and often we do meet those people. I do miss it though; I miss being able to meet somebody after a concert and going back to their place and have a coffee or sleep on their floor... I miss all that. At one stage I had thirteen people staying in my room when we toured through England. These people used to come out for the week or for the whole tour, and they'd be travelling, staying in all our rooms. It was amazing. Now we're getting a bit cut off from that. It's just the way of it, and I suppose we have accepted it, reluctantly."

Other topics that U2 discuss include American and European writers, the two paradoxical sides of America, and the mothers of the disappeared in Central America. When a guy asks Bono if he has experienced a personality change since the start of his career, Bono confesses: "Personality crisis... I have one every day. I don't know who I am. That's why I write songs. I think that's why any songwriter writes songs, 'cause he doesn't know who he is, so he tries to find himself in the songs he writes. There's a deep answer..."

Halfway into the show it seems that everyone has forgotten

they're on air. They sound more like a bunch of friends getting drunk in the pub, just enjoying themselves and letting go. It's a cosy sort of chaos and when people phone in, the band ask more questions than the callers. Towards the end U2 offer a hilarious version of the Donny Osmond hit *Puppy Love*, banging their fists on the table to the rhythm. The programme closes with the band successfully persuading Fanning to take his pants off out of solidarity.

JUNE 27, 28, 1987. DUBLIN, IRELAND, CROKE PARK

- Attendance: 114,000 sellout
- Support (first night): Light A Big Fire, The Dubliners, The Pogues, Lou Reed; (second night): Christy Moore, The Pretenders, Lou Reed, Hothouse Flowers
- Set first night: *Where The Streets Have No Name / I Will Follow / I Still Haven't Found / Gloria / A Sort Of Homecoming / MLK / The Unforgettable Fire / Sunday Bloody Sunday / Exit / In God's Country / Electric Co. / People Get Ready / Help / Bad / Springhill Mining Disaster / New Year's Day / Pride /* encore: *Bullet The Blue Sky / Running To Stand Still / With Or Without You / Party Girl / 40*

As at Self Aid, Dave Fanning has the honour of announcing the band. "Alright, listen: are you ready? OK, they have their clothes on. It's been two long years since Croke Park, so please welcome, back to Dublin, U2!" The press has built up excitement for the shows for weeks and with memories of their triumphant homecoming concert on these grounds two years ago still fresh, the audience go absolutely bonkers when U2 walk on stage. Expectations are so high that, although the show is good, it suffers a bit from tensions brought about by the occasion.

106

During the intro to *I Still Haven't Found* Bono looks back on the band's early days in Dublin: "When we started this group in 1977, I was 17, Edge was 15, Larry still is 15, Adam was 17 going on 70, a wise man. We didn't know where we were going, we just wanted to go there together. Ten years later, 1987: Croke Park! Our journey isn't over yet..."

A Sort Of Homecoming is performed for the last time this tour and hasn't been played since. During *Exit,* Bono plays a quick bit of Lou Reed's *Street Hassle* on guitar. After *Electric Co.* he sees a guy walking on the roof of the grandstand, and tries to persuade him to come down: "Some people get high on the music at our concert, not high on the roof, mister. Why dance with yourself when you can dance with all the rest of us? It's OK to have a hard neck, but it's not OK to have a broken neck. Get down there will you?!" It ends well.

"This is an old American gospel song we picked up along the way, called *People Get Ready.* Simple words, says, 'People get ready, there's a train coming, picking up passengers, coast to coast. Faith is the key to open the doors and the borders, you don't need no ticket, you just get on board.' There's only three chords in this song, so even I can play it. Some people down there are laughing when I pick up the guitar. You think you can play guitar better than me? I'm sure there's a young guitar player down there who could play the guitar better than me. Have we got a guitar player down there? C'mon, bring him up!" Someone is pulled up onstage and he plays well. Bono hopes the experience inspires the guy and the audience. "When we come back next time — hundred new bands in Dublin City, in Cork and Belfast and Derry and Limerick, Tipperary. It's not such a long way to the top."

During *Party Girl* Edge is introduced as Rory Gallagher and when at the end of the song Alison Hewson comes up to serve champagne, Bono hoots in admiration: "Imagine being married to that, whooo!"

- Set second night: same as Cologne, plus *Trip Through Your Wires* after *I Will Follow,* minus *Electric Co.,* plus *October,* and minus *Party Girl.*

For the second Dublin date the tension is gone and the band play more loosely and cheerfully. Since it rains, Bono sticks a snippet of *Rain* to *I Still Haven't Found* and at the end of *Bad,* the usually short snippet of *Walk On The Wild Side* is much longer. Lou Reed, support on both nights, comes on stage to add his dark voice to the song, marking a unique duet between Bono and one of his heroes.

JULY 1, 1987. LEEDS, ENGLAND, ELLAND ROAD STADIUM

- Attendance: 30,000; sellout
- Support: World Party, The Fall, The Mission, The Pretenders
- Set: *Stand By Me / C'Mon Everybody / I Will Follow / Trip Through Your Wires / I Still Haven't Found / MLK / The Unforgettable Fire / Sunday Bloody Sunday / Exit / In God's Country / Electric Co. / Help / Bad / October / New Year's Day / Pride /* encore: *Bullet The Blue Sky / Running To Stand Still / With Or Without You / Party Girl / 40*

"As I was growing up in Dublin City the kids on my street playing football talked with stars in their eyes about Leeds United Football Ground," says Bono to the crowd's delight. "I didn't myself but, you know..." Turning the concert into a request programme, he asks, "What do you wanna hear?" The crowd shout for several songs and cheer when Bono suggests, "How about *Electric Co.?*"

JULY 4, 1987. PARIS, FRANCE, HIPPODROME DE VINCENNES

- Attendance: 70,000; sellout
- Support: The Pogues, UB40
- Set: same as Leeds.

A few hundred tickets are again made available at the cash desk at the entrance gates to undercut scalpers and cater to fans travelling from afar. The venue is a huge horse racing track and with 70,000 tickets sold the show establishes an attendance record for a single performance in France. Island Records' 25th birthday celebrations are broadcast live on British TV and songs from the show are featured via a satellite link to the UK. Several TV cameras are positioned in front of the stage. When the tape of *Stand By Me* starts U2 take over live, all hell breaks loose. The huge crowd surge forward so hard that several people fall over and are almost trampled underfoot, and throughout the show hundreds of fans faint in a survival-of-the-fittest battle and have to be carried off. The band seem a bit intimidated by the TV cameras and the immense sea of people. Halfway through *With Or Without You* a tear gas bomb goes off in front of the stage and the audience jolt back a few metres. A big cloud of yellow smoke appears and people desperately cover their faces to avoid inhaling the stuff, while others panic and try to escape. Bono sees the chaos and is furious. "Hold it," he yells and the band stop. "I hope everything's OK down at the front here because nobody gets into trouble at a U2 concert, *nobody* gets hurt at a U2 concert! What is this stuff? Tear gas. I thought we had enough tears in this song." He sings an improvisation that seems to summarise his feelings about this concert: "I was strolling down this Paris way, I walked through the streets in the light of the day and knew that summer had arrived, when I saw your eyes, when I see you. Well I hope that it was good - as it was good for me if it was good for you, then it was good for me..."

Intimacy at Vorst Nationaal

JULY 8, 1987. BRUSSELS, BELGIUM, VORST NATIONAAL

- Attendance: 8,000; sellout
- Support: In Tua Nua
- Set: same as May 30, minus *A Sort Of Homecoming*, plus *Electric Co.* before *Help*.

In order to avoid playing nine stadium shows in a row, U2 scale things down with a concert at the relatively intimate Vorst. The show is one big celebration; a fantastic atmosphere with the band drawing strength from close contact with their audience. Bono dedicates *Bad* to Greg Carroll, whose burial took place exactly one year ago, and he recalls the Brussels shows of October 1984: "This is a song we filmed in this building, maybe two years ago. And the camera recorded a special concert. But the star of the camera was not the band. The star of the camera was a guy called Greg Carroll. He used to stand just there. On this day last year, a few of us arrived in New Zealand, in Wanganui. Greg Carroll was a member of the Maori tribe, and his tribe sent him off – forever. We were very proud to be guests at the burying of Greg Carroll this time last year, and we play this song for Greg Carroll, this year..."

JULY 10, 11, 1987. ROTTERDAM, HOLLAND, FEYENOORD STADIUM

- Attendance 92,000; sellout

- Support (first night): In Tua Nua, The Pretenders; (second night): In Tua Nua, Big Audio Dynamite, The Pretenders
- Set first night: *Where The Streets Have No Name / I Will Follow / I Still Haven't Found / MLK / The Unforgettable Fire / Sunday Bloody Sunday / Exit / In God's Country / Electric Co. / Help / Bad / October / New Year's Day / Pride / encore: Bullet The Blue Sky / Running To Stand Still / With Or Without You / Party Girl / 40*

World Party is originally announced as support act but In Tua Nua take their place. Shortly before the show Adam and Bono are interviewed for Dutch TV by Adam Curry at the side of the stage. Curry asks banal questions and has trouble maintaining the interest of the band members. Bono takes his guitar and sings two verses of *Lucille* to liven up the interview. "Just wrote that one this morning," he lies. When Bono hears the audience roar, he excitedly calls out, "Listen to that crowd!"

During the show, the excited audience jump up and down on the stands so heavily that the whole stadium shakes. Bono thanks everyone for buying tickets and acknowledges that these shows sold out quicker than those at Croke Park in their hometown.

- Set second night: same as Cologne, plus *Trip Through Your Wires* after *I Will Follow*, and *People Get Ready* replaces *Electric Co.*

This show benefits from beautiful summer weather and an eager crowd enjoy themselves doing waves and hurling beach balloons around the stadium all afternoon. Bono is very talkative. "What

about this place?" he asks over the intro of *I Still Haven't Found*. "Somebody said the best football team in Europe comes from this place. I don't know if they're right or wrong. I'll tell you after tonight. I always judge a football team by the way people rise to an occasion when on the football field. Coming back to this country and to the cities of Rotterdam and Amsterdam has a very good feeling for U2, because this country was the first in Europe to give U2 a break. When we came to play a little small place called the Milkyway, de Melkweg, we played to maybe one hundred people. I just hope the same hundred people are here. Anyway, here we are, 45, 50,000 people later, and it still feels the same for me, and I still haven't found what I'm looking for..."

There is an awkward moment after *Bad* when Bono cautiously announces he wants to sing a special song (hinting at *Springhill Mining Disaster*), but the audience happily embark on the typical Dutch "Olé olé olé" football chant. Bono is drowned out and, realising the audience are not ready for subtlety, laughs hopelessly. "Ah, you got your own song," he says while Adam retaliates with the opening notes of *New Year's Day*.

Before *Pride* Bono cheerfully asks, "You OK in the back?" Since there is no immediate response, he mumbles, "It takes about five minutes until they hear what you're saying," and tries again. "Yeaaahh!" Bono sees the people up in the high seats against the clear, dark-blue summer sky. "Have you seen the way people up in the top make this really nice silhouette? I really like that. Look at that, isn't that pretty? Oh dear, fair play to you Bono. Having a conversation with everybody. Isn't that what it's all about?"

Feyenoord Stadium

Rotterdam

Disaster after *October.*

This show wouldn't have happened had it not been for a girl who raised a petition with over 10,000 signatures requesting U2 to play. U2's management was impressed and arranged the show. It is only the second time that the horseshoe-shaped rugby stadium has been used for a rock concert (David Bowie a month before was the first). Having opened for U2 many times in 1982-1984, The Alarm are among the support acts for the only time this tour.

"I should tell you before we go any further that Cardiff Arms Park means a lot to an Irishman, but it means even more to a Welshman like The Edge," says Bono. "Edge's old man always said, 'One day my boy will play Cardiff Arms Park'. But he didn't mean rock & roll. He meant rugby football! So Edge is gonna play rugby football at Cardiff Arms Park!" Amid loud cries from the audience, Edge kicks a ball far into the audience. "Just as well as he plays electric guitar!" says Bono.

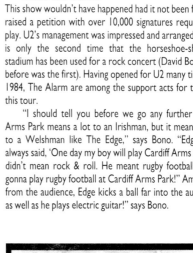

During *Party Girl* he thanks the audience for putting 'The Joshua Tree' at No 1 in the Dutch charts. However, the album has been at the top position for 13 consecutive weeks but now stands at No 2. Someone comes onstage to tell Bono. "Listen, there's been a big mistake," he says apologetically. "Somebody tells me Whitney Houston is No 1 in Holland!" The audience boo and Bono finishes, "Well, wait till next week..."

JULY 15, 1987. MADRID, SPAIN, ESTADIO SANTIAGO BERNABEU

- Attendance: 115,000; sellout
- Support: Big Audio Dynamite, UB40, The Pretenders
- Set: same as first Wembley Stadium show, with *Electric Co.* and *Help* replacing *Trip Through Your Wires,* and *Spanish Eyes* instead of *Gloria.*

U2's very first concert in Spain attracts the biggest audience of the whole 1987 tour and marks the second time that the band perform to well over a hundred thousand people. (The US Festival in 1983 was the first time.) The promoter assures U2's organisation that attendance is limited to 75,000, but another 40,000 tickets are put on sale illegally. Within three days all tickets are gone, even though U2 have never played in Spain before and thus have not been able to build up a following. Nevertheless, the audience go bonkers and sing along to virtually every song. Trying to break through to this huge audience, Bono uses an old trick and climbs to the roof of the stage during *Electric Co.* The highlight of the evening is the live première of *Spanish Eyes,* the B-side of the *I Still Haven't Found* single, which drives the Spaniards nuts. "I ask myself one question," Bono says before *40.* "Why have we not played here before?"

JULY 18, 1987. MONTPELLIER, FRANCE, ESPACE RICHTER

- Attendance: 35,000; sellout
- Support: World Party, UB40, The Pretenders
- Set: same as first show in Rotterdam, plus *Trip Through Your Wires* after *I Will Follow,* and *People Get Ready* replacing *Electric Co.* and *Help.*

During *Party Girl* a fan comes onstage and sings one or two lines. Before *40* Bono thanks the audience for coming from all over the country to see them.

JULY 21, 22, 1987. MUNICH, GERMANY, OLYMPIAHALLE

- Attendance: 24,000; sellout
- Support: In Tua Nua
- Set first night: *Where The Streets Have No Name / I Will Follow / Trip Through Your Wires / I Still Haven't Found / MLK / The Unforgettable Fire / Bullet The Blue Sky / Running To Stand Still / Exit / In God's Country / Sunday Bloody Sunday / People Get Ready / Bad / October / New Year's Day / Pride / encore: Party Girl / Spanish Eyes / With Or Without You / 40*

Two impressive concerts follow the disappointing show in Cologne. *Spanish Eyes* is played again and will appear only occasionally during the rest of the tour. Singer Leslie Dowdall of In Tua Nua serves the champagne during *Party Girl* on both nights. Before *40* Bono recalls memories of U2's first visit to Munich: "The first time we played here we played a small club called The Sugarshack. We walked onstage at about one o'clock in the morning and we had been drinking alcohol! Bavarian Schnaps. Because it was way past our bedtime we were all very drunk and in fact we fell asleep in the dressing room before we came on stage and our manager Paul McGuinness was shaking us saying, 'You have the whole of Germany outside, you must wake up!' And we said, 'No, no, we want to sleep...' But I didn't know it was gonna be like this! So, now when we drink Bavarian alcohol, we drink it *after* the gig, not before!"

- Set second night: *Stand By Me / C'Mon Everybody / I Will Follow / Trip Through Your Wires / I Still Haven't Found / MLK / The Unforgettable Fire / Exit / In God's Country / Sunday Bloody Sunday / Electric Co. / Help / Bad / October / New Year's Day / Pride / encore: Bullet The Blue Sky / Running To Stand Still / With Or Without You / Party Girl / 40*

During the section of *Pride* where Bono asks the audience to sing for Jimi Hendrix, Bob Marley, John Lennon, Janis Joplin et al, he adds Ian Curtis' name to the list of rock casualties. The singer of Joy Division, who committed suicide, originally performed the song *Love Will Tear Us Apart* which Bono often sings during *With Or Without You.*

JULY 25, 1987. CARDIFF, WALES, ARMS PARK

- Attendance: 45,000; sellout
- Support: The Silencers, The Alarm, The Pretenders
- Set: same as second show in Munich, plus *Springhill Mining*

JULY 29, 30, 1987. GLASGOW, SCOTLAND, SCOTTISH EXHIBITION CENTRE

- Attendance: 20,000; sellout
- Support (first night): Hoodoo Gurus; (second night): Hue & Cry
- Set first night: same as first show in Munich, with *Lucille* instead of *People Get Ready*.

Over the course of two inspired shows the band enjoy much horsing around. After *In God's Country* Bono imitates Barry McGuigan, the Irish boxer who is always thanking his manager in public. He mimics McGuigan's fast squeaking voice perfectly: "Well, you know, I just like to thank me manager Mr. Eastwood, you know, well I'm really looking forward to fighting at Glasgow, it's a great thing..." Then a crew member runs onstage to hand Bono a note. "Well, we just heard the news literally this second, this minute. Barry McGuigan's gone to No 1 in the United States with *I Still Haven't Found What I'm Looking For,* how about that?" The single marks U2's second consecutive No 1 on *Billboard's* Hot 100, three months after the *With Or Without You* single.

Lucille is played for the second time on the tour with Bono confessing that the band only allow him to sing U2's first ever country song on very special occasions. He says the song is named after B.B. King's guitar.

- Set second night: same as July 22, with *People Get Ready* replacing *Electric Co.* and *Help,* and minus *Party Girl.*

"How would you like it if I told you that we've got this mobile recording studio parked outside?" Bono announces. With the recording unit set to record the show anyway, U2 make use of it during the afternoon by taping their version of Phil Spector's *Christmas (Baby Please Come Home)* from the stage for a benefit album for the Special Olympics, which enables disabled athletes to stage their own Olympic Games. With some 1,500,000 athletes under its wing, the organisation needs money to continue and producer Jimmy Iovine has taken the initiative to seek artists willing to record a Christmas song for the album 'A Very Special Christmas'. Iovine also produces most of the tracks. The album will be released in the fall, and U2 are among fifteen artists to contribute. The album will raise several million dollars for the Special Olympics.

That night during the show Simple Minds guitarist Charlie Burchill comes onstage to play guitar on *40.*

AUGUST 1, 1987. EDINBURGH, SCOTLAND, MURRAYFIELD STADIUM

- Attendance: 58,000; sellout
- Support: Run Rig, Love & Money, The Mission, The Pogues
- Set: same as second show in Munich, plus *People Get Ready* before *MLK.*

"We've got to fight for the right to *Party Girl,*" Bono says, and introduces Edge as Carlos Santana. Kirsty McColl, Steve Lillywhite's wife, brings the champagne. "I don't even like champagne, but I like Kirsty McColl! I think I know what I want," Bono sings and chases after Kirsty. *40* is interrupted when two guys appear onstage and lift Bono up. Some security guards appear and guide the lads back into the audience.

AUGUST 3, 4, 1987. BIRMINGHAM, ENGLAND, NATIONAL EXHIBITION CENTRE

- Attendance: 22,000; sellout
- Support: Hoodoo Gurus
- Set first night: *Star Spangled Banner - Bullet The Blue Sky / Running To Stand Still / I Will Follow / Silver And Gold / Gloria / Sunday Bloody Sunday / Exit / In God's Country / Electric Co. / I Still Haven't Found / MLK / The Unforgettable Fire / Bad / October / New Year's Day / Pride / encore: Party Girl / Spanish Eyes / With Or Without You / 40*

Back at the NEC for two more shows, U2 open an exceptional first concert with a recording of Jimi Hendrix's interpretation of

the American national anthem, *The Star Spangled Banner,* as performed at Woodstock. In the meantime, U2 come onstage in the dark and before the tape is over crash into *Bullet The Blue Sky.* Another first is the performance of *Silver And Gold,* the song that Bono wrote for the 'Sun City' album and which has recently been re-recorded by them for release on the B-side of the *Where The Streets Have No Name* single. The band had been soundchecking the song in San Francisco and some stops in between. Bono announces, "This song is set in a South African prison, man at breaking point, says to himself... in the shithouse a shotgun..." The hard-hitting song is received well though the audience are not yet familiar with it.

"Holly came from Miami, Fla," Bono sings at the end of *Bad,* "Hitchhiked to Birmingham for the day; saw U2 at the NEC, pretty soon... what rhymes on NEC?"

- Set second show: same as July 21, minus *Spanish Eyes.*

During Edge's guitar intro of *I Still Haven't Found* Bono looks back at the growth of U2's audience: "Over the years we've seen from playing for 200 people to 2,000 to 20,000 people, and I wanna tell you I don't think we've changed. And it doesn't seem like you've changed either, at least not for the worse, and I hope a little bit for the better." At the end of the song Bono segues into Bob Marley's *Three Little Birds.* He dedicates *MLK* to Bob Marley instead of to Martin Luther King.

Before *People Get Ready* Bono strums his guitar and sings some lines of *Guantanamera* in perfect Spanish. "I'm having a great summer just being here. Any requests?" People shout U2 songs from all over the arena. "I got it, I got it: *People Get Ready*". After the first stanza a guy joins the band and Bono shows him the three chords. "Yeah, sing with me... faith is the key, if you wanna start a rock & roll band, you just need a lot of guts..." The guy gets to sing the final lines and doesn't want to leave the stage. "He doesn't wanna leave! For the first time in my life I feel like Jim'll fix it," Bono says, referring to Jimmy Saville's BBC TV show on which Saville makes people's wishes come true. "Just for a second I thought I was on 'Opportunity Knocks' meself... Is that programme still going?" "Yeaaaahh." "The guy who meant everything most sincerely, as far as I remember," Bono recalls, referring to presenter Hughie Greene.

"I wanna sing this for the cities of the North," Bono says during *Pride.* "For Birmingham and Liverpool and Newcastle and Manchester, places that mean so much to the memory of U2. I wanna thank you for coming tonight, look after yourselves on the way home. We'll see you again sooner, rather than later."

AUGUST 8, 1987. CORK, IRELAND, PAIRC UI CHAOIMH

- Attendance: 45,000; sellout
- Support: The Dubliners, The Subterraneans, UB40
- Set: same as second show in Munich, with *People Get Ready* instead of *Electric Co.,* and *Out Of Control* before *40.*

The European leg of the tour finishes in Ireland on Edge's 26th birthday. "Happy birthday Edge!" Bono shouts during *Stand By Me,* and pushes the microphone into Edge's face to force him to sing a few lines. U2 have strong bonding with the city. "The first time I felt like I was in a band was in Cork," Bono recalls. "We played in a place called the Arcadia Ballroom, and for the first time I saw queues around the block and I was made to feel like it was good to be in a rock & roll band!"

The show is full of inside jokes and most of the media regard this as better than the Dublin shows. After *People Get Ready* Bono introduces his guest guitarist. "He says his name is Eamon Mitchell and he wants to form a band but he can't find anyone to form a band with. Well, there's about 50,000 people that will be in a band tomorrow, OK? This is the one city in Ireland where there's more bands than pubs. In Dublin they're all in the pubs...!" During *Sunday Bloody Sunday* the audience repeatedly sing, "Wipe your tears away", while Bono asks to sing it for "Belfast, Derry, Cork, Dublin, Waterford, Galway City, Sligo!" They sing along so well that at the end Bono starts anew, actually stretching the song to twice its length.

Many of U2's regular road crew come from Cork, and Bono honours them during *Pride:* "I wanna sing this for Corkmen Joe O'Herlihy, for Tim Buckley, for Tom Mullally, for Sammy over here behind the drum kit... Steve Iredale. Because without these people, there'd be no rock & roll show. There's a lot of people working day in day out, putting up stages, taking down stages, putting them into trucks, driving the trucks, and all in the name of love..."

The big surprise of the evening is a huge birthday cake brought onstage during *Party Girl.* Bono calls out, "Anyone knows what The Edge wants? How about a birthday cake? So Edge, why don't you just give me the guitar here. And why don't you just try a slice of the birthday cake?" Out of the cake jumps

Close to the Edge. Dublin, August 6, 1987

Edge's wife Aisling, who showers everyone with a huge bottle of champagne. "My god, Edge, it's the missus! And what a beautiful party girl she is tonight! The best birthday present you can give Edge is his wife Aisling!" A wild version of *Out Of Control,* played for the first time this tour, completes the party and as usual *40* ends the show with the band members walking offstage one by one, leaving Larry to crash away alone on his drums. Finally, the crew up in the rigging release hundreds of ping-pong balls over Larry, who cracks up in laughter and shakes his fist at the culprits before he finishes the song, throws his sticks into the audience, and is off.

The 30 shows of the European tour are attended by 1,195,000 people, an average of 39,833 per show.

'THE JOSHUA TREE' TOUR LEG 3: AMERICA, FALL 1987

After a few weeks off in the South of France, the band embark on their most extensive American trek to date. The Spring tour has ignited even more interest to see U2. Fans go again, bring their friends, others come out of curiosity, having just discovered 'The Joshua Tree'. Six months after its release, the album is still in the Top 10, having already gone triple platinum on its way to quintuple platinum status (over 5 million sold) in the United States. With the U2 phenomenon still snowballing, there are twenty stadium shows booked, with thirty indoors. Hysterical scenes at ticket sales, as in Europe, occur Stateside as well, with most tickets selling out just hours after going on sale, and still leaving thousands ticketless. The 'Unforgettable Fire' tour had done very well for U2 financially, but now, with the move to stadiums, the amount of money generated from ticket and merchandising sales is immense, placing U2 among the biggest earners in the entertainment industry.

Having made plans earlier in the year, the band decide to make a concert movie of the tour. The 'Under A Blood Red Sky' video had captured the energy of a U2 performance, and continuing sales indicate public interest in owning a live U2 document. As they have progressed so much since that video's release four years ago, the band feel it's time to supercede Red Rocks. Phil Joanou, a 26-year old film maker, is hired over more experienced to direct the movie. They decide to shoot three types of film: colour 35mm concert footage, black & white 35mm concert footage and 16mm black & white documentary footage. U2 will pick one city on the tour each to film the b&w and colour material in, but Phil Joanou and a team of cameramen will follow the band around, operating 16mm cameras to capture all events that surround the concerts. Eventually

calling the movie 'Rattle And Hum', Paul McGuinness and the band finance the whole project themselves in order to maintain artistic control. They put up one million dollars each so they can produce the movie independently, thus preventing potential quarrels with movie companies wanting to exert their influence on the end result. Once they have finished the movie, U2 plan to find a distributor for the finished product. If no one wants to market it, it will be, as Adam put it, "the most expensive home video ever made".

SEPTEMBER 8, 1987. AMERICAN RADIO: 'TRIP THROUGH YOUR WIRES'

Two days before the start of the third leg of the tour, U2 are in a New York radio studio for a direct broadcast interview, syndicated by the DIR Radio Network and aired by over 50 local FM stations across North America. The number of requests for interviews in every city is so high that this nationwide interview seems to be a perfect way to satisfy the individual radio stations. The programme is dubbed 'Trip Through Your Wires' and the interview is conducted by WBCN Boston's Carter Alan with assistance from Linda Ryan of KUSF San Francisco. Listeners can phone in to put questions to the band.

U2 discuss the dilemma of playing stadiums, the frustration caused by ticket scalpers, John Lennon, U2's motivation for establishing their Mother Records company, as well as which places to visit while on holiday in Ireland. Larry is asked who inspired him as a drummer, Bono talks about the song *Silver And Gold* and his work with Keith Richards on that song. ("He's still in love with his music, and literally the lines disappear from his face when he picks up that guitar.") A funny moment occurs when Gina calls in. "Where are you from," asks Bono, and she says she lives in Tempe. "Tempe, Arizona? That's where we started the tour, I lost my voice down there," remarks Bono. "You lost your chin too, didn't you?" says Gina, referring to the fall Bono had there, and everyone in the studio cracks up with laughter. When asked if he's afraid of people making him into a rock icon, Bono answers, "I'm not afraid of them, but I don't like it. It's a good thing to be into music. I'm into rock & roll bands and I respect a lot of people, and I like to be respected. But when it goes further than that, when people wanna find out the meaning of life just because you can sing in tune, because you can write songs – well, then they got the wrong guy."

Serious subjects are intermingled with silly jokes by the band and the result is a very vivid and inspired interview. Live tracks from one of the May Meadowlands shows, and from the Amnesty show at Giants Stadium are played as well. In addition, Bono sings *Lucille* live in the studio, accompanying himself on guitar and Edge delivers his version of *Lost Highway*. Just before a live recording of *Sunday Bloody Sunday* is aired, Bono mumbles to the radio audience, "Turn on your tape recorders."

SEPTEMBER 10, 11, 1987. UNIONDALE, NY, NASSAU VETERANS' MEMORIAL COLISEUM

- Attendance: 34,899 (P); sellout
- Support: Mason Ruffner
- Set both shows: *Star Spangled Banner - Bullet The Blue Sky / Where The Streets Have No Name / I Will Follow / Trip Through*

Your Wires / I Still Haven't Found / MLK / The Unforgettable Fire / Exit - Silver And Gold / In God's Country / Sunday Bloody Sunday / Help / Helter Skelter / Bad / Running To Stand Still / New Year's Day / Pride / encore: *One Tree Hill / With Or Without You / Party Girl / 40*

U2 start the tour with two solid shows on Long Island. As The Beatles' *All You Need Is Love* fades out over the PA, the lights dim and, as in Birmingham a month before, Jimi Hendrix' *Star Spangled Banner* rings out as the band come onstage and crash into *Bullet The Blue Sky*. This is the first time *Bullet* is not followed by *Running To Stand Still*. U2 add a tight cover version of The Beatles' *Helter Skelter*. *Silver And Gold* is now linked to *Exit*, beautifully segueing into each other. The big surprise is the inclusion of *One Tree Hill*, the moving song about Greg Carroll's funeral, as Bono had expressed reservations about being able to overcome the emotional effort of performing it in public. The première of the song is solemn and sensitive. The audience hold their breath and explode into moving applause at the end.

SEPTEMBER 12, 1987. PHILADELPHIA, PA, SPECTRUM ARENA

- Attendance: 17,622 (P); sellout
- Support: Mason Ruffner
- Set: *Where The Streets Have No Name / I Will Follow / Trip Through Your Wires / I Still Haven't Found / MLK / The Unforgettable Fire / Bullet The Blue Sky / Running To Stand Still / People Get Ready / Sunday Bloody Sunday / Exit / In God's Country / Bad / October / New Year's Day / Pride /* encore: *One Tree Hill / With Or Without You / Party Girl / 40*

During *With Or Without You* a guy from the audience manages to get onstage and tries to grab the microphone. Bono is annoyed and stresses, "Not in this song! You can sing any other song but you can't sing this song, alright?!"

SEPTEMBER 14, 1987. EAST RUTHERFORD, NJ, GIANTS' STADIUM

- Attendance: 54,780 (P); sellout
- Support: Little Steven & The Disciples of Soul
- Set: same as Philadelphia, minus *Trip Through Your Wires*, and plus *Silver And Gold* linked to *Exit*.

The first stadium show of the fall tour manages to keep the huge crowd captivated, although many consider the show suffers from the absence of video screens to give those at the back a better view. Adam tries to start *New Year's Day* but fails. "Our bass player is struck by lightning," Bono says to fill up the gap, while Adam tries to figure out what's wrong. "So anyway, how's New York these days?"

SEPTEMBER 17, 18, 1987. BOSTON, MA, GARDENS

- Attendance: 31,018 (P); sellout
- Support: Little Steven & The Disciples of Soul
- Set first night: same as Uniondale, with *People Get Ready* instead of *MLK*, and minus *Helter Skelter*.

Bono's improvisational skills are tested when a sudden power failure blacks out all the lights during *I Will Follow*. "A man tells me that our lighting rig has broken down. Well, if the lights don't work, let's turn on the house lights, I don't care," says Bono. After the song he adds, "I don't know why at rock & roll concerts they bring all these expensive lights, smoke bombs and shit – we don't need it! Why? Because we have the spirit of Larry Bird within us!" (Larry Bird is a local hero, a basketball player with the Boston Celtics) U2 continue the show in a completely illuminated arena for an hour before their expansive lighting system works again and the 16 spotlight operators resume their jobs.

Steve Morse of the *Boston Globe* writes in next morning's newspaper: 'Where other superstars might have fallen flat without their lights, U2 carried on like troupers, forging an ever closer bond with the audience. Bono was infinitely more chatty, while still managing to convey the spiritual power of the band's music as the crowd spurred him on with long, majestic singalongs.'

■ Set second night: *Where The Streets Have No Name / I Will Follow / Trip Through Your Wires / I Still Haven't Found / MLK / The Unforgettable Fire / Bullet The Blue Sky / Running To Stand Still / Sunday Bloody Sunday / Exit / In God's Country /Help / Helter Skelter / Bad / October / New Year's Day / Pride /* encore: *One Tree Hill / With Or Without You / Spanish Eyes /* encore: *Out Of Control / 40*

Edge strikes the wrong notes at the start of *I Still Haven't Found*. Bono mocks, "Forgotten how to play this, Edge? Well gee, this is my big moment, right, I get to play guitar!" The audience sing as one, inspiring Bono to extend the song considerably. During *Running To Stand Still* he explains, "It's a true story about the city I grew up in, about two people so driven by a need to fill their veins with heroin, that they would do anything, risk anything. We're all addicted to something. Me? I'm addicted to being up here." Recalling the previous night, Bono asks for the house lights to be lit after *New Year's Day.* "Well, last night we had the house lights breaking down, tonight we had Edge's guitar breaking down, but does it matter?" "Noooooo!" yell the crowd. *Out Of Control* is a welcome surprise and for the rest of the tour will only be performed sporadically, usually in cities where U2 have a fanatical following. The song drives the crowd nuts. "Some kinds of chaos you can learn to love," Bono says.

SEPTEMBER 20, 1987. WASHINGTON, DC, ROBERT KENNEDY STADIUM

■ Attendance: 51,016 (P); sellout
■ Support: Little Steven & The Disciples of Soul
■ Set: *Where The Streets Have No Name / I Will Follow / Trip Through Your Wires / I Still Haven't Found / MLK / The Unforgettable Fire / Bullet The Blue Sky / Running To Stand Still / People Get Ready / Sunday Bloody Sunday / Exit / Help / Bad / October / New Year's Day / Pride /* encore: *Party Girl / With Or Without You / 40*

A video screen is installed behind the lighting tower after complaints about poor views at the Giants Stadium show. It rains throughout the concert. Bono praises the audience: "You've gone through so much trouble to make us feel at home, you even got it to rain this afternoon!" An Irish flag is thrown onstage during *Sunday Bloody Sunday.* "This flag – what colour do you see?" Bono asks, holding up the green part. "Green, yeah,

it's green." Holding up the orange part he then asks the audience the same, followed by the white part. "What colour do you see?" "White," scream the audience and Bono tears up the flag. "No, it's not white. Sometimes, all I see is red..." In his plea for no more bloodshed, Bono aggressively sings "No more!" with the crowd.

The stage is so wet from the rain that when Bono runs around during *Exit*, he slips and lands very hard on his left shoulder. He doesn't move for a minute. The rest of the band and the audience are not sure whether he's really hurt or if it's part of the show, and are relieved when the singer slowly stands up to finish the song. When the band come back for the encore, Bono has his arm in a sling and explains: "It may sound a bit stupid, and I feel a bit stupid, but the doctor says I might have dislocated my shoulder. Sorry about that."

Bono is rushed to hospital after the show. His wife accompanies him, as does Phil Joanou with his camera, who captures the ride and Bono's entrance to hospital. He causes some tension when he wants to film Bono being examined by the doctor and is refused admittance.

SEPTEMBER 21, 1987. BOSTON, MA, PARADISE THEATER

U2 hold a press conference exclusively for U2 fanzines. Hundreds of people all around the world are involved with publishing (usually photocopied) magazines devoted to U2 and related artists/topics, born out of the wish to write about their favourite band and share their opinions and experiences with others. Those based in North America are invited, but as many are unable to travel to Boston, only around 25 writers representing seven different fanzines attend. Joanou and his crew capture the event on film. Bono arrives late as he has been in the hospital having his left shoulder treated after the fall in Washington, but Edge, Adam and Larry answer all questions in the meantime. "Do you find fans are enjoying seeing you in stadiums?" somebody asks. Adam answers, "I agree there is a problem of visuals, but at least people get to come to a U2 concert. You're always faced with this dilemma of, do you tour an album for two years or do you do a tour in three months, playing the biggest places and then make another record. It's a time problem that you face constantly in this situation, plus driving up ticket prices, through scalping. There is no easy solution to it, I think. What we tried to do this time was mix and match the dates so that at least people had a choice where they wanna go to." Bono comes in with his arm wrapped in a sling. Obviously in pain, he sits down quietly and is not as talkative as

usual. When asked about the Foxboro show tomorrow, Bono says, "I've never dreamt of having to play a concert with one arm. It's hard enough to face 60,000 people, but it'll be interesting... I'll be singing for a change, instead of running around thinking I could fly."

SEPTEMBER 22, 1987. FOXBORO, MA, SULLIVAN STADIUM

■ Attendance: 55,378 (P); sellout
■ Support: The Pogues, Little Steven & The Disciples of Soul
■ Set: *Stand By Me / Where The Streets Have No Name / I Will Follow / Trip Through Your Wires / I Still Haven't Found / The Unforgettable Fire / Bullet The Blue Sky / Running To Stand Still / Exit / Sunday Bloody Sunday / Help / Helter Skelter / Bad / October / New Year's Day / Pride /* encore: *One Tree Hill / With Or Without You / 40*

Stand By Me opens the show for the last time this tour as the joke and surprise element have worn off. This is the first of twelve concerts that Bono has to endure with his arm in a sling. As a result, he isn't as physically active as usual, cannot play guitar and avoids doing anything that can possibly hurt his shoulder. A roadie stands in for Bono shining a spotlight on Edge during his guitar solo in *Bullet The Blue Sky.*

SEPTEMBER 23, 1987. NEW HAVEN, CT, COLISEUM

■ Attendance: 10,535 (P); sellout
■ Support: Mason Ruffner
■ Set: same as Foxboro, minus *Stand By Me*, plus *MLK* before *The Unforgettable Fire*, and *Party Girl* instead of *One Tree Hill.*

This is the smallest crowd of the fall tour. Bono angrily expresses his dissatisfaction with "the shit we hear on the radio", and during *Pride* he invites a black woman and a white man onstage to let them display their 'END APARTHEID' banner. "Well, I don't go to any Ivy League University, but it doesn't take a very smart man to work out that I cannot enjoy my freedom while there are others unfree," he states. Later on the show gets a more lighthearted air as Bono jokes, "This is a song from our latest album called 'Thriller', this is *Bad.*" During *Party Girl* he lets the audience in on the advantages of wearing a sling. "I'll tell you what – I think I'm gonna perform for the rest of my life in one of those. I'm getting a whole pile of sympathy from people, all spoiling me. 'You OK Bono, sit down Bono, you sure your arm isn't sore Bono?' Oh, it's really sore!"

words, I wrote those words'. So we went inside and we found The New Voices Of Freedom, a gospel choir. And they were singing this song..." At the end of *Party Girl* about 25 people take their place onstage and start singing along and dancing to the rhythm. Bono introduces them: "I told you about these people earlier on – they're The New Voices Of Freedom!" For the second time that night *I Still Haven't Found* is played, in an extended, gospel version with Bono duetting with the choir and soloists Dorothy Terrell and George Pendergrass. Adam and Edge abandon their instruments and watch from the other side of the stage.

Some days earlier, U2 had jammed with the New Voices in a church to shoot footage for the movie. Tonight's version of *I Still Haven't Found* will end up on the 'Rattle And Hum' album, but for the movie, footage from the church is used.

■ Set second night: same as Washington DC, plus *In God's Country* after *People Get Ready*, plus *Helter Skelter* after *Exit*, and minus *Party Girl*.

OCTOBER 1, 1987. MONTREAL, CANADA, OLYMPIC STADIUM

■ Attendance: 66,117 (P); sellout
■ Support: Little Steven & The Disciples of Soul, Los Lobos
■ Set: *Where The Streets Have No Name* / *I Will Follow* / *Trip Through Your Wires* / *I Still Haven't Found* / *MLK* / *The Unforgettable Fire* / *Exit* / *In God's Country* / *Sunday Bloody Sunday* / *Help* / *People Get Ready* / *Bad* / *October* / *New Year's Day* / *Pride* / encore: *Star Spangled Banner - Bullet The Blue Sky* / *Running To Stand Still* / *With Or Without You* / *40*

Bullet The Blue Sky and *Running To Stand Still* are moved to the encore and are preceded by the recording of *Star Spangled Banner* which, on the outdoor shows, is accompanied by a big fireworks display. The sound in the Olympic Stadium leaves a lot to be desired but U2 play a strong show, the first of only three Canadian dates this year. Bono thanks Gavin Friday before *40*.

OCTOBER 3, 1987. TORONTO, CANADA, CANADIAN NATIONAL EXHIBITION STADIUM

■ Attendance: 62,846 (P); sellout
■ Support: Little Steven & The Disciples of Soul, Los Lobos
■ Set: same as Montreal.

The audience suffer from extreme cold but Bono claims, "We're here to warm up your winter nights." This is the sixth stadium show of the tour with many more to come. "I remember

---

SEPTEMBER 25, 1987. PHILADELPHIA, JOHN F. KENNEDY STADIUM

■ Attendance: 86,145 (P); sellout
■ Support: Little Steven & The Disciples of Soul
■ Set: *Where The Streets Have No Name* / *I Will Follow* / *Trip Through Your Wires* / *I Still Haven't Found* / *MLK* / *The Unforgettable Fire* / *Bullet The Blue Sky* / *Running To Stand Still* / *People Get Ready* / *In God's Country* / *Exit* / *Sunday Bloody Sunday* / *Help* / *Bad* / *October* / *New Year's Day* / *Pride* / encore: *With Or Without You* / *Party Girl* / *Stand By Me* / *40*

The huge crowd that fill this gigantic, horseshoe-shaped stadium form the largest audience of the American tour. An option for a second show on the 26th is not taken up though the date is printed in the official tour book. As in Washington, a video screen is put up behind the lighting tower and this is now in place on most stadium dates. "Well, as you can probably see, it looks like I busted my shoulder up a little bit bad," Bono says. "But the joke around the band is that they busted my shoulder up to stop me playing guitar!" Two hysterical fans manage to get onstage during *The Unforgettable Fire* and as Bono is anxious about his fragile shoulder he gestures them to keep away until security lead them off. "I'd dance with you, my friends, only my arm is in a sling, you get the picture?"

Bono's rap during *Bullet The Blue Sky* changes during this period: "So I went walking through Philadelphia, to the streets and the side streets and on and off those little campuses et cetera. And then I found myself in this big, round open space made of concrete and steel called the J.F.K. And I said, if this is America, I like it! And I thought about my arm in a sling, and the way I feel walking up on to the stage in a rock & roll show, and I said it doesn't matter a shit. Because this is not Las Vegas, this is not show business, this is rock & roll. And that's when I knew that I had run... into the arms of America."

The big surprise of the night is saved for the encore when Bono says, "Anyone else like to play my guitar? Bruce Springsteen likes to play my guitar!" The audience chant "Brooooooce!!" as U2 start *Stand By Me* and The Boss comes on stage to sing and play along.

SEPTEMBER 28, 29, 1987. NEW YORK, NY, MADISON SQUARE GARDEN

■ Attendance: 39,510 (P); sellout
■ Support: The Pogues
■ Set first night: *Where The Streets Have No Name* / *I Will Follow* / *Trip Through Your Wires* / *I Still Haven't Found* / *MLK* / *The Unforgettable Fire* / *Bullet The Blue Sky* / *In God's Country* / *Sunday Bloody Sunday* / *Exit* / *Help* / *Bad* / *October* / *New Year's Day* / *Pride* / encore: *With Or Without You* / *Party Girl* / *I Still Haven't Found* / *Spanish Eyes* / *40*

"A few days ago we were in Harlem, and we heard these words coming out of a church hall," says Bono over the intro of *I Still Haven't Found*. "They said: 'I believe in the Kingdom come, then all the colours will bleed into one'. I said, 'Hey, those are my

Madison Square Garden. People Get Ready

thinking that the El Mocambo was too big for U2. I used to think that the Massey Hall was too big. You think this place is too big for U2?" he asks the audience. "Noooo!!" "You people must be cold out there. Are you cold?" Again, the entire crowd scream "Noooo!" "We made a big mistake playing only three dates in Canada," Bono admits. "Thanks for coming out here to see us play."

OCTOBER 6, 1987. CLEVELAND, OH, MUNICIPAL STADIUM

- Attendance: 50,081 (P); sellout
- Support: Little Steven & The Disciples of Soul, Los Lobos
- Set: same as Montreal, plus *Out Of Control* before *MLK*, and minus *People Get Ready*.

During a powerful performance, Bono is extremely talkative, reminiscing on many occasions about earlier shows in Cleveland. "One of the first songs we ever wrote," he says as the thundering intro of *Out Of Control* surprises the audience. "There was a time when U2 were not played on the radio," he says during the song and acknowledges the fact that Cleveland was one of the first cities to give U2 airplay in America. When it starts raining Bono sings some lines from *Rain*, which segue into *Help*. At the end of the show the rain stops. "Let me see the people in the back," he calls out during *40*, and there is no misty rain to prevent him from seeing everyone dancing on their seats. He sings, "I can see clearly now, the rain has gone, yeah!"

OCTOBER 7, 1987. BUFFALO, NY, MEMORIAL AUDITORIUM

- Attendance: 17,065 (P); sellout
- Support: Little Steven & The Disciples of Soul
- Set: same as Montreal, plus *Springhill Mining Disaster* after *In God's Country*, and minus *People Get Ready*.

Bono recalls memories of U2's first visit to Buffalo, when they played as support for some band whose name he has forgotten, but does remember it was the night John Lennon was murdered (December 8, 1980) *Springhill Mining Disaster* is played for the only time during the fall tour. During *Help* something snaps in Bono's voice. He sings hoarsely, the lower notes come out croaky and *Bad* is cut short. He apologises and the audience help him out the rest of the night. "Thank you so much," he says during *Pride*. "You sing so good! I've seen a doctor about my sore voice. He said, 'Where are you going next?' I said 'Buffalo'. And he said, 'Don't worry about singing in Buffalo, they're gonna sing for ya'."

During *Bullet The Blue Sky* a girl from the audience gets onstage and runs hysterically towards Bono, who jumps out of his skin and screams, "Don't touch my fucking arm tonight!" He quickly pulls himself together. "Normally I like to dance with girls. Excuse the bad language, ladies. Tonight's been a tough night."

OCTOBER 9, 1987. SYRACUSE, NY, CARRIER DOME

- Attendance: 39,157 (P); sellout
- Support: Little Steven & The Disciples of Soul, Los Lobos
- Set: same as Montreal.

"Action! Roll!" Bono shouts at the beginning of *Where The Streets Have No Name* to Joanou and his crew. The crowd in the university town of Syracuse are quiet compared to other cities and are not familiar with most of the pre-'Joshua Tree' material. Bono's voice is back in good shape.

OCTOBER 11, 1987. ROCHESTER, NY, SILVER STADIUM

- Attendance: 30,500 (P); sellout
- Support: Little Steven & The Disciples of Soul, Los Lobos
- Set: same as Montreal.

This show is originally planned for the 9,200-seat War Memorial Coliseum, but is moved to Silver Stadium due to enormous ticket demand. "We thought we were going to play a little club tonight," Bono says before *I Still Haven't Found*. "I suppose that's what this is, or what we want it to be. You want it to be like that?" "Yeaaaah!" the audience cry and are enthusiastic the whole night through, despite the cold and the pouring rain.

OCTOBER 13, 1987. PITTSBURGH, PA, THREE RIVERS STADIUM

- Attendance: 40,000
- Support: Little Steven & The Disciples of Soul, Los Lobos
- Set: same as Montreal.

Little Steven & The Disciples of Soul play their last show supporting U2. Bono's voice acts up again and he has to squeeze out the higher notes. A couple of days' rest follow.

OCTOBER 20, 1987. IOWA CITY, IA, CARVER-HAWKEYE ARENA

- Attendance: 15,846 (P); sellout
- Support: The BoDeans
- Set: same as Montreal.

The BoDeans join the U2 bandwagon and open for most of the remaining shows. U2's first appearance in Iowa since 1981 has no trouble selling out. The audience are rather quiet and aren't acquainted with most of the songs. Bono is relieved to finally be freed from his sling. "This is the first night in about three or four weeks that I've used two arms at a concert," he says and dedicates *Trip Through Your Wires* to "my once broken and now mended arm."

OCTOBER 22, 1987. CHAMPAIGN, IL, UNIVERSITY ASSEMBLY HALL

- Attendance: 16,193 (P); sellout
- Support: The BoDeans
- Set: same as Montreal.

Bono: "Why is it everyone keeps booing when I pick up this guitar? I don't play guitar too good but I play it kinda my way. Edge taught me three chords on this guitar: C, A-Minor, and an F. He said, Bono, with those three chords, you can change the whole world. Well, if not change the world, maybe get invited to a lot more parties, that's for sure. And if you practise real hard, The Edge said to me, maybe you could play Curtis Mayfield's *People Get Ready*." The guest-guitarist is great this night and before he leaves the stage he loudly proclaims his love to some girl in the audience.

OCTOBER 23, 1987. LEXINGTON, KY, RUPP ARENA

- Attendance: 22,815 (P); sellout
- Support: The BoDeans
- Set: same as Montreal, minus *40*.

"Let me tell you: if there's any ticket scalpers in this building –

they are *not* welcome. *We* decide what a U2 concert is worth," says Bono during *Pride*. Surprisingly, he sings "How long to sing this song", a couple of times at the end of *With Or Without You*, and *40* is left out.

OCTOBER 25, 1987. ST. LOUIS, MO, ARENA

- Attendance: 18,237 (P); sellout
- Support: The BoDeans
- Set: same as Montreal.

This night the St. Louis Cardinals baseball team play an important match against the Minnesota Twins and many in the audience follow the game through portable radios until the show. A banner draped over the balcony reads, 'Under a Cardinal Red Sky'. As U2 start their set, Bono walks on stage outfitted in a red Cardinals' jacket and baseball cap. "Well, as far as I'm concerned, St. Louis has already won the World Series," he calls out after *I Will Follow*. After *Help*, Bono pulls his hair back and confesses, "Gotta get a hair cut. That's what we used to do in Dublin, to stop being thrown out of class rooms: we'd tie our hair back and pretend we had short hair."

OCTOBER 26, 1987. KANSAS CITY, MO, KEMPER ARENA

- Attendance: 17,168 (P); sellout
- Support: The BoDeans
- Set: same as Montreal, with *Southern Man* replacing *People Get Ready*.

Southern Man is performed for the second time this tour. Bono sings, "We'd come into town, maybe five years ago. We played the Uptown Ballroom and put on a great show. I was nineteen and we were really good that night. I thought Kansas City was, out of sight, celebrate!" and then goes back to the original lyrics. Later in the songs he says, "We came to this city in 1981 or '82, and I think the band were the only people in the Uptown *under* the age of drinking. There were some people outside saying, 'Bono, I can't get in to see you, man!' I said, 'I can't even get in to see me, man!' Apart from that, Kansas City is pretty good..." The guy that gets onstage to jam along plays the song far better than Bono and gets a thunderous applause.

OCTOBER 28, 29, 30, 1987. CHICAGO, IL, ROSEMONT HORIZON

- Attendance: 51,998 (P); sellout
- Support: The BoDeans
- Set first night: same as Montreal, plus *Southern Man* after *In God's Country*, and minus *People Get Ready*.

A delirious audience sing every song word for word. "I hereby name Chicago the noisiest U2 city in the world," Bono states. Again *Southern Man* is played, with a lot of improvisation. After the first verse Bono says, "You know, we started playing our own songs because we couldn't play anybody else's songs... and we still can't. When I was 17 I just about learned to play this song on electric guitar. And I said, one day, maybe, if I learn the other chords, I'd go far. I thought these great singers and songwriters in rock & roll bands had some tricks up their sleeve, but there's no tricks at all – just three chords, and the truth." Tonight's guest guitarist does an extensive solo. "This guy is too good! Hey Edge, I think we better get him off quick!" Bono jokes. "He said his name is Big Dave. Hey, what was the name of the band again that you played for? Lost Luggage... Well, I still haven't found the luggage I'm looking for..."

- Set second night: *Where The Streets Have No Name / I Will Follow / Trip Through Your Wires / I Still Haven't Found / MLK / The Unforgettable Fire / Bullet The Blue Sky / Running To Stand Still / Silver And Gold / Out Of Control / Sunday Bloody Sunday / Exit / In God's Country / People Get Ready / Gloria / Pride /* encore: *Party Girl / With Or Without You / 40*

Chicago

Bullet The Blue Sky and *Running To Stand Still* are played early in the show, *Gloria* is inserted for the first time since Birmingham and the regular *Bad / October / New Year's Day* sequence is omitted. A rousing *Out Of Control* is included as well as a superb, full version of *Silver And Gold*. Bono talks about the song's development, how he originally wrote it for the 'Sun City' album, and about its contents: "A song about a man just at the point where he feels violence is the only way out. When we think of the life of the black man in South Africa, we can understand that. And I look into my own soul, and I can understand the wish and the want, to take up arms against those bastards. And yet, there is another way. There is another way to get these bastards by the balls. It's spelled M-O-N-E-Y. That's what brought them there in the first place, as they dug the earth for diamonds, for gold. And that's what's gonna get them out of there."

During the intro of *I Still Haven't Found* Bono explains, "About five or six years ago we came to this city for the first time, played a small club called the Parkwest. There was dancing on the tables and on the chairs. I remember that club felt like the biggest room in the whole wide world. And I said to Edge, 'How can we ever play to more than a thousand people?' A year later I said to him, 'How can we play to more than three-thousand, or

five thousand people'. Well, I think we've got the whole world in here tonight and it feels OK by me."

- Set third night: *Where The Streets Have No Name / I Will Follow / Trip Through Your Wires / I Still Haven't Found / Out Of Control / MLK / The Unforgettable Fire / Bullet The Blue Sky / Running To Stand Still / Sunday Bloody Sunday / Exit / In God's Country / Helter Skelter / Help / Bad / October / New Year's Day / Pride / encore: Party Girl / Spanish Eyes / With Or Without You / 40*

During Edge's guitar solo in *New Year's Day* Bono spots two girls holding a banner that says 'THERE IS BUT ONE FLAG – THE WHITE FLAG' and lets them drape it over the stage. The ladies go on to embrace Bono tightly but he grimaces with pain as they hurt his still fragile shoulder. Edge watches, pale-faced, but Bono recovers. In two hours it will be Larry's 26th birthday, and during *Party Girl* Bono briefly sings *Happy Birthday* while Larry cracks up laughing as he and his drum kit are showered with champagne.

NOVEMBER 1, 1987. INDIANAPOLIS, IN, HOOSIER DOME

- Attendance: 38,441 (P); sellout
- Support: The BoDeans, The Dalton Brothers, Los Lobos
- Set: same as Montreal, plus *Lucille* before *40*.

U2 carry out a prank they have planned for some time: to become their own support act. After The BoDeans an MC announces that there is an extra band on the bill called The Dalton Brothers, and U2 walk onstage dressed in silly wigs and cowboy gear. Adam wears a skirt and a blond curly wig; Bono's wig is red. With all four Daltons wearing sunglasses and assuming Texan accents, hardly anybody recognises them. Bono introduces his fellow players as "Luke, Duke and Betty Dalton", and sings *Lucille*, after which Edge (or rather Luke Dalton) sings Hank Williams' *Lost Highway*. During the song Bono talks about meeting the late country legend "a few years ago in Indianapolis", and hilariously recalls that Williams told him, "You can go far with country & western, not that rock & roll shit."

Two hours later U2 hit the stage as themselves and play a strong show. After *With Or Without You*, Bono says, "This is a little tune of a local band I met backstage called The Dalton Brothers. It seems to me a really good tune, it's only got three chords, so I can play it. Goes like this... Oh Lucille..." When they

hear the tune for a second time, many in the audience laugh heartily as they recognise it and suddenly realise U2 had fooled them earlier on.

NOVEMBER 3, 4, 1987. ST. PAUL, MN, CIVIC CENTER

- Attendance: 35,152 (P); sellout
- Support: The BoDeans
- Set first night: *Where The Streets Have No Name / I Will Follow / Trip Through Your Wires / I Still Haven't Found / Gloria / MLK / New Year's Day / Sunday Bloody Sunday / Exit / In God's Country / Help / Bad / October / With Or Without You / Pride / encore: Star Spangled Banner - Bullet The Blue Sky / Running To Stand Still / Out Of Control / 40*

New Year's Day is played early in the set and *With Or Without You* takes its place between *October* and *Pride*. The security in the hall is incredibly tight, with ushers constantly checking if people are in the right seats and in some cases fans who return from the toilet or the bar are refused admittance to their section. Bono has trouble connecting with the audience and as he is unhappy with the sound, invites a roadie up on stage to listen in order to adjust it. After *Out Of Control* Bono is slipped an orange envelope with a note from someone in the audience which prompts him to sing, "Like a Rhinestone Cowboy, getting cards and letters from people I don't even know..." After he has shone a spotlight on the audience during *40*, he aggressively starts to revolve the lamp vertically and rotates it very fast, scaring members of the band, the crew and the audience.

- Set second night: *Where The Streets Have No Name / I Will Follow / Trip Through Your Wires / I Still Haven't Found / MLK / Gloria / Spanish Eyes / Sunday Bloody Sunday / Exit - Silver And Gold / In God's Country / People Get Ready / Bad / October / New Year's Day / Pride / encore: Star Spangled Banner - Bullet The Blue Sky / Running To Stand Still / With Or Without You / 40*

The second night is completely different from the first as U2 play cheerfully and appear more inspired. *Spanish Eyes* opens with booming drums instead of guitar. Edge breaks a string and Bono sings, "Our love... needs a new guitar, in your Spanish eyes. I met The Edge, he hasn't changed a bit, he's still breaking guitar strings, like he used to do..." U2's guitar technician Fraser McAllister celebrates his birthday and is introduced by Bono to play guitar during *People Get Ready*. "Where's Fraser? He's gonna play these chords or else he's fired!" He doesn't play badly at all. "I wanna introduce you to one of the people that gets us ready... for you. Without this road crew, without these people hanging from lights, we are *nothing*, and never will be," Bono confesses, and after the song sings *Happy Birthday* with the audience before Fraser leaves the stage.

NOVEMBER 7, 8, 1987. DENVER, CO, McNICHOLS ARENA

- Attendance: 34,000 (P); sellout
- Support: The BoDeans
- Set both nights: *Where The Streets Have No Name / I Will Follow / Trip Through Your Wires / I Still Haven't Found / Gloria / MLK / The Unforgettable Fire / Sunday Bloody Sunday / Exit / In God's Country / Helter Skelter / Help / Bad / October / New Year's Day / Pride / encore: Star Spangled Banner – Bullet The Blue Sky / Running To Stand Still / Silver And Gold / Spanish Eyes / With Or Without You / 40*

During the soundcheck the band rehearse *She's A Mystery To Me*, a love song that Bono and The Edge wrote for Roy Orbison, which The Big O will later record for his 'Mystery Girl' album in 1989, shortly before he dies. They also play The Temptations' *My Girl*.

Denver is chosen for filming the 35mm black & white material that will make up a major part of 'Rattle And Hum'. Multiple cameras are set up in the arena, including two that cross the front on tracks between the audience and the stage.

The getaway car, Chicago

Betty and Alton Dalton

Camera units with steadycams walk on and off-stage to film the show from every angle possible. The first night U2 play a solid show. During *New Year's Day* Bono acknowledges the fans from Red Rocks. "You were there when the rain was coming down. Icy fingers, warm hearts... warm hearts!" The cameras film the show as well as possible but often block the audience's view, and the crew experience many technical difficulties.

The second night the cameras are less obtrusive and U2 play an explosive set. The show is fuelled by outrage, as U2 hear the news that on this day in Enniskillen, Northern Ireland, another Bloody Sunday occurs as thirteen innocent people are killed in a bombing by the Irish Republican Army during a Remembrance Day parade. U2 start *Sunday Bloody Sunday* and Bono expresses his disgust at today's bloodshed. "Let me tell you something," he begins in mid-song. "I've had enough of Irish-Americans who haven't been back to their country in 20 or 30 years who come up to me and talk about the resistance, the revolution back home... and the glory of the revolution and the glory of dying for the revolution. Fuck the revolution! They don't talk about the glory of killing for the revolution. What's the glory in taking a man from his bed and gunning him down in front of his wife and children? Where's the glory in that? Where's the glory in bombing a Remembrance Day parade of old age pensioners, their medals taken out and polished up for the day? Where's the glory in that, to leave them dying or crippled for life or dead under the rubble of a revolution that the majority of the people in my country don't want. NO MORE!"

The mood lightens towards the end of the show. *Spanish Eyes* is interrupted by Bono. "Who is this lady? Bring her to me!" A lady with a tambourine helps finish the song and hands over her tambourine to Bono when she leaves the stage. He starts hitting it, and leads an a capella chorus. "Wey hey hey, baby hang on," he sings. When the bass joins in, Bono stops cold. "I was just getting it together with the folks, Adam. I thought it was pretty good!" Adam laughs. "I think this beats standing in the rain, yeah? But standing in the rain didn't beat ya either," Bono says, referring to Red Rocks. He jokes, "At the moment we're really stuck for a place to go afterwards tonight. Has anyone got a house for us?" The audience roar and Bono says, "I didn't quite catch your name..."

Tonight's versions of *Helter Skelter*, *Silver And Gold* and *Pride* appear on the 'Rattle And Hum' album and in the movie. Other songs included in the movie from this show are *Exit*, *In God's Country* and *Sunday Bloody Sunday*.

NOVEMBER 11, 1987. SAN FRANCISCO, CA, JUSTIN HERMAN PLAZA

- Attendance: ca. 20,000
- Set: *All Along The Watchtower* / *Sunday Bloody Sunday* / *Out Of Control* / *People Get Ready* / *Trip Through Your Wires* / *Silver And Gold* / *Helter Skelter* / *Help* / *Pride*

In the spirit of the *Where The Streets Have No Name* video shoot on a rooftop in Los Angeles, where enthusiastic fans brought traffic to a standstill, U2 play a free impromptu show on Justin Herman Plaza in the middle of the financial district of San Francisco. After rumours early in the morning, radio stations confirm at 10am that U2 will perform around noon. Having walked out of classes, left work or whatever, some 20,000 people jam the Plaza, excited about the prospect of seeing U2 in the city where the idea of free rock & roll originated. It recalls the many free concerts twenty years ago during the Summer of Love. Concert promoter Bill Graham helped organise the gig at only 24 hours notice. Phil Joanou operates one camera that will supply documentary footage for the movie, and the show is also audiotaped by Jimmy Iovine.

When U2 start playing, passers-by join the crowd, business people from the area skip their lunch-break to attend, and hundreds of people driving along the Embarcadero freeway stop their cars to watch. Bono announces, "As the business sector is having such big problems, we decided to do a 'Save the Yuppies' concert," referring to the stock market crash the day before. Opening with a version of Bob Dylan's *All Along The Watchtower*, which they had played only once before (London, 1981), Bono improvises, "All I got is a red guitar, three chords and the truth. All I got is a red guitar, the rest is up to you". During *Sunday Bloody Sunday*, he sees someone waving an Irish flag with 'SF U2' written on it. He asks the guy if 'SF' is a girl's name or if it stands for Sinn Fein, the IRA's political wing. "I don't know how you can stand or stomach to wave that sign this week," Bono shouts, and berates the guy about the IRA's atrocities in Enniskillen four days ago until the poor lad puts the flag down. Though Bono's anger fuels an explosive version of the song, the general feeling among the crowd is that his outrage is misplaced, since it is so obvious that 'SF' stands for 'San Francisco'.

The incident is soon forgotten when the band continue their unusual set and Bono interacts with the crowd. "As you know, this is really a telethon," he quips after *Out Of Control*. "We're raising money for the business sector here – I'm wearing the hat because I'll be passing it around later." He announces *People Get Ready* as a song God has co-written with Curtis Mayfield. *Silver And Gold* is extended with a lengthy speech about what prompted Bono to write it. During *Pride*, he runs over to the nearby Vaillancourt Fountain and climbs up by a ladder to spray-paint on the statue, 'ROCK & ROLL STOPS THE TRAFFIC', as an acknowledgement of the power of rock & roll. Fans cheer and slowly disperse after the 45-minute concert.

Bono's spraying painting doesn't go down well with the local authorities. San Francisco Mayor Dianne Feinstein has been waging war on graffiti for years, and condemns Bono's action. She states, "I am disappointed that a rock star who is supposed to be a role model for young people chose to vandalise the work of another artist." San Francisco police hand Bono a misdemeanour charge for malicious mischief. His conviction could be anything between a $1,000 fine and one-year imprisonment. He is summoned to appear in San Francisco Municipal Court on December 16. The news spreads around the world. The Mayor of Dublin also offers criticism, and Bobby Hewson, Bono's father, comments in Irish papers that his son "deserves anything he gets convicted of."

Bono claims his action was an artistic expression and nothing more. He publicly apologises and picks up the tab for having the statue cleaned. U2's organisation try to convince the authorities that it was not a deliberate act of vandalism. A week later, all charges are dropped when the police realise this whole thing has been blown up out of proportion.

Save the Yuppies

Phil Joanou films U2 for 'Rattle And Hum'

All Along The Watchtower is included both on the 'Rattle And Hum' album and in the film. In the movie it is preceded by footage showing the band rehearsing the song in a camper just minutes before going onstage. The images of Bono spraying the Vaillancourt fountain, which occurred during *Pride*, are mixed in during *All Along The Watchtower*. Also included in the film are attractive aerial shots from the helicopter. On the album, many of Bono's improvisations are omitted.

NOVEMBER 12, 1987. VANCOUVER, CANADA, B.C. PLACE STADIUM

- Attendance: 54,254 (P); sellout
- Support: The BoDeans, Los Lobos
- Set: same as Montreal, minus *People Get Ready*.

This show is originally planned for Seattle, WA, but is then moved to Vancouver, making it the second consecutive tour that neglects the northwest of the United States. To compensate, over 10,000 tickets are put on sale in Seattle, Portland and other cities, with combined bus trips. *Trip Through Your Wires* is interrupted early in the song as Adam's instrument breaks down and he gets a replacement.

NOVEMBER 14, 15, 1987. OAKLAND, CA, STADIUM

- Attendance: 103,260 (P); (capacity: 119,000)
- Support: The BoDeans, The Pretenders
- Set first night: *Where The Streets Have No Name / I Will Follow / Trip Through Your Wires / I Still Haven't Found / Gloria / MLK / The Unforgettable Fire / Exit / In God's Country / Sunday Bloody Sunday / Help / Bad / October / New Year's Day / Pride / encore: Star Spangled Banner - Bullet The Blue Sky / Running To Stand Still / With Or Without You / People Get Ready / 40*

Dozens of fans wave flags saying, 'U2 STOP THE TRAFFIC', or something similar. "As you know I've been getting into a little bit of trouble here in San Francisco," Bono says early in the show. "A policeman called me up in my hotel room. He said he was collecting evidence concerning an 'act of violence' down at Vaillancourt Fountain. They said, Mr. Hewson, we take this thing very seriously in this city. I said, I take it very seriously too, but have you picked up a rock & roll band. I mean this is U2 – we're the Batman and Robin of rock & roll for God's sake. Anyway, I think it should be explained that there's a big difference because Armand Vaillancourt *himself* had spray painted his *own* sculpture, a few years ago, when he opened it. I mean, we put on a free concert for the city of San Francisco, I mean..." Bono sounds distraught over the whole affair, and wants to prove his innocence. He has invited the artist in question, Armand Vaillancourt, all the way from Quebec to explain onstage what he thought of Bono spraying his statue. Armand, walking with crutches, declares that he is glad to be here, and that he regrets that the graffiti has been washed off his work. Just for the record, Bono apologises to Armand and offers him to even the score. He gives Armand a spray can to graffiti U2's stage. He writes, 'STOP THE MADNESS!'

- Set second night: *Where The Streets Have No Name / I Will Follow / Trip Through Your Wires / I Still Haven't Found / Gloria / Out Of Control / Sunday Bloody Sunday / Exit / In God's Country / People Get Ready / Help / Bad / October / New Year's Day / Pride / encore: Star Spangled Banner – Bullet The Blue Sky / Running To Stand Still / With Or Without You / Stand By Me / 40*

Though the first show had sold out quickly, the second night leaves 15,740 tickets unsold. After *Gloria*, Bono introduces René Castro, the mural artist he met in San Francisco during the Amnesty tour. He comes onstage accompanied by his group of 20 community artists called Placa and they are invited to spray-

paint the stage backdrop. "And with any luck, we should be able to show Mayor Feinstein the difference between an act of vandalism and graffiti art," Bono says, still upset. The group of artists paint huge white doves of peace, illustrating their message: 'Peace in Central America'. After *Stand By Me*, he asks Castro and the group to sing along with *40*. Each holds a wooden cross, simulating the dead of strife-torn Central and South America. Bono expands on the 'disappeared' at length: "'Disappeared' is a euphemism that death squads use for taking you out in the middle of the night, putting a bullet through your head and not telling anyone about it." As he continues on the subject, some of the crowd shout things at him. "Will you SHUT THE FUCK UP while I'm talking," Bono sneers, but quickly offers his apologies for using bad language. His agitated reaction annoys many in the crowd, as do his remarks about how unjustly he has been treated following the graffiti incident. Thousands of fans leave the stadium with mixed feelings.

NOVEMBER 17, 18, 1987. LOS ANGELES, CA, MEMORIAL COLISEUM

- Attendance: 132,925 (P); (capacity 142,000)
- Support (first night): Steve Jones, The Pretenders; (second night): The BoDeans, The Dalton Brothers, The Pretenders
- Set first night: *Where The Streets Have No Name / I Will Follow / Trip Through Your Wires / I Still Haven't Found / One Tree Hill / Gloria / Sunday Bloody Sunday / Exit / In God's Country / People Get Ready / Bad / October / New Year's Day / Pride / encore: Star Spangled Banner - Bullet The Bullet Sky / Running To Stand Still / With Or Without You / 40*

The shows leave 9,075 tickets unsold, indicating that with four stadium shows in California the point of saturation has been reached. LA produces the highest box office result of the tour: with a ticket price of $19.50, the two shows gross $2,590,497. Referring to the shooting of the *Where The Streets Have No Name* video back in March, Bono dedicates *Trip Through Your Wires* to the Los Angeles Police Department downtown. "I think they know what we mean." *One Tree Hill* is back in the set for the first time since Foxboro. The Olympic flame is lit specifically for the show, marking only the fourth time this is done: it was lit twice for the Olympic Games, and once for the Pope.

- Set second night: *Where The Streets Have No Name / I Will Follow / Out Of Control / I Still Haven't Found / MLK / The Unforgettable Fire / Gloria / Sunday Bloody Sunday / Exit / In God's Country / Helter Skelter / Help / Bad / October / New Year's Day / Pride / encore: Star Spangled Banner - Bullet The Blue Sky / Running To Stand Still / With Or Without You / Party Girl / encore: Stand By Me / 40*

The second show is superior to the night before and includes four more songs. During a chilling version of *Bad*, Bono accepts a bunch of balloons from the audience and later releases them as he sings "Just let it go..." Bono's wife Alison brings the champagne during *Party Girl*.

As in Indianapolis, The Dalton Brothers make another hit-and-run appearance between the two support acts. After a grand introduction, The Daltons walk onstage and talk to the audience in thick Texan accents. "Right, we play two kinds of music: country, and western," the singer calls out. "This is a little tune I wrote back south, a tune I've labelled *Lucille*, hope ya like it!" The song starts and while half the audience recognise U2 and laugh their heads off, the other half is bewildered and look on silently. During the song the singer announces, "I'd just like to introduce you – we got Luke Dalton on guitar, ladies & gentlemen! This is my sister Betty Dalton, behind me here on the drums we got Duke Dalton. My name is Alton Dalton, don't you forget it!" The song finishes to a modest reception by the crowd, and Alton introduces his kid brother Luke: "I looked after him for, the last, oh, 20 or 30 years, he's gonna just sing a song for you." Luke comes forward: "Well, before we start my song, I'd just like to say it really is great to be back in Los Angeles. And whenever we come back to Los Angeles, my brother Alton, he says to me: 'Luke, it's great to be back in Los

Later that evening, U2 and a couple of crew members go to Antone's, Austin's most prominent blues club. Edge and Bono end up onstage jamming with Stevie Ray Vaughan, Dr. John and T-Bone Burnett and play a bunch of blues classics.

NOVEMBER 23, 24, 1987. FORT WORTH, TX, TARRANT COUNTY CONVENTION CENTER

- Attendance: 27,560 (P); sellout
- Support (first night): The BoDeans; (second night): B.B. King
- Set first night: same as November 15, plus *MLK* before *Gloria*, minus *Out Of Control*, *Helter Skelter* instead of *People Get Ready*, and *Spanish Eyes* replacing *Stand By Me*.

Bullet The Blue Sky is a high point in the show. Bono shares a surrealistic vision of watching television in "the same hotel where John F. Kennedy spent his last night", and finding news footage and TV evangelists and Miami Vice blurring to the point where fiction and reality are indistinguishable.

- Set second night: *Where The Streets Have No Name* / *I Will Follow* / *Trip Through Your Wires* / *Out Of Control* / *I Still Haven't Found* / *One Tree Hill* / *Sunday Bloody Sunday* / *Exit* / *Pride* / *People Get Ready* / *Bad* / *October* / *New Year's Day* / *Gloria* / encore: *Star Spangled Banner* – *Bullet The Blue Sky* / *Running To Stand Still* / *With Or Without You* / encore: *When Love Comes To Town* / *40*

Blues legend B.B. King opens for U2 and both Bono and Edge watch his set from beneath their customised stage. U2 and B.B. spend the afternoon rehearsing a song Bono wrote specifically for him. The sessions are filmed, as is the show that night. The show is also audio-taped. The atmosphere in the hall is alive with anticipation as the news about the rehearsal with B.B. travels fast. *Pride* is played exceptionally early in the show, leaving *Gloria* to close off the main set. "We're making a record tonight – there's a truck parked outside. The man in the truck tells me there's more microphones in the back of the hall than there is on the stage!"

During a frantic guitar solo in *Out Of Control* Bono points at the guitarist and gives him a warm introduction: "We're pleased to have him with us tonight. God bless him – we call him The Edge." Bono launches into a bitter attack on TV evangelists during his rap in *Bullet The Blue Sky*: "I see Jerry Falwell and I know he's looking just at me. I said Jerry, what do you want from me, Jerry – my *money*? Oral Roberts, what do you want from me, my *money*? And I see this hand coming out of the TV screen into the houses of the sick and the old, opening their bags, emptying their life savings. And I see those dollar notes disappearing back into the TV screen so it can build some glass cathedral. Fuck that! We don't need a glass cathedral from you; you're already a see-through soul!"

Audience speculation is fulfilled when B.B. King and his band come out for the second encore. Bono proudly introduces them and tells he saw B.B. in concert in Dublin. "I wrote this song for him, it's called *When Love Comes To Town*." Altogether they start playing the song, which is a direct result of U2's musical journey through America in search of the roots of rock & roll. It blends blues with rock music and contains, as B.B. calls it, "heavy lyrics". ("You're kinda young to write such heavy lyrics!" he says to Bono during the rehearsals.) Bono has written the song as a duet for himself and B.B. The performance includes B.B.'s typical guitar licks as well as his croaky but strong voice, while B.B.'s band, with its extensive brass section and soulful backing singers, provides a rich, warm sound. On this first public performance Bono sings slightly different lyrics from the studio version that will appear on the 'Rattle And Hum' album: "When the sun came up I was sleeping on the street, I felt the world was dancing and I was dirt beneath their feet. When I picked myself up, I saw the devil look down, but they could not play guitar the day love came to town..." During the song he says, "B.B. says you gotta know the blues to sing the blues. I got the first part of that..."

Footage of *When Love Comes To Town* during the show and the rehearsals end up in 'Rattle And Hum'.

Angeles!' So, here we go. This is a little tune we learned from Hank Williams, this is a little tune called *Lost Highway*." He sings, "I'm a rolling stone, all alone and lost..." and the crowd clap along. When a reporter for a local newspaper asks a spectator her opinion on The Daltons, she says, "They're OK, but I wish they'd bring U2 on."

NOVEMBER 22, 1987. AUSTIN, TX, FRANK ERWIN CENTER

- Attendance: 17,202 (P); sellout
- Support: The BoDeans
- Set: *Where The Streets Have No Name* / *I Will Follow* / *Trip Through Your Wires* / *I Still Haven't Found* / *One Tree Hill* /

Gloria / *Sunday Bloody Sunday* / *Exit* - *Silver And Gold* / *In God's Country* / *People Get Ready* / *Bad* / *October* / *New Year's Day* / *Pride* / encore: *Star Spangled Banner* – *Bullet The Blue Sky* / *Running To Stand Still* / *With Or Without You* / *Stand By Me* / *Spanish Eyes* / *40*

Before *People Get Ready* Bono confesses, "All you need is three chords and the truth... not that I know what that is!" His voice suffers from tour-exhaustion and he has to struggle to reach the high notes. Moreover, the show is marred by poor acoustics and monitor problems and at one point Edge even has trouble hearing the show, so Bono leans over to sing to him to help find the tempo. While Adam and Edge are switching their instruments in order to play *40*, Bono calls them over and they switch back. Two extra songs, *Stand By Me* and *Spanish Eyes*, are played to make up for the difficulties.

NOVEMBER 26, 1987. BATON ROUGE, LA, LOUISIANA STATE UNIVERSITY ASSEMBLY CENTER

- Attendance: 15,042 (P); sellout
- Support: The BoDeans
- Set: *Where The Streets Have No Name / I Will Follow / Trip Through Your Wires / I Still Haven't Found / MLK / The Unforgettable Fire / Gloria / Sunday Bloody Sunday / Exit - Silver And Gold / In God's Country / Help / Bad / October / New Year's Day / Pride /* encore: *Star Spangled Banner - Bullet The Blue Sky / Running To Stand Still / People Get Ready / 40*

This afternoon U2 videotape a promo-clip of their cover version of *Christmas (Baby Please Come Home)* which they had recorded in Glasgow for Jimmy Iovine's 'A Very Special Christmas' charity album for the Special Olympics. During the show Bono says he finds it remarkable that so many people have skipped their Thanksgiving dinner to attend the show. He points out Phil Joanou who is filming. "This guy here – when we get out of bed in the morning he's at the end of the bed. When we open the door, he's there too. He's omnipresent, this man! You may have heard we're making a movie. We're gonna make a little film clip from in here. This is a gospel song which is perfect for tonight," Bono says and begins *People Get Ready*. The atmosphere is exuberant and the crowd loudly clap along, but the song doesn't make it into the movie.

NOVEMBER 28, 1987. MURFREESBORO, TN, CHARLES M. MURPHY ATHLETIC CENTER

- Attendance: 11,619 (P); sellout
- Support: The BoDeans
- Set: *Where The Streets Have No Name / I Will Follow / Trip Through Your Wires / I Still Haven't Found / Gloria / Sunday Bloody Sunday / Exit – Silver And Gold / Helter Skelter / Help / Bad / One Tree Hill / New Year's Day / Pride /* encore: *Star Spangled Banner – Bullet The Blue Sky / Running To Stand Still / With Or Without You / Can't Help Falling In Love / People Get Ready / 40*

U2 do an extensive soundcheck and rehearse *Red Hill Mining Town* which they have never performed in concert. Larry has trouble remembering the drum track and claims he has to re-listen to the song in order to play it. *She's A Mystery To Me* is rehearsed once more but doesn't make it into the set.

This concert is added to the tour itinerary at the very last moment and is U2's first Tennessee show since they supported The J. Geils Band in March 1982. While in Tennessee, the band stop by Elvis Presley's Graceland estate and film their visit for inclusion in the movie. The experience inspires Bono to sing a quick, acoustic version of the Elvis classic, *Can't Help Falling In Love*. The audience sing and sway along to the romantic song. *People Get Ready* enjoys another guest appearance. "From The Judds, will you welcome Wynonna to take my guitar." Wynonna plays guitar and sings along but as she doesn't know the lyrics Bono has to guide her through the song. There are now four days off during which U2 record new tracks at Sun Studios in Memphis.

DECEMBER 3, 1987. MIAMI, FL, ORANGE BOWL

- Attendance: 54,111 (P); sellout
- Support: Buckwheat Zydeco, Los Lobos
- Set: same as Los Angeles, November 17.

There are three video screens in the stadium, one on each side of the stage and one behind the lighting tower. A guy called Joe plays along on *People Get Ready* and afterwards clings on to Bono: "You go change the world, man, you go change the world!" Bono jokes, "OK Joe, we change the world, you change your shirt!"

DECEMBER 5, 1987. TAMPA, FL, TAMPA STADIUM

- Attendance: 58,865 (P); sellout
- Support: Buckwheat Zydeco, Los Lobos
- Set: same as Los Angeles, November 17, plus *Spanish Eyes* before *40*.

"There's only one kind of audience that you can take out into a winter night, and they'll sing louder than any singer in any rock & roll band. And that's the U2 audience," Bono says proudly.

DECEMBER 8, 9, 1987. ATLANTA, GA, THE OMNI

- Attendance: 32,734 (P); sellout
- Support: The BoDeans
- Set first night: *Where The Streets Have No Name / I Will Follow / Trip Through Your Wires / I Still Haven't Found / MLK / The Unforgettable Fire / Bullet The Blue Sky / Running To Stand Still / People Get Ready / Bad / Out Of Control / Sunday Bloody Sunday / Exit / In God's Country / Pride /* encore: *With Or Without You / New Year's Day / 40 - Help - 40*

The songs are played in an unfamiliar order. *Bullet The Blue Sky* and *Running To Stand Still* are back in the main set and *New Year's Day* is in the encore. During the intro of *MLK* Bono says, "Seven years ago we got the news that John Lennon had been shot down. This is a song I dedicate to him and others whose lives are cut short by some violent motherfucker..." Thousands of lighters accompany a solemn version of *MLK*. *Pride* is dedicated to Coretta King and all in the Martin Luther King Peace Center. Bono sings a sensitive version of *Help* in the middle of *40*, after which *40* continues. "This one's for John Lennon," he whispers.

- Set second night: *Where The Streets Have No Name / I Will Follow / I Still Haven't Found / MLK / One Tree Hill / Gloria / Exit / In God's Country / Helter Skelter / Help / Bad / Star Spangled Banner – Bullet The Blue Sky / Running To Stand Still / Sunday Bloody Sunday / New Year's Day / Pride /* encore: *With Or Without You / People Get Ready / 40*

During *Pride* Bono recites some lines from Martin Luther King's "I have a dream" speech: "I have a dream: all God's children, black man and white man, Protestant and Catholic, will be able to join hands and sing, Free at last, free at last, thank God almighty, free at last..."

DECEMBER 11, 12, 1987. HAMPTON, VA, COLISEUM

- Attendance: 21,088 (P); sellout
- Support: The BoDeans
- Set first night: same as second show in Atlanta, but *Sunday Bloody Sunday* comes after *Gloria*, *People Get Ready* after *Running To Stand Still*, and a brief version of *Southern Man* replaces *Helter Skelter*.

- Set second night: *Where The Streets Have No Name / I Will Follow / I Still Haven't Found / MLK / 11 O'Clock Tick Tock / Sunday Bloody Sunday / Exit / In God's Country / Tequila Sunrise / Out Of Control / Bad / Bullet The Blue Sky / Running To Stand Still / New Year's Day / Pride /* encore: *Mothers Of The Disappeared / With Or Without You / Lucille / 40*

A night full of surprises. The BoDeans play their 26th and final show supporting U2, and for their last song, *Good Work*, The Edge is announced as special guest and jams along nicely. Then Larry comes onstage talking into a megaphone, followed by Bono who takes over the megaphone and repeatedly yells "The BoDeans, yeah!"

11 O'Clock Tick Tock is played for the only time this tour and for the first time since Cork, August 25, 1985, while *Mothers Of The Disappeared* is included again after a seven-month absence. After *In God's Country* Bono says, "Well, we started off about eleven years ago, when I was 16, Larry was 14, Edge was 15, Adam was 36. We just wanted to be in a band. And the person who owned the worst record collection got to be the drummer. He was particularly fond of The Eagles, do you remember them?" "Yeaah," the audience yell while Larry comes forward. "This is a favourite song of Larry's; it's another Peculiar Sunrise," introduces Bono, handing over the microphone to Larry. Edge plays the opening notes of The Eagles' song *Tequila Sunrise* and under the eyes of the frenzied fans Larry makes his début as a singer. His voice breaks and its shakiness indicates he is nervous as hell, and after two verses he gives up. "I don't know any more, sorry guys," Larry says. "It's really embarrassing, what can I say? You've been a lovely audience... uhm..." Bono comes to the rescue. "I want you to sing it for Larry but only if you mean it," he says and the audience sing along a few lines to help Larry out. *Out Of Control* follows during which Edge forgets to play his solo. "Edge – that's the guitar solo," Bono reminds him. When Edge

Duke Dalton, and I'm Luke. We're all from Galveston, Texas, except Duke here – he's from Dallas." They start to play *Lucille*, and Bono assumes his role as well. He changes the lyrics: "Oh Susanne, we know you're doing the best you can, come dance with me, until the morning sets you free..." As the motley crew leaves the stage Bono, or rather Alton, remarks, "My, Betty, do you grow prettier every day!"

DECEMBER 18, 1987. AMERICAN RADIO: KUPO, ARIZONA

U2 set up camp at Sun Devil Stadium in Tempe, Arizona, for the last two shows of the tour and briefly interrupt proceedings for a live interview on local radio. "See if you recognise this one, one of our early hits," Edge starts off, and plays the intro of the Led Zeppelin classic *Stairway To Heaven* on acoustic guitar. The interview is focused mainly on the upcoming shows and the forthcoming movie and album. "They're making a film *about* the film as well, it's really gotten a little bit out of hand," Bono sighs, sounding tired. "Hopefully we'll have two records: one of them will be live, the other one will be studio," he explains, and talks about the recording sessions in Sun Studios, the song he wrote for B.B. King, and the band's fascination with old American blues and country music. Edge sings and plays a full version of *Lost Highway* to illustrate that they always wanted to be a country band.

Some plans for the Tempe shows are revealed. "Normally we like to play around with the running order, but now we can't," Bono says. Edge adds, "We're gonna try something new with the last track on 'The Joshua Tree', *Mothers Of The Disappeared*. We have put some Spanish words together; we're so close to a Spanish speaking part of the world, we felt that maybe people at the concert might pick up on this lyric." Bono expands on this: "We've always ended our concerts with the song *40*, which is a refrain from *Sunday Bloody Sunday*: How long, how long must we sing this song. We recorded that on the 'Under A Blood Red Sky' film and record, and it's been a timepiece. At this concert we're hoping to actually put *Mothers Of The Disappeared* in place of *40* from now on. We're gonna make the chant a little more difficult: El pueblo vencera, which means: the people united will overcome." He says that these are the words that the actual mothers of the disappeared in Central and South America motivate themselves with in their struggle to find out what's happened to their children. Edge plays the melody of *Mothers* on the guitar and sings these words and Bono briefly joins in second voice. He says, "If the people of Arizona sing this, and if it goes into the film and onto the record, wherever we go in a way for the next few years, that will be taken up again. It'll be an interesting experiment; if it doesn't work, it doesn't work."

After the interview, the band go back to rehearse until 4am, generating around 300 complaints to the police as house windows in the vicinity of the stadium are shaking due to the high sound volume.

DECEMBER 19, 20, 1987. TEMPE, AZ, SUN DEVIL STADIUM

- Attendance: 110,450 (P); sellout
- Support: B.B. King
- Set first night: *Where The Streets Have No Name / I Will Follow / Trip Through Your Wires / I Still Haven't Found / Out Of Control / MLK / One Tree Hill / Gloria / Exit / In God's Country / Bad / Star Spangled Banner – Bullet The Blue Sky / Running To Stand Still / Sunday Bloody Sunday / New Year's Day / Pride /* encore: *With Or Without You / Mothers Of The Disappeared / People Get Ready / 40*

Originally U2 had intended filming the colour section for their movie in Buenos Aires, Argentina, on December 20 and 21, but when it becomes clear that it will be too complicated and expensive to ship their massive equipment there and organise the shows, Tempe, Arizona, the city where the tour started, is

corrects himself he overdoes it, going on far too long while Bono waits to start the next verse and it turns into a real mess. In the quiet part of the song Bono carries out his *you too* message: "Ladies and gentlemen – as living proof that *anyone* can make it to the top: Bono, Edge, Larry and Adam."

Bono's rap in *Bullet The Blue Sky* is riveting. He talks about the two different Americas he has discovered while travelling through the country: the one with "kids being ripped off, syringes stuck in their arms, and people inventing new drugs like crack so they can fuck 'm up even more", and the one "where 17,000 people can get together in one night and agree on rock & roll music, as rock & roll is the soundtrack to some kind of change... We got Amnesty International people over here, people working for Third World relief organisations over there. If this is America, I like it! And I feel a long way from the hills of San Salvador, where the sky was ripped open, and the rain pours

through a gaping wound, pelting the women and children, pelting the women and children, who run... and they run... into the arms... into your arms. Look after them."

At the end of the night, Bono thanks everybody in the U2 crew for all the trouble and hard work on the tour. "There's Joe O'Herlihy, he's going home to Ireland tomorrow, he's gonna have a baby! But there's one person I'd like to thank as without him this whole tour just wouldn't be possible, I'd like to introduce you to him now: Dallas Schoo Dalton, he's over here!" Guitar technician Dallas Schoo comes onstage outfitted in full Dalton gear. Bono continues, "Dallas is being one of our biggest influences, he started a legendary country band by the name of The Dalton Brothers, back in the late Sixties... this is his first... Oh my... oh shit," he laughs, as he sees three more roadies entering the stage. "Hi, y'all! We're the Dalton gang here!" says one of them. "This here is Betty Dalton, there's Alton Dalton,

chosen instead. Director Phil Joanou and producer Michael Hamlyn spare no expense: twelve cameras record the event from all angles and 80 extra hands are hired to operate them. A big Louma crane for filming the audience from above their heads moves across a long runway from the stage into the audience, and the show is also filmed from a helicopter .

To make sure both shows sell out and to encourage fans to travel from out of state, admission is set at a mere $5 and tickets go on sale throughout the country. The low price compensates for obstructed views as a result of the cameras. Merchandise prices are also substantially reduced. The plan works, as thousands of fans from all over America travel to Arizona to be part of the tour farewell and to be immortalised on celluloid. The first night the filming doesn't go as planned. The cameramen have trouble recording Bono's unpredictable capers as he rebels against the straitjacket the cameras impose on him, and he gives his all to the audience instead. Although it is not on the set list, Bono sings *Out Of Control* and a lighting technician rotates the windmill which is meant for *MLK*, following instructions to do it at the fifth song!

■ Set second night: same as previous night, minus *Out Of Control*, plus *Helter Skelter* and *Help* before *Bad*, and plus *Christmas (Baby Please Come Home)* before *40*.

The second night is U2's last chance to get footage for their film and they focus more on helping the camera crew. Bono keeps his wild stage antics within limits. At the intro of *I Still Haven't Found* he looks back on the year. "We've been all through the United States over the last year; from New York to Los Angeles,

from San Francisco to Arizona, from Chicago to Memphis. In Memphis we got to record some songs at Sun Studios. We went to see Graceland; got to root through Elvis Presley's record collection! And in there amongst these rock & roll records hang these old gospel tunes. This is a sort of a gospel song with a restless spirit."

For *Mothers Of The Disappeared* Bono explains what motivated him to write the song: "When we were on the Amnesty International tour, we were in San Francisco and I met some people who were very good to me. A guy called René Castro showed me an alleyway in the Mission district. It was covered for about 50 yards in the most beautiful kind of wall painting I'd ever seen. And that started a journey for me which ended up in El Salvador and Nicaragua, where I met some very beautiful people who are known to the world as the mothers of the disappeared. In this small building in San Salvador were about 25, 50, sometimes a hundred women. Outside there, a little small house, sometimes 500 police, sometimes the army, sometimes tanks and guns. They're really afraid of these women, so I'm gonna sing this song for them and for their bravery. These are women who have lost their sons and daughters, taken away in the morning light, taken away at dawn, never to be seen again. They only want to know if their sons or daughters are alive or dead. That's all they wanna know. To sing this song I'd like you to sing with me some Spanish: El pueblo vencera, which means: the people united will overcome." To rehearse the audience, Bono starts singing the Spanish words and when the audience sing along, Larry joins in and starts a version of the song that lasts close to nine minutes.

"Some of you know that Edge has been giving me some guitar lessons. He showed me these three chords here. C, A-Minor, F. He said, 'Bono, with those three chords you can change the whole world'. Well, maybe not change the whole world, but maybe you get to see the world anyway. You get to put on a concert in the desert in Arizona, how about that?" The crowd cheer. "Get your picture on *Time* magazine, how about that? Rock & roll is wonderful. Be a big hit with the opposite sex, how about that? Have people love ya *and* hate ya, even though they haven't met ya, how about that? Or maybe, if you're lucky, get to write a song as good as Curtis Mayfield's *People Get Ready*." For the last time this year, a member of the audience joins U2 and plays well. "First time lucky! And what a poseur, ladies and gentlemen!" The guy sings a few lines and is enjoying himself so much he can't be dragged off the stage. Bono remarks, "Listen, I know you feel comfortable up here, but, you know, we've got a movie to make. I mean, it's a bit of a distraction, but uhm..." The audience laugh. "What's your name again? Tom Willock. You're in a band? A band called Children. Well, we think your band are gonna make it to the big top, Tom! And if they do, get them to buy you a different hat, will ya!"

"There's only one song I think we can play now. We've never played it before in front of people," Bono announces, and starts singing, "The snow's coming down, I'm watching it fall..." U2 play a wonderful version of *Christmas (Baby Please Come Home)*, the song U2 contributed to the 'A Very Special Christmas' album. "Tomorrow I'm going home! Babe, I'm coming home to you!" Bono screams. And indeed, the day after, U2 will go back home to Dublin for Christmas and to rest after nine months of touring.

After the song Bono sings a line of *Jingle Bells* and the audience, now in the Christmas mood, sing the tune and laugh when Bono mocks, "Hey, listen, I just want you to know something: we've got a reputation to live down to, we're a very serious band! I mean, as the spokespeople for the generation, we've had a very hard year carrying the weight of the world on our shoulders, you know. I mean it's hard work: setting people free, looking after the homeless, tackling world hunger, and organising a summit between the world powers – this is hard work!" The audience cheer and seem to understand that Bono, with these words, is subtly attacking the press who overstressed U2's social and political significance. Bono continues on a quieter note: "No, it's not. It's not hard work at all. It's the best job I ever got, let me tell you. Have a happy Christmas and a wonderful New Year. I wanna tell you this has been some year for us. I wanna thank all our road crew: Joe O'Herlihy, Peter Williams, Tim, Steve. They're all here, all these faces. You can't see them. I see them every day, in fact, I'm sick of seeing them everyday, but anyway..." Bono gets keyboard technician Des Broadberry onstage and tells the audience he just had a baby boy back in Ireland, making him the third crew member to have a baby in the last six months on the road. Bono opens a bottle of champagne to spray all over Des and together they drink to this new life. *40* is extended with snippets of *Do they know it's Christmas?* and *We Are The World* and at the end Bono shouts, "I just like to thank Paul McGuinness, Ellen (Darst), and The Edge, Larry Mullen Junior and Adam Clayton for letting me be in their band. Good night!" One by one the band members leave the stage, and with 55,000 people in the audience singing "How long to sing this song" for several minutes after the final drumbeat, 'The Joshua Tree' Tour comes to an end.

Where The Streets Have No Name, MLK, With Or Without You, Bullet The Blue Sky and *Running To Stand Still* from the second Tempe show make it into 'Rattle And Hum' and form the colour section of the movie. *Mothers Of The Disappeared*, with the audience singing "El pueblo vencera" was considered for the closing sequence of the movie but rejected.

The fifty shows of the American fall tour are attended by a total of 1,576,518 people, an average of 31,530 per show. Another 20,000 people attend the free show in San Francisco. Only three concerts fail to sell out, leaving a mere 24,815 tickets unsold. With ticket prices ranging from $16.50 to $19.50, the total gross is a staggering $27,255,566.

FEBRUARY – JULY 1988. LOS ANGELES, CA / DUBLIN, IRELAND

Originally, the 'Joshua Tree' tour is scheduled to visit Australia early in 1988, but after nine months of touring the band are not up to it. The impressions from their journey through America leave them inspired to develop the musical and lyrical ideas they brought home and to examine the film material that Joanou has shot. The band decide to postpone the Australian tour till early 1989.

U2 spend six months working on the movie and the album. Studying over 160 hours of concert and documentary footage with Phil Joanou in Los Angeles, U2 assist in making editorial decisions to fit 90 minutes. They also record new songs at A&M Studios and STS Studios. In May, U2 hold camp in the Point Depot in Dublin, an old railway hall, where more songs are recorded and sessions are filmed to supply further footage for the movie. In June, the band are back in Los Angeles to do post-production work on the sound of both the album and the movie at A&M Studios.

SEPTEMBER 21, 1988. LOS ANGELES, CA, COLISEUM

■ Amnesty International's 'Human Rights Now!' Tour line up: Youssou N'Dour, Tracy Chapman, Peter Gabriel, Sting, Bruce Springsteen & The E Street Band.

Though U2 don't take part in Amnesty International's follow-up to the 1986 Conspiracy of Hope tour, Bono joins the all-star band at LA Coliseum for the finale of the Bob Dylan song *Chimes Of Freedom*, one of the theme songs of the tour, and gets a warm reception from the crowd. A version of Bob Marley's *Get Up, Stand Up* ends the show.

OCTOBER 10, 1988

The 'Rattle And Hum' album is released worldwide.

OCTOBER 16, 1988. LONDON, ENGLAND, DOMINION THEATRE

■ Attendance: 2,500; sellout
■ 'Smile Jamaica' benefit. Line up: Womack & Womack, Chris Rea, Ziggy Marley & The Melody Makers, Keith Richards, Robert Palmer, The Christians, U2
■ Set: *All Along The Watchtower / Angel Of Harlem / When Love Comes To Town / Love Rescue Me*

After rumours and speculation, U2 make a special 20 minute appearance at the Smile Jamaica benefit concert for the victims of Hurricane Gilbert, which destroyed one out of every five homes in Jamaica. The show is simulcast on UK radio and TV. U2 promote the event by including a small message in their press

AN INITIAL TELEVISION PRODUCTION FOR CHANNEL 4
IN AID OF
HURRICANE APPEAL
DOMINION THEATRE
TOTTENHAM COURT ROAD
SUNDAY 16TH OCTOBER
PERFORMANCES 10.00 - 12.30PM DOORS OPEN 8.45PM
NO ADMITTANCE AFTER 9.30PM
LIVE TELEVISION TRANSMISSION   SUBJECT TO CONDITIONS OVERLEAF

STALLS
Row N
Seat 42
PRICE
£10.00

advertisements for the 'Rattle And Hum' album: "Jamaica needs your help. Support the Hurricane Appeal. Smile Jamaica, on Channel 4 and ITV, Sunday October 16. Call to make your donation from 11th October. Or write..." It's U2's only official concert appearance of 1988 and for the first time since February 1985 they play for a small crowd. U2 are last on the bill and start with *All Along The Watchtower* in an arrangement similar to the version on 'Rattle And Hum'. The first live performance of *Angel Of Harlem* contains horns by The Rumour Horn Section. "Right,

which one of you hit the policeman?" Bono asks earnestly, referring to an incident that occurred at the box office when ticket went on sale. At the start of *When Love Comes To Town*, Bono wails, "Where's my mate, Keith Richards?" Keith is already onstage adjusting his guitar strap and throughout the song adds extensive guitar solos wherever he can. He stays onstage for *Love Rescue Me*, during which Ziggy Marley and The Melody Makers, who performed earlier, join in to sing a verse. The crowd sing "How long to sing this song" when U2 have left the stage.

This live version of *Love Rescue Me* becomes an extra track on U2's *Angel Of Harlem* single, released on December 1, 1988. All proceeds from the song, resulting from sales of the single and radio airplay, are donated to the Smile Jamaica Fund. The fund is further promoted by means of inclusion of their address on the record sleeve.

OCTOBER 27, 1988. DUBLIN, IRELAND, O'CONNELL STREET

■ Set: *When Love Comes To Town / I Still Haven't Found / Angel Of Harlem / Stand By Me*

The world première in Dublin of the 'Rattle And Hum' film is a big event with maximum hype, media attention and audience anticipation. Tickets to the première cost £50 with all proceeds, some £40,000, going to People In Need which benefits the homeless. An estimated 5,000 gather outside the cinema to catch a glimpse of the band and react ecstatically when, shortly before the movie is due to begin, U2 appear on a ramp between the Gresham Hotel and the Savoy cinema and play *When Love*

SAVOY 1 CINEMA
SAVOY 1 DUBLIN
GALA PREMIERE
EVENING 8.00
Stalls
D 17
GALA PREMIERE
EVENING 8.00
STALLS
D 17
TO BE GIVEN UP
Patrons should be seated before 8.00 p.m.
TO BE RETAINED

WORLD CHARITY PREMIERE

TO AID
PEOPLE IN NEED

Thursday October 27th 1988

At the
SAVOY CINEMA
O'CONNELL STREET
DUBLIN 1

Doors Open at 7.00

Please be seated by 7.45 pm

INFORMAL DRESS
FOLLOWED BY DRINKS AND FOOD
RECEPTION AT GRESHAM HOTEL
PLEASE RETAIN THIS TICKET TO GAIN ACCESS TO PARTY

THIS TICKET ADMITS ONE ONLY

Comes To Town and *I Still Haven't Found*, with Edge and Adam on acoustic guitars and Larry banging a tambourine. With people in the trees and on street lights, the impromptu performance becomes U2's long-awaited Millenium show to celebrate the 1,000th anniversary of Dublin City. After the movie ends, U2 enter the catwalk again and play loose versions of *Angel Of Harlem* and *Stand By Me* with Bono making up most of the words while the crowd act as a huge choir.

OCTOBER 29, 1988. MADRID, SPAIN, CINE GRAN VIA

U2 attend the Madrid première of 'Rattle And Hum', accompanied by tour manager Dennis Sheehan who stands in for Paul McGuinness. Proceeds of the Madrid and the three remaining premières are donated to Amnesty International. U2 make a speech on the cinema's stage, talking about the film and the charity they are supporting, after which Bono and Edge sing a verse of *I Still Haven't Found*. During the movie fans clap and sing along and many wave white flags.

OCTOBER 31, 1988. LONDON, ENGLAND, LEICESTER SQUARE

U2 attend the London première of 'Rattle And Hum' at the Empire Theatre but cannot perform live as the police refuse permission, fearing an impromptu performance will result in chaos in Leicester Square and people will get hurt. U2 are also refused permission to play live at the New York première on November 3.

NOVEMBER 4, 1988. LOS ANGELES, CA, CHINA THEATER

■ Set: *When Love Comes To Town / Stand By Me / I Still Haven't Found*

U2's last stop on their mini-tour of 'Rattle And Hum' premières is LA, where they manage to perform a few songs in front of the cinema on a small stage. Thousands of fans pack the streets and hear Edge strum a rough version of *When Love Comes To Town* with Larry even singing a few lines. The same day the movie opens in over 1,200 cinemas throughout North America. Glimpses of the performance and the première are shown on CNN's Entertainment News.

NOVEMBER, 1988. BRYAN FERRY: DUBLIN, IRELAND, RDS SIMMONS COURT

The Edge makes a surprise appearance at Bryan Ferry's show.

DECEMBER 16, 1988. DUBLIN, IRELAND, RTE STUDIOS

U2 appear on the 'Late Late Show' in a live broadcast on Irish TV. After a brief interview the band produce acoustic instruments and perform John Lennon's *Happy Christmas (War Is Over)*.

EARLY 1989

In early 1989 U2 decide to postpone the Australian tour to the second half of the year as they need some time for themselves after a year's work on the 'Rattle And Hum' album and movie and the promotional activities. Over the next two months members of the band will make several guest appearances. Bono writes some songs, among them one for Nina Simone called *Love Is Blindness But I Don't Want To See*. The band also record new material as well as cover versions for possible inclusion on the B-sides of upcoming singles.

EARLY 1989. NASHVILLE, TN

Adam, Bono and Cowboy Jack Clement are in a bar where a blues singer is playing. Cowboy Jack goes up onstage and sings, after which Bono and Adam join in and perform *Love Rescue Me* to around twenty people who have no idea who they are.

MARCH 11, 1989. B.B. KING: DUBLIN, IRELAND, NATIONAL STADIUM

As a consequence of his appearance with U2 in 'Rattle And Hum' and on the album, the audience at B.B. King's show are much younger than at his previous nine visits to Dublin. B.B. is greeted with a standing ovation and plays for close to two hours before he starts telling the audience about a special meeting he had backstage in Dublin a couple of years ago. For many in the audience this is the green light to leave their seats and rush to the front. B.B. talks about working with U2 and signals to Edge and Bono who make their way to the stage from the VIP box as the band launch into a ragged version of *When Love Comes To Town*. B.B. gracefully hands over Lucille, his guitar, to The Edge, who is honoured at being allowed to play it. Bono and B.B. duet on the song they first sang together 16 months earlier in Fort Worth, Texas. Bono improvises on Little Richard's *Lucille* which lasts a good ten minutes and has the band jamming along while B.B. and Bono sing and chat.

APRIL 27, 1989. DUBLIN, IRELAND, PINK ELEPHANT NIGHTCLUB

Gavin Friday launches his first solo album 'Each Man Kills The Thing He Loves' and Bono joins Gavin on stage doing versions of Queen's *We Are The Champions* and Paul Anka's *My Way*. Liam O'Maonlai of The Hothouse Flowers sings *Suspicious Minds* and Mary Coughlan croons *Heartbreak Hotel*.

APRIL 30, 1989. DUBLIN, IRELAND, ABBEY THEATRE

In a fundraising event for the continued existence of the 85-year old Abbey Theatre, Bono adapts two works by the Irish poet William Butler Yeats into musical pieces. Accompanied by a backing tape he has compiled, Bono sings the political poem *September 1913* and *Mad As The Mist And Snow*, marking his first live solo appearance.

JUNE 4, 1989. BOB DYLAN: DUBLIN, IRELAND, RDS SIMMONS COURT

Bono joins Dylan halfway through *Knocking On Heaven's Door*, the first encore, playing along on acoustic guitar and stealing a line or two from the master. It lightens up Dylan's otherwise predictable and disappointing performance and Dylan himself, who had seemed uninterested, appears to enjoy playing with Bono again. A rocking version of *Maggie's Farm* follows, during which Bono sings, "Well there ain't no work on Charley's farm no more", referring to Ireland's Prime Minister Charles Haughey.

JUNE 17, 1989. HOTHOUSE FLOWERS: GLASTONBURY FESTIVAL, ENGLAND

Adam joins in with The Hothouse Flowers, playing bass on *Feet On The Ground*. Later in the gig singers Maria McKee and Maria Doyle also make guest appearances.

JUNE 23, 1989. MARIA McKEE: DUBLIN, IRELAND, MOTHER REDCAP'S

Adam plays along on a few songs.

THE 'LOVETOWN TOUR' TOUR, LEG 1: AUSTRALASIA, 1989

In July, U2 start preparations for their long-awaited tour of Australia, New Zealand and Japan. With the tour having been postponed several times the band are now eager to play live again. They rehearse in Dublin throughout August, going through their repertoire and working out new songs. Meanwhile, René Castro, the Chilean mural artist whom U2 met on the Conspiracy Of Hope tour, is hired to design and produce backdrops for the new stage. Using the symbols of a guitar, a snake, Stars & Stripes and a hawkmoon, he designs three huge backdrops that will give U2's stage a more colourful and variable look than before.

Having first worked together in late 1987, B.B. King is asked to come along on tour as special guest and to warm up the audience before U2. B.B. accepts and U2 are honoured to be working again with the blues master, whose music has influenced some of their own recent songs. B.B. responds by saying he is honoured as well, and is thankful to U2 for giving him an opportunity to expose his music to an audience that are largely unfamiliar with his work.

With the tour already scheduled to commence in September, everything is suddenly jeopardised when on August 6 Adam is arrested by the police in the Blue Light pub in Glencullen, Ireland, and charged with possession of 19 grammes of marihuana and intent to supply. His trial is set for Sep-

tember 1. If Adam is convicted his visas to travel abroad could be revoked. The story makes the papers throughout the world and U2's fans, especially in Australia, are not amused. At the trial, Adam pleads guilty to possession and is fined £25,000, to be donated to the Women's Aid Refugee Centre. The Probation of Offenders Act applies in Adam's case, which means there is no conviction and Adam's record will remain clear of drug offences. Getting visas to travel is no problem and the tour is safe.

U2 arrive in Sydney on September 9 and start further rehearsals at the Homebush Sports Centre. The local press cover U2's every move, and report that in the week of final rehearsals they also record some demos at a local studio. U2-mania reigns over Australia, easily matching the euphoria that ruled Europe and America in 1987. Every show sells out instantly, and extra dates are being added all the time. In Melbourne a total of seven shows is booked. Taking over a city for a week appeals to U2; turning every city into a 'LoveTown' and playing multiple indoor shows so that all the fans get a chance to see the band in optimum conditions. With Love being the universal theme of the tour, the LoveTown show is low-key and, as it is the edge of a new decade, is meant to celebrate the first ten years of U2's career with a selection of songs that includes work from every phase. Realising that a significant number of fans will attend every show in town, the band have a number of basic sets that differ considerably. Each night in town will be different, with an average of 19 or 20 songs selected each night from no fewer than 35. Several songs will be inserted just once or twice on special occasions, which strengthens the sense of excitement and always surprise the audiences.

The *All I Want Is You* single, which came out in the rest of the world in April, is delayed until October to coincide with the tour. It will reach No. 1 in the Australian charts.

SEPTEMBER 15, 1989. SYDNEY, MERCANTILE HOTEL

U2 and B.B. King hold a press conference six days before the start of the tour. Asked about the group's collaboration with the blues singer, Bono says, "Working with B.B. is a mixed blessing because he's the only guy I know that when he moves back from the microphone his voice gets *louder*. I feel like a little girl when I'm singing with him." How did their working together come about in the first place? B.B. explains, "I met the group in Ireland about two or three years ago and as they were leaving I asked if Bono would write a song for me sometime, and he said yes. I thought maybe he might forget it." Is it exciting to be touching a whole new audience? B.B.: "Oh yes it is. Since 'Rattle And Hum' I've noticed a great change in my own audience and, of course, thanks to U2 that has happened. I'd like to add a little something: after hearing about the song *When Love Comes To Town* when my manager mentioned it to me, he didn't mention I was to sing it with U2. When Bono mentioned we'd do it together – really, it was one of the great things that's happened to me in my career."

Bono: "Organising this tour is a little devious of us. We just got the chance to have B.B. play with us so now we can learn from him. He comes from a generation of maybe six people of the order of B.B., and some of them are not around any more. I consider myself an apprentice around him. To actually have him on the road is an amazing thing." After the conference security tries to whisk the band away into a van, but there is a commotion when they seem more interested in socialising with the fans outside. A local shopkeeper watches the scene and comments, "You'd think it was The Beatles!"

SEPTEMBER 16, 1989. SYDNEY HARBOUR

B.B. King's 64th birthday is celebrated on a boat which U2 rent for the occasion. A live band play music while the entire tour entourage set out into Sydney harbour for the day. Inevitably, Birthday Boy himself ends up playing some blues on Lucille, and Bono accompanies him, as do several others.

SEPTEMBER 21, 22, 23, 1989. PERTH, ENTERTAINMENT CENTRE

- Attendance: 24,000; sellout
- Support: Weddings Parties Anything, B.B. King
- Set first night: *Hawkmoon 269 / Desire / All Along The Watchtower / All I Want Is You / Where The Streets Have No Name / I Will Follow / I Still Haven't Found / One Tree Hill / God Part II / In God's Country / People Get Ready / Bad / October / New Year's Day / Pride* / encore: *Star Spangled Banner – Bullet The Blue Sky / Running To Stand Still / With Or Without You* / encore: *Angel Of Harlem / When Love Comes To Town / Love Rescue Me / 40*

Australian band Weddings Parties Anything are hired for the tour and play for half an hour before B.B. King and his band take over to warm up the audience with a selection of blues spanning three decades. Their interest ignited by his appearance in 'Rattle And Hum', the audience are open to B.B.'s refined guitar playing and bluesy singing. During his last number B.B. urges the crowd, "When in a while the greatest band in the world come out, you are gonna make them happy, are you!?" At the end of his set he gracefully bows and gets enthusiastic applause. While U2's roadies clear the stage and prepare for U2's performance, Rolling Stones' and Beatles' music is played over the PA. Songs like *Love Me Do, I Saw Her Standing There, Stand By Me* and *All You Need Is Love* remind the audience of the theme for the night.

Edge introduces *Hawkmoon 269* with atmospheric, slowly swelling guitar before Larry bangs the song into motion. The Perth audience, most of whom are seeing U2 for the first time, are hysterical, setting a trend for the whole tour. A rousing

Is there love in the house tonight?

Desire moves fluently into *All Along The Watchtower*, which is much improved from the 'Save The Yuppies' version on 'Rattle And Hum'. Its new, fast-paced arrangement slows down before building to a climax with an attractive lighting design of yellow, orange, purple and green spotlights rhythmically circling across the stage. *All I Want Is You* is sung solemnly and offers the crowd an opportunity to bring out their lighters. The backdrop slowly lights up in red as the opening tones of *Where The Streets Have No Name* swell and bring the crowd to a complete frenzy. Houselights flash on early in the song to illuminate all present and establish a unity within the arena, enhancing the feeling of being part of an event rather than just watching a rock concert. Overall the lighting is more colourful than ever, with each song having its own design to match the feel of the music.

The live première of *God Part II* is a highlight of the show, with Bono doing a striptease, slowly removing his jacket, then pulling out his shirt until the song climaxes. *In God's Country* and *People Get Ready* are performed as in 1987, with the latter used as an opportunity for young guitar players to come onstage and enjoy five minutes of fame. The *Bad / October / New Year's Day / Pride* sequence is present again, and *Bullet The Blue Sky / Running To Stand Still* open the encore preceded by the recording of *The Star Spangled Banner*. Sixteen dark red spotlights swarm over the stage and around the arena during *Bullet*, with Bono again shining a spotlight on Edge. Scalpers do good business which prompts Bono to comment: "What's all this stuff about people paying $400 for a ticket? I mean, I'm in the band, and I know we're not worth $400!"

The second encore is the heart of the show. The three-piece horn section and the keyboard player of B.B. King's band come out again and add their rich sound to *Angel Of Harlem* and *When Love Comes To Town*, for which B.B. himself joins Bono in a sparkling duet. *Love Rescue Me* has B.B. sing a verse as well, taking over Bob Dylan's part from the studio version. U2 traditionally end the show with *40*.

The band are delighted by the audience's warm reception. Edge comments after the show, "I've been to a lot of shows, and I've never seen a crowd quite like a U2 crowd. It's almost like we are coming to their party, because it's such a great atmosphere!" "It felt good to be back," says Adam . "You forget how powerful it is to be in front of an audience. It's a great, great feeling."

■ Set second night: *Where The Streets Have No Name / I Will Follow / I Still Haven't Found / MLK / The Unforgettable Fire / Bullet The Blue Sky / Running To Stand Still / With Or Without You / God Part II / Desire / All Along The Watchtower / Help / Bad / October / New Year's Day / Pride / encore: Angel Of*

Harlem / When Love Comes To Town / Love Rescue Me

The set very much resembles a Joshua Tree tour setlist with the first seven songs played in the same order as two years ago. A bit of Bob Marley's *Exodus* is linked to *I Still Haven't Found*, while *Bad* has the usual snippets from *Ruby Tuesday* and *Candle In The Wind* at the end. In *Angel Of Harlem*, Elvis Presley's *Suspicious Minds* shows up, one of several new cover versions that will occasionally be played. "Help me, Edge," Bono says when he doesn't know how to move back to *Angel Of Harlem*, causing chaos as he starts another verse of *Suspicious Minds* just when everybody else is back to *Angel*. Bono gives B.B. a grand introduction: "Here he is: Monster of the blues... mister Beee Beee King!" Halfway through the song Bono raps, "B.B. King invented the blues, and then he found a cure for the blues..." B.B. takes over: "The cure is love – is there love in the house tonight? Is there enough love to make us not hurt each other? Is there enough love to make us wanna help each other?" The crowd respond affirmative. "Then there is love in this house tonight..."

Bono says, "When we heard that the tickets had all sold out, we threw a party back in Dublin, and we'd have invited y'all over there, but... So we're sort of throwing a party here..."

■ Set third night: *In God's Country / All Along The Watchtower / Bullet The Blue Sky / Running To Stand Still / All I Want Is You / Where The Streets Have No Name / I Will Follow / I Still Haven't Found / People Get Ready / Bad / With Or Without You / God Part II / Desire / New Year's Day / Pride / encore: Angel Of Harlem / When Love Comes To Town / Love Rescue Me*

The set is changed completely, with *In God's Country* an unusual opener for the show. Surprisingly, the first verse is sung a capella before the band join in. Edge makes a rare speech to introduce *I Still Haven't Found*, saying that he enjoys playing Australia again after five years and thanking the audience for coming. Later, Bono comments that this is the first time Edge has spoken to an audience anywhere in the world.

SEPTEMBER 27, 28, 29, 1989. SYDNEY, ENTERTAINMENT CENTRE

■ Attendance 37,500; sellout
■ Support: Weddings Parties Anything, B.B. King
■ Set first night: *Hawkmoon 269 / Desire / All Along The Watchtower / Bullet The Blue Sky / Running To Stand Still / All I Want Is You / Where The Streets Have No Name / I Will Follow / I Still Haven't Found / People Get Ready / Bad / With Or Without You / God Part II / New Year's Day / Pride / encore: Angel Of Harlem / When Love Comes To Town / Love Rescue Me / 40*

"I missed you!" Bono shouts as he opens the first of no fewer than eight concerts in Australia's biggest city. Snippets of The Byrds' *So You Want To Be (A Rock & Roll Star)* are included in *Desire* and will show up in most versions on the tour: "So you wanna be in a rock & roll band, better listen now to what I say. Just get yourself an electric guitar and in a week or two you'll know how to play..."

■ Set second night: *Where The Streets Have No Name / I Will Follow / I Still Haven't Found / MLK / The Unforgettable Fire / Bullet The Blue Sky / Running To Stand Still / All I Want Is You – With Or Without You / God Part II / All Along The Watchtower / Help / Bad / October / New Year's Day / Pride / encore: Angel Of Harlem / When Love Comes To Town / Love Rescue Me / encore: 40*

Bono sings only the first verse of *All I Want Is You* and has the audience sing the next verse, then starts *With Or Without You*. After the show, at the hotel, Bono surprises some fans waiting outside by playing guitar for them.

■ Set third night: *Where The Streets Have No Name / I Will Follow / I Still Haven't Found / One Tree Hill / God Part II /*

Welcome to LoveTown

Desire / All Along The Watchtower / Stand By Me / Bad / With Or Without You / Angel Of Harlem / When Love Comes To Town / Love Rescue Me / encore: Star Spangled Banner – Bullet The Blue Sky / Running To Stand Still / All I Want is You / New Year's Day / Pride

After All Along The Watchtower Bono plucks his guitar as if it is the first time he has ever played one. "What an invention eh, the electric guitar," he comments in admiration. "I like squeezing the notes like B.B. King does," he says and demonstrates this. "I like to take an acoustic guitar and play late at night outside the venue. Who were the girls that were there last night, that we were singing to? Some crazy people waiting outside; should've been in their beds!" Bono then starts to sing Stand By Me and halfway through says, "Larry Mullen, you can sing this too!" Larry is dragged up front and he sings while Bono takes Larry's place, debuting as U2's drummer! This is the first time since singing The Eagles' Tequila Sunrise in Hampton in December 1987 that Larry has sung in public and he sounds better than he did back then. Edge helps him out at the end, while Bono tries to finish the song with a drum solo but one of the sticks flies out of his hand and he desperately attempts to close with only one stick.

OCTOBER 2, 3, 4, 1989. BRISBANE, ENTERTAINMENT CENTRE

- Attendance: 24,000; sellout
- Support: Weddings Parties Anything, B.B. King
- Set first night: same as Sydney September 29, with MLK and The Unforgettable Fire replacing One Tree Hill, and Help instead of Stand By Me.

Brisbane is the next 'LoveTown' on the map. Things get hectic among the largely teenage audience and Bono says in concern, "I like to thank you all for coming here and going through so much trouble to get tickets. I think the thing about the U2 audience is that there is something that sets them apart: they look after each other. At least that's the way it's always been. So what I want you to do is just ease back a bit here. Some people up here got some breathing problems, so everybody try and ease back a bit. We can do that, can't we?"

During Bullet The Blue Sky Bono recalls an experience from the day before: "So anyway, I got into bed, and I must have fallen asleep for about an hour when suddenly an explosion went off in my head. It was the doorbell. I got down, fell over all my cassettes and records, and went to the door. I looked into the little hole that we have in our doors as paranoid rock & roll people, and on the other side of the door I saw myself, just about two years younger. And I thought, 'What's going on? What am I doing out there?' Anyway, it turns out it was some guy from a Bono lookalike competition, who managed to sneak in the hotel elevator, and was knocking on my room! He's gonna eat my porridge and watch my video tape recorder! Well, I felt really pissed off at the time; but tonight I thought, that's the sort of thing I might have done myself actually..."

- Set second night: Where The Streets Have No Name / Hawkmoon 269 / Desire / All Along The Watchtower / All I Want Is You / Where The Streets / I Will Follow / I Still Haven't Found / In God's Country / God Part II / People Get Ready / Bad / October / New Year's Day / Pride / encore: Angel Of Harlem / When Love Comes To Town / Love Rescue Me / encore: With Or Without You / 40

During Love Rescue Me Bono brings his baby daughter on stage.

"This is the first time she's ever seen U2 play. Her name is Jordan, she's four months old, by the way."

- Set third night: Where The Streets Have No Name / I Will Follow / I Still Haven't Found / MLK / One Tree Hill / God Part II / Desire / All Along The Watchtower / All I Want Is You / People Get Ready / Bad / October / New Year's Day / Pride / encore: Angel Of Harlem / When Love Comes To Town / Love Rescue Me / encore: Star Spangled Banner – Bullet The Blue Sky / Running To Stand Still / With Or Without You

Love Rescue Me is introduced on a sad note: "Two people have died on the way home from this concert, last night. You all take care of each other..." Like at some previous shows, 40 is omitted and is no longer the definite closing song.

OCTOBER 7, 8, 9, 12, 13, 14, 16, 1989. MELBOURNE, NATIONAL TENNIS CENTRE

- Attendance: 112,000; sellout
- Support: Weddings Parties Anything, B.B. King
- Set first night: Where The Streets Have No Name / I Will Follow / I Still Haven't Found / MLK / The Unforgettable Fire / God Part II / Desire / All Along The Watchtower / All I Want Is You / People Get Ready / Bad / October / New Year's Day / Pride / encore: Angel Of Harlem / When Love Comes To Town / Love Rescue Me / encore: Star Spangled Banner – Bullet The Blue Sky / Running To Stand Still / With Or Without You

In 1984 U2 played five concerts in Melbourne; this time it's seven in a venue twice as big. At first only two shows are cautiously put on sale, then another three, and another two; ticket demand seems inexhaustible. An eighth show for October

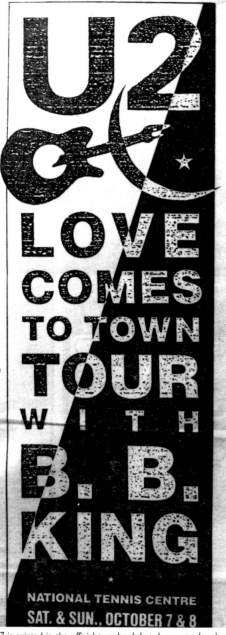

Set third night: *Stand By Me / In God's Country / Desire / All Along The Watchtower / All I Want Is You / Where The Streets Have No Name / I Will Follow / I Still Haven't Found / MLK / One Tree Hill / God Part II / Bullet The Blue Sky / Running To Stand Still / Van Diemen's Land / Bad / October / New Year's Day / Pride / encore: Angel Of Harlem / When Love Comes To Town / Love Rescue Me / encore: 40*

Like was often done in 1987, U2 enter the stage during the intro tape of *Stand By Me* and take over the song live with the house lights still on. Edge breaks a string during *All Along The Watchtower* and Bono sings, "No reason to get excited, Edge just broke a string, but he doesn't need that shit, he wants to do his thing..." At the end Bono causes feedback when he turns up the volume on his guitar and frenetically slides his hand up and down its neck. Bono and Adam leave the stage to leave Edge alone in the spotlight to sing *Van Diemen's Land* for the first time. Rumours abound that after the show the band will make a surprise appearance in an Irish pub downtown. Hundreds of fans go there but nothing happens.

Set fourth night: *Star Spangled Banner – Bullet The Blue Sky / Where The Streets Have No Name / I Will Follow / Gloria / I Still Haven't Found / MLK / The Unforgettable Fire / God Part II / Desire / All Along The Watchtower / All I Want Is You – Bad /*

17 is printed in the official tour book but does not take place. Bono dedicates *Bad* to a friend of the band who should have attended the show but has died in a car crash. During *Running To Stand Still* Bono substitutes the line "step out of the driving rain" with "can't get me no jet plane", referring to a pilots' strike which has thrown Australian air travel into chaos. At the end of the song he sings a brief chorus of *Waltzing Matilda*, which the audience finish for him.

Set second night: *Hawkmoon 269 / Desire / All Along The Watchtower / Bullet The Blue Sky / Running To Stand Still – All I Want Is You / Where The Streets Have No Name / I Will Follow / I Still Haven't Found / MLK / One Tree Hill / God Part II / Bad / October / New Year's Day / Pride / encore: Angel Of Harlem / When Love Comes To Town / Love Rescue Me / With Or Without You / 40*

Bono continues to change the rap in *Bullet The Blue Sky*: "So I cross the fields, I see the sky ripped open, and I find myself in the city of Melbourne, with enough powerful ammunition to blow the president of the United States to Kingdom Come... or the President of the Soviet Union... or the Prime Minister of Australia for that matter. There's another law that operates in this building... a law we call LOVE... and that isn't a 'flower in the hair' kinda love, it ain't the hippy dippy 1969 kinda love, it's a new hard as a stone, it's made of concrete and steel, and it's gonna change things in the future if we want it to..."

Van Diemen's Land / With Or Without You / People Get Ready / Angel Of Harlem / When Love Comes To Town / Love Rescue Me / encore: New Year's Day / Pride / encore: Out Of Control / Stand By Me / 40

Out Of Control is played for the first time on the tour, and with 23 songs, it's the longest show of the year. *All I Want Is You* halfway through segues into *Bad* with Bono singing the "isolation, dislocation" section before slipping back into *All I Want Is You*. During *People Get Ready* he sings, "Faith is the key, you gotta look to the future, don't look back, you can never look back!" In 1987 only male guitar players came onstage to take over Bono's guitar, but now it's time for a change. "Anybody else wanna join the band? Have we got any *ladies*, any rock & roll guitar women?" Unable to teach a girl the chords, he says, "I ask a woman up onstage and she tells me she can't play... I thought Melbourne was buzzing with music! I think we better give you a harmonica, OK? Just don't play it in the microphone, alright? Now, I'm looking for someone who plays electric guitar!" Another girl gets up but is too nervous to strap on the guitar and is sent straight back into the audience. Finally selecting a male guest, Bono shows him the chords but the guy gets carried away and does a Jimi Hendrix impersonation. Bono comments, "Man, this is like watching paint dry, you know what I mean? Play it man, play it!" He eventually gets it together while the girl works the harmonica. Looking at his two guests, Bono says, "Hey, you two should stick together, you sorta look good! Don't you think they look good together?" "Yeeaaaahhh!" the audience respond.

■ Set fifth night: *Hawkmoon 269 / Desire / All Along The Watchtower / All I Want Is You / Where The Streets Have No Name / I Will Follow / I Still Haven't Found / MLK / One Tree Hill / God Part II / Bullet The Blue Sky / Running To Stand Still / Bad / Van Diemen's Land / With Or Without You / New Year's Day / Pride / encore: Angel Of Harlem / When Love Comes To Town / Knocking On Heaven's Door / Love Rescue Me / encore: 40*

Bono forgets the words to *One Tree Hill* so Edge walks over and puts him right by singing them to him off mic. During *Bullet The Blue Sky* Bono adds the theme from 'Neighbours', the Australian TV soap. During *New Year's Day* a young boy runs onstage, Bono gives him his hat and takes him on his shoulders for the rest of the song. The big surprise of the evening is the inclusion of *Knocking On Heaven's Door* in the encore. B.B. plays the song for the first time ever and adds his squeaking guitar licks to the song. As *Love Rescue Me* starts, Bono says, "Anyway, you've been spoiling us rotten tonight, a great concert for us. For me it's like riding a wave or something, it's like surfing. The best concerts are just one big wave but even better than that is when you fall off the wave you get back upon a bigger one."

■ Set sixth night: *Where The Streets Have No Name / I Will Follow / I Still Haven't Found / All I Want Is You / MLK / The Unforgettable Fire / Exit / Gloria / Desire / All Along The Watchtower / Help / Bad / October / New Year's Day / Pride / encore: Angel Of Harlem / When Love Comes To Town / Love Rescue Me / encore: Star Spangled Banner – Bullet The Blue Sky / Running To Stand Still / With Or Without You*

During the Stones' intro music a guy in the stands does a Mick Jagger impersonation and attracts everyone's attention. *Exit* is played for the only time on the LoveTown tour and hasn't been performed since. The show seems to finish with *Love Rescue Me* as the spot operators climb down from the rigging and part of the audience starts to leave while others shout for more. Soon one of the crew is telling the lighting people to get back up there, and U2 come back for another three songs.

■ Set last night: *Hawkmoon 269 / Desire / All Along The Watchtower / Bullet The Blue Sky / Running To Stand Still / Where The Streets Have No Name / I Will Follow / Gloria / I Still Haven't Found / All I Want Is You / People Get Ready / Angel Of Harlem / When Love Comes To Town / Love Rescue Me / With Or Without You / God Part II / New Year's Day / Pride / encore: Party Girl / 40*

A small bunch of fans spend the afternoon outside the venue listening to U2 doing their soundcheck until Bono invites them inside to listen. Crew members guide the excited fans to seats at the back of the venue, get drinks for them and arrange tickets to the show for those who don't have any. The band rehearse *Where The Streets Have No Name, Bullet The Blue Sky*, as well as *Dancing Barefoot*, the Patti Smith song that U2 recorded for inclusion as an extra song on the *When Love Comes To Town* single. U2 never performed the song in concert. *She's A Mystery To Me*, the song Bono and Edge wrote for Roy Orbison, is also soundchecked as well as some unidentified blues songs. Edge sings *Van Diemen's Land* which receives applause from the tiny audience, upon which he bows gracefully.

The last show in Melbourne is powerful with another verbal jaunt during *Bullet The Blue Sky*. "Neighbours, everybody needs good neighbours... so Kylie Minogue comes up to me, see... so Jason Donovan comes up to me, see... so the President of the United States comes up to me and he wants to ask me a question. He says, 'Bono, we don't get 'Neighbours' over here in the USA... that's why I'm in such a bad mood across the border, see... that's why I don't think too much about what my panzer divisions are doing in Central America, Bono. If I could see Kylie and Jason, I would be happy, the world would be at peace tonight! I love that tune. I think that could be a big hit over here on the *Billboard* Hot 100.' And I look at The Edge, he looks into my eyes, and he says, 'Bono, I can see those fighter planes in your head.' Play them to me Edge, show me what you see..."

Prior to the show Bono's throat was examined by a doctor after complaints of soreness. During the intro to *I Still Haven't Found* Bono says, "There's a doctor backstage who says that I have the fever. Now, do I look like a man who has the fever? Well, tonight I take that as a compliment, actually." During Edge's guitar part in *Party Girl* Bono introduces him as Eddie van Halen, while the traditional champagne is brought out to end seven nights in Melbourne.

OCTOBER 20, 21, 1989. SYDNEY, ENTERTAINMENT CENTRE

■ Attendance: 25,000; sellout
■ Support: Wedding Parties Anything, B.B. King
■ Set first night: *Where The Streets Have No Name / I Will*

Follow / Gloria / I Still Haven't Found / MLK / The Unforgettable Fire / God Part II / Desire / All Along The Watchtower / All I Want Is You – Bad / Van Diemen's Land / New Year's Day / Pride / encore: Angel Of Harlem / When Love Comes To Town / Love Rescue Me / encore: Star Spangled Banner – Bullet The Blue Sky / Running To Stand Still / With Or Without You / 40

Thousands of teenagers scream hysterically whenever Bono announces a song or says anything at all, and often during quiet songs like *Running To Stand Still* loud shouts of "I love you Larry!" or "Kiss me Bono!" can be heard.

■ Set second night: *Star Spangled Banner – Bullet The Blue Sky / Desire / All Along The Watchtower / All I Want Is You / Where The Streets Have No Name / I Will Follow / I Still Haven't Found / MLK / One Tree Hill / People Get Ready / Bad / Van Diemen's Land / New Year's Day / Pride / encore: Angel Of Harlem / When Love Comes To Town / Love Rescue Me*

For days Bono has been suffering from a viral infection in his throat and he is under doctor's orders not to strain his voice. Before *Love Rescue Me* Bono thanks the audience for buying tickets and says, "We designed these to be special concerts, just for this part of the world and a few other places like our hometown. This is much better shit than the 'Joshua' Tree tour, anyway! I can tell it's good because if I've got a problem with my voice and I don't notice it, then it's good."

After the concert the band speed to Triple M studios for an interview on 'The Midnight Show', the country's main pop radio programme. Talking about Australian artists, Bono says Jason Donovan makes him wanna throw up, but thinks Peter Garrett of Midnight Oil is one of the great voices in Australia. Bono fiddles around on acoustic guitar while the interviewer announces that he will perform a new song live on the air. Bono says, "I wanna send this song to Willie Nelson. I think he's a great singer, and I want to write a great song for him. It's just been written recently, so I thought it might be nice to play it for people." It's a slow love song that starts, "My love is cruel as the night, she steals the sun and blots out the light, all of my colours turn to blue, when I'm with you. She does it slow dancing..." He sings one verse and the chorus and admits he hasn't written the second verse yet.

Coming back from the radio show, Bono has a burning pain in his throat which is diagnosed as laryngitis. He must take a week off to prevent any serious damage and, as a result, the remaining three Sydney shows planned for October 22, 24 and 25 have to be postponed. The press and the audience are shocked, but Adam assures them on MTV Australia that U2 will return to play the shows later. "If there's any way that Bono can sing, he will. It's very frustrating for him to be struck down by an illness." The U2 organisation and the concert promoter work overtime to reschedule the gigs.

OCTOBER 27, 28, 1989. ADELAIDE, MEMORIAL DRIVE STADIUM

- Attendance: 18,000; sellout
- Support: Wedding Parties Anything, B.B. King
- Set first night: *Where The Streets Have No Name / I Will Follow / I Still Haven't Found / MLK / The Unforgettable Fire / God Part II / Desire / All Along The Watchtower / All I Want Is You / People Get Ready / Bad / Van Diemen's Land / New Year's Day / Pride / encore: Angel Of Harlem / When Love Comes To Town / Love Rescue Me / encore: With Or Without You / 40*

These tennis stadium shows are U2's first Australian open-air concerts and benefit from lovely weather. The stage is visible from the hills outside so fans watch the band do their soundcheck in the afternoon. Bono and Edge greet them and direct their playing towards them. During the concert hundreds of people are listening outside. Bono slips during *I Will Follow* and falls, head first, off the stage. Everyone thinks he must have broken his neck, but he sings on as the security manage to catch him.

An experienced guitarist plays on *People Get Ready*. "That sounds like good shit to me!" Bono shouts, and inspires the guy to play lengthy solos. As the guy never stops, he stresses, "Don't go too far, alright?" After a week's rest Bono's voice has healed.

"How's the singing, is it alright?" he asks. "Yeaaahhh!" "Well, we better come back tomorrow then!"

- Set second night: *Where The Streets Have No Name / I Will Follow / Gloria / I Still Haven't Found / All I Want Is You / Desire / All Along The Watchtower / Help / Bad / October / New Year's Day / Pride / encore: Angel Of Harlem / When Love Comes To Town / Love Rescue Me / encore: Star Spangled Banner – Bullet The Blue Sky / Running To Stand Still / With Or Without You*

During *Love Rescue Me* Bono refers to the fans outside the stadium: "Even you people hanging on to the trees and down the back, sing with me: sha-la-la-la..." An impressive fireworks display accompanies *Bullet The Blue Sky*.

NOVEMBER 4, 1989. CHRISTCHURCH, NEW ZEALAND, LANCASTER PARK

- Attendance: ca. 40,000; (capacity 60,000)
- Support: B.B. King
- Set: *Where The Streets Have No Name / I Will Follow / Gloria / I Still Haven't Found / MLK / One Tree Hill / God Part II / Desire / All Along The Watchtower / All I Want Is You / People Get Ready / Bad / Van Diemen's Land / New Year's Day / Pride encore: Angel Of Harlem / When Love Comes To Town / Love Rescue Me / encore: Star Spangled Banner – Bullet The Blue Sky / Running To Stand Still / With Or Without You*

The day before, U2 and B.B. King held a press conference at Auckland Airport where several members of the press had not done their homework and excelled in asking banal questions. Press: "Would you ever do a Beatles cover?" Bono: "We already did. Go to the back of the class!"

When U2 played New Zealand in 1984, the four shows combined played to maybe 10,000 people. Five years later, U2 are booked for rugby stadiums only. The show at Lancaster Park is the biggest concert ever in Christchurch even though it doesn't sell out. "So, what's it like being Kiwi?" asks Bono, who on the whole has a bit of trouble establishing contact with the crowd, this being U2's first stadium show in almost two years. *All Along The Watchtower* includes bits of Neil Young's *Like A Hurricane*.

```
                                      14525
            U2               CLP924
    LOVE COMES TO TOWN TOUR
             WITH
         B.B. KING           ADMIT
        LANCASTER PARK             TNOBF1
   SATURDAY 4 NOVEMBER  7PM   $44.90
                                   017973
     GEN ADMIN          ADMIT      21Aug89
      017973           $44.90
```

NOVEMBER 8, 1989. WELLINGTON, NEW ZEALAND, ATHLETIC PARK

- Attendance: ca. 35,000; (capacity 50,000)
- Support: B.B. King
- Set: same as Christchurch, minus *God Part II, Gloria* is now played after *One Tree Hill*, and plus *40* closing the show.

People are squashed in the rough crowd and just prior to the show U2's production manager Steve Iredale comes onstage to stress that before the band will come on, everyone must take a step back. Several times throughout the show Bono asks the crowd to take it easy and look after each other. After *Pride* the band go backstage. Bono excuses himself: "Sorry, I have to take a piss!"

NOVEMBER 10, 11, 1989. AUCKLAND, NEW ZEALAND, WESTERN SPRINGS STADIUM

- Attendance: 80,000; (capacity: 120,000)
- Support: B.B. King
- Set first night: *Star Spangled Banner – Bullet The Blue Sky / Desire / All Along The Watchtower / All I Want Is You / Where The Streets Have No Name / I Will Follow / I Still Haven't Found / MLK / One Tree Hill / Bad / Van Diemen's Land / New Year's Day / Pride / encore: People Get Ready / Angel Of Harlem / When Love Comes To Town / Love Rescue Me / encore: With Or Without You / 40*

When 60,000 tickets for the November 11 show sell out, a second show is added for the 10th but only 20,000 people turn up. As a result, the first night is intimate and the audience are treated to a loose, informal concert as the band obviously feel at ease with the smaller crowd. *One Tree Hill* is heavy with sentiment, as the band had visited the grave of Greg Carroll on their arrival in New Zealand. Bono attempts to say something in Maori. After *When Love Comes To Town*, he shouts: "B.B. King! The man is 64 and he kicks ass! Or, as the English say, he 'kicks bottom'." On a more serious note, Bono comments on the current developments in communist countries like China and the Eastern Bloc where anti-Government protests aimed at change have been dominating world news for weeks. "I'd like to dedicate this song to the brave ones who have brought such great change to East Germany in the last few days, and for the brave ones who've lost their lives trying to bring about great change in China. The Eighties have been full of a lot of bullshit. But when they're writing the history books, 1989 is gonna be a very important year for the world..."

- Set second night: same as October 27, plus *Gloria* before *MLK* and *One Tree Hill* instead of *The Unforgettable Fire*.

The show lacks the intensity of the previous night. The audience are rough and hundreds of people faint in the pushing. Towards the end of the show some fights break out in the heart of the crowd.

Although the show on the 11th is the only one to sell out, the four New Zealand open-air shows draw 155,000 people which, in a country of 3.6 million people, means that one out of every 23 saw U2.

NOVEMBER 17, 18, 19, 1989. SYDNEY, ENTERTAINMENT CENTRE

- Attendance: 37,500; sellout
- Support: Weddings Parties Anything, B.B. King
- Set first night: *Star Spangled Banner – Bullet The Blue Sky / Desire / All Along The Watchtower / All I Want Is You / Where The Streets Have No Name / I Will Follow / I Still Haven't Found / MLK / The Unforgettable Fire / Gloria / God Part II / Help / Bad / Van Diemen's Land / New Year's Day / Pride / encore: Angel Of Harlem / When Love Comes To Town / Love Rescue Me / With Or Without You / 40*

U2 return to Sydney to make up the three shows that were cancelled in late October due to Bono's voice problems. "A few weeks back I had some real trouble trying to sing. I discovered you have some very psychedelic germs over here!" Two backing singers, Cheri and Zan, provide extra vocals for the encore with B.B. and will do so the next two nights. All three shows are filmed professionally by Australian director Richard Lowenstein for a documentary on the tour which will be aired in Australia and all over Europe later in the year. David Bowie and Tin Machine attend the show, after which they meet U2.

- Set second night: *Hawkmoon 269 / Desire / All Along The Watchtower / All I Want Is You / God Part II / Bullet The Blue Sky / Running To Stand Still / Gloria / I Will Follow / I Still Haven't Found / Knocking On Heaven's Door / Bad / Van Diemen's Land / New Year's Day / Pride / encore: Angel Of Harlem / When Love Comes To Town / Love Rescue Me / 40*

Shortly before the show is scheduled to start there is an

anonymous phone call to the venue stating that a bomb has been planted inside the building. The arena must be evacuated and Steve Iredale makes the announcement, assuring everyone that U2 *will* perform. "The band are going to play, don't worry about that. So, can people go towards the exit in an orderly fashion please, it's very important. There is no need to panic whatsoever but please take this seriously..." Fans are shocked and confused as no reason is mentioned. After 12,500 leave the building, there is a frantic 90-minute search for anything that looks suspicious but nothing is found.

"OK, ladies and gentlemen... I'd like to thank everybody on behalf of the U2 organisation and the Entertainment Center for your co-operation," says Iredale. The ominous tones of *Hawkmoon 269* fill the hall and the cameras zoom in on Bono's face, which shows nothing of the stress he must have been going through. "Thanks for sticking around, it wouldn't be the same without y'all," he says coolly halfway through the song. During *Desire* he tentatively refers to the bomb incident: "Turn on the lights Willie! Let me see who we're dealing with tonight! Let me tell you: everybody gets out of here ALIVE!"

The fearful thoughts of what could have happened if there really had been a bomb in the building push the band's adrenaline level to a peak, resulting in an explosive show that is one of the best of the tour. *Knocking On Heaven's Door* is highly emotional as Bono improvises on the theme of the people's struggle for freedom in China and behind the Iron Curtain. During *40* he sings snippets of *Give Peace A Chance*, a song which he hasn't dragged out of the closet in a long time.

- Set third night: *Where The Streets Have No Name / I Will Follow / I Still Haven't Found / MLK / God Part II / Desire / All Along The Watchtower / All I Want Is You / Bad / Van Diemen's Land / Star Spangled Banner– Bullet The Blue Sky / Running To Stand Still / With Or Without You / New Year's Day / Pride / encore: Angel Of Harlem / When Love Comes To Town / Love Rescue Me / encore: Party Girl / 40*

It's the final show of the Australian tour. "Thank you so much," Bono says. "We've been here for over two months now, you have worn us out! Somebody, somewhere, please make sure it's not five years till we're next back in Australia..." Anne-Louise Kelly of the U2 management team brings champagne on stage during *Party Girl*, after which Bono thanks everybody who has helped make this tour so successful, including the audience: "Thank you for the trouble you went through to get the tickets, sleeping out and all that shit. We won't forget you. Don't forget about us, now."

The 23 shows on the Australian tour sell a total of 278,000 tickets, an average of 12,086 per concert, and is one of the most successful rock tours ever in Australia. Another 155,000 attend the four shows in New Zealand.

NOVEMBER 23, 1989. YOKOHAMA, JAPAN, SPORTS ARENA

- Attendance: 10,000; sellout
- Set: *Where The Streets Have No Name / I Will Follow / I Still Haven't Found / MLK / The Unforgettable Fire / God Part II / Desire / All Along The Watchtower / All I Want Is You / Van Diemen's Land / New Year's Day / Pride / encore: Angel Of Harlem / When Love Comes To Town / Love Rescue Me / With Or Without You*

Though U2 had considered playing some other countries in Asia, their tour of the Far East visits Japan only. The jumbo 747 that transports the band's equipment is hit by a flock of seagulls on its way from Sydney to Yokohama and as a result the gear only arrives at the venue in the afternoon, just hours before the doors are scheduled to open. The crew work extra hard to install the sound and lighting systems and manage to get everything ready in time. The first of six shows is exactly six years and one day after U2's Japanese début. The audience are happy to see U2 but traditionally don't express much emotion.

NOVEMBER 25, 26, 1989. TOKYO, JAPAN, TOKYO DOME

- Attendance: 90,000; sellout
- Set first night: *Where The Streets Have No Name / I Will Follow / I Still Haven't Found / MLK / With Or Without You / God Part II / Desire / All Along The Watchtower / All I Want Is You / Bad / Van Diemen's Land / Star Spangled Banner – Bullet The Blue Sky / Running To Stand Still / People Get Ready / Angel Of Harlem / When Love Comes To Town / Love Rescue Me / encore: Pride / 40*

U2's popularity has grown vastly in this country and two shows at the Tokyo Dome, also known as 'The Big Egg' for its shape, have no trouble selling out. The enthusiastic crowd sing along to most of the songs and cheer when Bono greets them in their own language. A guy called Chica plays along to Bono's liking during *People Get Ready*. "Turn his guitar up, let me hear this man play!" he shouts. Though Japan is more than a thousand miles away from China, it's the closest U2 are playing to the country where thousands of students are rebelling against oppression by their government. At the start of *Love Rescue Me*, Bono says: "Rock & roll cannot change things. People change things. But rock & roll belongs to the people. People will make the changes. We play this song for East Berlin, for Czechoslovakia, for the people behind the Iron Curtain, who brought about change with no violence. Our music belongs to those people. We dedicate this next song to the people of China, to the brave ones who filled a square in Beijing..."

- Set second night: *Star Spangled Banner – Bullet The Blue Sky / Desire / All Along The Watchtower / All I Want Is You / Where The Streets Have No Name / I Will Follow / I Still Haven't Found / MLK / One Tree Hill / Help / Bad / Van Diemen's Land / New Year's Day / Pride / encore: Angel Of Harlem / When Love Comes To Town / Love Rescue Me / With Or Without You / 40*

NOVEMBER 28, 29, DECEMBER 1, 1989. OSAKA, JAPAN, CASTLE HALL

- Attendance: 60,000; sellout
- Set first night: *Star Spangled Banner – Bullet The Blue Sky / Desire / All Along The Watchtower / All I Want Is You / Where The Streets Have No Name / Gloria / I Still Haven't Found / Knocking On Heaven's Door / With Or Without You / God Part II / New Year's Day / Pride / encore: People Get Ready / Angel Of Harlem / When Love Comes To Town / Love Rescue Me / encore: 40*

Knocking On Heaven's Door is played for the third and last time this tour and gets a huge cheer of recognition from the audience.

Bono asks someone up for *People Get Ready* and gets angry when security manhandle fans who are struggling to get on stage. "Don't touch our fucking audience!" he shouts. The guy that eventually gets onstage is an accomplished guitarist and plays some fairly long solos.

- Set second night: same as Yokohama, but *Bullet The Blue Sky* replaces *God Part II*.

- Set third night: *Stand By Me / Pride / New Year's Day / I Still Haven't Found / People Get Ready / MLK / One Tree Hill / Where The Streets Have No Name / Gloria / Help / Bad / Van Diemen's Land / Star Spangled Banner – Bullet The Blue Sky / Running To Stand Still / Slow Dancing / Angel Of Harlem / When Love Comes To Town / Love Rescue Me / encore: Desire / All Along The Watchtower / All I Want is You / 40*

The remarkable, totally mixed-up order of the songs adds an exciting edge to the show. The surprise effect of coming on during the intro tape of *Stand By Me* again works well, but it's the last time U2 do this since the whole world has now seen it. U2 play so powerfully and soulfully that the crowd abandon their traditional restraint and are much more lively than the previous nights. During *I Still Haven't Found* several people leave their seats and dance their way up to the front, but one guy in the front row gets annoyed and tries to force the fans back to their seats. Bono acts rapidly: "At a U2 concert people do *not* push each other around! I don't care if you bought the front row or the back row... we're all the same in here!" The audience cheer. "I think that what we need right now is a love song," Bono says. The band perform *People Get Ready* much earlier in the set than usual as its peaceful lyrics befit the situation. The message does not get through and Bono has to act again to put the guy to a halt. "Listen guy: one more piece of shit out of you and you're

out of here!"

After *Running To Stand Still* Bono announces a new song, *Slow Dancing*, from which he sang some lines on Australian radio in October. Accompanying himself on guitar, he now premières the love song that he intends to send to American country singer Willie Nelson, hoping that he will record it. The song is tender and slow, dealing with the pain of a man in a passionate relationship with a stronger woman.

The show continues with an exuberant duet with B.B.. *Suspicious Minds* is included in *Angel Of Harlem*, and at the end of *Love Rescue Me* Bono sings part of *Amazing Grace*, which normally turns up in *Bad*. Hell-raising versions of *Desire* and *All Along The Watchtower* are followed by *All I Want Is You*, before *40* concludes U2's Japanese tour.

THE 'LOVETOWN' TOUR LEG 2: EUROPE, WINTER 1989/90

U2 decide to declare a few cities in Europe as LoveTowns as well, just for fun and good measure. Four cities are picked in which multiple shows will be played: Paris, Amsterdam, Dublin, and Dortmund, which is chosen because it houses the largest indoor arena in Germany, the 16,500 capacity Westfalenhalle. Rumours abound that U2 will play multiple shows at London's Wembley Arena, but it doesn't happen.

Unlike Australia and Japan, where all venues were fully seated, the European shows have no seats on the floor.

DECEMBER 11, 12, 1989. PARIS, FRANCE, PALAIS OMNISPORTS DE BERCY

- Attendance: 32,000; sellout
- Support: B.B. King
- Set first night: *Star Spangled Banner – Bullet The Blue Sky / Desire / All Along The Watchtower / All I Want Is You / Where The Streets Have No Name / I Will Follow / I Still Haven't Found / MLK / The Unforgettable Fire / God Part II / Bad / Van Diemen's Land / New Year's Day / Pride / encore: Angel Of Harlem / When Love Comes To Town / Love Rescue Me / encore: With Or Without You / 40*

A serious accident occurs in the early afternoon while the U2 crew are installing the lighting system in the Bercy arena. Due to faulty lifting equipment, one of the lighting trusses falls down and takes Steve Witmer, one of the riggers, along. Steve falls forty feet onto the solid concrete floor and has to be taken to hospital with a fractured pelvis.

At the beginning of *Bad* Bono sings a few lines of *Help* to a completely different melody. During *Angel Of Harlem*, *When Love Comes To Town* and *Love Rescue Me*, two girls named Claudia and Sophia sing background vocals and do so for the rest of the tour.

- Set second night: *Where The Streets Have No Name / I Will Follow / I Still Haven't Found / MLK / One Tree Hill / Gloria / God Part II / Desire / All Along The Watchtower / All I Want Is You / Van Diemen's Land / Star Spangled Banner –Bullet The Blue Sky / Running To Stand Still / People Get Ready / Angel Of Harlem / When Love Comes To Town / Love Rescue Me / encore: With Or Without You / Pride / 40*

The band are in excellent form and play a warm and dynamic

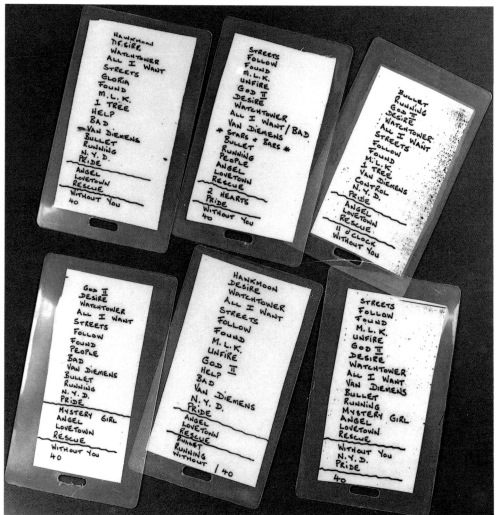

Different set-list every night

Claudia and Sophia. Dortmund, third night.

show. Bono gets B.B. King's band out for *People Get Ready* and declares, "We're on tour with these men, and we feel like we're at school, learning so much from these people!" During *People Get Ready* he has trouble finding a girl to play guitar. "I refuse to believe there's no young lady rock & roll guitar players in Paris!" he shouts. In the end a guy comes onstage, but Bono feels it's no problem: "Well, he looks like a woman, he'll do..."

DECEMBER 14, 15, 16, 1989. DORTMUND, GERMANY, WESTFALENHALLE

- Attendance: 49,500; sellout
- Set first night: *Where The Streets Have No Name / I Will Follow / I Still Haven't Found / MLK / The Unforgettable Fire / God Part II / Desire / All Along The Watchtower / All I Want Is You / Van Diemen's Land / Star Spangled Banner – Bullet The Blue Sky / Running To Stand Still / New Year's Day / Pride /* encore: *Angel Of Harlem / When Love Comes To Town / Love Rescue Me / With Or Without You / 40*

A big sign displaying U2's LoveTown logo is suspended over the entrance of the Westfalenhalle, with the text 'SOLD OUT – THANK YOU GERMANY' plastered over it. Tickets are sold exclusively by mail-order and after a string of advertisements in magazines, more than 220,000 orders rapidly come in from all over the country. This means U2 could fill Westfalenhalle thirteen times, but with only 49,500 tickets available for the three shows, all remaining orders are returned.

Despite heavy pushing in front of the stage, the atmosphere in the venue is excellent. Early in the show Bono says with croaky voice: "I must tell you that my voice is not so strong tonight, but your voice is strong tonight...?" The crowd make clear it's no problem and during many songs produce some first

rate community singing. Bono sings part of *Sexual Healing* during *All I Want Is You.*

- Set second night: *Star Spangled Banner – Bullet The Blue Sky / Desire / All Along The Watchtower / All I Want Is You / Where The Streets Have No Name / I Will Follow / I Still Haven't Found / MLK / One Tree Hill / Help / Bad / Van Diemen's Land / New Year's Day / Pride /* encore: *Angel Of Harlem / People Get Ready / When Love Comes To Town / Love Rescue Me / 40*

A more inspired show than the previous night as Bono's singing is more powerful and the band are physically more active. The crowd are delirious and the pushing in the front is unbearable, with many getting crushed. "You are noisy bastards, getting noisier every night," Bono remarks. *Like A Hurricane* shows up in *All Along The Watchtower, Bad* contains snippets of *Norwegian Wood* and during *Angel Of Harlem* Bono sings part of *Suspicious Minds.* The guy who comes on stage to play guitar during *People Get Ready* is no good so Bono searches for a girl instead. A girl from Holland gets onstage and plays along well. "I found me a young woman!" Bono calls out delightedly, and afterwards proudly laughs, "That just about put all those rock & roll animals back in their place. A young woman to beat the rest, thank you Gerian!"

- Set third night: *Where The Streets Have No Name / I Will Follow / Gloria / I Still Haven't Found / MLK / With Or Without You / Bullet The Blue Sky / Desire / All Along The Watchtower / All I Want Is You / Van Diemen's Land / New Year's Day / Pride /* encore: *White Christmas / Angel Of Harlem / When Love Comes To Town / Love Rescue Me*

With several changes in the set, this is a highly energetic show. The start of *All Along The Watchtower* is a complete mess as the band are out of synch. Bono turns to them, makes a cut-throat

gesture, then counts to three and they start anew. After *New Year's Day* a U2 flag is thrown on stage. Bono picks it up and performs a little trick, draping the flag over his outstretched forefinger and making Abracadabra gestures. When he removes the flag, his finger has gone.

Back on stage for the encore, he introduces B.B.'s band and wishes them a Happy Christmas. While Edge is aching to start *Angel Of Harlem,* Bono suddenly starts singing *White Christmas,* the title song of the movie starring Bing Crosby: "I'm dreaming of a white Christmas, just like the ones we used to know..." Edge looks on bewildered while the crowd pick up the song and Bono joins in again to bring it to an exhilarating end.

During *Love Rescue Me* Bono squeezes his throat and has difficulty singing. He misses lines, wanders about with a vulnerable look in his eyes and, when after the song the band members come forward to bow, he hugs everyone tightly. The emotional atmosphere changes character when the house lights are lit and the outro-music resounds over the PA. The audience stare at the stage, unable to believe that the show is over after only 75 minutes. Without *40* or at least one more song, the show has an unfinished feel to it and the cheering gradually changes into jeering and whistling. For one of the few times in U2's career, an angry audience walk away disappointed.

DECEMBER 18, 1989. AMSTERDAM, HOLLAND, RAI EUROPA HAL

- Attendance: 16,000; sellout
- Support: B.B. King
- Set: *Hawkmoon 269 / Desire / All Along The Watchtower / All I Want Is You / Where The Streets Have No Name / I Will Follow / I Still Haven't Found / MLK / The Unforgettable Fire / God Part II / Help / Bad / Van Diemen's Land / New Year's Day / Pride /* encore: *40*

Originally, three concerts are planned for Amsterdam, on December 18, 19 and 20, but everything goes wrong as Bono's voice problems continue to plague him. The first concert ends prematurely and the two remaining shows are postponed. There is much confusion among fans.

For the first time in U2 history, tickets are sold by lottery only because the number of tickets available will not come close to supplying demand. Advertisements are placed in all major newspapers along with a coupon to be filled out by anyone who wants to be in the running for two tickets for one show. A total of 24,000 coupons will be drawn. Realising that it will increase their chances of being chosen, thousands of fans send in many more coupons than just the one officially allowed, using names and addresses of neighbours and friends. Those drawn receive a letter informing them of where their tickets can be picked up. Many who sent in more than one coupon receive multiple letters and find themselves with surplus tickets and a lively exchange market in the classified sections of the papers follows, with people doing good business selling leftover tickets to those who have not been drawn, or swapping them for seats for different nights.

The city of Amsterdam lacks a proper arena to house big concerts, but as U2 insist on playing the Dutch capital instead of Rotterdam, the Europahal of the RAI Complex is chosen. There aren't any fixed stands, so small seating areas are built on the sides and in the back, but the majority of the 16,000 stand on the floor. The stage is set-up for a stadium concert, with a high stage and walls of speakers on each side rather than suspended from the ceiling. As fans rush to the front they experience another first: the section in front of the stage has been divided by barriers to function as shock absorbers to prevent fans from getting crushed in the pushing. Once the section is full, it is closed and those already in are given a wristband, so they can go to the toilet or get a drink without losing their spot up front. It proves effective and will be used on many more occasions to come.

The concert starts with an eerie *Hawkmoon 269* in a high spirited atmosphere. It's the only time this song is performed on the European tour. After *I Will Follow* Bono greets the crowd and

explains that his voice is not so strong tonight. The audience start singing *I Still Haven't Found* over its opening tones before Bono even begins. Larry comes in too soon and Bono cushions it: "We fucked up. That's alright, isn't it?"

U2 play vigorously and seem determined to give Amsterdam a few nights to remember. So Bono becomes very frustrated when his voice starts to act up during *God Part II*. This was the reason for the re-scheduled gigs in Sydney, and the problem also occurred in Dortmund. It is clear that Bono's voice is breaking and he is in serious pain. He performs with incredible aggression. He misses lines, grabs his throat, nervously trots the stage and starts whirling the microphone until it hits the stage with a huge bang. He demands that the last verse be repeated, which strains his voice even more. During *Help* he lets the audience sing the second verse, then attempts to sing *Bad* but sounds like a strangler's victim crying for help. "I'm sorry," he sighs powerlessly, and disappears backstage as the band finish the song and Edge takes the spotlight for *Van Diemen's Land*. Bono lets the audience take over *New Year's Day* as much as possible. "This city is a special city for U2," he says. "I wish we were feeling better, but I think you're feeling great. Thanks a lot, good night." *Pride* ends and the band leave the stage.

While the audience shout for more, the band discuss the situation backstage. A decision has to be made quickly. Bono returns onstage to announce, "Well, this has never happened to U2 before, but this is now a free concert in Amsterdam." The audience cheer but don't know quite how to interpret these words. "We have one more song to play for you," Bono says and *40* is started, which means that the whole set with B.B. King is skipped. Croaking and groaning Bono wrestles his way through *40* and it becomes clear that he is totally spent and cannot possibly sing any more.

While the audience sing "How long to sing this song," the concert promoter enters the stage. "Quiet please... you may have heard: Bono can't sing another note. With a hundred-thousand apologies, the best audience of the tour so far. His voice is gone, we have to end now." The crowd jeer and whistle. "One thing: hold on to your tickets," he adds and repeats this three times. Slowly but surely the jeering turns into applause since everybody realises that U2 will either refund the ticket price or, like everybody hopes, give an extra concert for tonight's crowd.

The next day there is great uncertainty about the two remaining shows on the 19th and 20th. The newspapers advise waiting for a radio announcement from the promoter in the afternoon. Bono's vocal cords are examined by a doctor who explains on the radio that the singer has strained his voice and needs to take a week off to prevent permanent damage. Then the concert promoter announces the outcome of many hours of frantic re-organising: the shows are re-scheduled for January 5, 6, 9 and 10 at the 8,000 capacity Ahoy Sports Palace in Rotterdam. All 16,000 tickets for December 19 are now valid for January 5 or 6, while those for December 20 grant admittance for January 9 or 10. The promoter also tries to present all 16,000 that went on the 18th with a brand new concert, but this isn't possible due to limited availability of U2, B.B. King and his band, as well as accommodations. In order for at least some of those 16,000 to see a complete show, fans can send their ticket to the promoter, who will draw 6,000 who can attend one of the new dates, 1,500 for each of the four shows. The remaining 10,000 get their money back.

Though Bono has been told to rest his voice, he takes out an acoustic guitar when he sees a few girls waiting in front of the hotel and quietly sings some songs while sitting on the stairs. He gives autographs and poses for photos, as do the other band members when they emerge later.

DECEMBER 26, 27, 30, 31, 1989. DUBLIN, IRELAND, THE POINT DEPOT

- Attendance: 20,000; sellout
- Support: B.B. King
- Set first night: *God Part II / Desire / All Along The Watchtower / All I Want Is You / Where The Streets Have No Name / Gloria / I Still Haven't Found / MLK / One Tree Hill / Van Diemen's Land / Star Spangled Banner - Bullet The Blue Sky / Running To Stand Still / New Year's Day / Pride / encore: Angel Of Harlem / When Love Comes To Town / Love Rescue Me / encore: With Or Without You / 40*

Rumours of the Dublin shows circulated as early as April 1989 and were confirmed by the promoter a few weeks later: U2 will play five shows at the Point Depot, the railway hall they used 18 months ago for 'Rattle And Hum' recording sessions, which has now been rebuilt as the proper concert venue that Dublin city lacked. When the shows were advertised in late September, there was a major controversy which filled newspaper columns and became the subject of heated discussions in the months to come.

The press and public are shocked at the ticket prices, £20.50 for standing and £25.50 for reserved seating. U2 are fiercely criticised for charging too much by a Catholic youth organisation that claims they have a responsibility to the people of Dublin, without whom they wouldn't be where they are now. Because U2 have pumped large amounts of money into the Irish economy in previous years, they are accused of hypocrisy for charging such prices.

The shows are U2's first indoor gigs in Dublin since December 1982. Where once the band were criticised for playing stadiums, now they are attacked by both media and fans because The Point is too small for everyone who wants to see them. Though such criticism has been following the band around all over the world since their rise to mega-success, the tone of the comments in their own country carries a venom and cynicism that is unparalleled elsewhere. U2 find themselves in a tricky situation: whatever they choose to do, the public and the press always find an angle to attack them.

They are both amazed and appalled by the situation. In response to the accusations, Paul McGuinness sends a statement by fax from Brisbane to *Hot Press* magazine for publication:

'The idea for U2 to play Dublin at the start of the new decade had been around for a long time. We wanted it to be a very special occasion and an opportunity for our hometown audience to see U2 in an intimate setting.

'It had often been said that U2 only perform nowadays in football stadiums. For these and many other reasons, we decided to play five shows at The Point Depot in the last week of this year in a mixed seating and standing configuration with a capacity of 4,500. We would bring in our stage, lighting, and sound production and we would make the venue the ideal environment in which to perform and the ideal environment for an audience to see the show. With the combined capacity limited to 22,500, supply could never meet demand (U2 performed to nearly 200,000 people in Belfast, Dublin and Cork on the Joshua Tree tour).

'U2 have had a policy over the years of giving good value: extra tracks on B-sides, special guests at our concerts, low ticket prices. Our reputation for fair play was so well established that we felt the proposed ticket prices were reasonable. In a town where it has cost up to £20.50 to see Bruce Springsteen in a field, £18.50 to see Simple Minds outdoors and £65 to see Frank Sinatra in a football stadium, we felt that people would be interested in paying to see U2 and B.B. King performing together in a comparatively intimate setting. We recognised that the ticket price was high and that was why we gave a couple of months' warning of the on-sale date. We felt that people would accept the prices proposed as fair for the circumstances.

'It seems that we have made a mistake. We will therefore be dropping the ticket prices to £16 standing and £18 seating. The configuration and therefore the capacity may have to be re-examined.

Bono's self-portrait

'As for the question of whether the shows are for charity or not, I will simply re-state U2's long-held policy of never discussing, with the media or other third parties, any charitable or philanthropic contributions we make. In any case, with the ticket prices at the new level the matter becomes academic: there may be no net profit to speak of on these shows.

'It must now be asked whether this peculiar coalition of priests and other commentators will be bringing their enormous influence to bear on the other more essential pricing issues of the day? Petrol? The cost of travel? Should the agricultural sector be subsidised? What about interest rates? Coal and butter?

'Best wishes from Brisbane on the LoveTown Tour (which we can't wait for you to see).' – Paul McGuinness, Manager U2.

In the meanwhile, excitement for the shows builds up regardless. The band plan to have the New Year's Eve show broadcast on TV worldwide, making it an extra special occasion. A few days before tickets go on sale, the promoter announces that the show originally planned for December 29 will not take place, probably to prevent Bono's voice from breaking down. As expected, tickets for the four remaining shows sell out instantly. Classified ads in the papers offer tickets at ridiculous prices.

With all the fuss over the shows in the past months, an uneasy tension hangs over the first night. The lights dim and the Stones' *Sympathy For The Devil* resounds over the PA, fading out as U2 enter the stage and start *God Part II* over incredible screaming from the crowd, who lap up the new tracks from 'Rattle And Hum'. At the intro of *Where The Streets Have No Name*, Bono kneels to read his notes about Samuel Beckett, the Irish novelist who had died four days earlier at the age of 83. "... The whole body of the man did seem, like one whom I had met in a dream. Sam Beckett dreamt of other roads, Sam Beckett dreamt of other lands, of another home... where the

streets have no name..."

After *Gloria*, Bono comments on an article that had appeared in the *Sunday Tribune* newspaper that implied that the main reason for the band for doing these shows was to make lots of money by selling the international TV rights to the New Year's Eve show. "I'd like to tell you the *real* reason why we're playing the Point Depot here. We're not playing here because we want to send it via satellite to the rest of the world. We're not here to make a pile of dough or anything. We've been playing for ten years in these big places, and we now wanted to play a small place. It's not really that complicated, is it?" During the guitar solo in *New Year's Day*, Bono jokes about the recent political changes in Eastern Europe and the fall of the Iron Curtain: "Czechoslovakia; East Germany; Poland; Romania; and all because of one man: The Edge!"

Most newspapers print extensive reviews under huge headlines like, 'BONO'S HOME' or 'WHEN U2 COME TO THEIR TOWN'. The show is generally well received, but some papers make awkward mistakes. The *Irish Independent* praises the way the show had started with *Hawkmoon 269*, which wasn't played at all. *The Star* prints a two-page spread in which they print a picture of The Babies' singer John Waite, captioning it, 'a young Bono'.

- Set second night: *Where The Streets Have No Name / I Will Follow / I Still Haven't Found / MLK / The Unforgettable Fire / God Part II / Desire / All Along The Watchtower / All I Want Is You / Bad / Van Diemen's Land / Star Spangled Banner – Bullet The Blue Sky / Running To Stand Still / People Get Ready / Angel Of Harlem / When Love Comes To Town / Love Rescue Me / encore: Two Hearts Beat As One / Pride / 40*

The second show is a relief for both band and audience as the nervous tension is gone. Bono teases the crowd, "It's great to be back in... uhm," making people cry out "Dublin!" Besides

Some of the Irish press

snippets of *Like A Hurricane* and The Stooges' *1969* being added to *All Along The Watchtower* and *Desire,* Bono sings a verse of *Dirty Old Town,* Ewan MacColl's Dublin song made famous by The Pogues, at the end of *Running To Stand Still.* He comments on the subject of Irish emigration: "Everybody wants to live in America. Not me. I love this city. I hate what some of those bastards have done to it: boring, unimaginative politicians, the arrogant architects, the back handed builders. Let them go to fuckin' America!"

Bono holds his guitar up in the air during *People Get Ready,* but instead of plucking someone from the audience, a special guest is waiting in the wings. "Anyone wanna play my guitar? Maria McKee wants to play my guitar!" The former Lone Justice singer, now a resident of Dublin, plays and duets with Bono for the fourth time within the last five years. "Remember, Coke is not the real thing; *this* is the real thing," Bono proudly shouts, and claims Maria is his second wife. "The queue for the third starts outside... so what's the problem? Dublin speechless for the first time!"

Bono causes concern when he explains before *Love Rescue Me,* "Well, I suppose this is a kind of going away party, because I think that's what we gotta do. We've had a great ten years. We're just throwing a party for ourselves and for you, and for the people that worked with us and those that believed in us along the way. We gotta do something else the next while, just gotta go away for a little bit..." "Noooo!" yell the crowd. Though Bono hints at a break between activities, many aren't so sure and fear U2 will call it quits. The next day the papers are full of 'U2 SPLIT'-type headlines and the exaggerated misinterpretation goes around the world and back in a matter of days.

A ragged version of *Two Hearts Beat As One,* which hadn't been played since Atlanta, April 29, 1985, is a great surprise and includes a line of *Billie Jean* at the end.

■ Set third night: *Star Spangled Banner - Bullet The Blue Sky / Running To Stand Still / God Part II / Desire / All Along The Watchtower / All I Want Is You / Where The Streets Have No Name / I Will Follow / I Still Haven't Found / MLK / One Tree Hill / Van Diemen's Land / Out Of Control / New Year's Day / Pride / encore: She's A Mystery To Me / Angel Of Harlem / When Love Comes To Town / Love Rescue Me / encore: 11 O'Clock Tick Tock / With Or Without You*

After two days off, U2 play an outstanding show which many regard as their finest ever in Ireland. Before *Running To Stand Still* Bono welcomes those from out of town and asks for silence so he can sing the Dublin ballad. One verse of *Dirty Old Town* is added. Bono parodies himself after *I Will Follow,* asking the audience, "Anything you want me to give out about? Sellafield? That's about 60 miles from here. It's a lot further to Margaret Thatcher's house..." Bono dedicates *I Still Haven't Found* to the Birmingham Six, the six Irishmen imprisoned for IRA crimes they didn't commit. During the guitar solo in *Out Of Control,* Bono raps in admiration: "Check out the boots! Check out the pants! The hairdo! The guitar player of his generation: The Edge!" Then the singer assumes a strong American accent and shares an awkward futuristic vision with the audience: "It's beautiful to be back in Las Vegas tonight. I remember playing Dublin on the turn of the decade, '89 to '90. Now, there was a special night..."

The encore sees the first ever public performance of *She's A Mystery To Me,* the song Bono and Edge wrote for Roy Orbison in 1987. In the fall of 1987 U2 had rehearsed it and also recorded it at Sun Studios, but their studio version has never been released. Live, the love song is sweetly sung and has a simple country-style backing with B.B.'s horn section and the background singers adding a warm feel. At the start of *Love Rescue Me* Bono sums up the last few months on the road.

"We've had a lot of fun, just getting to know the kinda music that we didn't know so much about. I was explaining to people the other night, but I might have gotten it a bit wrong, that this is just the end of something for U2, and that's why we're playing these concerts. We're throwing a party for ourselves and for you. It's no big deal, we have to go away and just dream it all up again."

11 O'Clock Tick Tock is played for the first time since Hampton, December 12, 1987, and is a reminder of the U2 of ten years ago, when they were beginning to be noticed outside Ireland, as they crossed the water to go to London, then Holland and the rest of Europe, followed by America, reaping sensational success. Back now in the city where they grew up, the band seem to have come full circle.

■ Set fourth night: *Where The Streets Have No Name / I Will Follow / I Still Haven't Found / MLK / One Tree Hill / Gloria / God Part II / Desire / All Along The Watchtower / All I Want Is You / Bad / Van Diemen's Land / Star Spangled Banner – Bullet The Blue Sky / Running To Stand Still / New Year's Day / Pride / encore: Party Girl / Angel Of Harlem / When Love Comes To Town / Love Rescue Me / 40*

As plans to air the New Year's Eve show on TV don't materialise, U2 arrange to have it broadcast on radio instead. Agreements are made with radio programmers of 21 countries across Europe that will air the show live and uninterrupted: Ireland, the United Kingdom, Holland, Belgium, France, Spain, Portugal, Italy, West and East Germany, Norway, Finland, Denmark, Sweden, Poland, Czechoslovakia, Yugoslavia, Hungary, Bulgaria, Rumania, and the USSR. Only a few countries prefer a later transmission. "It's a great thrill for us to know that so many people from east and west Europe will be hearing the show live on New Year's Eve," Paul McGuinness states in the papers. Where playing concerts behind the Iron Curtain have been impossible, the radio waves will cross borders to reach an audience of 300 million people.

RTE radio producer Ian Wilson tells *Hot Press* magazine, "No money changes hands on either side. U2 get the audience, we get the programme." There are no sponsors. The broadcast is a present for anyone who wants to listen. People are encouraged to record the show in order to have their own 'official bootleg' tape. U2 even buy advertising space in several music publications, among which *Hot Press* (Ireland), *Q* (UK), and *OOR* (Holland), to print a cut-and-fold cassette sleeve designed especially to store the tape in.

The U2 camp watch in amazement as the press goes completely over the top in their hyping of the New Year's Eve show, claiming that Bob Dylan, Keith Richards and Bruce Springsteen will all make guest appearances to celebrate the start of the new decade. Even Frank Sinatra is mentioned. To avoid expectations running wild, Paul McGuinness reacts by stating that B.B. King is *the* special guest .

The night is a big event regardless. While B.B. King delivers another sparkling set, there are still hundreds of fans without tickets queueing outside in the rain. A couple of minutes before midnight, the guards are instructed to open the gates to allow them in. It is New Year's Eve, after all.

Dave Fanning announces the countries that are taking the broadcast, with Eastern Europe especially greeted with cheers. "Alright everybody, say hello to welcome Europe to the Point Depot! Live from Dublin City, where the band who are gonna play for you tonight is the band that started out in this city ten years ago and who've dominated the Eighties!" Tension becomes unbearable as The Beatles' *All You Need Is Love* fades out over the PA and the house lights dim. The ethereal chords of *Where The Streets Have No Name* resound while Fanning and the 5,000 present count down the last fifteen seconds of the Eighties from a huge clock at the back of the stage. "...Three, two, ONE: HAPPY NEW YEAR! Happy new decade with U2!" The moment is high on emotion as everybody hugs and kisses their loved ones. The band enter the stage to deafening cheers, while the bells are ringing loudly and the music briefly segues into the traditional *Auld Lang Syne,* of which Bono sings two lines. The crowd are in a state of complete euphoria, with total strangers grabbing each other's hands in the air. "Here she comes: the

future," Bono speaks over Edge's guitar intro. "Happy Christmas, and Happy New Year to y'all. It's 1990. Forget about the past. We're gonna celebrate the future... where the streets have no name..." When the bright stage lights flash on to illuminate the arena, thousands of balloons are released from the ceiling to shower the crowd.

"So, how are you up there, are you OK?" Bono asks at the start of *I Still Haven't Found*. "Seeing as it's New Year's Day you probably expect me to get all sentimental, yeah? Well, you're exactly right. Here's to the future! The only limits are the limits of our imagination. Dream up the kind of world you wanna live in; dream out loud at high volume. That's what we do for a living. Lucky bastards!"

After an exhilarating start, the show falls back into routine and is unable to reach the energy level of the previous two shows. Obviously playing it safe, the band concentrate on delivering the best possible versions of their songs for the estimated radio audience of 300 million people, most of whom are hearing U2 for the first time. "Outside it's America," Bono raps during *Bullet The Blue Sky*, then refers to the show not being broadcast in the USA: "Not tonight it's not. Tonight it's the USSR; Germany, East *and* West; Italy; Yugoslavia; Rumania; and God knows where else they've got their tape recorders turned on. Well, Happy Christmas from U2 to you." With the countries behind the Iron Curtain in mind, Bono sings lines of Bob Dylan's *The Times They Are A-Changing*. "Over the last ten years, one of the things I feel the most proud of is that U2 got a chance to work with Amnesty International. I'd like to dedicate this song to those who work for Amnesty International and those who depend on Amnesty International," Bono tells the crowd before the band play a lengthy version of *Love Rescue Me*.

JANUARY 5, 6, 9, 10, 1990. ROTTERDAM, HOLLAND, SPORT PALEIS AHOY

- ■ Attendance: 38,000; sellout
- ■ Support: B.B. King
- ■ Set first night: *God Part II / Desire / All Along The Watchtower / All I Want Is You / Where The Streets Have No Name / I Will Follow / I Still Haven't Found / People Get Ready / Bad / Van Diemen's Land / Star Spangled Banner – Bullet The Blue Sky / Running To Stand Still / New Year's Day / Pride / encore: Angel Of Harlem / When Love Comes To Town / Love Rescue Me / encore: 40*

With the rest of the world thinking that the tour is over, U2 come back to Holland to play four concerts to make up for the two cancelled shows in Amsterdam. As in Dublin, the first show starts out with *God Part II*, with the band coming onstage in the dark and sudden bright white footlights flashing on when Bono starts singing. The atmosphere is elated and will remain so for the rest of the week. Bono's voice sounds fully mended. "I can sing, I can sing!" he calls out delightedly, and adds, "Or as they say in my hometown: that's a matter of opinion!"

Bono has great trouble finding someone who can actually play guitar during *People Get Ready*, as several people lie about their capabilities just for the kick of making it onto the stage. "Is rock & roll alive in Holland or what!? I want a guitar player!" After three failed attempts he gets desperate. "The last one's gonna need an ambulance if he's not telling the truth!" He nervously gives one more guy a chance and cries out "Hallelujah!" when his new guest really can play. After the song Bono kneels down and presses his hands together to praise him.

"As well as teaching me how to play guitar, B.B. King has

been helping me learn how to sing so that I don't screw up my voice," Bono says before *Love Rescue Me*. "We're playing these concerts because we're gonna go away for a while after these concerts, and start all over again, really," he explains. "We've had a great ten years, you've spoiled us rotten. And we're gonna have another great ten years, we're just going away for a while..." The audience listen carefully and applaud, making clear they respect Bono's words.

- ■ Set second night: same as second show in Dublin, minus *Bad, She's A Mystery To Me* replacing *People Get Ready*, and *With Or Without You* instead of *Two Hearts Beat As One*.

As Edge's guitar fails to work during *Desire* Bono sings, "With the red guitar, sometimes it don't work," while a roadie quickly jumps on stage to hand Edge a replacement. The band are in top kick-ass form, giving a far better performance than the previous night. During *Bullet The Blue Sky*, Bono jumps off the stage and runs to the audience in the stands to shake hands. A hysterical guy tries to hold on to him. "Relax, hey, buster, relax. Don't worry, be happy!" Bono tells him. While Edge plays his solo and is spotlighted by A.J., Bono runs over the slanting cycle track of the arena and holds on to someone while he tries to get A.J.'s attention. A.J. forgets about Edge, turns around and catches his cousin Bono in a bright beam of light, as he finds his way back on stage again. At the end of *Running To Stand Still* the audience sing along with "Still running" so well that when the song ends Bono motions to Larry to go on and improvises a whole extra verse that to this day remains unidentified. The show then moves into delicate mode when Bono announces *She's A Mystery To Me*, a song played only once before. In the encore he asks whether there are many people from Amsterdam. "I'm sorry I screwed

The jet arrives

up and you all had to come back. I think this is a good place to end our tour, because we kind of started out in a way over here."

■ Set third night: same as New Year's Eve concert in Dublin, minus *Bad* and *Party Girl*.

Bono mixes up the verses of *I Will Follow* and the band screw up completely as a result. *One Tree Hill* has its Dutch première, with the audience singing the last couple of lines in perfect harmony. *Bullet The Blue Sky* sees Bono running on to the cycling track again, and at the end of *Running To Stand Still* he sings part of *Dirty Old Town* and changes the lyrics: "I kissed my gal, in the Docker's pub..." When U2 come back onstage for the encore, Bono cracks a joke that hits home with the Dutch audience: "We've got people here tonight from all over the world, I believe. All over the world *and* Belgium."

■ Set fourth night: *Star Spangled Banner* – *Bullet The Blue Sky* / *Desire* / *All Along The Watchtower* / *Slow Dancing* / *All I Want Is You* / *Where The Streets Have No Name* / *I Will Follow* / *I Still Haven't Found* / *People Get Ready* / *Bad* / *Van Diemen's Land* / *New Year's Day* / *Pride* / encore: *Angel Of Harlem* / *When Love Comes To Town* / *Love Rescue Me* / *11 O'Clock Tick Tock* / *Out Of Control* / *40*

Scalpers do good business, selling tickets for five or six times face value outside the arena. Everybody realises tonight's show will be special and there are many people from Australia, America and all over Europe present to be part of U2's last night of the tour party. Just two hours before the show Bono comes out at the back entrance to sign some autographs. An extraordinary show begins with *Bullet The Blue Sky* during which

Farewell in Rotterdam

137

Bono takes to the cycling track again. While three roadies (instead of just one) are shining spotlights on Edge, Adam and Larry, security guards run after Bono but have great trouble following his unpredictable frolicking. He runs to and fro, shakes hands with people in the stands without stopping his singing, and doesn't go back to the stage until the start of *Desire*, during which he sings parts of *1969* as well as *So You Wanna Be (A Rock & Roll Star)*. People on the stands notice that drum technician Sam O'Sullivan is drumming along on snare drum hidden behind stacks of equipment! *All Along The Watchtower* has a climactic ending with Bono citing *In God's Country*. *Slow Dancing* is played partially after its début in Osaka, with the audience quietly listening to the unknown song. "A song for Willie Nelson," Bono announces, but to date, Nelson has not recorded the track.

"The future belongs to those who take it. Anybody out there like to take my guitar?" Bono holds up his guitar and waits for the first opportunistic soul to make his way through the audience and past the security guards to get a small taste of what it is like to be a rock star. He is pleased that the guy who comes on can actually play and drags him to the edge of the stage. "Bob Dylan, ladies and gentlemen!" he shouts.

"God bless rock & roll, the old encore thing is a great invention, what do you say?" Bono says. "You need that five minutes to get your shit together, you know what I mean? Let's party!" The encore is a moment of goodbye for both the audience and U2: it is the final show before the band take a long period of rest to decide what form the continuation of their career will take. Over the opening notes of *Love Rescue Me*,

Bono speaks of his admiration and gratitude for the band and the road crew, many of whom have been with U2 for several years. "B.B. King's a hero of mine; B.B. King's band are heroes of mine; The Edge, Larry Mullen, Adam..." Lighting designer Peter Williams, drum technician Sam O'Sullivan, sound engineer Joe O'Herlihy, and many more are all honoured. Bass technician Shelley, guitar technician Fraser McAllister, A.J.. Bono tries to drag someone on stage. "There's a man hiding down there, Paul McGuinness, manager of U2, he's a hero of mine. The list goes on and on, like we hope to do." Halfway through the song Bono thinks of some more people: "Sophia and Claudia are heroes of mine. Regine Moylett, hero of mine. Douglas, Dave, Steve, our tour manager Dennis Sheehan, Tim..." Even the audience aren't forgotten: "And while we're at it: you're all fucking heroes of mine!" The farewell is emotional. U2, B.B., his band and the backing singers form a chain and bow to the audience for the last time. Everybody hugs, kisses, thanks each other for the good times and wave at the audience.

U2 come back for a second encore and surprise the audience by playing energetic versions of both *11 O'Clock Tick Tock* and *Out Of Control*, during which they give everything they have left after four months on the road. Bono grabs a bucket of water from the security, drinks from it and empties it over the audience after a long, running start. In the meantime, the silhouettes of two crew members doing acrobatic tricks suspended on ropes appear on the white backdrop. A 'U2: A Celebration' flag is thrown on stage after the song. "You could call it that, all right," Bono shouts. As usual, he shines a spotlight over the outstretched arms of the audience before he waves goodbye.

JUNE 20, 1990. DAVID BOWIE: CLEVELAND, OH, RICHFIELD COLISEUM

After months in which U2 keep a low profile, Bono and Adam fly over to Cleveland to catch Bowie's greatest hits Sound + Vision tour. Peter Williams, U2's lighting designer since 1984, works this tour and Bono joins Bowie onstage when a rousing version of *Jean Genie* segues into Van Morrison's *Gloria*. "You know, this was a song written by an Irishman," Bowie says. "I get the impression it would sound even better if I had an Irishman singing with me. How about Bono?" The crowd react ecstatically. Bono comes on and hits the right chord with the audience as he sings, "Well, she comes around here, comes around at midnight. She makes me feel good, but Cleveland always makes me feel alright..." "Thank you Bono!" Bowie shouts after the song, mispronouncing his name. Adam watches the show from the wings.

A local newspaper claims that Bono and Adam had come to the show for a different reason. During his show, Bowie uses a transparent projection screen to illustrate some songs with pre-recorded video images. This wafer-thin screen is let down in front of the stage for some of the songs. The audience can see through it and at the same time see the images on the screen, creating a fascinating visual effect. The newspaper suggests that U2 are contemplating using this screen for their own forthcoming world tour.

An Irishman in Cleveland

NOVEMBER 1990 - SEPTEMBER 1991. BERLIN, GERMANY / DUBLIN, IRELAND

U2 work on their new album, with Daniel Lanois producing, starting in Berlin at the Hansa-by-the-Wall studios, laying down tracks and developing material written over the last year or so. In March 1991, the band move to Dublin for further recording at Dog Town, S.T.S., and Windmill Lane Studios. Brian Eno joins U2 for six weeks to help with production.

NOVEMBER 18, 1991.

'Achtung Baby', U2's 7th album, is released wordwide.

JANUARY 15, 1992. NEW YORK, NY, WALDORF-ASTORIA HOTEL

The Edge is invited to induct The Yardbirds into the Rock & Roll Hall Of Fame. He makes a speech and plays live on *Big River* with some of the world's guitar greats, including Neil Young, Keith Richards and Jimmy Page.

ZOO TV TOUR, LEG 1: NORTH AMERICA, WINTER/SPRING 1992

The year 1991 was the first year in U2's career that they didn't perform in public. As Bono had announced during the last few 'LoveTown' gigs, the band needed time to "dream it all up again". The result, 'Achtung Baby', was met with almost unanimous critical and public acclaim, with critics already hailing it as a classic of the Nineties. U2, as a band and as people, continued to develop. On 'Achtung Baby' much of their youthful idealism had made way for a healthy dose of reality. Several introspective songs tackled the darker sides of love and exuded a sense of confusion and loneliness. Musically, the album offered a wider variety of sounds than ever before, incorporating industrial noise and infectuous dance rhythms. The album was a crucial renaissance for U2 after almost two years out of the public eye. Commercially, it did spectacularly well, sky-rocketing to No. 1 in charts worldwide, and selling 7 million copies before the tour had even started.

Rumours about the next tour were circulating as early as November 1990. British music papers stated that U2 were about to embark on a two-year extravaganza that would be one of the biggest tours in rock history.

When the tour is finally announced in early 1992, it is met with unprecedented eagerness and anticipation. While between 1980 and 1987 U2 had toured America almost continuously, they have now been absent from the American live circuit for five years. Dubbed the 'Zoo TV Tour', the tour opens in Florida and includes 32 hit-and-run arena dates that function to announce their return in major cities while playing it safe as far as ticket sales are concerned.

For most shows, ticket sales are made by phone orders only, leading to much chaos and dissatisfaction as hundreds of thousands of people call up. Demand outstrips supply by over ten to one. It becomes clear that five years away has increased the demand to see U2 live, their reputation having inspired new fans to grab their first opportunity to see the band, while diehards who have followed the band for years continue to support them.

The Fly

Rehearsals

FEBRUARY 27, 1992. LAKELAND, FL, LAKELAND ARENA

After two weeks rehearsing the new show, U2 record a live version of *One*, live from their stage, for broadcast that evening on 'Top Of The Pops'. Being the third single off 'Achtung Baby', it is the first live performance of the song, and the first time the public get a glimpse of U2 playing live since the final LoveTown show over two years ago.

FEBRUARY 29, 1992. LAKELAND, FL, LAKELAND ARENA

- Attendance: 7,251 (P); sellout
- Support: The Pixies
- Set: *Zoo Station / The Fly / Even Better Than The Real Thing / Mysterious Ways / One / Until The End Of The World / Who's Gonna Ride Your Wild Horses / Trying To Throw Your Arms Around The World / Angel Of Harlem / Satellite Of Love / Bad - All I Want Is You / Bullet The Blue Sky / Running To Stand Still / Where The Streets Have No Name / Pride / I Still Haven't Found What I'm Looking For /* encore: *Desire / Ultra Violet / With Or Without You / Love Is Blindness*

An excited audience and the world's press await U2's first American concert since Tempe, December 20, 1987. Fans crowd the merchandise stands, which, besides tour books and T-shirts, offer 'Achtung Baby' condom packs that will become a best-selling item on the tour. (U2 will donate all revenues from these to AIDS research and charities that benefit its victims) The stage set up attracts much attention before the show has even started: six lavishly painted East German Trabant cars are suspended from the lighting rig, 36 TV monitors are draped across the stage, and a small remote stage sticks out into the audience from stage-right, connected by a slim catwalk. A dolly camera runs across tracks over the catwalk. Irish rock journalist / radio presenter B.P. Fallon is hired for the tour to act as DJ before the band begin. After The Pixies' performance, B.P. gets a grand introduction and takes his place in a seventh Trabant car which is positioned on the mini-stage and houses his CD player. After 30 minutes of music, B.P. leaves and the Trabant is hoisted up in the air.

When the house lights dim the crowd go crazy, screaming loudly as Bono enters the stage in the dark. While he repeatedly hollers, "Wheyhey, I could have lost you," in long, dramatic outbursts, the rest of the band assume their positions. As Edge plays the opening riff of *Zoo Station*, all the TV monitors on stage and the lighting system flash on, while four large Vidiwalls rise from the floor at the back and a large projection screen is lowered from the roof to center stage. The band are dressed in

glitzy outifts as in the video clip for *The Fly*, with Bono in a black plastic suit and wrap-around 'Fly' shades. He dances spasmodically, kicking one leg in the air and goose-stepping to the rhythm of the music. With the headlights of the Trabant cars functioning as spotlights, and the Vidiwalls flashing pre-recorded, distorted images of the band, U2 introduce their new approach to live performance, the most radical change yet in their live career: Zoo TV.

Where in the past U2's shows have been honest, spiritual, and minimalistic, Zoo TV is a coctail of contradictions, ironic and flippant. Utilising high-tech equipment, Zoo TV is U2's very own TV station that merges video and television with rock & roll. Making use of a multitude of images, Zoo TV is intended to portray the sensory overload that television has become. Hard action movies blend in with live CNN reports from wars raging across the globe; soap operas, game shows, sports and pornography battle for attention, while TV preachers and commercials compete to take your money. Eventually the viewer is left bored and numb. Developed by production designer Peter Williams, video directors Ned O'Hanlon, Carol Dodds, and Brian Eno, Zoo TV reflects all the seductive and destructive aspects of Nineties television, offering as much information as non-information until vision becomes wildly distorted. Pre-recorded images illustrating songs are intermingled with the live action on stage, filmed by four onstage cameras and the boom on the catwalk. In addition, images plucked out of the air by a satellite dish outside the venue are selected by the video editors at the control panels. "It's overload. We've got all this technology available and it's our duty to abuse it," Bono will say in interviews.

U2's stage demeanor has undergone an equally radical change. Dressed in leather, U2 use the exaggerated elements of Seventies glamrock to mock stardom, while at the same time taking advantage of this old but still potent formula. By adopting a trashy, flashy look, they are trying to shake off the myth of U2, which has pushed them into a corner over the years. For most of their career, the band's public image has been dominated by their social and political awareness. People identified with the band's ideas to the extent that their every word was weighed down by seriousness. The band were trapped by people's expectations and it stinted their artistic growth. To lose this straitjacket and free the way to the future, their image as starry-eyed idealists had to be confronted and reversed.

Both on and off stage, Bono becomes The Fly. Swearing to the press and behaving hedonistically, this alter ego relieves Bono of his over-earnest public image while at the same time enabling him to display previously neglected aspects of his personality. Irony and sex are the key to the Zoo TV show, Bono's raunchy moves recalling Elvis Presley's notorious hip shaking, and his silly humour offering throwaway entertainment. The band seem to be speaking indirectly to those who have

placed too much belief in U2. "I'm just showing the ridiculousness of being a pop star," Bono will say in an interview. "In general, people put too much faith in the rich, the famous, the politicians, and not enough faith in themselves."

Each song has its own specific visual presentation and lighting design. For *The Fly*, the audience are bombarded with a barrage of single words, one-liners and slogans in huge capital letters that flash by on the screens at such a dazzling pace that anyone trying to decipher ends up cross-eyed. Starting with "EVERYTHING YOU KNOW IS WRONG", texts like "TASTE IS THE ENEMY OF ART", "NOBODY-MOVE-AND-NOBODY-GET-HURT", "I'D LIKE TO TEACH THE WORLD TO SING", "DEATH IS A CAREER MOVE" and "IT'S-YOUR-WORLD-YOU-CAN-CHANGE-IT" are intermingled with single words. "NIGGER. BOMB. RACIST. JOB. JAPAN. WHORE. PUSSY. NOW. 69." The final message freeze frames as the song ends: "WATCH MORE TV."

The crowd are both amazed and confused by the band's new attitude and stage presentation. "What can I say? The tour starts here," Bono speaks to loud cheers. "Take a look at what we got for Christmas here -- we got a TV station." He shows off Zoo TV, switching channels on the screens by remote control. "Wanna watch this? Who needs this shit? Let's go, rock & roll!" he screams as Edge starts *Even Better Than The Real Thing*. The song's visuals click with the throwaway nature of the song. Fleeting images run by, everything from blabbering talkshow hosts to advertisements, with Bono's camcorder shots mixed in: he points it at his face, winks at the crowd via the screens, whirls

Mini-stage

around and opens his mouth as if to devour the camera. He also makes fun of the press photographers, reversing roles by sticking the camera into their faces.

Mysterious Ways has bizarre projections of a woman's head spinning like a pendulum with black bars covering eyes, ears or mouth. The live version is even funkier than the album version and includes a lengthy guitar solo. "Well, we got a satellite dish outside. We can beam all of us all over the world. But not tonight – this is a private party! Five years; too long," Bono states. "All week we've been playing with it, it's like the new toy, you know. During the week we got a message from a very special guy on the satellite. He's a cosmonaut floating out in space on Space Station Mir." The Russian cosmonaut should have returned to Earth six months earlier, but has been forgotten in the chaos of the revolution that has been developing as the USSR broke up to form a multitude of independent states. Attempts to contact him during the show fail. Bono dedicates *One* to him.

Bono takes off the shades for a tender version of *One*, its soothing melody prompting the crowd to bring out their lighters. Two screens show images of galloping buffalo, made by New York artist David Wojnarowicz. On the two other screens, the word 'one' appears in numerous languages, alternating with close ups of sunflowers. When the songs ends, an image of the buffalo falling over a cliff, Wojnarowicz' perception of the AIDS crisis, freeze frames. The screens read: 'Smell the flowers while you can.'

Until The End Of The World shows The Fly at his sleaziest, manipulating the audience in a most banal but effective way. Trotting along the catwalk, Bono teases the crowd, flirts with the camera on the Zoo TV boom and plants a wet, sloppy kiss on the lens, then pulls the camera into his crotch.

Trying To Throw Your Arms Around The World is the eighth new song in a row, and introduces a festive nature to the second half of the show in which audience participation and closeness to the crowd stand central. Briefly heading backstage, Bono loses the plastic jacket, thus shedding his Fly character, and returns with a bottle of champagne for a lighthearted drink-and-spray session with a girl from the crowd. He hands the girl the camcorder and instructs her to film him, a ritual that will occur every night and will lead to unpredictable and often obscene results. At the end of the song, Edge, Larry and Adam come over to the mini-stage for an 'unplugged' session with Larry on bongos. The mini-stage proves a clever physical link to the crowd, who clap and sing along to a cheerful version of *Angel Of Harlem*. While Edge starts *Satellite Of Love*, Larry swings the cable

hanging from the mirrored Trabant over their heads before going back to the main stage. Bono sings the Lou Reed song in a delicate falsetto. Halfway through, six spotlights illuminate the twirling Trabant, turning the car into a giant mirrorball as it reflects the light in tiny rays throughout the arena.

Bad is the first of a string of songs from 'The Unforgettable Fire' and 'The Joshua Tree' albums, adorned by a brief *All I Want Is You*. For *Bullet The Blue Sky*, the Vidiwalls rise up again to display fiery red, burning crosses that emphasise the song's sinister feel. Edge attacks the song more savagely than ever, adding a fierce guitar solo while Bono goes backstage to change. Wearing a utility vest, military cap and headmike, Bono returns ranting and raving across the stage, performing an act that he will later reveal is set in the Vietnam war. The Trabants, lowered now, sway to and fro to resemble an army of combat helicopters, and Bono bangs one of them while singing aggressively about the fighter planes. Combining the themes of drug abuse with the fear and madness of war, the song segues into a re-arranged version of *Running To Stand Still*, which has Bono nervously trotting the mini-stage, rolling up his sleeve as if to take drugs, then collapsing while yellow and red smoke bombs go off, symbolising flares fired in distress. Shrouded in smoke, he recovers and plays harmonica to the song's end as he walks back to the main stage.

The screens light up in red during the organ intro of *Where The Streets Have No Name*, which elicits huge cheers of recognition from the crowd. The houselights flash on to illuminate the hall, revealing everyone in the arena up on their feet, cheerfully clapping to the rhythm. "Hey you! I remember you," Bono shouts, pointing at his former self as footage of the Joshua Tree album sleeve photo shoot appears. *Pride* is still a crowd favourite and Martin Luther King's 'Promised Land' ideology appears on the screens. After the communal gospel twist of *I Still Haven't Found*, the band leave the stage and the crowd are treated to colourful images and bubbling underwater fishbowl sounds while waiting for the encores.

For *Desire*, Bono becomes the street preacher mentioned in the song. Dressed in a glitzy, golden Las Vegas cowboy outfit, he later says that it's a spoof of an Elvis impression done by country-rock singer Gram Parsons. "We call him the Mirror Ball man, because the original suit was made of mirror ball. He embodies a kind of learning-from-Las Vegas ethos that runs through the production – the idea that trash AND transcendence are not incompatible." Carrying a mirror onstage, he looks at and kisses him image: "You know something? You're fuckin' beautiful!" Cannons shoot out U2

funny money dollar bills, while the screens show images around the theme of desire and obsession, anything from gambling casinos to pornography.

Ultra Violet uses images of a woman doing sign language, her emotional expression adding a dramatic touch to the song. Ending the show with *With Or Without You* and *Love Is Blindness*, the band finally shed all their stage characters to show where they are really at right now: tangled up in the twilight of love, struggling with the contradictions that are inherent to loving relationships. The live version of *Love Is Blindness* is sultry, as the screens show a constellation map, giving the crowd a feeling of floating across the universe by the way it moves, transmitting a mood of distance and loneliness that corresponds with the nature of the song. Bono hauls another girl on stage to dance, a spotlight lit on the pair of them.

Leaving the hall, fans who have seen U2 before experience a different feeling than on previous tours. The happy, excited and optimistic feeling U2 installed in their audiences of yore has made way for a more emotional experience, a recognition of the band's state of mind, combined with a sense of confusion. There is no cheerful chanting of "How long to sing this song" in the parking lot. It is a quiet, almost solemn procession.

U2's return to the concert stage is triumphantly received by the media. Their new approach is a welcome relief to those who may have become bored with the band's 'save the world' aura of the mid-Eighties, and hits home with new fans of the MTV generation as well. Though most old time fans like the show and understand what the band are trying to do, many aren't so sure, and wonder whether Bono has really lost it or why the band utilise visual props they had previously resisted. Contrasting opinions will dominate the first few weeks on the road until the concept of Zoo TV sinks in and fans become acquainted with its many contradictions.

MARCH 1, 1992. MIAMI, FL, MIAMI ARENA

- Attendance: 15,000; sellout
- Support: The Pixies
- Set: same as Lakeland.

The show is somewhat better than Lakeland, but the band have still to find their rhythm. Mistakes show up in most of the new songs, leaving the band desperately improvising to cover up their out-of-synch playing. Belly-dancer Christina Petro makes her début tonight. A fan of U2, Christina had approached U2's management before the tour with an offer to dance during *Mysterious Ways* in much the same way as the belly-dancer appears metaphorically in the video. The management suggested she offer U2 a surprise performance, so Christina danced into their rehearsal. The band were very impressed, and Miami becomes her first opportunity to do it for real. During *Even Better Than The Real Thing* Christina, in an exotic outfit, is guided to the mini-stage in the dark. When the song starts, a blue spotlight flashes on, so she appears out of nowhere. Her act is highly choreographed to contain symbolic quality. While Christina dances gracefully, Bono, looking up in admiration, sings and gestures to her enlarged video image on one of the screens. As the song progresses, Christina dances her way along the catwalk towards the main stage where Bono stands on the edge, making desperate attempts to grab her. She teases him, dancing seductively but makes sure she remains out of his reach. After this show, Christina doesn't perform until she actually joins the tour in Boston.

Bono talks about the Russian cosmonaut. "Using our satellite dish, he sent down his best wishes. A whole revolution has taken place while he was up there." The start of *Where The Streets Have No Name* is a mess. Bono sings, "I wanna run... sunlight into my face..." Right.

MARCH 3, 1992. CHARLOTTE, NC, COLISEUM

- Attendance: 22,786 (P); sellout
- Support: The Pixies
- Set: same as Lakeland.

Though the largest of the spring tour, the crowd aren't as lively as in other cities. Before *Angel Of Harlem* a fan reaches out to Bono over the edge of the mini-stage, holding a dollar bill to play his favourite song. Bono responds, "You're offering me money? You've already paid me a fortune, man!" As he kisses the mirror during *Desire*, he calls his image "a hopeless case".

MARCH 5, 1992. ATLANTA, GA, THE OMNI

- Attendance: 16,336 (P); sellout
- Support: The Pixies
- Set: same as Lakeland.

Over two million phone calls were registered when tickets went on sale. A couple of shows into the tour, Bono is better acquainted with his alter-ego of The Fly and feels comfortable enough to stretch the nature of its character, producing tacky and sexy moves whenever he can. Larry steps forward to introduce a song. "Hello there! Adam, Edge and I would like to play a song for you, it's called *Arms Around The World*." The dance with a girl from the audience leaves Bono short of breath. He says, "It's getting hot in here. Whatever's going on in these pants, it's getting hotter!" "The Pixies were good, weren't they?" he asks, but the response is as meagre as it was during The Pixies' performance. "There's a band that's louder than America," Bono says.

MARCH 7, 1992. HAMPTON, VA, COLISEUM

- Attendance: 10,187 (P); sellout
- Support: The Pixies
- Set: same as Lakeland, but *The Fly* is played after *Mysterious Ways* instead of after *Zoo Station*, and *Love Is Blindness* is left out.

MARCH 9, 1992. UNIONDALE, NY, NASSAU COLISEUM

- Attendance: 17,397 (P); sellout
- Support: The Pixies
- Set: same as Lakeland.

"Welcome to Zoo TV, our very own soap opera," Bono says after *The Fly*. As in every city the tour visits, ticket prices run sky high on the black market. "I hope nobody paid too much, I heard somebody paid $500 to get in tonight. Let me tell you, we are not worth that price," Bono assures them.

MARCH 10, 1992. PHILADELPHIA, PA, SPECTRUM ARENA

- Attendance: 18,349 (P); sellout
- Support: The Pixies
- Set: same as Lakeland.

On leaving the stage, some guy from the audience runs up to grab Bono. Security tries to remove him but Bono hugs the guy, who in return gives him his boots. Like everywhere, the show gets a lot of attention in the local papers. *Philadelphia Daily News*: "The busiest mixed media since David Bowie's Glass Spider tour". *Courier Post* says it "wasn't quite the affair some over-enthusiastic reviewers in other cities made it out to be. Too many times, the band seemed to be overshadowed by its toys". *Philadelphia Inquirer* calls it "Powerful and effective enough to restore faith in rock & roll in this cynical 30-year old pop music critic".

MARCH 12, 1992. HARTFORD, CT, CIVIC CENTER

- Attendance: 16,438 (P); sellout
- Support: The Pixies
- Set: same as Lakeland, minus *Love Is Blindness*.

The show sells out in a Civic Center record of 40 minutes. Bono's voice is acting up, leaving him unable to sing the higher notes in many songs. After a troublesome *With Or Without You* he apologises. Frustrated at being unable to sing properly, he kicks over the microphone stand as he strolls off stage and omits the last song.

MARCH 13, 1992. WORCESTER, MA, CENTRUM

- Attendance: 13,835 (P); sellout
- Support: The Pixies
- Set: same as Lakeland.

"I love being in a rock & roll band in Massachusetts with The Pixies, on Adam Clayton's birthday!" Bono shouts. Adam turns 32, giving the show a festive feel. After *Even Better Than The Real Thing* a scantily clad woman dressed as a Playboy bunny arrives on stage. Bono introduces himself as the publisher of that best-selling magazine: "Hi, I'm Hugh Hefner, who are you?" "I'm a Bunnygram," says the girl and hands a big bunch of balloons to Adam as a present. She also drapes a purple boa around his neck. "Uhm, I'm just going away for a few minutes," Bono quips. "Please, no photographs," Adam mumbles, while the audience are in stitches.

Bono points at the huge stage-set behind him. "The greatest thing about all this shit, is that we don't need it. Is that right?" The audience cheer, agreeing that the size of the production does not overshadow the music. He yells, "I just need The Edge, play for me, Edge," but ironically the guitarist completely messes up in *Until The End Of The World*.

"Yo! This is usually the part of the show where I tell you about the next song," announces birthday boy Adam himself. "Yeeaaah!" "But I'm not going to do that tonight." "Ooohh," the audience sigh, but he tells them anyway: "This is a song about a Donegal man, coming back from the pub late at night, and when he gets back into his house, he can't put his key in the door. It's called *Trying To Throw Your Arms Around The World*." By the end of the song Bono calls the rest of the band over to the mini-stage and drops in lines of *Happy Birthday*. The band drink champagne in abundance. *Where The Streets Have No Name* is a mess as the band members are out of synch. "One sip of champagne, and the guy's down the drain, where the streets have no name," Bono sings.

Over a million orders have come in for the 59,165 available tickets for the four New England shows. Ticket touts were quick to take advantage. "I'd like to thank you all for the trouble you went through getting the tickets and everything," Bono says at the start of *I Still Haven't Found*. "I know you went through a lot of trouble, standing in line and queuing up and getting ripped off by the ticket touts, though we did our best to stop those

bastards." The audience cheer. Coming to the subject of the upcoming Presidential elections in America now that George Bush's fourth year is coming to a close, Bono comments, "We feel very lucky to be playing a sold-out show here in this time of recession, which is of course a polite word for depression. Anyway, it's election time. Maybe that's none of our business, seeing that we come from Ireland and all that... except that who you vote President of the United States, is *everybody's* business. So, while you got the vote, use it. I wish you well, I hope you find what you're looking for."

MARCH 15, 1992. PROVIDENCE, RI, CIVIC CENTER

- Attendance: 13,680 (P); sellout
- Support: The Pixies
- Set: same as Lakeland.

MARCH 17, 1992. BOSTON, MA, GARDENS

- Attendance: 15,212 (P); sellout
- Support: The Pixies
- Set: same as Lakeland, plus *Dirty Old Town* after *Angel Of Harlem*, and *Van Diemen's Land* after *Satellite Of Love*.

On St. Patrick's Day, the Irish holiday, U2 play in Boston where one out of four inhabitants are of Irish descent. Early in the day, Edge and Larry go into town to bar-hop in Irish pubs and come across a bar band playing U2 songs and play along. Joining the festivities, local radio station WZLX give away 25 pairs of tickets to people wearing original costumes or banners stating 'WZLX Welcomes U2'. Employees from WZLX select the most original 25 people and hand them their tickets at the venue but the situation gets out of hand when instead of a few hundred, as WZLX expects, no less than 8,000 people turn up on the streets around the Garden, all dressed in bizarre costumes, the text painted on themselves or on large banners. Though the carnivalesque mass of people provide a true sense of the absurd for an already special occasion, Boston city officials panic as rush-hour traffic is brought to a halt and police from all over the metropolitan area have to be called in to control the crowd and secure public safety. When his car is stopped in the streets, Paul McGuinness has trouble convincing a cop he's U2's manager and really needs to get through. [The city will later charge WZLX for cleanup crews and police overtime costs.] Though 600 tickets go on sale at the box office hours before the show, the large influx of ticketless fans is a scalper's paradise. Ticket prices range from $200 to $1,000 on the black market.

Inside, the atmosphere is sheer elation, with fans partying long before the show has started. Hundreds of reporters and photographers from all over Europe are flown in to report on the occasion. A pipe band march around the venue. Banners cover the balconies and green, the Irish national colour, dominates the audience's clothes. Even the beer is green!

"I've never been in Boston on St. Patrick's Day," Bono says after *The Fly*. "Now I know why – you bastards are louder than the band! We've been away for five years, feels like five minutes tonight... we're back!" A thunderous roar goes through the arena when Bono asks, "Any Irish out there tonight?" He touches upon the problem of unemployment amongst illegal Irish immigrants. "You can't all be Irish, this is America! Truth is, we all end up in Boston looking for work. And I got no green card either."

During *Trying To Throw Your Arms* Bono holds the microphone in front of Larry, who sings, "I dreamed I saw St. Patrick, played and scored a hat trick, and Larry Bird was throwing his arms around the world..." Larry Bird is the legendary basketball player of the Boston Celtics. [U2 have referred to him before: September 17th, 1987, also in this venue.]

Coming to the set on the mini-stage, U2 have some surprises in store. *Angel Of Harlem* is dedicated to "one of the greatest Irish singers of all time – Billy O'Holiday." Larry sings a verse of the song and afterwards Bono announces, "One more

St. Patrick's Day in Boston

from Larry Mullen, ladies & gentlemen, tonight for the first time ever!" Accompanied by Edge and Bono on guitar, Larry sings Ewan MacColl's *Dirty Old Town*, much to the crowd's delight, and sings hilariously out of tune. After *Satellite Of Love*, Edge sings *Van Diemen's Land* for the first time this tour. "I wanna sing a song for you about a man called John Boyd O'Reilly who left Ireland, unfortunately, on a prison ship heading for Australia, but managed to get out of there and head for a town in the United States of America called Boston. This song is about his leaving which I'm sure was not a happy one."

The band are overcome by the enthusiasm of the audience: "I really don't know what to say to y'all," Bono says. "It's an incredible feeling, it's a home away from home."

MARCH 18, 1992. EAST RUTHERFORD, NJ, MEADOWLANDS ARENA

- Attendance: 19,880 (P); sellout
- Support: The Pixies
- Set: same as Lakeland.

At the start of *With Or Without You*, Bono raps, "Let's go to Vegas, let's get married, for a while..." as he will do throughout the tour. 'Rattle And Hum' film director Phil Joanou attends the show and meets a woman called Katie. Inspired by Bono's words and the sense of let's-enjoy-this-ride-before-it's-too-late irresponsibility that surrounds the tour, Phil and Katie fly to Las Vegas to get married the next day.

MARCH 20, 1992. NEW YORK, NY, MADISON SQUARE GARDEN

- Attendance: 18,179 (P); sellout
- Support: The Pixies
- Set: same as Lakeland.

The show sold out in ten minutes. The extra tension of playing Madison Square Garden results in a hot show. Larry sings a verse of *Angel Of Harlem* and leaves Bono to bang away on the congas. The crowd, media and celebrities love the show. Now the Spring tour is halfway and U2's return to the American concert stage is proving hugely successful, preparations are well underway for a much bigger tour, which will see the band come back to America in August to play football stadiums. Though nothing is officially confirmed, Bono lets something loose during the show. "Maybe we should come back here at the end of the summer. In fact, we *are* coming back at the end of the summer," he says to loud cheers. "I know you've got your own problems in this city, I don't know much about them. This is election time. If you don't get the right President, we're all fucked!" Images of Phil Joanou's wedding, the day before in Las Vegas, are mixed in with the barrage of images during *Desire*.

MARCH 21, 1992. ALBANY, NY, KNICKERBOCKER ARENA

- Attendance: 16,258 (P); sellout
- Support: The Pixies
- Set: same as Lakeland.

U2 haven't played this city since 1983. A fan in the audience holds a large banner reading 'J.B. Scott's', the name of the Albany club where U2 played three concerts in 1981. During *Angel Of Harlem* Bono sees the sign, walks over, shakes the guy's hand and grabs the sign to drape it over the mini-stage. He jests, "I remember playing a club called J.B. Scott's in 1963. I can't play guitar now, either. The only difference is, you don't mind now."

MARCH 23, 1992. MONTREAL, CANADA, FORUM

- Attendance: 18,000; sellout
- Support: The Pixies

- Set: same as Lakeland, plus *Slow Dancing* after *Angel Of Harlem*.

The acoustic song *Slow Dancing*, which was performed in concert on two occasions during the LoveTown tour, pops up during the set on the mini-stage. "I'll sing you a song I've never sung before anywhere else," Bono announces. "This is a song myself and Edge wrote for Willie Nelson. I don't know if he likes it, but I really like it." Bono sings only two verses, then admits he hasn't finished the third yet.

MARCH 24, 1992. TORONTO, CANADA, MAPLE LEAF GARDENS

- Attendance: 16,015 (P); sellout
- Support: The Pixies
- Set: same as Lakeland.

A girl from the audience gets on stage during *With Or Without You* and finds a crew member chasing her. She runs over to Larry, Adam, kisses Bono, who lets her sing along with the song.

MARCH 26, 1992. CLEVELAND, OH, RICHFIELD COLISEUM

- Attendance: 18,083 (P); sellout
- Support: The Pixies
- Set: same as Lakeland.

MARCH 27, 1992. DETROIT, MI, PALACE OF AUBURN HILLS

- Attendance: 21,064 (P); sellout
- Support: The Pixies
- Set: same as Lakeland.

When switching channels after *Even Better Than The Real Thing*, Bono stops at a pizza advertisement and turns to the audience: "You want some pizza?" While the crowd roar, he picks up the phone and dials the number on the screen. "Hello? Is this Speedy Pizza? I'd like to order 10,000 pizzas for Detroit. We're at the Palace, you know the Palace? Yeah, I *am* serious, I'm very serious! You can't make 10,000? Just make as many as you can, OK? What? My name is Bono..."

As they wait for the encore, the crowd are confused when three men in blue uniforms wheel in a large cart, but cheer as one of the video screens zooms in to reveal what is *on* the cart: pizza. The crowd chant "Piz-za, piz-za", while a hundred pizza boxes are flung like Frisbees to those within reach, leaving the crowd exhilarated and well-fed. (Reports say it was pepperoni.)

The incident will prove one of the most notorious and much-quoted of the entire tour. For the 1993 tour, U2's merchandise company will print T-shirts with the text 'I'D LIKE TO ORDER 10,000 PIZZAS' on the front.

MARCH 30, 1992. MINNEAPOLIS, MN, TARGET CENTER

- Attendance: 18,256 (P); sellout
- Support: The Pixies
- Set: same as Lakeland.

MARCH 31, 1992. CHICAGO, IL, ROSEMONT HORIZON

- Attendance: 17,329 (P); sellout
- Support: The Pixies
- Set: same as Lakeland.

Though the hyper-enthusiastic crowd are generally well-behaved, the band have to deal with a couple of people whose fanaticism goes way over the top. As Bono walks along the catwalk to the mini-stage during *Trying To Throw Your Arms*, a guy yanks the towel off Bono's neck, leaving him with rug burns. Security guards move in, but Bono says it's OK and keeps them off. When, after the set on the mini-stage, Larry walks back, he stumbles over the rigging and a female fan grabs his leg and pulls him towards the crowd. Innumerable outstretched arms are grabbing at Larry's hair, his clothes, whatever is in reach. A security guard quickly wraps his arms around Larry's waist and barely prevents him from disappearing into the masses. Back on his feet, Larry tries to hide his disgust and proceeds with the show.

APRIL 5, 1992. DALLAS, TX, REUNION ARENA

- Attendance: 17,999 (P); sellout
- Support: The Pixies
- Set: same as Lakeland.

APRIL 6, 1992. HOUSTON, TX, THE SUMMIT

- Attendance: 16,342 (P); sellout
- Support: The Pixies
- Set: same as Lakeland.

Bono rams the microphone stand through one of the TV monitors on stage. *Love Is Blindness* is dedicated to a girl called Tiffany, who had a ticket for the show but died in a car crash some days before.

APRIL 7, 1992. AUSTIN, TX, FRANK ERWIN CENTER

- Attendance: 16,786 (P); sellout
- Support: The Pixies
- Set: same as Lakeland.

APRIL 10, 1992. TEMPE, AZ, ARIZONA STATE UNIVERSITY ASSEMBLY CENTER

- Attendance: 13,302 (P); sellout
- Support: The Pixies
- Set: same as Lakeland, minus *Desire* and *Ultra Violet*.

Playing Tempe brings back memories of the desert that is home to Joshua trees, of the opening shows of the 1987 tour, as well as the closing shows that were filmed for 'Rattle And Hum'. "I think we've been here somewhere before," Bono teases the crowd. "It's hot in here, we must be close to a desert or something, are we? Thanks for hanging around for five years."

When he drop-kicks a cup of water, it flies all the way to the mixing desk and spills down into the control panels. Bono looks startled and offers a sheepish mouthed apology, leaving the technicians to blow-dry the panels throughout the show. Someone in the stands wears a T-shirt reading 'Bono is a ticket scalper'; almost immediately after seeing it, Bono is wearing the shirt. Walking along the catwalk, Larry abruptly shakes off fans

trying to touch him and raises his hands out of reach.

"Hello, I think we've seen many of you before. Maybe we should come back and make a film or something," Adam jokes, and the crowd laugh as he announces, "We'd like to play an Irish song for you now... this is NOT a rebel song... this is *Trying To Throw Your Arms Around The World*," mocking the drama that used to introduce *Sunday Bloody Sunday*, back in 1983.

APRIL 12, 13, 1992. LOS ANGELES, CA, SPORTS ARENA

- Attendance: 31,692 (P); sellout
- Support: The Pixies
- Set first night: same as Lakeland.

"L.A. was the first place we ever felt like rock & roll stars. I feel embarrassed. Look at me: I'm a tart!" Bono remarks. *Angel Of Harlem* is dedicated to Quincy Jones.

- Set second night: same as Lakeland, plus *Dancing Queen* linked to *Angel Of Harlem*.

A quick, acoustic version of *Dancing Queen*, the 1976 smash hit by Abba, is linked to *Angel Of Harlem*. The crowd slowly recognise the song and react in surprise to U2's choice. Since Bono doesn't know the words very well, he presents Edge and Larry with the microphone but they crack up in laughter and only sing the melody.

APRIL 15, 1992. SAN DIEGO, CA, SPORTS ARENA

- Attendance: 13,824 (P); sellout
- Support: The Pixies
- Set: *Zoo Station / The Fly / Even Better Than The Real Thing / Mysterious Ways / One / Until The End Of The World / Who's Gonna Ride Your Wild Horses / Trying To Throw Your Arms Around The World / Angel Of Harlem–Dancing Queen / Satellite Of Love / Van Diemen's Land / Bad – All I Want Is You / Bullet The Blue Sky / Running To Stand Still / Where The Streets Have No Name / Pride / I Still Haven't Found / encore: With Or Without You / Love Is Blindness*

While zapping after *Even Better Than The Real Thing*, Bono comes to a jewellery ad on Home Shopping Club and unsuccessfully tries to order "a diamond the size of a belly-button". *Who's Gonna Ride Your Wild Horses* is stopped halfway through. "Would you mind if we do this acoustically?" Bono asks, starts anew, and proceeds to perform the song on his own, singing and playing acoustic guitar with Edge singing background vocals on the

chorus. This impromptu version highlights the show. *Van Diemen's Land* is performed for the second time on the tour.

APRIL 17, 1992. SACRAMENTO, CA, ARCO ARENA

- Attendance: 15,893 (P); sellout
- Support: The Pixies
- Set: same as Lakeland, plus *Dancing Queen* linked to *Angel Of Harlem*, and minus *Desire* and *Ultra Violet*.

Early in the show Bono says he feels sick and claims the doctor gave him some pills that are even better than the real thing. U2's performance is not as strong as usual and gets many bad reviews in the local press.

APRIL 18, 1992. OAKLAND, CA, OAKLAND COLISEUM

- Attendance: 14,431 (P); sellout
- Support: The Pixies
- Set: same as Lakeland, plus *Dancing Queen* linked to *Angel Of Harlem*.

The spirit of Freddie Mercury, who died of AIDS in November 1991, wanders through Oakland Coliseum. The show is taped for the Live For Life tribute to the late Queen singer on April 20 at London's Wembley Stadium. *Until The End Of The World* from this show will be shown on the video screens at Wembley and on TV worldwide between acts. Bono refers to Freddie throughout the show. *Dancing Queen* and *Satellite Of Love* are dedicated to him. "We're sending some of tonight's show down the wire to Freddie Aid in London. He was a very cool guy; he was exceptionally cool to me."

Bono teases the audience. "This is *Bohemian Rhapsody*... not!" Throughout the performance he refers to the show as being in San Francisco instead of in nearby Oakland.

A new gimmick evolving on the tour is Bono trying to get President George Bush on the phone before *Ultra Violet*. "Might be cool to call the President today, what do you think?" he asks wickedly, his gold lamé suit and cowboy hat glittering, while he dials the number. "Can I help you?" a female voice resounds. "Hello, is that the White House? Aah, God bless you! I'd like to speak to the President if that's possible." "That's not possible." "He's not home?" "He's not available." [The crowd jeer.] "So George doesn't want to speak to me – I guess I'm not as important as I thought I was! Can I leave a message? Just tell the President to watch more TV..."

APRIL 20, 21, 1992. TACOMA, WA, TACOMA DOME

- Attendance: 43,977 (P); sellout
- Support: The Pixies
- Set first night: same as Lakeland, plus *Dancing Queen* linked to *Angel Of Harlem*.

Originally, a concert has been planned for Portland, Oregon on April 20, but is replaced by a second show in Tacoma.

- Set second night: *Zoo Station / The Fly / Even Better Than The Real Thing / Mysterious Ways / One–Unchained Melody / Until The End Of The World / Who's Gonna Ride Your Wild Horses / Trying To Throw Your Arms / Angel Of Harlem / When Love Comes To Town / Slow Dancing / Bad–All I Want Is You / Bullet The Blue Sky / Running To Stand Still / Where The Streets Have No Name / Pride / I Still Haven't Found–Stand By Me /* encore: *Desire / Ultra Violet / With Or Without You / Love Is Blindness*

The show is outstanding with many firsts. After *One*, Bono sings a short, acoustic version of *Unchained Melody*, The Righteous Brothers' song that U2 covered for the B-side of the *All I Want Is You* single in 1989. It's sung quietly compared to the passionate rendering on record but is chilling enough to keep the audience captivated. Two more songs have their première on the tour: *When Love Comes To Town* is added to the acoustic set on the mini-stage, while *Stand By Me* is linked to *I Still Haven't Found*. *When Love Comes To Town* sees Bono sing a twisted improvisation about U2 starting out: "I was a boxer, or something like that. Edge said, 'You don't know the words, better eat your hat'. Larry played the drums, Adam played bass guitar. I guess I was a singer, boy, did we go far. I ran into a jukejoint when I heard the guitar play. Something about punk music and you didn't have to play. I said, 'Hey, I'll give up my job at the petrol station – get me over to the United States nation'..." *Slow Dancing* is another surprise to the crowd, and has Edge on background vocals and Larry on tambourine. Bono jokes about the song being influenced by the Seattle grunge scene.

APRIL 23, 1992. VANCOUVER, CANADA, PACIFIC NATIONAL EXHIBITION COLISEUM

- Attendance: 15,000; sellout
- Support: The Pixies
- Set: *Zoo Station / The Fly / Even Better Than The Real Thing / Mysterious Ways / One-Unchained Melody / Until The End Of The World / Who's Gonna Ride Your Wild Horses / Trying To*

Paul McGuinness, U2's manager

Throw Your Arms / Angel Of Harlem – Dancing Queen / Satellite Of Love / Bad–All I Want Is You / Bullet The Blue Sky / Running To Stand Still / Where The Streets Have No Name / Pride / I Still Haven't Found / encore: *With Or Without You / Love Is Blindness*

The Vancouver show finishes the first leg of the tour. The 32 shows of this American Spring tour sell 528,763 tickets, grossing $13,215,414.

Before the end of April, the first string of outdoor shows in August is announced, with over 500,000 tickets going on sale for two shows at Giants' Stadium in East Rutherford, two shows at RFK Stadium in Washington DC and three shows at Foxboro Stadium outside Boston. Meanwhile, the 'Achtung Baby' album has already gone triple platinum in the United States for sales over three million copies. Worldwide sales stand at eight million copies.

ZOO TV: EUROPE, SPRING 1992

With the first US swing a success and the world press raving about Zoo TV, U2 move into Europe with eagerness and confidence for a highly anticipated indoor tour that serves as a teaser for a major stadium tour in the summer of 1993. Ticket details are shrouded in secrecy. Sudden radio ads announce that tickets are on sale NOW, leaving only those lucky enough to be listening a chance to rush to the local box office before all tickets are gone. Because the production is expensive and crowds are relatively small, the European tour loses money. Paul McGuinness intends to include a few open air dates to make the books balance, but although big shows are scheduled for Berlin, Turin, Poland and Vienna, only the latter actually takes place.

MAY 7, 1992. PARIS, FRANCE, PALAIS OMNISPORTS DE BERCY

- Attendance: 16,000; sellout
- Support: Fatima Mansions
- Set: same as Vancouver.

Interviewed by MTV during the soundcheck, Edge remarks that "It's good to be back in a part of the world that's older than 200 years." Reporters and film crews from all over Europe are present. After *The Fly* Bono quips, "I ran into Jim Morrison the other night, and he said, buy as many U2 albums as you can afford and the world will be a better place," and raises his arms in innocence: "Just passing on the message..." The crowd are awed by the show. Since there are no seats on the floor, fans are jammed up against the barriers. As will happen at every show in Europe, pressure intensifies every time Bono parades down the catwalk and when the band come down to the mini-stage for the acoustic set.

MAY 9, 1992. GENT, BELGIUM, FLANDERS EXPO

- Attendance: 11,000; sellout
- Support: Fatima Mansions
- Set: *Zoo Station / The Fly / Even Better Than The Real Thing / Mysterious Ways / One – Unchained Melody / Until The End Of The World / Who's Gonna Ride Your Wild Horses / Trying To Throw Your Arms / Angel Of Harlem - Dancing Queen / Satellite Of Love / Bad-All I Want Is You / Bullet The Blue Sky / Running To Stand Still / Where The Streets Have No Name / Pride / I Still Haven't Found /* encore: *Desire / Ultra Violet / With Or Without You / Love Is Blindness*

The basic set as played in Lakeland is now extended with *Unchained Melody* linked to *One*, and *Dancing Queen* linked to *Angel Of Harlem*. A few hours away from his 32nd birthday, Bono strolls over the catwalk and picks up a girl from the crowd. "You wanna drink with me? Hell, it's my birthday!" She operates the camcorder and stays on the mini-stage for a couple of songs. Ending *Satellite Of Love* Bono says to her, "I want you for my birthday..."

MAY 11, 1992. LYON, FRANCE, ESPACE TONY GARNIER

- Attendance: 17,000; sellout
- Support: Fatima Mansions
- Set: same as Gent, minus *Dancing Queen*.

Prior to the show the audience sing *Happy Birthday* for Bono. During *All I Want Is You* three very similar looking girls come on stage. "All I want is... my three sisters," Bono sings, kisses them and leads them off. Zoo TV experiences technical problems: there is no satellite connection tonight, therefore the TV images that are usually live are from tape.

MAY 12, 1992. LAUSANNE, SWITZERLAND, PATINOIRE DE MALLEY

- Attendance: 10,000; sellout
- Support: Fatima Mansions
- Set: same as Gent.

During an inspired set Larry sings part of *Dancing Queen*, which is played almost in its entirety.

MAY 14, 1992. SAN SEBASTIAN, SPAIN, VELODROME ANOETA

- Attendance: 14,000; sellout
- Support: Fatima Mansions
- Set: same as Gent, plus *Spanish Eyes* after *Dancing Queen*.

This is U2's second ever show in Spain; the first was on July 15, 1987 in Madrid, when *Spanish Eyes* was performed for the first time. Here, after *Dancing Queen*, *Spanish Eyes* is played for the only time on the whole tour. The song ends prematurely as Bono struggles to remember the lyrics.

MAY 16, 18, 1992. BARCELONA, SPAIN, PALAU SANT JORDI

- Attendance: 32,000; (capacity 36,000)
- Support: Fatima Mansions
- Set first night: same as Gent, minus *Desire* and *Ultra Violet*.

Outside, fans sing and wave U2 flags in the hot afternoon sun. Venue security is tight, with a ban even on plastic bottles of mineral water. The audience have high expectations for U2's first visit to Barcelona. People storm to the seats close to the stage. On the left, a whole section of seats has been secured for VIP's and special guests. Bono's wife Alison, Larry's girlfriend Ann, and several friends and family of band and crew look on completely powerless as their seats are taken by over-excited fans who ignore the red tape. As security try in vain to clear the area, the lights dim and the show has begun.

Audience response is mixed. It becomes clear right away that many are unaware of U2's recent developments, as hundreds of 'War' banners and white flags are sticking out of the crowd. Though most are enthusiastic, many are not ready for U2's drastic change and look on confused at the bug-eyed creature amidst the video screens. During the set on the mini-stage, a huge amount of water is thrown over Bono by a guy in the crowd. Bono is outraged. He briskly jabs the culprit, takes his empty jerrycan and angrily throws it on the floor. A bizarre moment occurs when Bono, dripping wet, arms outstretched and a desolate look on his face, walks to the stands looking for sympathy, but only finds a mass of people hysterically screaming simply because he is moving closer. The show is ruined. The band play on, uninspired, cutting out two songs. After *Love Is Blindness*, a large part of the crowd shout in vain for *Sunday Bloody Sunday*.

■ Set second night: same as Gent.

Prior to the show the level of excitement is not as high as on the first night. The whole back section of the arena, around 4,000 seats, remains empty, making it the only concert of the European tour that doesn't sell out. U2 play a powerful show. It's a hot night. "So, who didn't pay the air-conditioning builders?" Bono asks. For *The Fly*, half the texts have been translated into Spanish. (Later on in the tour they will also be translated for the Italian and German audiences.) *Dancing Queen* is one of the highlights, with Bono encouraging the crowd to sing along. "Don't be embarrassed! Listen, *everybody's* got an Abba record in their collection."

At the start of *Bad* a guy throws water over Bono, who reacts by putting his fists up and shadow boxing. Back on the main stage water is throw at him *again*. He reacts impulsively, beckons come on, throw some, sticks his chest out and turns himself into a target. Water flies at him from everywhere. In revenge, Bono gets some water from security and, to release his aggression, throws it over the crowd .

Tonight, the last tones of *Love Is Blindness* are followed by Elvis' *Can't Help Falling In Love*, played over the PA while the crowd migrate towards the exits. This will remain the outro for the rest of the 1992/3 tour.

MAY 21, 22, 1992. MILAN, ITALY, FORUM DI ASSAGO

■ Attendance: 25,000; sellout
■ Support: Fatima Mansions
■ Set first show: same as Gent, with *Stand By Me*, played for the first time this tour, linked to *I Still Haven't Found*.

These shows were originally planned for May 20 and 21, but the first is postponed until the 22nd when one of the trucks breaks down on its way from Barcelona. Attempts to fly the contents to Milan fail.

On May 20, the crowd of 12,500 people, who had travelled from all over Italy, wait hours in the rain outside the Forum. Doors were due open at 7pm. When, at 8 o'clock gates are still closed and Forum employees are seen talking nervously, rumours that the show will not take place begin to fly around. There had been an earlier misunderstanding over whether the shows would take place at all, as 300,000 applications were received for the 25,000 available tickets, and the mayor feared that thousands of ticketless fans would cause troubles in his town. The situation becomes potentially explosive when the rain-drenched crowd becomes impatient and hundreds of carabinieri (armed policemen) are instructed to act as a buffer between entrance gates and venue doors. A Forum official announces by megaphone that the show will not take place. In a state of chaos and disappointment the crowd disperse without incident.

On the 21st, Edge and Bono tell fans at the hotel they were frustrated they couldn't play. "It was a real pain, we were ready to go," Edge says. That night, the crowd are ready to rock. Support act Fatima Mansions are booed, as at practically everywhere in Europe, after initial interest. During their ballad

Behind The Moon, the crowd even sing "How long to sing this song" so loudly that it drowns out the PA. U2's performance is dynamic and entertaining. Before *One*, Bono refers in Italian to the 1990 Italy-Ireland soccer match. Italy defeated Jack Charlton's team by 1-0 in the quarter-finals of the World Championships. "We forgive you that you were lucky," Bono says.

Towel and champagne in hand during *Trying To Throw Your Arms*, Bono goes onto the catwalk where a girl has already climbed onto the rails. He embraces her, opens the bottle with her, sprays those closest, and walks to the mini-stage. Bono gallantly offers her a seat on a monitor. "Edge, it's you she loves," he shouts. Together they serenade the girl, who is filming them as they argue about who is going to get her: "Woman, I will," they sing alternately, pushing each other around in mock-competition.

■ Set second night: *Zoo Station / The Fly / Even Better Than The Real Thing / Mysterious Ways / One / Until The End Of The World / Who's Gonna Ride Your Wild Horses / Trying To Throw Your Arms / Angel Of Harlem / When Love Comes To Town / Satellite Of Love / Bad – So Cruel / Bullet The Blue Sky / Running To Stand Still / Where The Streets Have No Name / Pride / I Still Haven't Found / encore: Desire / Ultra Violet / With Or Without You / Love Is Blindness*

Hoping to make up for the inconvenience of two days earlier,

U2 play an outstanding show. *Unchained Melody*, *Stand By Me* and *Dancing Queen* are left out, but *When Love Comes To Town* appears in the acoustic set and a quick version of *So Cruel*, performed for the very first time, replaces *All I Want Is You*. Before *Ultra Violet*, Bono makes a phone call to the speaking clock. "Hello? I got something I want to explain to you. You see, we had this truck, and it broke down, and we couldn't play the concert in Milano, and the people they travelled from Naples, they travelled from Florence, they travelled from all over. Listen, do you hear me, can you understand me?" he says to the recorded message.

MAY 24, 1992. VIENNA, AUSTRIA, DONAU INSEL

■ Attendance: ca. 60,000; (unlimited)
■ Support: Fatima Mansions
■ Set: same as Gent, with *Knocking On Heaven's Door* instead of *Dancing Queen*, minus *Satellite Of Love* and plus *Stand By Me* after *I Still Haven't Found*.

U2's first ever performance in Austria is their first open-air show since Auckland, November 11, 1989, and the only one on this European tour. The location is a big field on the strip of land between the old river Danube and the newly constructed waterway. The stage set-up is extended by three large video-screens at the sides of the stage and behind the lighting tower.

B.P. Fallon plays a new series of songs, including the German version of Bowie's *Heroes*, Guns n'Roses' *November Rain*, and, for the first time, *Television: The Drug Of The Nation* by The Disposable Heroes Of Hiphoprisy, which will replace *Be My Baby* as the last song before U2 come on stage for the rest of the tour.

Bono immediately moves to the mini-stage and gazes out at the immense audience. The visuals of the show lack impact due to the daylight. "Hello, wie geht's?" he asks. "Some of this bullshit is pretty cool, and some of it is just plain expensive. Sometimes there's just nothing doin'! We're here, we got our cars, we got our TV sets... hope you like the show... we love you..." His voice is dead, he seems to be just reeling off the words.

One is dedicated to "the men and the boys of Guns n'Roses." Gn'R had played here the night before and afterwards had gone drinking with U2. After *Angel Of Harlem*, Axl Rose comes on stage to sing *Knocking On Heaven's Door* with U2, who hadn't played it since Osaka, November 28, 1989, and this version sounds like Bono has forgotten even those few simple chords. When Axl starts in his nasal whining the crowd go wild, but chemistry between Axl and Bono is lacking, and the duet never takes off.

The show can easily be regarded as the worst of the European tour. The dynamics of Zoo TV had not been adjusted for an open-air crowd. Not having played outdoors for years, the band feel uncomfortable and seem out of place. This becomes painfully apparent when, during *Desire*, Bono angrily starts shouting, "For love or money, lotsa *money*, 'Let's do it outdoors,' more *money*." Evidently quoting someone, he takes a swipe at the U2 organisation for deciding to play outdoors to increase income.

MAY 25, 1992. MUNICH, GERMANY, OLYMPIAHALLE

- Attendance: 12,000; sellout
- Support: Fatima Mansions
- Set: same as Gent, with *Can't Help Falling In Love* replacing *Unchained Melody*.

U2 are deafeningly welcomed for their first of five shows in Germany. While zapping after *The Fly*, Bono greets every TV image with "Good evening", or "Good night!" if he doesn't like it. For the first time this tour he sings *Can't Help Falling In Love*, the romantic song made famous by Elvis, which he had done only once before (in Murfreesboro, November 28, 1987). While on the mini-stage, someone throws a hard-plastic cup right past Bono's head. "That was close," he says dryly. Edge's guitar malfunctions at the start of *Bullet The Blue Sky* and a roadie immediately runs up with a replacement. During this song there are different texts on the TV screens. First it was 'BOOM' which would appear in green throughout the entire song, but tonight the words change every few seconds, and it is different on every screen. The technicians keep working on the show as the tour progresses.

MAY 27, 1992. ZURICH, SWITZERLAND, HALLENSTADION

- Attendance: 10,000; sellout
- Support: Fatima Mansions
- Set: same as Gent, with *She's A Mystery To Me* replacing *Unchained Melody*.

One is followed by *She's A Mystery To Me*, played for the first time this tour. Bono sings it well but does only the first verse. While zapping, he comes to a fake TV commercial for U2's Greatest Hits. Though it seems as though the advertisement is actually on TV, it is put together by U2's production designer Peter Williams as an inside joke on the band. Talking to fans after the show, Bono says the band are considering incorporating *Acrobat*, the only song from 'Achtung Baby' that has not been played live, because it's his favourite track on the album.

MAY 29, 1992. FRANKFURT, GERMANY, FESTHALLE

- Attendance: 10,000; sellout
- Support: Fatima Mansions
- Set: same as Gent, but *When Love Comes To Town* replaces *Dancing Queen*, and *Stand By Me* is added to *I Still Haven't Found*.

"And now, ladies and gentlemen, would you please welcome: the craziest, zaniest, laziest man in show business; the most beautiful, the most gorgeous, the most sexy, all the way from Dublin Ireland, Mister Ramalama, King Boogaloo, the High Priest of Happiness, the man who likes to party but always tarty... ladies and gentlemen: Beee Peee Fallon!!" "Beep beep, beep beep, Yeaaahh!" Arms heroically held aloft, wearing the batcape, U2's 'Guru and Viber' comes on again and takes his place in the Trabant. "Guten abend, wie geht's? Sehr gut? Yeah?" he asks and introduces himself in a curious mixture of English and German. "OK, meine Name ist B.P. Fallon, and before U2 auf der Bühne kommt, werde ich etwas für euch spielen. I'd like to welcome you to a night of trash and Las Vegas flash, and sex and soul and magic and mystery." The German version of The Beatles' *She Loves You* follows after which he shows his concern about AIDS: "I just want to actually say something about sex, you know. I'll try and say it in German. Ich müsste etwas über Sex sagen, Sex ist sehr fantastisch, aber jetzt im Jahren '90, es ist anders. So if you're having wild, funky, dirty sex, or you're making beautiful, soft, tender love, what you've gotta do when du machts Liebe, you've got to use a condom. Gebrauch ein Kondome!"

Bono introduces *Satellite Of Love*: "I'd like to dedicate this song to the greatest blues and soul band that ever came out of Germany. They're here with us tonight, this is for Kraftwerk." By the encore, Bono is tired and worn out. "And the fever, I'm getting tired," he sings in *Desire* and omits a large part of the song. Edge takes over.

MAY 31, 1992. LONDON, ENGLAND, EARL'S COURT ARENA

- Attendance: 18,000; sellout
- Support: Fatima Mansions
- Set: Zoo Station / The Fly / Even Better Than The Real Thing / Mysterious Ways / One - Unchained Melody / Until The End Of The World / Who's Gonna Ride Your Wild Horses / Trying To Throw Your Arms / Angel Of Harlem – Dancing Queen / Satellite Of Love / Bad / All I Want Is You / Bullet The Blue Sky / Running To Stand Still / Where The Streets Have No Name / Pride / I Still Haven't Found - Stand By Me / encore: Desire / Ultra Violet / With Or Without You / Love Is Blindness

U2's first UK show since the Joshua Tree tour is preceded by controversy over the method of ticket sales, when the tried and true system of handing out wristbands to those first in line backfired. Long before the box office opened, hundreds of people pushed their way to the front of the queue, leading to frustration among those who were there earlier but remained without tickets. During the show Bono comments: "I'm sorry about the way all the tickets went on sale here at Earl's Court. We fucked up, it was a mess. Thanks for hanging around five years, that's pretty cool. Sometimes you do things that please yourself; we wanted to play indoors, we wanted to play small, before we go mega on you next year."

At the start of *Satellite Of Love* Edge briefly plays the intro of Led Zeppelin's *Stairway To Heaven*. Bono's phone call in the encore is to a sex line; he urges, "I wanna speak to my baby!" He blindfolds himself and his dancing companion during *Love Is Blindness*.

JUNE 1, 1992. BIRMINGHAM, ENGLAND, NATIONAL EXHIBITION CENTRE

- Attendance: 11,000; sellout
- Support: Fatima Mansions

- Set: same as London, with *Can't Help Falling In Love* replacing *Unchained Melody*, and *She's A Mystery To Me* instead of *Dancing Queen*.

"The first time we played Birmingham we played to about 22 people. It was great then, but we like this better," Bono remarks. "There's probably more Irish people in Birmingham than there are in Dublin, is that right? At least you built Birmingham properly! This is another Irishman, Lou O'Reed, who wrote this song." At the start of *Bad*, Bono quips, "Michael Jackson ripped me off, man! Now who's bad?" *Love Is Blindness* ends with Bono citing the poem *September 1913* by William Butler Yeats, which he had sung once at the Abbey Theatre in Dublin on April 30, 1989. He now quotes the first verse: "What need you, being come to sense / Having a finger in the till and adding the halfpence to the pence / And prayer to shivering prayer / Till you drive the marrow from the bone / Romantic Ireland's dead and gone / It's with O'Leary in the grave..."

JUNE 4, 5, 1992. DORTMUND, GERMANY, WESTFALENHALLE

- Attendance: 34,000; sellout
- Support: Fatima Mansions
- Set first night: same as London.

Two hours before show time, a bunch of fans hanging around the back entrance is let in to watch U2 soundcheck. Bono introduces *Can't Help Falling In Love* with, "This is a song from

Soundcheck

our next album, which features only Elvis songs," and sings a long, acoustic version. He walks over to the mini-stage to sing *She's A Mystery To Me* and at the end waves to the fans, "Enjoy the show," after which they are escorted out again.

- Set second night: Zoo Station / The Fly / Even Better Than The Real Thing / Mysterious Ways / One – Can't Help Falling In Love / Until The End Of The World / Who's Gonna Ride Your Wild Horses / Trying To Throw Your Arms / Angel Of Harlem / When Love Comes To Town / Satellite Of Love / Bad – All I Want Is You / Bullet The Blue Sky / Running To Stand Still / Where The Streets Have No Name / Pride / I Still Haven't Found – Stand By Me / encore: Desire / With Or Without You / Love Is Blindness

The crush at the front is rough. "I've just learned how to dance, and I want you to try it out. You need a bit of space, so please move back," Bono urges. Edge shows some funky moves during *Mysterious Ways*. Bono introduces *One* to a woman that he loves: "She also happens to be Adam Clayton's mother. She's here tonight; this is for you, Jo Clayton."

Milan, May 20, 1992. 12,500 fans wait in the rain

Kiel. The smallest crowd of the tour.

JUNE 8, 1992. GOTHENBURG, SWEDEN, SCANDINAVIUM

- Attendance: 8,000; sellout
- Support: Fatima Mansions
- Set: same as London.

Trying To Throw Your Arms is an erotic highlight. "Hey you – wanna drink with me? C'mon!" Bono encourages the girl of his choice. A ravishing blond girl steps onto the catwalk. "Woo, a good one, ah," he moans, shakes the bottle and bellows, "Oh yeah, I'm coming!" when the champagne lavishly flows. "I'm gonna run to you," he serenades the girl and when Edge appears he makes a U-turn and sings, "I'm gonna run from you, run from you." Edge supplies the subtlest "Pom pom pom's" of the tour on *Satellite Of Love*, while the audience excel in clapping out of time.

After the show Bono comes out to talk to fans and reveals that the band want to record a new album in the winter, to be released before the European summer tour in 1993 gets underway.

JUNE 10, 11, 1992. STOCKHOLM, SWEDEN, GLOBEN

- Attendance: 29,000; (capacity 30,000)
- Support: Fatima Mansions
- Set first night: same as London, with *She's A Mystery To Me* replacing *Unchained Melody*.

Sweden organises the European Soccer Championships and thousands of soccer fans swarm around town. On June 10, Sweden and France open the championships. Bono zaps to the match after *The Fly*, and the audience are delighted to see that their national team have already scored. Larry sings some lines of *Dancing Queen*, which Bono ends with "Sweden 5, France 0." (The real score would be 1-1.) "You've heard of Lou Reed?" "Yeeaaahh!!" "Good. He's heard of Stockholm, so it's kinda fair..." Anton Corbijn photographs the show off and on the stage. Around 1,000 tickets for seats behind the stage remain unsold.

- Set second night: same as London.

The square in front of the golfball-shaped Globe Arena bubbles with enthusiasm. Dealers selling illegal merchandise do good business. MTV film crews are interviewing fans for their report on the show, as tonight a satellite connection will be made between the venue and the living room of the winner of an MTV contest. Zapping along after *The Fly*, Bono finds MTV presenter Ray Cokes in the contest winner's house. "Hey, who's the dude with the ponytail?" Bono asks. "I'm John," says the winner amongst his cheering friends. The conversation isn't very elevated. "Where are you?" Bono asks. "I'm in Nottinghamshire." "Where's Nottinghamshire?" "That's in England," says John. "In England? Where's England? That's off the coast of Ireland, is it?" "England is in the European Championships," John answers. While John and friends watch U2's show on a screen in their living room, the image of them dancing to the show is shown on one of the screens in the Globe throughout the night.

Bono switches back after *Even Better*. "Hey John, what do you do for a living?" "I'm a factory worker, I don't make lots of money like you." "Oh, that's a shame," is Bono's mischievous answer. "What do you make?" "Tights and stockings... I don't wear them!" "Ah, you work in a knicker factory! Lingerie! That's OK. Well, in Sweden, we don't wear underpants." The crowd cheer. "Can you prove it?" asks John. "Well, I have other vices, I'm partial to belly-buttons myself," Bono says as cue to *Mysterious Ways*.

One is dedicated to "a great friend and one of the greatest photographers ever – this is for Anton Corbijn."

Bono turns to the screen. "John, what's your girlfriend's name?" "Dawn," he answers, and the lady goes wild. "AAAAAHHHHGGHH BONO, I LOVE YOU!" The pop of champagne at John's resounds through the Globe. Bono asks, "Hey can I have one of those?" Later in the show, he offers John

and his girlfriend a trip to America to see U2 play there in the fall.

The audience proudly sing along with *Dancing Queen*, and the show reaches its climax when Bono shouts "Björn, Benny", and turns to the main stage as a spotlight reveals two pudgy gentlemen on guitar and keyboard. Björn Ulvaeus and Benny Andersson from Abba are reunited on a concert stage for the first time in years to play in their hometown. The crowd scream emotionally. Bono goes over to the guests, embraces and serenades them and bows in 'Wayne's World' fashion: "We are not worthy!" As Björn and Benny walk off, the crowd sing the melody of *Dancing Queen* for several minutes.

When U2 go backstage, John and Co. start a wave which is quickly taken over by 15,000 people in the Globe. Bono thanks Stockholm for three great days. "I hope to see ya soon, maybe even next summer, if you'd like us to come back?"

JUNE 13, 1992. KIEL, GERMANY, OSTSEEHALLE

- Attendance: 6,500; sellout
- Support: Fatima Mansions
- Set: same as the second night in Dortmund.

B.P. Fallon continues to change his choice of pre-show music. "This is a group from Munich, this is The Freaky Fuckin' Weirdos," he announces, followed by an enormous noise. The Ostseehalle is so small that the mini-stage is almost at the back of the venue. With 6,500 people in attendance it's the smallest crowd on the entire 1992-3 tour.

U2 are in top form. Cursing, ranting and raving, Bono puts all his energy in the performance. After the zap-act, he sighs, "Ah, technology man; you wanna use it, I wanna abuse it. I think this is a great rock & roll gig. It's so hot, you can't breathe, that's kinda perfect for what we're doing right now. I'd like to thank you for lending us your country for the making of this album, this is a song called *One*." *Until The End Of The World* sees The Edge letting the beast out while the black light flickers and Bono yells to soundman Joe O'Herlihy: "Turn up that fucking guitar, Joe! Guitar Joe! Guitar Joe!"

A sexy girl calms Bono down during *Trying To Throw Your Arms*. She is self-assured and uninhibitedly bows down to zoom in on his crotch with the camcorder. "A woman needs a man, a man needs a belly-button," he sings lustily and praises the girl's confidence. "That's one cool lady! I'm still scared shitless when I walk on stage!" The girl is the subject of a long improvisation during *When Love Comes To Town*, that goes something like, "I was excited, I could turn on a thread, I wanted it up, and I don't know what I said. You want a fiver, buy some spare new pants, feel pretty stupid now, cause I got no chance..."

A few lines from *Walk To The Water*, one of the extra songs on the B-side of the 1987 *With Or Without You* single, which U2 have never performed live, are included in *Bad* ("He said he was an artist, but he really painted billboards") and, for the first time this tour, Bono sings a snippet from *Norwegian Wood*, before it segues into *All I Want Is You*. A sultry *Love Is Blindness* ends one of the best shows of the tour. "Good night Germany, thank you for a wonderful year."

JUNE 15, 1992. ROTTERDAM, HOLLAND, SPORT PALEIS AHOY

- Attendance: 10,800; sellout
- Support: Fatima Mansions
- Set: same as London, minus *Ultra Violet*.

Bono dedicates *One* to Patrick and Alison, two fans from Dublin who have travelled to this show on their honeymoon. When Bono zaps along the screens, he comes to the Holland v C.I.S. soccer game, which draws screams from the crowd, who embark on their traditional Olé, Olé chant. "What is this strange tribal ritual they call football? Holland 13, Russia 11; could that be right?" Later in the show, Bono inquires what the score is and makes a mischievous remark about the fact that the players of the former Soviet Union manage to keep the Dutch team from

scoring: "Zero-zero. Not good. I don't know – you give these people freedom and then they come and kick your ass..."

JUNE 17, 1992. SHEFFIELD, ENGLAND, ARENA

- Attendance: 11,250; sellout
- Support: Fatima Mansions
- Set: same as London.

JUNE 18, 1992. GLASGOW, SCOTLAND, SCOTTISH EXHIBITION CENTRE

- Attendance: 10,000; sellout
- Support: Fatima Mansions
- Set: same as second show in Dortmund, plus *When Love Comes To Town* after *Dancing Queen*.

Originally planned as the last show of the tour, U2 wanted to finish in Glasgow because their shows there always have a special atmosphere. Tonight is one big party with silly jokes and loose behaviour by band and crew. Seven crew members join the belly-dancer on the mini-stage, dressed in hilarious costumes to 'dance' during *Mysterious Ways*.

JUNE 19, 1992. MANCHESTER, ENGLAND, G-MEX CENTRE

- Attendance: 9,000; sellout
- 'Stop Sellafield' line up: Kraftwerk, Public Enemy, Big Audio Dynamite II, U2
- Set: same as London, minus *Ultra Violet*.

This 'Stop Sellafield' show is organised in collaboration with Greenpeace to protest against the proposed building of a second nuclear plant in Cumbria on the north-west coast of England. One of the biggest nuclear installations in the world, Sellafield re-processes nuclear waste to make plutonium for atomic bombs. In doing so, it has been releasing radio-active waste, including deadly plutonium, into the Irish Sea every day for the last 40 years. Radioactivity affects the DNA in all life forms. Sellafield's emissions have reached the coasts of Denmark, Norway, Iceland, Greenland, and have even been located under the ice of the North Pole. The nuclear waste affects all life in the sea and, with fish a major food source in those countries, people as well. The number of cancer sufferers or babies born deformed around Sellafield and the Irish Sea coast is up to ten times the national average.

Besides the regular emissions, vast amounts of radioactivity have leaked out through accidents and 'incidents' at the plant. Trains, trucks and ships carrying nuclear waste to Sellafield pass through some of the largest cities and busiest waterways in the world. The consequences of an accident are unthinkable.

British Nuclear Fuels Limited (BNFL) are planning to open a second nuclear plant, Sellafield 2, which would import nuclear waste from around the world to reprocess and would emit ten times as much radio-activity as Sellafield 1. It would be as if a disaster similar to Chernobyl occurred every two and a half years. Deadly Krypton gas is also likely to leak.

Greenpeace has been demonstrating against Sellafield since 1978. Together with CORE (Cumbrians Opposed to a Radioactive Environment), Greenpeace is determined to inform the British people about the enormous dangers to life and the environment posed by Sellafield 2. Massive public protest might force the British government to refuse a license for Sellafield 2. To help Greenpeace and CORE gain publicity, U2 step in.

The original plan was to stage a big open-air festival on June 20 at Manchester's Heaton Park that would at the same time be a protest rally against Sellafield 2. Between 50,000 and 100,000 people were expected. An advertisement for the show appeared in *Select* magazine, with £10 tickets going on sale on May 9. Eventually, the city of Manchester refused permission for such an big event because of damage and pollution that could be

caused to the park. The show was re-scheduled for the indoor G-Mex Centre for June 19.

Greenpeace and CORE still wanted to hold a large protest rally, and tried to organise one for June 20 at the gates of Sellafield. Earlier in the year, CORE had received permission from BNFL and local authorities to hold a demonstration at the site. BNFL did not object as a few hundred people were unlikely to attract much attention. Then U2 announced their intention to arrive at the site. Their official statement said: "BNFL have an annual advertising and public relations budget of several millions, which they spend on putting an acceptable face on the nuclear waste business. In an attempt to counter this massive propaganda, U2 are assisting Greenpeace in presenting the other side of Sellafield. U2 will be coming to Sellafield on June 20." The band had been inviting their audiences to join the demonstration ever since their London show on May 31. Instead of the line 'WATCH MORE TV', *The Fly*'s final slogan on the screens was 'BE AT SELLAFIELD 11 AM JUNE 20'.

U2's involvement scared BNFL. Realising the event would generate massive publicity that could turn public opinion against them, BNFL withdrew its permission for the demonstration, and even went to court to prevent it taking place. Their 'official' objection was hypocritical to say the least: they said U2's participation would attract a huge crowd and they were "concerned about public safety". BNFL won an injunction from the Supreme Court, forbidding the demonstration to take place. Anyone entering the Sellafield grounds on June 20 would be arrested.

Greenpeace, CORE, and U2 were outraged. Paul McGuinness stated: "It's quite ironic that British Nuclear Fuels, a company that produces raw materials for use in weapons of mass destruction, should be so concerned about public order."

The 'Stop Sellafield' show in Manchester could not be stopped though. Preceded by a press conference, Kraftwerk from Germany, Public Enemy from America and England's Big Audio Dynamite joined the show to help make the point that Sellafield is not just a local, but a global issue. For *The Fly*, the slogans are adapted to the occasion, including the words: 'LEUKEMIA – DEBT – CHILD – DETERRENT – WARHEAD – KRYPTON – PLUTONIUM – DECAY – MUSHROOM – FEAR – REACT OR DIE – START A CHAIN REACTION – E=MC2 – NOBODY IS PROMISED A TOMORROW – RADIATION SICKNESS – STOP SELLAFIELD NOW'. Bono comments after the song, "We were gonna invite you all down to the gates at Sellafield tomorrow. We had personal invitations; I guess when they found out you were coming, they didn't like it very much. I wonder what they've got to hide. They've cancelled a peaceful demonstration because they said they were worried about

'public safety'. These people are responsible for the deaths of innocent children, for God's sake; public safety doesn't come near them. Anyway, the whole farce has backfired on them; in the last week, they've given Greenpeace more publicity than they could ever want."

The anger-fuelled show has some sweet moments. To the crowd's surprise, Lou Reed joins Bono on the mini-stage to duet on *Satellite Of Love*. Lou struggles with the lyrics but it makes for a unique version. In the encore, Bono tries to reach Prime Minister John Major: "Let me see if I can get this man Major on the phone. It's 071-270-3000. You can try it yourself if you like. C'mon Johnny baby, don't let me down..." He doesn't get past the receptionist but leaves a message: "Could you tell him to watch more TV?"

After the show the band join the Greenpeace team on their ship Solo and sail secretly to the coast at Sellafield by night. The next day, June 20, at the crack of dawn, U2 disembark on Sellafield beach in inflatables. Out-smarting the court ban, they land on a stretch of beach beside the border with BNFL's land, below the high tide mark.

Dressed in white anti-radiation suits and wearing sunglasses and masks, the band symbolically roll out large drums with contaminated mud from the Irish Sea, and, standing on the drums, semaphore HELP, just like The Beatles on the cover of their album of that name. With an army of press photographers and reporters present, the action triggers a further stream of media attention that pressurises the government. "It's kind of absurd that we have to dress up like complete wankers to make this point," Bono says to one reporter, "but someone's got to do something." Asked why they are particularly involved with this, Edge answers, "Sellafield is our back garden. There's a particular school in Dundalk where a lot of girls have left and had Down's Syndrome babies. Over the years, time and time again, the finger gets pointed across the water. And the idea that this new plant would open up and increase emissions by 1,000% is completely outrageous." Edge declares that this isn't the end of actions against BNFL. On July 1, various environmental groups, political organisations and protesters deliver a petition to Prime Minister John Major. Later in the year, U2 and a host of other celebrities, including Michael Hutchence, Elvis Costello, Peter Gabriel, Sting and Annie Lennox, send protest letters to the government, hoping that many will follow their example in urging the government to stop the building of Sellafield 2.

Highlights of the show and documentary footage about the issue are released by Greenpeace as a 40-minute commercial video to promote the cause. All proceeds go to Greenpeace. *The Fly* and *Even Better Than The Real Thing* from U2's set are included, as are bits of interviews with Bono and Edge. Bono comments on their participation: "If people are interested in U2 and therefore become interested in the issues, that's all that matters."

ZOO TV – OUTSIDE BROADCAST – NORTH AMERICA, 1992

Zoo TV returns to North America to play outdoor venues only. Dubbed the Outside Broadcast, it becomes one of the most sensational and highest attended tours in US history. Peter Williams, U2's 'Head Of Taste', has re-designed the stage set in collaboration with Mark Fisher and Jonathan Park, who designed Pink Floyd's The Wall, and Rolling Stones' Steel Wheels sets. The concept of Zoo TV is adapted for outdoors. There is a broadcasting

tower on the left of the 248 by 80-foot stage, and the already large Vidiwalls are dwarfed by four mega-video screens big enough to enable those furthest away in any stadium to catch Zoo TV. Three dozen monitors are draped over the stage, and instead of seven there are now 13 Trabants, two of which are perched atop huge cranes positioned outside the stadium, which can move the cars up and out to fly over the stage and the audience. There are 1,200 tons of equipment in total. It takes 40 hours to set up the stage, requiring 180 construction builders and technicians in the travelling crew. In addition, around 200 labourers will be hired locally at each stop.

The tour maintains public interest in the 'Achtung Baby' album, which stays in the charts, pushing US sales to four million by late September, indicating that U2 continue to reach new audiences.

AUGUST 1 – 6, 1992. HERSHEY, PA, HERSHEYPARK STADIUM

U2 rehearse for Outside Broadcast in the small town of Hershey, Pennsylvania. The constant stream of trucks going in and out of the site and U2's one-million Watts sound system don't go by unnoticed. As word gets around, local people and thousands of loyal fans from all over the country congregate each night around the stadium to listen to the proceedings. Local papers print daily news updates. The rehearsals reveal several additions to the usual list of songs, including *Sunday Bloody Sunday*, *New Year's Day*, and *So Cruel*. *Acrobat*, the only song off 'Achtung Baby' not yet performed in concert, is extensively rehearsed, with Bono performing it acoustically, his guitar playing blending into ambient guitar feedback by The Edge near the end, which eventually segues into *Zoo Station*. Because this is done over and over again, it suggests that U2 are considering *Acrobat* for the opening song of the show. Other surprises are *Slow Dancing*, Beatles tunes like *She Loves You* and *Dear Prudence*, and a song called *Miracle Man*. The rehearsals cause dozens of complaints from residents, who feel that the volume is not loud enough for them to hear!

Rumours that the rehearsals will culminate in a try-out concert are fuelled by Bono who tells fans that they will be able to see what the band are doing by the end of the week. Sure enough, on August 5, tickets go on sale for a show on the 7th. The tickets say 'Outside Rehearsal' and are priced at $15. U2 will donate all proceeds to local charities.

AUGUST 7, 1992. HERSHEY, PA, HERSHEYPARK STADIUM

- Attendance: 25,000; sellout
- Support: WNOC
- Set: *Sunday Bloody Sunday* / *New Year's Day* / *Pride* / *Zoo Station* / *The Fly* / *Even Better Than The Real Thing* / *Mysterious Ways* / *One* – *Unchained Melody* / *Until The End Of The World*

Hersheypark Stadium, July 31, 1992

/ *Who's Gonna Ride Your Wild Horses* / *Van Diemen's Land* / *Trying To Throw Your Arms* / *Angel Of Harlem* / *When Love Comes To Town* / *All I Want Is You* / *Bullet The Blue Sky* / *Running To Stand Still* / *Where The Streets Have No Name* / *Pride* / encore: *Desire* / *Ultra Violet* / *With Or Without You* / *Love Is Blindness*

Local band WNOC play in support, after which B.P. Fallon acts as DJ until U2 appear. Functioning both as a try-out gig and as a way of saying 'thank you' to the town and its people, the show is great fun with the band in a loose and playful mood. *Sunday Bloody Sunday*, which had not been played in concert for almost five years, surprisingly opens the show. During *New Year's Day* Bono hands a big cake to Edge, whose 31st birthday is just a few hours away. After *Pride*, Zoo TV is switched on to present a major addition to the show's video production. "Ladies and gentlemen, the President of the United States." The earnest face of George Bush looks the crowd in the eye from the screens, and states, "We will, we will rock you", while the booming rhythm of the Queen song resounds. A hilarious example of image manipulation, the doctored footage is produced by the Boston-based company Emergency Broadcast Network. With atomic blasts mixed in to the beat of the music, Bush continues to whine, "Some may ask, why rock out now? The answer is clear: these are the times that rock man's soul. I instructed our military commanders to totally rock Baghdad. And I repeat this here tonight: we will, we will rock you... Let me say this for everyone listening to Washington tonight: may God continue to rock our nation, the United States of America." Bush's prelude to the show will bring laughter throughout the tour.

Bono acknowledges the fans who had been listening to the rehearsals: "Well, does it sound any better in here? All I know is you guys were having a lot more fun outside than we were inside trying to build this fucking thing!" The start of *Wild Horses* is a complete mess, as the singing doesn't run synch with the sequencer-produced organ intro sound. The machine is turned off, and Bono does the song acoustically instead, like he had

done in San Diego in April. *Van Diemen's Land* will not return in the set for the rest of the year.

There are several differences compared to the indoor shows. Instead of Christina Petro, another belly-dancer is hired, Morleigh Steinberg. Props added include a supermarket trolley with a big inflatable fish for *Trying To Throw Your Arms*. Instead of being linked to *Bad*, *All I Want Is You* stands on its own and is played in its full version by Bono on acoustic guitar. Sounds of helicopters flying over are added to the end of *Running To Stand Still*, completing the image of a war situation while Bono, in his military commander outfit, is shrouded in yellow and red smoke. During *With Or Without You*, a reclining nude woman appears at stage left, her image enlarged on the screens. Video tapes of her image will be used in subsequent shows for this song.

Proceeds of the show are eventually donated by U2 to five charitable organisations in the Hershey area: HELP Ministries of Christian Churches United, Channels Food Distribution, AIDS Assistance Network, Special Olympics of Pennsylvania and United Cerebral Palsy.

AUGUST 12, 13, 1992. EAST RUTHERFORD, NJ, GIANTS' STADIUM

- Attendance: 109,000 (P); sellout
- Support: Primus, Disposable Heroes Of Hiphoprisy
- Set first night: *Zoo Station* / *The Fly* / *Even Better Than The Real Thing* / *Mysterious Ways* / *One – Unchained Melody* / *Until The End Of The World* / *Who's Gonna Ride Your Wild Horses* / *Dirty Old Town* / *Trying To Throw Your Arms* / *Angel Of Harlem* / *When Love Comes To Town* / *Satellite Of Love* / *Bad - All I Want Is You* / *Bullet The Blue Sky* / *Running To Stand Still* / *Where The Streets Have No Name* / *Pride* / *I Still Haven't Found – Stand By Me* / encore: *Desire* / *Ultra Violet* / *With Or Without You* / *Love Is Blindness*

First night tickets are sold in 23 minutes, becoming the stadium's fastest sellout ever. The original date of August 11 is put forward one day to allow more time to set up the stage. The video and stage production include several new gadgets. The newsreel reads, 'SYSTEM CHECK... STAND BY FOR TRANSMISSION'. Stadium lights dim while red spots on the broadcasting tower flicker. Press photographers are up in a little tower on stage that says, 'PHOTO OPPORTUNITY'. The screens loudly flash on one by one, revealing Zoo TV bars which evolve into the George Bush footage. Bono is brought on stage by a hydraulic lift, his silhouette marking off against a background of static on the biggest screen. Edge sets in *Zoo Station*, while Bono does his kick-one-leg-with-outstretched-arm goose step. The opening night suffers from tension. As in Manchester, Lou Reed makes an appearance during *Satellite Of Love*.

The biggest gadget added to the show is the so-called 'Video Confessional', a portable toilet-like booth on the field, where fans can reveal all their sins to a video priest for 20 seconds. A selection of messages will be aired every night before the encore; anything is considered so long as it's silly, funny or perverted and thus fits Zoo TV standards.

- Set second night: *Zoo Station* / *The Fly* / *Even Better Than The Real Thing* / *Mysterious Ways* / *One - She's A Mystery To Me* / *Until The End Of The World* / *New Year's Day* / *Trying To Throw Your Arms* / *Angel Of Harlem* / *When Love Comes To Town* / *I Still Haven't Found* / *All I Want Is You* / *Sunday Bloody Sunday* / *Bullet The Blue Sky* / *Running To Stand Still* / *Where The Streets Have No Name* / *Pride* / encore: *Desire* / *With Or Without You* / *Love Is Blindness*

The second night is far better. There is a drizzle throughout the show with occasional lightning. *New Year's Day* and *Sunday Bloody Sunday* find a place in the set, crowd response indicating they are still two of U2's most popular songs. *I Still Haven't Found* is played in an acoustic version.

AUGUST 15, 16, 1992. WASHINGTON, DC, ROBERT F. KENNEDY STADIUM

- Attendance: 97,038 (P); sellout
- Support: Primus, Disposable Heroes of Hiphoprisy
- Set first night: Zoo Station / The Fly / Even Better Than The Real Thing / Mysterious Ways / One – She's A Mystery To Me / Until The End Of The World / New Year's Day / Trying To Throw Your Arms / Angel Of Harlem – Dancing Queen / When Love Comes To Town / I Still Haven't Found – Stand By Me / All I Want Is You / Sunday Bloody Sunday / Bullet The Blue Sky / Running To Stand Still / Where The Streets Have No Name / Pride / encore: Desire / With Or Without You / Love Is Blindness / Can't Help Falling In Love

The band are beginning to feel more confident and comfortable playing outdoors for large crowds. Bono overcomes the many mistakes that creep into the show with silly jokes that entertain the crowd and relieve the tension. The show is damp, the mist turning to heavier rain several times throughout the show. "So where are we? It's raining; must be DC! You know what happened the last time in DC in the rain", Bono says, referring to his fall on a wet stage here in 1987 when he dislocated his shoulder. He sings a verse of The Beatles' Rain before One, and snatches of Singing In The Rain are included in Until The End Of The World.

After Desire, in his silver Mirror Ball man suit, Bono makes a call to the White House. When he asks to speak to Barbara, the receptionist asks, "Barbara who?" Ms. Bush, Bono tells her. She is not available, but the operator kindly gives the number of Ms. Bush's direct line: "The number is 202-456-911. Call at 9am on Monday."

After Love Is Blindness, Bono tries a new ending to the show. "Edge, can you play a C chord?" he asks, and starts singing Can't Help Falling In Love from the mini-stage. He does the second half of the song in a high falsetto voice. The song fits the introspective mood of Love Is Blindness, and has the crowd still as a mouse, infected by its romantic and melancholic atmosphere. "Elvis is still in the building," Bono says at the end of the song, for it is the eve of the 15th anniversary of The King's death. As the lights dim and Bono walks offstage, Elvis' version comes over the PA.

Audience and media response to Zoo TV's first few stadium dates is almost unanimously positive. Critics state that while the overwhelming spectacle of Zoo TV offers sheer fun and sensation, the power and the subtlety of their songs still enable U2 to lyrically and musically touch people's spirit and emotions, regardless of how big is the audience.

- Set second night: Zoo Station / The Fly / Even Better Than The Real Thing / Mysterious Ways / One – Unchained Melody / Until The End Of The World / New Year's Day / Trying To Throw Your Arms / Angel Of Harlem / I Still Haven't Found / Satellite Of Love / Bad / Sunday Bloody Sunday / Bullet The Blue Sky / Running To Stand Still / Where The Streets Have No Name / Pride / encore: Desire / Ultra Violet / With Or Without You / Love Is Blindness / Can't Help Falling In Love

Phoning the White House, Bono gets the same operator on the line. He now asks for George himself. "George who?" asks the girl. "George the President; Mr. Bush, excuse me." He isn't there. "Could you just tell the President to watch more TV..." The experiment of ending the show with Can't Help Falling In Love proved successful and tonight a full version is played, which has the crowd softly singing along.

AUGUST 18, 1992. SARATOGA SPRINGS, NY, SARATOGA RACEWAY

- Attendance: 30,277 (P); (capacity 35,000)
- Support: Primus, Disposable Heroes of Hiphoprisy
- Set: same as August 13, plus Dirty Old Town after New Year's Day, Dancing Queen linked to Angel Of Harlem, and Ultra Violet after Desire.

The Saratoga horse race track in upstate New York is the first venue on the Outside Broadcast tour that doesn't sell out. Five thousand seats are set up in front of the stage, with the rest standing room only behind a big barrier. Adam watches The Disposable Heroes Of Hiphoprisy from the seated section practically unrecognised. Bono sings one stanza of the old Gershwin song Summertime before One: "Summertime, and the living's easy..." Larry steps forward for Dirty Old Town, "an Irish traditional song, I'll do a very bad rendition of it for ya now." Afterwards he confuses the crowd when he announces, "The next song is a song The Beatles stole from us – we're stealing it back." While the crowd scream and expect Helter Skelter, they don't hear Larry mumble, "it's called Trying To Throw Your Arms Around The World."

AUGUST 20, 22, 23, 1992. FOXBORO, MA, FOXBORO STADIUM

- Attendance: 148,736 (P); sellout
- Support: Primus, Disposable Heroes of Hiphoprisy
- Set first night: Zoo Station / The Fly / Even Better Than The Real Thing / Mysterious Ways / One – Unchained Melody / Until The End Of The World / New Year's Day / Whiskey In The Jar / Trying To Throw Your Arms / Angel Of Harlem / When Love Comes To Town / I Still Haven't Found / All I Want Is You / Sunday Bloody Sunday / Bullet The Blue Sky / Running To Stand Still / Where The Streets Have No Name / Pride / encore: Desire / With Or Without You / Love Is Blindness / Can't Help Falling In Love

When the first two shows sell out in one day, a third show is added, selling a total of 148,736 tickets. At $30 each, the gross is $4,427,100, which is two-and-a-half times as much as the entire American leg of the 'War' tour (48 shows) generated back in 1983. Bono asks, "Anybody who was here when we played the Paradise Theater in 1980?" A tremendous cheer goes through the stadium. "I think we've got 55,000 liars here!" Larry sings another Irish drinking song, Whiskey In The Jar, a song made famous by Thin Lizzy in the Seventies.

- Set second night: same as August 15, plus Wild Rover after New Year's Day, So Cruel instead of All I Want Is You, and plus Ultra Violet after Desire.

U2 do an extensive soundcheck in the afternoon. During Where The Streets Have No Name, Bono recites a verse of the Yeats poem September 1913. Larry does Wild Rover, yet another traditional Irish tune, which he will première tonight and will give him a third option for the rest of the tour. Bono rehearses So Cruel for a long time, but is hampered by technical problems. "Joe, this echo business," he enquires of his sound man, "is this the real world? I know I'm a nice bunch of guys, but there's about eight of me singing up here. So I don't know which one to play the guitar to. Which also might have been what was happening the other night on the B-stage."

That night, Bono's acoustic version of So Cruel chills the crowd. For Wild Rover, they supply well-timed hand claps in Irish tradition. While phoning the White House, Bono reads the number out loud and suggests everyone call it. As George isn't available, he asks for Barbara Bush, but she can't be reached either.

- Set third night: Zoo Station / The Fly / Even Better Than The Real Thing / Mysterious Ways / One – Unchained Melody / Until The End Of the World / New Year's Day / Dirty Old Town / Trying To Throw Your Arms / Angel Of Harlem – My Girl / When Love Comes To Town / I Still Haven't Found / Satellite Of Love / Bad / Bullet The Blue Sky / Running To Stand Still / Where The Streets Have No Name / Pride / encore: Desire / Ultra Violet / With Or Without You / Love Is Blindness / Can't Help Falling In Love

Larry dedicates Dirty Old Town to "33, the big bird," once again referring to basketball star Larry Bird, who had just retired. The crowd chant "Larry, Larry!" like they used to do at Celtic's games. Bono sings a brief version of The Temptations' classic My Girl after Angel Of Harlem. He praises the U2 road crew during I Still Haven't Found and mumbles he has been behaving like a jerk to them the past few days.

AUGUST 25, 1992. PITTSBURGH, PA, THREE RIVERS STADIUM

- Attendance: 39,586 (P); sellout
- Support: Primus, Disposable Heroes of Hiphoprisy
- Set: same as August 20, plus My Girl linked to Angel Of Harlem.

B.P. Fallon's birthday is celebrated when Michael Franti, lead singer of The Disposable Heroes Of Hiphoprisy, walks out with a cake to the Trabant where B.P. spins the records. Michael leads the crowd in singing Happy Birthday. Around 5,000 people without reserved seats are admitted to the floor, resulting in chaos as they hassle those already sitting there and try to take their seats. U2 seem tired and deliver an uninspired performance.

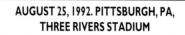
Hershey Outside Rehearsal

AUGUST 27, 1992. MONTREAL, CANADA, OLYMPIC STADIUM

- Attendance: 42,210 (P); (capacity 43,000)
- Support: Primus, Disposable Heroes of Hiphoprisy
- Set: same as August 20, minus *Whiskey In The Jar*, plus *Dancing Queen* linked to *Angel Of Harlem*, and *Ultra Violet* after *Desire*.

"U2! Zoo TV! Where rock & roll, hi-tech and trash collide!" runs a radio ad for the show. For *The Fly*, half the texts are in French. After a few songs, Bono quotes Axl Rose by saying, "What time is it? We gotta go," then quickly adds, "just kidding!" The Guns n'Roses show here earlier in the month ended prematurely, leading to an estimated 10,000 fans rioting in the streets of Montreal, looting shops and wrecking parked cars in their anger.

The highlight of the show is Daniel Lanois joining U2 on the mini-stage to play guitar. Producer of 'Achtung Baby' and co-producer with Brian Eno of 'The Unforgettable Fire' and 'The Joshua Tree', it's his first guest appearance at a U2 concert. He sings background vocals and adds some funk to the acoustic version of *I Still Haven't Found*. During *Desire* a fan breaks through the barriers and runs towards Bono. When a bouncer tries to tackle the fan, Bono grabs the guard, who is at least one foot taller and 100 pounds heavier than he is, puts him in a headlock and orders him to get the fuck off his stage. Bono sits down with the fan to finish the song.

AUGUST 28, 1992. AMERICAN RADIO: 'ROCKLINE'

U2 are interviewed by Dave Herman live in New York for 'Rockline', a syndicated radio show broadcast on some 300 local FM stations across the country. Listeners are invited to call in to ask a question. Edge and Bono perform *Can't Help Falling In Love*, which Bono has recently recorded for inclusion on the Elvis Presley tribute album 'Honeymoon In Vegas', the soundtrack to the movie which opens tonight. He comments, "Elvis does the kind of down-on-one-knee version; I do the sort of Irish-Catholic-guilt version."

Discussing phone calls to the White House, interviewer Dave Herman suggests Bono does it right now, live on the air. When he calls, the operator recognises him and hangs up before he can leave his message. Dave Herman suggests Bono may have better luck calling Democratic presidential candidate Bill Clinton. Another phone call comes in. Herman: "Our next caller is named Bill, he's from Little Rock, Arkansas. Hi Bill, what's your last name?" "Clinton." "Bill Clinton?! Sir, it's a pleasure having you on the air with us."

Though they act surprised, Herman and U2 knew beforehand that Clinton would call. Paul McGuinness would later reveal to the press that the phone call was Clinton's idea, inspired by Bono's onstage calls.

"I can't believe I've got U2 on the phone," Clinton says. "Hi, this is Bono here. How do you want us to call you; should we call you governor or Bill? Bill. Alright, you can call me Betty," he quips. After Bono mentions that he can't get through to George on the phone, Bill jumps in: "Well, he's not into music like I am." Bono says that being on a presidential campaign is very much like doing a rock tour: going from city to city, speaking in public, shaking hands, etc. Bono asks Bill what he feels is America's role in interfering with world issues. "I think the world doesn't want America to try to run it, but the world needs a strong America standing up for the right things," Bill says. Bono brings up the issue of censorship and putting warning stickers on 'raunchy' records. "Are politicians qualified to decide what is, and what isn't art?" he asks. Bill says he's against censorship, and compares the labelling of records with the age-category system used in the movie industry. He emphasises his commitment to preserving the National Endowment for the Arts.

Bill remarks: "I wanna say, as a middle-aged man, that I appreciate the fact that you made 'The Joshua Tree', and that record *Angel Of Harlem* at Sun Studios. You made me feel like I had a place in rock music, even at 46." Bono responds

mischievously, "Well Bill, if we got you into it, we must be doing something wrong..." Bill laughs. Bono concludes, "I have some problems imagining you pogoing to our music, but I'm very glad that you've listened to our records. Thanks for calling."

AUGUST 29, 30, 1992. NEW YORK, NY, YANKEE STADIUM

- Attendance: 104,100 (P); sellout
- Support: Primus, Disposable Heroes of Hiphoprisy
- Set first night: same as August 20, with *Wild Rover* instead of *Whiskey In The Jar*, *New York, New York* after *Angel Of Harlem*, and plus *Ultra Violet* after *Desire*.

U2 are only the second rock act to play this stadium. The shows are late additions to the tour schedule after the Giants' Stadium shows prove insufficient to satisfy U2's fans in the New York area. Having spoken to him the night before, the show is sprinkled with references to Bill Clinton. "What do you mean George Bush isn't available? Bill talked to us last night," Bono says during his call to the White House. He also refers to baseball legend Joe DiMaggio, an old hero of Yankee Stadium. The band embark on a hilarious version of Frank Sinatra's *New York, New York* in the acoustic set.

- Set second night: *Zoo Station / The Fly / Even Better Than The Real Thing / Mysterious Ways / One – She's A Mystery To Me / Until The End Of The World / New Year's Day / Whiskey In The Jar / Trying To Throw Your Arms / Angel Of Harlem / New York, New York / When Love Comes To Town / I Still Haven't Found / Satellite Of Love / Bad – All I Want Is You / Bullet The Blue Sky / Running To Stand Still / Where The Streets Have No Name / Pride / encore: Desire / With Or Without You / Love Is Blindness / Can't Help Falling In Love*

After *Trying To Throw Your Arms* the girl on stage goes back into the crowd. Bono sighs, "Bye, hello, goodbye... the story of my life!" and sings, "You say hello, and I say goodbye," (mis)quoting The Beatles song *Hello, Goodbye*, which will become a regular habit. During *Satellite Of Love*, pre-recorded images of Lou Reed singing parts of the song are shown on the screens, enabling Bono to duet with Lou even though he is not there. The footage was recorded the day after Lou appeared live at Giants' Stadium, and will be used every time the song is played for the rest of the tour. Tonight's version of *Love Is Blindness* appears as an extra

track on the *Stay (Faraway, So Close)* single, The Live Format, released in November 1993.

SEPTEMBER 2, 3, 1992. PHILADELPHIA, PA, VETERANS' STADIUM

- Attendance: 88,684 (P); sellout
- Support: Primus, Disposable Heroes of Hiphoprisy
- Set first night: *Zoo Station / The Fly / Even Better Than The Real Thing / Mysterious Ways / One – Unchained Melody / Until The End Of The World / New Year's Day / Wild Rover / Trying To Throw Your Arms / Angel Of Harlem / When Love Comes To Town / Satellite Of Love / All I Want Is You / Sunday Bloody Sunday / Bullet The Blue Sky / Running To Stand Still / Where The Streets Have No Name / Pride / I Still Haven't Found - Stand By Me / encore: Desire / With Or Without You / Love Is Blindness / Can't Help Falling In Love*

I Still Haven't Found is moved back to close the main set, and will remain there at most shows. Edge takes over singing *Stand By Me* halfway through.

- Set second night: same as August 30, with *Unchained Melody* instead of *She's A Mystery To Me*, minus *New York, New York*.

For his Irish traditional song, Larry is introduced as Marky Mark and receives some booing. Since it rains slightly, Bono sings a snippet of *Rain* at the end of *Bad*.

SEPTEMBER 5, 6, 1992. TORONTO, CANADA, CANADIAN NATIONAL EXHIBITION STADIUM

- Attendance: 108,043 (P); sellout
- Support: Primus, Disposable Heroes of Hiphoprisy
- Set first night: same as August 15, plus *Dirty Old Town* after *New Year's Day*, minus *Stand By Me*, and plus *Ultra Violet* after *Desire*.

Zoo TV malfunctions as Bono's zapping reveals nothing but blank screens but both shows are excellent with great atmosphere. The stadium is situated in a summer fair and amusement park, whose neon-lit Ferris wheel can be seen spinning from inside. Bono says it's the perfect setting for the glitzy concept of the show, calling it "the most Zoo location we've had!" The White House receives another call from Bono. "Hi there, I'm calling from Canada tonight, from Toronto. I've got 60,000 people here that would like to speak to George Bush... The President is not available for the people of Toronto?! Well!"

- Set second night: same as September 2, with *Whiskey In The Jar* instead of *Wild Rover*, plus *Bad* after *Satellite Of Love*, and minus *Sunday Bloody Sunday*.

Larry's version of *Whiskey In The Jar* is croaky. Bono sings during *Trying To Throw Your Arms*, "I'm gonna run to you, Larry be still," then holds the mike for Larry to finish, "Bono, I will". He changes the words to, "A woman needs a man, like an Edge needs a Handycam," while the girl on stage films both Edge and Bono. During *Desire* Bono picks a girl from the crowd who wears lamé pants that match his own outfit. When Bono does his Elvis-leg-shakes, she stands besides him and shakes right along.

SEPTEMBER 9, 1992. PONTIAC, MI, SILVERDOME

- Attendance: 36,740 (P); (capacity 40,680)
- Support: Primus, Disposable Heroes of Hiphoprisy
- Set: same as September 2, plus *My Girl* linked to *Angel Of Harlem*, and *So Cruel* instead of *All I Want Is You*.

A satellite link is made to Los Angeles where MTV hold their annual Video Awards show. U2's clip for *Even Better Than The Real Thing* is nominated for Best Group Video and Best Special Effects. Garth of 'Wayne's World' hosts the MTV Awards show and introduces U2. Zoo TV beams U2 to LA at the end of *The*

Fly. "Well, it's Zoo TV in Detroit, let's see if we can find some MTV," Bono says, and zaps along to find Garth on the vidiwalls. "We did it! It's Baaahno!" shouts Garth, jumping up and down. After a curious conversation, Bono invites Garth to play drums on *Even Better Than The Real Thing*. Garth shouts, "I'm not worthy!" and drums along on a rickety drum kit, his image on one of the screens and his drum sound mixed through U2's. "You're the real thing, dude!" Bono sings and drops to his knees to worship Garth. "Drum solo Garth!"

Later on in the MTV show, Annie Lennox and Peter Gabriel announce U2 as winner of Best Group Video and switch over to their dressing room at the Silverdome. While complimenting each other on their work, Gabriel mentions he's seen four Zoo TV shows and was very pleased. "You're a mad bastard, Peter," Bono calls, thanks everyone for voting for U2 and sprays champagne all over the MTV camera.

SEPTEMBER 11, 1992. AMES, IA, CYCLONE STADIUM

- Attendance: 48,822 (P); sellout
- Support: Primus, Disposable Heroes of Hiphoprisy
- Set: same as September 2, but *I Still Haven't Found* is played after *When Love Comes To Town*, and *Stand By Me* is left out.

Tell me all your sins

Though located in the sparsely populated farmlands of Iowa, Cyclone Stadium draws a capacity crowd. The show is attended by more people than actually live in Ames. During *Satellite Of Love* a fan throws his tour T-shirt to Bono, who responds, "You paid a fortune for this, what are you throwing it at me for, keep it," and throws it back. There are some remarkable 'confessions': since it's their last show on the tour, opening act Disposable Heroes Of Hiphoprisy do a rap thanking U2. Bass technician Stuart Morgan shouts, "Hey Adam, you thought I was on stage tuning your guitar; well, I'm not!"

SEPTEMBER 13, 1992. MADISON, WI, CAMP RANDALL STADIUM

- Attendance: 62,280 (P); sellout
- Support: Big Audio Dynamite II, Public Enemy
- Set: same as September 2, with *Whiskey In The Jar* instead of *Wild Rover*, minus *I Still Haven't Found – Stand By Me*, and plus *Ultra Violet* after *Desire*.

Big Audio Dynamite II and Public Enemy replace Primus and The Disposable Heroes Of Hiphoprisy as support bands. It's U2's first Wisconsin show since February 1982. Technical problems get on Bono's nerves as he shouts "Shut the fuck up!" after a

loud screech during *Mysterious Ways*. The 'confessions' contain another message from the bass technician: "Adam, I don't love you anymore, I want a divorce; but I'll still work for you." When phoning the White House, the operator asks who's calling. "This is Elvis here," says Bono. "Well I'm sorry Elvis, the offices aren't open." The crowd boo. "Could I leave a message for the President? I'd just like to say that I'm alive, and he's dead."

SEPTEMBER 15, 16, 18, 1992. CHICAGO, IL, WORLD MUSIC AMPHITHEATER

- Attendance: 89,307 (P); sellout
- Support: Big Audio Dynamite II, Public Enemy
- Set first night: same as September 2, minus *Unchained Melody*, *So Cruel* instead of *All I Want Is You*, and plus *Ultra Violet*.

For *Trying To Throw Your Arms*, Bono brings two girls up. After showering them with champagne, he motions Edge to come to his aid as they act too wild. One girl yanks Edge's cap off; he's not amused. Bono is knocked over by the girls who crawl over him and kiss his face as he lies on the catwalk. *So Cruel* makes another rare appearance, tenderly sung from the mini-stage. Calling the White House, Bono asks the operator her name. "Operator two." "Operator two? That's a lovely name. I think I love you."

- Set second night: same as August 30, minus *New York, New York* and *I Still Haven't Found*, and plus *Ultra Violet* after *Desire*.

The first two shows generate around 100 complaints about the sound volume from residents of nearby Country Club Hills. Its mayor, Dwight Welch, goes to court to force U2 to turn the volume down for the final show. U2 and the World Music Amphitheater win the case.

- Set third night: Zoo Station / The Fly / Even Better Than The Real Thing / Mysterious Ways / One – Can't Help Falling In Love / Until The End Of The World / New Year's Day / Wild Rover / Trying To Throw Your Arms / Party Girl / When Love Comes To Town / Satellite Of Love / Slow Dancing / Sunday Bloody Sunday / Bullet The Blue Sky / Running To Stand Still / Where The Streets Have No Name / Pride / I Still Haven't Found –Stand By Me / encore: Desire / Ultra Violet / With Or Without You / Love Is Blindness / Can't Help Falling In Love

The show is outstanding, with a remarkable set list. *Can't Help Falling In Love* is linked to *One* and also closes the show as usual. *Party Girl* is played for the only time of the year, replacing *Angel Of Harlem*, and has Edge singing a whole verse and the crowd participating nicely. *Slow Dancing* returns to the set after a six-month absence, in a complete version that stuns the crowd.

"There's been some people complaining about the noise," Bono says sarcastically, followed by the crowd producing their loudest noise possible. He continues, "I don't think they understand that the only thing louder than a U2 gig, is the people who come to a U2 gig! One lady said she could hear us from two miles off, turned up the television, but opened the window. Very strange behaviour. Well, I'm very sorry, and we've erected this whole stage here so we can play a little light folk acoustic set for Mrs. Chaka-Boom Chaka-Boom." *When Love Comes To Town* is played loud as hell.

For the ritual phone call, Bono asks, "Who do you want me to call? Let's try Mayor Welch, just in case they had any complaints! Hi, I'm in Country Club Hills and I am trying to find out if you had any complaints tonight. I'm here with a few friends, and we just can't get to sleep, you know what I'm saying? There's a rock & roll concert out there, I can't get to sleep!" The operator hangs up. "Can I leave a message? Tell 'em to open their windows and turn down the television sets!"

SEPTEMBER 20, 1992. ST. LOUIS, MO, BUSCH MEMORIAL STADIUM

- Attendance: 48,054 (P); sellout
- Support: Big Audio Dynamite II, Public Enemy
- Set: same as September 2, minus *I Still Haven't Found – Stand By Me*.

SEPTEMBER 23, 1992. COLUMBIA, SC, WILLIAMS-BRICE STADIUM

- Attendance: 28,305 (P); (capacity 40,136)
- Support: Big Audio Dynamite II, Public Enemy
- Set: same as September 2, with *Rain* replacing *Unchained Melody*, and *Slow Dancing* instead of *All I Want Is You*.

There is a slight drizzle, prompting Bono to sing lines of Albert Hammond's *It Never Rains In Southern California* after *Angel Of Harlem*. U2's first South Carolina show has the smallest turnout of the Outside Broadcast Tour. Phoning the White House, Bono finds the line is busy. Because White House operators have been so good handling the calls, U2 had offered to fly the entire staff to this show, but they didn't accept.

SEPTEMBER 25, 1992. ATLANTA, GA, GEORGIA DOME

- Attendance: 53,427 (P); sellout
- Support: Big Audio Dynamite II, Public Enemy
- Set: same as September 2, with *Slow Dancing* replacing *All I Want Is You*, and plus *Ultra Violet* after *Desire*.

At a band meeting in the afternoon, it is decided to postpone the Australian leg of the tour, which was already being prepared for the end of the year, to 1993. They feel they will be too tired to be able to put in a performance they'd be happy with.

U2 inaugurate the brand new Georgia Dome which opened a month earlier. At the start of the show they are distracted by the house lights staying on, and *Zoo Station* has to be performed in a fully illuminated stadium. Calling the White House, Bono asks why they declined the invitation of attending the Columbia show. "We would send our private aeroplane and everything to pick you up... why didn't you come?" The operator laughs and gets her colleague on the line. Bono grins, "Operator Two? She's my favourite – I'm getting to know their names! Is that Operator Two?" "Yes" "Hi, I just wanna say that I've got a crush on you." "Oh, thank you very much..." Bono assures her that U2 would put on a big show for the White House staff in South Carolina, but Operator Two admits that for now, lack of time does not allow such outings. "Well, darling, we really would like to see you at a U2 concert, so if you should change your mind, you just give us a call. In the meantime, if you could pass a message on to the President, just tell him to...", and the operator fills in: "watch more TV; thank you for calling us, bye."

The phone call is broadcast on MTV the next night, combined with a recent quote from George Bush. In a speech on his presidential campaign, he commented on Bill Clinton's phone conversation with U2 on 'Rockline': "So Governor Clinton doesn't think foreign policy is important, but anyway, he's trying to catch up. You may have seen this in the news, he was in Hollywood, seeking foreign policy advice from the rock group U2. Now, understand, I have nothing against U2. You may not know this, but they're trying to call me at the White House every night during the concert. But the next time we face a foreign policy crisis, I will work with John Major and Boris Yeltsin, and Bill Clinton can consult Boy George – I will stay with the experts."

OCTOBER 3, 1992. MIAMI, FL, JOE ROBBIE STADIUM

- Attendance: 45,244 (P); (capacity 46,000)
- Support: Big Audio Dynamite II, Public Enemy
- Set: same as September 2, but *Wild Rover* is played after *Mysterious Ways* instead of after *New Year's Day*.

Due to lack of security, a dozen fans manage to climb on the mini-stage. One guy persuades Bono to let him play guitar on

Angel Of Harlem. As the guy struggles through the song, Bono says he knows how he feels and takes back the guitar. During *With Or Without You,* another guy climbs up, puts his arm around Bono, shakes him hard and picks him up horizontally. Bono doesn't resist, just puts his glitter hat on the guy's head. A few weeks before the show, Hurricane Andrew had wrecked Florida state. Bono tells the crowd he hopes everyone hit by the hurricane is OK. "I thought Dublin got hit hard by the weather, but nothing like this."

Miami

OCTOBER 7, 1992. BIRMINGHAM, AL, LEGION FIELD

- Attendance: 35,209 (P); (capacity 41,632)
- Support: Big Audio Dynamite II, Public Enemy
- Set: same as September 2, with *My Girl* instead of *Unchained Melody,* and *Whiskey In The Jar* replacing *Wild Rover.*

U2's first ever show in Alabama state attracts a cheerful crowd unconcerned by occasional bursts of rain. Bono dedicates *One* to Eddie Kendricks, a founding members of The Temptations, who had died two days earlier, and sings part of their composition *My Girl.* At the Columbia show two weeks earlier, a 23-year old girl called Dail was found to be missing. A group of friends has been following the tour since. Wearing T-shirts with Dail's picture and passing out flyers, they hope to find anyone who saw her in Columbia and may supply information. At Legion Field, U2's crew help by projecting Dail's picture on the screens in between support acts. A $50,000 reward is offered for any information leading to the arrest of her kidnappers.

OCTOBER 10, 1992. TAMPA, FL, TAMPA STADIUM

- Attendance: 41,909 (P); (capacity 42,500)
- Support: Big Audio Dynamite II, Public Enemy
- Set: same as September 2, with *My Girl* instead of *Unchained Melody, Whiskey In The Jar* replacing *Wild Rover, Dear Prudence* instead of *All I Want Is You,* and *I Still Haven't Found – Stand By Me* and *Love Is Blindness* are left out.

It rains throughout the show. The chorus of *Singing In The Rain* introduces and finishes *Angel Of Harlem.* A slow and inspired version of The Beatles' *Dear Prudence* is played in the acoustic set for the only time on the 1992-3 tour. The show takes a highly unusual turn when, after *Pride,* a guy from the audience gets on stage and talks to Bono. "This dude here just crashed the stage," Bono explains. "He says he's a great songwriter; you wanna hear one of his songs or not?" The crowd cheer. Edge hands the guy a guitar. "It's good to finally be here," the guy shouts. "This is called *An Eye For An Eye Makes The Whole World Blind.*" The guy accompanies himself on guitar and confidently sings his powerful, socially-critical song that lasts six minutes. It's

the first time ever that a total stranger is allowed to perform a song on his own. During the song U2 go backstage and change; as a result, *I Still Haven't Found* and *Stand By Me* are not played and the video confessions are not shown. "God bless you, man, you have some guts!" Bono says as the band come back for the encore.

OCTOBER 14, 1992. HOUSTON, TX, ASTRODOME

- Attendance: 31,884 (P); (capacity 35,000)
- Support: Big Audio Dynamite II, Public Enemy
- Set: *Zoo Station / The Fly / Even Better Than The Real Thing / Mysterious Ways / One – Unchained Melody / Until The End Of The World / New Year's Day / Dirty Old Town / Trying To Throw Your Arms / Angel Of Harlem / When Love Comes To Town / Satellite Of Love / Redemption Song / Sunday Bloody Sunday / Bullet The Blue Sky / Running To Stand Still / Where The Streets Have No Name / Pride / I Still Haven't Found – Stand By Me /* encore: *Desire / Ultra Violet / With Or Without You / Love Is Blindness / Can't Help Falling In Love*

Yet another cover version is premièred in the acoustic set: *Redemption Song,* Bob Marley's song of freedom. Before singing it, Bono appeals for the return of his notebook which was stolen from the band's hotel in Houston in the spring. He croons lines of *My Way* before *With Or Without You:* "Regrets, I've had a few, but then again, too few to mention..." During *Ultra Violet* the video recording of the woman doing sign-language is replaced by the image of a woman doing the sign-language live on the side of the stage.

OCTOBER 16, 1992. DALLAS, TX, TEXAS STADIUM

- Attendance: 39,154 (P); sellout
- Support: Big Audio Dynamite II, Public Enemy
- Set: same as Houston.

Introducing *Redemption Song* Bono says you have to be either black or Irish to sing it. Calling the White House, Bono again declares his love to Operator Two.

OCTOBER 18, 1992. KANSAS CITY, MO, ARROWHEAD STADIUM

- Attendance: 37,867 (P); (capacity 40,000)
- Support: The Sugarcubes, Public Enemy
- Set: same as Houston, plus *My Girl* linked to *Angel Of Harlem,* and minus *Ultra Violet.*

U2 use their soundcheck to experiment with some unfinished songs. One is a trashy, grungy number with booming drums, another has Edge playing funky guitar on a very danceable song. Bono sings a new acoustic piece, then does an acoustic version of *Who's Gonna Ride Your Wild Horses.*

The Icelandic group The Sugarcubes ("We are the Icecubes from Sugarland") make their entry on the tour, replacing Big Audio Dynamite II. U2 play a loose show. Belly dancer Morleigh Steinberg celebrates her birthday and while she dances her way towards Bono during *Mysterious Ways,* she cracks up with laugher when she sees him trying to balance a big cake on his outstretched hand. The crowd sing *Happy Birthday.* Confessions include a girl claiming she was adopted and wonders if her real parents are in the stadium.

OCTOBER 21, 1992. DENVER, CO, MILE HIGH STADIUM

- Attendance: 54,450 (P); sellout
- Support: The Sugarcubes, Public Enemy
- Set: *Zoo Station / The Fly / Even Better Than The Real Thing / Mysterious Ways / One – Unchained Melody / Until The End Of The World / New Year's Day / Dirty Old Town / Trying To Throw Your Arms / Angel Of Harlem / When Love Comes To Town /*

Satellite Of Love / Bad – All I Want Is You / Bullet The Blue Sky / Running To Stand Still / Where The Streets Have No Name / Pride / I Still Haven't Found – Stand By Me / encore: *Desire / With Or Without You / Love Is Blindness / Can't Help Falling In Love*

Larry has microphone problems during *Dirty Old Town* and has to start anew. Bono adds some off-key lines of John Denver's *Annie's Song* ("You fill up my senses...") to the end of *Angel Of Harlem. Bad,* performed after an absence of ten shows, includes bits of Neil Young's *Old Man.* Bono's creed at the end of *Desire:* "I believe in love, love and money; I believe in poetry, electricity, cheap cosmetics; I believe in the sky over my head, and my silver shoes on my feet. I believe in you. I believe *for* you. I have a vision, I have a vision, now and forever, big time, prime time, all the time. I have a vision – television! That's all folks..." At later shows he will also include, "fruit juice, shampoo, James Brown's hairdo," or, "1-hour photo, 24-hour pizza, the smell of a new Sedan..."

OCTOBER 24, 1992. TEMPE, AZ, SUN DEVIL STADIUM

- Attendance: 35,177 (P); (capacity 40,000)
- Support: The Sugarcubes, Public Enemy
- Set: same as Denver, with *She's A Mystery To Me* replacing *Unchained Melody,* plus *Suspicious Minds* after *Angel Of Harlem,* and plus *Who's Gonna Ride Your Wild Horses* after *Satellite Of Love.*

Bono dedicates *One* to the "ex-governor of Arizona", referring to Ed Mechum who, back in 1987, had refused to honour Martin Luther King's birthday. MLK day is now recognised as a holiday in the state of Arizona.

The show is long, with 27 songs and contains several surprises. Bono sings an acoustic, full version of *Suspicious Minds,* the Elvis song which was occasionally played during the LoveTown tour, for the only time on the 1992-3 tour. He stops a few times to figure out the chords, and his voice cracks up here and there. *Who's Gonna Ride Your Wild Horses* enjoys its re-entry to the set, now played on the mini-stage by Bono in the acoustic version.

The phone call to the White House is somewhat bizarre. Bono: "Hello, this is me again, Mirror Ball man." Operator: "Miracle Man?" Bono: "No, we need miracles but I just have mirror balls." The operator promptly hangs up.

OCTOBER 27, 1992. EL PASO, TX, SUN BOWL

- Attendance: 35,564 (P); (capacity 39,500)
- Support: The Sugarcubes, Public Enemy
- Set: same as Denver, with *She's A Mystery To Me* replacing *Unchained Melody,* and plus *Who's Gonna Ride Your Wild Horses* after *Satellite Of Love.*

The level of anticipation is staggering for the first stadium show in this Texas/New Mexico/Mexico border town since Elton John in 1972. *The El Paso Times* prints a concert survival guide: 'If your seats are near the ramp, prepare to get wet. For the concert novice: bring earplugs, this show is LOUD.' The show is beamed to Sherry, the winner of the US MTV contest, in her home in Huntington Beach, California. Bono converses with her, courtesy of Zoo TV. She asks why, the more popular U2 gets, the tighter Bono's pants get. He says he has discovered apple pie since he came to America and claims he will break up the band to go solo and move to Las Vegas. He asks Sherry, "When I'm going through my fat Bono period, will you come and see me?"

Bono's voice sounds ragged, possibly due to the tequila he admits quaffing while across the border in Mexico. "How do you drink that shit?" The mood becomes sombre as he talks of coming back from Mexico: "We could see all the people standing at the border, could see their plight, could see the looks on their faces as they wanted to come into America, this supposed land of milk and honey. And, as an Irishman, I understood that feeling, that wish to leave your home to go far away to make something

Larry belts out an Irish drinking song.

of yourself. Well, what America turns out to be over the next ten years we'll wait and see. But I hope you find what you're looking for..."

OCTOBER 30, 31, 1992. LOS ANGELES, CA, DODGER STADIUM

- Attendance: 108,357 (P); sellout
- Support: The Sugarcubes, Public Enemy
- Set first night: same as Denver, with *Rain* instead of *Unchained Melody*, plus *Who's Gonna Ride Your Wild Horses* after *Satellite Of Love*, plus *Ultra Violet* after *Desire*.

As at most shows in the rain, a short version of *Rain* is played after *One*, and *It Never Rains In Southern California* introduces *When Love Comes To Town*.

- Set second night: same as Houston, with *She's A Mystery To Me* instead of *Unchained Melody*, minus *Ultra Violet*.

Larry's 31st birthday and Halloween night too make for a festive, exuberant show. Many in the crowd have come in monster outfits in true Halloween tradition. On some songs, Bono wears a sinister Freddie-from-'Nightmare On Elm Street' glove on one hand. Going through the channels, Elvira, a campy vampiresque sexpot who is the Mistress of the Night from nearby amusement park Magic Mountain, appears on the screens to congratulate Larry and leads the crowd singing *Happy Birthday*. She also expresses interest in running for President because "the voters want two boobs in the White House and they may as well be mine! I'd do ANYthing to get elected!" Larry thanks everyone for coming to his birthday party and dedicates *Dirty Old Town* to all young people in the stadium.

NOVEMBER 3, 4, 1992. VANCOUVER, CANADA, B.C. PLACE STADIUM

- Attendance: 77,448 (P); (capacity 83,000)
- Support: Sugarcubes, Public Enemy
- Set first night: same as Houston, minus *I Still Haven't Found – Stand By Me*.

"And now a word from our sponsor," the screens boast after *The Fly*. "Our sponsor is not Texaco or Ross Perot," Bono says. "Our sponsors tonight are the good people of Vancouver! Let's see what's on Zoo TV..." The satellite picks up Bill Clinton holding a speech. "Good luck, Bill, I hope you're a happy person," Bono says, as George Bush is busy being defeated for President. The band make a tired impression. At the start of *Pride*, Larry misses his cue and Bono is so angry that he throws his microphone straight at him, betraying signs of tour-madness. After the song the band rapidly leave the stage, thus omitting *I Still Haven't Found* and *Stand By Me*. Bono sings the encore from the mini-stage and, to make up, thanks Adam, Edge, "and especially Larry" for letting him be in their band.

- Set second night: same as Denver, with *She's A Mystery To Me* replacing *Unchained Melody*, *Wild Rover* instead of *Dirty Old Town*, and plus *Dancing Queen* linked to *Angel Of Harlem*.

It's election night in the United States. B.P. Fallon announces: "Ladies and gentlemen, the United States have a new President: Bill Clinton!" Just before Edge's solo in *Bullet The Blue Sky*, Bono mumbles, "Goodbye George Bush, I don't think we'll miss you that much..." The band deliver a spirited performance. Larry adds vocals to *Dancing Queen*, while Adam sings a whole verse of *When Love Comes To Town* far too fast for Larry and Edge to follow. Bono remarks that he's glad U2 added a second Vancouver show as it "fucked up the scalpers", leaving them stuck with bundles of tickets for the first night. Coming back for the encore, Bono, in his silver glitter suit, watches his image in the mirror and sighs, "You look like shit, man!" He tells the crowd in mid-song, "I don't wanna be Elvis tonight, I wanna be Bono tonight. You love me for who I am, don't you? I don't *have* to put on all this shit for you, do I? It's hard..."

NOVEMBER 7, 1992. OAKLAND, CA, OAKLAND STADIUM

- Attendance: 59,800 (P); sellout
- Support: The Sugarcubes, Public Enemy
- Set: same as Houston.

One is dedicated to the Needlepoint Exchange, the programme aimed at reducing AIDS among drug users. Bono dedicates *I Still Haven't Found* to San Francisco-based concert promoter Bill Graham, who died recently in a helicopter accident. Graham had been presenting U2's shows in the Bay Area ever since they first came to America. He was one of the key people responsible for getting the 1986 'Conspiracy of Hope' Tour off the ground, and also enabled U2 to perform the notorious 'Save The Yuppies' show with just 24-hours' notice. The show ends as Bono whispers, "Bill Graham is still in the building."

NOVEMBER 10, 1992. SAN DIEGO, CA, JACK MURPHY STADIUM

- Attendance: 33,575 (P); (capacity 55,000)
- Support: The Sugarcubes, Public Enemy
- Set: same as Houston, minus *Ultra-Violet*.

The stadium is almost half-empty. During *Trying To Throw Your Arms* Bono sees a girl in a wedding gown in the crowd. He asks, "Is this a fancy dress or did you really tie the knot here? You really did? Come over here." The girl, having married earlier in the day, is carried onto the catwalk by her husband. "Superman and his new wife! Well, all I can say is: the people of San Diego pronounce you man and wife!" Bono films the happy couple. "Superman IV, live on Zoo TV!"

Let's get married... for a while

Bono comments on the presidential election once again. "Well, you've got four years to see if you can turn the whole world around. I hope Bill Clinton is what he says he is, 'cause if he's not, we're *all* fucked, let's face it." He confesses that since he is a rich bastard from abroad, these elections were somewhat abstract for him, but says he ran into people from minority groups celebrating in a church in downtown San Francisco a few days ago and realised then the importance of the outcome of the election.

NOVEMBER 12, 1992. LAS VEGAS, NV, SAM BOYD SILVER BOWL

- Attendance: 27,774 (P); (capacity 37,011)
- Support: The Sugarcubes, Public Enemy
- Set: same as Denver, plus *Ultra Violet* after *Desire*.

"Thanks for coming out in the cold and seeing U2 play," Bono says as Edge starts *I Still Haven't Found*. He says the band have been enjoying this surreal and wonderful city very much. "This place is even more Zoo TV than Zoo TV!" Besides being famous for its huge gambling casinos, Las Vegas is also the wedding capital of the world. It has 24-hour chapels and drive-in weddings. Bono proceeds, "Last night Steve Iredale, who's

worked with us since the very beginning and is basically running the whole show here tonight, well, he took his babe down to a little desert church and got married there last night!" He dedicates the song to Steve and "his Duchess".

NOVEMBER 14, 1992. ANAHEIM, CA, ANAHEIM STADIUM

- Attendance: 48,640 (P); sellout
- Support: The Sugarcubes, Public Enemy
- Set: same as Denver, plus *My Girl* before *Angel Of Harlem*, and *Ultra Violet* after *Desire*.

The concert is added at the last moment when tour promoters sense they can fill another stadium in the LA area. It's the final show of the Outside Broadcast Tour. "We started off at Disney World, we've ended in Disneyland, it's perfect," Bono comments. He finds a football match on the screens. "Oh yeah, people dressed up as cars crashing into each other, that's perfectly Zoo. Next!"

The band are in a reflective mood. Stepping forward for *Dirty Old Town*, Larry says, "We're gonna go to Mexico for a few days. A couple of people aren't going to make it; truck drivers, bus drivers, caterers – I wanna sing this for their heavy duty. Hard to believe this is the last time I'm gonna sing this in the US." He mocks, "I know how disappointed you'll all be..."

"We've been on the road for a long time," says Bono. "This is our 100th concert, and we've had an amazing time, so much more than we expected." On the screens, all the cities the tour has played since Lakeland run by. "I don't know when we're gonna be back here, or if we'll ever be back to play like this again. I wanna thank our manager Paul McGuinness for helping to keep it together all these years, and Ellen Darst, his right-hand lady. Most of our organisation is run by women. We sort of work for them, really! We love them all. It's just too many names to mention. But thanks to Jake and Steve and Tim and Joe O'Herlihy on the sound, and the Reverend Willie out there at the lighting desk who makes this look so good. Also Carol and Monika with the videos have been really cool." The crowd applaud, then Bono continues: "I don't know why I feel so shit, but I really feel shit right now. Maybe it's because, for a performer, sometimes going home is harder than being on stage..."

"Let's call George one last time, waddaya say? That's 1-202-456-1414. Hello, is that the White House? Hi, can I speak to ex-president George Bush please? What? George isn't available? But it's our last night! Can I leave a message for George? Hello? I just wanna say I won't be bothering him anymore from now on. I'm gonna be bothering Bill Clinton now..."

The 42 Outside Broadcast shows and the unofficial rehearsal show in Hershey are attended by 1,847,971 and 25,000 people respectively, an average of 43,557 a night. A total of 79,329 tickets remain unsold. The total gross is $53,913,608.

NOVEMBER 21, 22, 24, 25, 1992. MEXICO CITY, MEXICO, PALACIO DE LOS DEPORTES

- Attendance: 83,068 (P); sellout
- Support: Big Audio Dynamite II
- Set second night: same as Denver, with *She's A Mystery To Me* replacing *Unchained Melody*, *Wild Rover* instead of *Dirty Old Town*, and *Can't Help Falling In Love* is left out.

With the stage and entourage shrunk to arena size, U2 play four indoor shows in Mexico City, their first in Central America, and the closest they've been to South America yet. Though tickets are relatively high priced at $51 and $22, all shows sell out the day tickets go on sale, grossing 13,035,390,000 Pesos, the equivalent of $4,148,756. Instead of the George Bush footage, the shows start with Bono doing his "I could have lost you" bit, like on the indoor tour. The shows attract young, enthusiastic crowds in their early twenties who although they rarely get to see foreign bands in their country, are fairly familiar with the songs.

DECEMBER, 1992. IRISH TV: 'LATE LATE SHOW'

Adam Clayton joins in on a tribute to Sharon Shannon, playing her song The Marguerita Suite together with Sharon, Liam O'Maonlai, Donal Lunny, and Philip King.

Thalia Theatre

JANUARY 20, 1993. WASHINGTON, DC

Adam and Larry team up with REM's Michael Stipe and Mike Mills to perform *One* at the MTV 1993 Rock & Roll Inaugural Ball for USA's new President Bill Clinton. MTV's bash is one of many unofficial events at which a wide variety of musicians team up to celebrate George Bush's defeat and the feeling that with Clinton, "rock & roll has arrived at the White House". The collaboration comes about when Adam and Larry run into the REM guys who have already decided to play *One* and invite them to join in. Merging the titles of the two bands' latest albums, bassist Mike Mills plays guitar as Adam plays bass in their one-off band Automatic Baby. It is aired on MTV.

JANUARY 30, 31, 1993. HAMBURG, GERMANY, THALIA THEATRE

Bono and Edge take part in the two-day Festival Against Racism, where some 50 artists, actors, writers and musicians perform dance, music, and hold speeches. The festival is organised to protest and give attention to the strong increase of hatred and aggression against minority groups in Germany. Tickets are priced at DM 200, all proceeds going to Unicef. The festival is attended mainly by scientists, historians, businessmen, artists and other VIPs. Under the creed, 'We will not forget – we will never let it happen again', victims of persecution by the Nazis, as well as contemporary Fascist victims like the mothers of the disappeared, tell their gruesome stories on the first day. Historians discuss the themes of xenophobia and racism, followed by speeches from artists such as John Trudell, Kris Kristofferson, Harvey Keitel and Bono.

Bono's speech is over five minutes long. "I should preface anything I say by stating the obvious, that I'm not a philosopher or a political thinker; I'm a singer in a rock & roll band," he starts. "We're here not just because this concerns us, but because we know we can do something. We're united not just because we're anti-Fascist, but because as artists, film makers, writers, we all work in the realm of imagination, and know that it's our best weapon." He says that people's inability to put themselves in

another's shoes is the core of intolerance, which is the basis of these problems and states that as artists, they need to paint pictures and see them move. "I think of the Berlin dadaists, whose movements unzipped the starch trousers of the Fascists, exposing them as serious, painfully serious, dickheads. Close to the poison, you'll find the cure. As well as an antidote, humour, laughter, is the evidence of freedom. Artists, scientists, writers, we are. Sometimes I wish we were comedians; we would probably have more effect. Mock the devil, and he'll flee from thee. Fear of the devil leads to devil worship."

He talks of the need to glimpse another way of being, to dream up the kind of world we *want* to live in, as well as describe the kind of world we *do* live in. "Rock & roll has given me a chance to imagine. It has stopped me from becoming cynical, in cynical times. Surely, it's the inherited cynicism, in our political and economic thinking, that contributes so much to the despair of the Nineties. The Fascists at least recognised the void. Their pseudo-strong leadership is a reaction to what feels like no leadership. Their simplistic racist analysis as to what ails the economy, and why there's so much unemployment, is a reaction to our government's reply, which even the smartest among us cannot understand."

He mentions seeing an interview with two of the world's economic experts on a TV show in America. Asked to explain what happened on Black Monday, when Wall Street crashed, they were puzzled and agreed it was like watching an aquarium where the goldfish all changed direction at exactly the same time, and for

Stoppt den Hass!

no apparent reason. "Does *anyone* know what the fuck is going on?" Bono continues: "Fascism is about control. They know what we won't admit: that things are *out* of control. We started the century with so many competing ideas, as to how we should live together. We ended with so few."

Our consumer society equates 'manhood' with spending power, Bono says. "Male-ness is an illusive notion; distorted but made accessible and concrete by the Nazis. We shouldn't underestimate this. The Fascists feed off youth culture, and if we're to overcome them, we must understand their sex appeal. And what, is *our* appeal? Theirs is a perverted idealism; but do we have any idealism? What is the ground we stand on, politically, economically, spiritually? I don't know, but I know this: in the history books, democracy is the oddity. Democracy is a fragile thing. Though the Greeks invented it, they never could live it. The Christian idea, that all men are equal in God's eyes, has been suppressed anywhere it raised its unique head. Obviously, this is not a German problem. The hundreds of thousands who took part in the candle-lit marches all over this country, sent a signal to the rest of us: that there *is* idealism in Germany, that it needs to be nurtured. And that while it is understandable to fight against the darkness with light, it is better to make the light brighter."

The next day, Bono and Edge perform *One*, together with Jo Shankar on violin, and Stefan Rager on percussion, the drummer of the German band Jeremy Days whom Bono had found willing to play drums for them just two hours before their appearance. After the song, more people come on stage to join in the theme song for the night, *We Will Never Forget.*

FEBRUARY 6, 1993. VAN MORRISON: DUBLIN, IRELAND, POINT DEPOT

Bono joins Van on stage for *Moondance* and *Gloria*, later joined by Bob Dylan, who played here the night before, Chrissie Hynde, Kris Kristofferson, Elvis Costello, Steve Winwood and others.

FEBRUARY 11, 1993. JOHNNY CASH & KRIS KRISTOFFERSON: DUBLIN, IRELAND, OLYMPIA THEATRE

In a show taped for RTE television, Edge, Larry and Bono play together with Cash and Kristofferson.

FEBRUARY, MARCH, APRIL 1993

Their adrenaline still pumping after having been on the road throughout the Zoo TV tour during the past year, U2 use the creative buzz to full advantage. They write and record songs for an intended five or six song EP to be released in spring or summer. As the work progresses, word goes out that the EP may well develop into a complete album.

ZOO TV: ZOOROPA 1993

"We've underplayed Europe for years," admitted manager Paul McGuinness in an interview with *Collectormania* magazine in June 1992. "The big outdoor shows next summer will be an opportunity for anyone who's interested in the band to see them."

Tickets for U2's first full stadium tour of Europe went on sale in late November, with many shows selling out instantly. Reaching many areas they have never

played before, often with multiple nights due to public demand, U2 will play to more than 2,100,000 people at 43 shows in Europe.

While the presidential elections featured in the shows in America, the Zoo TV Tour evolves into Zooropa as it is revised to reflect on the current state of affairs in Europe. During 1992 and 1993, Europe has turned into one big zoo, more divided than ever, where confusion and fear reign among people and politicians. In Eastern Europe, the fall of the Iron Curtain and communism has resulted in separatist movements as people fight to preserve ethnic identities suppressed for decades. The Soviet Union disbanded to form a multitude of states with borders drawn on historic lines. Czechoslovakia split in two. Yugoslavia fell apart as war broke out between Croats, Muslims and Serbs, whose programme of ethnic purification (read massacre) recalled Hitler's ideology. In Western Europe, opening the borders has not created the one big happy nation the European Community was supposed to be. Hundreds of thousands of refugees, fleeing from countries with unstable political situations, stream into the European Community looking for a better future. With the EC already suffering from massive unemployment and housing problems, millions of Europeans think more about self-preservation and become less tolerant to those coming in from the outside. Extreme right-wing political parties in Germany, France, Italy, Sweden, Holland and Belgium gain increasing support. Racist slogans are sprayed on city walls, and foreigners are intimidated, to the extent that their shops and houses are destroyed or burned down by extremists.

Having finished recording the new songs, U2 rehearse for the Zooropean trek in the last week of April before flying to Holland on May 6. A theatre group called Macnass from Galway, Ireland, are hired for the tour, to perform a play before the support acts.

MAY 7, 1993. ROTTERDAM, HOLLAND, FEYENOORD STADIUM

■ Rehearsal: *Zoo Station / The Fly / Even Better Than The Real Thing / Mysterious Ways / One – Unchained Melody / New Year's Day / Van Diemen's Land / Bullet The Blue Sky / Running To Stand Still / Where The Streets Have No Name / Pride / Desire*

U2 do a semi-dress rehearsal in front of a small group of fans that Bono has invited inside. The band go through most of the show, often taking short breaks to discuss technical aspects with the crew. The stage is somewhat smaller than on the Outside Broadcast tour, and only three Trabants are used, hanging from a rig behind the drum kit. Bono wears a red version of his plastic Fly-gear, which he will not use throughout the tour. Edge screws up *Van Diemen's Land* so badly that he and crew members can't suppress their laughter. Bono stops during *Running To Stand Still* because of "high frequency fucking up my ears." He is absent for *Pride*, so Edge fills in the vocals. After *Desire*, the fans on the stands see Bono parody himself in a campy, somewhat nasal voice: "The last time you saw me, I was waving a white flag; now look what you've done..." He tells about the "good old days", sings the tune of a Martini commercial, and rehearses the phone call. Though originally invited by Bono for "half an hour or so", the bunch of fans have been inside for two and a half hours, and upon leaving are all given a brand new Zoo Ecu funny money bill, which will be used for the show during *Desire*.

MAY 9, 10, 11, 1993. ROTTERDAM, HOLLAND, FEYENOORD STADIUM

■ Attendance: 135,104 (P); sellout
■ Support (first night): Utah Saints, Claw Boys Claw; (second night): Einstürzende Neubauten, Claw Boys Claw; (third night): Claw Boys Claw
■ Set first night: *Zoo Station / The Fly / Even Better Than The Real Thing / Mysterious Ways / One – Unchained Melody / Until The End Of The World / New Year's Day / Dirty Old Town / Trying To Throw Your Arms Around the World / Angel Of Harlem / When Love Comes To Town / Satellite Of Love / Bad – All I Want Is You / Bullet The Blue Sky / Running To Stand Still / Where The Streets Have No Name / Pride / encore: Desire / Ultra Violet / With Or Without You / Love Is Blindness / Can't Help Falling In Love*

Using the stage, mini-stage and part of the field, theatre group Macnass perform an anti-Fascist play in which a group of dictator-like doctors seek to suppress civilians by performing dubious treatments and feeding them into a gigantic Hoover. Eventually, good beats evil as the people break loose and toss the doctors into the Hoover themselves. This has the required cleansing effect – after absorbing the doctors, the Hoover spews out their rotten souls in the shape of black balloons which fade away into the sky. Involving 100 local people each night holding banners and wearing big misshapen heads, the 30-minute Macnass performance will precede the support bands at every show.

Though it has been sunny and warm all afternoon, a heavy thunderstorm erupts during the support bands and brings down the high-spirited atmosphere. After an hour of pouring rain, The Disposable Heroes Of Hiphoprisy's *Television: The Drug Of The Nation* indicates show time. Red lights flicker on and off, the opening notes of *Zoo Station* set in, and the screens flash on one by one. Starting with images of a young Hitler-Jügend drummer boy at the opening ceremony of the 1936 Olympics in Berlin, taken from Leni Riefenstahl's Nazi-propaganda movie 'The Triumph Of The Will', U2 hint at the parallel between Europe's current situation and its state in the mid-Thirties. Fanfare music, voices blasting out "It's very simple" and "What do you want?" in several languages, and Beethoven's *Alle Menschen Werden Brüder*, aka *Ode To Joy*, follow in succession. While the hydraulic lift brings Bono up from underneath the stage, the biggest screen displays the 12-star-circle-on-blue-logo of the European Community. One star symbolically falls off, then the logo

Zooropa

collapses altogether, while Edge strikes the savage guitar riff of *Zoo Station*, and the show is on.

First-night tension shows, but Larry's hilarious version of *Dirty Old Town* loosens things up a bit. A major addition to the video production occurs during *Bullet The Blue Sky*, when the burning crosses turn into swastikas, freeze frame for a few seconds, while Bono dramatically stresses, "We must never let it happen again..." The powerful, scary image of the swastikas functions as a slap in the face, to remind fans that the rise of racism and nationalism is a disturbing development in so-called 'united' Europe.

Two Trabant-fish swim across the screens while the crowd wait for the encore, followed by the 'confessions', recorded earlier in the day, which offer an opportunity for fans to propose to their loved ones, mock local or political issues, reveal sexual fantasies, or whatever else they want to share. Confessions that are too serious will generally not be shown. The crowd is then treated to an old Russian battle-hymn, which U2 took from an album called 'Lenin's Favourite Songs' and is seemingly sung by the manipulated image of the graffiti babyface printed on the 'Achtung Baby' compact disc [which will subsequently be used for the sleeve of the 'Zooropa' album].

While everyone is still gazing at the screens, the band return to the stage and crash into *Desire*, in which Bono premières his new alter-ego in a gold lamé suit, his face painted white with red lipstick, his hair combed-back and sporting red devil horns. Rather than sing, he speaks the text of *Desire* in a strong, ancient English accent. "What a night! What a show! What a life, what a way to go. I have a vision: Eurovision!", he shouts over the song's final notes. "Off with the horns, on with the show," he says in the same bizarre accent. "If you're feeling uptight, and things aren't right, then you've got a song it goes ding-ding-a-dong," he sings, quoting the Dutch winning entry of the 1975 Eurovision Song Contest by Teach In. "Well, it's the last Eurovision tomorrow night, isn't it? Yes, I feel a whole era has come to an end. Pop music just won't be so exciting again. I knew them all: Lulu, The Brotherhood Of Man. I taught them everything they knew. I know you young people like your pop stars to be exciting, so I bought these," he says, and lifts an ankle to display high glitter platform boots. When he accusingly says, "Look what you've done to me," and raises his arms, the crowd see a tarty, tired old rock star, blasé from success, and laugh as Bono's new character is being unveiled. "The last time I was here I was only 5 feet 8. Now look at me: I'm gigantic! You've made me very famous, and I thank you. Round about this time every night, I make a phone call. Sometimes to the President of the United States, but tonight I'm going to call a taxi to take me home." As he tries to order a taxi, he introduces himself: "My name is MacPhisto." When the girl on the line gets confused, he says, "Oh, you know me?" "Er, I don't know...?" "You know me very well, but I know you probably even better than you know yourself," he boasts, and starts singing *Ultra Violet*.

MacPhisto is the European equivalent of the 'preacher' with the glitter cowboy-hat and exaggerated American accent that Bono played on the Outside Broadcast tour. With MacPhisto, Bono delves into Berlin's decadent cabaret of the Thirties, his bleak facial expressions ranging from devilish grins to tragi-comic sadness. As Bono will later say in an interview, MacPhisto is The Fly when he's old and fat and playing Las Vegas.

Bono takes off the gold jacket, abandoning the MacPhisto character, to sing *With Or Without You*. Rain starts coming down again in buckets. While the security guards put on their raincoats and the crowd grasp for bits of plastic to cover themselves, Bono strolls down the catwalk, acting to the camera as he smudges his make-up, getting wetter every second but refusing to seek cover until the show is finished. The closing songs, *Love Is Blindness* and *Can't Help Falling In Love*, form the strongest part of tonight's show. When Bono quits the stage and Elvis' version comes over the speakers, the crowd leave the stadium quiet, cold, and soaking wet.

■ Set second night: Zoo Station / The Fly / Even Better Than The Real Thing / Mysterious Ways / One - Unchained Melody / Until The End Of The World / New Year's Day / Party Girl / Trying To Throw Your Arms Around The World / Angel Of Harlem - My Girl / I Will Follow / Satellite Of Love / Sunday Bloody Sunday / Bullet The Blue Sky / Running To Stand Still / Where The Streets Have No Name / Pride / encore: Desire / Ultra Violet / With Or Without You / Love Is Blindness / Are You Lonesome Tonight

There is disappointment for the winner of the video contest that *Nieuwe Revu* magazine had organised in collaboration with Ariola Records, the first prize of which is a one-minute airing on Zoo TV between support acts. The winner's home-made video for *Who's Gonna Ride Your Wild Horses* is announced, the music is heard over the PA... but the screens remain blank. German experimental band Einstürzende Neubauten, who play in support, are thrown off the stage and off the tour at once when one of the band members flings an iron bar into the booing crowd, almost injuring someone.

It is Bono's 33rd birthday, the show is loose and has several surprises. Edge does a splendid solo version of *Party Girl*, and sings a quick birthday song. During *Trying To Throw Your Arms*, two girls from the Dutch fan club enter the stage dressed up as a gigantic champagne bottle and birthday cake. Their appearance takes Bono by surprise and he reels off to the mini-stage while the cake collapses in the distance. Bono seeks a female companion to share a glass of the real thing and brings a pretty blonde girl on to the catwalk. After a sip of champagne, he tackles her and finishes the song sitting on top of her while she lies on her back laughing her brains out. The party continues on the mini-stage with Bono ad-libbing in *My Girl,* "You're my kind of crowd, so fucking loud." When he announces, "This is for the Paradiso", and Edge starts strumming the opening chords of *I Will Follow*, the stadium goes mad. They haven't performed the song since the LoveTown tour and tonight's version sounds semi-improvised but great.

"I'll sing you a song," MacPhisto announces after *Desire*: "Try a taste of Martini, the most beautiful drink in the world, it's the right one, it's the bright one, that's Martini!" The crowd cheer. "I love that one. Rock & roll is so wide, really, it's such a broad thing. Nobody really knows what it is," he says in the exaggerated slow, creepy voice. His phone call tonight goes out to the KLM Airline reservation office. "Tonight I'm going to call my travel agent, because I am very tired and need a break from all this," MacPhisto confesses. The audience boo. "Don't get me wrong; I love you. But I love myself as well." He dials the number, every button beeping loudly, blasted out into the stadium by a 1-million Watts sound system with 45,000 people listening in. "KLM reservations, there is one call ahead of you, please hold the line," a tape says, while the screens project MacPhisto's disappointed face. "Hello! Somebody pick up the phone," he shouts impatiently, but is put on hold and starts singing along to the waiting music. "Aah, they're playing my tune! Laladadaaadadaaa... Hello?" The crowd laugh. "I don't mind waiting, do you?" "Noooo!" scream the audience. "We've got all night, really, haven't we?" "Yeeess!" "We don't mind paying a £100,000 fine, now do we?" MacPhisto shouts, referring to the penalty for overrunning. "Anyway, off with the horns, I think I may have some more luck if they don't know who I am." As he takes off the horns, the call is immediately connected. A cheerful receptionist called Monique is very co-operative. "Hello, do you speak English?" "Yes sir, may I help you?" "Thank you very much, I am looking to leave Amsterdam tonight, and I'd like a flight out of Schiphol this evening. Is that at all possible?" "Where would you like to go to?" "Uhm, what flights have you left this evening?" "I don't think anything..." "Tomorrow morning then?" "Yeah, that would be better," Monique says relieved. "What have you got going, I don't really mind, as long as it's sunny." "Well, it's supposed to be sunny here, in Holland," Monique says, extracting a tremendous cheer from the crowd. MacPhisto is quick: "Well, that's what they said yesterday, and there was this terrible thunderstorm, and it ruined my hair!" "Oh really?", Monique laughs heartily. "Have you nowhere exotic, like Singapore?" "Of course! Let me see..." "You wouldn't be taking the mickey out of an old man, now would you?" MacPhisto asks suspiciously. "A mickey? I don't know what's a mickey." "Oh, it's a colloquialism." "It's a joke – no sir, no joke, I'm very serious! We have a flight tomorrow, at 15:05 to Singapore." "Well, thank you, I just might make it. You're a very nice lady, what is your name?" "My name is Monique." "I'd like to sing you a song, Monique." "Oh, that would be nice!" "If you just stay on the line, there's a good girl," MacPhisto says, while the music swells and he starts singing *Ultra Violet* through the telephone. Monique listens, not knowing what the hell is happening. (After the show, U2's management will phone her to explain and to present her with two VIP tickets for tomorrow night's show as a token of appreciation for her spontaneous participation.)

Tonight's show ends with another Elvis cover, *Are You Lonesome Tonight*, performed by U2 for the first time. Bono sings, "Will your heart feel the same, will you come back again..." "YES!!" the stadium shouts. "Then my dears, I'm not lonesome tonight," Bono concludes.

The MacPhisto act forces Bono to stretch his imagination to extremes and he obviously enjoys it immensely. "I don't know where this thing is taking me," he tells Gavin Martin of *New Musical Express* after the show. "What happened tonight you couldn't plan. It was exciting but scary at the same time."

■ Set third night: same as May 9, but *Wild Rover* replaces *Dirty Old Town*, with *Slow Dancing* and *I Still Haven't Found* instead of *When Love Comes To Town*.

The last Rotterdam show is rather peculiar. In *Zoo Station*, there is a technical failure as the screens suddenly start reeling off the texts for *The Fly*; then someone pulls the plug and the screens go blank. In *The Fly*, Bono embarrassingly shouts "Achtung y'all!" far too early and gets lost in some unintelligible rap. Word has it that the band are hung over from a wild birthday party at the Dutch seashore the night before. Although they mess up quite a few other songs as well, it doesn't seem to matter, for tonight U2 display a new sensitivity undetectable on previous shows.

During *New Year's Day* Bono disappears into the First Aid pit at the side of the stage and the cameraman has trouble locating him. Larry comes forward to do *Wild Rover*, with the crowd nicely filling in hand claps. Bono cheerfully strolls along the catwalk with a girl during *Trying To Throw Your Arms*, while he rambles, "Don't worry about a thing, every little thing is gonna be all right, little off-key tonight, that's all right, there's no tomorrow night..." The acoustic set is superb, with a moving version of *Slow Dancing* and an extended *I Still Haven't Found*.

Queen Beatrix is MacPhisto's next victim. "Shall we give her a call to find out whether she is into rock & roll or not?" The receptionist does not appreciate the joke and hangs up. "Well now!" MacPhisto blurts out: "The last time royalty hung up on me I sent the House of Windsor up in flames!"

Bono leaves out his waltz routine with a girl during *Love Is Blindness*. He's too busy trying to handle a lighter somebody has thrown on stage. It doesn't work properly, the flame only flickers for a couple of seconds. All of a sudden, thousands of people imitate his attempts with their lighters, producing a breathtaking sight: lighters switching on and off in the stadium for the rest of the song.

MAY 15, 1993. LISBON, PORTUGAL, ESTADIO JOSE ALVALADE

- Attendance: 63,500; sellout
- Support: Utah Saints
- Set: same as May 9.

After a festival appearance in 1982, this is only U2's second show in Portugal. The girl that gets on stage for *Trying To Throw Your Arms* is called Maria, and when she tells Bono it's her birthday, he sings *Happy Birthday* for her with the crowd. The show is regarded as an historic event by the Portuguese press. Throughout the month of May, U2 will continue to work on the final stages of mixing their new album, flying in just hours before the gig, and going back to Dublin straight afterwards.

MAY 19, 1993. OVIEDO, SPAIN, ESTADIO CARLOS TARTIER

- Attendance: ca. 30,000
- Support: Utah Saints, The Ramones

With just two shows in Spain, Barcelona is left out this year because in 1992, the second night did not sell out. Twenty minutes into their supporting show, The Ramones have to quit after blowing up their amplifiers in the rain.

MAY 22, 1993. MADRID, SPAIN, ESTADIO VICENTE CALDERON

- Attendance: 60,000; sellout
- Support: Utah Saints, The Ramones
- Set: same as May 9, with *Wild Rover* instead of *Dirty Old Town*.

The enthusiastic crowd laugh when MacPhisto complains that the Ritz Hotel in town has "a problem with rock stars", and picks up the phone. He explains to the Ritz manager that he wants to stay at his hotel but has heard they have a problem with the dress code. "You will need a tie and jacket," states the hotel manager. "But I've got a very special jacket, and I have some horns. Will that be a problem?" When told it's no problem, MacPhisto spews, "So you'll have MacPhisto, but you won't have the group U2; that's fine, thank you!"

MAY 26, 1993. NANTES, FRANCE, STADE DE LA BEAUJOIRE

- Attendance: ca. 30,000; (near-sellout)
- Support: Urban Dance Squad, Utah Saints
- Set: same as May 9.

A shiny hawkmoon going down over the small stadium illuminates the clear blue sky. Bono finds the Champions League Euro Cup soccer final between Olympique Marseille and AC Milan on the screens and announces that the French team are leading 1-0. Instead of Morleigh Steinberg, a substitute belly dancer performs during *Mysterious Ways*. MacPhisto phones a taxi to take him home. Asked which stadium exit he has to be picked up from, MacPhisto confuses the operator by saying that it doesn't matter, since he is "everywhere."

MAY 29, 1993. WERCHTER, BELGIUM, FESTIVAL GROUNDS

- Attendance: 73,000; (capacity: 75,000)
- Support: Stereo MC's, Urban Dance Squad
- Set: same as May 9, with *Party Girl* instead of *Dirty Old Town*.

A second show is announced for May 30, moved to May 31, then cancelled altogether because of a parade through the area on that date. With 10,000 tickets already sold, fans are given refunds or can attend the show on the 29th. With 73,000 inside, the field is chock-full. It's the same site where U2 performed three times (1982, 1983 and 1985) at the annual Werchter Festival. After being introduced by Bono as Bob Dylan, Edge comes forward to sing *Party Girl*, and pronounces his thanks to "everybody who was here in 1982". As they are still hard at work mixing their new album in Dublin, the band seem somewhat absent-minded. Lack of adequate parking facilities leads to chaotic scenes after the show, with traffic being jammed in the village for four hours after the show has ended.

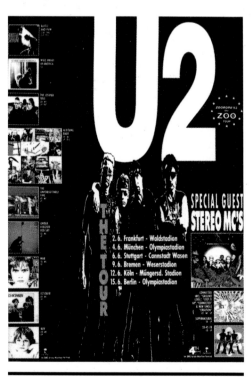

JUNE 2, 1993. FRANKFURT, GERMANY, WALDSTADION

- Attendance: 50,000; (capacity: 54,000)
- Support: Stereo MC's, Die Toten Hosen
- Set: same as May 9, with *Sunday Bloody Sunday* instead of *Bad – All I Want Is You*.

The German dates take place in the wake of another racist incident. Three days earlier, on May 29, a right-wing extremist

had thrown a fire-bomb into the house of the Turkish family Genc in the city of Solingen, killing two women and three young children. It is the umpteenth racist attack in Germany in the last two years. At several earlier assaults, residents had come out on the street to watch houses owned by foreigners burn down, clapped in approval, ignoring the screams of those trapped inside. The Solingen incident triggers a shock-wave through Germany and the rest of Europe, leading to a series of demonstrations and candle-marches in many cities that attract hundreds of thousands of people. "Achtung Helmut Kohl!" Bono screams in *The Fly*, referring to Chancellor Kohl's claim that the Solingen attack was a one-off incident unrelated to increasing racism in his country. The crowd applaud emotionally when Bono dedicates *One* to the murdered women and children of the Genc family. "Broken bottles under Turkish feet," he sings in *Sunday Bloody Sunday*, and runs towards the crowd in the stands screaming, "Stoppt den Hass! Stoppt den Hass! Sing: no more!" When the burning crosses in *Bullet The Blue Sky* turn into swastikas, and Bono stresses, "We must never let it happen again," it sends an impressively tangible shiver of fear and realisation throughout the entire crowd.

JUNE 4, 1993. MUNICH, GERMANY, OLYMPIASTADION

- Attendance: 56,000; sellout
- Support: Stereo MC's, Die Toten Hosen
- Set: same as May 9, plus *Redemption Song* after *Satellite Of Love*, *I Will Follow* instead of *When Love Comes To Town*, and *Sunday Bloody Sunday* replaces *Bad – All I Want Is You*.

The audience are generally aggressive, pushing heavily and booing the Macnass performance. The section of their act which features Bono and Edge caricatures climbing out of smoke-filled containers now includes Larry and Adam caricatures as well. Larry holds giant drum sticks, while the Adam caricature has a huge cigarette. At the German shows, those in the blocked-off sections next to the catwalk cannot get wristbands and are therefore unable to go to the toilet or buy food with the assurance they will be let back in.

One is again dedicated to the Genc family, and Bono urges the crowd to attend the anti-racism demonstration the next day at the Marienplatz. He sings *Redemption Song* on the mini-stage for the first time in Europe. MacPhisto phones Chancellor Helmut Kohl, who is out of the office, but leaves a message: "I'm back!"

JUNE 6, 1993. STUTTGART, GERMANY, CANNSTATTER WASEN

- Attendance: 53,800; (capacity: 55,000)
- Support: Stereo MC's, Die Toten Hosen
- Set: same as May 9, with *Party Girl* instead of *Dirty Old Town*.

Hundreds of policemen are present because Guns n'Roses incited crowd riots on this site, but there are no disturbances during U2's show. The show is inspired. *Party Girl* is performed on the mini-stage, with Edge singing and Adam and Larry playing while sitting on the monitors.

JUNE 9, 1993. BREMEN, GERMANY, WESERSTADION

- Attendance: 45,000; sellout
- Support: Stereo MC's, Die Toten Hosen
- Set: same as May 9, plus *Redemption Song* after *Satellite Of Love*, and *Sunday Bloody Sunday* instead of *Bad – All I Want Is You*.

With the show a near-sellout, a second Bremen date is announced for June 10, then cancelled as sales stagnate at 12,000. With a few thousand seats remaining for the 9th, tickets for the 10th are made valid for the 9th or are refunded. In the end, more people attend than stadium capacity allows, leading to

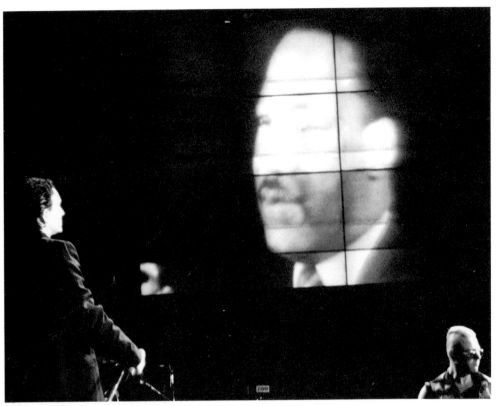

Martin Luther King: We'll get to the Promised Land

The Wild Rover

Estadio Vicente Calderon, Madrid

irritation as the field and many sections in the stands are over-crowded. The fans are grateful to U2 for coming to their town for the first time, and are immensely enthusiastic throughout the show. Bono congratulates local soccer team Werder Bremen, which has just become champions of the German Bundesliga. MacPhisto phones a taxi to take him to Chancellor Helmut Kohl. "I've got to go and see him now. He needs me, I put him to sleep at night." The taxi-operator reacts shocked: "But that is very far away, that's in Bonn, it's about 600 kilometres from here! It's very expensive, and takes a long time!" "I don't mind travelling that far, he needs to see me and I'd like to thank him for letting me back into the country..."

JUNE 12, 1993. COLOGNE, GERMANY, MÜNGERSDORFERSTADION

- Attendance: 62,000; sellout
- Support: Stereo MC's, Die Toten Hosen
- Set: same as May 9, plus *Redemption Song* after *Satellite Of Love*, and *Sunday Bloody Sunday* instead of *Bad – All I Want Is You*.

During the soundcheck, U2 surprise the queuing crowd at the entrance gates by playing full versions of *I Will Follow* and *11 O'Clock Tick Tock*, which hasn't been played since the LoveTown tour. Though it leads to speculation, U2 don't play them during the show. *One* is dedicated to "the still divided Germany", and prompts thousands of people to bring out their lighters, as do all the slow songs. Bono dedicates *Satellite Of Love* to his childhood mate Guggi and his new bride Sylvia.

JUNE 15, 1993. BERLIN, GERMANY, OLYMPIASTADION

- Attendance: ca. 40,000; (capacity: 76,000)
- Support: Stereo MC's, Die Toten Hosen
- Set: same as May 9.

With plans for shows in 1985 and 1992 not materialising, this is U2's first Berlin concert since November 1981. In the former capital of Adolf Hitler's Third Reich, the opening footage of the drummer boy, recorded in this very stadium in 1936, lends the show a sinister atmosphere. As Bono noted weeks before in an interview, that boy may well be alive still and could even be in the audience. Though the show is far from sold out, with the

second ring completely empty, it's the first chance for people from the East side of Berlin, and from former East Germany, to see U2.

JUNE 23, 1993. STRASBOURG, FRANCE, STADE DE LA MEINAU

- Attendance: 33,000; sellout
- Support: Stereo MC's, The Velvet Underground
- Set: same as May 9, plus *I Still Haven't Found – Stand By Me*

after *Pride*.

After having opened solo for U2 several times in 1987, Lou Reed plays in support as a member of the reunited Velvet Underground for five Zooropa shows. Larry commences *Sunday Bloody Sunday* just after Bono has picked up a guitar intending to play *Redemption Song*, leaving him dumbfounded and forced to put down the guitar again. As several European politicians are holding a summit in Strasbourg, MacPhisto phones the hotel where they are staying and asks for Jean Marie Le Pen, leader of the French extremist Front National party. He is not available, and neither is Helmut Kohl.

JUNE 26, 1993. PARIS, FRANCE, HIPPODROME DE VINCENNES

- Attendance: 75,000; sellout
- Support: Belly, The Velvet Underground
- Set: same as May 9, with *Wild Rover* instead of *Dirty Old Town*.

Since the Parc des Princes stadium is not available, the inferior Hippodrome is booked. Initial plans to limit the capacity to 40,000 and play two nights fail to materialise. As a result, the field is over-crowded with heavy pushing at the front and hundreds of people fainting in the heat. Bono dedicates *Satellite Of Love* to Ellen Darst, one of the key people in U2's management team, as she has quit working for U2 after ten years.

JUNE 28, 1993. LAUSANNE, SWITZERLAND, STADE DE LA PONTAISE

- Attendance: 45,000
- Support: The Velvet Underground

MacPhisto phones Benedict Hentsch, who is believed to have been Adolf Hitler's personal banker, but he doesn't get him on the phone. The following day, Hentsch hears about the call and tries to phone Bono in the hotel to offer him his financial advice.

JUNE 30, 1993. BASEL, SWITZERLAND, ST. JAKOB'S STADION

- Attendance: 50,000
- Support: The Velvet Underground
- Set: same as May 9, with *Sunday Bloody Sunday* instead of *Bad – All I Want Is You*.

As it rains throughout the show, Bono includes lines of *Rain* after *Angel Of Harlem*.

JULY 2, 3, 1993. VERONA, ITALY, STADIO BENTEGODI

- Attendance: 90,000; sellout
- Support: An Emotional Fish, Pearl Jam
- Set first night: same as May 9, plus *My Girl* linked to *Angel Of Harlem*, and plus *I Still Haven't Found – Stand By Me* after *Pride*.

This is the first of eight shows in Italy, where U2 are immensely popular. The hot-blooded Italians are highly enthusiastic, chanting Bono's name and greeting his attempts to speak Italian with fervour. A new pre-recorded video to accompany *One* is premièred. It shows blood cells rushing through veins in microscopic close-up and will alternate with the sunflower/buffalo video for the rest of the tour.

The crowd are quiet during MacPhisto's "Look what you've done to me" act, not participating in the question/answer game and failing to understand Bono's role-playing. He phones Irish group Clannad, who are celebrating their 20th anniversary back home in Dublin. On the phone he gets singer Maire Ni Bhraonain, with whom Bono had recorded the 'In A Lifetime' duet in early 1986. Maire immediately recognises her old mate, and laughs as she hears a 45,000-strong choir sing *Happy Birthday* to her by phone.

- Set second night: *Zoo Station / The Fly / Even Better Than The Real Thing / Mysterious Ways / One - Unchained Melody / Until The End Of The World / New Year's Day / Satellite Of Love / I Still Haven't Found / I Will Follow / Redemption Song / Sunday Bloody Sunday / Bullet The Blue Sky / Running To Stand Still / Where The Streets Have No Name / Pride / encore: Desire / Ultra Violet / With Or Without You / Love Is Blindness / Can't Help Falling In Love*

In the afternoon, Bono is interviewed by an American film maker called Bill Carter, who works in a relief camp in Sarajevo, the Bosnian city in former Yugoslavia which is besieged by the Serbs in the war between the Serbs, Croats and Muslims. After *Mysterious Ways*, Bono tells the crowd that the people of Sarajevo built a dance club under the ground where, three nights a week, they play rock & roll and dance music as loudly as possible to drown out the sound of bombs and shells in an attempt to forget about the war.

After *New Year's Day*, Bono goes to the mini-stage to start *Satellite Of Love*, omitting *Trying To Throw Your Arms* and *Angel Of Harlem*. It seems the ritual of inviting a girl on stage and spraying champagne has run its course. Since it's the anniversary of Jim Morrison's death, Bono adds lines of The Doors' *The End* to *Running To Stand Still*. During the encore, the crowd are again quiet in MacPhisto's act, as he rambles on about show business being a great idea and even the Pope doing a world tour. He picks up the phone: "Let's see if we can wake the good fellow up." While dialling the Vatican number, he sings a line of Stevie Wonder's *I Just Called To Say I Love You* and Blondie's *Hanging On The Telephone*. There is no connection. "All I was going to ask him was, would he need some Zoo TV equipment when we've finished with our world tour, for his next."

After the show, Bill Carter tells Bono and Edge more about the atrocities occurring in their city, and leave them with a feeling that they have to do something.

JULY 5, 1993.

U2's 'Zooropa' album is released worldwide.

JULY 6, 7, 1993. ROME, ITALY, STADIO FLAMINIO

- Attendance: 84,000; (capacity: 70,000)
- Support: An Emotional Fish, Pearl Jam
- Set first night: same as May 9, minus *Trying To Throw Your Arms*, and *Van Diemen's Land* instead of *Dirty Old Town*.

Edge sings *Van Diemen's Land* in concert for the only time in 1993. The stadium is overcrowded, leading to suspicions within U2's management that the promoter has offered extra tickets for sale above the agreed limit. The promoter claims to have issued 35,000 per show, as agreed, but Paul McGuinness instructs crew members to manually count all the torn-off ticket strips collected at stadium entrances, and finds that 42,000 attended the first night. It appears that the promoter has illegally sold a combined 14,000 tickets too many.

- Set second night: same as July 3, with *She's A Mystery To Me* instead of *Unchained Melody*, plus *Numb* after *New Year's Day*, minus *Can't Help Falling In Love*.

During *Even Better Than The Real Thing*, the winner of an MTV contest briefly operates one of the Zoo TV cameras onstage. With the 'Zooropa' album just in the shops, *Numb* is premièred tonight with Edge performing it alone, reading the text from a stand, while the screens display images of factory workers enduring the monotony of their jobs.

JULY 9, 1993. NAPLES, ITALY, STADIO SAN PAULO

- Attendance: 70,000
- Support: The Velvet Underground
- Set: *Zoo Station / The Fly / Even Better Than The Real Thing / Mysterious Ways / One – Unchained Melody / Until The End Of The World / New Year's Day / Numb / Satellite Of Love / Angel Of Harlem / When Love Comes To Town / Redemption Song / Sunday Bloody Sunday / Bullet The Blue Sky / Running To Stand Still / Where The Streets Have No Name / Pride / encore: Desire / Ultra Violet / With Or Without You / Love Is Blindness / Can't Help Falling In Love*

While constructing the stage at San Paulo, U2's crew find that their local storage depot has been broken into and a fork-lift truck stolen. Bono sings lines of *Daddy's Gonna Pay For Your Crashed Car* in *When Love Comes To Town*, and bits of *Lemon* are included in *Desire*.

JULY 12, 1993. TURIN, ITALY, STADIO DELLE ALPI

- Attendance: 60,000
- Support: An Emotional Fish, Ligabue
- Set: same as Naples, minus *Sunday Bloody Sunday* and *Can't Help Falling In Love*, plus *I Still Haven't Found – Stand By Me* after *Pride*.

Hundreds of stallholders do great business selling illegal U2 T-shirts outside the stadium, as there are no official merchandise stands either outside or inside. (The next day, newspapers reveal that the stadium manager demanded 40% of all profits from U2's merchandise sales which Paul McGuinness rejected.) MacPhisto points out the Trabant cars and claims they used to have many more, but those three are the last ones in existence. "Do you think if I called Mr. Agnelli, he would help me? I just wanted to know if we could have some Fiat Bambinis for our stage..." The cheerful crowd embark on a rapturous round of swear words. When he calls the Fiat office, the receptionist hangs up hastily when Bono sings, "I just called to say I love you; I just called to say how much I care..."

JULY 14, 1993. MARSEILLE, FRANCE, STADE VELODROME

- Attendance: 55,000; sellout
- Support: An Emotional Fish
- Set: same as Naples, minus *Sunday Bloody Sunday*, plus *My Girl* linked to *Angel Of Harlem*.

July 14 is a holiday in France, as on this day in 1789 the Bastille was stormed, and triggered the beginning of the French Revolution. Bono zaps to the military parade on the Champs Elysées. "Liberté, Egalité, Fraternité; but not in Sarajevo, not in Bosnia-Herzegovina," he says, and phones Bill Carter, the American film maker whom he had met in Verona, live in Sarajevo. Bono invites Bill to tell him and the crowd about conditions in the besieged city. "Well, the situation is desperate, without the basics of water, food, electricity," says Bill. Bono asks, "How do the people of Sarajevo feel about Europe? Do you feel we have let you down?" Bill says that the people feel that Sarajevo's problems concern the rest of Europe as well. Bono concludes, "Bill, we are ashamed tonight to be Europeans and turn our back to you and your people. We wish you well, and we will call again."

The conversation confuses and annoys the crowd somewhat, as Bono speaks of "you and your people" while the person in question is an American, and not an inhabitant of Sarajevo struggling to survive.

In the encore, MacPhisto holds a replica of the Euro Cup that soccer team Olympique Marseille had won on the night of the Nantes concert, touching local pride as the crowd embark on a tribal bellowing of the "Olé, olé, olé", chant. MacPhisto phones Bernard Tapie, president of Olympique Marseille, but the call remains unanswered.

With the 'Zooropa' album at Number 1 in the charts, U2's four shows in France ignite such public interest that sales of their back catalogue rise impressively, to the extent that 'War' becomes the fifth best-selling album in the country, albeit ten years after its release.

JULY 17, 18, 1993. BOLOGNA, ITALY, STADIO COMUNALE

- Attendance: 64,000; sellout
- Support: An Emotional Fish, Galliano
- Set first night: same as Naples, plus *My Girl* linked to *Angel Of Harlem*, minus *Sunday Bloody Sunday*.

"We're about 500 kilometres here from a city very different to this city. We're gonna try and get through to the people of Sarajevo, using our high-tech shit." In order to do something in a more confrontational way than in Marseille, Bono sent a satellite dish to Sarajevo for direct reports on everyday life in the war-torn city on the rest of the tour. Bill Carter appears on the screens, explaining that just an hour ago, two bombs killed one child and injured five people. "People are eating grass; to get water you have to walk two to three hours. Today I went to the hospital and saw a friend of mine: while he was getting water, a grenade fell and hit him on the head. He has two daughters, who will now have to get their own water. Did you know that, if I get on a plane right now, I could be at your concert before it's over? I'm less than an hour away from Bologna." Bono comments, "We just wanted you to know that here in Bologna, at this moment, we're thinking about you and we pray that Europe will take the people of Sarajevo more seriously than they are doing right now. They're ignoring you, we are betraying you..."

Many in the crowd do not feel this section is appropriate to the rock & roll character of the show. Critics observe that while Zoo TV parodies information overload on TV, where live CNN reports of human atrocities merge with action-packed series like Miami Vice, U2 are now doing the same. Bono comments before *Redemption Song*, "There's something obscene about having pictures from across the water in Sarajevo, in a rock & roll concert. Something doesn't quite fit. This is a Bob Marley song that might say things a whole lot better..."

MacPhisto phones Luciano Pavarotti, who obviously expected the call as he asks how the show is going. "Well, the people of Bologna are splendid this evening! How's the maestro's voice, is it fine? I believe you're losing a lot of weight, but I love you just the way you are!" MacPhisto asks him to sing a song, but Pavarotti laughs and just wishes everyone health and happiness.

Girl linked to *Angel Of Harlem*.

Set second night: *Zoo Station / The Fly / Even Better Than The Real Thing / Mysterious Ways / One – She's A Mystery To Me / Until The End Of The World / New Year's Day / Numb / Angel Of Harlem – Dancing Queen / When Love Comes To Town / Satellite Of Love / Bad – All I Want Is You / Bullet The Blue Sky / Running To Stand Still / Where The Streets Have No Name / Pride / encore: Desire / Ultra Violet / With Or Without You / Love Is Blindness / Can't Help Falling In Love*

Bono expresses joy over the 'Zooropa' album being the best selling album in Italy. *Dancing Queen* is played for the first time since Vancouver, November 1992. At the beginning of *When Love Comes To Town*, Bono gives a screaming introduction as he had given B.B. King on the LoveTown tour: "Will you welcome, mayor of LoveTown, King of the Blues... only joking!"

The satellite link-up with Sarajevo now occurs after *Satellite Of Love*. "I suppose the thing with TV is that you don't know if what you see is real. You can't tell the difference any more between the adverts and CNN. You can't ask the TV questions. Well, this is Zoo TV and we're gonna try and ask the TV some questions." Bill Carter tells us that there has been little fighting in Sarajevo today, but 12 kilometres away, 15,000 refugees are being attacked by artillery and have nowhere to go. He says that his friend that had the piece of grenade in his head died this morning. Having decided with U2 to let the people of Bosnia speak for themselves, Bill introduces a local man called Darko. "Thanks to Bill, U2, and all you people, we don't feel so alone this night as we usually do the last few months," Darko says. He tells, "The hardest thing of the war for me personally is being separated from my family, my wife and kids. They live and they grow up somewhere abroad, without me, with no opportunity to contact them. Even more shocking is the fact that my parents live just four kilometres from this place, and I am not able to contact them for a year now..." It's the first time in 17 months of war, that a Bosnian speaks live to the outside world.

Rock star with a conscience one moment, Bono transforms

Oslo

into MacPhisto the devil again for the encore. He refers to Italy's former Fascist leader Benito Mussolini: "Do you think Il Duce would like a gold lamé suit like mine? I do miss him, do you?" "Nooo!!" scream the audience. "I believe he has a very nice granddaughter," he says, and phones Alessandra Mussolini, who has walked in her grandfather's footsteps to form the National Party. MacPhisto leaves a message on her answering machine: "I was a close friend of your grandfather; you're doing a wonderful job. I'll be leaving Italy tomorrow, but I will be with you forever in spirit..."

JULY 23, 1993. BUDAPEST, HUNGARY, NEP STADION

- Attendance: 60,000; sellout
- Set: same as July 18, with *Unchained Melody* instead of *She's*

A Mystery To Me, My Girl replacing *Dancing Queen*, and *Let It Be* instead of *All I Want Is You*.

A late addition to the tour, the Budapest date is not printed on the official tour T-shirts or in the programme booklet. With plans to stage shows in Poland and Prague not coming through,

Satellite link-up with Sarajevo

this is the first and only time U2 perform in a former Eastern Bloc country. Bono welcomes the crowd in Hungarian, but when he talks about Sarajevo, his words are, sentence by sentence, translated by an interpreter on stage. Bill Carter says that 3,000 grenades were fired on the city in the last few days. A guy from a local band says he hasn't slept for two weeks, and that three of his friends were killed recently by one bomb. Bill plays a pre-recorded video showing images of Sarajevo, accompanied by the sound of a small child singing The Beatles' song *Let It Be*. The crowd softly clap and whisper the words. Bono includes lines of the song at the end of *Bad*, ending with, "There must be an answer, don't let it be..."

JULY 27, 1993. COPENHAGEN, DENMARK, GENTOFTE STADION

- Attendance: 32,000; sellout
- Support: P.J. Harvey, Stereo MC's
- Set: same as July 18, with *Unchained Melody* instead of *She's A Mystery To Me, Dear Prudence* replacing *Dancing Queen*, and *Let It Be* instead of *All I Want Is You*.

Originally planned for August 2, the show is U2's first in Denmark since 1982 and is highly anticipated. Huge ticket demand results in black market prices around five times face value. With 'Zooropa' the biggest selling album in the world since its release three weeks ago, U2 are starting to incorporate more new material in the set. The first verse of *Daddy's Gonna Pay For Your Crashed Car* is included at the end of *When Love Comes To Town*. A bit of The Beatles' *Dear Prudence* is sung after *Angel Of Harlem* for the only time this year.

JULY 29, 1993. OSLO, NORWAY, VALLE HOVIN STADION

- Attendance: 35,000; sellout
- Support: P.J. Harvey, Stereo MC's
- Set: same as July 18, with *Unchained Melody* replacing *She's A*

Mystery To Me, Norwegian Wood instead of *Dancing Queen*, plus *I Will Follow* after *When Love Comes To Town*, *Let It Be* instead of *All I Want Is You*, and minus *Can't Help Falling In Love*.

During the soundcheck new songs off the 'Zooropa' album are rehearsed, including *Babyface, Stay* and *Daddy's Gonna Pay For Your Crashed Car*, but none are played that night. In the encore, MacPhisto inquires about the controversy concerning Norway's whale hunts, which are forbidden by the European Union. "What have the whales ever done for us, eh? They're unemployed, they don't pay taxes, and they take up a lot of room, don't you think?" He phones Jan Henri Olsen, the Minister of Fishery. Olsen explains that as long as there are large quantities of whales, he feels there's no harm in catching them to supply food. "I'm sure that if you catch them, you'll eat them all yourself; you like to munch on a whale-steak, don't you mister Olsen?" Olsen: "I take a bit, yes, I'm gonna have one tomorrow; you wanna come and have dinner with me?" "Mister Olsen: I think you and I will get on just fine!"

Love Is Blindness, performed in an exceptional, mainly spoken version with Bono including two verses of *All Along The Watchtower*, ends the show.

JULY 31, 1993. STOCKHOLM, SWEDEN, STOCKHOLMS STADION

- Attendance: 33,410 (P); sellout
- Support: P.J. Harvey, Stereo MC's
- Set: same as July 18, with *Unchained Melody* instead of *She's A Mystery To Me*, plus *Stay* after *New Year's Day*, and *Rain* instead of *Dancing Queen*.

The crowd includes 4,000 from Finland, where Stockholm tickets were sold with boat trips. Having been extensively rehearsed earlier in the day, *Stay*, from the 'Zooropa' album, is premièred, with Bono starting out acoustically and Edge on background vocals. Bono briefly goes into *Daddy's Gonna Pay For Your Crashed Car* during *When Love Comes To Town*. During the satellite link-up, a Sarajevo fireman sends his love to his girlfriend Tanya who is in the crowd tonight, and tells her he is all right, and so is her family. Shortly before the Martin Luther King speech in *Pride*, Bono remarks to the crowd that they know what it means to have a great man killed by an assassin's bullet, referring to their former Prime Minister, the late Olof Palme.

While the cannons shoot out Zooropa Ecus during *Desire*, Bono sings lines of Abba's *Money, Money, Money*. MacPhisto tries to call Ian Wachtmeister, leader of the racist New Democratic Party. Although he fails to get through to Wachtmeister, the woman taking the call babbles on and even sings along with *I Just Called To Say I Love You*.

AUGUST 3, 1993. NIJMEGEN, HOLLAND, GOFFERT PARK

- Attendance: 54,844 (P); (capacity: 60,000)
- Support: P.J. Harvey, Stereo MC's
- Set: same as July 18, with *Unchained Melody* instead of *She's A Mystery To Me*, plus *Stay* after *New Year's Day*, minus *Dancing Queen*, and *I Will Follow* instead of *When Love Comes To Town*.

A fourth date in Holland is announced shortly after the Rotterdam shows and, after extensive advertising, the field comes close to selling out. Bono announces that *Stay* is being played for the second time only, and apologises in case they fuck up. MacPhisto remarks, "Call me old-fashioned, but I miss the good old days: the Third Reich." MacPhisto says he has a friend here and phones Hans Janmaat, leader of the right-extremist party Centre Democrats. He reads the phone number out loud; his "I just called to say I love you" message is immediately hung up on.

AUGUST 7, 8, 1993. GLASGOW, SCOTLAND, CELTIC PARK

- Attendance: 70,000; sellout
- Support (first night): Utah Saints, P.J. Harvey; (second night:) Utah Saints, Stereo MC's
- Set first night: same as July 18, with *Unchained Melody* instead of *She's A Mystery To Me*, plus *Stay* after *New Year's Day*, minus *Dancing Queen*, and *I Will Follow* instead of *When Love Comes To Town*.

The Glasgow crowd are receptive to the satellite connection with Sarajevo. Bill Carter says that after 17 months of war, people are expecting Europe to act instead of just talk. A local woman says, "We are not afraid of dying – we are afraid of what will happen after this, how to live with this experience. The Europeans decided 50 years ago that Fascism and genocide won't happen again, but it is here, as you can see..."

"Did you know that MacBeth – the man, not the play – died 400 years ago this evening?" MacPhisto asks. "I know another great actor: Ian Lang, Her Majesty's Secretary for Scotland." The crowd boo. "I thought he was such a fine man! He has everybody thinking he's Scottish, but he's not, he's a Tory, like me." When he calls, Lang is not there. "My name is Mister MacPhisto, and I am a personal friend, a fellow thespian, and he knows exactly who I am and I am surprised he hasn't told you I was going to call! I just like to say that he's doing a jolly good job up north, and these Scots are a rowdy bunch. I just like to tell him: out, out, damned Scot!"

- Set second night: *Zoo Station / The Fly / Even Better Than The Real Thing / Mysterious Ways / One – Unchained Melody / Until The End Of The World / New Year's Day / Numb / Zooropa / Stay / Angel Of Harlem – Rain / When Love Comes To Town / Satellite Of Love / Bad – The First Time / Bullet The Blue Sky / Running To Stand Still / Where The Streets Have No Name / Pride / encore: Desire / Ultra Violet / Love Is Blindness / Can't Help Falling In Love*

The show is excellent, with great crowd participation and several surprises in the set list. *Zooropa* is played for the first time, performed without the opening piano sequence on the album version. Bono skips the first three verses, starting the song with, "And I have no compass, and I have no map..." He wears a blue military jacket that he casts off after the song. The version is shaky and needs more rehearsal. Bono confesses, "Well, it's one thing writing a few songs while you're on the road, and putting them on record – now we gotta try and play the fuckin' things!" After *Stay* Bono and the crowd sing *Happy Birthday* for Edge's 33rd birthday. After singing part of *Rain*, Bono boasts, "Special surprise – Edge is gonna sing *Lost Highway*!" Edge looks at Bono completely bewildered. Bono, Adam and Larry sit down on the monitors and giggle while they watch Edge panic. Edge can hardly remember the chords, but manages to play and

sing one verse of the Hank Williams song. Instead of a brief snatch of *All I Want Is You*, Bono sings part of *The First Time* at the end of *Bad* before *Bullet The Blue Sky* crashes in.

Before the Sarajevo satellite link-up, Bono tells the crowd, "Somebody from Sarajevo came to see us a few weeks ago, and asked us to come and play. He called back later and said, 'Don't come, because things have gotten too bad for you to come and play; not that I'm worried about your safety, but the people who wanna come to the concert might be picked off by the snipers...'."

There are several obscene and politically tinted confessions. An American fan says: "You Scots are great people, but I can't understand a word you're saying!" MacPhisto claims Lady Diana, and his friend John Major, are into showbusiness, and calls the latter "an exciting fellow, he ran away from the circus to become an accountant." He phones him at No. 10 Downing Street, but he is not in. "John Major is not available?! My name is MacPhisto, and I'm calling from the top of the country – he may have heard of it, it's called Scotland." The crowd boo when he finishes the call by saying Major is doing a marvellous job for the people of Scotland.

The shows receive mixed reviews in the UK press. Because of the Sarajevo satellite link-up, many reviewers suggest that U2 are still the same old rockers with a conscience as in the mid-Eighties, though this tour was partly about shedding their over-serious and over-conscious image.

AUGUST 11, 12, 1993. LONDON, ENGLAND, WEMBLEY STADIUM

- Attendance: 144,000; sellout
- Support: P.J. Harvey, Big Audio Dynamite II
- Set first night: same as August 8, plus *Babyface* after *Zooropa*, minus *Angel Of Harlem – Rain* and *When Love Comes To Town*.

The first of four Wembley shows is tight but has its moments. *Zooropa* sounds better than in Glasgow, complete with the buzzing sound, but still proves instrumentally difficult to perform live. *Babyface*, a song about practising obsessive love for a celebrity on TV by manipulating the image with a machine, is premièred tonight. Bono doesn't know whether to sing it in a low or high-pitched voice, and spends the whole song trying to make up his mind. Halfway through Bono picks a girl from the crowd to operate the handycam. While she dances on the catwalk, Bono slowly drops to the floor, motions the girl to move closer, and she ends up sitting on top of him before the song is over. "That's Linda, she's from Argentina."

The band move to the mini-stage for *Stay* and *Satellite Of Love*, after which the link-up to Sarajevo is made. Bill Carter introduces three women, one Muslim, one Croat and one half-Serb, half-Croat. They have been friends for 25 years and they want to live together in peace instead of in a country split into

three different nations.

"What's all the fuss – Salman Rushdie can't be English, can he?" MacPhisto asks, referring to Rushdie's attempt to have the British government take him into protection. Since January 1989, when the Ayatollah Khomeini issued a *fatwah* on Rushdie for offending Islamic fundamentalists in his book *The Satanic Verses*, he has been living in hiding. "Shall I give him a telephone call?" When someone picks up, the words "Yes, this is Salman Rushdie speaking," sound too clear for a phone link. With his macabre humour, MacPhisto says heartily, "Salman, it's been a long time! Tell me, how miserable are you these days? Do you get out and about much?" "Oh yes, now and again. I have to be careful, of course. I have even more trouble with the critics than you do," Salman answers. "Maybe not. Well, I don't want to make you too jealous because we're having an absolutely fabulous evening here at Wembley Stadium." While the crowd cheer, Salman says, "Yes, I know that, because I'm here too!" "I beg your pardon?" "I'm much closer to you than you could ever imagine. In fact, I can see you now: you're wearing a ridiculous gold suit, and you're standing in front of the loudest people I've ever heard in my life." MacPhisto challenges him: "I don't believe you're here. Come out if you're not afraid!"

Arms outstretched, it is indeed Salman Rushdie who comes walking on stage from the wings. While he goes over to hug Bono, Salman's face is enlarged on the screens, and the crowd produce a tremendous cheer as they realise his appearance is an historic occasion. It is almost unbelievable that for almost five years this man, embracing Bono in front of 72,000 people, has been unable to simply walk down the street for fear of being killed by Muslim extremists.

"I think you might need these, Salman," says MacPhisto, and puts his red devil horns on Salman's head. "I'm not afraid of you; real devils don't wear horns," Salman says. The next day newspapers all over the world print photos of their embrace, and in many countries it makes the TV news. In an interview with *The Irish Times*, Salman will later say: "I owe U2 a debt of gratitude for the gesture of solidarity and friendship they made by inviting me to join them on stage at Wembley Stadium. Not many novelists ever experience what it's like to face an audience of over 70,000 people – and, fortunately for everyone, I didn't even have to sing."

- Set second night: same as August 8, with *She's A Mystery To Me* instead of *Unchained Melody*, plus *Babyface* after *Zooropa*, plus *I Will Follow* after *Stay*, minus *Angel Of Harlem – Rain* and *When Love Comes To Town*.

While zapping, Bono comes across a news bulletin reporting on the war in Bosnia and comments, "I think we've got a theme going, don't you? Sometimes it feels like 1933, not 1993." Bono misses the first verse of *One* as his microphone doesn't work and he has to wait for a new one. Edge's mumble-rap of *Numb* is hardly intelligible, but is well received by the crowd who

Linda from Argentina

Wembley Stadium, August 11, 1993

participate enthusiastically throughout the show. The girl who comes on stage for *Babyface* does her best to arouse Bono sexually, wiggling her body while sitting on his crotch and uninhibitedly licking his face, causing Bono to sing the wrong lines at the wrong moment. After the song she whispers something in Bono's ear. He mumbles, "You've come from Sicily all the way for me?" A powerful performance of *I Will Follow* drives the crowd crazy and has Bono jumping around and striking poses reminiscent of the days of the Marquee.

"Sarajevo is all over the news," Bono says. "It's supposed to be really complicated so mere mortals like us are not supposed to be able to understand what's going on over there. Systematic rape, the bombing of civilians... The truth is, it's just a bunch of Fascists trying to divide up a small country around ethnic lines. And this smoke screen of complexity is just an excuse for politicians to do nothing." While the crowd applaud, Bono hints at press criticism of the Glasgow shows: "Now, we're just a rock & roll band, and maybe we should shut the fuck up; on the other hand, maybe we shouldn't."

The screens show two young Sarajevo women who paint a clear picture of their situation: "Hello U2, hello Wembley. My name is Layla, and this is my sister Selma. Two years ago we were living like all teenagers: listening to music, going out, we had schools, friends, plans for the future. Now, we have shells, we have screams of children, our schools are burned down. We will never see many of our friends; they are gone forever. You have read in your history books about Fascism. The same one that destroyed your London, 50 years ago. And now, we are living that history again, here in Bosnia. Before the war, we didn't know who Major and Mitterand were. But now, our lives depend on them. I think they're trying to ease their conscience, sending us humanitarian aid. We are thankful for their food. But as long as there is war in Bosnia, they're only feeding the graveyards. I know that you can't exert influence on their decisions, but at least ask yourselves, who leads you. I hope you enjoy your concert tonight, but you should realise that your politicians are letting you, and us, down."

The crowd applaud with respect; Bono thanks the girls for taking the time to talk. *Bad* sets in, and has a guest appearance by violinist Jo Shankar, with whom Bono and Edge played at the anti-racism festival in Hamburg in January. Tonight's version of *Bullet The Blue Sky* is angrier than ever, as the song not only criticises American politically-motivated military intervention in El Salvador, but now also attacks America and the European Community for not intervening in Bosnia for humanitarian reasons. Bono screams highly aggressively, "Outside it's America... America... where the fuck are you?! United Kingdom: fuck you! Fuck you Germany! Fuck you France! Zoo-nited Nations, Zoo-nited Nations!"

AUGUST 14, 1993. LEEDS, ENGLAND, ROUNDHAY PARK

- Attendance: 80,000; sellout
- Support: Marxman, Stereo MC's
- Set: same as August 8, with *Babyface* instead of *Zooropa*, minus *Rain*, and *All I Want Is You* replaces *The First Time*.

Zooropa is dropped from the set, as is the Sarajevo link-up, which has generated enough attention to the issue. A second show on this bowl-shaped field on August 15 was announced, then cancelled shortly afterwards. Bono mentions that the site is so big that "it makes Wembley Stadium look like a bowling green." He dedicates *Satellite Of Love* to catering company Flying Saucers ("not the ones in the sky, but the ones that feed us"), whose twelve employees are travelling with the tour to prepare three meals for 400 people every day. Confessions include: "I had a shit on my neighbour's car," and a girl seductively revealing one of her breasts as she says, "I just wanted to get something off my chest..." MacPhisto refers to the Sellafield nuclear plant, which is less than 100 miles away, saying that the people of the North are generous for taking the nuclear waste of the world. He calls the home of the Minister of Environment, Mr. Gummer, but his wife tells him he's not in.

AUGUST 18, 1993. CARDIFF, WALES, ARMS PARK

- Attendance: 50,000; (capacity 53,000)
- Support: Utah Saints, Stereo MC's
- Set: same as August 8, with *Babyface* instead of *Zooropa*, *Stay* and *Angel Of Harlem* switch places, *Dancing Queen* replaces *Rain*, minus *When Love Comes To Town*.

MacPhisto claims Margaret Thatcher likes to go shopping in Wales and has sold the trains and coal mines of the UK to finance her hobby. When trying to reach her by phone, Thatcher's secretary advises him to write instead of call.

AUGUST 20, 21, 1993. LONDON, ENGLAND, WEMBLEY STADIUM

- Attendance: 114,000; (capacity 144,000)
- Support (first night): Utah Saints, Stereo MC's; (second night): Bjork, Stereo MC's.
- Set first show: same as August 8, with *Babyface* instead of *Zooropa*, *Stay* is played after *Angel Of Harlem*, minus *Rain* and *When Love Comes To Town*, plus *With Or Without You* after *Ultra Violet*.

These shows were added when the August 11 and 12 dates sold out instantly. As people want to attend the final UK show, tickets for August 21 sell out, but over 30,000 seats for August 20 remain unsold. Days before the show, U2 announce that unemployed people who do not have money to buy tickets will be admitted free if they have a UB40 card. Although a few thousand people take up on this offer, the stadium is little over half-full.

Wembley

MacPhisto's act in the encore: "Rock & roll: don't you love it. It's the new religion, I think. Some of my best friends are religious leaders: the Ayatollah, the Pope, even the Archbishop of Canterbury. I think he's fabulous. They're doing my job for me, aren't they? Putting all the children off God. I'm a little bit concerned about George Cary because he wants to let women into the church. Then again, you'll all just become Catholic, won't you?" MacPhisto gives the Archbishop a call and leaves his "I just called to say I love you" message.

- Set second show: Zoo Station / The Fly / Even Better Than The Real Thing / Mysterious Ways / One – Unchained Melody / Until The End Of The World / New Year's Day / Numb / Trying To Throw Your Arms Around The World / Angel Of Harlem – Dancing Queen / Stay / Satellite Of Love / Bad – The First Time / Bullet The Blue Sky / Running To Stand Still / Where The Streets Have No Name / Pride / encore: Desire / Ultra Violet / With Or Without You / Love Is Blindness / Can't Help Falling In Love

Trying To Throw Your Arms returns to the set for the first time since Verona. *Babyface* and *Zooropa* are out and will not be played for the rest of the year. U2 are the fourth act to play four

nights at Wembley Stadium on one tour; only Michael Jackson (7), Rolling Stones (5) and Genesis (4) have played more or as many shows. U2's last UK show of the year is one of their best. Though it rains, the atmosphere is excellent. Bono drops lines of *Singing In The Rain* here and there. He dedicates *One* to Joseph, a friend of the band who died of AIDS, and introduces *Stay* as "a song Wim Wenders stole from The Beatles; we're stealing it back."

For the encore, MacPhisto delves into Wembley's past: "What a theatre, Wembley Stadium! All the history of this place. Live Aid; the FA Cup; the 1966 World Cup when England won. They haven't been winning much lately, now have they?" MacPhisto asks, referring to the English soccer team's efforts to qualify for the 1994 World Cup in the United States. "What's happened to this noble country? Almost out of the World Cup. The Smiths have split up. There is only one man who can save us. Shall I give Graham Taylor a telephone call?" An immense cheer goes through the stadium, as MacPhisto phones the much criticised manager of the national team. The 72,000-strong Wembley crowd join MacPhisto singing into Taylor's answering machine, "Walk on with hope in your heart, and you'll never walk alone..."

The UK tour has a tremendous impact on U2's album sales. With 'Zooropa' at No. 2 in the *Music Week*/Gallup chart, 'Achtung Baby' jumps to 17, and three catalogue albums, 'The Joshua Tree', 'Rattle And Hum' and 'War', re-enter at Nos 27, 34 and 38 respectively.

AUGUST 24, 1993. CORK, IRELAND, PAIRC UI CHAOIMH

- Attendance: 39,000 (capacity: 40,000)
- Support: Engine Alley, Utah Saints
- Set: same as August 21, minus *Trying To Throw Your Arms* and *Dancing Queen*.

U2's return to the Irish concert stage is preceded by much hassle and controversy. Not wanting to be criticised again, as on the LoveTown tour, for not issuing enough tickets and prices being too high, in November 1992 U2 had announced a massive open-air show at Phoenix Park, which would be either free or low-priced. Planned as the final European show of the tour for August 28, around 100,000 people were expected. Since Dublin's cultural committee did not want to absorb part of the cost of organising such a mega-event, U2 decided to charge £10 per ticket just to cover expenses (installing toilets, catering, cleaning of the park, etc.). Having expected the show to be free, the majority of the public was offended, and critics attacked U2 for not paying the costs, an estimated £1.5 million, themselves. They stated that £10 is too much money for people to fork out, and that many among the poor and unemployed would be unable to attend the show.

A few months later, U2 announced that the Phoenix Park plan was off. Three Irish dates are organised instead. Deciding on a smaller venue than the 57,000-capacity Croke Park, two shows at the relatively small RDS Showgrounds are booked, and one in Cork. Tickets are regularly priced at £20 and £25, as in the UK. There are no more complaints.

Sales for Cork are initially slow, but pick up in the last few weeks and sell out but for a thousand. The Cork show is preceded by another controversy, when Cork County secretary Frank Murphy of the highly conservative Gaelic Athletics Association, who own the stadium, bans the sale of U2's 'Achtung Baby' condoms from their merchandise stands. U2 manager Paul McGuinness reacts by handing out handfuls of condoms for free to an eagerly accepting crowd. His action is criticised by the Lord Mayor of Cork, who is upset "because there were also 13-year olds in the audience".

Of course, Bono uses his MacPhisto character to take a sneer at Frank Murphy's decision. "Civilisation is crumbling, who can take it back from the brink? The GAA, that's who! We're their guests tonight, so there'll be no sale of condoms, no rubber Johnnies." The crowd laugh as he continues to ridicule Murphy: "We don't want the young people carried away on a sea of seed and desire, now do we? They'll be at it like rabbits, slaves to the devil's monument, delivered to the gates of hell in latex jackets! Contraception, safe sex, AIDS: it's not their problem. No homo's, junkies or Haitians here tonight; just castrated, abstemious, happy families! Fine and dandy, not a willie in sight. And we got the GAA to thank for that." MacPhisto delivers a brief rendition of an old Eurovision Song Contest entry, Dana's *All Kinds Of Everything*, when he calls Frank Murphy but nobody picks up. Murphy is in the stadium watching the show.

AUGUST 27, 28, 1993. DUBLIN, IRELAND, ROYAL DUBLIN SOCIETY SHOWGROUNDS

■ Attendance: 72,000 (P); sellout
■ Support first night: Marxman, The Golden Horde; (second night): Scary Eire, Stereo MC's
■ Set (first night): same as August 21, with *Dirty Old Town* instead of *Dancing Queen*, plus *I Will Follow* before *Stay*.

Days before the Dublin shows, the Department of Health announces that it will be taking legal action against U2 for their promotional concert posters in which Bono has a small cigar in his mouth. They say the posters are in breach of legislation, which prohibits the use of tobacco products in advertisements.

Ever since being elevated to national hero status after their triumphs at Croke Park and Live Aid in the summer of 1985, U2's live appearances in Ireland have been surrounded by controversies that have more to do with expectations and opinions about how the band should behave than anything else. Responsibilities thrown at U2 from the outside have, for years, distracted attention from the music and have contributed to their frequent uneasiness when performing in their own country. The first night in Dublin is a good example. The show starts out tense, with the band hiding behind their routine and not really opening up their box of tricks as at other shows. It loosens up somewhat during the acoustic set. With Larry drumming while sitting on a monitor on the mini-stage, Bono holds the microphone for him to sing a cheerful version of *Dirty Old Town*. Larry's fun is ruined during *I Will Follow* when he is hit on the side of his face by a big shoe that comes flying from the crowd.

"What a night," MacPhisto shouts. "Home with the people who love us more than anybody else in the whole world! Home with the people who see through all the trappings and the hype. Home with the people who know the real me. Home with the people who don't see me as a glamorous pop star." The crowd are quiet, unsure how to interpret his speech. MacPhisto continues on a personal note: "Home with the people who call me 'dad'. I'm going to sleep in my *own* bed tonight. Perhaps I should warn them; I know they're excited to see me, after so long. I'm so tired hassling people," he says, dialling his own home number. On the answering machine is the voice of his four-year old daughter Jordan: "Hellooo, we're on holidaaaay. Daddy, if that's you: we're not coming home until you take the horns off! Byeeee!"

■ Set second night: same as August 21, with *When Love Comes To Town* instead of *Dancing Queen*, plus *Help* after *Desire*

The second show is transmitted live on radio in America, Ireland, the UK and most European countries, reaching an estimated total audience of 400 million. As with the New Year's Eve show in 1989, U2 encourage fans to tape the show and *Hot Press* magazine prints a specially designed cassette cover for the purpose. Being a big radio event, as well as U2's last concert on European soil for quite some time, the level of anticipation and pre-show excitement is enormous. As usual when U2 play their hometown, thousands of fans from all over the world, especially America, Italy and Holland, are in attendance. Over 2,000 guests of the band cram the VIP box, including Salman Rushdie, David Bowie, Paul McCartney, Jim Kerr, Bob Geldof, Mick Jagger and Nastassia Kinski.

Days before the show, U2 find themselves in a row with the manufacturers of Foster's lager. Having made an agreement with the concert promoters, Foster's are running adverts in which

they proudly proclaim they are serving at the U2 shows. Throughout their career, U2 have always refused to link their name to any product or engage in corporate sponsorship for large amounts of money. Appalled that Foster's are associating their name with U2 in a manner that suggests U2 are endorsing their beer or being sponsored by it, the band withdraw the agreement and choose another beer.

U2's video technicians react promptly. After *The Fly*, a huge Foster's lager can appears on the screens, captioned: 'Official sponsor of the tour'; then, after a few seconds, 'NOT!' appears over the can in big, red capital letters.

Bono welcomes the crowd and those tuning in on Zoo Radio. The show is powerful, free of any tension, and contains a few surprises. Adam's girlfriend Naomi Campbell comes onto the catwalk during *Trying To Throw Your Arms*. As Bono hands her the Handycam and instructs to film him, Naomi ignores Bono and walks to the main stage to focus on Adam, who has trouble repressing his laughter. "A woman needs a man, like Clayton needs a Handycam," Bono sings. During the intro to *Bad*, Bono says hello to Michael Jackson if he's out there listening, and expresses his disbelief over the much reported allegations that Jackson sexually abused a 13-year old boy.

Tonight's confessions are from members of U2's crew and their organisation only, and include many inside jokes and personal remarks about the past few months on the road. "Zooropa is all over," sighs MacPhisto. "So many have turned out to see us, I don't know what to say..." He thanks everyone in the audience and some heavenly spirit in particular: "There is someone who used to come and see us all the time, and who hasn't been around for a while. We used to be so close. People think I've forgotten about him, but I haven't. I used to find him so inspiring back then; he invented me. I was his most magnificent creation; the brightest star in his sky. Now look at me: a tired old pop star in platform shoes... I tried to speak to him all the time but he won't take my calls. But I can't blame him for

everything; all the wars, all the famine, all the trouble in the world; I get blamed for it. Even the *Evening Herald* slags me off. Who can I get to help me make peace with him? Who will mediate for me? Shall I call the United Nations? Maybe they can help me. Off with the horns, on with the show."

He phones the United Nations; it's a hoax. The tape on the answering machine states that they're out for lunch but leaves another number to report any new wars or massacres. MacPhisto looks distressed and the audience sigh as one in sympathy. The crowd join in as MacPhisto sings an unaccompanied version of *Help*.

U2 donate £315,000, their profits from ticket sales, merchandising and catering at the three Irish shows, to several charity organisations: Dublin Aids Alliance, Alone, the Rape Crisis Centre, the Simon Community, the Focus Point Centre for the Homeless, and the Hospice Foundation.

SEPTEMBER 3, 1993. LOS ANGELES, CA, UNIVERSAL AMPHITHEATER

Edge makes his first ever solo live appearance, performing *Numb* at the annual MTV Video Awards show. Dressed in a blue military jacket with beret and sunglasses, Edge plays guitar in front of an improvised mini-version of Zoo TV, with a stack of video monitors piled up at the back of the stage.

OCTOBER 1, 1993. DUBLIN, IRELAND, CLARENCE HOTEL

At the wedding reception of long-time friend Gavin Friday, U2 do a brief performance, playing a version of Thin Lizzy's *The Boys Are Back In Town*, after which Edge and Naomi Campbell do some karaoke numbers.

Dublin, RDS

ZOO TV: ZOOMERANG / NEW ZOOLAND

The final leg of the tour is dubbed 'Zoomerang' for Australia, 'New Zooland' for New Zealand and just 'Zoo TV Japan' for Japan. Only six shows are booked for the sparsely populated Australia, two for New Zealand and two for Japan. Playing the biggest cities only, Perth is not visited and in Japan, only Tokyo is booked. When ticket sales start in August, steep prices obstruct instant sell-outs, and the Adelaide show is almost cancelled due to poor ticket sales.

NOVEMBER 12, 13, 1993. MELBOURNE, CRICKET GROUND

- Attendance: 95,000; (capacity 110,000)
- Support: Kim Salmon and The Surrealist, Big Audio Dynamite II
- Set first night: *Zoo Station / The Fly / Even Better Than The Real Thing / Mysterious Ways / One - Unchained Melody / Until The End Of The World / New Year's Day / Numb / Trying To Throw Your Arms / Angel Of Harlem / Stay / Satellite Of Love / Dirty Day / Bullet The Blue Sky / Running To Stand Still / Where The Streets Have No Name / Pride / encore: Daddy's Gonna Pay For Your Crashed Car / Lemon / With Or Without You / Love Is Blindness / Can't Help Falling In Love*

As Bono promised the last time U2 were in Australia, it hadn't taken them five years to return. It was four years, this time. Having postponed the Australian swing to the very end of the Zoo TV trek, Bono exaggerates the figures a bit: "Over 1.2 million miles; 13 million punters; 192 nations; several US Presidents; and finally we make it through just here. The latest, the greatest in hardware, software, and men's wear: welcome to Zoo TV, y'all." The Australian fans have followed Zoo TV's development via the media, from the first Lakeland reports to inhabitants from Bosnia talking about the war during the show. "People don't like it when you get rock & roll mixed up with politics," Bono remarks. "People don't like it when you get rock & roll mixed up with religion, sex, anything like that. I thought that was our job."

The basic set list is the same, with *Bad, Desire,* and *Ultra Violet* making way for songs from the 'Zooropa' album. *Dirty Day* evolves into a loud and savage song after its quiet start. After the confessions and the cartoons, the band start *Daddy's Gonna Pay For Your Crashed Car* while Bono is still in the dressing room. The screens show him adding the final touches to his MacPhisto make-up, singing and miming the first verses to his mirror image. He then puts on his gold jacket and the camera follows him making his way on stage. Two Trabants hanging from the roof crash into each other as they sway to and fro.

MacPhisto shows his boots to the crowd. "You need a good gimmick these days to compete with Michael Jackson or Madonna," he says. The crowd boo, then sympathise with him. "Before I became a celebrity, nobody found me attractive at all. Now, everybody loves me. All the glitz and the glamour make you very sexy. You like celebrities, don't you? What are you doing with poor old Derryn Hinch then?" Hinch is a controversial journalist who had just been sacked from his own current affairs show by Network Ten. When he calls him, he offers Derryn work at Zoo TV if he's not doing anything else.

Bono does flamenco dance moves to the swinging beat of

Lemon, which he sings faultlessly in the high-pitched 'fat lady' voice as on the record. Edge sings along with the Talking Heads-style backup vocals that is played from tape.

- Set second night: same as first show, with *She's A Mystery To Me* instead of *Unchained Melody*, plus *Dancing Queen* after *Angel Of Harlem*.

Some 15,000 seats remain empty for the second show. MacPhisto tries to phone the Queen Mother to inquire about her health but gets a woman who bewilderedly states, "I'm sorry darling, you have the wrong number. Who's calling?" "I'm an Australian royalty, I'm very famous, my name is MacPhisto." "Are you the popular singer?" she asks, and as the conversation progresses it appears the woman is Dame Edna Everage. MacPhisto asks if she would take the place of the Queen Mother

if she is unwell. MacPhisto sings a stanza of *God Save The Queen* but substitutes "queen" for "Dame". Before the song is over, Dame Edna gets in a quick plug her upcoming shows in town.

NOVEMBER 16, 1993. ADELAIDE, FOOTBALL PARK

- Attendance: 30,000
- Support: Kim Salmon and The Surrealists, Big Audio Dynamite II
- Set: same as November 12.

Ticket sales have picked up in the last few weeks after a slow start. The winner of the MTV Australia U2 contest is beamed into the show after *The Fly* for a quick conversation.

NOVEMBER 20, 1993. BRISBANE, ANZ STADIUM

- Attendance: 50,000; sellout
- Support: Kim Salmon and The Surrealists, Big Audio Dynamite II
- Set: same as November 12.

It rains throughout the show but it doesn't dampen spirits among the cheerful crowd. "Did you know I used to baby-sit the Queen of England? We're related," says MacPhisto. He claims that the British are responsible for cricket, Australia's most popular sport, and phones Allan Border, the long-serving captain of the Australian XI. Having asked who's calling, Border responds, "MacPhisto? Sounds like a hamburger!"

NOVEMBER 26, 27, 1993. SYDNEY, FOOTBALL STADIUM

- Attendance: 95,000; (capacity: 104,000)
- Support: Big Audio Dynamite II, Kim Salmon and The Surrealists
- Set both nights: same as November 12.

The first night marks U2's first ever performance without one of its members. Lying in bed with a virus, Adam tells the rest of the band he feels too sick to perform. Bass technician Stuart Morgan, who has been working for U2 for two years, takes Adam's place. The audience are bewildered over Adam's absence and chant his name after The Fly. Bono explains that though Adam is ill, they didn't want to cancel the show. Morgan doesn't play faultlessly, but the others cover up his few mistakes. Since earlier in the year Adam had hinted vaguely to several journalists that he finds his being in U2 is getting too demanding, his non-appearance results in rumours and press speculation that Adam is about to leave the band.

Running to the mini-stage at the end of Bullet The Blue Sky, Bono trips, doesn't bother to stand up and sings Running To Stand Still lying flat on his back. MacPhisto phones Dame Edna Everage, who again uses the opportunity to advertise her Sydney performances later that week.

The second night is aired live to America on Thanksgiving on pay-per-view TV, and is broadcast in 46 other countries in the weeks to follow. Titled 'Zoo TV Live From Sydney', the show is eventually released commercially on home video in April 1994, making for a valuable document of the 1992/93 tour. The show stands alongside Red Rocks and Live Aid as U2's most televised and globally exposed concert footage.

Some 9,000 tickets were unsold for the first night, but with it being such a big TV event, the second show rapidly sells out. Adam is back but looks a bit pale and doesn't smoke as many cigarettes as he normally does. The show is excellent, as is the editing of the TV special. MacPhisto announces his time among us is about to end and that Zoo TV must descend to take its place with all the other satellites.

DECEMBER 1, 1993. CHRISTCHURCH, NEW ZEALAND, LANCASTER PARK

- Attendance: 25,000; (capacity 60,000)
- Support: Big Audio Dynamite II
- Set: same as November 12, with One Tree Hill replacing Unchained Melody, and My Girl is added to Angel Of Harlem.

It is the first day of summer in New Zealand and is terribly cold. Adam is dressed for an Antarctic expedition. One Tree Hill is played acoustically by Bono on both New Zealand dates only. The stadium is not even half-full. In 1989, U2 played to 155,000 people on four stadium dates in New Zealand. This time, two shows draw a combined 67,000 people with 53,000 tickets unsold. During Where The Streets Have No Name hundreds of people manage to sneak into the stadium for free.

DECEMBER 4, 1993. AUCKLAND, NEW ZEALAND, WESTERN SPRINGS STADIUM

- Attendance: 42,000; (capacity: 60,000)
- Support: Three D's, Big Audio Dynamite II
- Set: same as November 12, with One Tree Hill instead of Unchained Melody.

Auckland.

Stuart Morgan stands in for Adam

The temperature is bearable again. In the city of One Tree Hill, the crowd sing along with the song of the same name. Zapping after The Fly, Bono finds a soap commercial that uses Unchained Melody as its tune, and briefly joins in. MacPhisto phones a house on the hill opposite the stadium, where the owner is charging admission to watch the show.

DECEMBER 9, 10, 1993. TOKYO, JAPAN, TOKYO DOME

- Attendance: 90,000; (capacity 100,000)
- Support: Big Audio Dynamite II
- Set both nights: same as November 12.

Since many people find ticket prices too high, and students skip the mid-week first night and go to the second show instead, the third ring of the stadium is practically empty during the first show. Marred by bad acoustics, U2 play uninspired for a relatively quiet, non-participating audience. Edge's guitar transmitter malfunctions during Even Better Than The Real Thing, leaving the song bare without his guitar. Fans are not allowed to stand up from their seats on the floor as security is incredibly tight, so much so that the girl chosen by Bono to join him for Trying To Throw Your Arms is thoroughly frisked before she is allowed on stage. MacPhisto phones Akebono, a famous Sumo wrestling champion, and invites him for an arm wrestling match.

The second show is much better, with improved sound quality, and the band lash out all their energy on their last night on tour. During Where The Streets Have No Name Bono jumps off the stage to run along the cycling track of the stadium, anxiously followed by a dozen Japanese security guards who panic over his unexpected leap. Madonna watches the show from the sound desk, accompanied by a portable phone. MacPhisto tries to phone her during the encore but there is no connection.

The December 10 show is the final, 157th Zoo TV performance. Starting out in Lakeland, Florida on February 29, 1992, U2 have been on the road with their Zoo TV station for nearly 20 months, interrupted by six months during which they wrote and recorded the 'Zooropa' album. Using their technical toys for the last time, the Tokyo show closes down a phase which began in November 1990, when they moved to Berlin to commence work on what was to become 'Achtung Baby'. U2 and their entourage hold a final crew party that lasts all night. Back in familiar surroundings in Dublin, the band take nine months off to contemplate their future.

To be continued...

JANUARY 19, 1994. NEW YORK, NY, WALDORF-ASTORIA HOTEL

At the annual Rock & Roll Hall Of Fame ceremony, Bono inducts Rita Marley, wife of the late Bob Marley, and sings One Love together with Rita, her son Ziggy, and Whoopi Goldberg.

Tokyo Dome

Listed below are all the songs that U2 have performed live, with a reference to the page on which the song is first mentioned. Not all of the songs listed below have actually been performed in concert. Several songs have been rehearsed at soundchecks but failed to make it into a show. Cover versions, artists guesting with U2 and members of U2 performing with other artists are all detailed in a similar way.

Also included is a listing of original songs U2 have never performed in concert, and an overview of the total number of concerts the band have played, with specifications as to the countries where they took place.

1) ORIGINAL U2 SONGS

A Celebration: 31
A Day Without Me: 10
A Sort Of Homecoming: 56
Acrobat: 151
All I Want Is You: 124
An Cat Dubh: 14
Angel Of Harlem: 124
Another Day: 10
Another Time, Another Place: 7
Babyface: 56
Bad: 55
Boy-Girl: 7
Bullet The Blue Sky: 79
Cartoon World: 8
Daddy's Gonna Pay For Your Crashed Car: 166
Desire: 124
Dirty Day: 171
Electric Co.: 15
Even Better Than The Real Thing: 140
Exit: 78
False Prophet: 7
Father is An Elephant: 16
Fire: 23
Gloria: 24
God Part II: 124
Hawkmoon 269: 124
I Fall Down: 22
I Still Haven't Found What I'm Looking For: 79
I Threw A Brick Through A Window: 24
I Will Follow: 14
In God's Country: 78
In Your Hand: 8
Indian Summer Sky: 55
Inside-Out: 7
Into The Heart: 14
Jack In The Box: 10
Lemon: 171
Like A Song: 38
Love Is Blindness: 140
Love Rescue Me: 123
Lucille: 80
MLK: 55

Mothers Of The Disappeared: 97
Mysterious Ways: 140
New Year's Day: 35
Numb: 166
October: 24
One Tree Hill: 111
One: 140
Out Of Control: 7
Party Girl: 38
Pete The Chop: 10
Pride: 52
Red Hill Mining Town: 119
Rejoice: 24
Running To Stand Still: 79
Scarlet: 26
Seconds: 38
Shadows And Tall Trees: 8
She's A Mystery To Me: 115
Silver And Gold: 99
Silver Lining: 8
Slow Dancing: 128
So Cruel: 147
Spanish Eyes: 109
Stay (Faraway, So Close): 167
Stories For Boys: 7
Street Missions: 7
Sunday Bloody Sunday: 35
Surrender: 35
The Cry: 16
The Dream Is Over: 10
The First Time: 168
The Fly: 140
The Fool: 8
The King's New Clothes: 8
The Magic Carpet: 7
The Ocean: 15
The Speed Of Life: 8
The Unforgettable Fire: 53
Things To Make And Do: 15
Tomorrow: 30
Touch: 13
Trevor: 10
Trip Through Your Wires: 74
Trying To Throw Your Arms Around The World: 141
Twilight: 10
Two Hearts Beat As One: 38
Ultra Violet: 140
Until The End Of The World: 140
Van Diemen's Land: 127
Walk To The Water: 150
When Love Comes To Town: 118
Where The Streets Have No Name: 79
Who's Gonna Ride Your Wild Horses: 140
Wire: 54
With A Shout: 24
With Or Without You: 80

Womanfish: 74
Zoo Station: 140
Zooropa: 168
11 O'Clock Tick Tock: 13
40: 38

2) OFFICIALLY RELEASED U2 SONGS NEVER PERFORMED LIVE IN CONCERT

Though some of the songs below have been considered and rehearsed at soundchecks, none have actually been performed in concert or elsewhere.

Album Tracks:

From 'October': Stranger In A Strange Land, Is That All?
From 'War': Drowning Man, The Refugee, Red Light
From 'The Unforgettable Fire': Promenade, 4th Of July, Elvis Presley And America
From 'The Joshua Tree': Red Hill Mining Town
From 'Rattle And Hum': Heartland
From 'Achtung Baby': Acrobat
From 'Zooropa': Some Days Are Better Than Others, The Wanderer

Single B-sides

J. Swallow
Treasure (Whatever Happened To Pete The Chop)
The Three Sunrises
Love Comes Tumbling
Bass Trap
Luminous Times
Walk To The Water
Deep In The Heart
Race Against Time
The Sweetest Thing
Hallelujah, Here She Comes
A Room At The Heartbreak Hotel
Alex Descends Into Hell For A Bottle of Milk/Korova 1*
The Lady With The Spinning Head

3) COVER VERSIONS: SONGS BY OTHER ARTISTS PERFORMED LIVE BY U2:

Part One: full versions:

The artists who originally performed these songs is in brackets.

All Along The Watchtower (Bob Dylan): 18
A Hard Day's Rain's Gonna Fall (Bob Dylan): 47
Are You Lonesome Tonight (Elvis Presley): 162
C'Mon Everybody (Eddie Cochran): 74
Can't Help Falling In Love (Elvis Presley): 119
Christmas (Baby Please Come Home) (Phil Spector): 110
Dear Prudence (The Beatles): 156

Glad To See You (The Ramones): 8
Happy Chriatmas (War Is Over) (John Lennon): 122
Heart Of Gold (Neil Young): 6
Help (The Beatles): 76
Helter Skelter (The Beatles): 111
I Shall Be Released (Bob Dylan): 76
Knocking On Heaven's Door (Bob Dylan): 36
Let It Be (Beatles): 78
Lost Highway (Hank Williams): 97
Mad As The Mist And Snow (William Butler Yeats): 123
Maggie's Farm (Bob Dylan): 74
Mannequin (Wire): 6
My Hometown (Bruce Springsteen): 71
New York, New York (Frank Sinatra): 154
Nights In White Satin (Moody Blues): 6
People Get Ready (Curtis Mayfield): 78
Rain (The Beatles): 70, 104
Redemption Song (Bob Marley): 156
Satellite Of Love (Lou Reed): 140
September 1913 (William Butler Yeats): 123
Show Me The Way (Peter Frampton): 6
Southern Man (Neil Young): 30
Springhill Mining Disaster (Peggy Seeger): 79
Stand By Me (Ben E. King): 99
Sun City (Little Steven): 76
Sweet Jane (Velvet Underground): 77
Tequila Sunrise (The Eagles): 119
Vicious (Lou Reed): 77
Whiskey In The Jar (Traditional): 153
Wild Rover (Traditional): 153

Part Two: Snippets

Snatches of other artists' songs have appeared during many U2 songs, with Bono often incorporating one or two verses of songs into their own songs or adding them afterwards. Several of the songs listed below have become linked to specific U2 songs for years, while some have only been performed once or twice.

A Hard Day's Night (The Beatles): 47
Amazing Grace (Traditional): 58
Annie's Song (John Denver): 156
Are You Lonesome Tonight (Elvis Presley): 162
Auld Lang Syne (Traditional): 68
Be Bop A LuLa (Gene Vincent): 48
Biko (Peter Gabriel): 76
Billie Jean (Michael Jackson): 39
Blaze Of Glory (The Alarm): 40
Break On Through (Doors): 40
Candle In The Wind (Elton John): 69
Cold Turkey (John Lennon): 74
Dancing In The Street (Martha & The Vandellas): 79
Dancing Queen (Abba): 145
Dear Prudence (The Beatles): 45
Dirty Old Town (Ewan McColl): 135
Do They Know It's Christmas (Band Aid): 63
Ein Bisschen Frieden (Nicole): 50
Exodus (Bob Marley): 19
Give Peace A Chance (John Lennon): 17

Glittering Prize (Simple Minds): 44
God Save The Queen (Traditional): 171
Guantanamara (Sandpipers): 110
Hanging On The Telephone: (Blondie) 166
Happy Birthday (Traditional): 38
Hello Goodbye (Beatles): 154
I Can See Clearly Now (Johnny Nash): 114
I Just Called To Say I Love You (Stevie Wonder): 166
I Left My Heart In San Francisco (Tony Bennet): 29
If You Love Somebody, Set Them Free (Sting): 77
It Never Rains In Southern California
    (Albert Hammond): 155
Jingle Bells (Traditional): 52
John. I'm Only Dancing (David Bowie): 80
Let's Twist Again (Chubby Checker): 23
Light My Fire (Doors): 60
Like A Hurricane (Neil Young): 129
Like A Rhinestone Cowboy (Glen Campbell): 115
Loch Lomand (Traditional): 40
Love Will Tear Us Apart (Joy Division): 80
Love To Love You Baby (Donna Summer): 58
Midnight Hour (Wilson Picket): 50
Molly Malone (Traditional): 65
Money, Money, Money (Abba): 167
My Girl (The Temptations): 115
My Way (Paul Anka): 156
New York, New York (Frank Sinatra): 24
Norwegian Wood (Beatles): 63
Old Man (Neil Young): 156
Puppy Love (Donny Osmond): 106
Riders On The Storm (The Doors):
Ruby Tuesday (Rolling Stones): 62
Satellite Of Love (Lou Reed): 63
Send In The Clowns (Steven Sondheim): 29
Sexual Healing (Marvin Gave): 51
She Loves You (Beatles): 151
Singing In The Rain (Gene Kelley): 48
So You Wanna Be A Rock & Roll Star (Byrds): 125
Someone, Somewhere, In Summertime (Simple Minds): 49
Stairway To Heaven (Led Zeppelin): 120
Street Hassle (Lou Reed): 107
Summertime (George Gershwin): 153
Suspicious Minds (Elvis Presley): 125
Sympathy For The Devil (Rolling Stones): 62
Take Me To the River (Al Green): 62
The Boys Are Back In Town (Thin Lizzy): 170
The Cutter (Echo & The Bunnymen): 38
The Times They Are A'Changing (Bob Dylan): 136
Three Little Birds (Bob Marley): 79
Too Shy (Kajagoogoo): 38
Unchained Melody (Alex North/Hy Zaret): 146
Waiting For The Man (Velvet Underground): 35
Walk On the Wild Side (Lou Reed): 70
Waltzing Matilda (Traditional): 127
We Are The World (USA For Africa): 65
White Christmas (Bing Crosby): 42
Wooden Heart (Elvis Presley): 61
Yankee Doodle Dandy (Traditional): 41
1969 (Stooges): 135

4) GUEST APPEARANCES: U2 MEMBERS AT OTHER ARTISTS' CONCERTS.

Listed below are the bands and artists with whom members of U2 have made guest appearances. All-star finales at big festivals with a multitude of artists are not counted.

The Alarm (Bono): 36, 51
Tuesday Blue (Adam): 78
The BoDeans (Edge, Bono, Larry): 119
David Bowie (Bono): 138
Johnny Cash (Bono, Edge, Larry): 160
Bob Dylan (Bono): 52, 123
Brian Ferry (Edge): 122
Gavin Friday (Bono): 123, 170
Hothouse Flowers (Adam): 123
B.B. King (Bono, Edge): 123
Simple Minds (Bono): 60, 78
Van Morrison: (Bono): 160
The Police (Bono): 35, 77, 78
Maria McKee (Adam): 123

5) GUEST APPEARANCES II: OTHER ARTISTS AT U2 SHOWS

The following artists have performed live at U2 shows. Anyone coming on stage but not singing or playing is not included, nor are all-star events.

Stuart Adamson: 40
The Alarm: 47
Mike Peters: 38, 40, 52
Benny Anderson + Björn Ulvaeus: 150
Charlie Burchill: 57, 110
Bob Dylan: 99
Garland Jeffries: 32
Busta Jones: 24
Wynonna Judd: 119
Jim Kerr: 49
B.B. King and his band: 118, 124
Daniel Lanois: 154
Annie Lennox: 49, 50
Ziggy Marley and The Melody Makers: 122
Maria McKee: 68, 97, 105, 135
The New Voices of Freedom: 113
Lou Reed: 76, 77, 107, 150, 152
Keith Richards: 122
The Red Rockers: 65
Axl Rose: 148
The Rumour Horn Section: 122
Jo Shankar: 159, 169
Bruce Springsteen: 113
Steve Wickham: 37, 40, 48, 50, 72
Pete Wylie: 18

U2 CONCERTS – 1976-1994 PER COUNTRY

Guest appearances at shows by others, radio and TV specials and impromptu sessions are not included. Festival appearances are included. U2 played many shows in Ireland during their formative years which remain unlogged.

Australia: 44
Austria: 1
Belgium: 18
Canada: 22
Denmark: 3
Finland: 1
France: 23
Germany: 32
Holland: 31
Hungary: 1
Ireland: 69 (known)
Italy: 16
Japan: 14
Mexico: 4
New Zealand: 10
Norway: 4
Portugal: 2
Spain: 6
Sweden: 9
Switzerland: 8
United Kingdom: 194
United States Of America: 360

U2 CONCERTS 1976 — 1994

This list covers official U2 concerts only – short live sessions performed during radio interviews or appearances at other artists' shows are not counted. Many shows between 1976 and 1980 are unrecorded, and are not included here.

1976-1979: 45 (known)
1980:   97
1981:   142
1982:   64
1983:   91
1984:   50
1985:   63
1986:   7
1987:   110
1988:   1
1989:   47
1992:   104
1993:   53

TOTAL: 877

RADIO BROADCASTS OF LIVE MATERIAL:

I: Radio Sessions:

Richard Skinner, BBC, September 1980: 15
KRO Dutch Radio, October 14, 1980: 16
BBC In Concert, August 23, 1981: 25
Kid Jensen, BBC, October 14, 1981: 26

II: Radio Interviews that include live sessions:

Dave Fanning Show, RTE, June 25, 1987: 105
Trip Through Your Wires, September 8, 1987: 111
KUPO, Arizona, December 18, 1987: 120
Early Morning Radio Show, October 21, 1989: 128
Rockline, USA radio, August 28, 1992: 154

III: Live Concerts (live or delayed, partly or wholly)

Cork, Opera House, October 5, 1979: 8
Dublin, February 26, 1980: 11
The Hague, February 12, 1981: 18
Boston, March 6, 1981 (1st show): 20
Denver, May 11, 1981: 23
Geleen, June 8, 1981: 24
Amsterdam, October 30, 1981: 27
Boston, November 14, 1981: 28
Cleveland, December 8, 1981: 29
Lido Beach, December 13, 1981: 29
Hattem, May 14, 1982: 32
Werchter, July 4, 1982: 34
London, December 6, 1982: 36
Glasgow, March 24, 1983: 40
Boston, May 6, 1983: 42
Philadelphia, May 14, 1983: 44
Devore, May 30, 1983: 45
Denver, June 5, 1983: 45
Werchter, July 3, 1983: 49
St. Goarshausen, August 20, 1983: 50
London, July 13, 1985: 72
Dublin, May 17, 1986: 74
East Rutherford, June 15, 1986: 78
London, October 16, 1988: 122
Dublin, December 31, 1989 / January 1, 1990: 135
Dublin, August 28, 1993: 169

TV BROADCASTS:
I: Sessions / TV Shows:

These incorporate live sessions for television, usually in TV studios in front of a small studio audience, or live events specifically organised by the TV broadcasters for the purpose.

Late Late Show, January 15, 1980: 10
Belfast, January, 1981: 18
Mandagsbörsen, February 9, 1981: 18
Old Grey Whistle Test, February 28, 1981: 19
The Tomorrow Show, May 30, 1981: 24
Rockpalast', November 4, 1981: 27
Countdown In Concert, May 14, 1982: 32
Something Else, May 15, 1982: 33
Get Set For Summer, May 1982: 33
Top Of The Pops, January 1983: 38
The Tube', March 16, 1983: 40
Top of the Pops, March 31, 1983: 41
Rockpalast, August 20, 1983: 50
Japanese TV, November 1983: 51
RockPop In Concert, November 21, 1984: 58
TV Gaga, January 30, 1986: 74
Old Grey Whistle Test, March 11, 1987: 78
Late Late Show, March 16, 1987: 79
Tube TV, April 14, 1987: 97
Countdown, July 10, 1987: 108
Late Late Show, December 16, 1988: 122

II: Live Concerts

This incorporates TV airings of live concerts, partly or wholly. Several of these were simulcast on radio. (See Radio.)

Cork, October 5, 1979: 8
Brussels, February 10, 1981: 18
The Hague, February 12, 1981: 18
Geleen, June 8, 1981: 24
Roskilde, July 2, 1982: 33
Werchter, July 4, 1982: 34
Gateshead, July 31, 1982: 35
Devore, May 30, 1983: 45
Denver, June 5, 1983: 45
New York, June 29, 1983: 48
Werchter, July 3, 1983: 49
Chicago, March 21, 1985: 65
East Rutherford, April 12, 1985: 67
London, July 13, 1985: 72
Dublin, May 17, 1986: 74
East Rutherford, June 15, 1986: 78
Paris, July 4, 1987: 107
London, October 16, 1988: 122
Dublin, Dec. 31, 1989 / Jan. 1, 1990: 135
Oakland, April 18, 1992: 145
Paris, May 7, 1992: 146
Stockholm, June 11, 1992: 150
Pontiac, September 9, 1992: 154
Atlanta, September 25, 1992: 155
Sydney, November 27, 1993: 172